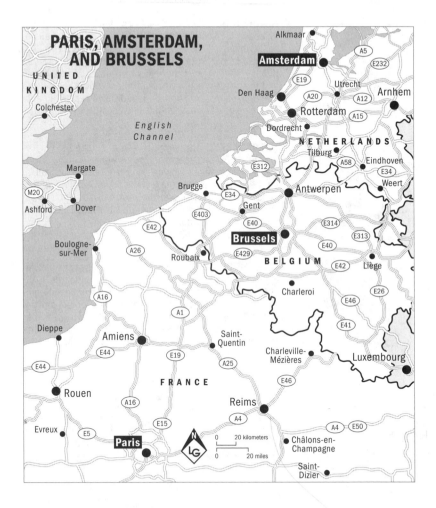

PARIS, AMSTERDAM, AND BRUSSELS

UNITED KINGDOM

Colchester

English Channel

Margate

M20

Ashford   Dover

Boulogne-sur-Mer

Dieppe

Rouen

Evreux

E5

Paris

Amiens

E44

E44

A26

A16

A16

E15

E19

A25

A1

Roubaix

E42

A4

E403

E34

Brugge

Gent

E40

Brussels

E429

BELGIUM

Charleroi

Saint-Quentin

Charleville-Mézières

E46

Reims

A4

Châlons-en-Champagne

Saint-Dizier

FRANCE

Alkmaar

Amsterdam

A5

E232

E19

Utrecht

Arnhem

Den Haag

A20

A12

Rotterdam

A15

Dordrecht

NETHERLANDS

Tilburg

A58

Eindhoven

E34

Weert

Antwerpen

E312

E314

E313

E40

Liège

E42

E26

E46

E41

Luxembourg

E46

A4   E50

0   20 kilometers

0   20 miles

RESEARCHER-WRITERS

HEATHER BUFFO. Armed with a few choice French phrases ("Bonjour!" "Merde!"), Heather ran a marathon sprint through Paris and Brussels before retiring to the south of France. With a trusty traveling gnome at her side, Heather briefly joined the ranks of France's Most Wanted and befriended some shockingly deceptive bartenders. She eventually wound up on a paradisiacal beach, tan and scheming how to smuggle Nutella crepes back into the US.

TAYLOR NICKEL. This *Let's Go* veteran returned to France to conquer Paris's streets and woo its women with his savvy wit. When he wasn't sipping on a demi-pêche or resting up in his apartment in the 14ème, Taylor was finding the perfect local hangouts and the best bargains. Though it's slightly more stressful than the French countryside, Paris will always be Taylor's home away from home.

KATHARINE VIDT. From providing X-rated research notes to cycling around on her bicycle, Kat embraced the true spirit of Amsterdam. She proved she could pry information from anyone, whether a stony-faced hostel owner or just a plain stoner. Though Kat could probably write books solely on Electric Ladyland, Albert Heijns, and stroopwafel ice cream, she conquered the whole city, and did it with swag.

PARIS, AMSTERDAM & BRUSSELS

At first glance, grouping Paris, Amsterdam, and Brussels together may seem as odd and unlikely as a lunch date between Brigitte Bardot, Vincent Van Gogh, and Tintin. But with rich political, artistic, and culinary legacies, these three cities continue to be major destinations for young travelers looking to experience everything from the classic beauty of Paris's wide boulevards to the reefer-clouded progressiveness of Amsterdam to the famous waffles, chocolates, and beer of Brussels. Students might go to Paris to discover the secrets that inspired the likes of Claude Monet and Ernest Hemingway, the latter of whom once declared the grand city "a moveable feast." From the sweet aromas drifting out of the corner *boulangeries* to that famous French snobbery, Paris is a city that will charm and bitchslap you with equal gusto. But don't fret—the gleam of bronze balconies and the buzz of a good €2 bottle of wine are worth crossing cultural divides, and by your third or fourth sincere attempt at *s'il vous plaît*, even the waiters will soften up. While the City of Lights has a tendency to outshine its peers—indeed, Brussels's Manneken Pis certainly lacks the grandeur and poise of the Eiffel Tower, and wooden clogs aren't exactly a hot commodity on the Champs-Élysées—Amsterdam and Brussels offer their own varieties of folksy, earnest charm. Like your ex-hippie high school history teacher, Amsterdam somehow manages to appeal to both tulip-loving grandmas and Red-Light-ready students. Come to this city to gawk at coffeeshops and prostitutes, then take some time to cultivate an appreciation for canals and the Flemish masters. While visiting Brussels, tap into your middle school nerd and admire the comic book characters that abound in the city's museums and on the sides of many buildings. If cartoons aren't your thing, head over to the European Parliament and mingle with Eurocrats while plotting future world domination. Diverse as they may be, these three cities each have a unique character that, if probed beyond that surface, offers a little something for everyone.

when to go

Spring weather in Paris is fickle and brings rainy and sunny days in equal numbers. June is a notoriously wet month, while July and August see temperatures rise; heat waves during the summer can be uncomfortable, and muggy weather aggravates the city's pollution problem. By fall, a fantastic array of auburn brightens up the foliage in the city's parks, and the weather is dry and temperate. Mild winter months tend to see more rain than snow. In Amsterdam and Brussels, you can expect moderate weather; here, temperatures rarely rise to intolerable levels, although rainy, gray skies are fairly characteristic of the Low Countries' fluctuating climate. The Netherlands are also graced by a classic ocean fog that almost always dissolves by midday.

Everyone loves Paris and temperate weather in the springtime, but summer sees droves of tourists move in as Parisians depart for their vacations. Many of the city's best festivals are held during the summer (see Festivals), although smaller hotels, shops, and services usually close for the month of August. The Low Countries reach their tourist peak during the summer (July and August), when the weather is sunniest, the days are longest, and most people are on vacation. Spring is another time to hit the region, especially if you're a flora fanatic dying to see Holland's tulips in bloom or a jazz junkie hoping to soak up some jams at Brussels's Jazz Marathon.

top five places to go dutch

5. MANNEKEN PIS: Answer nature's call and pay a visit to Brussels's favorite public urinator.

4. ANNE FRANK HOUSE: You read her diary in eighth grade; now see the building where her inspiring story was written.

3. LEIDSEPLEIN: Bike your way home after a late night spent partying in this neighborhood that never sleeps. You'll earn more local street cred than the bros on the Leidseplein Pub Crawl will ever possess.

2. JARDIN DU LUXEMBOURG: It's the Central Park of Paris. Lounge like a local or jog like an expat.

1. TOUR EIFFEL: Beautiful and awe-inspiring, a visit to Paris's most iconic monument is never a waste, no matter how cliché (or phallic) it is.

what to do

LET'S (VAN) GOGH

Forget Italy and its Renaissance—the Dutch Golden Age inspired serious strides in architecture, literature, and painting. Leonardo, Donatello, Raphael, and Michelangelo? The Ninja Turtles should have been named Rembrandt, Vermeer, Hals, and Brueghel. Amsterdam even has more canals than Venice. In all seriousness, were you to put Italian and Dutch art up against one another in a cage match, there'd be no decisive winner (probably because the Dutch side would either find a way to subsidize itself out of the problem or wouldn't pass the drug test, but that's beside the point). Dutch art may be "quieter" than its Italian counterparts, but after studying it in places like the Rijksmuseum, you'll agree that it's got a certain something.

But Amsterdam isn't the only city outdoing Italy for the top artistic spot. The city of Paris itself is something of a work of art, with its wide boulevards and buildings that don't exceed more than six stories, *pour que tout le monde ait du soleil* ("so that all have sunshine"). Having served as inspiration for artists from Monet to Rodin to the painters who crowd the streets of Montmartre, Paris is home to art museums that house some of the world's most famous works. Belgium may not be as well known for its artwork, but Brussels still boasts a few museums worth visiting.

- **THE LOUVRE:** Do we even need to tell you why to come here? (Paris; p. 62).

- **MUSÉE RODIN:** Contemplate the universe alongside *The Thinker* (Paris; p. 75).

- **MUSÉE DE L'ORANGERIE:** A gallery of Impressionist and post-Impressionist paintings that include the works of Monet, Matisse, and Picasso (Paris; p. 64).

- **THE RIJKSMUSEUM:** *The* museum of Dutch art. Come here to marvel at *Night Watch*, Rembrandt's gargantuan tableau that rivals Leonardo's *Last Supper*, and the blank-verse poetry of Vermeer's intimate domestic scenes (Amsterdam; p. 219).

- **VAN GOGH MUSUEM:** Compared to the Rijksmuseum, this collection of Van Gogh masterpieces is far more intimate and manageable. Due to the chronological arrangement of the master's works, a tour through the exhibit can help enrich your understanding of Van Gogh's biography (Amsterdam; p. 218).

- **THE HORTA MUSEUM:** Although a bit out of the way, this museum showcases the work of Art Nouveau architect, Victor Horta. It was declared an UNESCO World Heritage Site in 2000 (Brussels; p. 280).

A CASE OF THE MUNCHIES

Counterbalance all that walking and sightseeing you've been doing with a taste of Paris's, Amsterdam's, and Brussels's best cuisine.

- **FRITLAND:** Forget about arteries—we'll gladly wash down as many fistfuls of creamy, mayonnaise-dipped French fries with as many cans of blonde Belgian beer as we like, *merci beaucoup* (Brussels; p. 287).

- **VAN DOBBEN:** This old-school deli offers the best value in pricey Rembrandtplein, hands down (Amsterdam; p. 229).

- **EAT PARADE:** The sandwiches here taste like cake and are so good, you might just cry of happiness (Brussels; p. 290).

- **LE JIP'S:** Add a little spice to your life and enjoy some cheap and authentic Cuban/African/Brazilian food (Paris; p. 100).

MIDNIGHT IN PARIS, AMSTERDAM, AND BRUSSELS

When the clock strikes midnight, you might not find yourself transported to the 1920s (or a Woody Allen film), but after hours in these cities can still provide you with a magical (if somewhat drunken) time.

- **DELIRIUM:** Ask for the Beer Bible of more than 2000 beers of the world, gather around beer barrels downstairs with friends, and drink up (Brussels; p. 294).

- **STUDIO 80:** Full of the coolest Dutch kids, techno fanatics, and a few in-the-know tourists, this is the place to be on a Saturday night (Amsterdam; p. 242).

- **LE FIFTH BAR:** One of the best places to party in the Latin Quarter (Paris; p. 138).

- **FUSE:** Proudly proclaiming itself the "Best Belgian Club Ever," Fuse is certainly Brussels's biggest and liveliest club (Brussels; p. 297).

- **BANANA CAFÉ:** This GLBT-friendly establishment has all-night dance parties that draw all kinds of patrons (Paris; p. 132).

- **SUGAR FACTORY:** A sweet place to dance with friends on a Saturday night (Amsterdam; p. 241).

BEYOND TOURISM

If you're interested in more than a plate of *frites* and a snapshot of the Eiffel Tower, we suggest that you take some time to travel more extensively in Paris, Amsterdam, or Brussels as a student or volunteer. Future revolutionaries, imagine the social justice issues to be tackled in a place where pot and prostitution are two of the biggest tourist draws. Food snobs, prepare to discover the secrets behind a perfect souffle. Romantics, picture the pretty face of those cute Belgian kids you'll be looking after if you take an au pair position. Given the region's visible social conscience and the frequency of spoken English throughout the Netherlands, the

student superlatives

- **MOST EMBARRASSING MUSEUM TO VISIT WITH YOUR FAMILY (ESPECIALLY CREEPY UNCLE FLOYD):** The Amsterdam Sex Museum (p. 211).

- **BEST PLACE TO CONSIDER CUTTING OFF YOUR EAR:** The Van Gogh Museum (p. 218).

- **BEST PLACE TO GET HIGH:** The Atomium; ride the world's fastest elevator to the top of Brussels's celebrated monument (or biggest eyesore, depending on who you ask) (p. 284).

- **BEST PLACE TO FINISH A SCHOOL PROJECT:** The Parc des Buttes Chaumont, the birthplace of Plaster of Paris (p. 96).

- **BEST PLACE TO INDULGE YOUR INNER BLAIR WALDORF:** The Champs-Élysées, where you can splurge at high-end stores and cafes (p. 79).

- **MOST LIKELY TO GIVE YOU A SUGAR RUSH:** Angelina's, where you can sip smooth *chocolat chaud* and indulge in the mirrors and gold-dripped décor (p. 100).

- **MOST LIKELY TO EXPAND YOUR WAISTLINE:** Antoine's *friterie*, the oldest in Brussels (p. 292).

- **BEST PLACE TO PULL OUT YOUR LEG WARMERS AND PRETEND THE '80S NEVER ENDED:** Studio 80 in Amsterdam (p. 242).

Low Countries provide ample opportunity for visitors to travel as volunteers or students. And although volunteer work in Paris is harder to come by for foreigners, the city's study abroad programs really have their act together and involve intensive language immersion programs, placement with host families, and cross-enrollment with partner French institutions. In any one of these three cities, you can also turn your native tongue into a money-making asset by setting up shop as an English tutor or au pair.

- **CHANTIERS HISTOIRE ET ARCHITECTURE MÉDIÉVALS:** Participate in masonry work and excavations through restoration projects in Paris (p. 341).

- **LA CUISINE PARIS:** Tap into your inner Julia Child and learn the art of French cooking at this culinary school (p. 340).

- **GREAT AU PAIR:** Perfect your French language skills with the aid of small children (p. 344).

suggested itineraries

BEST OF PARIS, AMSTERDAM, AND BRUSSELS IN 9 DAYS

Experience everything from the style and romance of Paris to the internationalism and progressivism of Amsterdam to the cuisine and fine living of Brussels in just over a week.

- **PARIS (4 DAYS):** Use your first day to see some of Paris's most celebrated sights, including the Eiffel Tower, Notre Dame, and the Louvre. Day two can be spent getting to know the city better; take a stroll through the Jardin du Luxembourg, then head over to the Champs-Élysées and Place de la Concorde to see the shops and the Arc de Triomphe. Spend your third day visiting Paris's historical sights; don't miss the Bastille (or what's left of it, anyway), Hôtel de Ville, and the Grand Palais. Spend your last day visiting some of the city's lesser-known sights: the Cimetière du Père-Lachaise, where Oscar Wilde and Jim Morrison are buried; the Catacombs, where you can navigate your way through the city of tunnels in this underground graveyard; and the Musée du Vin, where your tour ends with a complimentary class of wine.

- **AMSTERDAM (3 DAYS):** Hit the Rijksmuseum and the Van Gogh Museum first thing. Follow them up with some time in Vondelpark before a night in Leidseplein. Start day two early to

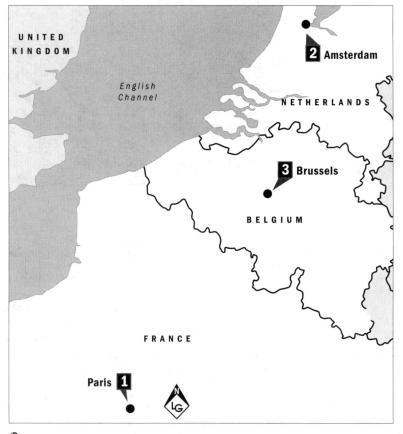

beat the crowds at the Anne Frank House; check out Westerkerk as you head for Nieuwmarkt and onward to the Red Light District for some early evening entertainment. Pack day three with a morning at Zuiderkerk and Museum Het Rembrandt, an afternoon at the Jewish Historical Museum, and a full night in Rembrandtplein.

- **BRUSSELS (2 DAYS):** On your first day, explore the Grand Place and the Magritte Museum, then take a trip to the Cathédral des Saints Michel ed Gudule to see one of the city's grandest churches. Tour the European Parliament on day two before heading over to the Musée du Cacao et du Chocolat to indulge your inner Augustus Gloop. Return to Brussels's center for a beer in the evening, and keep an eye out of Tintin and other comic book characters that may pop up in the murals that are scattered throughout the city.

PARDON MY FRENCH

Anchor your week in Paris before heading out to explore some of the nearby areas.

- **PARIS (3 DAYS):** On your first day, take time to see some of the city's most iconic sights, including the Eiffel Tower, Notre Dame, and the Arc de Triomphe. Day two can be spent appreciating Paris's rich artistic culture; visit the Louvre, the Centre Pompidou (the largest museum in Europe, it's basically an epic game of shoots and ladders), and the Musée d'Orsay, whose core works were originally Louvre rejects (which really says something about the Louvre). Spend your last day outside, experiencing the city. Stroll through the Jardin du Luxembourg, the Jardin des Tuileries, and the Place des Vosges.

- **VERSAILLES (1 DAY):** Sun King Louis XIV's sumptuous palace is pretty much the visual equivalent of gorging yourself on cotton candy. Don't miss a walk through the gardens or a trip out to Marie Antoinette's cottage.

- **CHARTRES (1 DAY):** Chartres's majestic cathedral is celebrated for its beautiful stained glass and is also home of a cloth that the Virgin Mary supposedly wore when she gave birth to Jesus.

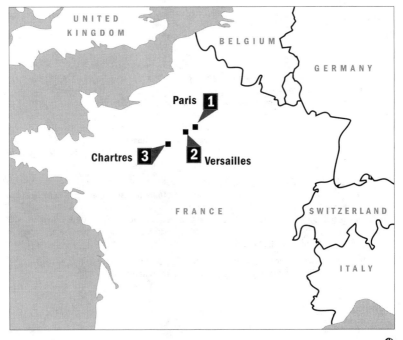

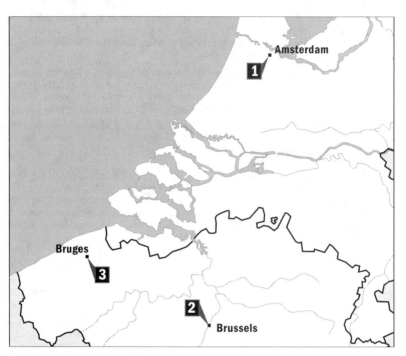

NORTHERN NICETIES

Indulge your taste buds and practice your Dutch in this six-day tour of the Low Countries.

- **AMSTERDAM (3 DAYS):** After a few days here, you'll be saying Amster-damn. Take day one as an opportunity to tour the plentiful selection of coffeeshops in the Nieuwe Zijd and Jordaan neighborhoods, then head to the Electric Ladyland for a psychedelic trip before filling up on grub at one of the many restaurants in Scheepvaartbuurt. Spend your second day in the De Pijp neighborhood, getting kitschy at the Heineken Experience, browsing the eclectic collection at Albert Cuypstraat's outdoor market, and enjoying the neighborhood's cheap eats and hipster nightlife. Culture yourself on day three with visits to the Canal Ring's FOAM and Van Loom Museums, an exploration of the Golden Bend, and an evening excursion to either the Concertgebouw or Muziektheater for first-rate opera, ballet, or classical music.

- **BRUSSELS (2 DAYS):** Delight in the delicious delicacies of this culinary capital (there's even a charming chocolate museum) and appreciate its elegant architecture in a day spent wandering about the Grand Place and environs, making sure not to miss the Manneken Pis; the nearby Sablone area also has a lot of chocolate shops and antique stores. On your second day, spend the morning at the Musical Instrument Museum and the afternoon at the Belgian Center for Comic Strip Art.

- **BRUGES (1 DAY):** Continue your Fatty McFat-Fat ways with a stop in Bruges. Splurge on mussels, and admire the city's canals and northern Renaissance buildings.

PASSAGE DU NORD

LESSER-KNOWN WONDERS

If you've had enough of the Eiffel Tower and the Manneken Pis, explore some of Paris's, Amsterdam's, and Brussels's lesser-known wonders.

- **PARIS (2 DAYS):** Get to know Paris a bit more intimately at the Musée Carnavalet, where you can trace the city's history from its origins to Napolen III. Later, when everyone else is flocking to Notre Dame and the Louvre, spend some time at the Eglise Saint-Eustache, where Louis XIV was baptized, and the Musée de l'Orangerie, home of Monet's *Water Lilies*. On day two, spend the morning exploring Mahlia Kent, an artisan workshop that weaves the intricate fabrics that eventually become garments for labels like Dior and Chanel. Although Paris isn't known for its test tubes, a visit to the Cité des Sciences et de l'Industrie in the afternoon will provide a great break from all those art museums. End the day with a stroll around the city's oldest public square, the Place des Vosges.

- **AMSTERDAM (2 DAYS):** On your first day, visit Oude Kerk, Amsterdam's oldest church (built in 1306) that has survived everything from the Protestant Reformantion to the growth the Red Light District. For some more modern history, spend some time at the Verzetsmuseum, which chronicles the Netherlands' five years of Nazi occupation during WWII. Finish the day with a climb up Westerkerk, an 85m tower that offers the best views of the city. Start off day two with a visit to Electric Ladyland; if the name alone isn't enough to tempt you, this "First Museum of Fluorescent Art" is an unforgettable exploration into the history, science, and culture of florescence. For a little afternoon delight, head over to Vondelpark (where, we might add, it's legal to have sex in the park, as long as you clean up after yourself).

- **BRUSSELS (1 DAY):** Begin your day with a trip to the Horta Museum, which was once the home of famed Art Nouveau architect Victor Horta. In the afternoon, indulge your inner Jay Leno with a visit to AutoWorld. Cap off the day in true Belgian style with a beer at La Fleur en Papier Doré.

discover paris, amsterdam & brussels

how to use this book

CHAPTERS

In the next few pages, the travel coverage chapters—the meat of any *Let's Go* book—begin. First, head to **Paris,** where you can experience the Eiffel Tower, Louvre, and just about every other famous sight you've seen on postcards. Next, take a trip north to **Amsterdam** in the Netherlands to see the stomping grounds of Rembrandt and Van Gogh. Finally, embrace the French and Dutch influences from the first two legs of your trip in **Brussels,** where there's a whole lot more to do than eat french fries, chocolate, and waffles. (Though you'll inevitably spend quite some time on those culinary delights, as well.)

But that's not all, folks. We also have a few extra chapters for you to peruse:

CHAPTER	DESCRIPTION
Discover Paris, Amsterdam & Brussels	Discover tells you what to do, when to do it, and where to go for it. The absolute coolest things about any destination get highlighted in this chapter at the front of all *Let's Go* books.
Essentials	Essentials contains the practical info you need before, during, and after your trip—visas, regional transportation, health and safety, phrasebooks, and more.
Beyond Tourism	As students ourselves, we at *Let's Go* encourage studying abroad, or going beyond tourism more generally, every chance we get. This chapter lists ideas for how to study, volunteer, or work abroad with other young travelers to get more out of your trip.

LISTINGS

Listings—a.k.a. reviews of individual establishments—constitute a majority of *Let's Go* coverage. Our Researcher-Writers list establishments in order from **best to worst value**—not necessarily quality. (Obviously a five-star hotel is nicer than a hostel, but it would probably be ranked lower because it's not as good a value.) Listings pack in a lot of information, but it's easy to digest if you know how they're constructed:

ESTABLISHMENT NAME type of establishment $$$$

Address ☎phone number website

Editorial review goes here.

⇄ Directions to the establishment. ***i*** *Other practical information about the establishment, like age restrictions at a club or whether breakfast is included at a hostel.* [$] *Prices for goods or services.* ⏰ *Hours or schedules.*

ICONS

First things first: places and things that we absolutely love, sappily cherish, generally obsess over, and wholeheartedly endorse are denoted by the all-empowering 👍**Let's Go thumbs-up.** In addition, the icons scattered at the end of a listing (as you saw in the sample above) can serve as visual cues to help you navigate each listing:

👍	*Let's Go* recommends	☎	Phone numbers	⇄	Directions
i	Other hard info	[$]	Prices	⏰	Hours

OTHER USEFUL STUFF

Area codes for Paris, Amsterdam, and Brussels are indicated in the boxes titled "Call me!" at the beginning of those cities' respective chapters. The area codes for excursions appear opposite the name of the city and are denoted by the ☎ icon.

PRICE DIVERSITY

A final set of icons corresponds to what we call our "price diversity" scale, which approximates how much money you can expect to spend at a given establishment. For **accommodations,** we base our range on the cheapest price for which a single traveler can stay for one night. For **food,** we estimate the average amount one traveler will spend in one sitting. The table below tells you what you'll *typically* find in Paris, Amsterdam, and Brussels at the corresponding price range, but keep in mind that no scale can allow for the quirks of all individual establishments. The prices for France and Belgium are indicated on the left; the Netherlands shows up on the right.

ACCOMMODATIONS	RANGE		WHAT YOU'RE LIKELY TO FIND
$	under €25	under €30	Campgrounds and dorm rooms, both in hostels and actual universities. Expect bunk beds and a communal bath. You may have to provide or rent towels and sheets.
$$	€26-45	€31-50	Upper-end hostels and lower-end hotels. You may have a private bathroom, or a sink in your room with a communal shower in the hall.
$$$	€46-70	€51-75	A small room with a private bath. Should have some amenities, such as phone and TV. Breakfast may be included.
$$$$	over €71	over €76	Large hotels, chains, and fancy boutiques. If it doesn't have the perks you want (and more), you've paid too much.
FOOD			**WHAT YOU'RE LIKELY TO FIND**
$	under €10	under €10	Street food, fast-food joints, university cafeterias, and bakeries (yum). Usually takeout, but you may have the option of sitting down.
$$	€11-20	€11-19	Sandwiches, pizza, low-priced entrees, ethnic eateries, and bar grub. Either takeout or sit-down service with slightly classier decor.
$$$	€21-32	€20-29	A somewhat fancy restaurant. Entrees tend to be heartier or more elaborate, but you're really paying for decor and ambience. Few restaurants in this range have a dress code, but some may look down on T-shirts and sandals.
$$$$	over €33	over €30	Your meal might cost more than your room, but there's a reason—it's something fabulous, famous, or both. Slacks and dress shirts may be expected.

MAP LEGEND

You'll notice that our maps have lots of crazy symbols. Here's how to decode them.

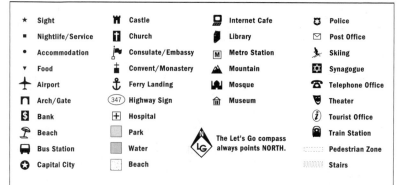

★ Sight	♖ Castle	🖵 Internet Cafe	🞖 Police
■ Nightlife/Service	🏛 Church	📖 Library	✉ Post Office
• Accommodation	⚑ Consulate/Embassy	M Metro Station	🎿 Skiing
▼ Food	✝ Convent/Monastery	⛰ Mountain	✡ Synagogue
✈ Airport	⚓ Ferry Landing	🕌 Mosque	☎ Telephone Office
⌂ Arch/Gate	(347) Highway Sign	🏛 Museum	🎭 Theater
$ Bank	✚ Hospital		(i) Tourist Office
🏖 Beach	▨ Park		🚆 Train Station
🚌 Bus Station	▨ Water	The Let's Go compass always points NORTH.	⠿ Pedestrian Zone
✪ Capital City	▨ Beach		⠿ Stairs

PARIS

Paris leaves an impression on everyone, from students perfecting their langue française to tourists who wonder why the French don't pronounce half the consonants in each word. This city has been home to countless films, revolutions, and kings named Louis, and, in case you hadn't heard, it's a really big deal. Nearly everyone in the world idealizes Paris, whether it's for the Eiffel Tower, the grand boulevards, or the fact that there are more miles in the Louvre than in many towns. Don't let yourself be content with ideals. If you want to know the danger of that, do some research on Paris Syndrome. This city can be rough, and, yes, the waiters are judging you. When you get Englished for the first time (when someone responds to your mangled-French inquiry with an English response), you'll realize that you maybe weren't prepared for all this. But Paris and its people pull through spectacularly for those who can appreciate the sensory experiences around every corner—the sweet tastes to be found in a patisserie, the resonating bells of Notre Dame, the springtime greens in the Jardin des Tuileries. This city will charm and bitchslap you with equal gusto, but don't get too le tired—by your third or fourth sincere attempt at s'il vous plaît, even those waiters will soften up.

greatest hits

- **"METAL ASPARAGUS," INDEED.** Lord knows the Eiffel Tower wasn't popular at first, but it's done pretty well for itself since then (p. 75).

- **PORT IN A STORM.** Foodies and gluttons alike shouldn't miss the Martiniquais fare at Chez Lucie. Shark and rum are on the menu—can you find a more nautical combination? (p. 112).

- **MONET MADNESS.** Wade among the lily pads of the celebrated painter's massive masterpiece Les Nymphéas at the Musée de l'Orangerie (p. 64).

- **MUSIC TO YOUR EARS:** Known as "Le VD" to the locals, Violin Dingue (Crazy Violin) has some of the cheapest happy hour drinks in Paris and is open until 5am. Play on (p. 138).

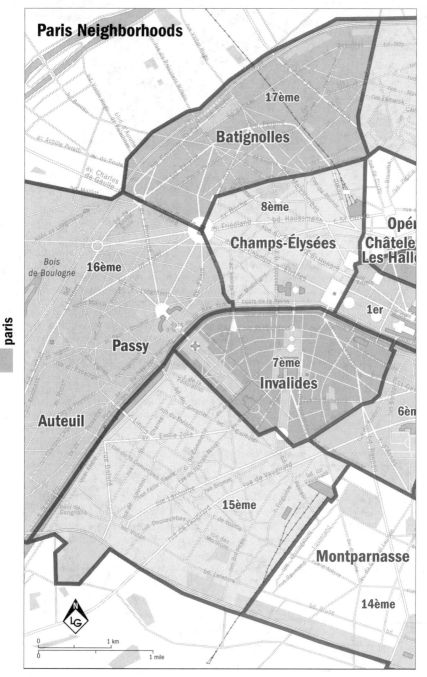

Paris Neighborhoods

17ème

Batignolles

8ème

Champs-Élysées

Opé

Châtele
Les Hall

Bois
de Boulogne   16ème

1er

Passy

7ème

Invalides

6èn

Auteuil

15ème

Montparnasse

14ème

0   1 km

0   1 mile

paris

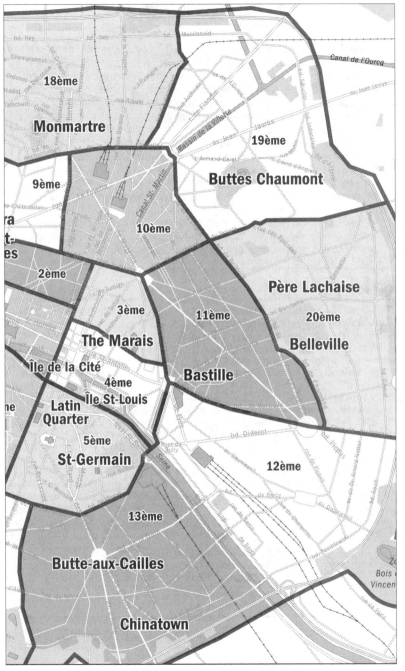

paris neighborhoods map

Students have been wandering the **Latin Quarter** and **St-Germain** in cap and gown since the 12th century, making Paris the world's second-oldest university town. Though the language of the Romans may no longer be spoken here, the city still teems with universities and deals aimed specially at drawing in student dollars, especially on the Left Bank. You might just find yourself stumbling back from **rue Mouffetard** after a series of happy hour specials and English trivia nights, but students fleeing the tourist-heavy areas of the city can also be found in the cheap brasseries and restaurants of **Montparnasse** and Southern Paris. Paris wouldn't be Paris, however, without a little youthful romance: when the sun sets, the banks of the Seine fill up with young Frenchies clutching bottles of wine and picnic blankets. Others gather on the marble staircase in front of **Sacre-Cœur,** which boasts spectacular views of Paris' monuments and hosts live music nightly during the summer. Throw away your images of pristine boulevards and suited waiters; modern student life in Paris is gritty, ethnically diverse, and often quite activist. If cooking classes and museum tours aren't really your thing, try volunteering with one of France's varied political parties; you may even meet the next Sarkozy.

orientation

paris

Despite all the invasions, revolutions, and riots throughout French history, Paris was still meticulously planned. The Seine River flows from east to west through the middle of the city, splitting it into two sections. The *Rive Gauche* (Left Bank) to the south is known as the intellectual heart of Paris, while the *Rive Droite* (Right Bank) to the north is famous for fashion, art, and commerce. The two islands in the middle of the Seine, the Île de la Cité and Île St-Louis, are the geographical and historical center of the city. The rest of Paris is divided into 20 *arrondissements* (districts) that spiral outward from the islands. These *arrondissements* are numbered; for example, the Eiffel Tower is located in *le septième* (the seventh), abbreviated 7ème.

If the simplicity of this layout sounds too good to be true, it is. Neighborhoods frequently spread over multiple *arrondissements* and are often referred to by name rather than number. The Marais, for example, is in both the 3ème and the 4ème. Neighborhood names are based on major connecting hubs of the Metro or train (Montparnasse, Bastille) or major landmarks and roads (Champs-Élysées, Invalides). Streets are marked on every corner, and numerous signs point toward train stations, landmarks, and certain *triomphant* roundabouts. You can try to walk through it all, but the size of the city is deceiving. So when your feet start to fall off, remember that buses and the subway go almost everywhere in the city, and your hostel is just a short ride away.

call me!

The phone code for Paris is ☎01.

ÎLE DE LA CITÉ AND ÎLE ST-LOUIS

Some 2000 years ago, the French monarchy claimed Les Îles as the geographic center of its kingdom as well as the governmental and royal seat of power. The islands were perfectly located and easily defendable in the middle of the Seine—think castles, drawbridges, fire-breathing **dragons**, and then don't because you're probably thinking of a bad *Shrek* sequel. Today, you can see how Paris grew outward, both physically expanding beyond the islands and politically distancing itself from the monarchy.

Île de la Cité, the larger of the two islands, is still considered the city's center and is home to Paris's *kilomètre zéro*, from which distances are measured and where France's major roads originate. Here you will find **Notre Dame** and the **Palais du Justice**, along with the obligatory daily onslaught of photo-snapping tourists. Most restaurants here are tourist traps, particularly the closer you get to Notre Dame, but it is possible to find a few hidden gems tucked in the nooks and crannies of this island. Although the physical center of the city sounds like an ideal place to stay, most accommodations are overpriced, and once the tourist traffic clears out after sunset, the islands tend to become uncomfortably quiet, with the exception of the plaza in front of Notre Dame. St-Louis, the quiet younger sister of the two islands, sits peacefully beside its impressive big brother and welcomes the wealthier tourists who are willing to drop a pretty penny on cheese and wine. The only Metro stop on the islands is in the center of Île de la Cité, but several other stops are located just across the bridges that connect the islands to the mainland of the city, including Paris' largest stop, Châtelet.

CHÂTELET-LES HALLES (1ER, 2ÈME)

Les Îles are the geographic center of the city, but, with the exception of the Eiffel Tower, Paris's 1er and 2ème arrondissements are the fountainhead from which everything flows. Most famously, the **Louvre** and **Les Halles** marketplace draw crowds from far and wide to Paris's belly button. Naturally, this area is tourist-heavy during the daytime, especially in the summer. Unfortunately, Les Halles and the Jardin des Halles have been under serious renovation and reconstruction since 2011 and are currently an unsightly block of cranes and concrete; the project is expected to be finished in bits and pieces through 2016. ⓂChâtelet-Les Halles is the city's main transportation hub and is located in the southeast corner of these neighborhoods; three RER and five Metro lines can be accessed between here and the two connecting stations, ⓂChâtelet and ⓂLes Halles. The ⓂOpéra stop is a prominent point in the northwest corner of the neighborhood, topped off by **boulevard Haussmann/ Montmartre/Poissonnière** and hugged in the east by **boulevard de Sébastopol.** The closer you are to the Louvre, the more likely prices are to be unnecessarily high, so make the effort to go a few blocks farther north, east, or west to get away from the loud crowds and equally annoying prices. **Rue St-Denis** runs parallel to bd de Sébastopol and is generally a dependable strip for good but pricey nightlife and more reasonable food and accommodation options.

THE MARAIS (3ÈME, 4ÈME)

The Marais embodies the ultimate ugly duckling tale. Originally a bog (*marais* means "marsh"), the area became livable in the 13th century when monks drained the land to build the **Right Bank.** When Henri IV constructed the glorious **place des Vosges** in the early 17th century, the area suddenly became the city's center of fashionable living, and luxury and scandal soon took hold. Royal haunts gave way to slums and tenements during the Revolution, and many of the grand *hôtels particuliers* fell into ruin or disrepair. In the 1950s, the Marais was revived and declared a historic neighborhood; since then, decades of gentrification and renovation have restored the Marais to its pre-Revolutionary glory. Once palatial mansions have become exquisite museums, and the tiny twisting streets are crowded with hip bars, avant-garde galleries, and one-of-a-kind boutiques.

Boulevard de Sébastopol divides the Marais from Les Halles in the west, while **Boulevard Bourdon** and **Boulevard Beaumarchais** cap the eastern end where they meet at **la Bastille.** The **Hôtel de Ville** is the iconic monument at the forefront of the area and is a good place to get your bearings once you've braved the Châtelet Metro stop. Today, the Marais is known as a center of Parisian diversity. **Rue des Rosiers,** in the heart of the 4ème, is the center of Paris's Jewish population, though the steady influx of hyper-hip clothing stores threatens its identity. Superb kosher delicatessens also neighbor Middle Eastern and Eastern European restaurants, and the Marais remains livelier on Sundays than the rest of the city. The Marais is unquestionably the GLBT center of Paris, with the community's hub at the intersection of **rue Sainte-Croix de la Brettonerie** and **rue Vieille du Temple.** Though the steady stream of tourists has begun to wear on the Marais's eclectic personality, the district continues to be a distinctive mix of old and new, queer and straight, cheap and chic.

LATIN QUARTER AND ST-GERMAIN (5ÈME, 6ÈME)

The Latin Quarter and St-Germain are two of Paris's primary tourist neighborhoods, second only to the areas around the Louvre, Notre Dame, and the Hôtel de Ville. The Latin Quarter, however, got its name from the many institutions of higher learning in the area, including the famous **Sorbonne,** where Latin scriptures and studies were more prevalent than kissing couples along the Seine. To this day, these neighborhoods—the Latin Quarter in particular—are the student hubs of Paris, mixing overpriced tourist traps with budget-friendly student hangouts. **Boulevard St-Michel** divides the two areas, with St-Germain to the west and the Latin Quarter to the east. Meanwhile, **Boulevard du Montparnasse** and **Boulevard de Port Royal** separate both areas from southern Paris, with the **Jardin du Luxembourg** and the **Panthéon** being the central icons of each *arrondissement.* As tempted as you may be to shell out your money in St-Germain-des-Prés, your wallet will thank you if you head to the 5ème and roam **rue Monge** and **rue Mouffetard** for affordable food, nightlife, and accommodations.

INVALIDES (7ÈME)

Given the plethora of museums and famous tourist attractions in the 7ème, this area is more of a day-trip destination for the budget traveler. The most outstanding landmark in Invalides (and all of Paris) is by far the **Eiffel Tower.** Looking over the 7ème from the west on the Seine, the **Champs de Mars** stretches southeast, covering the western end of this neighborhood. Moving east you will find Ⓜ**Invalides** on the northern end of the Esplanades des Invalides, which boasts a handful of museums, including the **Musée de l'Armée,** running north-south in the middle of the neighborhood. Continue east to find the **Musée d'Orsay** on the banks of the Seine. Starting at Ⓜ**Rue du Bac** and running south, bd Raspail divides the 7ème in the east from St-Germain in of the 5ème.

CHAMPS-ÉLYSÉES (8ÈME)

The Champs-Élysées is a whole other kind of Paris, where even the Metro stops seem to sparkle with glamor. This is the Paris where the daughters of American millionaires throw their bachelorette parties and where fashion moguls wipe their you-know-whats with only the finest of hand-woven silks. It's a fun place to window shop and daydream about the finer things in life, but the buck stops there.

Avenue des Champs-Élysées is the heart of this area, pumping life from the **Arc de Triomphe** through the rows of designer shops and out-of-this-world expensive restaurants and nightclubs. If you want to continue to immerse yourself in all the beautiful things you will probably never have, head for **Avenue Montaigne, rue du Faubourg St-Honoré,** or the side streets around **La Madeleine.** The #2 Metro line separates the 8ème from the 16ème in the north, but the closer you get to this area, the fewer tourists you will find.

OPÉRA (9ÈME) AND CANAL ST-MARTIN (10ÈME)

Although they follow the spiral pattern from the center of the city along with the other *arrondissements*, the 9ème and 10ème feel a bit ambiguously plopped in the middle of the *Rive Droite*. The 9ème can be particularly difficult to navigate, especially since its namesake Metro stop and tourist site, the Paris Opéra, is positioned at its southern tip rather than at the center. The 9ème is roughly surrounded by the #2 Metro line in the north along bd de Clichy, Gare St-Lazare in the west, and ⓂOpéra in the south. Navigating the Opéra neighborhood by Metro generally requires savvy maneuvering of the #12, 7, and 9 lines. The #7 runs under **rue Lafayette** which cuts Opéra on a diagonal, while **rue des Martyrs** runs almost due north-south through the center of the neighborhood, which is best explored on foot. Bd Haussman cuts through the southern portion of the area and tends to be Opéra's most lively area by night.

Right next to the 9ème, the 10ème is known (and named for) the **Canal Saint-Martin,** which runs along the eastern border of the *arrondissement*. Stray too far from this "mini-Seine" (i.e., anywhere west of bd Magenta) and you'll find yourself smack in the middle of the sketchy area that surrounds the **Gare du Nord** and **Gare de l'Est.** If the gun armories and cash-for-gold stores didn't give you a hint, we'll tell you now: stay clear of this area at night.

BASTILLE (11ÈME, 12ÈME)

The Bastille is home to the famous prison where the French Revolution kicked things off with a bang on July 14, 1789. A few centuries later, Parisians still storm this neighborhood nightly in search of the latest cocktails, culinary innovations, and up-and-coming musicians in the city. Five Metro lines converge at ⓂRépublique and ⓂNation, and three lines at ⓂBastille, making this district a busy transport hub. Although the area is still a bit worn around the edges, the Bastille is a neighborhood that is becoming increasingly known for its ethnic food, nightlife, and hot shopping. The highest concentration of all three is in the area between **rue de Charenton,** in the south of the 11ème, and **rue de la Roquette,** running northeast away from the Bastille. The Algerian community offers countless dining options at the **Place d'Aligre,** where the weekly outdoor market sets up. The **Viaduc des Arts** and **Promenade Plantée** (see **Sights**) will lead you toward the more expensive shops and galleries in the 12ème.

MONTPARNASSE AND SOUTHERN PARIS (13ÈME, 14ÈME, 15ÈME)

These three *arrondissements*, which make up nearly one-sixth of Paris, lack the photo-ops and famous sights that attract tourists elsewhere in the city. They do, however, tend to comprise Paris's so-called better half, where locals dominate the tourists and the pace of life is more relaxed. The neighborhoods spread east to west in ascending order, with Montparnasse somewhere in between the 14ème and 15ème in the area immediately surrounding the **Montparnasse Tower** and the **Cimetière du Montparnasse** in the 14ème. Your best mode of transportation between here will be the #6 Metro line, which runs aboveground along bd du Grenelle and bd Garibaldi on the northern edge of the 15ème, then cuts a bit farther down into the 14ème and 13ème along bd St-Jacques and bd Vincent. The 15ème and 14ème are divided by the train tracks that stem from the SNCF station behind the Montparnasse Tower, and **rue de la Santé** roughly divides the 14ème and the 13ème. The 13ème has a strange combination of characters thanks to **Chinatown,** nestled near rue de Tolbiac, and the small hippie enclave surrounding **rue de la Butte aux Cailles,** which avoids the capitalist drive to overcharge for meals or entertainment. The bank of the River Seine along the 13ème is home to a series of floating bars and restaurants, especially opposite the Parc de Bercy, though many travelers don't make it this far south or east.

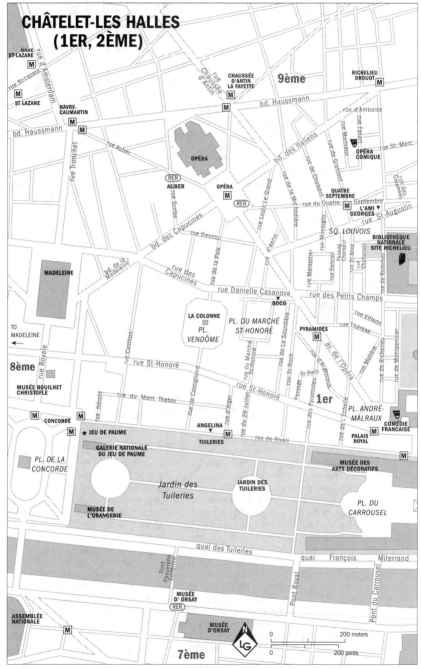

CHÂTELET-LES HALLES
(1ER, 2ÈME)

GARE
ST-LAZARE
Ⓜ

rue St-Lazare

Ⓜ
ST LAZARE

rue d'Amsterdam

rue Chaussée d'Antin

CHAUSSÉE
D'ANTIN
LA FAYETTE

9ème

RICHELIEU
DROUOT
Ⓜ

HAVRE-
CAUMARTIN
Ⓜ
Ⓜ

Ⓜ

bd. Haussmann

rue d'Amboise

rue Favart

rue Marivaux

OPÉRA
COMIQUE

rue St-Marc

bd. Haussmann

rue Auber

bd. des Italiens

rue de Gramont

rue Tronchet

rue Scribe

OPÉRA

rue de Choiseul

rue de la Michodière

QUATRE
SEPTEMBRE
rue du Quatre Septembre
Ⓜ
L'AMI ▼
GEORGES

rue des Colonnes

RER
AUBER

OPÉRA
Ⓜ
RER

rue Louis-le-Grand

rue St-Augustin

bd. des Capucines

rue Daunou

rue d'Antin

rue Monsigny

rue Ste-Anne

SQ. LOUVOIS

rue de Richelieu

BIBLIOTHÈQUE
NATIONALE
SITE RICHELIEU

MADELEINE

bd. de la Madeleine

rue des Capucines

rue de la Paix

rue Danielle Casanova

rue Marsollier

rue Dalayrac

Passage Choiseul

rue Chabanais

rue des Petits Champs

BOCO

rue Villedo

TO
MADELEINE
◄

8ème

rue Royale

LA COLONNE
■
PL.
VENDÔME

PL. DU MARCHÉ
ST-HONORÉ

PYRAMIDES
Ⓜ

rue Thérèse

rue de Montpensier

MUSÉE BOUILHET
CHRISTOFLE

rue Cambon

rue St-Honoré

rue du Marché St-Honoré

rue de la Sourdière

av. de l'Opéra

rue Ste-Anne

rue de Richelieu

rue du Mont Thabor

rue de Castiglione

rue St-Honoré

rue St-Roch

Passage St-Roch

rue des Pyramides

1er

PL. ANDRÉ-
MALRAUX

COMÉDIE
FRANCAISE

Ⓜ
CONCORDE
Ⓜ

rue d'Alger

rue du 29 Juillet

rue de l'Échelle

PALAIS
ROYAL

rue Hérold

ANGELINA
▼
Ⓜ

rue de Rivoli

Ⓜ

★ JEU DE PAUME

TUILERIES

PL. DE LA
CONCORDE

GALERIE NATIONALE
DU JEU DE PAUME

MUSÉE DES
ARTS DÉCORATIFS

Jardin des
Tuileries

JARDIN DES
TUILERIES

MUSÉE DE
L'ORANGERIE

PL. DU
CARROUSEL

quai des Tuileries

quai   François   Miterrand

Pont Passerelle Solférino

Pont Royal

Pont du Carrousel

MUSÉE
D'ORSAY
RER

ASSEMBLÉE
NATIONALE
Ⓜ

MUSÉE
D'ORSAY

N
LG

0   200 meters
0   200 yards

7ème

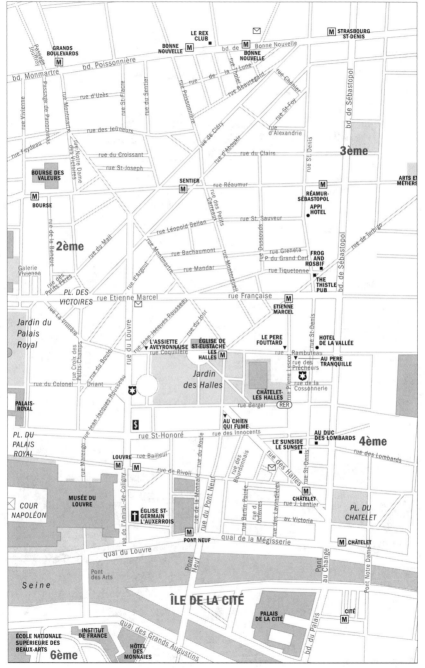

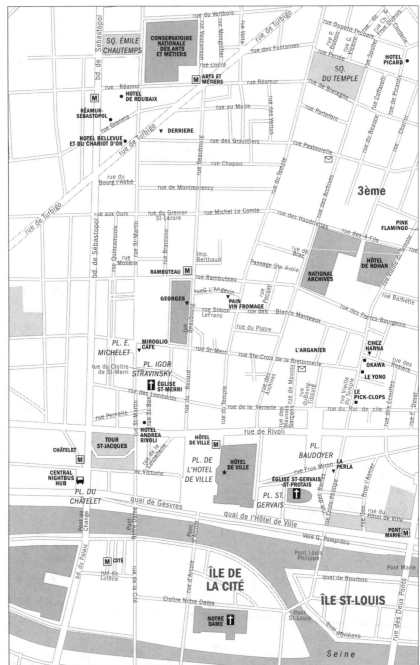

paris

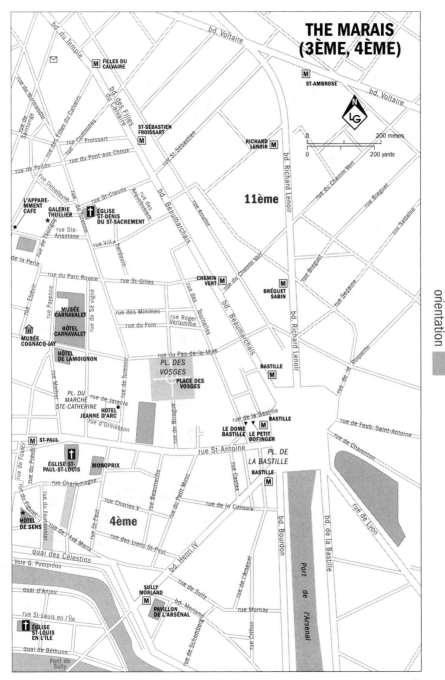

THE MARAIS (3ÈME, 4ÈME)

orientation

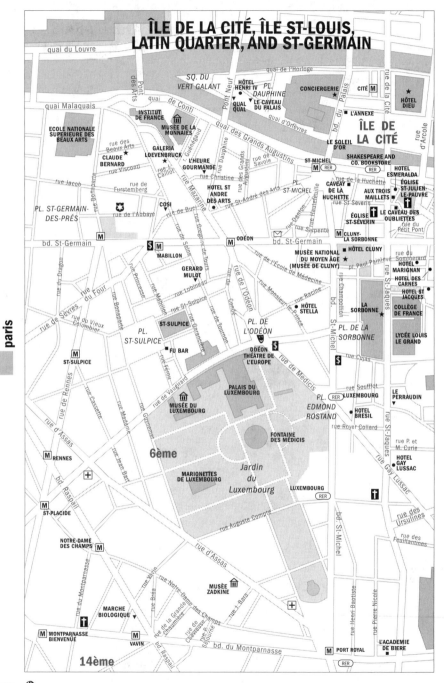

ÎLE DE LA CITÉ, ÎLE ST-LOUIS, LATIN QUARTER, AND ST-GERMAIN

quai du Louvre

quai de l'Horloge

SQ. DU VERT GALANT

HÔTEL HENRI IV

PL. DAUPHINE

CONCIERGERIE

CITÉ M

HÔTEL DIEU

Pont des Arts

quai de Conti

Pont Neuf

QUAI QUAL

LE CAVEAU DU PALAIS

bd. du Palais

rue de la Cité

quai Malaquais

INSTITUT DE FRANCE

quai d'Orfèvres

L'ANNEXE

ÎLE DE LA CITÉ

rue d'Arcole

ECOLE NATIONALE SUPÉRIEURE DES BEAUX ARTS

MUSÉE DE LA MONNAIES

quai des Grands Augustins

LE SOLEIL D'OR

rue des Beaux-Arts

GALERIA LOEVENBRUCK

SHAKESPEARE AND CO. BOOKSTORE

CLAUDE BERNARD

L'HEURE GOURMANDE

rue de Christine

rue de Savoie

ST-MICHEL M RER

RER

HOTEL ESMERALDA

rue Visconti

rue Jacob

rue de Furstemberg

HÔTEL ST ANDRE DES ARTS

PL. ST-MICHEL

rue de la Huchette

CAVEAU DE LA HUCHETTE

AUX TROIS MAILLETS

ÉGLISE ST-JULIEN-LE-PAUVRE

COSI

rue de Buci

rue St-André-des-Arts

rue St-Séverin

ÉGLISE ST-SÉVERIN

LE CAVEAU DES OUBLIETTES

PL. ST-GERMAIN-DES-PRÉS

rue de l'Abbaye

rue Danton

rue Serpente

CLUNY-LA SORBONNE

rue du Petit Pont

bd. St-Germain

M

ODÉON

bd. St-Germain

M

MABILLON

MUSÉE NATIONAL DU MOYEN ÂGE (MUSÉE DE CLUNY)

HÔTEL CLUNY

rue du Sommerard

HOTEL MARIGNAN

GERARD MULOT

rue de l'École de Médecine

pl. Paul Painlevé

HOTEL DES CARNES

HOTEL ST JACQUES

rue Monsieur-le-Prince

rue Racine

LA SORBONNE

COLLÈGE DE FRANCE

HÔTEL STELLA

ST-SULPICE

PL. DE L'ODÉON

PL. DE LA SORBONNE

LYCÉE LOUIS LE GRAND

PL. ST-SULPICE

FU BAR

ODÉON THÉÂTRE DE L'EUROPE

rue de Médicis

rue Cujas

M ST-SULPICE

rue de Vaugirard

PALAIS DU LUXEMBOURG

rue Soufflot

LUXEMBOURG RER

LE PERRAUDIN

MUSÉE DU LUXEMBOURG

PL. EDMOND ROSTAND

HOTEL BRESIL

rue Royer-Collard

FONTAINE DES MÉDICIS

rue P. et M. Curie

HOTEL GAY LUSSAC

M RENNES

6ème

Jardin du Luxembourg

rue Gay Lussac

MARIONETTES DE LUXEMBOURG

LUXEMBOURG RER

M ST-PLACIDE

NOTRE-DAME DES CHAMPS M

rue d'Assas

rue des Ursulines

rue des Feuillantines

bd. St-Michel

MUSÉE ZADKINE

MARCHE BIOLOGIQUE

MONTPARNASSE BIENVENUE

VAVIN

bd. du Montparnasse

M PORT ROYAL

RER

L'ACADEMIE DE BIERE

14ème

paris

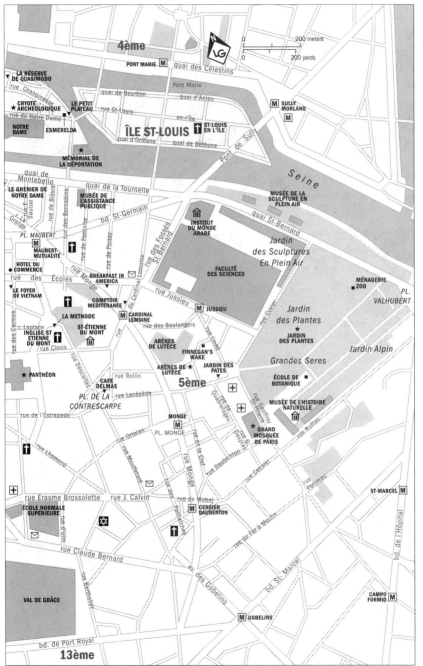

4ème

PONT MARIE Ⓜ quai des Célestins

0   200 meters
0   200 yards

▼ LA RÉSERVE
DE QUASIMODO
rue Chanoinesse

Pont Marie

quai de Bourbon

quai d'Anjou

Ⓜ SULLY
MORLAND

★ CRYOTÉ
ARCHÉOLOGIQUE   ▪ LE PETIT
PLATEAU   rue St-Louis

rue du Notre Dame

en-l'île

Ⓜ

NOTRE
DAME   ▪ ESMERALDA

ÎLE ST-LOUIS   ✝ ST-LOUIS
EN L'ÎLE

quai d'Orléans   quai de Béthune

Seine

★ MÉMORIAL DE
LA DÉPORTATION

quai de
Montebello

quai de la Tournelle

MUSÉE DE LA
SCULPTURE EN ▪
PLEIN AIR

LE GRENIER DE ●
NOTRE DAME

rue de Poissy

rue des Bernardins

MUSÉE DE
L'ASSISTANCE
PUBLIQUE

bd. St-Germain

quai St-Bernard

rue de Pontoise

🏛 INSTITUT
DU MONDE
ARABE

Jardin
des Sculptures
En Plein Air

PL. MAUBERT

Ⓜ MAUBERT
MUTUALITÉ   ✝

rue de Bièvre

rue des Fossés
St-Bernard

FACULTÉ
DES SCIENCES

MÉNAGERIE
▪ ZOO

HOTEL DU ●
COMMERCE

rue   des   Écoles

▼ LE FOYER
DE VIETNAM

BREAKFAST IN ▪
AMERICA

rue du Cardinal Lemoine

rue Jussieu

Ⓜ JUSSIEU

rue Cuvier

PL.
VALHUBERT

COMPTOIR ▪
MÉDITÉRANÉE   ✝

rue Monge

Ⓜ CARDINAL
LEMOINE

Jardin
des Plantes

LA MÉTHODE

ST-ÉTIENNE
DU MONT

rue des Boulangers

★ JARDIN
DES PLANTES

INGLISE ST
ETIENNE
DU MONT   ✝

rue des Carmes

🏛

Jardin Alpin

rue Clovis

ARÈNES DE
LUTÈCE

rue Linné

rue Descartes

▪ FINNEGAN'S
WAKE

Grandes Seres

★ PANTHÉON

CAFÉ
DELMAS

rue Rollin

ARÈNES DE ★
LUTÈCE

JARDIN DES
PÂTES ▼

5ème

ÉCOLE DE ▪
BOTANIQUE

PL. DE LA
CONTRESCARPE

rue Lacépède

✚

rue de l'Estrapade

rue Ortolan

MONGE
Ⓜ
PL. MONGE

rue de la Clef

rue Geoffroy
St-Hilaire

rue Quatrefages

✚

MUSÉE DE L'HISTOIRE ▪
NATURELLE

🏛

rue Buffon

✝

rue Lhomond

rue Mouffetard

rue Monge

★ GRAND
MOSQUÉE
DE PARIS

rue Daubenton

rue du Fer à Moulin

rue de Mirbel

rue des Patriarches

✉

rue Erasme Brossolette   rue J. Calvin

✝ CENSIER
DAUBENTON

ÉCOLE NORMALE
SUPÉRIEURE

✚

rue d'Ulm

✡

✝

rue Censier

rue Poliveau

ST-MARCEL Ⓜ

bd. de l'Hôpital

rue Claude Bernard

rue Berthollet

av. des Gobelins

bd. St-Marcel

CAMPO
FORMIO Ⓜ

VAL DE GRÂCE

Ⓜ GOBELINS

bd. de Port Royal

13ème

orientation

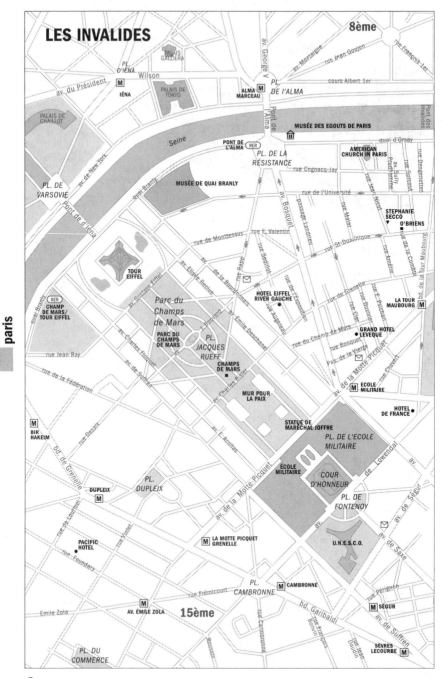

LES INVALIDES

8ème

PALAIS GALLIERA

PL. D'IENA

av. du Président Wilson

PALAIS DE TOKYO

IÉNA M

PALAIS DE CHAILLOT

av. de New-York

Seine

PL. DE VARSOVIE

Pont de d'Iéna

quai Branly

TOUR EIFFEL

RER CHAMP DE MARS/ TOUR EIFFEL

rue Jean Ray

rue de la Fédération

M BIR HAKEIM

bd. de Grenelle

rue Desaix

DUPLEIX M

PL. DUPLEIX

rue du Lourmel

rue Viollet

PACIFIC HOTEL

rue Foundary

Emile Zola

M AV. ÉMILE ZOLA

15ème

PL. DU COMMERCE

av. George V

av. de Mortagne

rue Jean-Goujon

rue François 1er

PL. D'IENA

cours Albert 1er

ALMA MARCEAU M

PL. DE l'ALMA

Pont de l'Alma

Pont des Invalides

MUSÉE DES EGOUTS DE PARIS

quai d'Orsay

PONT DE L'ALMA RER

PL. DE LA RÉSISTANCE

AMERICAN CHURCH IN PARIS

av. Cognacq-Jay

rue Sully Prudhomme

rue Surcout

rue des Desgenettes

MUSÉE DE QUAI BRANLY

rue de l'Université

rue Jean-Nicot

av. Bosquet

STEPHANIE SECCO

O'BRIENS

rue de Montessuy

rue E. Valentin

rue du Sedillot

av. Rapp

av. de la Bourdonnais

rue Cler

rue St-Dominique

rue Amélie

rue de Grenelle

bd. de la Tour Maubourg

LA TOUR MAUBOURG M

HOTEL EIFFEL RIVER GAUCHE

av. Elisée-Reclus

av. Gustave Eiffel

av. de Suffren

av. Charles Floquet

av. Joseph Bouvard

av. Emile-Deschanel

av. de l'Exposition

rue du Champ-de-Mars

rue de Grenelle

GRAND HOTEL LEVEQUE

av. de la Motte-Picquet

Pass. de la Vierge

rue de la Vierge

Parc du Champs de Mars

PARC DU CHAMPS DE MARS

PL. JACQUES RUEFF

CHAMPS DE MARS

av. Charles Risler

MUR POUR LA PAIX

av. E. Acollas

STATUE DE MARECHAL JOFFRE

M ECOLE MILITAIRE

HOTEL DE FRANCE

PL. DE L'ECOLE MILITAIRE

ÉCOLE MILITAIRE

COUR D'HONNEUR

PL. DE FONTENOY

av. de Lowendal

av. de Ségur

av. de Saxe

av. de la Motte-Picquet

M LA MOTTE PICQUET GRENELLE

U.N.E.S.C.O.

PL. CAMBRONNE

M CAMBRONNE

rue Frémicourt

bd. Garibaldi

rue Pétignon

M SÉGUR

av. de Suffren

rue Cambronne

rue François Bonvin

rue Jean Daudin

SÈVRES LECOURBE M

paris

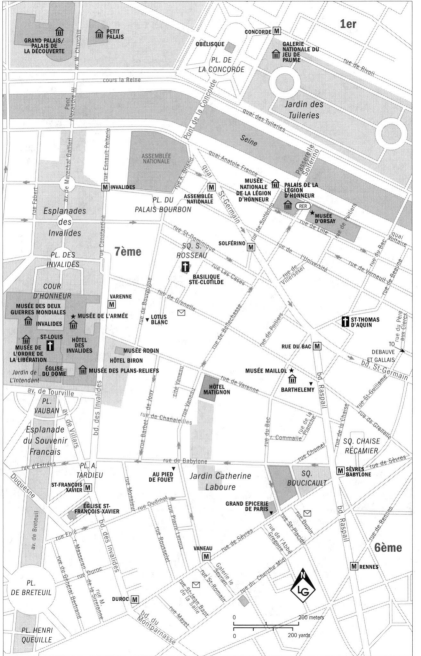

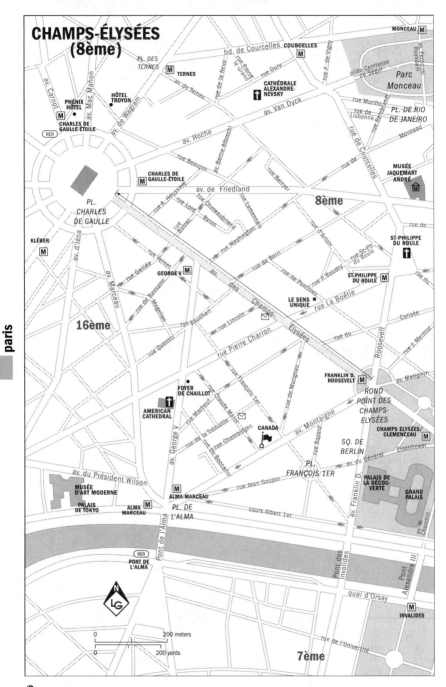

CHAMPS-ÉLYSÉES (8ème)

MONCEAU Ⓜ

bd. de Courcelles   COURCELLES Ⓜ

PL. DES TERNES   TERNES Ⓜ

av. de Ternes

Parc Monceau

av. Carnot

av. Mac Mahon

PHÉNIX HÔTEL Ⓜ
HÔTEL TROYON

CHARLES DE GAULLE-ÉTOILE RER

av. de Wagram

rue de la Neva
rue Pierre le Grand
rue Daru

CATHÉDRALE ALEXANDRE-NEVSKY

rue P. de Vigny

allée Comtesse de Ségur

av. de la Faisanderie

av. Van Dyck

av. Hoche

rue de Lisbonne
rue de Monceau

PL. DE RIO DE JANEIRO

rue Murillo

av. de Messine

Monceau

CHARLES DE GAULLE-ÉTOILE Ⓜ

rue Beaujon

rue de Berri Albrecht

rue Balzar

MUSÉE JAQUEMART ANDRÉ 🏛

PL. CHARLES DE GAULLE

av. de Friedland

8ème

KLÉBER Ⓜ

av. d'Iéna

av. Marceau

rue A. Houssaye
rue Lord Byron
rue Chateaubriand
rue Washington
rue la Tremoille

ST-PHILIPPE DU ROULE 🕆

rue de

rue Galilée
rue Vernet

GEORGE V Ⓜ

rue de Bassano

av. des Champs-Élysées

rue de Berri

rue de Ponthieu

rue de P. Boudry

rue St-Ph. du Roule

ST-PHILIPPE DU ROULE Ⓜ

rue La Boétie

16ème

rue de Magellan

rue Quentin

rue Bauchart

rue Lincoln

rue Pierre Charron

LE SENS UNIQUE ■ ✉

rue du

av. de Friedland

Colisée

rue J. Mermoz

FRANKLIN D. ROOSEVELT Ⓜ

av. Matignon

FOYER DE CHAILLOT

rue François 1er

rue Marbeuf
rue Clauda-Mesnil

rue du Colisée

rue de la Tremoille

rue Chambiges

rue du Bocador

CANADA ⚑

rue Jean Goujon

av. Montaigne

av. Bayard

ROND POINT DES CHAMPS-ÉLYSÉES

CHAMPS ELYSÉES/ CLEMENCEAU Ⓜ

Eisenhower

AMERICAN CATHEDRAL 🕆

av. George V

SQ. DE BERLIN

PL. FRANÇOIS 1ER

av. du Général

Eisenhower

av. du Président Wilson

MUSÉE D'ART MODERNE

PALAIS DE TOKYO

ALMA MARCEAU Ⓜ

ALMA-MARCEAU Ⓜ

PL. DE L'ALMA

cours Albert 1er

av. Franklin D. Roosevelt

PALAIS DE LA DÉCOUVERTE

GRAND PALAIS

av. W. Churchill

Pont de l'Alma

RER
PONT DE L'ALMA

Pont des Invalides

quai d'Orsay

Pont Alexandre III

INVALIDES Ⓜ

paris

N
LG

0   200 meters
0   200 yards

7ème

rue de l'Université

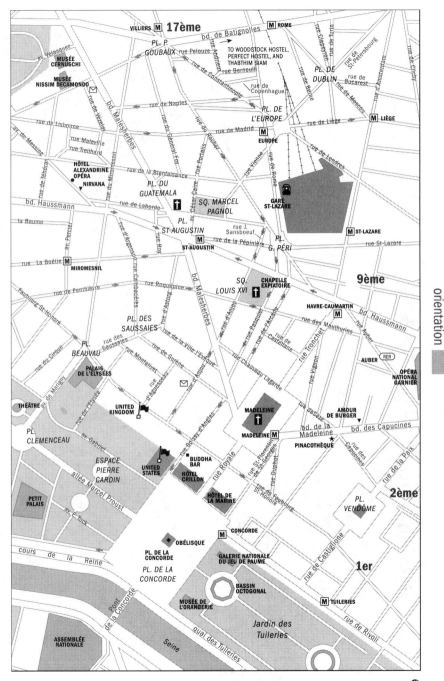

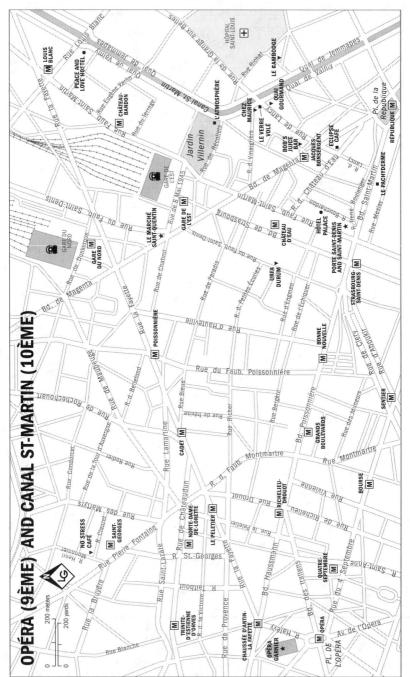

OPÉRA (9ÈME) AND CANAL ST-MARTIN (10ÈME)

paris

0 200 meters
0 200 yards

Ⓜ LOUIS BLANC

PEACE AND LOVE HOSTEL ●

Ⓜ CHÂTEAU-LANDON

Rue Louis Blanc

Quai de Valmy

Rue du Faub. Saint-Martin

Rue Eugène Varlin

Rue des Récollets

Quai de Jemmapes

HÔPITAL SAINT-LOUIS ✚

Rue Bichat

LE CAMBODGE ▶

QUAI GOURMAND ■

ATMOSPHÈRE ■

CHEZ MAURICE ▶

LE VERRE VOLÉ ▶

Rue de Lancry

Quai de Jemmapes

Pl. la République

Ⓜ RÉPUBLIQUE

Canal St. Martin

Jardin Villemin

BOB'S JUICE BAR ■

JACQUES BONSERGENT **Ⓜ**

ECLIPSE CAFÉ ■

R. d. Vinaigriers

R. du Château d'Eau

Bd. de Magenta

GARE DE L'EST **𝄞**

GARE DE L'EST **Ⓜ**

Rue du 8 Mai 1945

LE MARCHÉ SAINT-QUENTIN ★

Rue du Faub. Saint-Denis

GARE DU NORD **𝄞**

GARE DU NORD **Ⓜ**

Rue de Chabrol

Bd. de Strasbourg

CHÂTEAU D'EAU **Ⓜ**

Rue du Château d'Eau

HOTEL PALACE ●

PORTE SAINT-DENIS AND SAINT-MARTIN ★

Rue Boulenger

LE PACHYDERME ■

Bd. Saint-Martin

Bd. de Magenta

Rue de Dunkerque

Rue du Faub. Saint-Denis

Rue de Paradis

R. d. Petites Écuries

URFA DURUM ▶

Rue d'Enghien

Rue de l'Échiquier

STRASBOURG-SAINT-DENIS **Ⓜ**

Bd. de Magenta

Ⓜ POISSONNIÈRE

Rue La Fayette

Rue d'Hauteville

Rue du Faub. Poissonnière

BONNE NOUVELLE **Ⓜ**

Rue de Cléry

Rue d'Aboukir

Rue du Faub. Poissonnière

Rue Bleue

Rue de Trévise

Rue Richer

Rue Bergère

Bd. Poissonnière

GRANDS BOULEVARDS **Ⓜ**

SENTIER **Ⓜ**

Rue des Jeuneurs

Bd. de Magenta

Rue de Maubeuge

Rue de Belzunce

R. d. Petits-Hôtels

Rue de Rochechouart

Rue de Maubeuge

Rue Condorcet

Rue de la Tour-d'Auvergne

Rue Rodier

CADET **Ⓜ**

Rue Lamartine

Rue Montmartre

GRANDS BOULEVARDS

BOURSE **Ⓜ**

Rue Vivienne

Rue de Richelieu

RICHELIEU-DROUOT **Ⓜ**

Rue Drouot

Rue de Richelieu

Rue des Martyrs

NO STRESS CAFÉ ▶

SAINT-GEORGES **Ⓜ**

R. Clauzel

R. Henri Monnier

Rue Pierre Fontaine

Rue de Châteaudun

NOTRE-DAME-DE-LORETTE **Ⓜ**

LE PELETIER **Ⓜ**

Rue le Peletier

Rue Laffitte

Rue de la Victoire

Rue de Provence

Rue La Fayette

R. St.-Georges

Rue Saint-Lazare

Rue Taitbout

Rue de la Chaussée-d'Antin

Bd. Haussmann

Bd. des Italiens

QUATRE-SEPTEMBRE **Ⓜ**

Rue du 4 Septembre

Rue Sainte-Anne

Rue de la Bruyère

Rue Blanche

TRINITÉ-D'ESTIENNE D'ORVES **Ⓜ**

CHAUSSÉE D'ANTIN-LA FAYETTE **Ⓜ**

OPÉRA GARNIER ▰

OPÉRA **Ⓜ**

R. Halévy

PL. DE L'OPÉRA

OPÉRA **Ⓜ**

Av. de l'Opéra

BASTILLE (11ÈME)

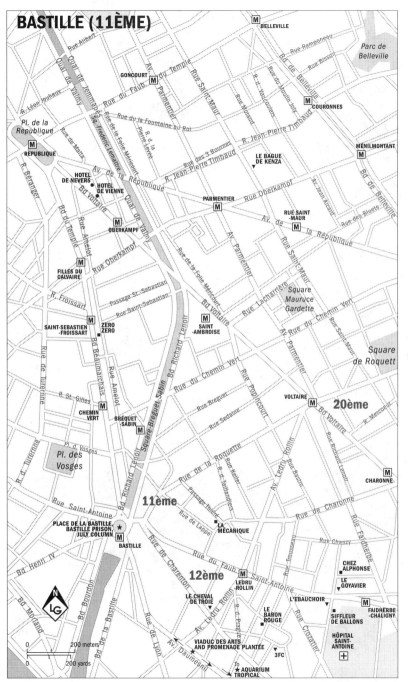

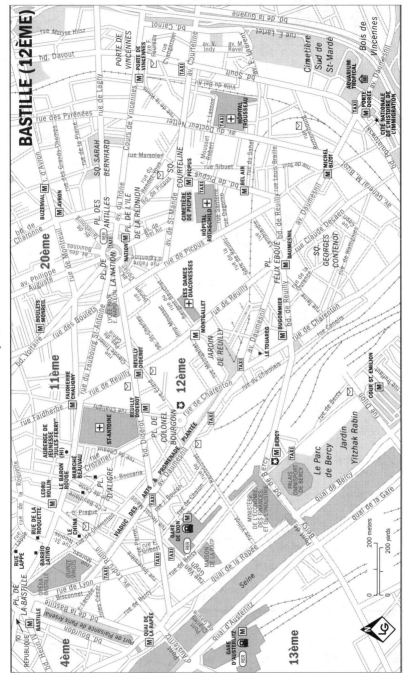

BASTILLE (12ÈME)

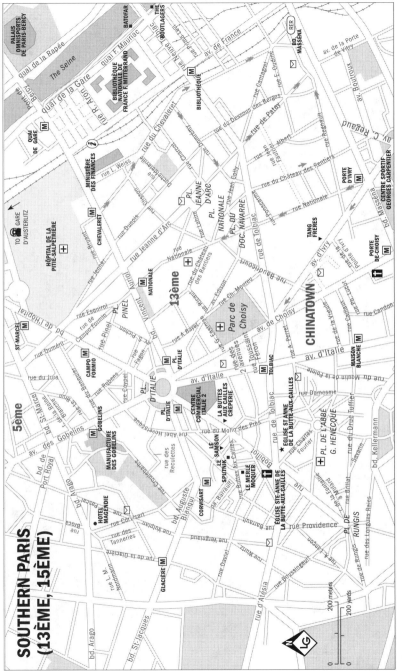

SOUTHERN PARIS (13ÈME, 15ÈME)

MONTPARNASSE (14ÈME)

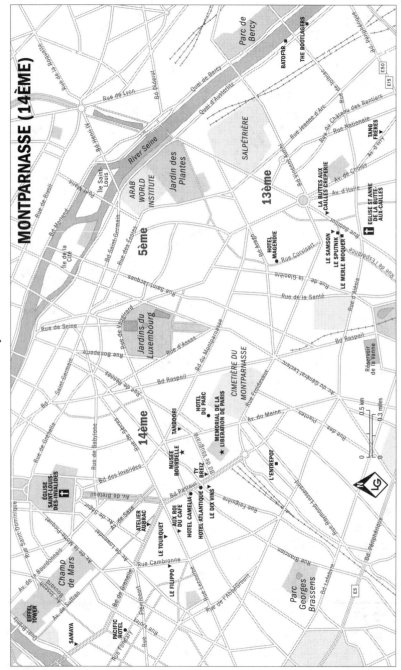

Parc de Bercy

THE BOOTLAGERS ■
BATOFAR ■

Quai de Bercy

Bd. Diderot

Rue de Lyon

Quai d'Austerlitz

River Seine

Rue de Rivoli

Bd. Henri IV

Pont Marie

Île Saint Louis

Bd. Morland

Île de la Cité

Pont de la Tournelle

Rue de la Harpe

Bd. Saint-Germain

Rue des Écoles

ARAB WORLD INSTITUTE

Jardin des Plantes

SALPÉTRIÈRE

13ème

Rue Jeanne d'Arc

Rue du Château des Rentiers

Rue Nationale

TANG FRERES ▼

Av. de Choisy

Av. d'Italie

LA BUTTES AUX CAILLES CREPERIE ▶

ÉGLISE ST ANNE DE LA BUTTE AUX-CAILLES

5ème

Rue Saint-Jacques

Rue Corvisart

HOTEL MAGENDIE ●

Bd. Arago

LE SAMSON ● LE SPUTNIK ▶ LE MERLE MOQUER ■

Rue de la Glacière

Rue de la Santé

Rue d'Alésia

Rue de Seine

Rue de Vaugirard

Jardins du Luxembourg

Rue d'Assas

Bd. du Montparnasse

Bd. Raspail

Rue de Rennes

Bd. Raspail

Réservoir de la Vanne

CIMETIÈRE DU MONTPARNASSE

Rue Froidevaux

Av. du Général Leclerc

HOTEL DU PARC ●

MÉMORIAL DE LA LIBERATION DE PARIS ★

Av. du Maine

Rue des Plantes

TANDOORI ▶

MUSÉE BOURDELLE ●

TY BREIZ ▶

Bd. de Grenelle

Rue de Babylone

Bd. des Invalides

Av. de Breteuil

Av. de Saxe

ÉGLISE SAINT-LOUIS DES-INVALIDES

AUX ROI DU CAFÉ ●

HOTEL CAMELIA ●

HOTEL ATLANTIQUE ●

LE DIX VINS ▶

L'ENTREPOT ●

Rue Falguière

Rue Raymond Losserand

ATELIER AUBRAC ●

LE TOURQUET ▶

Rue Cambronne

LE FILIPPO ▶

Champ de Mars

Av. de la Bourdonnais

Av. de Suffren

Av. de la Motte-Picquet

EIFFEL TOWER

SAMAYA ▼

PACIFIC HOTEL ●

Rue Volta

Rue Fondary

Parc Georges Brassens

Rue de l'Abbé Groult

Rue Blanche

Bd. Lefebvre

0.5 km

0.3 miles

0

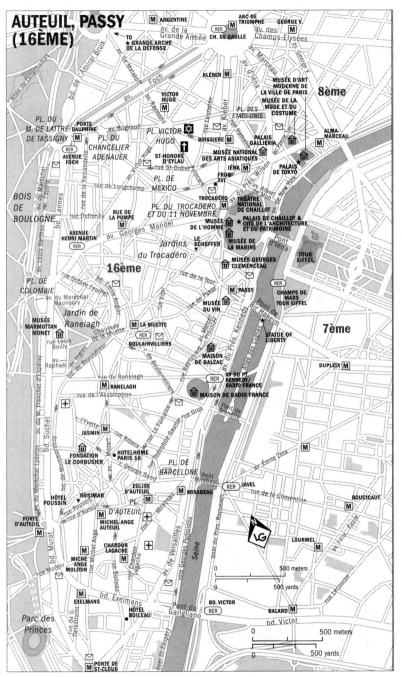

AUTEUIL, PASSY (16ÈME)

8ème

7ème

16ème

BOIS DE BOULOGNE

Jardins du Trocadéro

Jardin de Ranelagh

Parc des Princes

TO ★ GRANDE ARCHE DE LA DÉFENSE

ARGENTINE Ⓜ
av. de la Grande Armée
ARC DE TRIOMPHE
CH. DE GAULLE RER
GEORGE V. Ⓜ
av. des Champs-Elysées

KLÉBER Ⓜ
MUSÉE D'ART MODERNE DE LA VILLE DE PARIS
MUSÉE DE LA MODE ET DU COSTUME

VICTOR HUGO Ⓜ
PL. DES ETATS-UNIS
PALAIS GALLIERA

PL. DU M. DE LATTRE DE TASSIGNY
PORTE DAUPHINE Ⓜ
av. Bugeaud
PL. DU CHANCELIER ADENAUER
PL. VICTOR HUGO ✡
BOISSIÈRE Ⓜ
ALMA-MARCEAU Ⓜ

RER
AVENUE FOCH
ST-HONORÉ D'EYLAU
rue St-Didier
MUSÉE NATIONAL DES ARTS ASIATIQUES
IÉNA Ⓜ
PALAIS DE TOKYO

rue de Longchamp
PL. DE MEXICO
FROG XVI
TROCADÉRO Ⓜ
THÉÂTRE NATIONAL DE CHAILLOT

RUE DE LA POMPE
rue Dufrenoy
PL. DU TROCADÉRO ET DU 11 NOVEMBRE
av. Georges Mandel
MUSÉE DE L'HOMME
PALAIS DE CHAILLOT & CITÉ DE L'ARCHITECTURE ET DU PATRIMOINE

AVENUE HENRI MARTIN RER
LE SCHEFFER
MUSÉE DE LA MARINE
Pont d'Iéna
TOUR EIFFEL

PL. DE COLOMBIE
rue Octave Feuillet
av. du Maréchal Maunoury
MUSÉE GEORGES CLÉMENCEAU
PASSY Ⓜ
CHAMPS DE MARS TOUR EIFFEL

MUSÉE MARMOTTAN MONET
rue Louis Boilly
MUSÉE DU VIN
STATUE OF LIBERTY

LA MUETTE Ⓜ
RER
BOULAINVILLIERS
MAISON DE BALZAC
DUPLEIX Ⓜ

rue du Ranelagh
RANELAGH Ⓜ
rue de l'Assomption
AV. DU PT KENNEDY/ RADIO FRANCE RER
MAISON DE RADIO FRANCE

r. l'Yvette
JASMIN Ⓜ
Pont de Grenelle

FONDATION LE CORBUSIER
HOTELHOME PARIS 16
PL. DE BARCELONE
Pont Mirabeau
JAVEL RER
rue de la Convention
BOUCICAUT Ⓜ

ÉGLISE D'AUTEUIL
ROSIMAR
HÔTEL POUSSIN
PL. D'AUTEUIL
MIRABEAU Ⓜ

PORTE D'AUTEUIL Ⓜ
MICHEL-ANGE AUTEUIL
av. Émile Zola Ⓜ
LOURMEL Ⓜ

CHARDON LAGACHE
MICHE ANGE MOLITOR Ⓜ
av. Georges Pompidou
Seine

EXELMANS Ⓜ
bd. Exelmans
HÔTEL BOILEAU
Pont du Garigliano
BD. VICTOR RER
BALARD Ⓜ
bd. Victor

PORTE DE ST-CLOUD Ⓜ

0 500 meters
0 500 yards

orientation

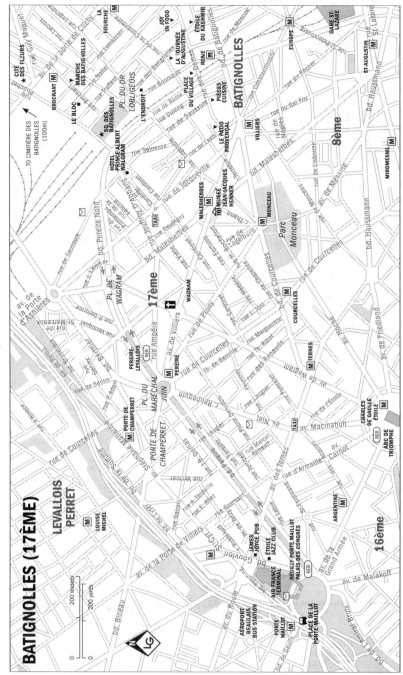

BATIGNOLLES (17ÈME)

LEVALLOIS PERRET

BATIGNOLLES

17ème

8ème

16ème

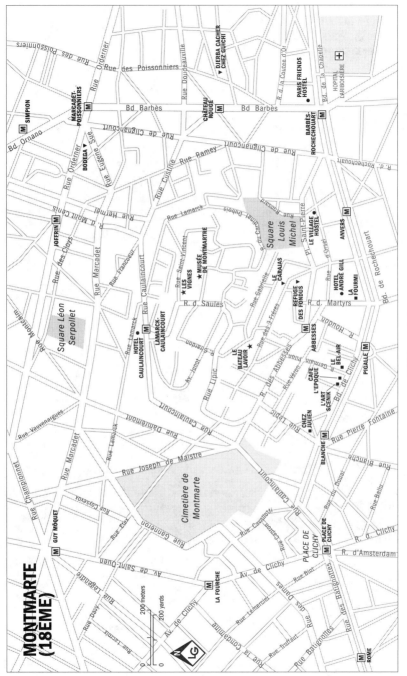

MONTMARTE (18EME)

Rue des Poissonniers
Rue des Poissonniers
Rue Ordener
Rue Doudeauville
DJERBA CACHER CHEZ GUICHI ▸
R. de la Goutte d'Or
PARIS FRIENDS HOSTEL ●
Bd. de la Chapelle
HOPITAL LARIBOISIÈRE ✛

SIMPION M
MARCADET-POISSONNIERS M
Bd Barbès
CHÂTEAU ROUGE M
Bd Barbès
BARBÈS-ROCHECHOUART M

Bd Ornano
Rue de Chateauville
Rue Ordener
BODEGA ▸
Rue Eugène Sue
Rue de Clignancourt
Rue de Clignancourt
R. de Rochechouart

Rue Custine
Rue Ramey

JOFFRIN M
R. du Mont Cenis
Rue Hermel
Rue des Cloys
Rue Marcadet
Rue Francoeur
Rue Lamarck
Impasse Dubois
R. du Chevalier de la Barre
Square Louis Michel
Rue Lamarck
rue Poulbot
Rue Saint-Pierre
LE VILLAGE HOSTEL ●
ANVERS M
Bd. de Rochechouart

Square Léon Serpollet
Rue Marcadet
Rue Caulaincourt
Rue Lamarck
R. de Saules
Rue Saint-Vincent
✭ LES VIGNES
✭ MUSÉE DE MONTMARTRE
Rue Gabrielle
LE CARJAS ✭
REFUGE DES FONDUS ▸
Rue d'Orsel
HOTEL ANDRÉ GILL ●
LA FOURMI ●
R. d. Martyrs

Rue du Mont-Cenis
HOTEL CAULAINCOURT ●
LAMARCK-CAULAINCOURT M
Av. Junot
Impasse G. Bratton
Rue Lepic
Rue des 3-Frères
LE BATEAU LAVOIR ✭
Rue des Abbesses
Rue Germain Pilon
Bd. de Clichy
ABBESSES M
Bd. de Clichy
PIGALLE M

Rue Vauvenargues
Rue Caulaincourt
Rue Damrémont
Rue Caulaincourt
Rue Véron
Rue Germain
CAFE L'ÉPOQUE ●
L'ART SCÉNIK ■
LE BEL-AIR ■
Rue Pierre Fontaine

Rue Championnet
Rue Marcadet
Rue Lamarck
Rue Joseph de Maistre
Rue Lepic
CHEZ JULIEN ●
BLANCHE M
Rue Blanche

GUY MOQUET M
Rue Coysevox
Rue Etex
Rue Ganneron
Cimetière de Montmarte
Rue Caulaincourt
Rue Cavallotti
Rue du Douai
Rue Ballu

Rue Montcalm
Av. de Clichy
Rue Vaugirard-St-Ouen
LA FOURCHE M
Av. de Clichy
PLACE DE CLICHY
PLACE DE CLICHY M
R. d'Amsterdam
R. d. Clichy

Rue Legendre
Rue Dautancourt
Rue Lamandé
Rue la Condamine
Av. de Clichy
Rue Lemercier
Rue Biot
Rue Truffaut
Rue des Dames
Rue des Batignolles
ROME M

200 meters
200 yards
0
0

orientation

www.letsgo.com **Ꝑ 37**

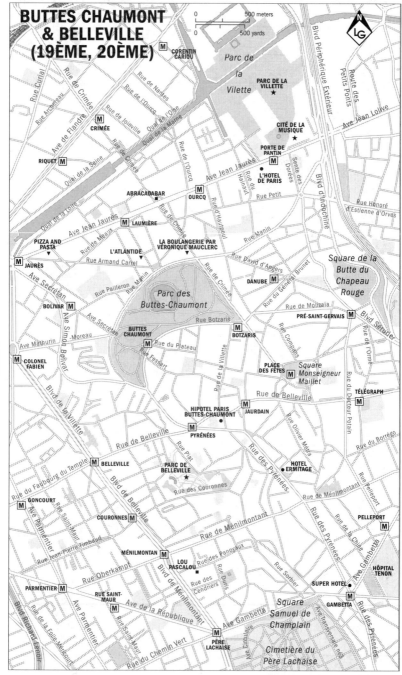

BUTTES CHAUMONT & BELLEVILLE (19ÈME, 20ÈME)

0   500 meters
0   500 yards

N LG

CORENTIN CARIOU Ⓜ

Rue Curial
Rue Archereau
Rue de Crimée
Rue de Nantes
Rue de l'Ourcq
Rue de Joinville
Quai de l'Oise
Quai de la Marne

Parc de la Vilette
PARC DE LA VILLETTE ★

Blvd Périphérique Extérieur
Route des Petits Ponts
Ave Jean Lolive

Ⓜ CRIMÉE

Ave de Flandre
Quai de la Seine
Rue de Crimée

CITÉ DE LA MUSIQUE ★

RIQUET Ⓜ

PORTE DE PANTIN

Rue de l'Ourcq
Ave Jean Jaurès

Sente des Dorées
Blvd d'Indochine

L'HOTEL DE PARIS ●
Rue du Hainaut

ABRACADABAR ■
OURCQ Ⓜ

Rue Petit

Rue Honoré d'Estienne d'Orves

Quai de la Loire
Ave Jean Jaurès
Ⓜ LAUMIÈRE
Rue de Crimée
Rue de l'Ourcq
Rue d'Hautpoul

Rue Manin

PIZZA AND PASTA ▼
Rue de Meaux

L'ATLANTIDE ▼

LA BOULANGERIE PAR VÉRONIQUE MAUCLERC ▼

Rue David d'Angers

Square de la Butte du Chapeau Rouge

Ⓜ JAURÈS
Rue Armand Carrel

DANUBE Ⓜ

Rue du Général Brunet

Ave Secrétan
Rue Pailleron
Rue Manin

BOLIVAR Ⓜ

Parc des Buttes-Chaumont

Rue de Crimée

Rue de Mouzaïa

PRÉ-SAINT-GERVAIS Ⓜ

Blvd Sérurier

Ave Secretan
Ave Simon Bolivar
Ave Mathurin Moreau

BUTTES CHAUMONT
Rue Botzaris

Rue du Plateau
Rue Fessart

BOTZARIS

Rue Compans

Rue de l'Orme

Ⓜ COLONEL FABIEN

Rue de la Villette

PLACE DES FÊTES Ⓜ
Square Monseigneur Maillet

Rue du Docteur Potain

TÉLÉGRAPH ●

Blvd de la Villette

Rue de Belleville

HIPOTEL PARIS BUTTES-CHAUMONT ●

JAURDAIN ●

Rue Olivier Métra

Ⓜ PYRÉNÉES

Rue du Borrégo

Rue de Belleville
Rue Piat
Rue des Pyrénées

HOTEL ERMITAGE ●

Ⓜ BELLEVILLE

PARC DE BELLEVILLE ★

PELLEPORT ●

Rue du Faubourg du Temple
Rue Saint-Maur
Blvd de Belleville

Rue des Couronnes

Rue de Ménilmontant

Rue de la Chine
Ave Gambetta
Rue des Pyrénées

GONCOURT Ⓜ
Ave Parmentier

COURONNES Ⓜ

Rue de Ménilmontant

Rue Pelleport

HÔPITAL TENON

MÉNILMONTAN Ⓜ

LOU PASCALOU ■

Rue des Panoyaux
Rue Duris

Rue Sorbier

SUPER HOTEL ●

Rue Jean-Pierre Timbaud
Rue Oberkampf

Rue des Cendriers

GAMBETTA Ⓜ

PARMENTIER Ⓜ

RUE SAINT-MAUR Ⓜ

Ave de la République

Square Samuel de Champlain

Rue des Pyrénées

Blvd Richard Lenoir
Rue de la Folie Méricourt
Ave Parmentier
Rue Saint Maur
Ave de Ménilmontant
Ave Gambetta

PÈRE LACHAISE Ⓜ

Cimetière du Père Lachaise

Rue du Chemin Vert

paris

slight redistricting

Paris wasn't always divided into 20 *arrondissements;* strange references to *anciens* arrondissements on old churches and random street corners come from the city's old organization. While his uncle controlled most of Europe, Napoleon III conquered the internal structure of Paris, doubling the area of the city and subsequent reorganizing it all. It's no surprise Napoleon I remains the more famous of the two: as great as sensible municipal organization is, it's no match for continental domination.

AUTEUIL, PASSY & BATIGNOLLES (16ÈME, 17ÈME)

The 16ème and 17ème are almost devoid of tourists. More residential, these neighborhoods are home to ladies who lunch, their beautiful children, and their over-worked husbands. The 16ème is frequented by Parisian elites who have money and are willing to spend it in the expensive boutiques and cafe lounges lining the main roads around Ⓜ**Trocadéro.** The 17ème, meanwhile, is far more relaxed in terms of its residents and prices. Its sheer size and lack of notable sights make this area a retreat for working class citizens and overly earnest teenagers who take leisurely strolls or sit in the many cafes.

The 16ème covers the area west of the 8ème, where the Seine dives sharply south. Auteuil and Passy are loosely defined, if at all, but Auteuil generally covers the southern half of the *arrondissement*, while Passy makes up the northern half (although you probably won't hear many Parisians refer specifically to either one). Most tourist traffic converges at Ⓜ Trocadéro at the **Palais de Chaillot;** many major sights are scattered about the banks of the river, especially near Ⓜ**Passy** (between the **Musée du Vin** and **Maison de Radio France**), where you can find some of the best views of the Eiffel Tower. The northern border of this area is generally marked by the **Arc de Triomphe.**

The 17ème consists of the area directly north of the Arc de Triomphe and the 8ème. Batignolles tends to refer just to the eastern corner of this *arrondissement*, around the **Square des Batignolles.** It is in and around the square that most of the best bars and restaurants in the neighborhood can be found, especially along and just off **rue des Dames.** Pl. du Maréchal Juin anchors the other side of town and is connected to bd des Batignolles and bd de Courcelles by av. de Villiers.

MONTMARTRE (18ÈME)

Montmartre is easily the most eccentric of Paris's *arrondissements*, with religious landmarks like the **Basilique du Sacré-Cœur** looming over historic cabarets like the infamous 🖼**Moulin Rouge** and the land of the scantily-clad, the **Red Light District.** The 18ème has recently exploded with youth hostels that keep bars full at night but also attract pickpockets. The neighborhood sits on top of a huge hill that is a bit of a hike, so plan your sightseeing accordingly. The bottom of the hill is lined by **boulevard de Clichy** and **boulevard de Rochechouart,** under which the #2 Metro line runs and where you can find a lot of those great bars. **Boulevard Barbès** roughly borders the eastern end of this area, and the Cimetière de Montmartre borders it to the west.

BUTTES CHAUMONT & BELLEVILLE (19ÈME, 20ÈME)

The Buttes Chaumont and Belleville neighborhoods cover a huge area. The lack of visible landmarks makes it difficult to navigate on foot, so it's better to take the Metro during the day and a taxi at night (if for some reason you end up here after

orientation

dark). The main places worth visiting are the **Parc des Buttes Chaumont** ([M]Buttes Chaumont, Botzaris, or Laumière) and **Père Lachaise** cemetery ([M]Père Lachaise, Gambetta, or Philippe Auguste). Running along the northern edge of the 19ème is **avenue Jean Jaurès,** which leads straight to the Museum of Science. From av. Jean Jaurès, any turn up the hill leads to the park. **Boulevard de Belleville** connects the two *arrondissements* and has some of the best (and cheapest) African and Asian restaurants in the city. As soon as the sun sets, however, this place turns into a Parisian mini-Marseille, and that's not where you want to be after dark.

accommodations

Budget accommodations (or budget anything, for that matter) can be difficult to find in Paris. Hostels and hotels generally get cheaper the farther you journey from the center of the city into the less trafficked *arrondissements*. Once you get to the 17ème, though, you're looking at a pretty long Metro ride, and an inconvenient location doesn't always translate to a decent price. But there are still deals for savvy travelers who know where to look. Both the Châtelet-Les Halles and Bastille neighborhoods are home to youth hostels with rock-bottom prices and locations ridiculously close to Paris's main attractions. When it comes to hotels, be on the lookout for exceptionally good two-star options, especially in the 5ème and 6ème. Expect to pay about €40-60 for the best budget hotels, which can be anywhere from very quirky to very forgettable but are always cleaner and more peaceful than the alternatives. Free Wi-Fi and cheap breakfasts (you shouldn't pay more than €6 for breakfast unless you're a sucker) are almost always provided, and it's not uncommon for hotels and hostels to have adjoining bars. But if you're doing Paris on the cheap, be warned that you can't always count on having your own bathroom or shower, even if you shell out for a single, so be sure to ask what you're getting yourself into.

ÎLE DE LA CITÉ AND ÎLE ST-LOUIS

Unless you're feeling like it's about time you dropped another daily €100 on your ever-growing collection of fine cheeses, les Îles are not the most practical areas for accommodations. Even though this area is technically the geographic center of the city, the crowds virtually disappear at night, so don't stay here if you're looking to stay within drunk-crawling distance of good nightlife.

HOTEL HENRI-IV HOTEL $$$

25 pl. Dauphine ☎01 43 54 44 53 henri4hotel.fr

Located on the beautiful, leafy pl. Dauphine, Hotel Henri-IV has the unique advantage of being one of the only (affordable) accommodations in Paris's geographic center. Not only are two of city's biggest attractions, the Louvre and the Notre Dame, just minutes away, but the hotel is located on the quiet western corner of the island that tourist traffic tends to miss. Every room is bright and comfortable and has a view of the breezy plaza below. Although the history of this area dates back to King Henry IV, recent history has kept the hotel in the family since 1937. That and the warm fuzzy feeling you experience upon entering a room will have you feeling more at home here than at most of the centrally located hotels in Paris.

 # [M]Pont Neuf. Cross Pont Neuf to the Île de la Cité and turn left into the park. ℹ Breakfast included. Best to book 2-3 months in advance. [$] Singles with shower €67, with full bath €72; doubles €78/82; triples with full bath €88. June-Aug add €8. ⏰ Reception 7am-midnight.

CHÂTELET-LES HALLES

While affordable hotels in this trendy neighborhood are usually hard to come by, there are a few high-quality budget locations that are worth checking out. Be sure to make reservations far in advance; cheap spots in such a central location fill up quickly year-round.

CENTRE INTERNATIONALE DE PARIS (BVJ): PARIS LOUVRE　　　　HOSTEL $$
20 rue Jean-Jacques Rousseau　　　　　　　☎01 53 00 90 90　www.bvjhotel.com
This monstrous 200-bed hostel has clean rooms. (Even the lofts are clean—they must have high-reaching dusters.) In the summer, it's packed with international youths and backpackers. Despite the hostel's location next to the old Parisian stock market, you won't pay much for a huge entry, glass ceiling foyer, and the free language lessons you get when conversing with your bunkmates.

⚧ ⓜLouvre-Rivoli. *Walk north on rue du Louvre and turn left onto rue St-Honoré. Turn right onto rue Jean-Jacques Rousseau.* ⓘ *Breakfast included. Lockers €2. Wi-Fi in dining hall €2 per hr., €3 per 2hr. Reservations can be made no more than 2 months in advance Jul-Aug, no more than 15 days in advance Sept-June.* ⓢ *Dorms €29; doubles €70. Cash only.* ⓠ *Reception 24hr. 3-night max. stay; extensions can be arranged upon arrival.*

HOTEL DE LA VALLÉE　　　　　　　　　　　　　　　　HOTEL $$$
84-86 rue St-Denis　　　　　　　　☎01 42 36 46 99　www.paris-hotel-lavallee.com
Hotel de la Vallée is discretely tucked between two restaurants on the busy rue St-Denis. While the exterior and stairs seem deceptively small, the rooms themselves are much roomier than your average budget hotel, and prices are extremely reasonable given the hotel's excellent location. The cheaper rooms have rather small shared showers, so you may form some more intimate relationships with your neighbors here than you normally would.

⚧ ⓜChatelet-Les Halles. *Walk east toward rue St-Denis and turn left; the hotel is on the right.* ⓘ *Free Wi-Fi in reception area. Breakfast €6.* ⓢ *Singles with sink €49-65, with separate shower €69-85; doubles €59-75/79-95.* ⓠ *Reception 24hr. Check-in 2pm. Check-out 11am.*

APPI HOTEL　　　　　　　　　　　　　　　　　　　　HOTEL $$
158 rue St-Denis　　　　　　　　　☎01 42 33 35 16　www.appihotel.com
Appi Hotel will welcome you into a cozy atmosphere that's so homey you won't remember you just walked by at least two sex shops to reach your destination. Despite the dark, wall-to-wall carpeting and wine-red paint, this hotel will leave you feeling surprisingly light and happy inside. The rooms themselves are much brighter than the reception area and have large windows that look out onto the busy rue St-Denis. The Châtelet-Les Halles Metro and RER stop is a short walk down the street and is the jumping off point for just about every other part of Paris.

⚧ ⓜRéaumur: Sébastopol. *Walk west on rue Réaumur and turn left onto rue St-Denis; the hotel is on the left.* ⓘ *Free Wi-Fi. Breakfast €6.* ⓢ *Singles with sink and shared shower €30-40; doubles with sink and shared shower €45-50, with ensuite shower €60-65; triples with ensuite shower €75-80.* ⓠ *Reception 9am-1pm and 4-11pm.*

HÔTEL MONTPENSIER　　　　　　　　　　　　　　　HOTEL $$$
12 rue de Richelieu　　　　　　　☎01 42 96 28 50　www.hotelmontpensierparis.com
One of few affordable hotels in the area, Hôtel Montpensier doesn't skimp on amenities, offering marble bathrooms and large beds. It has a convenient location up the street from the Place du Palais Royal, and the rooms will remind you of the Belle Époque.

⚧ ⓜPalais Royal-Musée du Louvre. *Facing la Comédie Française, turn left and walk up rue de Richelieu. The hotel is 1½ up blocks on the right.* ⓘ *Free Wi-Fi. Breakfast €9.* ⓢ *Singles €60, with bath €70; doubles with shower €99, with full bath €100; triples €149; quads €159.* ⓠ *Reception 24hr.*

accommodations

HOTEL TIQUETONNE

HOTEL $$

6 rue Tiquetonne   ☎01 42 36 94 58   www.hoteltiquetonne.fr

Extremely close to the center of the 1er, Hotel Tiquetonne is a very confused one-star budget hotel: it serves breakfast in your room, but charges €6 for shower tokens if you are in a single *sans-douche*.

♯ ⓜ*Étienne-Marcel. Walk against the traffic on rue de Turbigo and turn left onto rue Tiquetonne.* *i* *Breakfast €6. Hall showers €6. Must reserve in advance. Parking available.* Ⓢ *Singles €40, with bath €50; doubles with bath €60.* Ⓩ *Reception 24hr.*

HÔTEL DES BOULEVARDS

HOTEL $$$

10 rue de la Ville Neuve   ☎01 42 36 02 29   www.hoteldesboulevards.com

Hôtel des Boulevards is a simple hotel that clearly couldn't afford a decorator. If you aren't looking for more than clean, cheap rooms and complimentary breakfast, then you won't be disappointed. Rooms cost the same if you're solo or traveling with someone else, so find a friend and split the cost.

♯ ⓜ*Bonne Nouvelle. Walk 2½ blocks down rue de la Ville Neuve. The hotel is on the right.* *i* *Free Wi-Fi. Breakfast included.* Ⓢ *Singles and doubles €55, with toilet €63, with full bath €68.*

---

bike it out

You may notice a number of gray bikes scattered around the city. These are part of a city wide bike-sharing program called **Vélib**. If you're going to be in Paris for a while and have a credit card with an EMV-chip (few US cards currently have them; most European ones do), it may be worth getting a subscription. Bikes are €1 per day and you can take unlimited 30min. trips. Longer rides face extra charges, but, as long as you're staying in the central part of Paris, you'll rarely need it for more than half an hour.

THE MARAIS

The Marais is generally overpriced, but there are a number of budget accommodations that won't leave you completely drained for cash. Otherwise, there is still a handful of hotels that have lots of personality for a reasonable price and are worth the couple extra euro.

🏨 LE FAUCONNIER

HOSTEL $$

11 rue du Fauconnier   ☎01 42 74 23 45   www.mije.com

Le Fauconnier is an ivy-covered, sun-drenched building just steps from the Seine and Île St-Louis. Clean rooms have beds arranged in every possible way: lofts, bunks, and even Tetris-inspired arrangements. But don't worry; you'll get to know your neighbors after soaking in the sun on the terrace.

♯ ⓜ*Pont Marie. Walk east on quai des Célestins and turn left onto rue du Fauconnier.* *i* *Breakfast included. Lockers €1 deposit. MIJE membership required. Reserve 45 days before arrival online or 1 week ahead if by phone. Ages 18-30 only. Internet €0.50 initial connection fee, €0.10 per min. thereafter.* Ⓢ *Dorms €30; singles €49; doubles €72; triples €96. MIJE membership €2.50.* Ⓩ *Curfew 1am; notify in advance if returning later. Lockout noon-3pm. 1-week max. stay.*

🏨 MAUBUISSON

HOSTEL $$

12 rue des Barres   ☎01 42 74 23 45   www.mije.com

Run by the same company as Le Fauconnier, Maubuisson is in a former 17th-century convent on a quiet street by the St-Gervais monastery. In a move that would make Mother Superior nervous, the hostel only accommodates individual travelers between the ages of 18 and 30, but and the quality of the hostel benefits from the lack of foot traffic.

⚡ ⓜSt-Paul. *Walk against traffic on rue François Miron for several blocks and turn right onto rue des Barres.* *i* *Breakfast included. Lockers €1 deposit. Internet €0.50 initial connection fee, €0.10 per min. thereafter. MIJE membership required. Reserve 45 days before arrival online or 1 week ahead if by phone. Ages 18-30 only.* Ⓢ *Dorms €30; singles €49; doubles €72; triples €96. MIJE membership €2.50. ⓔ Lockout noon-3pm. Curfew 1am; notify in advance if returning later. 1 week max. stay.*

⬛ HÔTEL JEANNE D'ARC   HOTEL $$$
3 rue de Jarente   ☎01 48 87 62 11 www.lesvoixdejeanne.com

Hotel Jeanne d'Arc will brighten up any traveler's day with fun and artistic decor in the lobby and common area. The rooms themselves may seem a bit disappointing after walking by the huge mosaic mirror in the breakfast room or passing through a common room with funky flower lamps and purple leaves on the walls. Not to worry, though—this lovely boutique hotel is alive with color and the cheery staff won't leave you feeling blue.

⚡ ⓜSt-Paul. *Walk against traffic onto rue de Rivoli; turn left onto rue de Sévigné, then right onto rue de Jarente.* *i* *Breakfast €8. Reserve 2-3 months in advance (earlier for stays in Sept-Oct).* Ⓢ *Singles €65; 1-bed doubles €81-96, 2-bed €119; triples €149; quads €164.*

HÔTEL DE ROUBAIX   HOTEL $$$$
6 rue Greneta   ☎01 42 72 89 91 www.hotel-de-roubaix.com

With countless pixelated cityscapes and comic-strip prints throughout the hotel, Hôtel de Roubaix will leave you feeling like you're living in a cartoon. Walk up the beautiful, carpeted marble stairs and BAM!—find your room with a bright red door and heavy brass knob. Enjoy the view of the picturesque street and French buildings across the way, or KA-POW!—hang out in the breakfast room that's decorated with rows of posters and advertisements for vintage French cartoons. But when it comes time to clean up, SKERRRRT!—lock your bathroom door, as none of the showers have shower curtains.

⚡ ⓜRéaumur-Sébastopol. *Head east on rue Réaumur, take the 1st left onto rue St-Martin, then turn left again.* *i* *Free Wi-Fi. Breakfast €7. Telephone €0.30.* Ⓢ *Singles €78; doubles €82-84; triples €92-96. ⓔ Reception 24hr.*

HÔTEL ANDRÉA RIVOLI   HOTEL $$$$
3 rue St-Bon   ☎01 42 78 43 93 www.andreahotel.fr

With purple walls and grey leopard print lining the stairs, this hotel has plenty of flair. Better yet, most rooms here are quite spacious and bathrooms are clean and bright. This hotel also has a great location, nestled on a quiet street just a couple blocks from the Hôtel de Ville.

⚡ ⓜHôtel de Ville. *Head west with traffic on rue de Rivoli and turn left onto rue St-Bon. The hotel is on the left.* *i* *Free Wi-Fi. Breakfast €9. Best to book 2 months in advance. All singles in back of hotel; extra for balcony in front of building.* Ⓢ *Singles €74-86; doubles €92-128; triples €154. ⓔ Reception 24hr. Check-in 1pm. Check-out 11:30am.*

HOTEL DE LA HERSE D'OR   HOTEL $$$
20 rue St-Antoine   ☎01 48 87 84 09 www.parishotelherseor.com

Quiet, peaceful rooms can be difficult to find in the Marais. The Hotel de la Herse d'Or, though, provides a tranquil place to crash just a block from the pl. des Vosges. Though not the best budget option for a couple nights' stay, the lavish doubles and apartment-sized triples create a bohemian escape that can be affordable for stays over one week.

⚡ ⓜBastille. *Walk back toward the Marais on rue St-Antoine for 1½ blocks.* *i* *Discounts up to 20% for stays of 1 week or longer.* Ⓢ *Singles €69; doubles €79, with bath €109; triples with bath €139.*

HÔTEL DU SÉJOUR HOTEL $$$$

36 rue du Grenier St-Lazare ☎01 48 87 40 36 www.hoteldusejour.com

Bringing the spirit of minimalism to the hotel industry (read: no TV or air-conditioning), Hôtel du Séjour features 20 basic rooms decorated with Pop Art of Parisian landmarks and colorful stripes. It's a little loud, but worth the price for the ideal location one block away from Les Halles and the Centre Pompidou.

Ⓜ Étienne-Marcel. Walk 3 blocks down rue aux Ours, turn left onto rue St-Martin, and right onto rue du Grenier St-Lazare. i Reserve 2-3 weeks in advance. Ⓢ Singles €82; doubles €87, with shower and toilet €97. Reception 7:30am-10:30pm.

HÔTEL BELLEVUE ET DU CHARIOT D'OR HOTEL $$$

39 rue de Turbigo ☎01 48 87 45 60 www.hotelbellevue75.com

Come to the Bellevue, darling, where you might like to sip a cup of tea in the salon or smoke a cigar with your fellow patrons after dinner. Although no one smokes indoors anymore and the Bellevue doesn't actually host tea time, the building's timeless architecture and charm will have you feeling like you've taken a trip back to the good ol' days you never knew. The rooms are contemporary, in contrast to the old lobby, and don't quite evoke nostalgic daydreams, but they are very spacious and have pleasant views of either the courtyard or the street. If you feel it's about time for your 5 o'clock tumbler of scotch, the bar downstairs unfortunately is out of commission, but reception will be happy to serve you upon request.

Ⓜ Arts et Métiers. Walk southwest on rue de Turbigo about 2½ blocks. i Free Wi-Fi. Breakfast €7. Ⓢ Singles €65; 1-bed doubles €81-96, 2-bed €119; triples €149; quads €164.

HOTEL PICARD HOTEL $$$

26 rue de Picardie ☎01 48 87 53 82 www.hotelpicardparis.com

Hotel Picard doesn't feel very special, and for the most part, it's not. The rather plain rooms feature a white decor accented by delicate blue flowers on the bedspread. Rooms on the front side of the building offer nice views of the street that will unfortunately be obscured until 2014, when the showroom being built is completed. The major inconvenience of this hotel is that here, hygiene comes at a cost: shared showers only turn on after you insert €3 token into a slot, and even then you will only get 10min. of water. While this may encourage you to take shorter showers and conserve water, it's still pretty annoying.

Ⓜ République. Follow bd du Temple and turn right onto rue Charlot. Take a slight right onto rue de Franche Comte, which becomes rue de Picardie. The hotel is on the left. i Breakfast €6. Shower €3 for 10min. Reserve 1 week ahead in summer and 2 weeks ahead the rest of the year. Ⓢ Singles with sink €58-68, with bath €79-93; doubles €59-74/89-112; triples with both €132-155.

LATIN QUARTER AND ST-GERMAIN

Hotels in these neighborhoods are generally a bit overpriced due to their central location. Secret gems, however, are still accessible to budget travelers—they're usually located down quiet alleys right around the corner from some of the most popular spots. Even better, they're all near the Metro, in case your drunken escapades take you a bit far from home.

YOUNG AND HAPPY HOSTEL HOSTEL $$

80 rue Mouffetard ☎01 47 07 47 07 www.youngandhappy.fr

A funky, lively hostel with 21 clean (if basic) rooms, some with showers and toilets, Young and Happy Hostel is where you want to stay in the 5ème. It's a great option if you're young, fun, and on a budget, as it's on rue Mouffetard and in the center of the cheapest student watering holes in Paris. While impromptu, their reception doubles as a bar and serves drinks if you ask for them.

Ⓜ Place Monge. From rue Monge, walk behind the pl. Monge on rue Ortolan and turn left onto rue Mouffetard. The hostel is on the right. i Breakfast included. Internet €2 per 30min. Ⓢ High-season dorms €28-45.

HÔTEL DE NESLE

HOTEL $$$

7 rue du Nesle ☎01 43 54 62 41 www.hoteldenesleparis.com

Hôtel de Nesle is a phenomenal place to stay. Each room is unique and represents a particular time period or locale. The Molière room is ideal for the comically minded, and a Colonial room is available for undying proponents of the good ol' days of the Scramble for Africa (don't let that be you). Reserve in advance, because space fills up quickly, especially in the summer.

⇄ [M]Odéon. Walk toward the church on bd St-Germain and turn right onto rue Mazarine. Turn right onto rue Dauphine and head toward the river. Rue de Nesle is the 1st street on the left. i Laundry facilities on-site as well as a Turkish bath (Le Hammam). [S] Singles €55-65; doubles €75-100. Extra bed €12.

HÔTEL DU COMMERCE

HOTEL $$$

14 rue de la Montagne ☎01 43 54 89 69 www.commerceparishotel.com

With the friendly feel of a hostel and the privacy of a hotel, Hôtel du Commerce gives you the Hannah Montana best of both the worlds. The kitchen and common room offer space to socialize, while the private bedrooms allow for some alone time, too. Newly painted hallways add some zest in different shades of purple, green, and orange, while the decor in the white rooms is far simpler. Come to the Hôtel du Commerce for hotel-quality rooms at (nearly) hostel-quality prices.

⇄ [M]Maubert-Mutualité. Walk with traffic on rue St-Germain, turn left onto rue Monge, then turn left onto rue de la Montagne. i Free Wi-Fi. Luggage storage and kitchen available. [S] Singles or doubles with sink €44-54, with shower €64; twins with shower and toilet €74; triples with sink €74; quads with shower and toilet €144. Sept 1-Oct 31 add €4. Shared showers €2 per day for unlimited use or €2 per shower if you don't plan to shower every day (you nasty). ⏰ Reception 24hr.

HÔTEL STELLA

HOTEL $$

41 rue Monsieur-le-Prince ☎01 40 51 00 25 http://site.voila.fr/hotel-stella

Designed in the style of Old World Paris, Hôtel Stella has no place for TVs or even an elevator. The rooms are huge and boast high ceilings, exposed beams, the occasional piano, and oriental rugs. With a location down the street from the Jardin de Luxembourg, Hôtel Stella could charge twice as much for their rooms, so thank God they don't.

⇄ [M]Odéon. Walk up rue Danton in the direction of traffic past Université René Descartes Paris V, and turn left onto rue Monsieur-le-Prince. The hotel is just past the intersection with rue Racine. [S] Singles €30-50; doubles €60; triples €80; quads €100.

HÔTEL ESMERALDA

HOTEL $$$$

4 rue St-Julien-le-Pauvre ☎01 43 54 19 20 www.hotel-esmeralda.fr

The shadowy Hotel Esmeralda has been taking in travelers for 350 years. Despite its age, however, the hotel and its rooms maintain a charming antique feel without the common dysfunctions of centuries-old buildings. Black wallpaper with pink and green *fleurs-de-lis* give the hallways and rooms a classic touch, while white French boudoirs add some extra panache. If that's not enough, most of the rooms have a clear view of Notre Dame. This air-tight hotel even manages to drown out the noise from the busy St-Michel Metro stop nearby. Be warned: Esmeralda's structure calls for more limber travelers, as the hallways are be dangerously narrow and the tight spiral staircase difficult to maneuver.

⇄ [M]St-Michel. Walk toward the Seine, then turn right onto quai St-Michel, then right onto rue St-Julien. i Free Wi-Fi. Breakfast €7. [S] Singles €75-95; doubles €100-115; triples €140; quads €150. ⏰ Reception 24hr.

HÔTEL MARIGNAN

HOTEL $$$

13 rue du Sommerard ☎01 43 54 63 81 www.hotel-marignan.com

This family-owned hotel has some valuable and rare finds for accommodations in Paris: 5-person rooms and special rates for travelers who move in packs; free laundry for those explorers who are extra-dirty extra-often; and a fully-outfitted kitchen for patrons who are too cheap to buy their meals at restaurants (we're looking at you, *Let's Go* reader). All this is accompanied by a friendly atmosphere and rooms with funky, decorative touches (it's not every day you find faces popping out of trees painted on the wall over your bed). The breakfast area is reasonably large and occupied by people on their computers.

 # [M]Maubert-Mutualité. Walk down the rue des Carmes and take the 1st right onto rue du Sommerard. i Free Wi-Fi. Breakfast included. Laundry and kitchen available. Reserve 2 weeks-1 month ahead. Group and other promotions available depending on the season, call for details. [S] Apr-July singles €59-68, doubles €75-105, triples €102-127, quads €123-145, quints €138-159; Aug-Oct €54-64/€68-95/€95-119/€115-130/€125-150; Nov-Feb €50-78/€64-87/€93-112/€108-125/€120-145; Mar €54-66/€68-93/€96-113/€116-130/€127-145.

HÔTEL BRÉSIL HOTEL

10 rue Le Goff ☎01 43 54 76 11 www.bresil-paris-hotel.com

Easy, breezy, beautiful Hôtel Brésil will keep you comfortable in the midst of the busy 5ème. While the small rooms make it a bit difficult to turn around, if you're looking to explore the Latin Quarter's hoppin' bar scene, you shouldn't expect to spend much time in your room anyway. If that isn't enough consolation for you, then the potential of sleeping in the same chamber as one of the hotel's former occupants, Sigmund Freud, may appeal to your subconscious.

 # RER: Luxembourg. Walk north on bd St-Michel along the edge of the Jardin du Luxembourg; at the roundabout, turn right onto rue Soufflot and take the 1st right. i Free Wi-Fi. Breakfast €6. [S] Singles €85; doubles €95-110; triples €135; quads €145.

HÔTEL GAY LUSSAC HOTEL $$$

29 rue Gay Lussac ☎01 43 54 23 96 www.paris-hotel-gay-lussac.com

Although an elderly couple runs this equally aged hotel, this is a great place to mix and mingle with a younger crowd. With a location in the student-heavy Latin Quarter, a no-frills dining room, and rock-bottom prices, this hotel attracts patrons of all ages but is particularly popular with the youngsters. The combination of French doors and an old-school style are so charming you might not even notice all the creaky floorboards.

 # RER: Luxembourg. Walk north on bd St-Michel along the edge of the Jardin du Luxembourg; just before the roundabout, take a hard right onto rue Gay-Lussac. i Wi-Fi €3 per 24hr., €5 per 48hr. Breakfast €5. [S] Singles €55-65; doubles €70-85; triples €100; quad €110.

HÔTEL ST-ANDRÉ DES ARTS HOTEL $$$$

66 rue St-André-des-Arts ☎01 43 26 96 16

A combination of stone- and wood-beam walls make this place feel like a country inn in the heart of Paris. Originally constructed in the 16th century, Hôtel St-André des Arts offers modern comfort in old digs. Some rooms are much larger than others, but all are fitted with beautiful antique furniture, big windows, and an attentive staff.

 # [M]Odéon. Walk 1 block up rue Mazarine and turn right onto rue St-André-des-Arts. i Free Wi-Fi. Breakfast included. [S] Singles €76; doubles €96-103; triples €121; quads €134.

HOTEL ST-JACQUES HOTEL $$$$

35 rue des Écoles ☎01 44 07 45 45 www.paris-hotel-stjacques.com

This elegant hotel will satiate your appetite for the fancy-schmancy as long as you're willing to shell out the dough for a truly classic hotel. Audrey Hepburn and Cary Grant fans may recognize this chic hotel from the 1963 romantic murder-mystery *Charade.* Rooms are decorated with ocean-blue walls, brass teapots, and *trompe-l'oeil* accents. All these trimmings are further fancied-up with chandeliers and Belle-Epoque frescoes. It's not quite Versailles, but it's pretty good for €160.

 # [M]Maubert-Mutualité. i Free Wi-Fi. Breakfast €14. Online discounts available. [S] Singles €160; doubles €175-230; triples €278.

DELHY'S HÔTEL   HOTEL $$$

22 rue de l'Hirondelle   ☎01 43 26 58 25 www.delhyshotel.com

This might be the easiest hotel to find in the Latin Quarter. It's close to pl. St-Michel and the Seine, yet tucked away from the hustle and bustle down a quiet cobblestone alleyway. Cheaper rooms have just a sink, but we would advise against bathing in the St-Michel fountain.

✈ Ⓜ*St-Michel. Facing the St-Michel fountain, turn to your right and walk through the passage to the left of La Rive Gauche cafe. The hotel is on the right.* ⓘ *Breakfast included. Check website for promotions.* Ⓢ *Singles €58, with shower €73; doubles €76/83; triples €119. Extra bed €15.*

HOTEL DES CARMES   HOTEL $$$$

5 rue des Carmes   ☎01 43 29 78 40 www.hoteldescarmesparis.com

It is quite possible that a village of Smurfs exploded all over Hotel des Carmes, where everything—the walls, the carpets, even the elevator—is blue. Inside, the bedspreads throw in a splash of yellow to liven things up. Although the accommodations here are rather simple compared to other hotels in this price range, the rooms and bathrooms are exceptionally spacious for the area (some even feature a large tub for you to soak in at the end of the day). The Metro and Notre Dame are also only a short walk away, meaning the location is also a steal.

✈ Ⓜ*Maubert-Mutualité or RER: Cluny-la Sorbonne. Walk straight down rue des Carmes; the hotel is on the left.* ⓘ *Free Wi-Fi. Breakfast €6.* Ⓢ *Singles €97-112; doubles €107-122. Extra bed €34.*

INVALIDES

Budget travel isn't exactly synonymous with the elegant 7ème. If you absolutely must stay here, there are a couple of options that are easy to get to and affordable by local standards. Outside the touristy areas, all you will likely find are expensive apartments. You have been warned.

GRAND HÔTEL LÉVÊQUE   HOTEL $$$$

28 rue Cler   ☎01 47 05 49 15 www.hotel-leveque.com

With an unbeatable location on a cobblestone, restaurant-heavy street halfway between the Champs de Mars and the Hôtel des Invalides, the Grand Hôtel Lévêque is on the high end of budget, but rightfully so. Recently renovated rooms have a dark contemporary coolness to them and are quiet, keeping the noise from neighboring restaurants at a minimum.

✈ Ⓜ*École Militaire. Walk up av. de la Motte-Picquet (away from the Champs de Mars and toward the esplanades) and turn left onto rue Cler.* ⓘ *Free Wi-Fi. Lobby computer €1 per 10min. Breakfast €9.* Ⓢ *Singles €75-85; doubles €149-179; triples €180-190.* ⏰ *Reception 24hr.*

HOTEL EIFFEL RIVE GAUCHE   HOTEL $$$$

6 rue du Gros-Caillou   ☎01 45 51 51 51 www.hotel-eiffel.com/hotel-rive-gauche

With a view of the Eiffel Tower from anywhere on this street, you know you've found prime real estate. Rooms at the Hotel Eiffel are on split levels for added privacy. The bright yellow walls of the courtyard contrast with the more toned down reds in the interior hallways and bedrooms. Reception is friendly and will help you find an accommodation whether or not you stay at their hotel. If you're staying in the city for a more extended period, their apartment may be a good option.

✈ Ⓜ*École Militaire. Walk up av. Bosquet and turn left onto rue de Grenelle, then right onto rue du Gros-Caillou.* ⓘ *Free Wi-Fi. Breakfast €12. All prices are negotiable; check online for promotions or call for the best rates. 1-bedroom apartment is available in a building around the corner; call for details.* Ⓢ *Singles from €87; doubles from €90; triples from €114; quads from €162.* ⏰ *Reception 24hr.*

accommodations

HÔTEL DE FRANCE HOTEL $$$$

102 bd de La Tour Maubourg ☎01 47 05 40 49 www.hoteldefrance.com

Everything at the Hôtel de France is pretty steep, from the prices to the unbeatable views of the Hôtel Invalides. However expensive, Hôtel de France will ensure that you get what you pay for. Taking pride in its customer service (something that doesn't really exist for budget accommodations), this place goes the extra mile to make your stay more comfortable. The breakfast buffet has a spread suitable for hungry travelers: eggs, scones, baguettes, sliced deli meat, and grapefruit will greet your grumbling stomach in the morning. Rooms have vibrant, jazzy colors that will make your stay even brighter.

 # [M]École Militaire. With your back to the Musée de l'Armée, take the diagonal to the right of the traffic semi-circle. The Hôtel de France is on the corner. *i* *Free Wi-Fi. Breakfast buffet €12. Best to book at least 1 week in advance.* *[$] Singles €95-140; doubles €120-140; twin or queen €160-180; triples €180-270.*

HÔTEL DE TURENNE HOTEL $$$

20 av. de Tourville ☎01 47 05 99 92 www.france-hotel-guide.com/h75007turenne.htm

Centrally located Hôtel du Turrene offers little more than what you would expect from every forgettable hotel you've ever stayed at. What you do get is the much sought-after air-conditioning, full bath, and satellite TV in every room.

 # [M]École Militaire. Exit the Metro facing away from the Eiffel Towerand walk down av. Tourville. Hotel is at the intersection of Tourville and rue Chevert. *i* *Breakfast €9.* *[$] Singles €69; doubles €85-100; twins €105; triples €140.*

CHAMPS-ÉLYSÉES

The 8ème has a few good options for those looking to stay in Paris for a longer period of time.

PHÉNIX HÔTEL HOTEL $$$

5 rue du Général Lanrezac ☎01 44 09 05 05 www.hotelphenix.fr.st

The location of the Phénix Hôtel, just a few steps away from the Arc de Triomphe, will leave you feeling hoity-toity rich no matter how many pennies you've got in your pocket. Yellow walls and red and blue bedspreads leave the rooms here feeling bright and cheery. While the bathrooms are so small that you have to take care not to step in the toilet on your way out of the shower, the money you'll save here is worth the extra precaution.

 # [M]Charles de Gaulle-Étoile. Walk up av. Carnot and turn right onto rue du Général Lanrezac. *i* *Free Wi-Fi. Breakfast €7.* *[$] Singles €72-78; doubles €84-95.*

FOYER DE CHAILLOT FOYER $$

28 av. George V, 3rd fl. ☎01 53 67 87 27 www.foyer-galliera.com

With its unbeatable address, the Foyer provides upscale dorm rooms and midbrow apartments that welcome female students, or *stagiaires*. The rooms, which come well-equipped with sinks and showers, are outdone by the communal facilities: a full kitchen is available for breakfast and weekend meals, and the large common rooms are replete with stereos and TVs. Toilets and additional showers are in each hall.

 # [M]George V. In a high-rise silver office building called Eurosite George V; on the 3rd fl. *i* *Cash and checks only. For women ages 18-25 only; residents must be working, studying, or holding an internship. Dinner included M-F. Full computer lab with internet. Fitness room and laundry service available. Bulletin boards advertise apartments for rent, theater outings, and other activities.* *[$] €350 deposit required to reserve a room; applications on the website. Reserve 1-2 months ahead, especially Sept-Nov. €35 application/booking fee. Monthly doubles €515, monthly singles €585. For students and foreign interns €600/670.* *⏰ 2-month min. stay, 2-year max. stay. Guests permitted 9am-9pm.*

HÔTEL ALEXANDRINE OPÉRA   HOTEL $$$$

10 rue de Moscou   ☎01 43 87 62 21 www.alexandrineopera.com

Hôtel Alexandrine Opéra is a nice little place that keeps things comfortable without trying too hard. Tucked on a quiet street, this hotel boasts rooms with autumn colors that create a nice, warm atmosphere for guests. Although the red polka-dotted carpet in the hallway might not be your style, a night here will be an all-around enjoyable experience in the 8ème.

⚥ Ⓜ*Liège. Walk with traffic down rue de Moscou.* ℹ *Breakfast €9.* ⑤ *Singles €80-120; doubles €90-170.*

HÔTEL TROYON   HOTEL $$$$

10 rue Troyon   ☎01 43 80 14 09 www.hotel-troyon.com

Hôtel Troyon will pleasantly surprise you with its beautiful paintings of canals and harbors (a vague attempt to help you forget you're staying in an expensive, land-locked city); the rooms are clean and spacious enough for the price range. Just don't expect to spend a lot of time trolling around online (though we don't know why you'd stick your face behind a computer screen rather than behind a camera aimed at the Eiffel Tower), as the Wi-Fi rates here are *très* out of control.

⚥ Ⓜ*Charles de Gaulle Étoile.* ℹ *Wi-Fi €1 per 30min., €13 per hr., €20 per 24hr.* ⑤ *Singles €82-106; doubles €129-135; triples €164.*

UNION CHRÉTIENNE DE JEUNES FILLES (UCJF/YWCA)   FOYER $$

22 rue de Naples   ☎01 53 04 37 47 www.ucjf.net

Although it's the YWCA for *jeunes filles*, men can stay here too. During the summer, the stay is one month minimum, which makes it feel like a shared apartment. The simple rooms have sinks, desks, and hardwood floors. Features like the oak-paneled common room with cozy fireplace, theater space, and family-style dining room help build a sense of community.

⚥ Ⓜ*Europe. Walk down rue de Madrid away from the train tracks and turn right on rue du Rocher. Walk 1 block and turn right onto rue de Naples.* ℹ *Ages 18-25 only. Kitchen and laundry available. Free Wi-Fi in the lobby. Guests permitted until 10pm. Shared bathrooms.* ⑤ *Monthly singles, doubles, and dorm-style triples €390-505. 1 month rent deposit required.* ⌚ *Reception M-F 8am-12:25am, Sa 8:30am-12:30pm and 1:30pm-12:25am, Su 9am-12:30pm and 1:30pm-12:25am. No curfew, but ask for key ahead of time. 1-month min. stay; 1-year max. stay.*

accommodations

money-making decision

When Disney proposed the construction of its multi-million dollar theme park in Paris, many locals scoffed at the idea. They called it "cowboy colonialism" saying that the park would threaten French culture. But when the French government realized how much revenue the park could rake in, it gave Disney the green light. Thus began the era of **Disneyland Paris,** whose 15 million annual visitors make it the most popular tourist attraction in France. Sorry to disappoint you, Walt, but money has a lot more pull than Mickey Mouse.

OPÉRA AND CANAL ST-MARTIN

You should know better than to stay in a hotel close to the **Gare du Nord.** Whether it's because you're coming in late and don't want to go far or you're only in Paris for a night (shame on you), resist the urge to park yourself there. However, there are a few budget options in the north that feel a bit more like Montmartre than Opéra, so spend some time with a map before making any decisions.

HÔTEL PALACE HOTEL $$

9 rue Bouchardon ☎01 40 40 09 45

Try as we might, we cannot figure out why this recently renovated (in November 2011) hotel has such low prices. Its quiet location and brand new breakfast terrace in the inner courtyard make this a hard place to leave, even with the Metro stop less than two blocks from this wannabe-Art Deco hotel. People are catching on to this deal, so book well in advance.

 # [M]Strasbourg-St-Denis. Exit Metro and walk east on bd St-Martin for 1 block. Walk through the roundabout and turn left onto rue René Boulanger, and rue Bouchardon is your 1st left. The hotel is on the left. ⏰ Free Wi-Fi. Breakfast €4. [$] Singles €23-35; doubles €28-45; triples €60; quads €70. Prices increase with each additional bathroom accoutrement (sink, sink and toilet, full bath).

HOTEL DE MILAN HOTEL $$

17 rue de St-Quentin ☎01 40 37 88 50 www.hoteldemilan.com

If you have an unusual affinity for salmon (the color, not the fish), Hotel de Milan will satisfy your chromatic desires. All of the rooms are newly renovated and fitted with brown doors, pink bedspreads and walls, and warm carpeting. Aside from the bold color statement made by the rooms' walls, the digs here are comfortable and rather spacious for an old building in an old neighborhood. The hotel is conveniently located near Paris's biggest train station, but it is tucked back on a street quiet enough that you won't be bothered by the nearby bustle.

 # [M]Gare du Nord. From the front of the station, walk straight down rue de St-Quentin. ℹ Wi-Fi €2 for 1hr., €3 for 2hr., €5 for 3hr. Breakfast €5. Showers (for rooms without one) €4. [$] Singles €38-42, with bath €63; doubles €53/70-76; triples with bath €96. Extra bed €17. ⏰ Reception 24hr. Check-in 2pm. Check-out 11am.

PERFECT HOTEL & HOSTEL HOTEL, HOSTEL $$

39 rue Rodier ☎01 42 81 18 86 www.paris-hostel.biz

Perfect Hotel & Hostel is just a little bit less than perfect. Rooms aren't very remarkable, but for the price, location, and relative luxury of only having to share a room with one or two people, it's hard to turn down (almost) Perfect. With both shared and private rooms, Perfect is home to the young and the old, but travelers are always vibrant and energetic no matter what their age.

 # [M]Anvers. Turn left out of the Metro, walk through the park, and walk straight down rue Rodier on the right. Perfect Hotel is 1½ blocks down on the right. ℹ Free Wi-Fi. Breakfast, towel, and linens included. [$] Shared facilities per person: doubles €26-30; triples €26-28. Private facilities per person: singles €52-56; doubles €35-37; triples €28-30. Extra bed €24. ⏰ Reception 24hr.

PEACE AND LOVE HOSTEL HOSTEL $

245 rue La Fayette ☎01 46 07 65 11 www.paris-hostels.com

This is one of the only hostels in this neighborhood, but the low prices come with some drawbacks. The reception doubles as a bar and stays open until 2am serving the cheapest pints (€3.80) around for mostly Anglo-backpackers. But the limited hours for Wi-Fi, cash-only policy, and strict adherence to check-in times (read: they will give away your bed if you are more than 3hr. late) make this a hostel for those who can stick to a schedule. That's what backpacking, peace, and love are all about, right?

 # [M]Jaurès. Like, right there. Or from Gare du Nord, it's a 10min. walk up rue la Fayette, and the hostel is on the left. ℹ Ages 18-35 only. Wi-Fi 8am-6pm only. Cash only. [$] High-season dorms €23; private rooms €30. Low-season dorms €18; private rooms €26.

CAMBRAI HOTEL HOTEL $$$

129 bis bd Magenta ☎01 48 78 32 13 www.hotel-cambrai.com

Bright green walls in every room give the otherwise generic decor a minty kick. Located on a busy and accordingly noisy main road just steps from the Gare du Nord, Cambrai Hotel is probably not for light sleepers. Nonetheless, reception will warmly welcome you and ensure that your stay is comfortable.

⇄ [M]Gare du Nord. Exit Gare du Nord at the front of the station and go right, then turn right onto bd Magenta; the hotel is on the left. i Free Wi-Fi in the lobby. Breakfast €6. [S] Singles €59-65; doubles €65-69; triples €100; quads €110. Extra bed €15. ⏰ Reception 24hr.

WOODSTOCK HOSTEL HOSTEL $

48 rue Rodier ☎01 48 78 87 76 www.woodstock.fr

Woodstock Hostel brings in a clientele that is as colorful as the trip your parents may or may not have taken at Woodstock back in '69. Consistently young, international, and always interesting, Woodstock hosts backpackers that want to see Paris on a budget. Rooms are a squeeze, and there is only one shower on each floor. If you are going to stay at Woodstock, make sure your TSA lock fits your luggage; some travelers report that the "safes" in the room aren't so safe.

⇄ [M]Anvers. Turn left out of the Metro, walk through the park, and walk straight down rue Rodier on the right; it's 1½ blocks down on the left. i Free Wi-Fi and internet access from 3 lobby computers. Breakfast included. [S] Mar 2-Sept dorms €25-28; doubles €28-31. Oct-Mar 1 €22less. €1 deposit on sheets, returned at check-out. ⏰ Lockout 11am-3pm. Curfew 2am (although your room key card will let you into the building at any time).

BASTILLE

Littered with hotels (and other things), the 11ème offers something for everyone, including many quality budget hotels. The neighboring 12ème offers relatively inexpensive and simple accommodations, which work hard to make up for their remote location. Look to **Gare de Lyon** for the best budget options.

AUBERGE INTERNATIONALE DES JEUNES (AIJ) HOSTEL $

10 rue Trousseau ☎01 47 00 62 00 www.aijparis.com

The AIJ attracts a steady stream of 20-somethings with what it claims are the cheapest dorms in Paris (we believe them). Clean bathrooms are located in the hallways, and vending machines provide late-night snacks for those sober enough to sort through their coins. Guests really just get the basic amenities, but AIJ does throw in a free map of Paris, which has to be worth something.

⇄ [M]Ledru-Rollin. Walk 3 blocks away from Bastille down rue du Faubourg St-Antoine and turn left onto rue Trousseau. AIJ is on the right. i Breakfast included. Under 30 only. [S] Dorms €18; doubles €40. ⏰ Lockout 11am-4pm.

AUBERGE DE JEUNESSE "JULES FERRY" (HI) HOSTEL $$

8 bd Jules Ferry ☎01 43 57 55 60 www.fuaj.org/Paris-Jules-Ferry

Located on the Seine in the 11ème, Jules Ferry provides the perfect location for Bastille bar hopping. The hostel's colorful rooms with sinks, mirrors, and tiled floors match the carefree atmosphere.

⇄ [M]République. Walk down av. de la République, cross over Canal St-Martin, and turn left onto bd Jules Ferry. i Wi-Fi €5 per 2hr. Breakfast included. Kitchen available for guest use. [S] Dorms from €25. ⏰ Reception 2pm-10:30am. Lockout 10:30am-2pm.

PARIS ABSOLUTE HOSTEL $$

1 rue de la Fontaine au Roi ☎01 47 00 47 00 www.absolute-paris.com

Paris Absolute is made popular by its location a few blocks from the party center of Oberkampf. Clean, lime green dorms will welcome you after a long night out, when you'll be grateful there's no curfew.

⇄ [M]République. Walk toward Canal St-Martin on rue du Temple and cross the canal. The hostel is on the right. i Breakfast included. [S] Dorms €29; doubles €75-85.

HÔTEL DES ARTS BASTILLE
HOTEL $$$

2 rue Godefroy Cavaignac   ☎01 43 79 72 57 www.paris-hotel-desarts.com

If you're traveling in a small group, this hotel can be cheaper than a hostel. Bright rooms with large windows light up the already-arresting orange color scheme. Reserve online for almost 60% off listed prices; take an additional €10 off if you book a three-night stay.

✚ ⓂCharonne. Walk down bd Voltaire away from ⓂVoltaire and turn right onto rue de Charonne. Walk for 200m and turn right onto rue Godefroy Cavaignac. ⓢ If booking online, singles €55; doubles €55; twins €60; quads €89. By phone or in person, €90/99/109/130.

L'HÔTEL BAUDELAIRE BASTILLE
HOTEL $$$

12 rue de Charonne   ☎01 47 00 40 98 www.paris-hotel-bastille.com

A nicer option for those who outgrew hostels not too long ago, this hotel greets you with ensuite bathrooms and modern art in the breakfast room. The deluxe room goes all out with a plush black-tiled bathroom and bathtub.

✚ ⓂLedru-Rollin. Walk 1 block toward Bastille on rue du Faubourg St-Antoine and turn right onto rue de Charonne. The hotel is on the right. 𝒊 Free Wi-Fi. ⓢ Singles from €55; doubles €60; triples €71; deluxe room €89. Book online a month in advance and get 10% off. ⓩ Reception 24hr.

HÔTEL DE NEVERS
HOTEL $$

53 rue de Malte   ☎01 47 00 56 18 www.hoteldenevers.com

You can find better rooms in other parts of Paris for the same price as Hôtel de Nevers, but if you're looking for a good location in the Bastille area near the busy République Metro stop, this will do. Rooms here have seen better days, as some have torn wallpaper and tired bathrooms, but most are clean and have bright decorations that keep the mood light.

✚ ⓂRépublique. Walk down av. de la République and turn left onto rue de Malte. 𝒊 Free Wi-Fi. High season May-June and Sept-Dec. High-season breakfast €6, low-season €5. ⓢ High-season singles €50-62; doubles €69; triples and quads €80. Low-season singles €30-40/49/60. Extra bed in high season €9, low season €5.

HÔTEL DE VIENNE
HOTEL $$$

43 rue de Malte   ☎01 48 05 44 42 hoteldevienne@gmail.com

The rooms at the Hôtel de Vienne are uninspiring at best, the only attempt at decoration being a splash of flavor on the bright, bronze-colored bedspreads. This isn't the kind of hotel where you'll be dying to spend your day, but hopefully you'll be out and about in Bastille anyway. After sightseeing and stuffing your face with cheap food, you won't even notice how unremarkable your room is when you finally drag yourself back to bed at night.

✚ ⓂRépublique. Walk down av. de la République and turn left onto rue de Malte. 𝒊 Free Wi-Fi. ⓢ Singles €50-78; doubles €55-85. ⓩ Reception 24hr.

MONTPARNASSE AND SOUTHERN PARIS

Montparnasse and southern Paris are a lot more spread out than the center of the city but remain comfortably quiet and less expensive. It's probably best to stay near a Metro stop so you don't have to journey too far to reach your bed after dark.

🏨 OOPS!
HOSTEL $$

50 av. des Gobelins   ☎01 47 07 47 00 www.oops-paris.com

Why it's named Oops!, we have no idea. Maybe it's the creative use of bright colors and patterns that vary by room (and sometimes by wall). Both private rooms and dorms are remarkably clean and have balconies that overlook av. d'Italie. Book well in advance for the summer months, as Oops! is very popular among young backpackers.

✚ ⓂLes Gobelins. Walk south on av. des Gobelins toward pl. d'Italie. The hostel is 3 blocks from the Metro, on the right. 𝒊 Breakfast included. Reserve online. ⓢ High-season dorms €30; private rooms €70. Low-season dorms €23; private rooms €60.

FIAP JEAN-MONNET HOTEL $$$

30 rue Cabanis ☎01 43 13 17 00 www.fiap.asso.fr

With a bar, two restaurants, an outdoor terrace, and regular parties on Wednesdays and Fridays, this student-friendly hotel definitely has a vibrant social scene. The rooms match the '60s-meets-modern-art-museum feel. This is one of the only hotels we've ever heard of that allows six people in one room, although those six people don't have air-conditioning and have to check out at the ungodly hour of 9am.

⇆ [M]Glacière. Walk down bd Auguste Blancqui and turn left onto rue Dareau. Walk 2 blocks and turn left onto rue Broussais, and then left onto rue Cabanis. ℹ Lockers €3 per day. Reserve at least 1 month in advance. [$] Singles €59; doubles €79; triples €105; quads €140; 5- and 6-person rooms €136-162. ⏰ Reception 24 hr.

HOTEL DU PARC HOTEL $$$$

6 rue Jolivet ☎01 43 20 95 54 www.hotelduparc-paris.com

Hotel du Parc enjoys a central location in the 14ème, nestled between the Montparnasse Tower and the Cimetière du Montparnasse. The view over the quiet park in front of the hotel provides a nice balance to the sometimes noisy bar and cafe scene of the surrounding streets. Rooms have modern decor with soft brown bedspreads and red and pink accents, and the walls are adorned with beautiful, up-close print of roses (budget romantics take note). Be sure to book well in advance, as there is often a steep difference in price between seasons.

⇆ [M]Edgar Quinet. Walk west on bd Edgar Quinet and turn left against traffic onto rue du Montparnasse. Turn right onto rue du Maine, then turn right onto rue Jolivet. ℹ Free Wi-Fi. Breakfast €12. Best to book at least a month in advance, especially in summer. [$] Singles €70-250; doubles €80-300; triples €90-300. ⏰ Reception 24hr.

PACIFIC HÔTEL HOTEL $$$$

11 rue Fondary ☎01 45 75 20 49 www.pacific-hotel-paris.com

Don't expect an ocean view or the sound of crashing waves if you stay here. With its mural of a lively garden and green wicker chairs welcoming guests, the lobby of the Pacific Hôtel will try to make you forget you are in a rather empty neighborhood. Despite this futile guise, we appreciate the effort. Rooms range from small and gray to spacious (by Parisian standards) and brightly colored, so ask to see another room if you're unhappy with yours.

⇆ [M]Dupleix. Walk south on rue de Lourmel, away from the Eiffel Tower, then turn left onto rue Fondary; the hotel is on the left. ℹ Free Wi-Fi. Breakfast €8. [$] Singles €75; doubles €86; triples €140. ⏰ Reception 24hr. Check-in 2pm. Check-out 11am.

HÔTEL CAMÉLIA HOTEL $$$$

24 bd Pasteur ☎01 47 83 76 35 www.hotelcamelia.fr

While dragging your suitcase up the narrow spiral staircase may be a drag, this hotel is conveniently located just one block from the Metro and a stone's throw from a collection of eateries and shops. The white rooms, accented by blue curtains and bedspreads, are a bit claustrophobic, so we recommend that you pack lightly.

⇆ [M]Pasteur. If the tower is on your left, you will see it across from the metro. ℹ Free Wi-Fi. Breakfast €6. [$] Singles and doubles €75-95; triples €130. ⏰ Reception 24hr. Check-out 11:30am. Check-in 1:30pm.

HOTEL MAGENDIE HOTEL $$$$

2-4 rue Magendie ☎01 43 36 13 61 www.belambra.fr

A standard two-star hotel with fake plants and whitewashed concrete walls, Hotel Magendie offers clean and box-like rooms that are comfortable, if somewhat forgettable. The lobby is more welcoming, with warm yellow walls adorned with several different maps of Paris. While lacking in excitement, this hotel is appropriate for the quiet, mostly residential area where it is nestled.

⇆ [M]Les Gobelins. Walk down bd Arago (it's bd St-Marcel in the other direction) and turn left onto rue Corvisart. ℹ Free Wi-Fi. Breakfast included. Garage €12. [$] Singles €118; doubles €140; triples €160. ⏰ Check-in 2pm. Check-out noon.

HOTEL ATLANTIQUE HOTEL $$$$

54 rue Falguière ☎01 43 20 70 70 www.hotel-atlantique-75.fr

The bright, robin's-egg-blue doors at this otherwise lackluster hotel may be the most exciting part of your stay, but at least it's something. The rooms are typically small, and some are awkwardly arranged in an impressive manipulation of geometric furniture; nevertheless, the beds are clean, comfortable, and just boring enough to put you to sleep at night.

 # [M]Pasteur. i Free Wi-Fi. Breakfast €6. [$] Singles €79; doubles €89-95; triples €120. ⏰ Reception 24hr.

THREE DUCKS HOSTEL HOSTEL $

6 pl. Étienne Pernet ☎01 48 42 04 05 www.3ducks.fr

It's always happy hour at the Three Ducks Hostel—the concierge desk doubles as a bar. They're so laid-back that they haven't gotten around to painting the walls or trimming the plants in the garden recently. If the frequency of people coming and going makes you feel more uneasy than social, you can ask to store your belongings in the safe at reception.

 # [M]Félix Faure. Exit the Metro across from St-Jean Baptiste Church and follow the street to the left. i Reserve at least 1-2 months in advance. Free Wi-Fi and computer. [$] High-season dorms €23; doubles €52. Low-season dorms €18; doubles €46. Beer €2.20-7. ⏰ Reception 24hr.

HÔTEL DE BLOIS HOTEL $$$

5 rue des Plantes ☎01 45 40 99 48 www.hoteldeblois.com

Those who get a thrill from finding a bargain should try their hand at the website for this 25-room boutique hotel. Prices vary between €65 and €200—it takes a bargain hunter's will and determination to nab one of the cheaper rooms. The pastel-colored rooms are in good shape and the neighborhood is peaceful.

 # [M]Alésia. Walk 2 blocks toward the Tour Montparnasse on rue du Maine and turn left onto rue de la Sablière. Turn right onto rue des Plantes. i Breakfast €12. Reserve at least 1 month in advance. [$] Prices vary depending on availability; check the website for current prices. ⏰ Reception 7am-10:30pm.

ALOHA HOSTEL HOSTEL $$

1 rue Borromée ☎01 42 73 03 03 www.aloha.fr

Although Aloha serves cheap cocktails, the lockout and 2am curfew might put a damper on your wild side. Then again, it does ensure that you don't have to take a taxi back, since the Metro will still be open, and the bar stays open late enough for you to get your nightcap on. There's free computer access, and the dorms and bathrooms are nothing to quibble with.

 # [M]Volontaires. Walk with traffic on rue des Volontaires. Turn left onto rue Blomet and walk 2 blocks to the corner of rue Blomet and rue Borromée. i Breakfast included. Reserve a few weeks in advance. [$] Dorms €28; doubles €64. Reserve with a credit card, pay in cash. ⏰ Curfew 2am. Lockout 11am-5pm.

ASSOCIATION DES FOYERS DE JEUNES: FOYER TOLBIAC HOSTEL $

234 rue de Tolbiac ☎01 44 16 22 22 www.foyer-tolbiac.com

If you're a woman aged 18-25 coming to work or study in Paris, Foyer Tolbiac is the place for you. This hostel reminds us of college dorms without the boys, and it's very affordable if you meet the narrow requirements.

 # [M]Glacière. Walk south on rue de la Glacière for 2 blocks and turn left onto rue de Tolbiac. The hostel is on the right. i Women ages 18-25 only; must "come to Paris with a professional project" like job hunting, training, or studies. Reserve by email at least 2 months in advance. Application and deposit required. Arrival fee €5. [$] Dorms €20. Monthly singles €411; doubles €600. For stays more than 3 nights, deposit of €46 required.

AUTEUIL, PASSY & BATIGNOLLES

Don't say we didn't warn you about this posh area. In the 16ème, you'll find a few "budget" options, while the 17ème has slightly more affordable digs (emphasis on the slightly). Only stay here if you're looking to experience the quiet, local, secluded, very pretty but rather boring side of Paris. If suburbia isn't really your scene, walk uphill to the 18ème, where hostels abound and budget hotels (the kind that don't rent by the hour) line the Red Light District and surround the Sacré-Cœur.

👍 **HOTELHOME PARIS 16** APARTMENTS $$$$

36 rue George Sand ☎01 45 20 61 38 www.hotelhome.fr

Nestled in a quiet residential neighborhood, HotelHome allows its guests to live like true Parisians during their time in the city. Each of the 17 apartments here is decorated with creative wallpaper designs that range from butterflies and leaves to world maps and cityscapes. All rooms have warm colors that truly give this place a home-away-from-home feel.

➡ [M]Jasmin. Walk south on av. Mozart and turn left onto rue George Sand. ℹ Free Wi-Fi. Breakfast and A/C included. All rooms have a separate bedroom, living room, and kitchenette. Discounts for early bookings. Services like shopping, meal delivery, laundry, babysitting, and guided tour scheduling available à la carte on request. [$] Junior suite (1-3 people) 30 sq. m €123-260; twin suite (1-4 people) 35 sq. m €180-345; double suite 45 sq. m (1-4 people) €207-385; family suites (1-6 people) 60-65 sq. m €288-580. ⏰ Reception open M-F 9am-2pm and at scheduled arrival and departure times.

HÔTEL POUSSIN HOTEL $$$$

52 rue Poussin ☎01 46 51 30 46 www.hotelpoussin.com

The Hôtel Poussin's prices are a bit steep, though not outrageous for this area, and the charming and comfortable atmosphere here is well worth the extra money. Rooms can be small but are brightly decorated with beautiful furniture and big windows. Watch an old film on the TV in the lobby with the gentle sound of water splashing from the fountain in the background; if you're in the mood for some fresh air, explore the flower market across the street or the gardens on the other side of the main boulevard.

➡ [M]Michel Ange Auteuil or [M]Porte d'Auteuil. Just in from the corner of rue Poussin and bd Montmorency. ℹ Free Wi-Fi. Breakfast €11 buffet in dining room, €15 in room. Ask about promotional prices, usually cheaper on weekends. [$] Singles €109-159; doubles €139-179; triples €179-259. ⏰ Reception 24hr.

HÔTEL PRINCE ALBERT WAGRAM HOTEL $$$$

28 passage Cardinet ☎01 47 54 06 00 www.hotelprincealbert.com

Given the yellow walls and green trim that adorn the lobby, hallways, and rooms of this hotel, you may feel like you're sleeping inside a key lime pie. Although you have not, in fact, wandered into a baked good, Hôtel Prince Albert Wagram is still a pretty sweet place. Tucked in the back of a quiet alley in the less frequented part of Batignolles, this hotel has rooms that will satisfy your appetite for comfort.

➡ [M]Malesherbes. Walk northwest up bd Malesherbes. Turn right onto rue Cardinet and then left onto passage Cardinet. ℹ Free Wi-Fi. Breakfast €6. A/C €10 per day. [$] Singles €75-102; doubles €90-110. Extra bed €20. ⏰ Reception 24hr. Check-in 2pm. Check-out noon.

HÔTEL BOILEAU HOTEL $$$$

81 rue Boileau ☎01 42 88 83 74 www.hotel-boileau.com

The newly renovated Hôtel Boileau promises a stay as charming as the neighborhood it's in. Your room may be up a stairway lined with framed photos and paintings or up a covered spiral staircase outside, which leads to more secluded rooms with floral walls and high ceilings. Regardless, prepare for a quiet, cozy, and flowery accommodation.

➡ [M]Exelmans. Walk down the right side of bd Exelmans and turn right onto rue Boileau. ℹ Free Wi-Fi. Breakfast €9 in dining room, €11.50 in room. [$] Singles €70-95; doubles €90-130; twins €100-135; triples €130-160. Extra bed €15. ⏰ Reception 24hr.

HÔTEL CHAMPERRET HELIOPOLIS HOTEL $$$$

13 rue d'Héliopolis ☎01 47 64 92 56 www.champerret-heliopolis-paris-hotel.com

This brightly lit boutique hotel with quiet, flowery (as in full of flowers) inner courtyard and private wooden balconies is perfect for grandparents, or those who appreciate the "homey" feel. Just make sure you can speak French, since the reception doesn't speak English.

[M]Porte de Champerret. [$] Singles €77; doubles €90, with bath €96; twin €96; triples with bath €120.

HÔTEL DE L'EUROPE HOTEL $$$

67 rue de Moins ☎01 53 31 01 20 hotel.europe75@gmail.com

Close to the 18ème, this Art Deco hotel explodes with random colors and patterns and has a room to suit just about anyone, from a long backpacker's single with just a sink to a large room with a kitchenette and bathroom for families or friends. Not to worry if you prefer to rough it: there are shared toilets on every floor and a shared kitchen on the ground floor.

[M]Brochant. With your back to the post office, walk 1 small block and turn left on rue de Moins. The hotel is ½ a block down on the left. [$] Singles €55, with shower €65, with full bath €75; doubles €65/75/88. Email reservations for triples and quads with kitchenette and bathroom; prices vary with availability and season but hover around €20-30 per person.

HOTEL RIVIERA HOTEL $$$$

55 rue des Acacias ☎01 43 80 45 31 www.hotelriviera-paris.com

Since it just went through an extensive makeover, the Riviera has rooms that actually smell brand new. Rooms have impeccable marble or tiled bathrooms with painted faux finishes on the walls; some even have large beds and day beds to convert a double into a triple or quad.

[M]Ternes. Exit Metro and walk toward the church St-Germaine until you cross where av. Mac Mahon turns into av. Niel. Make a slight left onto Acacias. The hotel is immediately on the right. Alternatively, [M]Étoile. With your back to the Arc de Triomphe, walk down av. Mac Mahon until you hit Acacias. Turn left and the hotel is immediately on the right. i Breakfast €7. [$] Singles €79; doubles €86-136; triples €120; quads €150.

don't get stuck

If you need a break from hectic city life, visit rue du Chat-qui-Pêche, the narrowest street in Paris. Built in 1540, the road contains only a few windows and no doors. The street's name, "Street of the Fishing Cat," comes from an ancient tale about a cat who fished in the flooded cellars of houses during monsoon season before the harbor was built on the Seine. A word of caution to prospective visitors: walking through the 1.8m wide street is not for the claustrophobic or faint of heart—it wasn't named for the stealthiest and most flexible of mammals for nothing.

MONTMARTRE

There are a lot of great budget hostels in Montmartre, and this area is a great place to meet other backpackers and (safely) gallivant about the Red Light District with your newfound friends.

PLUG-INN BOUTIQUE HOSTEL HOSTEL $

7 rue Aristide Bruant ☎01 42 58 42 58 www.plug-inn.fr

Recently opened, this hostel is named for the unlimited free Wi-Fi and computer use. The brand new rooms and untouched bathrooms make you feel slightly cleaner after being in the cabaret- and sex-shop-infused neighborhood, and the views of Paris from the roof are stunning. Check out their blog for details on *soirées* and various discounts.

⇆ Ⓜ Blanche Sarl. Face the Moulin Rouge and walk 5 blocks up rue Lepic. Turn right onto rue des Abbesses. Rue Aristide Bruant is the 1st right. ℹ Breakfast included. Free Wi-Fi and computer use. $ Dorms €25; doubles €60; triples €90. ⏰ Lockout 10am-3pm.

LE VILLAGE HOSTEL HOSTEL $$

20 rue d'Orsel ☎01 42 64 22 02 www.villagehostel.fr

With flags from around the world all over the walls and ceiling of the lobby, Le Village welcomes a young and international crowd looking for fun. Rooms are adorned with bright red walls and the even more colorful personalities of your hostelmates. Expect a good time during your stay, and don't be surprised if the lobby suddenly turns into a dance floor with flashing lights and bumpin' music.

⇆ Ⓜ Anvers. Turn right out of the Metro (there is only 1 exit here), then turn right again onto rue d'Orsel; the hostel is down the block on the left. ℹ Free Wi-Fi. Breakfast included. No curfew or lockout. $ Dorms €28-40; doubles €70-100; triples €96-117; quads €112-152. ⏰ Reception 24hr.

LE MONTCLAIR HOSTEL HOSTEL $$

62 rue Ramey ☎01 46 06 46 07 www.montclair-hostel.com

Complete with funky striped walls, a foosball table, and vending machines, Le Montclair is a standard young and hip hostel. Clean dormitories have shared bathrooms, but Montclair offers doubles with either a shower or full bath for those looking for more privacy.

⇆ Ⓜ Jules Joffrin. Follow rue Ordener and turn right onto rue Hermel and rue Ramney is the first left. ℹ Breakfast included. Computer €1.50 per 30min., €2.50 per hr. $ Dorms €29, with bath €35; doubles €76, with toilet €80, with full bath €88. ⏰ Lockout 10am-3pm.

PARIS FRIENDS HOSTEL HOSTEL $

122 bd de la Chapelle ☎01 42 23 45 64 www.paris-hostels.com

Located on the busy bd de la Chapelle right across from the Metro, the Paris Friends Hostel has some rooms that fall victim to the noise of the bustling nearby streets, but there are others that remain surprisingly quiet. While navigating your way to those back rooms may take some wiggling and several turns through the long hallways, the digs are worth it. The rooms here are cheap without being a total drag, and a place as big as this is filled with plenty of potential friends, meaning you won't run out of ways to meet new people.

⇆ Ⓜ Barbès Rochechouart. On the north side of the Metro stop. ℹ Free Wi-Fi, though some travelers have reported that it isn't entirely reliable. Breakfast €1. $ Dorms €16-18. ⏰ Reception 24hr.

HOTEL CAULAINCOURT HOTEL, HOSTEL $$

2 sq. Caulaincourt ☎01 46 06 46 06 www.caulaincourt.com

Hotel Caulaincourt doubles as a hotel and hostel, which means you can enjoy the comfort of a private room without sacrificing the fun and social aspects of hostel life. An upbeat tempo, zebra-striped lobby, and crew of fun-loving backpackers keep this place young. Dorm rooms are cozy, so expect to get to know your roommates well if you don't opt for a single room. Although this place has a strict no-alcohol policy inside or opened containers outside, the bar in the basement is open every night until 2am, which means there's always a place to party close to home.

⇆ Ⓜ Lamarck-Caulaincourt. Walk east, with the park on the left, down rue Caulaincourt. ℹ Free Wi-Fi. Breakfast included. Max. stay 7 days. Computers in lobby. Full payment due upon arrival; no refunds. Room key deposit €1. Towels and sheets €1. $ Dorms €31-33; singles €62-72; doubles €74-86; triples €99. Extra bed €15. Wine and pints €3.50 at Metro Bar. ⏰ Check-in 4pm. Check-out 11am. 2am curfew. Metro Bar downstairs open daily 7pm-2am.

HOTEL ANDRÉ GILL   HOTEL $$

4 rue André Gill   ☎01 42 62 48 48

Newly renovated as of 2012, Hotel André Gill offers its guests (essentially) brand spankin' new rooms for the price of the old ones. The bathrooms here have spotless colorful tiles, and the bed linens come in a soft, rosy color scheme. Tucked on a side street near some of Montmartre's busier bars, this place offers a great location for those looking to go out at night but still manages to keep things quiet. Young people frequent this affordable hotel, so spend some time in the breakfast room and make a few new friends.

🏳 ⓂPigalle. Exit the Metro and continue straight; turn right onto rue des Martyrs, then right again onto the short dead-end. *i* Free Wi-Fi. Breakfast €5. Ⓢ July-Aug singles €29-45; doubles €89-120. Sept-June €70/89-120. ⓚ Reception 24hr. Check-in 2pm. Check-out 10am.

BUTTES CHAUMONT & BELLEVILLE

This area is devoid of tourist accommodations, and it's not a place you want to be stumbling home to after bar hopping; be sure to call a cab if you over-indulge on your night out. You shouldn't stay this far out unless you want to be near the **Gare Routière International**.

L'HÔTEL DE PARIS   HOTEL $$$

188 av. Jean Jaurès   ☎01 42 39 41 37 info@hotel-de-paris.org

With warm yellow walls, colorful bedspreads, and small but charming water-color paintings, l'Hôtel de Paris won't disappoint. The halls and rooms are deceptively quiet considering this place's location on the busy av. Jean Jaurès, but if you're a light sleeper, it's probably best to ask for a room in the back of the building or on the top floor (don't worry, there's an elevator).

🏳 ⓂPorte de Pantin. Walk down av. Jean Jaurès with the park on your right. *i* Free Wi-Fi. Ⓢ Singles €55-65; doubles €65-75; triples 85. ⓚ Reception 24hr.

AUBERGE DE JEUNESSE "LE D'ARTAGNAN"   HOSTEL $

80 rue Vitruve   ☎01 40 32 34 56 www.fuaj.org

A healthy walk from the Metro and a stone's throw from the Cimetière du Père Lachaise, this is everything you'd expect from FUAJ: clean rooms (around 440 beds), a bar, a majority of French or non-Anglophone clients, and a totally relaxed atmosphere. Mingle with French transients and pregame at the bar before heading out.

🏳 ⓂPorte de Bagnolet. Exit onto bd Davout and take the first right onto rue Vitruve. The hostel is on the left. *i* Max. stay 4 nights. Breakfast included. Lockers €2-4 per day. Wi-Fi €2 per hr. Reserve online. Ⓢ Beds from €27. Discounts for International Youth Hostels Association members. ⓚ Lockout noon-3pm.

HÔTEL DE LA PERDRIX ROUGE   HOTEL $$$$

5 rue Lassus   ☎01 42 06 09 53 www.hotel-perdrixrouge-paris.com

Next to the Saint Jean-Baptiste de Belleville church and just steps from the Metro, Hôtel de la Perdrix Rouge offers a pricey, peaceful home base away from the clamor of central Paris. Surrounded by a bank, a grocery store, and several bakeries and restaurants, patrons will find the neighborhood tourist-free and generous when it comes to the necessities. Thirty clean, red-carpeted rooms come with bathrooms, hair dryer, telephones, and TV.

🏳 ⓂJourdain. Facing the church, the hotel is on the left side of the street. Ⓢ Breakfast €7.50. ⓚ Singles €73; doubles €79-92; triples €101. Book 30 days in advance to save €6 per night.

HIPOTEL PARIS BUTTES CHAUMONT   HOTEL $$$

7 rue Jean-Baptiste Dumay   ☎01 46 36 64 22 www.hipotel.fr

The Hipotel Paris Buttes Chaumont is one of six two-star "Hospitality in Paris" hotels. The Buttes Chaumont location has rooms that are a bit worn with age but offer the comfort of home with warm colors and big windows.

✚ ⓂPyrénées. *Walk down rue des Pyrénées and turn left onto rue Jean-Baptiste Dumay. Hipotel is on the left.* **i** *Free Wi-Fi. Prices usually lower on weekends.* Ⓢ *Singles €60-100; doubles and twins €80-120.* Ⓩ *Reception 24hr.*

SUPER HOTEL   HOTEL $$$

208 rue des Pyrénées   ☎01 46 36 97 48 www.superhotelparis.fr

Super Hotel has an exciting lobby with blue halogen lights lining the purple walls and the diner-like breakfast area. Unfortunately, that's the most super part of this hotel, given that the rooms are otherwise consistently boring. Mismatched bedspreads, curtains, and carpets add color if nothing else, and free A/C also keeps rooms cool in the summer, a rare find in Paris.

✚ ⓂGambetta. *The hotel is right off pl. Gambetta on rue des Pyrénées.* **i** *Free Wi-Fi. Breakfast €8. A/C.* Ⓢ *July 15-Sept 1 singles €60-70; doubles €75-90; triples €130. Sept 2-July 14 singles €80-95; doubles €100-120; triples €140. Extra bed €15.*

HÔTEL ERMITAGE   HOTEL $$$

42 bis rue de l'Ermitage   ☎01 46 36 23 44 www.hoteldelermitage.com

Hôtel Ermitage provides room with beds in them and a place to rest your head. That's about all there is to say about this comfortable but forgettable hotel. Rooms are separated from the stairwell for added privacy.

✚ ⓂJourdain. *Walk down rue de Jourdain and turn left onto rue des Pyrénées, then left onto rue de l'Ermitage. The hotel is on the right.* **i** *Free Wi-Fi.* Ⓢ *Singles €45-50; doubles €65.* Ⓩ *Reception 24hr.*

sights

Seeing everything in Paris is exhausting if not impossible (even we struggled a bit). For a short trip, visiting the main attractions can mean waiting in lines, fighting the urge to add the annoying couple in front of you to the body count at the Catacombs, and becoming completely desensitized to some of mankind's greatest feats of engineering and art. Give yourself a break. Before heading off to see something because you saw it on a postcard, check this section and decide what's really worth it. Some of Paris's most interesting sights are devoid of tourists. To save money and give yourself a more authentic Parisian experience, picnic in a park that once housed a palace; go to a less famous museum when the line for the Louvre is more than the flight time to CDG; and realize that some of the best (and cheapest) history lessons can be discovered at the city's churches, squares, and public landmarks. When you can appreciate the small things, the Louvre and the Eiffel Tower will be even more awe-inspiring.

ÎLE DE LA CITÉ AND ÎLE ST-LOUIS

Île de la Cité boils with tourists on the daily, especially those hungry for picture-perfect Kodak moments with the Notre Dame. The former seat of the French monarchy and the current seat of the French government make for a rich history that is worth learning about.

▨ NOTRE DAME   CATHEDRAL

Île de la Cité   ☎01 53 10 07 00

Centuries before it witnessed Quasimodo's attempts to rescue Esmeralda, Notre Dame was the site of a Roman temple to Jupiter. Having decided that a pagan temple would be a good place for some Catholic infusion, Rome began building churches, the last of which was Notre Dame in 1163. Taking a liking to the high Gothic ceilings and explosion of color from the large stained glass windows, the French nobility claimed it for most of their weddings (we can only assume Maui was booked at the time.) Among those who took their vows were François II to Mary Queen of Scots and Henri of Navarre to Marguerite de Valois. On the other side of the happiness spectrum, this is also where **Joan of Arc** was tried for heresy. She was only 19 at the time of her trial and subsequent barbecue. To make up for that tiny injustice, she was made a patron saint of France (after almost 500 years) and has her own shrine next to the Treasury.

The revolution had the same effect on Paris, and especially Notre Dame, as a drunken weekend in Vegas has on the individual. Everyone woke up five years later to discover that Notre Dame had been renamed the Temple of Reason and covered with a Neoclassical facade. It was later reconsecrated and served as the site of **Napoleon's** famed coronation in 1804. However, the building fell into disrepair, and for two decades it was used to shelter livestock. **Victor Hugo** cleared away the donkeys and pigs when he wrote his famed novel *The Hunchback of Notre Dame* in 1831, which revived the cathedral's popularity and inspired Disney to introduce the French idea of "gypsycide" to children all over the world. Restorations (read: major changes) by **Eugène Viollet-le-Du** included a third tower, gargoyles, and a statue of himself admiring his work. Most of the 20th century included more praying against German invasion (we know how that ended up) and famous masses for the funerals of both Charles de Gaulle and François Mitterrand.

If you've read this far, stay with us for a little longer. Here is what you need to see and do when visiting Notre Dame. First, as you enter, notice the headless figures above the doors. Revolutionaries thought that the King of Judah was somehow related to the French monarch (he's not) and decapitated him. From the entrance, you'll see massive crowds. Keep to the right and follow the arrows past Joan of Arc to the Treasury, where you can see Napoleon's sweet emperor cloak as well as relics like St. Louis's tunic. Jesus's thorny crown rests here too, but it's only revealed on the first Friday of the month at 3pm. Round the church and get a good look at the stained-glass window in the back and the altar from the priest's point of view. For the towers, you'll have to brave a line that only lets in 20 people at a time and a 422-step climb to the bell towers to take in the views of the Latin Quarter and the Marais. The *crème de la crème* is the 13-ton bell in the South Tower that requires eight men—or one hunchback—to ring.

✠ ⓜCité. Ⓢ *Free. Audio tour €5, includes treasury visit. Treasury €3, ages 12-25 €2, 5-11 €1.* ⓩ *Cathedral open daily 7:45am-6:45pm. Towers open daily 10am-5:30pm, last entry 4:45pm. Free tours in French M-F 2 and 3pm; English W-Th 2pm, Sa 2:30pm. Treasury open M-Sa 9:30am-6pm, Su 1:30-5:30pm; last entry 15min. before close. Su mass 8:30am (French), 10am (Gregorian Chants), 11:45am (international i.e. easy French with some English thrown in), 12:45pm, and 6:30pm.*

🏛 SAINTE-CHAPELLE   CHURCH
6 bd du Palais   ☎01 53 40 60 97 www.monuments-nationaux.fr
Everybody needs the occasional diversion to get through a service. Take the 13th-century equivalent of TVs in church: the stunning floor-to-ceiling stained-glass windows in the **Upper Chapel** of Sainte-Chapelle, illuminating dreamscapes of no fewer than 1113 individual Biblical stories. They really tried, but you just can't squeeze that many depictions onto stained glass and make it understandable without a priest (or tour guide) explaining each one. The easiest to make out is the Passion of the Christ, located at the apex of the Chapel. Originally designed to house the Crown of Thorns and an actual piece of the crucifix, Sainte-Chapelle has a good reason for its smaller size: most of the budget was blown

on the crown itself, purchased for the ungodly sum of UKE135,000 (adjust that puppy for about 800 years of inflation). They lost out anyway, since the crown now resides in Notre Dame. The **Lower Chapel** has a blue vaulted ceiling dotted with the golden symbol of the French monarchy, the *fleurs-de-lis*, and contains a few "treasures"—platter-sized portraits of saints. This was where mortals served God, while royalty got to get a little closer in the Upper Chapel.

⇆ [M]Cité. Within Palais de la Cité. $ €8, ages 18-25 €5, under 18 free. Twin ticket with Conciergerie €12.50, ages 18-25 €8.50, under 18 free. ⏰ Open daily Mar-Oct 9:30am-6pm; Nov-Feb 9am-5pm. Last entry 30min. before close. Guided tours in French 11am, 3pm, and 4:40pm; in English 3:30pm.

CONCIERGERIE PALACE, PRISON

2 bd du Palais ☎01 53 40 60 97 www.monuments-nationaux.fr

The Conciergerie is Paris's historical benchmark. Long before the palace/prison was built in 1302, the Île de la Cité was established as the French monarchy's playground for government business as well as a symbolic urination spot to mark their royal territory, if you will. When Charles V decided to relocate his royal residence from the island, he put a royal *concierge* in charge of running the palace and the prison. Despite all this, the Conciergerie is best known as the prison where revolutionary celebrities like Robespierre and the unforgettable Queen Marie Antoinette were put behind bars; it's also where over 2000 executions took place over the course of a single year. If you have a common French last name, check the list of executed prisoners to see if you have any long-lost guillotined relatives. Reconstructed prison cells show the difference between the common, dungeon-like image of medieval layman's quarters and the sweet digs criminal notables could buy to pimp out their cell—Marie Antoinette's room has a bed, a wall tapestry, a throw rug, and a table and chair for reading and writing. We bet Lindsay Lohan couldn't pull that off.

⇆ [M]Cité. $ €8.50, students €5.50, EU citizens ages 18-25 and under 18 free. Combined ticket with Sainte-Chapelle €12.50, students €8.50, EU citizens ages 18-25 and under 18 free. ⏰ Open daily 9:30am-6pm. Last entry 5:30pm. Tours in French 11am, 3pm.

PALAIS DE JUSTICE COURTHOUSE

4 bd du Palais ☎01 44 32 51 51

The Palais has witnessed the German spy Mata Hari's death sentence, Sarah Bernhardt's divorce from the Comédie Française, and Alfred Dreyfus's guilty verdict and subsequent declaration of innocence. Learning from the Joan of Arc mistake of the past, the court managed to declare Dreyfus innocent while he was still alive, but only after 12 years of solitary confinement on the hard-labor penal colony Devil's Island. While the courtrooms and legal consultants are open to the public, "public" does not mean foreigners. For those without an EU passport, you'll have to settle for the massive 1760 sq. m colonnade **Conciergerie** (above), through which every prisoner with a death sentence was marched (when they still did that).

⇆ [M]Cité. Within Palais de la Cité. ⏰ Open daily Mar-Oct 9:30am-6pm; Nov-Feb 9am-5pm. Last entry 30min. before close.

PONT NEUF BRIDGE

Though its name might suggest otherwise, the bridge cutting through the western tip of Île de la Cité is the oldest in Paris. Completed in 1607, it would have been the busiest street in Paris for tourists in the 17th century. Today the bridge is lined with lip-locked lovers, seated in the many romantic enclaves overlooking the Seine. That's about it, though: youthful romance and the occasional gargoyle (which you can find at just about every Gothic building in Paris) are all that Point Neuf has to offer nowadays.

⇆ [M]Pont Neuf.

CRYPTE ARCHEOLOGIQUE   MUSEUM

7 parvis Notre-Dame, pl. Jean-Paul II   ☎01 55 42 50 10 www.crypte.paris.fr

Hidden beneath the feet of the countless tourists traipsing about the plaza in front
of Notre Dame lies the Crypte Archeologique. The exhibit takes visitors through a
tour of ancient ruins that were excavated in the late 1960s. Here, visitors can take
a look at the history of Paris and its development beyond its geographical center
at the Île de la Cité. The oldest ruins date back to the Roman Empire, proving the
island's importance even 2000 years ago. The authenticity of the remains feels a
bit ruined by the rather industrial ceiling separating it from the Notre Dame plaza
above, but the exhibit is nonetheless a great historical find.

🍴 Ⓜ️Cité. *There is a set of stairs at the end of the plaza in front of Notre Dame that looks like an
entrance to the Metro.* Ⓢ *€4, seniors €3, ages 14-27 €2, under 14 free. Audio guides €3.* Ⓣ *Open
Tu-Su 10am-6pm, last entry 5:30pm.*

HÔTEL-DIEU   BUILDING, HOSPITAL

1 pl. Parvis Notre-Dame   ☎01 42 34 82 34

Upon realizing that it might be helpful to save actual people in addition to their
Christian souls (this was the Dark Ages, it was a pretty revolutionary idea), Bishop
St. Landry built this hospital in 651 CE. If you're wondering why you want to
visit a hospital, we would probably share your skepticism. However, the open air
colonnade and impeccably kept gardens are open to the public and are worth a
look for multiple examples of irony, including memorial plaques to Louis Pasteur
(in a country that doesn't pasteurize most of its milk and cheese) or doctors and
nurses using the garden as a smoking lounge.

🍴 Ⓜ️Cité. Ⓢ *Free.* Ⓣ *Open M-F 8am-8pm, Sa-Su 10am-5pm.*

QUAI D'ANJOU   ROAD

This quiet road along the northeastern side of Île St-Louis is a picturesque and
romantic summary of Paris. The walk along this part of the island in and of
itself is a nice, quiet getaway from the tourist traffic. The houses along this road
were once home to some big names, such as Voltaire, Daumier, and the Three
Mountains Press that published works by Hemingway and Ford Madox Ford.
Reading the placards (in French) along the way is a fun little walk of fame in
Paris. If none of this means anything to you, you will at least be able to enjoy the
view of the Seine and some of Paris's oldest and most beautiful hotels.

🍴 Ⓜ️Pont Marie. *The road wraps around the northeast edge of the island to the left after the Pont
Marie.* Ⓢ *Free.*

CHÂTELET-LES HALLES

Châtelet-Les Halles is perhaps Paris's densest tourist area, and that's saying something.
From the commercial indulgence of the pl. Vendôme to the mind-numbing grandeur
of the Louvre to the bizarre trends on display at the Musée des Arts Décoratifs, the
1er and 2ème arrondissements certainly have it all.

🖼 MUSÉE DU LOUVRE   MUSEUM

rue de Rivoli   ☎01 40 20 53 17 www.louvre.fr

Try as you might, it's impossible to see everything in the Louvre. The museum's
miles (yes, miles) of galleries stretch seemingly without end, and their collections
span thousands of years, six continents, countless artistic styles, and a vast range of
media. It's no wonder that the Louvre sees an average 8.5 million visitors per year.
Like most of Paris's spectacular sights, the Louvre was initially commissioned by
kings and intended as a tribute to…themselves. Thinking that those tributes should
be shared with everyone, revolutionaries made the museum permanent after
kindly asking the monarchy to leave. Napoleon filled the Louvre with plundered
goods from just about everywhere he went, and its massive bankroll has allowed
the museum to continue acquiring pieces that make Jean Paul Getty look like a

stamp collector. Successful trips to the Louvre require two things: a good sense of direction and a great plan of attack. If you're looking for detailed tours, the Louvre's website describes several thematic trails you can follow.

The museum sprawls four floors and three main wings: **Sully, Richelieu,** and **Denon.** To make this easier for you, we'll give you the breakdown of the floors, as the wings really have nothing in common other than to tell you where you are. The basement is where you'll be shuffled to buy tickets and make the daunting selection of which wing to enter first. Here you'll see the medieval foundations of the Louvre as well as its history, which reads like a European History 101 textbook. Appropriately, this is where some of the Louvre's oldest pieces are stored, which include sculptures from the 10th and 11th centuries and the first items from the Egyptian collection.

The **ground floor** houses some of the works that people flock to Paris to see. The *Venus de Milo* is in room 16 in the Sully wing, while the *Law Code of Hammurabi* is stored with the Near Eastern Antiquities in Room 3 of Richelieu. You can find the full extent of the Egyptian collection as well as Greek and Roman sculpture sprawled out on this level.

The biggest crowds are located on the **first floor,** and rightfully so. The most impressive halls of the museum are rooms 77 and 75 in the Denon wing, which house Théodore Géricault's *Raft of the Medusa*, Eugène Delacroix's *Liberty Leading the People*, Jacques-Louis David's *Coronation of Napoleon*, and Paolo Veronese's *The Wedding at Cana.* These paintings are all gigantic, which makes the crowds seem less of a hassle, as everyone can get a good view. We wish we could say the same for Leonardo's **Mona Lisa** (*La Jaconde* for those of you who like to sound lofty and enlightened). The tiny painting has an entire wall to itself, and there is almost always a crowd surrounding it. In the Richelieu wing, the museum has more Jesus-inspired paintings from the Renaissance as well as Napoleon III's fully furnished apartments.

On the **second floor,** only Sully and Richelieu are accessible. In Sully, all of the rooms are filled with French paintings that typically require some background in art history to fully appreciate. Richelieu is filled with student groups and more obscure tours checking out the remaining Belgian, Dutch, German, Russian, and Scandinavian works. These are pretty to look at, but you may be better off spending a little more time getting friendly with your favorites from earlier. At the Louvre, unless you're planning on bunking up next to the *Venus de Milo*, seeing everything is impossible. Just getting a glimpse of what's in front of you, though, is a pretty good start.

⇆ [M]Palais Royal-Musée du Louvre. ℹ The Carte Louvre Jeunes entitles the owner to 1 year unlimited access without waiting in line and free access for the owner and a guest W and F after 6pm. $ €10, under 18 and EU citizens ages 18-25 free. Special exhibits €11. Combined ticket €14. Carte Louvre Jeunes ages 18-25 €15, 26-29 €30. 1st Su of every month (does not include special exhibits) free. F after 6pm free for under 26 of all nationalities. Audio tour €6, under 18 €2. ⏰ Open M 9am-6pm, W 9am-10pm, Th 9am-6pm, F 9am-10pm, Sa-Su 9am-6pm. Last entry 45min. before close; rooms begin to close 30min. before museum. "Discovery trails" tours in English, French, or Spanish daily 11am, 2, and 3:45pm; sign up at the info desk.

poor francis

Francis I wasn't the most successful king. Among his failures were failing to become the Holy Roman Emperor, losing a series of wars in Italy, and being captured by the actual Holy Roman Emperor. He was captured and held in Madrid until he agreed to sign over all claims to Milan and Naples and hand over his two sons as payment for the ransom. Having done this, he returned to his comfy Palais du Louvre, only to invade Italy again and again until he ran out of money. Perhaps his only success was picking up a portrait for the palace during his conquests: The *Mona Lisa.* You win some, you (mostly) lose some.

JARDIN DES TUILERIES GARDEN

pl. de la Concorde, rue de Rivoli

Covering the distance from the Louvre to the pl. de la Concorde, the Tuileries are a favorite of tourists during the summer, and Parisians when there aren't too many tourists to scare them off (read: annoy them). In the tradition of matching garden size to house size, the Tuileries are a massive complex of hedges, trees, and a very large fountain. Originally built for Catherine de' Medici, the garden was modeled after her native Florence to make her feel more at home—or to take her mind off the fact that her husband, Henry II, was much more infatuated with his mistress. The gardens grew as each successive king added something to call his own. Today, the Tuileries are filled with food stands, merry-go-rounds, and a huge Ferris wheel near the rue de Rivoli entrance, quite different from the Tuscan sanctuary Henry imagined.

⇄ [M]Tuileries. $ Free. ⏰ Open daily June-Aug 7am-11pm; Sept 7am-9pm; Oct-Mar 7:30am-7:30pm; Apr-May 7am-9pm. Amusement park open June to mid-Aug.

MUSÉE DE L'ORANGERIE MUSEUM

Jardin des Tuileries ☎01 44 77 80 07 www.musee-orangerie.fr

Once the greenhouse of the Jardin des Tuileries, l'Orangerie opened as a museum in 1927. Today, it displays works by Impressionist and post-Impressionist painters including Monet, Matisse, Picasso, and Renoir. Since its conversion into a museum, L'Orangerie has become home to Monet's *Water Lilies* and received the collection of renowned art collector Paul Guillaume in the 1960s. This impressive list probably explains why it's impossible to enter the museum without waiting in line, even on weekdays. On weekends the wait can last up to two hours. Show up at 9am or on Free Sunday (the first Sunday of every month) if you don't want to roast in the sun for most of the day. If you're okay with a quick visit, the admission fee is reduced for the last hour it's open.

⇄ [M]Concorde. $ €7.50, students and after 5pm €5. Combined ticket with Musée d'Orsay €13. Free 1st Su every month. ⏰ Open M 9am-6pm, W-Su 9am-6pm.

ÉGLISE SAINT-EUSTACHE CHURCH

2 rue du Jour ☎01 42 36 31 05 www.saint-eustache.org

What do Cardinal Richelieu, Molière, Louis XIV, and Mme. de Pompadour have in common? Église St-Eustache is where each of them was baptized. As a result of some poor fundraising (surprising, since their marketing plan was to tax baskets of fish from the market at Les Halles), the church took over a century to build. You can still see the impact of this dearth of funds on its two towers, one of which is complete while the other is nothing more than a stump. The interior houses a pipe organ larger than that of Notre Dame, paintings by Peter Paul Rubens, and a silver sculpture dedicated to the victims of the AIDS epidemic. Église St-Eustache sees few tourists, allowing the intrepid few to enjoy the silence and grandeur of the 34m vaulted Gothic ceilings.

*⇄ [M]Les Halles. **i** Audio tours available in English, ID required. $ Free. Audio tour suggested donation €3. ⏰ Open M-F 9:30am-7pm, Sa 10am-7pm, Su 9am-7pm. Mass Sa 6pm; Su 9:30, 11am, 6pm.*

JEU DE PAUME MUSEUM

1 pl. Concorde ☎01 47 03 12 50 www.jeudepaume.org

Originally designed to house Napoleon III's *jeu de paume* courts in 1861, this building was transformed into an art museum in 1909. During WWII, the Nazis used the building as a storage area for confiscated paintings by Jewish artists and eventually sold most of this so-called degenerate art on the black market. Unsold art was unceremoniously burned in a bonfire near the museum. Since then, the museum has changed its focus a number of times and is currently dedicated exclusively to photography and cinematography. Exhibits change at least three times a year, and each one is usually accompanied by a series of related events, like talks and guided tours, so make sure to check the website before visiting.

✢ [M]Concorde. ℹ Students and ages 26 and under free last Tu every month from 5-9pm. Free guided tours W and Sa at 12:30pm. Check website for other guided tours. $ €8.50, students and under 26 €5.50, under 10 free. ⏰ Tu 11am-9pm, W-Su 11am-7pm.

PALAIS-ROYAL PALACE

25 rue de Valois ☎01 49 27 09 09

This palace has a history plagued with death, bad luck, and low funding. Cardinal Richelieu, who commissioned it, died the same year it was finally completed. Queen of England Henrietta Maria called the palace home after being kicked out of her own country for being Catholic. (The French reaction to her showing up was apparently "You're Catholic? Move into this palace!") Finally, in 1781, the broke Duke of Orléans had to rent out the space to raise money. It's a place to wander and window-shop, while the interior is occupied by government offices.

✢ [M]Palais Royal-Musée du Louvre. $ Free. ⏰ Fountain, galleries, and garden open daily June-Aug 7am-11pm; Sept 7am-9:30pm; Oct-Mar 7:30am-8:30pm; Apr-May 7am-10:15pm.

MUSÉE DES ARTS DÉCORATIFS MUSEUM

107 rue de Rivoli ☎01 44 55 57 50 www.lesartsdecoratifs.fr

Fashion-conscious Francophiles could easily spend a full day perusing the Musée des Arts Décoratifs. The complex is comprised of three different museums in addition to many smaller exhibits. **Arts Décoratifs** (Interior Design), **Mode et Textile** (Fashion and Fabric), and **Publicité** (Advertisement) are all dedicated to *haute couture* designs that the average tourist has probably never experienced. In the Arts Décoratifs, you'll find sheep-shaped chairs, elephant-shaped fountains, and chairs whittled into birds. The Mode et Textile has exhibits on the evolution of fashion from the '70s to the '90s and features small exhibits on prominent fashion designers, including Yves Saint Laurent. The jewelry collection, **Galerie des Bijoux,** will make anyone's engagement ring look embarrassing.

✢ [M]Palais Royal-Musée du Louvre. $ All 3 museums €9, ages 18-25 €7.50, under 18 and EU citizens 18-25 free. ⏰ Open Tu-W 11am-6pm, Th 11am-9pm, F-Su 11am-6pm. Last entry 30min. before close.

you say you want a revolution?

Paris was the center of one of the most violent and bloody revolutions in history. Here are some key revolutionary sites that can still (sort of) be seen today.

- **CAFE DE FOY:** Appropriately located in front of the Palais-Royal in the center of the city, this was where Camille Desmoulins supposedly sparked the first revolt, ending a speech against Louis XVI with the call "Aux armes!" If only your valedictorian speech stirred up that much commotion.
- **BASTILLE:** Thanks to its storming and subsequent destruction, the infamous fortress isn't there anymore. If you're lucky, there might be a carnival in the open *place* where the mighty armory once stood, where rioting Parisians freed a grand total of seven innocent civilians from tyrannical and unjust imprisonment in 1789.
- **TUILERIES:** This palace was also destroyed, but not by angry peasants. It was purposefully burned down in 1871 during the suppression of the Paris Commune. In its place is a huge garden where you can try to picture Marie Antoinette crying, after she was forced here from the Palais du Versailles.

THE MARAIS

You'll see more here than just strolling rabbis and strutting fashionistas. The eastern section of this *arrondissement* is a labyrinth of old, quaint streets dotted with churches and some of Paris's most beautiful mansions (particularly around the **place des Vosges**). The **Centre Pompidou,** the Marais's main attraction, breaks up the beige monotony in the western half (or maybe it's just a tourist eyesore). Though the Pompidou, quite like a spoiled child, steals the show, there are a number of other museums that are just as entertaining. If you aren't the museum-going type, **rue Vieille du Temple** and **rue des Rosiers** are great streets to explore.

CENTRE POMPIDOU — MUSEUM, LIBRARY

pl. Georges Pompidou, rue Beaubourg ☎01 44 78 12 33 www.centrepompidou.fr

Though describing the exterior of the Pompidou in words is almost impossible, we'll give it a shot: it features a network of yellow electrical tubes, green water pipes, and blue ventilation ducts. You have to see it to really get it. The center's functions are as varied as its colors; it serves as a sort of cultural theme park of ultra-modern exhibition, performance, and research space. It is home to the famous **Musée National d'Art Moderne,** whose collection spans the 20th century. TVs display what can be characterized as Andy Warhol's drug-induced visions alongside amorphous tie-dye colored statues, a giant mushroom, and a wall of globes with layered tape to represent the cancerous growth of wars and violence. The second floor features pre-1960s art with less provocative pieces but just as famous names: Duchamp, Picasso, and Miró. Temporary exhibits on international modern art fill the top floors. Other parts of the complex to explore include **Salle Garance,** which runs an adventurous film series; **Bibliothèque Publique d'Information,** a free, non-circulating library; **Institut de la Recherche de la Coordination Acoustique/Musique (IRCAM),** an institute and laboratory for the development of new technology; and the rooftop restaurant, **Georges.**

⇆ Ⓜ Rambuteau or Hôtel de Ville. $ Museum €12, under 26 €9, under 18 and EU citizens ages 18-25 free. Library and forum free. ⏰ Center open M 11am-9pm, W-Su 11am-9pm. Museum open M 11am-8:50pm, W 11am-8:50pm, Th 11am-11pm, F-Su 11am-8:50pm. Last entry 1hr. before close. Library open M noon-10pm, W-F noon-10pm, Sa-Su 11am-10pm.

paris

MUSÉE CARNAVALET — MUSEUM

23 rue de Sévigné ☎01 44 59 58 58 www.carnavalet.paris.fr

Located in Mme. de Sévigné's beautiful 16th-century *hôtel particulier* and the neighboring Hôtel Le Peletier de St-Fargeau, this meticulously arranged and engaging museum traces Paris's history from its origins to Napoleon III. The city's urban development is conveyed through paintings, furniture, and sculptural fragments. Highlights include Marcel Proust's fully reconstructed bedroom and a piece of the Bastille prison wall. (We tried, but shouting "*Vive la Revolution!*" doesn't entitle you to touch it.)

⇆ Ⓜ Chemin Vert. Take rue St-Gilles, which becomes rue du Parc Royal, and turn left onto rue de Sévigné. $ Free. ⏰ Open Tu-Su 10am-6pm. Last entry 5:15pm.

MUSÉE DE LA CHASSE ET DE LA NATURE — MUSEUM

62 rue des Archives ☎01 48 87 40 36 www.chassenature.org

The collection may be quirky, but it's sure to elicit some sort of response—whether it's fascination or disgust. The museum displays hunting-themed art, weaponry, and stuffed animals from several continents in lavish, elegantly arranged rooms that would bring a tear to Allan Quatermain's eye. While the Trophy Room is the most impressive section of the museum, it's basically a what's what of endangered species, the most arresting of which are a polar bear on its hind legs and a pair of cheetahs in a glass case.

⇆ Ⓜ Rambuteau. Walk against traffic on rue Beaubourg, turn right onto rue Michel le Comte, and left onto rue des Archives. $ €6, ages 18-25 and seniors €4.50, under 18 free. 1st Su of each month free. ⏰ Open Tu-Su 11am-6pm.

PLACE DES VOSGES   PARK

Paris's oldest and perhaps snootiest public square has served many generations of residents, from the knights who clashed swords in medieval tournaments to the hipsters who swap bottles during picnics today. All 36 buildings that line the square were constructed by Baptiste du Cerceau in the same architectural style; look for pink brick, slate roofs, and street-level arcades. The quaint atmosphere attracted **Cardinal Richelieu** (who lived at no. 21 when he wasn't busy mad-dogging musketeers), writer **Alphonse Daudet** (who lived at no. 8), and **Victor Hugo** (no. 6). It was also the venue for one of seven-year-old prodigy **Mozart's** concerts, inspiring every "My Child is an Honor Student" bumper sticker. Come here to people-watch, nap in the grass, and wish you were friends with Molière or Voltaire.

⚑ ⓜ*St-Paul or Bastille. Follow rue St-Antoine and turn onto rue de Birague.*

NATIONAL ARCHIVES   MUSEUM

60 rue des Francs-Bourgeois   ☎01 40 27 62 18 www.archivesnationales.culture.gouv.fr/arn

The most famous documents of the National Archives are on display in the Musée de l'Histoire de France, ensconced in the plush 18th-century **Hôtel de Soubise.** Two to three annual rotating exhibits feature such transformative documents as the Treaty of Westphalia, the Declaration of the Rights of Man, Marie Antoinette's last letter, and letters between Benjamin Franklin and George Washington. Louis XVI's diary entry for July 14, 1789, the day the Bastille was stormed, reads simply *"Rien"* ("nothing")—a reference to the hunt that day at Versailles rather than the riots in Paris. Also open to visitors are the apartments of the Princess de Soubise, which were sculpted with mythological motifs and feature works by Boucher. Call for information on current exhibits as well as occasional performances by foreign dance companies. The Archives's second location at **Hôtel de Rohan** (87 rue Vieille-du-Temple) is currently closed but is still worth a glance from the outside.

⚑ ⓜ*Rambuteau. Walk with traffic down rue Beaubourg and turn left onto rue Rambuteau.* *i* *2nd location at 87 rue Vieille du Temple is currently closed.* Ⓢ *€4, reduced €2, under 26 free. Temporary exhibits €6/4/free.* ✆ *Open M 10am-5:30pm, W-F 10am-5:30pm, Sa-Su 2-5:30pm.*

HÔTEL DE VILLE   GOVERNMENT BUILDING, PLAZA

pl. de l'Hôtel de Ville   ☎01 42 76 43 43
Information office: 29 rue de Rivoli

The Hôtel de Ville has been the location of Paris's city hall since 1357. Although the current building only dates back to 1882 after the original burned down in an eight-day blaze in 1871, the historic significance of the building and the pl. de Hôtel de Ville have withstood the test of time. Originally called the pl. de Grève, for centuries this area had been a gathering spot for both general community revelry and public execution until 1830 (you know, common French pastimes). Today, Hôtel de Ville is the most extravagant and picture-worthy non-palace edifice in the city, and the pl. de Grève is a center of community life. In the winter you may be able to (attempt to) ice skate on an impromptu rink, and in the summer you can watch tennis star Rafael Nadal dominate the clay courts on a big screen set up in the middle of the plaza during the French Open. Tours of the interior are only available by pre-arranged appointments, and occasionally temporary exhibits earn the distinct honor of displaying work inside the Hôtel.

⚑ ⓜ*Hôtel de Ville.* *i* *Tourist office entrance on rue de Rivoli. Special exhibit entry on rue de Lobau. Free group and individual tours available with advance reservation.* ✆ *Open M-Sa 9am-6pm; special exhibits Ma-Sa 9am-7pm.*

MAISON DE VICTOR HUGO   MUSEUM

6 pl. des Vosges   ☎01 42 72 10 16 www.musee-hugo.paris.fr

Dedicated to the father of French Romanticism and housed in the building where he lived from 1832 to 1848, the museum displays memorabilia from his pre-exile, exile, and post-exile days, including his family's little-known paintings and the desk where he wrote standing up. On the first floor, the collection reveals paintings of scenes from *Les Misérables* and other works. Upstairs, you'll find Hugo's apartments, a recreation of the bedroom where he died, and the *chambre chinoise*, which reveals his flamboyant interior decorating skills and just how romantic he really was.

⚓ ⓜSt-Paul or Bastille. Follow rue St-Antoine and turn onto rue de Birague. ⓢ Free. Special exhibits €7-8, seniors €5, under 26 €3.50-4. Audio tour €5. 🕐 Open Tu-Su 10am-6pm. Last entry 5:40pm.

FAIT AND CAUSE   GALLERY

58 rue Quincampoix   ☎01 42 74 26 36 www.sophot.com

This gallery draws large crowds with its award-winning exhibits dedicated to increasing humanist and humanitarian consciousness through documentary, photography, and other media. The most recent exhibit was on post-earthquake Haiti.

⚓ ⓜÉtienne Marcel. Follow rue Étienne Marcel and turn right onto bd de Sébastopol. Turn left onto rue Rambuteau and then right onto rue Quincampoix. ⓢ Free. 🕐 Open Tu-Sa 1:30-6:30pm.

ÉGLISE SAINT-PAUL SAINT-LOUIS   CHURCH

99 rue St-Antoine   ☎01 42 72 30 32

Dating from 1627, when King Louis XIII laid its first stone, the Église St-Paul is an imposing fixture on the colorful rue St-Antoine. Its large dome—a trademark of Jesuit architecture—is unfortunately currently covered for renovation. Paintings inside the dome, however, are on full display and depict four French kings: Clovis, Charlemagne, Robert the Pious, and St-Louis. The embalmed hearts of Louis XIII and Louis XIV were kept here in ruby red boxes before they were destroyed during the Revolution. The church's Baroque interior is graced with three 17th-century paintings of the life of St-Louis and Eugène Delacroix's dramatic *Christ in the Garden of Olives* (1826). A work by Lebrun is also on display, as are the holy-water vessels that were gifts from Victor Hugo.

⚓ ⓜSt-Paul. Walk against traffic on rue St-Antoine; the church is on the right. ⓢ Free tours in French at 3pm every 2nd Su of the month or upon request. 🕐 Open M-F 8am-8pm, Sa 8am-7:30pm, Su 9am-8pm. Mass Sept-June M 7pm, Tu-F 9am and 7pm, Sa 6pm, Su 9:30, 11am (official service) and 7pm; July-Aug Sa 6pm, Su 11am and 7pm. Confession Tu-F 10am-12:30pm, 5-7pm; Sa 4:30-6pm.

GALERIE THULLIER   GALLERY

13 rue de Thorigny   ☎01 42 77 33 23 www.galeriethuillier.com

One of Paris's most active galleries, Galerie Thullier has exhibits that rotate every two weeks, which means that is always something new to see when you visit. The art displayed here ranges across all styles, and the gallery exhibits a number of different artists at any given time. Although there is no real permanent exhibit, some artists have close relationships with the gallery and show their work here as often as possible.

⚓ ⓜSt-Sébastien-Froissart. Walk down rue du Pont aux Choux and turn left onto rue de Turenne, then right onto rue de Thorigny. 🕐 Open Tu-Sa 1-7pm.

MUSÉE DE LA POUPÉE   MUSEUM

7 Impasse Berthaud   ☎01 42 72 73 11 www.museedelapoupeeparis.com

Nestled in a cul-de-sac, the Musée de la Poupée is the ultimate fantasy fulfillment for those who occasionally still play with Ken and Barbie. With three small rooms of dolls that depict historical figures and styles from antiquity to the 1960s, the museum begs questions like: would Matel have had more luck marketing

paris

Napoleon and Louis XVI dolls to nerdy boys? Or, would it have been acceptable for your older brother to set fire to the Joan of Arc figurine?

🚏 ⓂRambuteau. Walk with traffic on rue Beaubourg and take a left onto Impasse Berthaud. $ €8, ages 12-24 and seniors €5, ages 3-11 and handicapped €3, under 3 free. Free 2nd F of each month 10am-noon. ⏰ Open Tu-Su 10am-6pm. Last entry 5:30pm.

MUSÉE D'ART ET D'HISTOIRE DU JUDAÏSME — MUSEUM

71 rue Vieille du Temple — ☎01 53 01 86 53 www.mahj.org

Displaying a very select portion of Jewish history in Europe and North Africa, with a focus on community traditions throughout the Diaspora, the Musée d'Art et d'Histoire du Judaïsme begins with the cut-and-dry aspect of circumcision (apparently Abraham did it to himself at the age of 99—that's commitment). Modern testimonials on Jewish identity are interspersed with exquisite ancient relics. While they have extensive collections of art and relics looted by the Nazis from Jewish homes, don't expect to learn anything about the horror of the Vélodrome d'hiver. History buffs, prepare to be appalled.

🚏 ⓂRambuteau. From the Metro, turn right onto rue Rambuteau, and then left onto rue Vieille du Temple. $ €6.80, ages 18-26 €4.50, under 18 and art students free. Special exhibits €5.50, ages 18-26 €4. Combined ticket €8.50/6. Guided tours €9/6.50. ⏰ Open M-F 11am-6pm, Su 10am-6pm. Last entry 5:30pm.

IGOR STRAVINSKY FOUNTAIN — FOUNTAIN

pl. Igor Stravinsky

This fountain's multicolored elephants, lips, mermaids, and bowler hats are inspired by Stravinsky's works and have been known to squirt water at unsuspecting bystanders. This is a good stepping stone to brace yourself for the Pompidou, or to adjust back to the real world after being mentally assaulted by it.

🚏 ⓂHôtel de Ville. Adjacent to the Centre Pompidou on rue de Renard.

LATIN QUARTER AND ST-GERMAIN

Sights, sights, and more sights. There's more to see in the 5ème and 6ème than there is time to do it in. If you're only in Paris for a short while, there are a few things you can't miss. The **Jardin du Luxembourg** is magnificent and, alongside the Tuileries, one of the best relaxation spots in the city. If you want museums with more than just paintings and sculptures, the **Musée National du Moyen Âge** and the massive **Musée de l'Histoire Naturelle** are two of Paris's most important collections. If you're the artsy type, don't miss the slew of galleries in the **Odéon/Mabillon** area. And if you're in the mood to walk in the footsteps of Jean-Paul Sartre, Simone de Beauvoir, and Ernest Hemingway, make sure to visit **Saint-Germain-des-Prés** and the **Shakespeare and Co. Bookstore.**

👍 **PANTHÉON** — HISTORICAL MONUMENT, CRYPT

pl. du Panthéon — ☎01 44 32 18 04 http://pantheon.monuments-nationaux.fr

If there's one building that doesn't know the meaning of antidisestablishmentarianism, it's the Panthéon. Because the Neoclassical building went back and forth between a church and a "secular mausoleum" over the years, it contains some surprising grave mates. Within the crypt, tombs alternate between Christian heroes such as St. Louis and Enlightenment thinkers like Voltaire, who would probably object to being placed so close to icons of church dogma. What's worse, both Foucault's pendulum and revolutionary statues lie above the remains of Joan of Arc and St. Geneviève. The trip up the dome has three stops with 360-degree views of the Marais and Latin Quarter, and you can meander the colonnade at the top for the allotted 10min. before being herded back down.

🚏 ⓂCardinal Lemoine. Head away from the river on rue du Cardinal Lemoine and turn right onto rue Clovis. Walk until you reach pl. du Panthéon. ℹ Dome visits Apr-Oct in Dutch, English, French, German, Russian, and Spanish. $ €8, ages 18-25 €5, under 18 free. Oct-Mar 1st Su of each month free. $ Open daily Apr-Sept 10am-6:30pm; Oct-Mar 10am-6pm. Last entry 45min. before close.

JARDIN DU LUXEMBOURG   GARDEN
Main entrance on bd St-Michel

As with most ornate things in Paris, these gardens used to be exclusively for royalty. When the great expropriation occurred around 1789, the fountains, statues, rose gardens, and well-kept hedges were opened to the public, ensuring a quick picnic spot for every student in the Latin Quarter and St-Germain. The Palais is still off-limits, but the best and most sought-after spot in the garden is the **Fontaine des Médicis**, a vine-covered grotto east of the Palais complete with a murky fish pond and Baroque fountain sculptures.

⚡ ⓂOdéon or RER B: Luxembourg. *i* Guided tours in French Apr-Oct 1st W of each month 9:30am. Tours start at pl. André Honorat behind the observatory. Ⓢ Free. 🕐 Open daily in summer from 7am to 1hr. before sunset; in winter from 8am to 1hr. before sunset.

GALERIE CLAUDE BERNARD   GALLERY
7-9 rue des Beaux-Arts   ☎01 43 26 97 07 www.claude-bernard.com

Claude Bernard is one of the oldest and most prestigious galleries in Paris, particularly on rue des Beaux-Arts and surrounding streets, where the galleries seem to occupy every other storefront. Founded in 1957, Claude Bernard is famous for hosting exhibits by famous artists such as DuBuffet, Kandinsky, and some guy named Picasso.

⚡ ⓂSt-Germain de Prés. Walk with traffic down bd St-Germain, turn left onto rue de Seine, then left onto rue des Beaux-Arts. Ⓢ Catalogues from past exhibits €8-30. Posters €8. 🕐 Open Tu-Sa 9:30am-12:30pm and 2:30-6:30pm.

MUSÉE ZADKINE   MUSEUM
100B rue d'Assas   ☎01 55 42 77 20 www.zadkine.paris.fr

Installed in 1982 in the former house and studio of Russian sculptor Ossip Zadkine (1890-1967), the pleasantly tourist-free Musée Zadkine houses a collection of his work along with contemporary art exhibits. While most artists, tend to stick to one area, Zadkine worked in 12 different styles, from Primitivism to Neoclassicism to Cubism, and the museum's collection represents all 12 of his creative periods. Zadkine's tremendous artistic range is the collection's greatest strength; visitors pore over his classical masterpiece *L'hommage à Apollinaire*, then immerse themselves in his more modern, emotionally raw *Maquette du Moment de la Ville Detruite*. The tiny forested garden, realized by landscape painter Gilles Clément, is a welcome retreat from the busier northern part of the 6ème.

⚡ ⓂVavin. At the intersection, turn left onto rue de la Grande Chaumière, then right onto rue Notre-Dame des Champs. Turn left onto rue Joseph Bara, then left onto rue d'Assas. *i* Guided tours available by reservation. Ⓢ Permanent exhibit free; temporary exhibits vary. 🕐 Open Tu-Sa 10am-6pm.

ARÈNES DE LUTÈCE   PARK, HISTORIC MONUMENT
49 rue Monge

Back in the days of the Romans in the first and second centuries, this arena was used for spectacles like ⚔**gladiator battles** and animal fights attended by as many as 15,000 people. Tamer audiences came for the plays and comedies, but we bet the place only filled up for the blood baths. There were actual baths here, too, but those aren't around anymore. Since the site was discovered and excavated in 1869, seating around the amphitheater has been restored and opened to the public. Occasionally there are summertime performances that feature music, comedy, theatre, and dance, but generally this circular sandpit is used for pick-up soccer games and various other forms of public folly (some things never change).

⚡ ⓂPlace Monge. At the intersection of rue de Navarre and rue des Arènes; the Metro stop is beneath it. *i* Occasionally hosts outdoor performances. 🕐 Opening times vary according to season.

paris

MUSÉE D'HISTOIRE NATURELLE

MUSEUM

57 rue Cuvier

☎01 40 79 30 00 www.mnhn.fr

Three science museums constitute the Museum of Natural History, all situated within the **Jardin des Plantes**. The four-floor **Grande Galérie d'Evolution** is the most impressive of the three. The center of the gallery is on the ground and first floors, where you'll discover Mother Nature's great intelligence and sometimes equally great sense of humor. The next two levels of the museum are an educational journey through the evolution of life and man's not-so-positive role in it. These parts are a little less interesting but do manage to educate without being too pessimistic. Next door, the **Musée de Minéralogie** displays rubies, sapphires, and other minerals—nothing terribly exciting. The **Galeries d'Anatomie Comparée et de Paléontologie** are at the other end of the garden.

🕈 Ⓜ*Jussieu. Walk down rue Jussieu with the Faculté des Sciences on your left until you hit the garden, then follow signs for the museums.* Ⓢ *Grande Galerie de l'Evolution €7, reduced €5, under 26 free; temporary exhibit €9, reduced €7, under 4 free. Galéries d'Anatomie Comparée et de Paléontologie €7, reduced €5, under 26 free.* 🕗 *Grande Galerie de l'Evolution open M 10am-6pm, W-Su 10am-6pm. Galéries de Paléontologie et d'Anatomie Comparée open Apr-Sept M 10am-5pm, W-F 10am-5pm, Sa-Su 10am-6pm. Last entry for all museums 45min. before close.*

ÉGLISE SAINT-ÉTIENNE DU MONT

CHURCH

30 rue Descartes

☎01 43 54 11 79

The smaller and less frequented Église St-Étienne once vied with the Panthéon for cryptic fame. Ste-Geneviève, the patron saint of Paris, is buried in the crypt of the nearby **Abbaye-Sainte-Geneviève**. As visitors started flocking to pay homage to Geneviève, chapels were built to satisfy the demand until the 16th century, when construction on St-Étienne du Mont began. The church has the French Revolution to blame for its disintegrated status: during the Revolution, it was closed and turned into a "Temple for Brotherly Piety." Mathematician Blaise Pascal and dramatist Jean Racine are buried here today. The structure's atypical façade blends Gothic windows, an ancient belfry, and a Renaissance dome and nave. Inside, the church's unique central attraction still inspires awe. Sculpted from stone and flanked by spectacular spiral staircases, the choir screen is among the last of its kind in Paris. To the right of the nave, check out a Herculean Samson holding up the wood-carved pulpit.

🕈 Ⓜ*Cardinal Lemoine. Walk against traffic on rue du Cardinal Lemoine, then turn left onto rue Clovis. The church is on the right.* Ⓢ *Free.* 🕗 *Open Tu-F 8:45am-7:30pm, Sa 8:45am-noon and 2:30-7:45pm, Su 8:45am-12:15pm and 2:30-7:45pm.*

LA SORBONNE

UNIVERSITY

45-47 rue des Écoles

www.english.paris-sorbonne.fr

France's most famous place of higher learning was founded in 1257 by theologist Robert de Sorbonne as a dormitory for poor theology students. The smartly located Sorbonne has since diversified its curriculum and earned a place among the world's most celebrated universities. Its sheer age makes American celebrations of its university bicentennials (or, you know, America's bicentennial) seem quite insignificant. Today, the French government officially controls the Sorbonne, having incorporated the university into its extensive, convoluted, and much-disdained public education system. Of the University of Paris's 13 campuses, the Sorbonne comprises four: Paris I, Paris III, Paris IV, and Paris V. Students studying at Paris IV take classes at the original 13th-century complex. Befitting its elite status, the Sorbonne remains closed to the public indefinitely, although the Chapelle de la Sorbonne might re-open after restoration. Cafes, students, and all the wonderful things that result from mixing cafes with students (PDA, hipsters, self-importance, etc.) are in the nearby pl. de la Sorbonne, making it a favorite destination for chilling and people-watching.

🕈 Ⓜ*Cluny-La Sorbonne. Walk with traffic on bd St-Germain, turn right onto rue St-Jacques, then turn right onto rue des Écoles.* 𝒊 *Closed to the public.*

sights

MUSÉE NATIONAL DU MOYEN ÂGE (MUSÉE DE CLUNY) MUSEUM

6 pl. Paul Painlevé ☎01 53 73 78 00 www.musee-moyenage.fr

Originally occupied by Gallo-Roman baths and then by the 15th-century Hotel of the Abbots of Cluny, the Musée National du Moyen Âge sits on one of the prime pieces of historic real estate in Paris. The main attraction, *La Dame à la licorne*, is a collection of tapestries featuring every little girl's dream pet: the unicorn. The horned animal paradoxically represented both a Christ figure and a profane abomination, depending on how it was depicted through the ages. In addition to making you nostalgic for My Little Pony, the museum hosts many exhibitions, including one on medieval sword fighting.

➜ ⓂCluny-La Sorbonne. Walk up bd St-Michel and turn left onto rue du Cluny. $ €8, ages 18-25 €6, EU citizens under 26 free; includes audio tour. 1st Su of the month free. ⏰ Open M 9:15am-5:45pm, W-Su 9:15am-5:45pm. Last entry 5:15pm.

JARDIN DES PLANTES GARDEN, MUSEUM, ZOO

57 rue Cuvier ☎01 40 79 30 00 www.mnhn.fr

This one is a doozy. Within the Jardin des Plantes, you can find a whopping five museums, a garden, and a zoo. The **Museum of Natural History,** divided into three separate institutions, is housed here. Of its constituent parts, the four-floor **Grande Galérie d'Évolution** is the best; while not striking in and of itself, it looks better alongside its positively horrible comrades. The exhibit illustrates evolution with a series of stuffed animals (Curious George not included) and numerous multimedia tools. Next door, the **Musée de Minéralogie** displays rubies, sapphires, and other minerals. The **Galeries d'Anatomie Comparée et de Paléontologie** are at the other end of the garden. Inside is a ghastly cavalcade of femurs, ribcages, and vertebrae from prehistoric animals (all the ingredients to create your own Frankenstein). Despite some snazzy new placards, the place doesn't seem to have changed much since it opened in 1898; it's almost more notable as a museum of 19th-century grotesquerie than as a catalogue of anatomy. The largest part of the garden is taken up by the **menagerie,** which houses an impressive reptile terrarium as well as a huge ape house with orangutans.

➜ ⓂJussieu. $ Musée de Minéralogie €8, students under 26 €6. Galéries d'Anatomie Comparée et de Paléontologie €7, under 26 free. Grande Galerie de l'Évolution €7, students under 26 free. 2-day passes for the 3 museums and the menagerie €25. ⏰ Museums open W-Su 10am-5pm. Last entry for all museums 4:15pm.

SHAKESPEARE AND CO. BOOKSTORE BOOKSTORE

37 rue de la Bûcherie ☎01 43 25 40 93 www.shakespeareandcompany.com

Sylvia Beach's original Shakespeare and Co. at 8 rue Dupuytren (later at 12 rue de l'Odéon) is legendary among Parisian Anglophones and American literature nerds alike. An alcoholic expat crew of writers gathered here in the '20s; Hemingway described the bookstore in *A Moveable Feast.* After closing during WWII, George Whitman—no relation to Walt—opened the current rag-tag bookstore on the shores of the Seine in 1951, dubbing it "a socialist utopia masquerading as a bookstore." You're free to grab a book off the shelves, camp out, and start reading. This isn't your run-of-the-mill, money-machine bookstore; they're in it for the love of the game.

➜ ⓂSt-Michel. Take quai de Montebello toward Notre Dame and turn right onto rue St-Jacques. Rue de la Bûcherie is on the left. ⏰ Open daily 10am-11pm.

ÉGLISE SAINT-GERMAIN-DES-PRÉS CHURCH

3 pl. St-Germain-des-Prés ☎01 55 42 81 33 www.eglise-sgp.org

The Église St-Germain-des-Prés is the oldest church in Paris, and it shows. A popular place to store loot from the Holy Land, this church was sacked by the Normans and was the trial run for revolutionaries looking to hone their storming abilities before the Bastille. Apparently this didn't send a strong enough message the first time, so the revolutionaries returned in 1792 to kill 186 priests (it probably wasn't fairest fight). The abuse continued after, with someone missing the "No Smoking" sign next to 15 tons of gunpowder in 1794, and the church suffered complete devastation when urban planner Georges-Eugène Haussmann extended rue des Rennes in the 1850s, tearing down what was left of the abbey. It has since been refurbished with frescoes, mosaics, and, oddly enough, the interred heart of René Descartes.

✝ Ⓜ*St-Germain-des-Prés.* Ⓢ *Free.* 🕐 *Open daily 8am-7:45pm. Information office open M 2:30-6:45pm, Tu-F 10:30am-noon and 2:30-6:45pm, Sa 3-6:45pm.*

LA FONTAINE DE SAINT-SULPICE   HISTORIC MONUMENT
pl. St-Sulpice

Situated adjacent to the church in the middle of the pl. St-Sulpice, this fountain by sculptor Louis Visconti is often known as *La Fountaine des Quatre Points Cardinaux.* The rather bitter nickname is to deride the four ambitious bishops—Bossuet, Fénelon, Massillon, and Fléchier—who grace its four sides. None of these men ever became cardinals. How hard you choose to mock them should be based on whether you think becoming a cardinal or being enshrined on a monumental fountain is a bigger achievement.

✝ Ⓜ*St-Sulpice.*

MUSÉE DELACROIX   MUSEUM
6 rue de Furstemberg   ☎01 44 41 86 50 www.musee-delacroix.fr

If you really like the Romantic era, you'll have a blast here. Painter Eugène Delacroix, the artistic master behind the famous *Liberty Leading the People* (which is actually housed in the Louvre), lived in this three-room apartment. It has since been turned into a museum filled with his watercolors, engravings, letters to Théophile Gautier and George Sand, sketches for his work in the Église St-Sulpice, and souvenirs from his journey to Morocco.

✝ Ⓜ*St-Germain-des-Prés. Walk toward Odéon and turn left onto rue Cardinale. The museum is straight ahead as the street bends left.* 𝒊 *Free same-day entry with a Louvre ticket.* Ⓢ *€5, students and under 18 free.* 🕐 *Open June-Aug M 9:30am-5pm, W-Su 9:30am-5:30pm; Sept-May M 9:30am-5pm, W-Su 9:30am-5pm. Last entry 30min. before close.*

found underground

Paris is a city of appearances, and this extends to the aesthetic effort that the city has put into decorating its Metro stations. With artful posters and complimentary graffiti, certain stops are tourist destinations themselves.

- **ABBESSES.** This Montmartre station has a winding staircase that lets the athletically inclined trek seven stories to the exit. Although there's an elevator, take the stairs to appreciate the mural depicting abstract scenes of Paris.

- **SAINT-GERMAIN-DES-PRÈS.** This station holds a collection of famous poetry books in glass cases. Not only that, projectors blow up quotes from French poets onto the walls, making for some higher quality reading during the morning commute than the usual tabloids.

- **CONCORDE.** This one's for people who love both history and Scrabble. The station has what looks like a gigantic word search, and the letters spell out the Declaration of the Rights of Man penned during the French Revolution.

- **ARTS ET MÉTIERS.** Redesigned in 1994 with inspiration from the Conservatory of Arts and Crafts Museum above, this stop looks like a submarine, complete with metallic walls and portholes. Don't forget your oxygen tank.

sights

GRANDE MOSQUÉE DE PARIS   MUSEUM, MOSQUE

39 rue Geoffroy St-Hilaire   ☎01 43 31 38 20 www.mosquees-de-paris.net

The Grande Mosquée de Paris was built in 1920 to honor the contributions of North African countries during WWI. Given the nature of the times, the North Africans had to build it themselves, but the French did at least finance the construction. While prayer and worship spaces are closed to the public, all visitors are welcome to wonder at the 33m minaret, sweat it out in the hammam's marble steam baths, and sip mint tea in the cafe.

⚡ ⓂCensier Daubenton. ⑤ Guided tour €3, students €2. Hammam (steam bath), 10min. massage, and black tea €38. ⌚ Cafe open daily 9am-11:30pm. Restaurant open daily noon-evening. Hammam open for women M 10am-9pm, W-Th 10am-9pm, F 2pm-9am, Sa 10am-9pm; open for men Tu 2-9pm, Su 10am-9pm.

GALERIE LOEVENBRUCK   GALLERY

6 rue Jacques Callot   ☎01 53 10 85 68 www.loevenbruck.com

This gallery displays contemporary art of every medium—sculpture, painting, photography, and some interesting mixed-media pieces like wood and blown glass. Most artists exhibited here are French, although the gallery occasionally showcases work from Belgium and other parts of Europe. Exhibits change every month, which is appropriate, as the gallery comprises a single room.

⚡ ⓂMabillon. Walk with traffic down bd St-Germain. Turn left onto rue Mazarine, then left onto rue Jacques Callot. ⌚ Open Tu-Sa 11am-7pm.

CAFÉ DE FLORE   HISTORIC CAFE

172 bd St-Germain   ☎01 45 48 55 26

Legend has it that when Jean-Paul Sartre dined here, he and his friends (with benefits, if we're talking Simone de Beauvoir) sat on the opposite side of the cafe from communist Marguerite Duras and company. If the coffee at Fouquet's was too rich for your taste, you can get the Left Bank's version for almost half the cost and feel just as spiffy and a little bit more intellectual.

⚡ ⓂSt-Germain-de-Prés. ⑤ Coffee €4.10. Cocktail "Le Flore" €15. ⌚ Open daily 7:30am-1:30am.

LES DEUX MAGOTS   HISTORIC CAFE

6 pl. St-Germain-des-Prés   ☎01 45 48 55 25

Attracting intellectuals and those who just like to be seen, Les Deux Magots was a lot cheaper back when Hemingway, Camus, and Picasso visited, which may have been why it almost went bankrupt in 1913. Today it's far from broke, although the coffee is 10 cents cheaper than at neighboring Le Café de Flore.

⚡ ⓂSt-Germain-des-Prés. ⑤ Coffee €4. Mixed drinks €13. ⌚ Open daily 7:30am-1am.

MUSÉE DU LUXEMBOURG   MUSEUM

19 rue Vaugirard   ☎01 40 12 62 00 www.museeduluxembourg.fr

The Musée du Luxembourg is housed in a small segment of the historic Palais du Luxembourg. There is no permanent exhibit at this museum, but the temporary exhibit changes twice a year and alternates between modern and Renaissance art. If Renaissance Venetians like Cima de Conegliano are your thing, go for it. Otherwise, this whole museum can be seen in an hour or less and isn't necessarily worth the money. Unless it's a rainy day, your time will be better spent enjoying the great outdoors of Paris in the Jardin du Luxembourg.

⚡ ⓂSt-Sulpice. Walk away from rue de Rennes on rue Madames until you hit the garden. Or RER Luxembourg; enter the garden and follow signs to the museum. ⓘ Guided tours available by appointment. ⑤ €11; ages 13-25, art professors, professional artists, and unemployed €7.50; under 13 and handicapped free. Audio guides €4, reduced €3. ⌚ Open M-Th 10am-7:30pm, F 10am-10pm, Sa-Su 10am-7:30pm.

INVALIDES

Visit this *arrondissement* more than once if you can. Unsurprisingly, the *Tour Eiffel* towers over all of the 7ème attractions, but this posh neighborhood also hosts the French national government, a number of embassies, and an astonishing concentration of famous museums. Be sure to stop by the **Musée Rodin** and **Musée d'Orsay.**

▓ EIFFEL TOWER
TOWER

Champs de Mars, closest to the Seine   ☎01 44 11 23 23 www.tour-eiffel.fr

In 1937, Gustave Eiffel said, "I ought to be jealous of that tower; she is more famous than I am." The city of Paris as a whole could share the same lament, especially since the Eiffel Tower has come to stand for Paris itself. Gustave Eiffel designed it to be the tallest structure in the world, intended to surpass the ancient Egyptian pyramids in size and notoriety. Apparently hard to impress, Parisian society continues to shrug in disappointment; the response they'll give is usually, "*c'est honteux*" (it's shameful). Despite the national love-hate relationship, over 150 million Parisians and (mostly) tourists have made it the most visited paid monument in the world, proving once again the French ability to make a fuss and do nothing about it.

    Still, at 324m—just a tad shorter than New York City's Chrysler Building—the tower is a tremendous feat of design and engineering, though wind does cause it to occasionally sway 6 to 7cm (nobody's perfect). The unparalleled view from the top floor deserves a visit. The cheapest way to ascend the tower is by burning off those *pain au chocolat* calories on the world's tallest stairmaster, although the third floor is only accessible by elevator. Waiting until nightfall to make your ascent cuts down the line and ups the glamour. At the top, captioned aerial photographs help you locate other famous landmarks; on a clear day it is possible to see Chartres, 88km away. From dusk until 2am (Sept-May 1am) the tower sparkles with light for 10min. on the hour.

    ✟ Ⓜ*Bir-Hakeim or* Ⓜ*Trocadéro.* Ⓢ *Elevator to 2nd fl. €8.20, ages 12-24 €6.60, 4-11 and handicapped €4.10, under 4 free; elevator to top €13.40/11.80/9.30/free; stair entrance to 2nd fl. €4.70/3.70/3.20/ free. Buy your ticket online and pick your time to climb and cut down the wait. Champagne bar on top, €10 per glass (don't say we didn't warn you).* ☾ *Elevator open daily June 17-Aug 28 9am-12:45pm; Aug 29-June 16 9:30am-11:45pm; last entry 45min. before close. Stairs open daily June 17-Aug 28 9am-12:45pm, last entry at midnight; Aug 29-June 16 9:30am-6:30pm, last entry 6pm.*

▓ CHAMPS DE MARS
PARK

Lined with more lovers than trees, the expansive lawn that stretches from the École Militaire to the Eiffel Tower is called Champs de Mars (Field of Mars). Close to the neighborhood's military monuments and museums, it has historically lived up to the Roman god of war for whom it was named. The open field has been used for military boot camp and as a convenient place for violent demonstrations, including but not limited to civilian massacres during the Revolution. At the end toward the Military School is the "Wall of Peace," a glass structure that has 32 languages worth of the word "peace" in an attempt to make up for the field's bloody past.

    ✟ Ⓜ*La Motte Picquet-Grenelle or* Ⓜ*École Militaire.*

▓ MUSÉE RODIN
MUSEUM

79 rue de Varenne   ☎01 44 18 61 10 www.musee-rodin.fr

According to Parisians in the know, this museum is one of the city's best. During his lifetime, Auguste Rodin (1840-1917) was among the country's most controversial artists and was considered by many to be the sculptor of Impressionism. Today, the art world considers him the father of modern sculpture and applauds him for imbuing stone with a downright groovy level of "psychological complexity." While most of his lesser known sculptures are inside the former Hôtel Biron, the 18th-century building where he lived and worked, the two absolute museum must-sees are *Le Penseur (The Thinker)*, and *La Porte de L'Enfer (The Gates of Hell)*. These

two are rightfully displayed side by side: *The Thinker* is Dante contemplating the *Divine Comedy*, which is portrayed in the *Gates of Hell*, a bronze mess of lustful pairs swirling in the violent turbulence of the second ring of Hell.

✈ ⓂVarenne. *i Temporary exhibits housed in the chapel, to the right as you enter. Touch tours for the blind and educational tours available (☎01 44 18 61 24). ⑤ Museum €9, ages 18-25 €5, under 18 and EU citizens under 26 free. Joint ticket with Musée d'Orsay €12. Garden €1/1/free. 1st Su of the month free. Audio tours in 7 languages €4 each for permanent and temporary exhibits, combined ticket €6. ⑤ Open Tu-Su 10am-5:45pm; last entry 5:15pm.*

🖼 MUSÉE D'ORSAY   MUSEUM
62 rue de Lille   ☎01 40 49 48 14 www.musee-orsay.com

Aesthetic taste is fickle. When a handful of artists were rejected from the Louvre salon in the 19th century, they opened an exhibition across the way, prompting both the scorn of stick-up-their-arses *académiciens* and the rise of Impressionism. Today, people line up at the Musée d'Orsay to see this collection of groundbreaking rejects. Originally built as a train station, the Musée d'Orsay opened as President Mitterrand's gift to France. It gathered works from the Louvre, Jeu de Paume, Palais de Tokyo, Musée de Luxembourg, provincial museums, and private collections to add to the original collection the Louvre had refused. On the ground floor, you can see the pre-Impressionist paintings, and it only gets weirder as you go up. In the back sits a model of the Parisian Opera cut in two to reveal the inside. Despite our best efforts, we were unable to find the elusive Phantom. The top floor includes all the big names in Impressionist and Post-Impressionist art: Degas, Manet, Monet, Seurat, and Van Gogh. Degas's famed "dancers" are a particular highlight.

✈ ⓂSolférino. *Access to visitors at entrance A off the square at 1 rue de la Légion d'Honneur. ⑤ €8, ages 18-25 €5.50, under 18 and EU citizens 18-26 free. 🕐 Open Tu-W 9:30am-6pm, Th 9:30am-9:45pm, F-Su 9:30am-6pm. Visitors asked to leave 30min. before close.*

MUSÉE DE L'ARMÉE MUSEUM

129 rue de Grenelle ☎01 44 42 37 64 www.invalides.org

Americans in favor of the Second Amendment, European empire enthusiasts, and war buffs will all find a visit to the Musée de l'Armée a sure-fire good time. Housed inside the grand Hôtel des Invalides and built by Louis XIV for his war veterans, the Musée de l'Armée is comprised of six main parts. The elegant **Église du Dôme** is the most recognizable part of the museum from the outside and famously holds the tomb of Napoleon that was ornately erected in the very center of the dome. The dome and the **Saint-Louis des Invalides Chapel** are flanked by the Charles de Gaulle historial and collections covering Louis XIV to Napoleon III in the East wing and the WWI and WWII exhibit and ancient armor and arms collections in the west wing. The historial will test your audiovisual sensibilities with a thrilling account of Charles de Gaulle's unforgettable stamp on the 20th century, while a combination of objects, videos, interactive maps, and propaganda will keep you on your toes in the exhibit on WWI and WWII.

🚶 Ⓜ Invalides or Ⓜ La Tour-Maubourg. The museum is located in the center of the park. ℹ The Charles de Gaulle Historial and chapel are currently under renovation but are still open to the public. $ Admission to all museums €9, students under 26 €7, EU citizens and under 18 free; after 5pm and late on Tu €7. Temporary exhibits €8. Entrance to both permanent and temporary €11. Audio guides €6, under 26 €4. ⏰ Open Apr-Sept M 10am-6pm, Tu 10am-9pm, W-Su 10am-6pm; Oct-Mar daily 10am-5pm. Closed 1st M of each month. Charles des Gaulle Historial closed every M.

MUSÉE DE LÉGION D'HONNEUR MUSEUM

2 rue de la Légion d'Honneur ☎01 40 62 84 94 www.musee-legiondhonneur.fr

The Légion d'Honneur is the French military hall of fame, awarding members admittance for courage, military finesse, and patriotism since its founding by Napoleon Bonaparte in 1802. The museum displays glorious military decorations and artifacts of war and requires only a brief (and free) visit. The audio guides give each piece meaning and lead visitors through the well-organized collection. Have a chat with the unusually cheerful museum guards and they will be excited to point out some highlights. One of the collection's prized pieces is Napoleon's Collier de la Légion d'Honneur, made by Biennais in gold and enamel, which the emperor wore at his coronation and is often pictured with when painted in imperial costume.

🚶 RER Musée d'Orsay or Ⓜ Solférino. ℹ Handicapped entrance at 1 rue de Solférino. $ Free entrance and audio guide. ⏰ Open W-Su 1-6pm.

INVALIDES MUSEUM

Esplanade des Invalides ☎08 10 11 33 99 www.invalides.org

This is a must see for history buffs. A comprehensive collection of all things war-like and French (yes, including the defeats), this building is more than just a pretty gold dome. Although you have to pay to enter the various military museums as well as **Napoleon's tomb,** the majority of the complex is accessible for **free,** including the inner courtyard (tip: it's about 15 degrees cooler in the shade), upper walkway, and the St-Louis des Invalides Chapel, all of which have samples of what's inside the museums, including a battery of 60 cannons. Also check out the Charles de Gaulle *Historial* (film), which outlines the famed president/general's efforts during the Nazi resistance. There are also a number of rotating exhibitions that highlight particular times in French military history, from Louis XI "The Spider King," to the wars in Indochina.

🚶 Ⓜ Invalides. $ €9, under 18, EU citizens 18-25 free. ⏰ Open Apr-Sept M 10am-6pm, Tu 10am-9pm, W-Su 10am-6pm; Oct-Mar daily 10am-5pm. Closed 1st M each month. Charles de Gaulle Historial closed M. Films show every 30min. Dome open Jul-Aug until 7pm.

MUSÉE DU QUAI BRANLY MUSEUM

37 quai Branly ☎01 56 61 71 72 www.quaibranly.fr

A gift to the French people from Jacques Chirac, this adventure/time machine/museum sucks you in with its overgrown gardens of exotic plants under the shade of the raised modern building. Don't let the architecture fool you: this museum houses a huge collection of ancient artifacts from tribal cultures around the world. Organized into four areas (Africa, Asia, Americas, and Oceania), the museum has anticipated your impending boredom and made itself as visually and auditorily stimulating as possible. Timothy Leary would be so proud. In case you can't tell the difference between a Nepalese tunic and an African one, look at the floor: the color under your feet corresponds to what section of the world you are in. Be sure to sit in one of the many hidden sound caves to take in some tribal noises in solitude, but beware of local high school students using the dark spaces as personal make out rooms.

 # Ⓜ Alma-Marceau. Cross Pont de l'Alma and follow quai Branly toward the Eiffel Tower. $ €8.50, under 18 and EU citizens 18-25 free. ⏰ Open Tu-W 11am-7pm, Th-Sa 11am-9pm, Su 11am-7pm.

ÉCOLE MILITAIRE GOVERNMENT SITE

1 pl. Joffre

Demonstrating the link between sex, war, and power, Louis XV founded the École Militaire in 1751 at the urging of his mistress, Mme. de Pompadour, who hoped to make officers of "poor gentlemen." In 1784, 15-year-old Napoleon Bonaparte enrolled. A few weeks later, the cocky teen presented administrators with a comprehensive plan for the school's reorganization. Teachers foretold he would "go far in favorable circumstances." Little did they know. While you can't go inside the building, standing behind the Wall of Peace makes the word "peace" appear to be written on the sides of the still-used military school, making for a pretty ironic photo-op.

 # Ⓜ École Militaire.

MUSÉE MAILLOL MUSEUM

61 rue de Grenelle ☎01 42 22 59 58 www.museemaillol.com

One could argue that Aristide Maillol has an artistic style akin to Georgia O'Keefe, except instead of ambiguous "lady" flower images that devote an unspoken appreciation for the female figure, Maillol is pretty straight forward. Crotches, butts, and breasts abound in paintings and sculptures that would make the immature giggle. Maillol's inspiration started with Dina Vierney, who became his model and muse at age 15 and eventually found her own calling as an art collector. The museum's permanent collection presents Maillol's work that Vierney devoted years of effort to make available to the public after his sculptures were donated to the state in 1964. Maillol's pieces are accompanied by names such as Matisse, Kandinsky, and Gauguin, but many visitors come especially for the temporary exhibits.

 # Ⓜ Rue du Bac. Walk south down rue de Bac and turn left onto rue de Grenelle. The museum is on the right. $ €11; ages 11-25, unemployed, and handicapped €9; under 11 free. Audio guide €5. ⏰ Open M-Th 10:30am-7pm, F 10:30am-9:30pm, Sa 10:30am-7pm. Last entry 45min. before close.

MUSÉE DES EGOUTS DE PARIS MUSEUM, SEWER

Pont de l'Alma ☎01 53 68 27 81 www.egouts.tenebres.eu

If you stop to think about it—"I'm paying to go see sewers"—you might hold on to those €3. But make no mistake—you are in fact paying for symbolic submersion into the city of Paris, even if you are walking around with feces rushing underfoot. Some of the posters here look like something out of a high school civics project, and at times the museum smells pretty bad. Still, it is cool to see the literal underbelly of the city, and the guided tours provide food for thought (already digested, of course). Did you know that there are twice as many rats as people in Paris, and they eat three times their body weight in waste?

 # [M]Alma-Marceau. Opposite 93 quai d'Orsay. $ €4.30, students €3.50, under 6 free. ⏰ Open May-Sept M-W 11am-5pm, Sa-Su 11am-5pm; Oct-Apr M-W 11am-4pm, Sa-Su 11am-4pm.

LA PAGODE CINEMA, HISTORIC SITE

57 bis rue de Babylone ☎01 45 55 48 48 www.etoile-cinemas.com

Some men buy flowers; others build pagodas. The Japanese temple, built by Bon Marché department store magnate M. Morin as a gift to his wife in 1895, endures as an artifact of the Orientalist craze that swept France in the 19th century. When Mme. Morin left her husband for his associate's son just prior to WWI (a pagoda just wasn't enough), the building became the scene of Sino-Japanese *soirées* despite tensions between the two countries. La Pagode opened its doors to the public in 1931, and after closing several times it was re-opened under private ownership in November 2000. La Pagode's cinema continues to draw hipsters and middle-aged crowds to screenings of smaller, independent films. The cafe in the bamboo garden outside is particularly pleasant.

*# [M]St-François-Savier. **i** Reduced prices M and W nights. $ Tickets €9, students and under 18 €7.50. ⏰ Cafe open daily between shows.*

CHAMPS-ÉLYSÉES

There's a reason that the 8ème has remained popular with tourists for so long. The neighborhood harbors more architectural beauty, historical significance, and shopping opportunities than almost any other in the city and remains an exhilarating—if hectic—place to spend a day. Champs-Élysées is also home to a variety of art museums in its northern corners; they are often located in *hôtels particuliers*, where they were once part of private collections.

ARC DE TRIOMPHE HISTORIC MONUMENT

pl. Charles de Gaulle-Étoile www.arc-de-triomphe.monuments-nationaux.fr

Probably the second most iconic structure in the whole city, the Arc de Triomphe dominates the Champs-Élysées and remains strikingly powerful even when viewed from a distance. The original architect imagined an unparalleled tribute to France's military prowess in the form of a giant, bejeweled elephant. Fortunately, Napoleon had the more restrained idea of building an arch. You could probably pull together an exhibition of French history since the arch's 1836 completion based purely on photos of the Arc's use in ceremonial celebrations. It stands both as a tribute to French military triumphs and as a memorial to those who have fallen in battle. The Tomb of the Unknown Soldier, added in 1920, lies under the arch. The Arc is spectacular to look at, and it returns the favor by being spectacular to look from. The observation deck offers a brilliant view of the Historic Axis, which stretches from the Louvre to the Grande Arche de la Défense.

*# [M]Charles de Gaulle-l'Étoile. You will die (and face a hefty fine) if you try to dodge the 10-lane merry-go-round of cars around the arch, so use the pedestrian underpass on the right side of the Champs-Élysées facing the arch. **i** Expect long waits, although you can escape the crowds if you go before noon. Buy tickets in the pedestrian underpass. $ €9.50, ages 18-25 €6, under 18 and EU citizens 18-25 free. ⏰ Open daily Apr-Sept 10am-11pm; Oct-Mar 10am-10:30pm. Last entry 30min. before close.*

AVENUE DES CHAMPS-ÉLYSÉES SHOPPING DISTRICT

From pl. Charles de Gaulle-Étoile to pl. de la Concorde

There's a reason we included it here and not in **Shopping:** you can't afford it. The Champs-Élysées seems to be a magnificent celebration of the elite's pomp and fortuitous circumstance, but it's mostly filled with flashy cars, expensive cafes, rich foreigners, and kitschy shops. On the plus side, it does have some of the best people-watching in Europe. The avenue also hosts most major French events: on **Bastille Day** the largest parade in Europe takes place here, as does the final stretch of the **Tour de France.** While the Champs itself may be deteriorating in class (with the invasion of chain stores), many of its side streets, like **avenue Montaigne,** have picked up the slack and ooze sophistication.

✚ ⓂCharles de Gaulle-l'Étoile. ⓂGeorge V, ⓂFranklin D. Roosevelt, or ⓂChamps-Élysées-Clemenceau

PLACE DE LA CONCORDE   PLAZA
pl. de la Concorde

Constructed by Louis XV in honor of himself, the Place de la Concorde quickly became ground zero for all public grievances against the monarchy. During the Reign of Terror, the complex of buildings was renamed pl. de la Révolution, and 1343 aristocrats were guillotined here in less than the span of one year. Louis XVI met his end near the statue that symbolizes the French town of Brest, and the obelisk marks the spot where Marie-Antoinette, Charlotte Corday (Marat's assassin), Lavoisier, Danton, and Robespierre lost their heads. Flanking either side of Concorde's intersection with the wide **Champs-Élysées** are reproductions of Guillaume Coustou's **Chevaux de Marly;** also known as *Africans Mastering the Numidian Horses,* the original sculptures are now in the Louvre to protect them from pollution. At night, the Concorde's dynamic ambience begins to soften, and the obelisk, fountains, and lamps are dramatically illuminated. On ◾**Bastille Day,** a military parade led by the President of the Republic marches through the Concorde (usually around 10am) and down the Champs-Élysées to the Arc de Triomphe, and an impressive fireworks display lights up the sky over the plaza at night. At the end of July, the **Tour de France** finalists pull through the Concorde and into the home stretch on the Champs-Élysées. Tourists be warned: between the Concorde's monumental scale, lack of crosswalks, and heavy traffic, crossing the street here is impossible at best and fatal at worst.

✚ ⓂConcorde.

OBÉLISQUE DE LUXOR   HISTORIC MONUMENT
pl. de la Concorde

In the center of Paris's largest and most infamous public square, the 3300-year-old Obélisque de Luxor stands at a monumental 72ft. The spot was originally occupied by a statue of Louis XV (after whom the square was originally named) that was destroyed in 1748 by an angry mob. King Louis-Philippe, anxious to avoid revolutionary rancor, opted for a less contentious symbol: the 220-ton red granite, hieroglyphic-covered obelisk presented to Charles X from the Viceroy of Egypt in 1829. The obelisk, which dates back to the 13th century BC, recalls the royal accomplishments of Ramses II and wasn't erected until 1836. Today, it forms the axis of what many refer to as the "royal perspective"—a spectacular view of Paris from the Louvre, in which the Place de la Concorde, the Arc de Triomphe, and the Grande Arche de la Défense appear to form a straight line through the center of the city. The view serves as a physical timeline of Paris's history, from the reign of Louis XIV all the way to the celebration of commerce.

✚ ⓂConcorde.

CHAPELLE EXPIATOIRE   CHURCH
29 rue Pasquier   ☎01 44 32 18 00

This massive church is set in the charming park of pl. Louis XVI, where Parisians stop to relax with their toy dogs and exhausting children. Originally the burial place of Louis XVI and Marie Antoinette, Louis XVIII (XVI's brother)

had the bodies exhumed and moved to St-Denis in 1815. He had this church built to be a place of "prayer and commemoration" for the king and his tragic wife. White marble statues under the naturally lit dome of this church show Marie Antoinette kneeling before Jesus and King Louis XVI being supported by an angel. The king's last will and testament is engraved on the front of his statue while Marie Antoinette's last letter to the king's sister is engraved on hers.

🚷 Ⓜ*Madeleine,* Ⓜ*Havre-Caumartin, or* Ⓜ*St-Lazare. Chapel inside pl. Louis XVI, just below bd Haussmann.* **i** *English-language pamphlets available at entrance.* Ⓢ *€5.50, ages 18-25 €3.50, under 18 and EU Citizens 18-25 free.* 🕐 *Open Th-Sa 1-5pm. 45min. tours in French available most Saturdays, 1:30 and 3:30pm.*

CATHÉDRALE ALEXANDRE-NEVSKY   CATHEDRAL

12 rue Daru   ☎01 42 27 37 34 www.cathedrale-orthodoxe.com

Napoleon III approved the construction of this church in 1847 after the Russian community in Paris demanded its own orthodox place of worship. Russian Emperor Alexander II made a personal contribution of 150,000 gold francs to start the process, and donations from Catholics and Protestants in the area helped complete the project. Named for one of the Russian orthodox church's most beloved of the beatified, St. Alexander, this five-domed cathedral features an immaculate interior that is a colorful array of golds, reds, blues, and greens and includes portraits of countless religious idols.

🚷 Ⓜ*Courcelles. Turn right onto rue Daru just past the intersection.* **i** *No shorts or uncovered shoulders.* 🕐 *Open to visitors Tu, F, and Su 3-5pm. Vigils Sa 6pm. Divine liturgy Su 10am.*

MUSÉE JACQUEMART-ANDRÉ   MUSEUM

158 bd Haussmann   ☎01 45 62 11 59 www.musee-jacquemart-andre.com

Nélie Jacquemart's passion for art and her husband Edouard André's wealth were combined to create this extensive collection, which is housed in their gorgeous late 19th-century home. During the couple's lifetime, Parisian high society admired their extravagant, double-corniced marble and iron staircase; only very special guests, however, got a glimpse of their precious collection of English, Flemish, French, and Italian Renaissance artwork, which included a *Madonna and Child* by Botticelli, *St-George and the Dragon* by Ucello, and *Pilgrims at Emmaeus* by Rembrandt. Today, you can wander through the mansion—a sight in itself, with its wealth of gold embellishments, towering windows, and marble columns—and peruse a collection worthy of the most prestigious museums. The museum hosts rotating temporary exhibits several times a year. Make sure you get all the way through the museum to see the *Musée Italien* and the *Chambres de Madame et Monsieur,* the couple's private apartments. We bet you don't have a queen-sized bed decked out in gold threads and matching drapery.

🚷 Ⓜ*St-Philippe-du-Roule. Go behind the church, walk 1 block and turn right onto bd Haussmann.* **i** *Credit card min. €9.50.* Ⓢ *€11, students and ages 7-17 €9.50, under 7 free. 2nd child free. Audio guides for permanent exhibit free with admission.* 🕐 *Open daily 10am-6pm. Open until 9pm M and Sa during temporary exhibits. Last entry 30min. before close.*

PINACOTHEQUE   MUSEUM

28 pl. de la Madeleine   ☎01 42 68 02 01 www.pinacotheque.com

A young contender in Paris's competitive museum scene, Pinacotheque has held its own since it opened in 2007. Director Marc Restellini was working at the Musée du Luxembourg (see **Sights,** Latin Quarter) when he decided to open his own gallery to display an eclectic, less traditional mix of artwork. The museum organizes large exhibitions dedicated to a few artists, usually highlighting less recognized collectors. Most recently, it gathered more than 250 works by Edvard Munch, selected to highlight the difference between his general work and his iconic masterpiece, *The Scream.* Another recent exhibit featured Jonas Netter and a slew of Modigliani's work. Easily-distracted museum-goers may enjoy the opportunity to look closely at one artist's oeuvre or scan the permanent collection for big names like Monet and Delacroix.

✚ Ⓜ*Madeleine. Facing the front of the church, turn around to the left, and the museum is on the corner.* ⓘ *Audio guides available for download online.* Ⓢ *€10, ages 12-25 and students €8, under 12 free. Special group and university group rates available.* Ⓩ *Open M-Tu 10:30am-6:30pm, W 10:30am-9pm, Th 10:30am-6:30pm, F 10:30am-9pm, Sa-Su 10:30am-6:30pm. Last entry 45min. before close.*

PARC MONCEAU   PARK
58 bd de Courcelles

The signs say *"Pelouse interdite"* (keep off the lawn), but on sunny days, everyone pretends to be illiterate. Protected from the chaos of the city by gold-tipped, wrought-iron gates, this storybook park has all the clichés: shady brooks, arched stone bridges, and a colonnade made to look like ruins that will have even the coldest of hearts aching for their yet-to-be-discovered prince or princess. Few tourists make it out this far, so it's perfect for family picnics.

✚ Ⓜ*Monceau or* Ⓜ*Courcelles.* Ⓢ *Free.* Ⓩ *Open daily Apr-Oct 7am-10pm; Nov-Mar 7am-8pm. Last entry 15min. before close.*

GRAND PALAIS   PALACE
3 av. du Général Eisenhower   ☎01 44 13 17 17 www.grandpalais.fr

Designed for the 1900 World's Fair, the Grand Palais and the accompanying Petit Palais across the street were lauded as exemplary works of Art Nouveau architecture. Since the novelty of a then-modern building has worn off in the past century, most of the Grand Palais houses a 20th-century fine art exhibit and a children's science museum, **Palais de la Découverte** (see below). Most of the building's beauty can be admired outside for free, especially at night when its 6000 metric ton glass ceiling glows, lighting up the French flag that flies above it.

✚ Ⓜ*Champs-Élysées-Clemenceau.* Ⓢ *€11.50, students €8. For special exhibits, admission varies; expect €8-16, students €6-9, art students free.* Ⓩ *Open M-Tu 10am-8pm, W 10am-10pm, Th-Su 10am-8pm. Last entry 45min. before close.*

PETIT PALAIS   MUSEUM
av. Winston Churchill   ☎01 53 43 40 00 www.petitpalais.paris.fr

The Petit Palais showcases a hodgepodge of European art from Christian orthodoxy to 20th-century Parisian artists. If you are really into obscure works by famous artists, go for it. Otherwise you might be burnt out after d'Orsay and the Louvre. But hey, the Petit Palais is free for the permanent collection, so it's got that going for it.

✚ Ⓜ*Champs-Élysées-Clemenceau or* Ⓜ*Franklin D. Roosevelt. Follow av. Winston Churchill toward the river. The museum is on the left.* Ⓢ *Permanent collection free. Special exhibits €5-11, ages 14-27 half price, under 13 free. Audio tour €4. Credit card min. €15.* Ⓩ *Open Tu-Su 10am-6pm. Special exhibits open Tu-W 10am-6pm, Th 10am-8pm, F-Su 10am-6pm. Last entry 1hr. before close.*

MADELEINE   CHURCH
pl. de la Madeleine   ☎01 44 51 69 00; www.eglise-lamadeleine.com

While this famous church is worth a visit to admire its immensity and large sculpture of Mary Magdalene, there isn't much else to see, though there are frequent chamber and music concerts. Today, pricey clothing and food shops line the square surrounding Madeleine, including the famous macaroon boutique, **Ladurée.**

✚ Ⓜ*Madeleine.* Ⓩ *Open daily 9am-7pm. Regular organ and chamber concerts; contact church for schedule and tickets. Mass M-F 12:30 and 6:30pm at the nearby chapel; Sa 6pm; Su 9:30, 11am, and 7pm with organ and choir.*

PALAIS DE LA DÉCOUVERTE
MUSEUM

av. Franklin D. Roosevelt, in the Grand Palais   ☎01 56 43 20 20 www.palais-decouverte.fr

Children tear around the interactive science exhibits in the Palais de la Découverte, and it may be hard not to join them—nothing brings out your inner child like buttons that start model comets on their celestial trajectories, spinning seats that demonstrate angular motion, and displays of creepy-crawlies. What's more, both adults and children are likely to learn a surprising amount about physics, chemistry, astronomy, geology, and biology. The temporary exhibits (four per year) are usually crowd-pleasers; one of the most recent, entitled "Dinosaur Diet," featured real-sized animated dinosaurs. The planetarium has four shows per day; arrive early during school vacation periods.

⚑ ⓜFranklin D. Roosevelt or ⓜChamps-Élysées-Clemenceau. Ⓢ €7; students, seniors, and ages 5-17 €4.50; under 5 free. Planetarium €3.50. ⚅ Open Tu-Sa 9:30am-6pm, Su 10am-7pm. Last entry 30min. before close. Planetarium shows 11:30am, 2, 3:15, 4:30pm.

OPÉRA AND CANAL ST-MARTIN

While the 9ème and 10ème don't offer much in the way of landmarks or museums, there are a few sights that you might want to check out. **Le Marché Saint-Quentin,** in particular, is worth a longer perusal.

MUSÉE GUSTAVE MOREAU
MUSEUM

14 rue de La Rochefoucauld   ☎01 48 74 38 50 www.musee-moreau.fr

Provided that its workers aren't on strike (a recreational activity in France), the Musée Gustave Moreau is one of the finest and most intimate museums that Paris has to offer. Located within spitting distance of the Opéra district, the museum offers the premier collection of Moreau paintings, sculptures, and drawings on the site of the eccentric artist's home in the 9ème. The first floor of the museum offers a peek into Moreau's dining room, boudoir, bedrooms, and office, all richly decorated in 19th-century style. The second and third floors, bridged by a uniquely-shaped, beautiful spiral staircase, showcase the diverse artistic tones and masterpieces of the multi-talented and multi-faceted Moreau.

⚑ ⓜTrinité. Turn right onto rue St-Lazare and left onto rue de La Rochefoucauld. Ⓢ €5, under 26 and Su €3, under 18 and 18-25 EU members free. 1st Su of the month free. ⚅ Open M 10am-12-:45pm and 2-5:15pm, W-Th 10am-12:45pm and 2-5:15pm, F-Su 10am-5:15pm.

CAFÉ DE LA PAIX
HISTORIC RESTAURANT

12 bd des Capucines   ☎01 40 07 36 36 www.cafedelapaix.fr

With prices fit for Louis XIV, Café de la Paix is not so much about eating as it is about history (at least for the budget traveler). When you're too poor for an €82 brunch, you might as well get educated. Celebrating its 150th birthday in 2012, Café de la Paix has been a glamorous pillar of the Opéra neighborhood since 1862 and has hosted pretty much every famous character in *Midnight in Paris* (just don't expect Gertrude Stein or F. Scott Fitzgerald to pop up when you visit). Oscar Wilde thought he hallucinated the reflection of the statue on top of the Opéra, and Georges Clemenceau watched victory celebrations from the balcony of the cafe in 1914. If you come at an off-meal time when the only patrons of the cafe are on the patio, you may be able to marvel at the immaculate carpets, pillars, and ceiling frescoes that are official members of the French Supplementary Inventory of Historic Monuments.

⚑ ⓜOpéra. Ⓢ Daytime menu breakfast €4-12. Sandwiches €13-30. Finger food €21-35. Evening menu entrées €19-72 (for caviar). Fish and meat plats €31-41. Su brunch €82, under 12 €41, under 3 free. ⚅ Open M-F 7-10:30am, noon-3pm, and 6:15-11:30pm; Sa 7-11am, noon-3pm, and 6:15-11:30pm; Su 7-11am, 12:15-3:30pm, and 6:15-11:30pm.

OPÉRA GARNIER
pl. de l'Opéra

THEATER

☎08 92 89 90 90 www.operadeparis.fr

The Opéra Garnier was formerly known as the Opéra National de Paris before the creation of the Opéra Bastille became world famous when its main six-ton chandelier crashed to the ground in 1896, killing one person. This incident inspired the longest running musical on Broadway and a weird sex idol for drama kids everywhere. Yes, we're talking about the *Phantom of the Opera*, and its songs may run through your head throughout your visit. Today, visit the Opéra (when it's not sporadically closed due to performances) and see the grand staircase, foyer, and stage—all decorated with frescoes and ornate stone and marble designs that often leave visitors speechless.

⚡ Ⓜ️*Opéra.* Ⓢ *€9, under 25 €5. Guided visit €12, over 60 €10, students €9, under 13 €6.* ✆ *Open 10am-4:30pm; may be closed on performance days, so check the website.*

NOTRE DAME DE LORETTE
18 bis rue de Châteaudun

CHURCH

☎01 48 78 92 72 www.notredamedelorette.org

Built between 1823 and 1836 by architect Hippolyte Le Bas, Notre Dame de Lorette is a remarkably ornate Neoclassical church in an otherwise average residential neighborhood. At the time of its construction, the church pushed the limits of socially acceptable extravagance and even compelled a cadre of church officials, journalists, and other *Parisiens* to disapprove of its borderline-vulgar opulence. The four massive and intricately carved pillars that support the church's blackened entrance will remind you of the Parthenon; splendid frescoes adorn the ceilings of each of the four chapels and portray the Virgin Mary and the four principal sacraments in detail. Though a must-see for lovers of art and architecture, Notre Dame de Lorette remains an active neighborhood church, so try to avoid showing up during mass unless, of course, you want to go to partake in the service. Given some serious disrepair, the future of the church's renovation is up in the air. Catch it while it's still here.

⚡ Ⓜ️*Notre-Dame-de-Lorette.* ✆ *Mass M 12:30 and 6:45pm; Tu-Sa 8am, 12:30, and 6:45pm; Sa 11am and 6:30pm; Su 9:30 (except Jul-Aug), 11am, 6:30pm. Reception M-F 2:30-6:30pm, Sa 5:00-6:30pm. Open for visitors daily 9am-7:30pm.*

LE MARCHÉ SAINT-QUENTIN
Corner of rue de Chabrol and bd Magenta

COVERED MARKET

The largest covered market in Paris, Le Marché St-Quentin is an overwhelming combination of the finest cheeses, fish, and meats. Even if you're not shopping, come just to experience the mix of aromas and mingle with veteran foodies who spend their days browsing for the perfect Camembert. There's a bistro in the middle of the market for those who can't wait until they get home to chow down on their produce.

⚡ Ⓜ️*Gare de l'Est.* ✆ *Open M-Sa 8:30am-1pm and 4-7:30pm, Su 8:30am-1pm.*

PORTE SAINT-DENIS AND SAINT-MARTIN
bd St-Denis

MONUMENT

It's tough being a stone arch in Paris, especially when you're so easily over-shadowed by another, larger arch on better real estate. Unfortunately, that's the lot of these two nearly adjacent monuments. In the words of surrealist André Breton, *"C'est très belle et très inutile"* ("It's very beautiful and very useless").

⚡ Ⓜ️*Strasbourg-St-Denis is in between the two arches.*

BASTILLE

Aside from the **place de la Bastille,** there are few monumental sights left in this neighborhood. Still, the symbolic historical value remains, and this lively area provides many contemporary diversions. The 12ème boasts monoliths of modern architecture like the **Opéra Bastille.** While the formerly working-class neighborhood is now mostly commercialized, a bit of idiosyncratic charm can be seen in and around the funky **rue de Roquette,** where clubs and bars sit alongside boutiques and cafes.

MALHIA KENT FASHION

19 av. Daumesnil ☎01 53 44 76 76 www.malhia.com

Fulfilling every Project Runway fantasy, this workshop gives an up-close, behind-the-scenes look at fashion. The store gets leftover fabrics from high-end designers like Chanel and either sells them at half the price or reworks these hot threads into new vestments. Malhia Kent also debuts a number of up-and-coming designers from France and other countries around Europe. You will mostly find clothes here, but you can also browse through Hector Saxe backgammon sets and accessories up the wazoo. If there is something in particular that attracts your attention, ask about it, as everything in this store is for sale, including the furniture.

[M]Bastille. In the Viaduc des Arts. $ Items usually run from €75-300. ⏰ Open Tu-Sa 10am-7pm.

VIADUC DES ARTS AND PROMENADE PLANTÉE PARK, SHOPPING STRIP

1-129 av. Daumesnil ☎01 44 75 80 66 www.viaducdesarts.fr

Paris's contemporary artists occupy the shops under the heavy archways of the **Viaduc des Arts,** a former old railway viaduct and current hive of creative activity. You can find everything from flashy *haute couture* to workshops that use leather, wood, copper, and glass to create trendy art collections that scream, "Look at me! I'm artistic!" from the windows. There are also restorers here who will make your old stained incense jar (because we know you have one of those) shiny and new. Located above the swanky shops is the Promenade Plantée; this is Paris's version of the New York City Highline, but with more greenery and a little more trash. Still, the plants make for an enjoyable afternoon stroll, and the view level with the tops of the French buildings lining the avenue offer even more to look at.

[M]Bastille. The viaduct extends from rue de Lyon to rue de Charenton. Entrances to the Promenade are at Ledru Rollin, Hector Malot, and bd Diderot. ⏰ Park opens M-F 8am, Sa-Su 9am; closing hours vary, around 5:30pm in winter and 9:30pm in summer. Stores open M-Sa; hours vary, with many taking a 2hr. lunch break at noon.

CITÉ NATIONALE DE L'HISTOIRE DE L'IMMIGRATION MUSEUM

293 av. Daumesnil ☎01 53 59 58 60 www.histoire-immigration.fr

It's both appropriate and ironic that this recently opened museum on immigration is housed in the Palais de la Porte Dorée, which was built during France's colonial expansion and thus features not-so-politically-correct friezes of "native culture" on its walls. Presented chronologically, the permanent collection traces the arrival and subsequent attempts at integration of immigrants from all over the world. The message is driven home with stories of Algerians separated from families and a model of a six-person bunk bed. After seeing this, you'll definitely have to stop complaining about how cramped your hostel room is.

[M]Porte Dorée. In the Palais de la Porte Dorée, on the western edge of the Bois de Vincennes. $ €5, ages 18-26 €3.50, under 18 and EU citizens ages 18-26 free. 1st Su of every month free. ⏰ Open Tu-F 10am-5:30pm, Sa-Su 10am-7pm. Last entry 45min. before close.

AQUARIUM TROPICAL MUSEUM

293 av. Daumesnil ☎01 44 74 84 98 www.aquarium-portedoree.fr

This tropical aquarium is modest in size but offers an enjoyable display of a variety of fish from around the world. Don't miss the unicorn fish in the back (because who would ever want to miss out on that semi-magical experience?) or the crocodiles. Keep in mind that going on the weekend means you'll avoid the droves of school children huddled around the clown fish tank looking for Nemo.

[M]Porte Dorée. In the Palais de la Porte Dorée, on the western edge of the Bois de Vincennes. $ €4.50, reduced €3, students €1.50, families €6. First Su of the month free. Cité Nationale de L'Histoire de l'Immigration and Aquarium joint ticket €8. ⏰ Open M-F 10am-5:30pm, Sa-Su 10am-7pm. Ticket office closes 45min. before close.

BASTILLE PRISON HISTORIC SITE

Visitors to the prison subsist on symbolic value alone—it's one of the most popular sights in Paris that doesn't actually exist. On July 14, 1789, an angry Parisian mob stormed this bastion of royal tyranny, sparking the French Revolution. They only liberated seven prisoners, but who's counting? Two days later, the Assemblée Nationale ordered the prison demolished. Today all that remains is the fortress's ground plan, still visible as a line of paving stones in the pl. de la Bastille. But it was hardly the hell hole that the Revolutionaries who tore it down imagined it to be. Bastille's elite inmates were allowed to furnish their suites, use fresh linens, bring their own servants, and receive guests; the Cardinal de Rohan famously held a dinner party for 20 in his cell. Notable prisoners included the **Man in the Iron Mask** (made famous by writer Alexandre Dumas), the Comte de Mirabeau, Voltaire (twice), and the Marquis de Sade. The anniversary of the storming is July 14th, which (much like a certain celebration 10 days earlier across the Atlantic) is a time of glorious fireworks and copious amounts of alcohol, with festivities concentrated around pl. de la Bastille.

[M]Bastille.

PLACE DE LA BASTILLE SQUARE

Though the revolutionary spirit has faded, a similar fervor still manifests itself nightly in fits of drunken revelry, most marked on Bastille Day. At the center of the square, a monument of winged Mercury holding a torch of freedom symbolizes France's movement (albeit a slow one) from monarchy to democracy.

[M]Bastille.

JULY COLUMN MONUMENT

Towering above the constantly busy pl. de la Bastille, this light-catching column commemorates many groups of French freedom fighters—though, somewhat illogically, not the ones who stormed the Bastille. It celebrates the *Trois Glorieuses*, the "three glorious" days that toppled Charles X's monarchy in favor of a free republic…just kidding, it was another monarch, Louis-Philippe, who took over. When Louis-Philippe was in turn deposed in 1848, the column was rededicated to those fighters as well, and 200 additional bodies were buried under it. Apparently thinking it was a revolutionary good luck trinket, the Communards used the tower as a rallying point for their 1871 uprising, but, after three successful months, the French army came in and deported nearly 7500 and executed 20,000. Sheer numbers prevented any additional burials under the column.

[M]Bastille. In the center of pl. de la Bastille.

OPÉRA BASTILLE PERFORMANCE HALL

130 rue de Lyon ☎08 92 89 90 90 www.operadeparis.fr

The "People's Opera" has been not-so-fondly referred to as ugly, an airport, and a huge toilet, due to its uncanny resemblance to the coin-operated *pissoirs* on the streets of Paris. Yet the opera has not struck a completely sour note, as it helped renew local interest in the arts. The guided tours offer a behind-the-scenes view of the colossal theater. The modern granite and glass auditorium, which seats 2723, comprises only 5% of the building's surface area. The rest of the structure houses exact replicas of the stage (for rehearsal purposes) and workshops for both the Bastille and Garnier operas.

[M]Bastille. Look for the box office (billetterie). ***i*** *Call in advance to arrange English tour.* *[$] €11, students and over 60 €9, under 18 €6.* *Box office open M-Sa 10:30am-6:30pm. 1hr. guided tours in French fall-spring daily at 1 and 5pm.*

ITHEMBA SHOWROOM

67 av. Daumesnil ☎01 44 75 88 88 www.ithemba.fr

A colorful, funky showroom filled with sparkling beads and light bulbs, Ithemba has upped its street cred since 2003. In that year it committed itself to the fight against HIV/AIDS in Africa by donating proceeds from the sale of Africa-inspired lampshades, cloth bags, and beaded jewelry, which are then handmade by HIV/AIDS victims in South Africa and Swaziland. With good intentions come high prices. ⚑ Ⓜ*Gare de Lyon.* ⏲ *Open M-Sa 11am-7pm.*

MONTPARNASSE AND SOUTHERN PARIS

There are few monuments in Montparnasse and Southern Paris. Diverse, residential, and pleasantly odd, these neighborhoods remain uninterrupted by the troops of pear-shaped tourists in matching fanny packs that plague the more popular *arrondissements*. Though short on medieval cathedrals, this area is home to hidden gems from Paris's recent waves of immigration and perturbed *bo-bos* (bohemian bourgeoisie).

▨ CATACOMBS   HISTORIC LANDMARK

1 av. du Colonel Henri Roi-Tanguy   ☎01 43 22 47 63 www.catacombes-de-paris.fr
The Catacombs were the original site of Paris's quarries, but they were converted into an ossuary in 1785 to help alleviate the stench rising from overcrowded cemeteries (perfume only goes so far). Not for the claustrophobic or faint of heart, this 45min. excursion leads visitors down a winding spiral staircase to a welcoming sign: "Stop! Here is the Empire of Death." Stacks of skulls and femurs line the walls, and the remains of six million people make you feel quite insignificant in the grand scheme of things. Try to arrive before the opening at 10am; hordes of tourists form extremely long lines hoping to escape the beating sun. The visitors' passage is well marked, so don't worry about getting lost. Try trailing behind the group a little for the ultimate creepy experience—you won't be disappointed.
⚑ Ⓜ*Denfert Rochereau. Cross av. du Colonel Henri Roi-Tanguy with the lion on your left.* Ⓢ *€8, over 60 €6, ages 14-26 €4, under 14 free.* ⏲ *Open Tu-Su 10am-5pm. Last entry 4pm.*

MÉMORIAL DE LA LIBÉRATION DE PARIS   MEMORIAL, MUSEUM

23 allée de la 2ème DB, Jardin Atlantique   ☎01 40 64 39 44 www.ml-leclerc-moulin.paris.fr
Opened in 1994 for the 50th anniversary of the liberation of Paris from Nazi control, this memorial is composed of the **Mémorial du Maréchal LeClerc** and the **Musée Jean Moulin,** named for two celebrated WWII heroes. The whole memorial is located above the SNCF station where LeClerc set up his command post in 1944 and in the neighborhood where Moulin lived under the artist guise *Romanin* prior to his military success. The two galleries are symbolically connected by the Liberation Gallery, which is meant to represent the remarkable unification of resistance forces to fight the Nazi regime and liberate France. The Gallery contains an impressive array of 13 screens that play a harrowing series of video footage chronicling the tragedies and victories Paris experienced over the course of Nazi occupation and liberation.
⚑ Ⓜ*Montparnasse-Bienvenue. Follow signs for the Memorial Leclerc from the Metro stop to the Memorial; the museum is on top of the SNCF terminal.* Ⓢ *Permanent collection free. Rotating exhibits vary, usually €4, ages 14-26 €2.* ⏲ *Open Tu-Su 10am-6pm.*

MUSÉE BOURDELLE   MUSEUM

16 rue Antoine Bourdelle   ☎01 49 54 73 73 www.bourdelle.paris.fr
No, this is not a museum of whorehouses, you dirty, dirty traveler—you're thinking of *bor*delle. For the Philistines among us, Antoine Bourdelle was a French sculptor whose work was extremely influential in the early 1920s; this museum is located at the site of his former home and workshop. Make sure to come to the museum on a nice day so you can enjoy the gardens outside. Some of the museum's most beautiful offerings are in the gardens, including the enormous *Aphrodite ou La Naissance de la Beauté* and a commanding

sculpture of an American soldier dedicated to the memory of US aid in WWI. Inside, the central room of this museum is decorated with colossal sculptures, and both Bourdelle's original *atelier* (workshop) and bedroom have been preserved. This museum also houses an extensive archive and rotating exhibits of modern art for you nerds in Paris doing research (or for you few who like modern art).

✦ Ⓜ*Montparnasse-Bienvenue. Take av. du Maine heading away from bd Montparnasse; the museum is on the left.* Ⓢ *Permanent exhibit free. Rotating exhibits vary, but reduced rates apply and under 14 are free. Audio guide €5.* ⏰ *Open Tu-Su 10am-6pm. Last entry 5:45pm.*

TOUR MONTPARNASSE   TOWER
33 av. du Maine   ☎01 45 38 52 56
Built in 1969, this modern tower stands 196m tall and makes Paris look like a miniature model. The elevator is allegedly the fastest in Europe (moving at 5.12m per sec.—not a lot of time to clear the pressure in your ears) and spits you out to a mandatory photo line on the 56th floor. After being shoved in front of a fake city skyline and forced to smile for a picture that you probably don't want, you're finally allowed up to the 59th floor to take in the beauty and meticulous planning of Paris's historic streets. Thankfully, the city ruled that similar eyesores could not be constructed in Paris's downtown shortly after this one was built.

✦ Ⓜ*Montparnasse-Bienvenue. Entrance on rue de l'Arrivée.* Ⓢ *€10, students €7.* ⏰ *Open M-Th 9:30am-10:30pm, F-Sa 9:30am-11pm, Su 9:30am-10:30pm. Last entry 30min. before close.*

CIMETIÈRE MONTPARNASSE   CEMETERY
3 bd Edgar Quinet   ☎01 44 10 86 50
Paris certainly has a lot of cemeteries. Despite the repetitiveness of buried celebrities, there are some unique features that make Montparnasse's worth visiting. Because it's secluded from the main tourist areas, this cemetery is more of a local park during the day, but one where you can stroll past Jean-Paul Sartre and Simone de Beauvoir (the two are buried together—how cute). Watch out for older kids from the *banlieues* bumming cigarettes off tourists and the occasional homeless drunk. Nonetheless, the cemetery showcases some delightful architecture and an impressive list of tenants.

✦ Ⓜ*Edgar Quinet, opposite the Square Delambre.* Ⓢ *Free.* ⏰ *High season open M-F 8am-6pm, Sa 8:30am-6pm, Su 9am-6pm; low season open M-F 8am-5:30pm, Sa 8:30am-5:30pm, Su 9am-5:30pm.*

ÉGLISE DE STE-ANNE DE LE BUTTE-AUX-CAILLES   CHURCH
189 rue de Tolbiac   ☎01 45 89 34 73 www.paroissesainteanne-paris.fr
Glory to God in the Highest! Finally, a church that won't bore you to tears. Built in 1861, the Église de Ste-Anne is beautifully decorated with colorful tiles and mosaics adorning each of the three *chapelets* behind and on either side of the central altar. In the right-hand *chapelet*, the Virgin mother and her child are backed by an array of *fleurs-de-lis* and surrounded by cobalt-blue stones and pearly white mosaics. The bright, transparent stained glass high up on the walls of the church makes for an impressive kaleidoscope of color on a sunny day. Although we think these decorations may be in some violation of the church's stance on vanity, it certainly adds some dazzle to a potentially somber setting. Tourists take note: this church is an active place of worship, and parishioners' prayers should not be disturbed by camera flashes or poorly-stifled "oohs" and "aahs."

✦ Ⓜ*Tolbiac. Walk east on rue de Tolbiac. Church is unmissable.* *i* *Wheelchair-accessible entrance 11 rue Martin Bernard.* Ⓢ *Free.* ⏰ *Open M-F 10am-noon and 4-6:45pm, Sa 10am-noon and 4-6pm. Mass M 7pm, Tu 9am and 7pm, W 9am and noon, Th 9am and 7pm, F 9am and noon, Sa 9am.*

paris

CITÉ INTERNATIONALE UNIVERSITAIRE   UNIVERSITY

17 bd Jourdan   ☎01 44 16 64 00 www.ciup.fr

Built in the 1920s to nurture cultural exchange between international students, the Cité Internationale Universitaire teaches students of over 140 different nationalities. The university's architecture is pretty impressive—the roof of Le Corbusier's Pavillon Suisse housed anti-aircraft guns during WWII—but the best thing to do here is grab a drink at the Maison Internationale's cafe and head to the back deck, where students blend languages, bend accents, and study a whole lot of nothing. There's always at least one soccer game and one picnic happening on the big lawn. The university welcomes all ages; whether you're a student yourself or an aging Boomer looking for your own hot tub time machine, this is a great place to make some new friends.

⚔ ⓂPorte d'Orléans. *i* Guided tours 1st Su of the month at 3pm. Ⓢ Free. Guided tours €8, students €3. 🕘 Grounds open daily 7am-10pm. Cafe at Maison Internationale open daily 8am-7pm. Tour at 3pm.

BIBLIOTHÈQUE NATIONALE DE FRANCE: SITE FRANÇOIS-MITTERRAND   LIBRARY

quai François-Mauriac   ☎01 53 79 59 59 www.bnf.fr

With its wide windows and towering steel frame, this library is an imposing piece of architecture worthy of its 13 million volumes. Highlights include a complete, first-edition **Gutenberg Bible** displayed in rotation with the Galerie des Donateurs. The reading room is straight out those old movies that required lawyers to stay up all night delving into old books, and the lounge on the large deck is a decent spot to survey the Seine with (or without) a cigarette in your hand.

⚔ ⓂQuai de la Gare. Ⓢ Day pass to reading rooms €3.30. Tours €3. Exhibits €7, students and ages 16-30 €5, under 16 free. 🕘 Open M 2-5pm, Tu-F 9am-5pm, Sa 9am-4pm. Exhibits open Tu-Sa 10am-7pm, Su 1-7pm. Tours Tu-F 2pm, Sa-Su 3pm.

QUARTIER DE LA BUTTE-AUX-CAILLES   NEIGHBORHOOD

Intersection of rue de la Butte-aux-Cailles and rue des 5 Diamants

Traces of the district's original counterculture from the 1968 riots are alive and well here: dreadlocks are the hairstyle of choice, the walls are covered in graffiti, and the fashionably unaffected are armed with guitars at all times. Here you can find some of the cheapest cafes and restaurants, which (as expected) only accept cash. Basically, this neighborhood makes Haight-Ashbury look like Silicon Valley, and it provides a good chance for you to get cheap eats and free entertainment from carefree hippies.

⚔ ⓂPlace d'Italie. Take rue Bobillot south a few blocks and turn right onto rue de la Butte-aux-Cailles.

QUARTIER CHINOIS   NEIGHBORHOOD

Just south of rue de Tolbiac

Spread out over four Metro stops just south of rue de Tolbiac, Paris's Chinatown should really be called Paris's Indo-Chinatown. Thanks to years of colonialism, some of the most authentic and talented chefs have flocked to this region from Cambodia, Laos, Vietnam, and Thailand to provide super cheap food. A walk here (especially in the sweltering summers) will transport you to Ho Chi Minh City.

⚔ ⓂTolbiac, Maison Blanche, Porte de Choisy, or Porte d'Ivry.

AUTEUIL, PASSY & BATIGNOLLES

Fortunately for tourists, all of the museums in this neighborhood are within walking distance of each other. But even if you are tempted to hit all these sights at once, take your time and savor each one. We suggest that you head to the wine museum first, get a buzz going, then hike up the road to **Trocadéro.**

MUSÉE DU VIN — MUSEUM

rue des Eaux ☎01 45 25 70 89 www.museeduvinparis.com

Formerly a 15th-century monastery, the Musée du Vin's underground tunnels and vaults take visitors through the history of wine production, including the tools that till the soil, the harvesting techniques in different regions of France, and how they make champagne. The exhibits integrate history with models of Louis Pasteur, who cured wine disease by heating the wine in a vacuum, and Napoleon, who cut his wine with water (you know, to stay sharp on the battlefield). The tour ends with a tasting of one of three types of wine (rosé, white, or red—we recommend the last one), but only after a thorough explanation of where each came from. Be patient, and for goodness' sake let them pour it for you.

[M]Passy. Go down the stairs, turn right onto pl. Albioni, and then right onto rue des Eaux; the museum is tucked away at the end of the street. [$] Self-guided tour and 1 glass of wine €12; students, seniors, and visitors with disabilities €9.70. ⏰ Open Tu-Su 10am-6pm.

LA GRANDE ARCHE DE LA DEFENSE — MONUMENT

pl. de la Défense ☎01 49 07 27 27 www.grandearche.com

When French president François Mitterand created an international design competition for Paris's newest monument, those who entered the artistic fray faced some intimidating predecessors—who, after all, wants to compete with Gustave Eiffel? Danish architect Johan Otto Von Spreckelsen took the plunge in 1983 and submitted his design for an arch that now towers over the business section of the city and has become one of Paris's defining monuments. Made of 300,000 tons of white marble and standing taller than the Notre-Dame, the arch was inaugurated on July 14, 1989, at the 15th G7 summit on the bicentennial of the French Revolution. Today you can take a glass elevator 360ft. in the air to see a stunning panorama of Paris that extends as far as the Louvre and the Eiffel Tower. Inside the arch, you can enjoy more modern wonders like the Musée de l'Informatique (Museum of Computers), a movie about the construction of the arch, a 3D gallery of Dimitri, and a bar and restaurant with free Wi-Fi.

[M]La Defense. [$] €10, students and ages 6-17 €8.50, under 6 and handicapped free. Groups of 10 or more €8 for adults, €7 for students. [i] ISIC accepted. ⏰ Open daily Apr-Aug 10am-5pm; Sept-Mar 10am-7pm. Last admission 30min. before close.

PALAIS DU CHAILLOT — MUSEUMS, HISTORIC BUILDING

1 pl. du Trocadéro ☎01 58 51 52 00 www.hotelpalaisdechaillot.com

The Palais du Chaillot was commissioned by the French government in 1936 for Paris's last World Exhibition. The Palais and the Paris Museum of Modern Art were the first gems of this project, but today the Palais is home to three museums: the Maritime Museum for the kiddos, the Paris Aquarium for the fishes, and the Cité de l'Architecture et du Patrimoine (see below) for the nerds. The Palais is also famous for its spectacular head-on view of the Eiffel Tower from across the Pont d'Iéna.

[M] Trocadéro.

CIMETIÈRE DE PASSY — CEMETERY

2 rue du Commandant-Schloesing ☎01 53 70 40 80

Opened in 1820, this cemetery is home to some of Paris's most notable deceased, including the fashionable Givenchy family, composer Claude Debussy, Impressionist Berthe Morisot, and painter Édouard Manet. The idiosyncrasies and enduring rivalries of these figures continue even in death: the graves here look more like miniature mansions than tombstones. The tomb of the Russian artist Marie Bashkirtseff is a recreation of her studio and stands at an impressive 40 ft. tall. Morisot and Manet are buried in a more modest tomb together; we suspect that Morisot's husband would not have approved. Well-groomed and quiet, the graveyard is more like a shadowy garden, with a wonderful view of the Eiffel Tower.

✝ ⓂTrocadéro. Follow av. Paul Doumer right. The cemetery is on the right. Ⓢ Free. ⌚ Open Mar 16-Nov 5 M-F 8am-6pm, Sa 8:30am-6pm, Su and public holidays 9am-6pm; Nov 6-Mar 15 M-F 8am-5:30pm, Sa 8:30am-5:30pm, Su and public holidays 9am-5:30pm. Last entry 30min. before close. Conservation office open M-F 8:30am-12:30pm and 2-5pm.

CITÉ DE L'ARCHITECTURE ET DU PATRIMOINE   MUSEUM
1 pl. du Trocadéro   ☎01 58 51 52 00 www.citechaillot.fr

The Cité de l'Architecture et du Patrimoine features a walk through France's architectural heritage from the 12th to 18th century, with additional exhibits on more contemporary architecture. The museum is split up into three parts: a gallery of casts, a gallery of modern and contemporary architecture, and a gallery of wall paintings and stained glass. For those with a particular interest in architecture, the casts and the modern and contemporary exhibits are a real treat (check out the head-on view of the Eiffel Tower here), while the wall paintings appeal to a wider audience. And while the limited stained glass exhibits are a bit disappointing, the temporary exhibits on the lower two floors are very interactive and interesting for museum-goers of any age, particularly youngsters.

✝ ⓂTrocadéro. Inside the Palais du Chaillot. Ⓢ Permanent exhibits €8, ages 12-25 and handicapped €5, under 12 free. Temporary exhibits €5-8, ages 12-25, groups of 10 or more, and handicapped €3-5; under 12 free. Video guides €3. ⌚ Open M-W 11am-7pm, Th 11am-9pm, F-Su 11am-7pm. Last entrance 45min. before close.

MUSÉE DE LA MODE ET DU COSTUME   MUSEUM
10 av. Pierre 1er de Serbie   ☎01 56 52 86 00 www.galliera.paris.fr

There's no denying it—the French dress to impress. This museum elegantly displays the history of fashion from the 18th to 20th century. With 30,000 outfits, 70,000 accessories, and not much space in which to display them, the museum organizes its exhibits by century and rotates them more swiftly than a Lady Gaga costume change. The museum will be closed for renovations until spring 2013.

✝ ⓂIéna. Walk down av. Pierre 1er de Serbie. Entrance is on the right side of the street. *i* Entrance on Place Rochambeau. Ⓢ €7, students and seniors €5.50. ⌚ Open Tu-Su 10am-6pm. Last entry 5:30pm.

CIMETIÈRE DES BATIGNOLLES   CEMETERY
8 rue St-Just   ☎01 53 06 38 68

Cemeteries are much like budget hotels: they all look the same, and it's often a struggle to find something notable about them. On the surface, this cemetery is no exception to the rule, but the real intrigue here lies six feet underground. Cimetière des Batignolles holds some famous headstones, including those of Admiral Albert Grasset, journalist Samuel London, and Russian painter Alexandre Benois. If you take the time to walk around and look closely past the countless bouquets brightening up the mossy gravestones, you may find some other interesting memorials, such as the grave markers of WWI soldiers or victims of the Holocaust. Regardless, the cemetery is a nice green respite from the busy Paris streets on a sunny day, even if you can still hear the rumble of the highway to the north.

✝ ⓂPort de Clichy. Exit Metro and turn right at the corner, then right again onto av. du Cimetière des Batignolles; the entrance is straight ahead at the end of the road. *i* Request free map and list of famous graves at the info booth at the entrance. ⌚ Open Mar 16-Nov 5 M-F 8am-6pm, Sa 8:30am-6pm, Su and holidays 9am-6pm; Nov 6-Mar 15 M-F 8am-5:30pm, Sa 8:30am-5:30pm, Su and holidays 9am-5:30pm. Conservation Bureau open M-F 8am-noon and 2-5:30pm. Last entry 5:15pm.

SQUARE DES BATIGNOLLES PARK

Square des Batignolles is one of several English-style parks in the city that were commissioned by Napoleon III after he acquired a taste for British leisure during his exile in England until 1848. Monet once sat here to paint the Gare St-Lazare train tracks. Today, a less illustrious crowd of screaming children scrambles through the playground while canoodling couples and picnickers gather in the grass around the romantic little pond.

 # [M]Brochant. Walk southwest down rue Brochant, away from av. de Clichy. $ Free. ⏰ Open M-F 8am-9:30pm, Sa-Su and holidays 9am-9:30pm.

MAISON DE BALZAC MUSEUM

47 rue Raynouard ☎01 55 74 41 80 www.balzac.paris.fr

When he wasn't sleeping his way through Paris, Honoré de Balzac hid from the world in this three-story house where he wrote most of *La Comédie Humaine.* Today, the house features drafts of his most famous work and various paintings, sculptures, and books related to his life. Visitors can also see the heavy-set desk where he worked. If you've never read Balzac, check out the select quotes lining the walls for a quick introduction to his style. If you have no interest at all in this literary figure, benches scattered among bushy trees and Wi-Fi make the accompanying garden a beautiful and practical place to sit for a bit.

 # [M]Passy. Walk west away from the Seine and turn left onto av. Marcel at the big intersection which turns into rue Raynouard. ℹ Free Wi-Fi. Call ahead for guided tours. $ Permanent collection free. Temporary exhibits €4. ⏰ Open Tu-Su 10am-6pm. Last entry 5:30pm. Library open M-F 12:30-5:30pm, Sa 10:30am-5:30pm.

MUSÉE MARMOTTAN MONET MUSEUM

2 rue Louis Boilly ☎01 44 96 50 33 www.marmottan.com

Even for the artistically challenged, this is worth a visit. Less crowded than any other popular museum in Paris, the gold-detailed, ornately decorated museum brings you back to the Belle Époque. Housing Monet's *Water Lilies* as well as Berthe Morisot's works of the same Impressionist genre, this museum also throws a bone to the iconography of the Middle Ages.

 # [M]Muette. Walk through the Jardin de Ranelagh on av. Jardin de Ranelagh. The museum is on the right on rue Louis-Boilly. $ €10, under 25 €5. ⏰ Open Tu-W 11am-6pm, Th 11am-10pm, F-Su 11am-6pm. Last entry 30min. before close.

MUSÉE D'ART MODERNE DE LA VILLE DE PARIS MUSEUM

11 av. du President Wilson ☎01 53 67 40 00 www.mam.paris.fr

Rooms here are organized according to artistic movements like Fauvism, Cubism, Realism, and abstraction. Try as we could, we couldn't tell you which was which. Exhibits additionally showcase the works of major figures like Duchamp, Mondrian, and Picasso. The highlight—especially if you don't like art—is the large room entirely covered with an explosively colorful mural of scientists and inventors from around the world, from Archimedes to Tesla. During the summer, the museum cafe opens up to a gorgeous terrace with a river view.

 # [M]Iéna. Cross the street to av. du President Wilson and walk with the Seine to your right. $ €10, students €5. ⏰ Open Tu-Su 10am-6pm. Last entry 5:45pm. Special exhibits open Tu-W 10am-6pm, Th 10am-10pm, F-Su 10am-6pm.

MUSÉE NATIONAL DES ARTS ASIATIQUES (MUSÉE GUIMET) MUSEUM

6 pl. d'Iéna ☎01 56 52 53 00 www.museeguimet.fr

The Musée Guimet houses one of the largest collections of Asian art (stone sculptures) outside of (read: stolen during colonial times from) the Orient. Over 45,000 works from 17 different countries occupy the five-floor labyrinth of rooms. Free audio guides enhance the museum experience.

 # [M]Iéna. $ €7.50; students €5.50; under 18, EU residents 18-25, visitors with disabilities, and unemployed free. Special exhibits €8, students €6. Combined ticket €9.50, students €7. ⏰ Open M 10am-6pm, W-Su 10am-6pm. Last entry 5:45pm.

JARDINS DU TROCADÉRO   PARK
The ultimate tourist hub, the gardens provide the perfect "I've been to Paris" photo-op, with one of the clearest views of the Eiffel Tower. The fountain and sprawling, sloping lawns are great for a picnic or watching the many street performers working for your spare change.
💠 ⓜ*Trocadéro.*

PALAIS DE TOKYO   MUSEUM
13 av. du President Wilson   ☎01 47 23 54 01 www.palaisdetokyo.com
Come to this modern and contemporary art museum with an open mind. Palais de Tokyo hosts the kind of exhibits that will either leave you completely befuddled or have you breaking a serious mental sweat trying to figure out just what it is you're looking at. Even if you're not so refined as to understand more esoteric art, this place is worth the visit if for no other reason than to experience the strange, mixed feeling of both confusion and amazement. The Musee d'Art Moderne de la Ville de Paris next door may be a more comfortable, familiar museum experience for traditionalists, but Palais de Tokyo is far more interesting.
💠 ⓜ*Iena.* ⓘ *Free admission to general public 1st M of every month from 6pm.* Ⓢ *€8; under 26 and teachers €6; under 18, seniors, and handicapped free.* Ⓩ *Open M noon-midnight, W-Su noon-midnight.*

STATUE OF LIBERTY   STATUE
Allée des Cygnes
This replica of France's famous gift to the US is not nearly as grand as the statue that watches over New York Harbor, but then again, who would dare challenge the majesty of the Eiffel Tower from this side of the Seine? To reach this sight, take your time and start at the top of the Allée des Cygnes (the man-made strip stretching from the Pont de Bir Hakeim to the Pont de Grenelle), then stroll down to the statue at the end. If you're in Paris on a warm summer's day, you may catch a few wedding photoshoots on the Pont de Bir Hakeim; regardless, you should take a minute to snap a few shots of yourself with the monument in the background.
💠 ⓜ*Passy. Walk down rue d'Albioni toward the Seine and cross av. du President Kennedy to the Pont Bir-Hakeim. Turn right onto Allee de Cygnes if you want a closer look.*

MONTMARTRE

Most people come to Montmartre to see the **Moulin Rouge** or **Sacré-Cœur,** but those aren't the only memorable sights in this area. With a rich history of wining, dining, and dancing, the Musée Montmartre is definitely worth a stop for the culturally conscious. Pickpockets are well aware of Montmartre's tourist appeal, so hold tight to your things around the cheap clothing stores and stands by the Metro stops. Remember, the whole neighborhood is draped over a large hill, so plan some extra time for getting from one place to the next.

🏛 BASILIQUE DU SACRÉ-CŒUR   CHURCH
35 rue du Chevalier-de-la-Barre   ☎01 53 41 89 00 www.sacre-coeur-montmartre.fr
Situated 129m above sea level, this splendid basilica was first planned in 1870. Its purpose? To serve as a spiritual bulwark for France and the Catholic Church, which were under the weight of an imminent military defeat and German occupation. The basilica was commissioned by the National Assembly and was initially meant to be an assertion of conservative Catholic power, but the only people that assert themselves on the steps today are the scammers offering "free" bracelets, so beware. The basilica sees over 10 million visitors per year and offers a free, spectacular view of the city. On a spring day, grab some ice cream and marvel at the view.
💠 ⓜ*Lamarck-Caulaincourt. Take rue Caulaincourt and turn right onto rue Lamarck. Follow rue Lamarck until you reach the basilica.* Ⓢ *Free.* Ⓩ *Basilica open daily 6am-10:30pm. Dome open daily Mar-Nov 9am-7pm; Dec-Feb 9am-6pm. Mass M-F 11:15am, 6:30, 10pm; Sa 10pm; Su 11am, 6, 10pm.*

sights

HALLE SAINT-PIERRE   MUSEUM

2 rue Ronsard   ☎01 42 58 72 89 www.hallesaintpierre.org

Halle St-Pierre is a one-of-a-kind (read: weird) abstract art museum located right down the street from the Sacré-Cœur. Exhibits change constantly, so the museum is hard to pin down. In general, the art tends to be a bit far out. The most recent exhibition, on display until March 4, 2012, is on "Modern Art and Pop Culture," and displays paintings such as Mickey Mouse smoking a cigarette and (to the dismay of Christendom) three pumas being crucified.

✦ ⓂAnvers. *Follow rue de Steinkerque up the hill and turn right onto pl. St-Pierre. Walk 1 block and turn left onto rue Ronsard.* Ⓢ *€7.50, students €6.* Ⓩ *Open Sept-July daily 10am-6pm; Aug M-F noon-6pm.*

MUSÉE MONTMARTRE   MUSEUM

12 rue Cortot   ☎01 49 25 89 37 www.museedemontmartre.fr

Located on the site of the former home of Claude de La Rose (Molière's successor) and in the building that housed the ateliers of Van Gogh and Renoir, this museum is dedicated entirely to the diverse and fascinating history of the 18ème. Although the building itself is rather small and feels more like a nicely-decorated house than an actual museum, it will no doubt keep you entertained. The top floor is dedicated to the French can-can, and your audio guide will tell you some fun stories about the Moulin Rouge. You can also see the original iconic *Chat Noir* poster and hear the history of the world-famous cabaret and shadow theater. The pristine gardens in the back of the museum, renovated in 2012, are definitely a highlight, so come on a sunny day if you can.

✦ ⓂLamarck-Caulaincourt. *Walk east down rue Caulaincourt, turn right onto rue des Saules, then left onto rue Cortot, it's on the left.* 𝒊 *Audio guides free with admission.* Ⓢ *€8; students ages 18-25, adult groups, and handicapped €6; ages 10-17 €4; under 10 free.* Ⓩ *Open daily 10am-6pm.*

CIMETIÈRE DE MONTMARTRE   CEMETERY

20 av. Rachel   ☎01 53 42 36 30

The vast Cimetière de Montmartre, stretching across a significant proportion of the 18éme, lies below street level on the site of a former quarry. It is the resting place of multiple acclaimed artists: writer Émile Zola, painter Edgar Degas, saxophone inventor Adolphe Sax, and ballet dancer Marie Taglioni are among the long-term residents. If you have an extra pair in your backpack, you can leave pointe shoes on Taglioni's grave. The other dead celebs prefer coins on their gravestones. One of the most infamous killers in French history is also buried here: the Charles Henri Sanson, Royal Executioner, who executed nearly 3000 people, including Louis XVI himself.

✦ ⓂPlace de Clichy. *Head up bd de Clichy, which becomes rue Caulaincourt. The entrance is at the intersection of rue Caulaincourt and av. Rachel.* Ⓢ *Free.* Ⓩ *Open May 16-Nov 5 M-F 8am-6pm, Sa 8:30am-6pm, Su 9am-6pm; Nov. 6-May 15 M-F 8am-5:30pm, Sa 8:30am-5:30pm, Su 9am-5:30pm.*

CLOS MONTMARTRE   HISTORIC SITE, GARDEN

Intersection of rue des Saules and rue St-Vincent

Way back in the Middle Ages, Montmartre's primary income came from vineyards that covered the hill. In the words of one very unflattering 17th-century saying, "It's Montmartre wine of which you drink a pint and piss out a quart." We're not sure then how this practice lasted for over a century in this area, but needless to say, Montmartre wine is now a thing of the past. This garden of vines was planted in 1933 as a commemoration of the good ol' days. Some 18th-century bottles are on display in the 18ème's town hall. The garden is closed to the public, but most of it can be seen from the foot of the slope it sprawls over or from the back of the Musée Montmartre. The vines only really get public attention once a year, during the harvest celebrations in mid-October, when the garden's produce is harvested and auctioned off for charity.

✈ Ⓜ*Lamarck-Caulaincourt. Walk east on rue Caulaincourt and turn right onto rue des Saules. The garden is right across the street from the Lapin Agile and behind the Musée Montmartre.* *i* *Closed to public, except during the Fête des Vendanges, usually the 2nd Sa of October; see www. fetedesvendangesdemontmartre.com for scheduling information.*

LE BATEAU LAVOIR
HISTORIC SITE

11 bis pl. Émile Godeau

Le Bateau Lavoir is not a boat. In fact, it's not really anything except a façade, the only remaining part of a building that burned down in 1970. It wasn't just any building, though. Beginning in 1889, it housed the studios of some serious names in art and poetry, including Henri Bovet, Modigliani, Max Jacob, and some guy name Picasso (apparently this is where Pablo painted *Les Demoiselles d'Avignon*). Sadly, the building was almost entirely destroyed 1970 fire but was reconstructed in 1978 and is still home to artists' studios. There really isn't anything to see here, though, unless the thought of gracing the same ground as long-dead poets and painters gives you tingles.

✈ Ⓜ*Abbesses. Walk away from rue d'Orsel and continue uphill just past rue des 3 Fréres. The building is at the top of some steps next to a hotel.* *i* *Closed to public.*

PIGALLE
NEIGHBORHOOD

This famous, seedy neighborhood has a bad reputation for a reason. Home to strip clubs, sex shops, and fake designer clothing and handbags, Pigalle turns a dark corner at night. Travelers report that you shouldn't take the Metro at night around here; instead, opt for a taxi. Now that the disclaimer is out of the way, the **Moulin Rouge** (82 bd de Clichy ☎01 53 09 82 82; www.moulinrouge.fr) cabaret show is definitely worth the €90 you have lying around, as it's the classiest titty show you'll ever see. The neighborhood is improving as young bohemians take advantage of the low rent rates, so there is a growing rock and hip-hop scene, especially at **Elysée Montmartre** (72 bd de Rochechouart ☎01 44 92 45 36; www. elyseemontmartre.com).

✈ Ⓜ*Pigalle.*

BUTTES CHAUMONT & BELLEVILLE

🏛 PARC DES BUTTES CHAUMONT
PARK

Not your average Parisian park, the Buttes Chaumont was modeled after Hyde Park in London, but it seems more like Pandora from *Avatar*. Despite the barrier of trees around the park and walkways, there is more than enough sun for a picnic or laying out on the steep grassy slopes that overlook the high cliff. Bridges lead over the surrounding lake to the top, where designer Adolphe Alphand decided (why? we don't know) to build a small Roman Temple. In the 13th century, this area was the site of a gibbet (an iron cage filled with the rotting corpses of criminals), a dumping ground for dead horses, a haven for worms, and a gypsum quarry (the origin of the term "plaster of Paris"). Thankfully, it's come a long way since then.

✈ Ⓜ*Buttes Chaumont.* Ⓢ *Free.* 🕐 *Open daily May-Sept 7am-10:15pm; Oct-Apr 7am-8:15pm.*

🏛 CIMETIÈRE DU PÈRE LACHAISE
CEMETERY

16 rue du Repos
☎01 55 25 82 10

After Pasteur and his germ theory totally messed with the zoning regulations of the Cimetière des Innocents (right next to the Les Halles food market), Père Lachaise was opened as a place to bury the dead. Parisians have buried over one million bodies here, despite there being only 100,000 graves. Highlights include elbowing your way past leather-studded jackets at Jim Morrison's grave where people have taken to "madly loving" their rock/drug idol; kissing Oscar Wilde's grave (we passed on that one); or just getting utterly lost in the maze of headstones, Tim Burton-esque mausoleums, and cobblestone paths.

🍴 ⓂPère Lachaise or ⓂGambetta. *i* Free maps at the Bureau de Conservation near Porte du Repos; ask for directions at guard booths near the main entrances. For more info on "theme" tours, call ☎01 49 57 94 37. Ⓢ Free. 🕐 Open from mid-Mar to early Nov M-F 8am-6pm, Sa 8:30am-6pm, Su 9am-6pm; from Nov to mid-Mar M-F 8am-5:30pm, Sa 8:30am-5:30pm, Su 9am-5:30pm. Last entry 15min. before close. Free 2½hr. guided tour from Apr to mid-Nov Sa 2:30pm.

🏛 CITÉ DES SCIENCES ET DE L'INDUSTRIE   MUSEUM
30 av. Corentin Cariou   ☎01 40 05 12 12 www.cite-sciences.fr

If art isn't your cup of tea and you have a passion for the sciences, welcome to your Louvre. This massive complex has anything that would make Bill Nye giggle like a school girl. Permanent exhibits on energy use, optical illusions, and human genetics all have videos and interactive games to make those subjects palatable for those who couldn't stay awake in biology class, and the constantly rotating temporary exhibits keep up with what's interesting in scientific news. Recent exhibits have tackled climate change, the ocean, and new transport technology (complete with a flight simulator). Carl Sagan would cry tears of joy while watching their planetarium show on the history of the universe, projected onto a nearly 11,000 sq. ft. dome. If you're low on cash, the aquarium is free.

🍴 ⓂPorte de la Villette. Ⓢ €8-20. Admission price depends on which exhibits you want to see. 🕐 Open Tu-Sa 10am-6pm, Su 10am-7pm. Health info center open Tu-Su noon-6pm.

PARC DE LA VILLETTE   PARK
211 av. Jean Jaurès   ☎01 40 03 75 75 www.villette.com

Parc de la Villette is more than a park; it's a normal park's multi-tasking, overachieving, sometimes excessive but always impressive older sibling. Oh, so you're a park and you have nice picnic areas and a garden? Well Parc de la Villette has nine restaurants more than 12 individually landscaped and themed gardens—including a mirror garden, a bamboo garden, an acrobatic garden, and a 🐲dragon garden. Okay, so you're a park with a nice museum and some outdoor concerts? Parc de le Villette has a museum dedicated to music (Cité de la Musique, see below), a science and technology museum (Cité des Sciences et le l'Industrie), countless concerts, a cabaret, and theaters dedicated to circus arts, street performances and puppet shows, contemporary French plays, and film screenings. Not to mention the equestrian park behind the cabaret and the submarine in the Canal de l'Ourcq that runs through the middle of the park. Do you see where we're going with this? Start at the information office at the Porte de Pantin entrance to grab a map that includes a list and brief description of all the goodies you can find in this park of endless entertainment.

🍴 ⓂPorte de Pantin or ⓂPorte de la Villette brings you right to the edges of the park. 🕐 Info office open M-Sa 9:30am-6:30pm. Garden open Sa-Su 3-7pm.

CITÉ DE LA MUSIQUE   MUSEUM
221 av. Jean Jaurès   ☎01 44 84 44 84 www.citedelamusique.fr

The highlight of the Cité de la Musique is the Musée de la Musique, although it is also home to concerts halls, practice rooms, a media library, and workshops. The museum takes visitors on a tour of music from the 17th century to the present and includes everything from 16th-century Venetian pianos (a must see) to early 20th century radios. Take a free audio guide with you to listen to music clips and descriptions of nearly 1000 instruments, including a tortoise guitar and instruments formerly owned by greats like Frédéric Chopin.

sights

Temporary exhibits hit the museum's lower levels twice a year. Exhibits cover a range of musical styles and time periods; a recent exhibit was dedicated entirely to Bob Dylan.

🍴 Ⓜ️*Porte de Pantin.* 𝒊 *Extra charges may apply for temporary exhibits.* Ⓢ *Concerts €8-39. Museum €8, with guided tour €10; group of 10 or more, music professors, and ages 26-28 €6.40/8; under 26 €5; handicapped and EU members under 26 free/€5.* 🅘 *Info center open Tu-Sa noon-6pm, Su 10am-6pm. Musée de la Musique open Tu-Sa noon-6pm, Su 10am-6pm; last entry 5:15pm. Médiathèque open Tu-Sa noon-6pm, Su 1-6pm. Musicians daily Sept-June, 2-5pm, July-Aug 3-4:30pm. Concerts, workshops, and special guests 2nd Su each month.*

PARC DE BELLEVILLE   PARK
27 rue Piat

Parc de Belleville is the place to get lost in a book; get lost in a meal of baguettes, cheese, apples, and wine; get lost in a game of badminton; or get lost just wandering about the terraces and smelling the endless colorful flowers. From the top of the park you can enjoy a wonderful view of Parisian landmarks like the Eiffel Tower and the Panthéon. Gently bubbling fountains decorate different parts of the park and add a pleasant ambient soundtrack to the landscape. The park is divided into terraces and different grassy areas that are used for pick-up soccer games or picnics. Although Parc de Belleville closes after dark and many patrons clear out by late evening, fences are low and often breached by bored teenagers looking for a place to rendezvous after hours. (*Let's Go* does not recommend hopping fences like a hoodlum).

🍴 Ⓜ️*Pyrénées. Walk west on rue de Belleville, then turn left onto rue Piat.* 𝒊 *Entrances on rue Piat, rue des Couronnes, rue Bisson, and rue Jouye-Rouve.* Ⓢ *Free.* 🅘 *Open daily dawn-dusk.*

food

Say goodbye to foot-long subs and that sticky pre-sliced cheese they sell at Costco; you're not in Kansas anymore. Food is an integral part of French life—while world-famous chefs and their three-star prices are valued Parisian institutions, you don't have to break the bank for excellent cuisine, especially if you come at lunchtime (when prices are nearly half what they are at dinner). Brasseries are even more casual and foster a lively and irreverent atmosphere. Most places, no matter the category, will offer a *menu* or *formule* at lunch or dinner that includes an *entrée* and *plat*, *plat* and dessert, or all three for a set price. The least expensive option is usually a creperie, which specializes in thin Breton pancakes filled with meat, vegetables, cheeses, chocolate, or fruit. Creperies might conjure images of yuppie brunches and awkward first dates for Americans, but here in Paris you can often eat a crepe for less than you'd pay at the great Golden Arches. Specialty food shops, including *boulangeries* (bakeries), *patisseries* (pastry shops), and chocolatiers, provide delicious and inexpensive picnic supplies. A number of cheap kebab and falafel stands around the city also serve quick, inexpensive fare. *Bon appetit!*

ÎLE DE LA CITÉ AND ÎLE ST-LOUIS

The islands are expensive. Period. Forage all you want, but the cheapest meal you can put together here is a crepe and maybe some ice cream. If you want an actual meal, head to Île St-Louis, where the tourist crowds (and the prices) tend to diminish. Of course, if you do happen to be loaded, there are a lot of dimly lit, intimate (read: expensive) restaurants where you will pay for the privilege of eating in the true center of Paris.

MA SALLE À MANGER   RESTAURANT, COCKTAIL BAR $$
26 pl. Dauphine   ☎01 43 29 52 34

This cafe in the quiet pl. Dauphine gains curb appeal from its funky explosion of
color. The establishment is a quirky combo of Corsican posters, old movies, and
old French adverts. Think of a French hippie's garage sale, but throw in cheap
lamb, *moules-frites*, and a selection of (relatively) affordable cocktails for an
early start to the night.

🍴 ⓂCité or Pont Neuf. Ⓢ Entrées €6-10. Menu du jour (entrée and plat, or plat and dessert) from
€13. Mixed drinks €8. ⓩ Open M-F 11am-3:30pm and 7-10:30pm, Sa-Su 11am-10:30pm.

CAFÉ MED   RESTAURANT, CREPERIE $$
77 rue St-Louis-en-l'Île   ☎01 43 29 73 17

Come here for a fix of Moulin Rouge, where the Red Windmill is the central theme
of this usually packed cafe. The most affordable meal is a traditional Bretagne
crepe/cider combo, but for a healthy dose of carbs, go for the lunch or dinner
menu, where most of the main dishes are pasta with *herbes de Provence*.

🍴 ⓂPont Marie. Ⓢ Galette/crepe/cider combo €10.50. Lunch menu €12. Dinner menu €18.
ⓩ Open M-F 11am-3:30pm and 7-10:30pm, Sa-Su 11am-10:30pm.

BERTHILLON   ICE CREAM $
31 rue St-Louis-en-l'Île   ☎01 43 54 31 61 www.www.berthillon.fr

If you are the ice cream aficionado who has made pilgrimages to the Ben and
Jerry's or Blue Bell factories, this should probably be on your bucket list. While
it may not offer the tours or free samples of larger factories, one similarity
remains: the ice cream is phenomenal. The sweet dessert is served (mixed with
fresh fruit on demand) minutes after it's made in the old parlor room.

🍴 ⓂPont Neuf. Ⓢ 1 scoop €2.50; 2 scoops €3.50; 3 scoops €5. ⓩ Open Sept to mid-July W-Su
10am-8pm. Closed 2 weeks in Feb and Apr.

LE PETIT PLATEAU   CAFE $$
1 quai aux Fleurs   ☎01 44 07 61 86

Le Petit Plateau is tucked away from the Notre Dame, but foot traffic between
here and St-Louis can cause this truly *petit* cafe to fill up quickly, especially at
lunchtime. Quiches are made fresh every day and are usually included in the
generous lunch special. Following a quiche or salad with dessert is a must here.

🍴 ⓂCité. On the eastern tip of the island, before the bridge to St-Louis. Next to Esmeralda.
Ⓢ Quiches €8.50. Salads €10-11.50. Sandwiches €5-15. Lunch €12-16. Dessert €3.50-7. ⓩ Open
daily 10am-6pm.

LA RÉSERVE DE QUASIMODO   WINE, CAFE $
4 rue de la Colombe   ☎01 46 34 67 67

Conversation will flow freely here, just as it has for the last seven centuries.
Each dish pairs perfectly with wine from the small cellar, which operates in
conjunction with the restaurant and is packed with bottles floor to ceiling. Bring
your friends for an intimate evening or bring a date for a romantic dinner that
may very well turn into an even more romantic evening.

🍴 ⓂCité. Ⓢ Entrees €5. Salads €10-13. Plats €9.50-12.50. Lunch special €16. ⓩ Open M-Sa
10:45am-late.

BRASSERIE DE L'ÎLE ST-LOUIS   BRASSERIE $$$
55 quai de Bourbon   ☎01 43 54 02 59

Don't let the exterior fool you: this is not the stock brasserie that it appears to
be. Step inside and go back to the colonial period, where you would stare at
the hunting trophy horns on the walls if it weren't for the giant old-fashioned
coffee maker that towers four feet over the bar. Come for the double espressos
for €2.80 (cheap for the islands) or a more filling *cassoulet* (a casserole of meat
and beans; €18).

🍴 ⓂPont Marie. Ⓢ Entrées €6-10. Plats €17-45. Desserts €7-11. ⓩ Open daily noon-11pm.

LE CAVEAU DU PALAIS   TRADITIONAL $$$

17-19 pl. Dauphine   ☎01 43 26 04 28 caveaudupalais@wanadoo.fr

With its dark brick interior, Le Caveau du Palais is aptly named. Although you won't be lighting cigars and sipping bourbon here, you can still feel fancy eating hearty, traditional French food that will be worth having to starve yourself the next day to stay within budget.

✢ ⓜPont Neuf. *Cross the bridge to the island, then turn left toward pl. Dauphine.* ⓢ *Lunch €9-15. Entrees €9.50-16. Plats €19-26. Fish €25-31.* ⓩ *Open daily 12:15-2:15pm and 7:30-10:15pm.*

CHÂTELET-LES HALLES

Food in Châtelet caters to tourists and is unabashedly overpriced. While you can get a lot of bang for your buck at the many pizza and pasta places in the center of the area, once you go farther up **rue St-Honoré** or past Les Halles, you'll find quirkier places that aren't crowded with hungry shoppers and tourists.

⬛ LE JIP'S   FUSION $$

41 rue St-Denis   ☎01 42 21 33 93

Le Jip's has some of the cheapest and most authentic Cuban/African/Brazilian food in Paris (wrap your head around those flavor combos). You could spend the whole day chowing down on chicken creole in coconut milk, melt-in-your-mouth lamb, and desserts like *crème de citron vert* (lime green custard) and caramelized pineapple. Tapas platters and mojitos with a choice of four kinds of rum can warm you up in the afternoon until the bar explodes with salsa dancing until 2am.

✢ ⓜChâtelet. *i Salsa dancing Su 3-5pm; call ahead to reserve.* ⓢ *Tapas platters €12. Lunch menu €15. Mojitos €10. Salsa dancing €10; includes 1 drink.* ⓩ *Open daily 11am-2am.*

ANGELINA   TEA HOUSE $$$$

226 rue de Rivoli   ☎01 42 60 82 00 www.angelina-paris.fr

A hot chocolate at Angelina will make you feel like Eloise at the Plaza. Located right across from the Jardin des Tuileries, this *salon de thé* will be celebrating its 110th year in 2013, and bright frescoes, mirrored walls, and white tablecloths have immortalized Angelina's status as a Parisian classic. Given its popularity, you can expect to wait during peak lunch hours in the summer, but if you come just for hot chocolate or mid-afternoon tea, you may be able to get seated right away. The hot chocolate is an Angelina staple that many travelers say is worth the price (€7.90), even in the heat of the summer. All food items are available for takeout, and the patisserie is set apart from the restaurant, although there's often a line for that as well. Again, worth the wait.

✢ ⓜTuileries. ⓢ *Set breakfast menu €20-29. Brunch €39. Entrées €14-17. Plats €23-35. Pastries €5-13. Tea and coffee €4-7.50.* ⓩ *Open M-Th 7:30am-1pm, F-Sa 8:30am-7pm, Su 7:30am-1pm.*

BOCO   CAFE, ORGANIC $$

3 rue Danielle Casanova   ☎01 42 61 17 67 www.boco.fr

Boco is riding the wave of green, organic, health-conscious eating and riding it well. Five nationally-renowned French chefs decided it was about time there was an easy, affordable option for healthy eaters, and so Boco was born. The chefs' own recipes are prepared daily and pre-packaged in heavy-duty glass jars. Take your pick of pasta, soup, or eggs (each with a fancier French twist, of course), and either bring it to the counter to be heated up, eat it as is, or take it home to prepare it as you please. The jar is an added bonus that you can reuse for storing more food or for growing your own. If that all sounds too complicated to you, Boco guarantees a daily special menu that includes an *entrée, plat,* and dessert for just €15.

✢ ⓜPyramides. *Walk north on av. de l'Opéra toward the Opéra and turn left onto rue Danielle Casanova. Boco is on the left near the corner.* ⓢ *Entrées €5-6.50. Plats €7-9.50.* ⓩ *Open M-Sa 11am-10pm.*

AU CHIEN QUI FUME   SEAFOOD, TRADITIONAL $$$$
33 rue du Pont Neuf   ☎01 42 36 07 42 www.auchienquifume.com
Au Chien Qui Fume has been a Parisian favorite for more than a century. The
name, "The Dog Who Smokes," comes from the 1920s and the original owner
who had a poodle and a terrier with a penchant for cigars and pipes. Although
there won't be any nicotine-addled mutts eating your leftovers under the table,
the large paintings of well-dressed business hounds near the bar keep the laid-
back spirit of this restaurant alive in a setting that is often abuzz with tourists
and Parisians alike. Seafood is the specialty here, but the traditional French
dishes are nothing to sniff at, either. You will have to take a crowbar to your
wallet to really enjoy Au Chien Qui Fume's fine dining options, but it will be a
meal and an experience to remember.

꓿ Ⓜ*Les Halles.* ꀇ *Reservations recommended, especially for dinner F-Sa.* Ⓢ *Entrée or plat with*
drink and coffee €19, noon-5pm. Entrées €8.50-14. Plats €18-28.50. ⏰ *Open M-F noon-midnight,*
Sa noon-1am, Su noon-midnight.

L'AMI GEORGES   BRASSERIE $$$
5 rue du Quatre-Septembre   ☎01 42 97 48 80
L'Ami Georges is where locals congregate for prime traditional French food that
is best shared with friends. The interior of the restaurant looks a lot like other
brasseries in Paris: charming, intimate seating, menus on chalkboards, and a few
pieces of art strewn about on the walls. But unlike other brasseries, especially
the touristy ones where you can buy bite-sized sandwiches for the price of your
first-born child in a cramped room full of Anglophones, L'Ami Georges has big
plates, small prices, and plenty of French to go around. Try the ham and cheese
omelet for breakfast or a special like the pork filet mignon for dinner.

꓿ Ⓜ*Quatre Septembre. Walk east down rue du Quatre-Septembre; the brasserie is on the right*
on the corner. Ⓢ *Entrees €5. Salads €12-15. Plats €13.50-17.* ⏰ *Open daily 7am-11pm for food,*
until late for drinks.

AU PÈRE TRANQUILLE   BRASSERIE $$$
16 rue Pierre-Lescot   ☎01 45 08 00 34
Au Père Tranquille is as chill as its name suggests. Although this large restaurant
fills up quickly, the tables inside are set up as if they were on a terrace: small
round tables for light conversation over coffee with family or a few close friends.
The second level offers a shift from faux-marble tables to big leather chairs and
an area full of books (because who doesn't want to read when they're trying to
eat?). No matter where you sit, you will surely be relaxed, especially knowing
that you won't be paying a fortune to have a nice meal close to the city's main
attractions.

꓿ Ⓜ*Châtelet-Les Halles. Exit the station on the eastern side of the mall; Au Père is to the left on*
the corner. Ⓢ *Brunch daily €12.50. Tartines and croques €8.50-10.50. Plats €10-15.50.* ⏰ *Open*
daily 9am-midnight.

LE PÈRE FOUETTARD   TRADITIONAL $$$
9 rue Pierre Lescot   ☎01 42 33 74 17
Le Pere Fouettard will serve up a satisfying meal for just a little bit less than its
neighbors in this busy tourist neighborhood. The seating areas here are a bit
cramped, but you can still enjoy the fresh air on the terrace or take shelter on
the second floor if the weather's bad. The atmosphere is laid-back but cheerful, a
refreshing respite from the bustling and sometimes overbearing crowds at other
restaurants.

꓿ Ⓜ*Châtelet-Les Halles. Exit the station on the eastern side of the mall; the restaurant is to the*
left on the corner. ꀇ *Reservations recommended.* Ⓢ *Entrées €4-15. Salads €14-16. Plats €12-24.*
Lunch entrée, plat, coffee €15 or plat, dessert, coffee €20. ⏰ *Open daily noon-12:30am. Lunch*
noon-3pm.

food

LE STADO
150 rue St-Honoré

BASQUE $$
☎01 42 60 29 75

Don't let the rugby jerseys or Olympic photos make you think Le Stado is a sports bar, because it's almost the opposite. The upscale Basque restaurant serves *canard*, *salade paysanne*, and regional cakes. Come here for a three-course lunch on a weekday, as it's difficult to afford the dinner menu (€28).

✠ Ⓜ*Louvre-Rivoli.* Ⓢ *Salads €8-11. Plats €10-25. Lunch menu €13.* Ⓣ *Open daily 11:30am-2:30pm and 7-11pm.*

RIZ QUI RIT
142 rue St-Denis

KOREAN, VEGETARIAN $$
☎01 40 13 04 56 www.rizquirit.wordpress.com

This hip Korean restaurant will maintain your Zen (or at least try to explain to you what Zen is) with their eco-friendly meat dishes and vegetarian options. Bento Zen lunch boxes combine a whole meal into one partitioned tray and can be taken to go for those in a hurry.

✠ Ⓜ*Étienne Marcel. Walk against traffic on rue de Turbigo and turn left onto rue St-Denis.* Ⓢ *Bento Zen lunch box €12. Vegetable and meat dishes €8-16.* Ⓣ *Open daily 9am-7pm.*

FLAM'S
62 rue des Lombards

CAFE $
☎01 42 21 10 30 www.flams.fr

Flam's is a basic cafe chain that has taken the Alsatian recipe for *flammekueche* ("cake baked in flames"; a thin pizza topped with cheese and cream) and made it available for next to nothing. The bright orange exterior makes the restaurant easy to find, and the cheap beer and cocktails make it hard to leave. While this isn't the chain's only location in Paris, it's most attractive here thanks to being one of the cheapest places around.

✠ Ⓜ*Châtelet.* Ⓢ *Flammekueche €5.50-8. Prix-fixe menu €17. Beer €2.50-3.50. Mixed drinks €4.50-7.* Ⓣ *Open M-Th 11:45am-midnight, F-Sa 11:45am-11:30pm, Su 11:45am-midnight.*

1979
49 rue Berger

TRADITIONAL $$
☎01 40 41 08 78

Appropriately decorated with Pop Art, Mardi Gras masks, and the odd faux polar bear mounted on the wall, 1979 serves traditional French foods with a twist, like clams, prawns, and smoked salmon combined with *ravettes de foie gras.*

✠ Ⓜ*Louvre-Rivoli. Take rue du Louvre north and turn right onto rue Berger.* Ⓢ *Prix-fixe menus €9-16.* Ⓣ *Open M-Th noon-2:30pm and 8-10:30pm, F noon-2:30pm and 8-11pm, Sa 8-11pm.*

THE MARAIS

Many Parisians avoid dining in this area due to prices that are often marked up for the tourist rush. However, there are several quality dinner options hidden throughout the neighborhood, and with lunch specials that usually include an *entrée* and a *plat* or a *plat* and dessert for a fixed price, these options allow you to eat here on a budget. **Rue Vieille du Temple** is lined with bars that are occupied any night of the week with casual drinkers but also serve reasonable and aromatic meals. Even if these prices are outside of your ideal budget range, the few extra euro will be money well spent. If you're still not convinced, head to **rue des Rosiers** for some cheap falafel from just about every other storefront on this street.

🔲 DERRIÈRE
69 rue des Gravilliers

TRADITIONAL $$$$
☎01 44 61 91 95 www.derriere-resto.com

When you walk into the Derrière (we're giggling, too) you may be confused as to whether you're at a restaurant or in the home of someone who just likes to have a lot of dinner parties. The courtyard preceding the restaurant has plain tables and green chairs, but the interior is another story. First, you are greeted by a motorcycle, then by a ping-pong table. If you're feeling fancy, order the

€75 *côte de boeuf* for two and sit at the long table with elegant cream-colored antique chairs and *fleurs-de-lis* adorning the cushions. Otherwise, you can keep it casual and head for the low, leather chairs that surround a coffee table. ♯ Ⓜ️Arts et Métiers. *Walk south on rue Beaubourg, then turn right onto rue des Gravilliers.* Ⓢ *Entrées €10-19. Plats €18-28.* Ⓞ *Open M-F noon-2:30pm and 8pm-midnight, Sa-Su noon-4pm and 8pm-midnight.*

PAIN VIN FROMAGE   TRADITIONAL $$$
3 rue Geoffrey L'Angevin   ☎01 42 74 07 52 www.painvinfromage.com
This rustic Parisian hidden gem certainly serves up a unique French cuisine experience. If you can handle the rich smell of cheese and hot fondue for an evening, it will be worth it. With a selection of fine cheeses from seven different regions in France and the perfect wine selection to pair them with, the gentlemen might as well twist their handle-bar mustaches with a *hoh hoh hoh* while the ladies puff on their long cigarette handles with an *ooh là là!* ♯ Ⓜ️Rambuteau or Ⓜ️Hôtel de Ville. *i Reservations recommended.* Ⓢ *Entrées €4-9.50. Plats €8.50-10.50. Fondue €14.50-16.50. Cheese plates by region €18.* Ⓞ *Open daily 7-11:30pm.*

L'AS DU FALAFEL   FALAFEL $
34 rue des Rosiers   ☎01 48 87 63 60
L'As du Falafel has become a landmark, and with good reason. Get a view into the kitchen and you'll see giant tubs of freshly cut veggies and the chef frying falafel as fast as it's ordered. Patrons line up outside for the famous "falafel special"—we saw it as more of a magic trick, because we still don't know how they managed to fit everything into that pita. Seriously, it's huge, especially for only €5. ♯ Ⓜ️St-Paul. *Take rue Pavée and turn left onto rue des Rosiers.* Ⓢ *Falafel special €5. Shawarma €7.50.* Ⓞ *Open high season M-Th noon-midnight, F noon-7pm, Su noon-midnight; low season M-Th noon-midnight, F noon-5pm, Su noon-midnight.*

CHEZ JANOU   BISTRO $$
2 rue Roger Verlomme   ☎01 42 72 28 41 www.chezjanou.com
Tucked into a quiet corner of the 3ème, this Provençal bistro serves affordable ambrosia to a crowd of enthusiasts. The duck practically melts in your mouth, and the chocolate mousse (€6.60) comes in an enormous self-serve bowl, though Parisians count on self-control. For those without it, the choice of more pastis (over 80 varieties) than food items will have you channeling your inner Fitzgerald—just don't drive home. ♯ Ⓜ️Chemin-Vert. *Follow rue des Tournelles south until the intersection with rue Roger Verlomme.* *i Reservations recommended, as this local favorite is packed every night of the week.* Ⓢ *Plats start at €14. Prix-fixe menu €14.* Ⓞ *Open daily noon-midnight. Kitchen open M-F noon-3pm and 7:45pm-midnight, Sa-Su noon-4pm and 7:45pm-midnight.*

PINK FLAMINGO   PIZZA $$
105 rue Vieille-du-Temple   ☎01 42 71 28 20 www.pinkflamingopizza.com
The Pink Flamingo will have you wondering how pizza came from Italy and not from this lawn decoration-inspired Parisian hole-in-the-wall. The smells here alone will make your mouth water just enough that you might even be able to finish the massive pizzas. For a unique dining experience, call ahead and book a table in the Pink Flamingo van, an old school VW where you and four to five of your closest friends can share a pizza in hippie heaven. ♯ Ⓜ️Rambateau. *Walk against traffic on rue Beaubourg and turn right onto rue Michel le Comte, then left. Or, from Ⓜ️St-Sebastien-Froissant, walk down rue du Pont aux Coux and turn left.* Ⓢ *Pizzas €10.50-16.* Ⓞ *Open M-F noon-3pm and 7-11:30pm, Sa-Su noon-4pm and 7-11:30pm.*

MICKY'S DELI   KOSHER $$
23 bis rue des Rosiers   ☎01 48 04 79 31
Thanks to Rabbi Rottenberg, every slice of meat and beef patty at this deli is pure to the standards of the Torah. One of the last traditional holdouts of the

food

3ème, Micky's Deli gets a lot of traffic, so head in early or toward closing to get a hold of its monster-sized hot pastrami or burger, or go for the famous Micky's Burger, which blasphemously combines the two.

✚ ⓜSt-Paul. Take rue Pavée and turn left onto rue des Rosiers. Ⓢ Burger and fries with drink €7. Deli sandwiches €11-17. Ⓚ Open M-Th 11:30am-3pm and 7-11pm, F 11:30am-3pm, Sa 8pm-midnight, Su noon-11pm.

L'ARGANIER   MOROCCAN $$$
19 rue Ste-Croix de la Bretonnerie   ☎01 42 72 08 25 www.larganier-marais.com
L'Arganier is a local hotspot in an area that is generally full of overpriced tourist traps. Authentic Moroccan fare catches your nose as your survey the huge buffet that lines the entire right wall of the main dining room. The front seating rooms are dimly lit and full of colorful chairs and tables. For an even more authentic dining experience, head to the back of the restaurant to eat at a low table with couches or floor cushions, and enjoy the West African vibes.

✚ ⓜHôtel de Ville. Walk against traffic on rue du Renard and turn right onto rue Ste-Croix. Ⓢ Buffet €18. Entrées €6-10. Plats €14-20. Salads €12. Couscous €17-26. Lunch €13 for entrée and plat or plat and dessert. Entrée, plat, and coffee €21. Entrée, plat, dessert, and 0.25L wine €25. Ⓚ Open daily noon-3pm and 7:30pm-midnight.

MIROGLIO CAFFE   ITALIAN $$$
88 rue St-Martin   ☎01 42 71 21 24 www.miroglio-caffe.com
Welcome to Little Italy. With a daily all-you-can-eat buffet composed of assorted hot and cold dishes, Miroglio Caffe offers a slew of options. Parisians frequent this quaint Italian eatery for the unlimited buffet, a staff with the warmth only Italians can offer, and serious bang for your buck. The menu changes regularly, so the dishes are always interesting, and plates here are almost always licked clean.

✚ ⓜChâtelet or Hôtel de Ville. Walk down rue du Rivoli and turn onto rue St-Martin in the opposite direction of the river. Behind Centre Pompidou. Ⓢ Brunch Sa-Su noon-3pm €18. M-F lunch menu €11 or complet €14.50. Buffet €15-19. Ⓚ Open daily 8am-midnight. Lunch noon-3pm. Happy hour 4-7pm. Buffet 7-10:30pm.

LA PERLA   MEXICAN $$$
26 rue Francois Miron   ☎01 42 77 59 40 www.cafepacifico-laperla.com
Get your sombreros and fill your stomachs with as much cheesy nachos and quesadillas as you can—the tequila packs a real punch here. Best known for its wild cocktails, La Perla is a Mexican staple in Paris, with other locations in London, Amsterdam, and Sydney. If you're planning to eat dinner here, you might as well plan to park it for the night; no matter how much you ingest, you'll soon be headed for one tequila, two teguila, three qetuila, floor.

✚ ⓜSt-Paul. Walk with traffic down rue de Rivoli; rue F. Miron branches off the south side of rue de Rivoli and toward the river. Ⓢ Entrées €6.60-9.50. Plats €9.20-10.80. Beer €6. Mexican mixed drinks €10. Tropical mixed drinks €10. Happy hour drinks €4. Ⓚ Open M-Th noon-midnight, F-Sa noon-2am, Su noon-midnight. Happy hour M-F 5-8pm.

CHEZ HANNA   FALAFEL
54 rue des Rosiers   ☎01 42 74 74 99 www.restaurant-chezhanna.com
Rue de Rosiers has some pretty stiff competition on the falafel front, and in this battle of the best pitas in Paris, Chez Hanna holds its own. A much more pleasant dining experience than the usual push-and-shove lines in the street, Chez Hanna's dim purple lighting and white stone walls will highlight your night. Piping hot pitas accompany plates stacked high with falafel, so make sure to arrive on an empty stomach.

✚ ⓜSt-Paul or ⓜHôtel de Ville. Walk along rue de Rivoli and turn away from river onto rue Vieille du Temple, then turn right. Ⓢ Entrées and salads €5-10. Plats €16, come with rice or potatoes and green beans. Ⓚ Open Tu-Su noon-midnight.

PETIT BOFINGER
BRASSERIE $$$$

6 rue de la Bastille ☎01 42 72 05 23 www.bofingerparis.com

The Petit Bofinger is the more modest younger brother to the Bofinger across the street, with only slightly more moderate prices. The Bofinger opened in 1864 and was the first bar in Paris to serve beer on tap, catering to a largely Alsatian crowd. Business thrived after Prussia annexed Alsace and Lorraine and refugees flooded the St-Germain area of Paris; the restaurant's popularity hasn't relented since. The Petit Bofinger offers a calmer, family-friendly setting to the high-energy high-rollers of the Bofinger while still allowing you to feel as fancy as the next (rich) guy.

✦ Ⓜ Bastille. Restaurant is very close to the Metro stop directly off of bd Beaumarchais. Ⓢ Entrée and plat or plat and dessert from limited menu €24.50. All three €28.50. Daily specials €20. Ⓩ Open daily noon-3pm and 7pm-midnight.

LE DÔME BASTILLE
BISTRO, SEAFOOD

2 rue de la Bastille ☎01 48 04 88 44

Le Dôme Bastille caters to an elegant crowd with similarly upscale prices. But with a long menu of specialty fish dishes and port-themed decor, this bistro feels a bit more laid back without losing any class. Try one fish, two fish, a red fish, or grilled sardines (sorry, no bluefish here).

✦ Ⓜ Bastille. Walk down rue St-Antoine and turn right onto rue des Tournelles. Ⓢ Salads €9.50-16. Plats €23-27. Dessert €7.50-8.50. Ⓩ Open daily 12:15-1:30pm and 7:15-10pm.

GEORGES
CAFE, UPSCALE $$$$

Centre Pompidou, 6th fl. ☎01 44 78 47 99 www.maisonthierryc.com

Georges is a posh cafe lucky enough to have one of the best views of Paris, although the view may be the best thing it has going for it. With prices only fat pockets can afford for and modern chairs uncomfortable enough to make your butt go numb, it may not be worth the €60 meal to spend a stiff evening here. Then again, the picture of the city is so breathtaking, you could be gnawing the fat off a fried chicken wing and not care enough to miss out on this view. And if you're looking to show off to your date with your hard-earned bonus (you dog, you), the single roses on every table add a romantic touch to the modern architecture.

✦ Ⓜ Rambuteau or Ⓜ Hôtel de Ville. Walk to down rue du Renard/rue Beaubourg until you reach the Centre Pompidou. Take the elevator in the back of the Pompidou on the left (if prior to 8:50pm, otherwise take the escalators). 𝒊 Reservations recommended for dinner, required to reserve rooms for groups of 10 or more. Ⓢ Plats €13-43. Beer €8. Mixed drinks €12-18. Ⓩ Open W-Su noon-midnight.

ROBERT ET LOUISE
FRENCH $$$

64 rue Vieille du Temple ☎01 42 78 55 89 www.robertetlouise.com

Defined by a firm belief that chicken is for pansies (let's not even talk about vegetarians), Robert et Louise offers a menu that's wholeheartedly carnivorous—we're talking veal kidneys, steak, prime rib, and lamb chops. The only concession to white meat is the *confit de canard*. There's a definite homey vibe here; you'll feel like you've been taken in by a generous French family who found you abandoned and shivering on their way home from a hunt.

✦ Ⓜ St-Paul. Follow the traffic on rue de Rivoli and turn right onto rue Vieille du Temple. 𝒊 Reservations recommended. Ⓢ Entrées €5.60-8. Plats €12-63. Lunch menu €12. Desserts €5.60-6. Ⓩ Open Tu-Su noon-2:30pm and 7-11pm.

LE LOIRE DANS LA THÉIÈRE
PATISSERIE, CAFE $$

3 rue des Rosiers ☎01 42 72 90 61

If we were to rename this cafe, we'd call it "Just Desserts"—and not in the bad-karma sense. Almost like a hip cafe in New York's SoHo, Le Loire dans la Théière serves pies, cakes, tartes, and meringue with a tea for under €10. It's so popular that it closes at 7pm. The walls are covered with ads for jazz and rock concerts, and they serve omelets at Sunday brunch with mint and goat cheese.

❖ Ⓜ*St-Paul. Take rue Pavée and turn right onto rue des Rosiers.* Ⓢ *Pot of tea and dessert €9.50.* ⓧ *Open daily 10am-7pm.*

BREAKFAST IN AMERICA
DINER $$

4 rue Malher   ☎01 42 72 40 21   www.breakfast-in-america.com

BIA promises to be one thing: "an American diner in Paris." It sure delivers—from the shiny red booths to the delicious fries, shakes, bottomless mugs o' joe, and the expected post-meal tips, it doesn't get more American than this.

❖ Ⓜ*St-Paul.* Ⓢ *Burgers and sandwiches €9-12. Student menu (burger, fries, and drink) €8. All-you-can-eat-brunch Su €20. Milkshakes €5.* ⓧ *Open daily 8:30am-11pm.*

PAGE 35
CREPERIE $$

4 rue du Parc Royal   ☎01 44 54 35 35   www.restaurant-page35.com

Instead of picking which type of French restaurant to go to, check out this hip, modern art gallery/restaurant/creperie that serves anything under the red, white, and blue banner. Page 35 sums up the spirit of the Marais with its extensive menu of sirloin, tartare, *confit de canard*, poached egg on foie gras, and pasta with Provençal herbs. For those who haven't tried them yet, they also serve traditional buckwheat crepes from Brittany. Come toward the end of lunch to avoid the heavy crowds.

❖ Ⓜ*St-Paul. Take rue de Sévigné to the intersection with rue du Parc Royal.* ⓘ *Flash your Let's Go guide for a free Kir.* Ⓢ *Lunch menu €13. Dinner menu €24.* ⓧ *Open Tu-F 11:30am-3pm and 7-11pm, Sa-Su 11:30am-11pm.*

MARCHÉ DES ENFANTS ROUGES
MARKET $

39 rue de Bretagne

Paris's oldest covered market is a foodie's paradise of hidden restaurants and chaotic stands where you can grab a meal for under €10. Parisians often stop by for lunch at the wooden tables or heated patios. Since you can find French *boulangeries*, *fromageries*, and *patisseries* almost anywhere, your best bet is to go for the more exotic (like Moroccan *tagines* or Japanese sushi bento boxes), since they are much cheaper than in specialty restaurants.

❖ Ⓜ*Filles du Calvaire. Turn left onto rue Froissart, which becomes rue de Bretagne.* ⓧ *Open Tu-Th 9am-2pm and 4-8pm, F-Sa 9am-8pm, Su 9am-2pm.*

LA PAS-SAGE OBLIGÉ
VEGETARIAN $$

29 rue du Bourg Tibourg   ☎01 40 41 95 03   www.lepassageoblige.com

Seemingly defying French culture, this restaurant manages to present traditional dishes without meat. The general VG burger (pronounced VEH-jee) and the more authentic *terrine de champignons* are both satisfying, and carnivores are kept happy with *entrecôte* and tartare.

❖ Ⓜ*Hôtel de Ville. Walk against traffic on rue de Rivoli and turn left onto rue du Bourg Tibourg.* Ⓢ *Plats €11-15. Su brunch buffet €19.* ⓧ *Open daily noon-2pm and 7-10:30pm.*

LATIN QUARTER AND ST-GERMAIN

These neighborhoods have just as many good finds as they do overpriced tourist traps. The big, flashy restaurants and cafes take up entire street corners and are usually packed to the gills, but their options are inevitably overpriced and not worth your while. Venture as far as you can onto some of the side streets, and you'll be more likely to find something just as tasty but more reasonable for your traveler's budget. As a general rule, restaurants between the Seine and bd St-Germain are not as authentic as those south of St-Germain. **Rue Mouffetard** has some smaller, cheaper options that are popular with students and budget travelers, while **rue de la Huchette** is lined end-to-end with bars and gyro joints if you're looking to satisfy your late night cravings.

COSÌ   SANDWICHES

54 rue de Seine   ☎01 46 33 35 36

The original inspiration for the popular American chain, this place is just like the chain—except the food here is actually good. Fresh-baked bread and unique sandwich combinations (try the Naked Willy with ricotta cheese, cucumbers, walnuts, and roasted red peppers) make for a more-than-satisfying lunch option. And when you can get a huge sandwich with a drink and a dessert for under €11, well, we're happy. Order from the big counter on the ground floor that fronts the deep kitchen and take your food upstairs to eat by open windows; otherwise, you can grab your sandwich to go.

❦ ⓂMabillon. *Walk north on rue de Buci and take a slight left onto rue du Seine.* Ⓢ *Sandwiches €5.50-8.50. Salads €4-8. Menus €9.50-11.50 for a sandwich or salad, drink, and dessert.* 🕐 *Open daily noon-11pm.*

BREAKFAST IN AMERICA (BIA)   DINER $$

17 rue des Écoles   ☎01 43 54 50 28 www.breakfast-in-america.com

Feeling homesick? Feel like you're just not getting enough cholesterol in your carbilicious, baguette-heavy French diet? Come to Breakfast in America, where the owners will satisfy all of your greasy spoon needs. Owner Craig Carlson opened this BIA in 2003 (and a second across the river in 2006) after moving to Paris to work in the film industry. Like just about everyone else, he fell in love with the city but couldn't take his mind off what he missed most about home—a "good ol' American breakfast." So with some help from his buddies in the film business, Carlson opened BIA with huge success. With hunks of meat stacked high with lettuce, onions, tomatoes, pickles, and all of your favorite sandwich stuffers and accompanied by a healthy helping of "French" fries, you won't leave here hungry (although you may just be a little more homesick than you were before).

❦ ⓂCardinal Lemoine. *Walk up rue Monge and turn left onto rue des Écoles; the restaurant is on the left.* Ⓢ *Lunch menu M-F noon-3pm. Burger and soda €10, students €8. Breakfast €7-11 all day. Lunch and dinner €7.50-11.50 noon-close. Beer and wine €3-5.50.* 🕐 *Open daily 8:30am-11pm.*

JARDIN DES PÂTES   PASTA $$

4 rue Lacépède   ☎01 43 31 50 71

If the forbidden fruit was a plate of pasta, then the Garden of Eden would have been called the *Jardin des Pâtes.* Creative combinations of veggies and fruits mixed with fresh pasta offer new alternatives to the ol' spaghetti-and-meatballs standby. While hanging and potted green plants decorate the bright white walls, the dishes themselves are what add real color to the place. Bring a date, your mom, or your petulant child who insists she won't eat anything besides noodles with butter and cheese—this will surely change her mind.

❦ ⓂJussieu. *Walk away from the Faculté des Sciences (the blocky building) down rue Linné, then turn right onto rue Lacépède. The restaurant is on the right.* Ⓢ *Entrees €4.70-6. Pasta €10-13.* 🕐 *Open daily noon-2:30pm and 7-11pm.*

FOYER MON VIETNAM   VIETNAMESE $$

24 rue de la Motagne Ste-Genevieve   ☎01 46 34 12 02

In a city with brasseries and cafes on every corner, Foyer Mon Vietnam brings a diverse flavor to the Latin Quarter. Scents of beef and hot vermicelli flood your nose upon entering this modest restaurant, but like at many Vietnamese restaurants, vegetarian options abound. The decor is simple and the atmosphere relaxed, aptly self-described as *"ambiance conviviale."* Families, students, locals, and tourists frequent this popular spot for a flavorful meal that will please any budget.

❦ ⓂMaubert Mutalité. *Head south on rue Monge, turn right onto rue des Écoles, then left onto rue de la Montagne; the restaurant is on the right.* Ⓢ *Menus €12 for entrée and plat or plat and dessert. All three €15.50. Entrées €5-6. Plats €7.50-11.* 🕐 *Open daily 11:30am-2:30pm and 7-11pm.*

food

CAFÉ DELMAS CAFE $$

2 pl. de la Contrescarpe ☎01 43 26 51 26

With a perfect view of the plaza's fountain and trees, Café Delmas is the ideal French cafe. Inside, you will find dark colors and comfortable leather chairs, but even on a cold day you will want to sit out on the terrace where you can watch teens take their crepes to go or couples stroll hand in hand around the small cobblestone plaza. Enjoy a hot coffee, a fresh-squeezed and very pulpy orange juice, a perfectly runny egg, toast, and a croissant for just €11.

[M]Cardinal Lemoine. Walk south against traffic on rue du Cardinal Lemoine until you reach the small, circular plaza. [$] Lunch special €11. Entrées €6.50-9.50. Salads €14-16. Plats €11-25. Sandwiches €12.50-17.50. Wine €5.40-9.60. ⏰ Open daily 7:30-11:30am and noon-2am. Brunch Su 10am-5pm. Happy hour 7-9pm.

LE PERRAUDIN TRADITIONAL $$$$

157 rue St-Jacques ☎01 46 33 15 75 www.restaurant-perraudin.com

Take a trip to the French countryside without leaving Paris. This restaurant serves up real French classics that you only see people eating in the movies, like snails and duck liver. Join the French locals here for their lunch break or bring a date for impressive food in a modest setting that features checkered tablecloths, vintage French posters, and food fit for Louis XIV.

RER: Luxembourg. Walk north on bd St-Michel along the garden, then turn left onto rue Soufflot. Turn left onto rue St-Jacques. [$] Lunch menu M-F €17.50 for entree, plat, cheese, or dessert and coffee. Dinner menu €32. Entrées €8.50-13. Plats €17-25. ⏰ Open daily noon-2:30pm and 7-10:30pm.

LE GRENIER DE NOTRE-DAME VEGETARIAN $$$

18 rue de la Bûcherie ☎01 43 29 98 29 www.legreniernotredame.fr

A peaceful combination of hanging plants, white walls, and soft lighting make this vegetarian sanctuary feel like a little earthen alcove in the city. With vegetarian takes on classic dishes like lasagna as well as some expected veggie favorites like tofu, Le Grenier offers a diverse menu that caters to any vegetarian's (or open-minded carnivore's) palate. Even when the place is full, the crowd here remains subdued, making this a great place for a peaceful night away from the rowdy St-Michel stop and the always busy rue de la Huchette.

[M]St-Michel. Walk against traffic along the river and turn right onto rue Lagrange, past the small park, then take an immediate left; the restaurant is on the left, about halfway down the block. [$] Entrées €6-7.50. Plats €15.50-18. Salads €14.50-16.50. ⏰ Open daily noon-2:30pm and 6:30-11pm.

L'HEURE GOURMANDE TEA HOUSE $$

22 Passage Dauphine ☎01 46 34 00 40

L'Heure Gourmande is easy to miss, tucked away as it is on a quiet little street. Unlike at many other *salons de thé* in Paris, the main attraction here actually is the tea. Share a pot with a few friends on the quiet patio, inside the bright yellow walls below ground, or on the second level overlooking the street. Decorative teapots adorn the walls and make the environment here all about the hot beverages.

[M]Odéon. Walk against traffic on bd St-Germain and turn right onto rue Mazarine. Passage Dauphine is then on the right. [$] Tea €6-7. Brunch served all day; €27 for beverage, toast, jam, smoked salmon, tarts, and a cheese plate or dessert. Salads €13-15. Mixed drinks €7.80. Wine €4-5. ⏰ Open daily 11:30am-7pm.

GÉRARD MULOT PATISSERIE $$

76 rue de Seine ☎01 43 26 85 77 www.gerard-mulot.com

This romantic little patisserie has been a Parisian favorite since it opened in 1989. *Pâtissier, chocolatier,* and *artisan authentique,* Gérard Mulot opened his self-named patisserie to share his love for traditional and quality French desserts. Mulot was met with much success that he has since opened patisseries in the Marais and la Butte aux Cailles. We can understand why this little shop on rue de Seine has become so popular—the chocolates and fresh fruit will make your mouth water just looking at them. If you're in need for something a little more substantial than dessert, Gérard Mulot also offers a selection of prepared foods, priced by the kilogram.

⚜ Ⓜ*Odéon. Walk against traffic on bd St-Germain and turn left onto rue de Seine.* Ⓢ *Chocolate €11.50 for 125g. Cheesecake €4.20. Taboule €23.50 per kg.* ☪ *Open M 6:45am-8pm, W-Su 6:45am-8pm.*

CRÊPERIE DES CANETTES   CREPERIE $
10 rue des Canettes   ☎01 43 26 27 65 www.pancakesquare.com

Creperies are ubiquitous; however, this one uniquely prepares affordable crepes in the traditional way—square and crispy, not round and soft. The goat cheese and walnut crepes (€7) are a good choice, as is the "Typhoon" (salmon, crème fraiche, and lemon; €9), which appropriately goes with the sailing theme.

⚜ Ⓜ*Mabillion. Walk down rue de Four and turn left onto rue des Canettes.* Ⓢ *Crepes €3.50-9. Lunch and dinner menus €12.* ☪ *Open M-Sa noon-11pm.*

LA METHODE   PROVENÇAL $$
2 rue Descartes   ☎01 43 54 22 43

This Provençal restaurant takes French dishes and gives them a southern flair, creating an upscale meal that won't leave you broke. One of the best starters is the artichoke salad and duck foie gras, or, for the less adventurous, the salmon and ratatouille *entrée* is pretty damn good. The most difficult decision will be where to sit: the terrace overlooks the small plaza while the dark converted wine cave from the 17th century is perfect for a glass of wine (from the restaurant's own winery).

⚜ Ⓜ*Cardinal Lemoine. Walk uphill on rue du Cardinal Lemoine and turn right onto rue Clovis. Walk 1 block and turn right onto rue Descartes. The restaurant is on the left in the square.* Ⓢ *Plats €11-14. Lunch menu €14. Dinner menu €15.* ☪ *Open Oct-Aug M-Sa noon-2pm and 7-10pm, Su noon-10pm.*

snack attack

Parisians prefer traditional patisseries, *boulangeries,* and *fromageries* to supermarket chains that sell pre-packaged cheese and baguettes. But Paris's supermarkets still treat taste buds better than their equivalents in most other cities. Hop into any Carrefour, Monoprix, or Franprix to get ahold of these unique snacks.

- **SPECULOOS BISCUITS.** Based with a Nutella-like spread, this alternative to graham crackers was featured on pastry chef David Lebovitz's famous Parisian food blog.

- **PIMM'S COOKIES.** These crunchy treats based on the British drink are filled with orange or raspberry jelly. Though they won't give you a buzz, the sugar high might make up for your sobriety.

- **KINDER BARS.** This Italian candy bar is highly popular in France. Try a Bueno bar for its wafery goodness with a tongue-numbing hazelnut cream filling. The Duplo bar is a classier alternative with nougat cream, whole walnuts, and milk chocolate. A word of caution: avoid the candy aisle after schools let out, or you'll be duking it out with hungry French children for these treats.

- **FLAVORED YOGURT.** The French love being daring with dairy, so take advantage of the interesting yogurt varieties sold in most grocery stores. Among the unique flavors are citrus *(citron)* and hazelnut *(noisette).* Quality (read: expensive) brands come in glass jars.

food

LE VIEUX BISTRO

54 rue Mouffetard

BISTRO $$

Visit Le Vieux Bistro for one of the cheapest three-course meals in the 5ème, served by a staff that won't rush you. The bistro serves traditional Savoy faire with *escargot*, onion soup, and tenderloin that melts in your mouth. The local youth make Le Vieux their hangout spot, despite the somewhat cheesy baskets, pots, and spices that hang from the ceiling.

✠ ⓂPlace Monge. Walk down rue Monge and turn right onto pl. Monge. Keep going as it turns into rue Ortolan and turn right onto rue Mouffetard. The restaurant is on the left. Ⓢ 3-cheese fondue €14. Lunch menu €10. Dinner menu €16. ☾ Open daily noon-3pm and 6pm-midnight.

DANS LES LANDES

119 bis rue Monge

TAPAS $$

☎01 45 87 06 00

This bistro will have you thinking it's Spanish with their tapas happy hour (cocktail and choice of *tapa; €*8). The terrace is tempting, but the inside draws you in with its curvy stone-finish walls, Southern European wine that doubles as decoration, and huge shared tables that encourage chatting with your neighbors.

✠ ⓂCensier-Daubenton. Walk down rue Monge. The restaurant is on the left. Ⓢ Plats €7-21. Happy hour special €8. ☾ Open daily noon-11pm. Happy hour 5-7:30pm.

LE BISTROT D'HENRI

16 rue Princesse

TRADITIONAL $$

☎01 46 33 51 12

For a really impressive meal—or to impress your date—this Old World bistro serves some reasonably priced traditional French food. The chef recommends the lamb, which is expertly marinated in prune juice for 7hr. (this may strike you as over the top, but he's an artist), or the duck breast covered in honey. Landing a table at this Art Deco joint can be difficult, so call ahead for reservations or hop on La Fourchette (www.lafourchette.com) to nab a table and get discounts on *entrées* or drinks.

✠ ⓂMabillon. Walk down rue du Four and turn left onto rue Princesse. Ⓢ Entrées €7-11. Plats €14-23. ☾ Open M-Sa noon-2:30pm and 7-11:30pm.

BOTEQUIM

1 rue Berthollet

BRAZILIAN $$

☎01 43 37 98 46

If you're looking for an escape from traditional Parisian cuisine, enter Botequim and be transported to Brazil. Statues of Catholic saints stand alongside tribal boa headdresses on the shelves. Without a knowledge of Portuguese, it will be a little hard to navigate the menu. Never fear: go for anything, from the coconut shrimp to the *salade tropicale* (hearts of palm, shrimp, cashews, and pineapple) or the salmon with mango sauce. Just be prepared for the culture shock when you leave and discover you're back in France.

✠ ⓂCensier-Daubenton. Walk down rue Monge and turn right onto rue Claude Bernard. The restaurant is at the corner with rue Berthollet. Ⓢ Entrées €8-9. Plats €15-17. ☾ Open M-Sa noon-3:30pm and 8pm-2am.

L'ASSIETTE AUX FROMAGES

25 rue Mouffetard

FONDUE $$

☎01 43 36 91 59 www.lassietteauxfromages.com

This Swiss establishment is the answer to your authentic-fondue prayers. The smiling cow in the window hints at the wide variety of French cheeses you can order to accompany any salad or melon and ham dish. Choose between the two *formules* (one more expensive than the other) that include *confit de canard* or lamb with rosemary.

✠ ⓂPlace Monge. Walk down rue Monge and turn right onto pl. Monge. Keep going as it turns into rue Ortolan and turn right onto rue Mouffetard. The restaurant is 1½ blocks down on the right. Ⓢ Fondues €15-17. Formules €16 or €26. ☾ Open daily noon-2:30pm and 6:30-11:30pm.

AUX DOUX RAISINS

29 rue Descartes

BISTRO $$

☎01 43 29 31 13

While most of the items on the menu of this winery-inspired bistro may be as basic as you'd pack for a picnic in the Jardin du Luxembourg, they do serve popular dishes that would be familiar to any French farmer: *bœuf bourguignon*, foie gras, and *confit de canard* (€13-14). For an impressive spread of meats and cheeses for two, split the *planche doux raisins* (€13).

₮ ⓂCardinal Lemoine. Walk uphill on rue du Cardinal Lemoine and turn right onto rue Clovis. Walk 1 block and turn left onto rue Descartes. Ⓢ Entrées €7-8.50. Plats €13-14. Desserts €7-8. ⓐ Open daily 11:30am-1am.

CAVE LA BOURGOGNE BRASSERIE $$
144 rue Mouffetard ☎01 47 07 82 80

Whether you go for beer or a full meal, this brasserie's terrace is usually packed (even on Sunday), and its location in the middle of a roundabout makes it great for people watching. If you don't want to wait for outside seating, the interior is decorated with wine barrels and empty wine bottles that clue you into what should be paired with your affordable steak tartar (€15).

₮ ⓂCensier-Daubenton. Walk down rue Monge and turn right onto rue Censier. Walk until you reach the Square St-Médard. It's on the other side of the roundabout. Ⓢ Salads €7-10. Meat dishes €14-18. ⓐ Open daily noon-3pm and 7:30-11pm.

COMPTOIR MÉDITERRANÉE LEBANESE $
42 rue du Cardinal Lemoine ☎01 43 25 29 08 www.comptoirmediterranee.fr

Savannah Café's little sister, Comptoir Méditerranée is a small, order-and-eat sort of place sitting quietly on the corner of Cardinal Lemoine and rue Monge. The stone- and yellow-walled restaurant is a pleasant place to sit down with your food, but taking your meal home is also a good option. The servings are surprisingly small but appropriately filling and accordingly priced.

₮ ⓂCardinal Lemoine. Walk north on rue du Cardinal Lemoine; the restaurant is on the left. Ⓢ Sandwiches €4.50. 4 items for €7, 8 items for €13. Tea €1.50-2.50. ⓐ Open M-Sa 11am-10pm.

MARCHÉ BIOLOGIQUE MARKET
bd Raspail between Cherche-Midi and Rennes

Under the leafy shelter of bd Raspail, French New Age marketers peddle everything from seven-grain bread to olives to tofu patties. The selection caters to but is not limited by its largely vegan clientele; fish, meat, and cheese are still available en masse.

₮ ⓂRennes. ⓐ Open Tu 9am-2pm, F 9am-2pm, Su 9am-2pm.

SAVANNAH CAFÉ LEBANESE $$
27 rue Descartes ☎01 43 29 45 77 www.savannahcafe.fr

A contradictory mix of Lebanese cuisine and French flavors makes Savannah all the rage with Parisian restaurateurs. One of the best deals is the mix of six Lebanese appetizers for €17. The bright yellow interior is covered with stuffed toy zebras, photos of the Middle East, and framed recommendations.

₮ ⓂCardinal Lemoine. Walk uphill on rue du Cardinal Lemoine and turn right onto rue Clovis. Walk 1 block and turn left onto rue Descartes. The cafe is on the left. Ⓢ Entrées €7-14. Plats €14-16. Desserts €6-7.50. ⓐ Open M-Sa 7-11pm.

INVALIDES

The chic 7ème is low on budget options, but there are a number of quality restaurants that are worth the extra euro. **Rue Saint-Dominique, rue Cler,** and **rue de Grenelle** feature some of the best gourmet bakeries in Paris. The steaming baguettes and pastries make for an ideal picnic under the Eiffel Tower. If you're really in a pinch, **rue de Baby-lone** offers a number of reasonably priced, aromatic cafes and themed restaurants.

▧ **BARTHÉLÉMY** FROMAGERIE $
51 rue de Grenelle ☎01 45 48 56 75

Although this probably goes without saying, brace yourself for the distinctly sharp scent of cheese as soon as you open the door to Barthélémy. Your tongue will later thank your nose for withstanding the abuse for such a luxurious treat.

food

Although the shop is tiny, a full staff of lab coats and cheese doctors occupy half the space to ensure that you don't have to wait to cure your craving for dairy. Every type of cheese is available here, from young to aged and soft to hard. If you describe what variety you like, the experts here will be happy to give their professional opinion on what cheese is best for you.

✚ ⓂRue de Bac. Walk south down bd Raspail and turn right onto rue de Grenelle; the shop is on the right, just before the next corner. Ⓢ Boulamour raisins €6.50. ☪ Open Tu-F 8:30am-1pm and 4-7:15pm, Sa 8:30am-1:30pm and 3-7pm.

CHEZ LUCIE   CREOLE $$
15 rue Augereau   ☎01 45 55 08 74

Specializing in dishes from Martinique, this creole hole in the wall will make you abandon your Eurotrip for a sailboat in the French Antilles. The owner prides himself on his conversation skills; he shoots the breeze with customers and will even show you pictures of his wife while you dine on gumbo, spicy catfish, or—for the more adventurous—shark. The portions are enormous for such a low price, and the *ti' ponch* (rum punch) will knock you on your ass.

✚ ⓂÉcole Militaire. Walk toward the Eiffel Tower on av. de la Bourdonnais, turn right onto rue de Grenelle, and then take an immediate left onto rue Augereau. The restaurant is on the right (with a bright yellow awning). Ⓢ Entrées €7. Plats €10-30. 3-course lunch special €16. Dinner special €16-25. ☪ Open daily noon-2pm and 7-11pm.

LES COCOTTES   RESTAURANT $$
135 rue St-Dominique   ☎01 45 50 10 31 www.maisonconstant.com

Christian Constant, a famed Parisian chef, realized that not everyone wants to pay an arm and a leg for a good meal. He then opened Les Cocottes and began serving quick gourmet salads (poached egg and dried meat on greens with vinaigrette) and dishes cooked in the famed metal kettles (like caramelized potatoes and pork) for up-and-coming, business-casual French as well as intrepid tourists.

✚ ⓂÉcole Militaire. Walk toward the Eiffel Tower on av. de la Bourdonnais, turn right onto rue de Grenelle, followed by an immediate left onto rue Augereau. Walk to St-Dominique and turn right. The restaurant is on the right. Ⓢ Mousseline d'artichaut €16. Salads €10-12. Mousse au chocolate €7. ☪ Open M-Sa noon-4pm and 7-11pm.

LE SAC À DOS   TRADITIONAL $$$
47 rue de Bourgogne   ☎01 45 55 15 35 www.le-sac-a-dos.fr

This hidden gem makes up for generic French fare with personality that will make you blush. Or was that because the sun-bleached owner's shirt is unbuttoned to his navel? Choose from one of the main dishes written on chalkboards, and make room for the *mousse au chocolat* that is served in a cookie bowl.

✚ ⓂVarenne. Walk away from Pont d'Alexandre III on bd des Invalides, turning left onto rue de Varenne. Walk 1 block, past the Musée-Rodin, to rue de Bourgogne and turn left. The restaurant is on the right. Ⓢ Plats €17. Desserts €6. ☪ Open M-Sa 11am-2:30pm and 6:30-11pm.

DEBAUVE & GALLAIS   CHOCOLATIER $
30 rue des Sts-Pères   ☎01 45 48 54 67 www.debauve-et-gallais.com

Any doctor that prescribes chocolate as the elixir to your woes is fine by us. Opening his first shop in 1800, chemist Sulpice Debauve goes down in history as the most brilliant chocolatier of all time. Serving the courts of Louis XIII, Louis XVI, Charles X, and Philippe III, Debauve quickly earned a reputation for producing France's (and arguably the world's) best chocolate. In 1823 Debauve brought his nephew and fellow chemist, A. Gallais, into the business, and together they invented the best things since sliced bread (seriously), including chocolate milk, almond milk, a machine for finely crushing cocoa, and hot chocolate. If that wasn't enough, the pair was also renowned for their medicinal work, prescribing treatments for cholera prevention and anxiety. Although the business left the family after Debauve's and Gallais's deaths, the name persisted and the reputation never faltered. Prices are now a bit steeper than when Mr. Hugon pioneered the effort to make quality chocolate available to all budgets in 1858, but the legendary sweets are definitely worth the splurge.

🚇 Ⓜ St-Germain-des-Prés. *Walk west on bd St-Germain and turn right onto rue des Sts-Pères.* Ⓢ *Boite de Pistoles de Marie-Antoinette €34.* 🕐 *Open M-Sa 9am-6:30pm.*

AU PIED DE FOUET
CAFE, TRADITIONAL $$
45 rue de Babylone　　　　　　　🕾01 47 05 12 27 www.aupieddefouet.com

In an otherwise *riche* neighborhood, Au Pied de Fouet offers traditional French food at affordable prices. Generic red-checkered tablecloths and vintage signs on the walls don't make this place look any different from other French cafes, but the warm family feel and regular clientele give this place that extra special touch. And with traditional duck confit at just €12, it's hard to pass up this neighborhood favorite.

🚇 Ⓜ Saint-Francois-Xavier. *Walk east on rue de Babylone away from the esplanade; the cafe is on the right.* 𝒊 *Other locations at 3 rue St-Benoit, 6ème (🕾01 42 96 59 10) and 96 rue Oberkampf, 11ème (🕾01 48 06 46 98). Credit card min. €15.* Ⓢ *Entrées €4-5. Plats €9-12.50. Desserts and cheese plates €3-4.* 🕐 *Open Sept-July M-Sa noon-2:30pm and 7-11pm.*

STÉPHANE SECCO
BOULANGERIE, PATISSERIE $
20 rue Jean-Nicot　　　　　　　　　　　🕾01 43 17 35 20

With mint green and baby pink hues coloring the façade, the interior, the shopping bags, and even the business cards of this *boulangerie-patisserie*, Secco adds a feminine touch to already knee-weakening sweet treats. The macaroons are worth putting up a fight for, but if you're feeling something savory, Secco also offers a wide selection of prepared foods like salads and pastas.

🚇 Ⓜ La Tour-Maubourg. *Walk away from the park and turn right onto bd de la Tour-Maubourg, left onto rue St-Dominique, then right onto rue Jean-Nicot.* 𝒊 *Another location at 25 bd de Grenelle, 15ème.* Ⓢ *Croquet €1.15. Large macaroon €2.40.* 🕐 *Open Tu-Sa 8am-8:30pm.*

LOTUS BLANC
VIETNAMESE $$
45 rue de Bourgogne　　　　　　　　　🕾01 45 55 18 89

This small restaurant serves small dishes that are nonetheless packed with big flavor. Both the lower level and the loft are cramped and narrow and make the room as hot as your pork balls, but this place is well worth a little sweat. After all, if Antonio Banderas and other notable clients can take the heat here, then it must be the real deal.

🚇 Ⓜ Varenne. *Walk away from the park down rue de Varenne and take the 1st left onto rue de Bourgogne. Lotus is halfway down the block on the left.* Ⓢ *Entrées €7-9. Plats €8-17.* 🕐 *Open M-Sa noon-2:30pm and 7:30-11pm.*

EL SOL
IBERIAN $$
147 rue Ste-Dominique　　　　　　　🕾01 45 55 84 09 www.el-sol.fr

While it looks like a butcher shop (well, it is, but stay with us), this quick Iberian restaurant will literally slice your meal from the hanging meat on the ceiling and prepare it for you. If meat isn't your thing, you can at least avoid looking at it and sit at one of the two barrel tables outside. The restaurant also sells cut meats as well as Spanish wine (think picnic and Champs de Mars).

🚇 Ⓜ École Militaire. *Walk in the direction of traffic down av. Bosquet. Continue past rue de Grenelle and turn right onto rue Ste-Dominique. The restaurant is immediately on the right.* Ⓢ *Plats €6-9.* 🕐 *Open M-F 11am-3pm and 5-11:30pm, Sa 11am-11:30pm.*

CAFÉ DES LETTRES
CAFE $$$
53 rue de Verneuil　　　　　　　　　　🕾01 42 22 52 17

Close to the Musée d'Orsay, this quiet French restaurant provides a shady escape in the courtyard behind the street. Dessert tarts and *entrées* (try the tuna *rillets;* €8) are the best flavor bang for your buck, but if you want a more filling experience, shell out more for the beef fillet or curry madras.

➡ [M]Rue de Bac. Walk towards the Seine on rue de Bac, keeping left when the road forks. Cross rue de l'Université, and turn left once you get to rue de Verneuil. The cafe is on the left. $ Entrées €8-13. Plats €16-50. ⏰ Open June M-F noon-2:30pm and 8-10:30pm, Sa-Su noon-7pm; July-May M-F noon-2:30pm and 8-10:30pm.

CHAMPS-ÉLYSÉES

Once the center of Paris's glamorous dining scene, the 8ème's culinary prowess is on the wane, but its prices are not. We don't recommend eating on the Champs-Élysées, but we do suggest visiting the bakeries, *épiceries*, and cafes for small (but expensive) treats. **Thabthim Siam** is an exception—eat there for a great and affordable meal. There are also cheaper establishments around **rue la Boétie, rue du Colisée,** and **pl. de Dublin.**

👍 NIRVANA — INDIAN $$$

6 rue de Moscou ☎01 45 22 27 12 www.restaurant-indien-paris-nirvana.fr

One of the Champs-Élysées's ethnic gems, this Indian eatery is clamoring with scraping cutlery and busy mouths inside. With pristine wooden chairs, red booths with colorful beaded pillows, and waiters in silver and gold vests, Nirvana will make you feel like you own a bank without breaking the bank. The food is as delicate and refined as the decor, so if you prefer a spicy Indian meal, ask for extra zest.

➡ [M]Liège. $ Entrées €8-9.50. Plats €11-16. Naan €3.50-4. ⏰ Open M-Sa noon-2:30pm and 7-11:30pm.

👍 THABTHIM SIAM — THAI $$

28 rue de Moscou ☎01 43 87 62 56

Thabthim Siam is where locals come to get their curry fix. The changing menu allows patrons to sample a wide range of Thai cuisine. Linguistically challenged customers beware: authentic Thai names like "keng kiew wan kai" (chicken in green curry) only have French translations, so if those aren't in your repertoire, just point to a neighboring table and order what they're eating—it's most likely delicious.

➡ [M]Rome. $ Entrées €8. Plats €13-17. 2-course lunch menu with drink €15. ⏰ Open M-Sa noon-2pm and 7-10:30pm.

👍 LADURÉE — TEA HOUSE $

18 rue Royale ☎01 49 60 21 79 www.laduree.com

Opened in 1862, Ladurée started as a modest bakery but has since become so famous that a *Gossip Girl* employee was flown here to buy macaroons so Chuck could offer his heart to Blair properly. On a more typical day the Rococo decor of this tea salon—the original location of a franchise that now extends to 13 countries—attracts a jarring mix of well-groomed shoppers and tourists in sneakers. Along with the infamous mini macaroons arranged in pyramids in the window (beware: the rose flavor tastes like bathroom freshener), most items will induce a diabetic coma. Dine in the salon or queue up an orgasm to go.

➡ [M]Concorde. $ Macaroons €1.70. ⏰ Open M-Th 8:30am-7:30pm, F-Sa 8:30am-8pm, Su 10am-7pm. Other locations at 75 av. des Champs-Elysées, 21 rue Bonaparte, and 64 bd Haussmann.

AMOUR DE BURGER — BURGERS $$

7 rue Godot de Mauroy ☎01 53 30 09 72 www.amourdeburger.com

Amour de Burger will have you falling in love with burgers all over again. Set up like an American greasy spoon, this French burger joint still maintains a European air, with most patrons sipping white wine or watching a soccer match on the TV above the bar. The portions, however, are not quite as French and will leave you both stuffed and head-over-heels in love with this Parisian anomaly.

➡ [M]Madeleine. Facing the church, turn around to the left toward Pinacotheque, pass Pinacotheque, and take the 1st left. Amour de Burger is on the left. $ Burgers €12-18.50. Dinner menu €10 and 13. ⏰ Open daily noon-3pm and 7-11pm.

white is the new yellow

The McDonald's on av. des Champs-Élysées is not your typical grab-and-go fast food. While taking a bite of your *Croque McDo* (grilled ham and cheese sandwich) and sipping a can of Kronenbourg 1664 in the spacious restaurant, you'll notice that the famous golden arches in front of the store look unusually pale. Apparently, Parisians considered the traditional Mickey D's yellow to be too tacky—the city enforces a regulation that requires shops on this posh avenue to flaunt classy white signs only.

TY YANN CREPERIE $

10 rue de Constantinople ☎01 40 08 00 17

The ever-smiling Breton chef and owner, M. Yann, cheerfully prepares outstanding and relatively inexpensive *galettes* (€7.50-11) and crepes in a tiny, unassuming restaurant—the walls are decorated with his mother's pastoral paintings. Creative concoctions include La Vannetaise (sausage sautéed in cognac, Emmental cheese, and onions; €10). Create your own crepe (€6.40-7.20) for lunch.

⇄ [M]Europe. [$] Crepes €7.50-11. Credit card min. €12. ⏰ Open M-F noon-2:30pm and 7:30-10:30pm, Sa 7:30-10:30pm.

MOOD ASIAN, BURGER BAR $$

114 av. des Champs-Elysées and 1 rue Washington ☎01 42 89 98 89 www.mood-paris.fr

Like the Asian woman's nipple that greets you at the door (don't get too excited; it's only a photograph), Mood is a matter of personal taste, and you may or may not think the restaurant warrants all the fuss. The sensuous mélange of Western decor and delicate Japanese accents reflects the fusion cuisine that revisits the classic American hamburger. The *prix-fixe* lunch (€17-21) might be the only affordable way to finagle your way into the beige upper dining room.

⇄ [M]George V. [$] Entrées €10-19. Plats €17-35. Mixed drinks €15. ⏰ Restaurant open M noon-2:30pm, Tu-F noon-2:30pm and 7pm-1am, Sa 7pm-1am, Su noon-2:30pm and 7pm-1am. Bar open daily 5pm-1am. Happy hour daily 5-8pm.

FOUQUET'S CAFE $$$$

99 av. des Champs-Élysées ☎01 47 23 50 00

Restaurants can only dream of this kind of fame. This sumptuous, red velvet-covered cafe once welcomed the likes of Chaplin, Churchill, Roosevelt, and Jackie Onassis. While it's past its glory days, the people-watching on the Champs-Élysées alone is worth the €8 coffee. Just so you know, you're paying to sit among the rich, not for your beverage. Still, it's an experience of quintessential old-time Parisian glamour, easy on the eyes and devastating for the bank account (*entrées* start at €30).

⇄ [M]George V. [$] Plats €20-55. ⏰ Cafe open daily 8am-2am. Restaurant open daily 7:30-10am, noon-3pm, and 7pm-midnight.

FAUCHON FOOD STORE $$$

26-30 pl. de la Madeleine ☎01 47 42 60 11 www.fauchon.com

If you didn't blow all your euro at Ladurée, then you might be able to afford this pricey and equally upper-class *épicerie*. Splurge on nougat (€8-13) or *pâte de fruit* (fruit paste; €6.50) to add some class to your picnic, or buy teas and chocolates (€10-145) as a gift for your connoisseur friend.

⇄ [M]Madeleine. ⏰ Épicerie and confiserie open M-Sa 9am-8pm. Boulangerie open 8am-9pm, eat-in 8am-6pm. Traiteur and pâtisserie open 8am-9pm. Tea room open 9am-7pm.

OPÉRA AND CANAL ST-MARTIN

It's not a challenge for the average tourist to find the famous places in the 9ème, most of which are located around **Saint-Georges.** Here, we're throwing out some harder-to-find but equally good restaurants. The unknown secret is the 10ème, which easily outshines the 9ème in terms of quaint, cheap establishments, especially around the canal area. Passage Brady, two blocks north of 🍴**Strasbourg Saint-Denis,** has a wealth of Indian and Pakistani restaurants that serve up the best cheap curries in Paris.

🍴 **CHARTIER** TRADITIONAL $$

7 rue du Faubourg Montmartre ☎01 47 70 86 29 www.restaurant-chartier.com

A restaurant this old with a dinner rush that would put any fat camp to shame, Chartier could easily charge out the you-know-what for its menu that changes on a daily basis. Located in a two-story, high-ceilinged old building as elegant as the Bofinger (see **Food,** Chatelet) but with a family-friendly atmosphere like Breakfast in America (see **Food,** Latin Quarter), Chartier is the epitome of excellence. If luxury budget dining were a thing, Chartier would be legendary. Did we mention the food is awesome? Well, the food is awesome.

⇆ Ⓜ Grands Boulevards. Walk with traffic down bd Poissonnière and turn right onto rue du Faubourg Montmartre. ***i*** *Reservations recommended for larger groups. $ Menu €18. Entrées €2-7. Fish €8.50-13. Plats €8.50-11.50. Cheese plates €2-2.50. Desserts €2-4.50. ⏰ Open daily 11:30am-10pm.*

🍴 **L'OSTERIA DAL GOBO** ITALIAN $$$

26 rue Bergère ☎01 47 70 79 75

If ever there were a true family restaurant in the world, it's L'Osteria dal Gobo. Chef and 76-year-old owner Luigi opened his restaurant in 1949, and the long history of this place has been carefully documented by the photographs that cover the walls. Though a bit cramped, the restaurant is opened up a bit by a tall ceiling and mirrored walls. Only come to L'Osteria if you have the energy for a lively dinner, as Luigi is not shy about taking the (invisible) mic and dueting with Andrea Bocelli as he scurries about cooking and schmoozing. You can watch him throw together some salads and appetizers at the front of the restaurant, where he has ingredients ready to go.

⇆ Ⓜ Grands Boulevards. Walk with traffic down bd Poissonnière and turn right onto rue du Faubourg Montmartre, then right again onto bd Bergère. $ Entrées €6-8. Plats €12-20. ⏰ Open daily 11am-3pm and 6pm-2am.

🍴 **BOB'S JUICE BAR** SMOOTHIES, BAGELS $

15 rue Lucien Sampaix ☎09 50 06 36 18

This small hippie, eco-conscious smoothie and bagel shack is usually filled with backpackers sharing long tables and snacking on homemade baked goods (€1-3) and bottomless coffee brewed all day.

⇆ Ⓜ Jacques Bonsergent. Walk up bd Magenta toward Gare du Nord, and turn right on rue Lucien Sampaix. Juice Bar is ½ a block up on the left. $ Smoothies €5-6. Bagel sandwiches €5.50. ⏰ Open M-F 8am-3pm.

🍴 **CHEZ MAURICE** BISTRO $$

26 rue des Vinaigriers ☎01 46 07 07 91

Finally, a real French meal for dirt cheap. If the old-fashioned wooden interior doesn't transport you to the turn of the century, a carafe of wine from the tap will help. Hold out for the desserts, where you'll be hard pressed to choose between crème brûlée or chocolate fondue, even after stuffing yourself with *escargot* or steak tartare.

⇆ Ⓜ Jacques Bonsergent. Walk up bd Magenta toward Gare du Nord, and turn right onto rue Lucien Sampaix. Walk 1 block to rue des Vinaigriers and turn right. The restaurant is on the right. $ Menu formule €11-16. Cash only. ⏰ Open M-F noon-3pm, Sa 6:30-11pm.

parisian bistro?

Think that bistros are a French invention? Think again. The word "bistro" originated during the occupation of Paris by the Russian army. In the 1814 Montmartre neighborhood, Cossack Russians set up a cafe that aimed to serve food quickly, or быстро (Russian for "quickly," pronounced "BEE-struh"). French linguists, however, dismiss this claim and say "bistro" is was a shortening of the word *bistrouille,* meaning brandy and coffee.

SAVEURS ET COÏNCIDENCES TRADITIONAL, FUSION $$$$

6 rue de Trévise ☎01 42 46 62 23 www.saveursetcoincidences.com

Saveurs et Coïncidences serves hearty food in a light atmosphere. Traditional French with Italian, Japanese, and other worldly twists make the menu a bit more interesting than your standard *croque monsieur* and *onglet de boeuf.* The small but not cramped dining room has bright white walls and hardwood floors with blue water glasses and abstract canvas art on the walls that give the place a lot of color without much effort. Expert chef Jean-Pierre Coroyer is no slouch with a knife and a pan, and satisfied, laughing customers will confirm his prowess.

⇄ [M]Grands Boulevards. Walk with traffic on bd Poissonnière and turn right onto rue du Faubourg Montmartre, then right again onto rue St-Cécile. The restaurant is on the 2nd corner. [$] Menus €26-29. Entrées €9-16. Plats €20-30. Dessert €9-10. ⏰ Open M-Th 11:30am-2:30pm and 7-10:30pm, F-Sa 11:30am-2:30pm and 7-11pm. Happy hour 6-8:30pm.

KASTOORI INDIAN $$

4 pl. Gustave Toudouze ☎01 44 53 06 10

Likely the most lively place in the weirdly quiet St-George's area, pl. Gustave Toudouze offers several good dinner options, and Kastoori is no exception. The spices will light up your nose upon entering the restaurant, and when it gets busy, fuggettaboutit. The menu is traditional Indian and Pakistani, and the prices are untraditionally reasonable. Word on the patio is that the lassis (yogurt- and milk-based drinks) and milkshakes are must-haves.

⇄ [M]St-Georges. Walk north with traffic down rue Notre-Dame de Lorette and turn right onto rue Henry Monnier. Kastoori is on the corner of rue Clauzel. [$] Lunch menu €10 and 17. Dinner menu €17. Entrées €4. Plats €11-13. Lassis €4. Milkshakes €5. ⏰ Open Tu-Sa 11am-2:30pm and 7-11pm.

LA CANTINE DE QUENTIN MARKET, DELI $$

52 rue Bichat ☎01 42 02 40 32

Has it been too long since the last time you enjoyed a good picnic? The answer is yes, it has. Right next to the Canal St-Martin, eating lunch at La Cantine de Quentin, is a picnic in and of itself, but we suggest you grab a basket and head for the Champs de Mars. With just enough room for a few tables and a small patio, the restaurant offers a cozy dining experience, while the boutique boasts a hearty selection of sauces, jams, olives, cheeses, and wine. Whether you eat in or take your spread for the road, you will enjoy a genuine French eating experience.

⇄ [M]Jacques Bonsergent. Walk northeast up rue de Lancry toward the canal, cross the canal, and walk left along the canal. La Cantine is the 1st right. [$] Entrées €6-8. Plats €13-18. Dessert €8. ⏰ Boutique open daily 10am-7:30pm. Restaurant open Tu-Su noon-3:30pm.

NO STRESS CAFE TAPAS, CAFE $$
24 rue Clauzel ☎48 78 00 27
The huge terrace and quiet plaza give this funky cafe its namesake vibe. While you can skip most of the food, No Stress has a killer happy hour (Tu-Th 6-8pm) with cheap cocktails (€5) and tapas (€3.50) that draw a young crowd that quickly evaporates once the deal ends, only to reappear for one last drink before closing.
⇆ [M]St-Georges. Walk up rue Notre Dame de Lorette in the direction of traffic until you reach rue H. Monnier. Turn left and the cafe is in the pl. G. Toudouze. [$] Formule midi (plat and dessert) €13. Plats €14-18. Woks €15-18. Salads €14-16. Desserts €7.50-8.50. ⏰ Open Tu-Su 11am-2am.

QUAI GOURMAND PASTA, CAFE $
79 quai de Valmy ☎01 40 40 72 84
This super cheap, albeit tacky, cafe serves the type of food that you could probably prepare yourself in a hostel kitchen. But its location right on the canal and tempting selection of Magnum Bars for dessert will help you withstand the bright pink and green interior and NRJ pop music soundtrack.
⇆ [M]République. Walk toward the canal on rue de Faubourg (the one that bisects pl. de la République). Turn left once you get to the canal and walk 3 blocks. The cafe is on the left. [$] Sandwiches €4.50. Formule midi (until 3:30pm) €8. To-go pasta bowls €6. Crepes €3, additional ingredients €1. ⏰ Open daily 10am-8pm.

URFA DURUM KURDISH $
58 rue Faubourg St-Denis ☎01 48 24 12 84
In a city full of kebabs and faux Middle Eastern fast food, Urfa Durum stays true to its Kurdish roots. Cheap lamb sandwiches are served in bread baked to order. Top off the experience by eating at the traditional (read: miniature) wooden tables and stools outside the shop.
⇆ [M]Château d'Eau. Exit onto bd de Strasbourg. Facing the Gare de l'Est at the intersection of bd de Strasbourg and rue du Château d'Eau, walk left and take the 1st left onto rue Faubourg St-Denis. [$] Sandwiches €6. ⏰ Open daily noon-8pm.

BASTILLE

Bastille has a pleasantly diverse array of ethnic food, much of which is upscale and far exceeds the gyro joints that dot the streets of the city. Fortunately for you, quality doesn't come at a ridiculous price, and you can find plenty of great meals for affordable rates. The Algerian community in the 11ème also offers tons of awesome kebab and meat options.

RESTAURANT 3FC KEBABS, ALGERIAN $
16 rue d'Aligre ☎01 43 46 07 73
If you're totally starving, only have a meager supply of coins jangling in your pocket, and don't want to eat out of the garbage, hit 3FC. Not only is the food cheaper than dirt (€0.70 per kebab—we estimate that the current market price for dirt is at least €0.90 per handful), it's bangin' delicious. Choose from a selection of raw kebabs in the front freezer, take them to the kitchen, and wait for the fresh-grilled meat to be brought back to your seat. This place is packed on a nightly basis (note: kebabs are particularly popular among the drunk-munchies crowd), but the beauty of food on a stick is that it's just as mobile as you are.
⇆ [M]Ledru-Rollin. Walk east on rue du Faubourg St-Antoine away from Bastille, take the 3rd right onto rue du Cotte, and turn left onto rue d'Aligre. [$] Kebabs €0.70. Couscous €7. Entrées €3.50. Plats €6. ⏰ Open daily 11am-midnight.

LE GOYAVIER CREOLE $$$
4 rue St-Bernard ☎01 43 79 61 41
Hailing from the Réunion Island in the Indian Ocean, the chef here knows how to cook up a real ethnic meal and cooks it damn well. The place itself is tiny, unmarked, and tucked behind scaffolding as if trying to hide itself. And perhaps with good reason: the place is always so packed that there isn't much room for

more traffic. Inside, the uninspiring beach-like decor is forgotten after your first bite. Served straight from the pot, the food here drips with flavor and texture, whether you eat in or take your meal to go.

[M]Ledru Rollin. Walk east on rue du Fauberge St-Antoine and turn left onto rue St-Bernard. The restaurant is on the right behind the scaffolding. [$] Entrées €6-9. Plats €20-22. Desserts €4-5. Open M-Tu 8pm-midnight, Th-Su 8pm-midnight.

AUGUSTE SANDWICHES $

10 rue St-Sabin ☎01 47 00 77 84 www.augusteparis.com

A tiny hole in the wall whose clientele look like throwbacks to the days of the Paris Commune, this *sandwicherie* is packed at lunchtime with students and penny-pinchers looking to get at simple—but huge—sandwiches like the salmon and avocado or goat cheese and honey.

[M]Bréguet-Sabin. Cross Canal St-Martin on rue Sedaine and turn right onto rue St-Sabin. [$] Sandwiches €2-4. Soups €3-5. Cash only. Open M-Sa 11am-4pm.

VILIA ITALIAN $$$

26 rue de Cotte ☎339 80 44 20 15

The Italian chef here clearly knows what he's doing, with a permanent menu of cheeses and tapas-like dishes accompanied by a menu of appetizers and a main dish that changes daily. Come for a succulent bowl of oysters one night and a steaming plate of pasta the next. This restaurant is small and fairly new, but its popularity is growing quickly, so consider making a reservation for a weekend dinner.

[M]Ledru Rollin. Walk west on rue du Faubourg St-Antoine and turn right. [$] Entrées €8-9. Plats around €22. 4-course meal €32. Alimentari €8-12. Mixed drinks €6-7. Open Tu-Sa 10am-11pm, Su 10am-2pm.

LE CHEVAL DE TROIE TURKISH $$$

71 rue de Charenton ☎01 43 44 24 44 www.chevaltroie.com

A romantic date here will expose you to the colorful and flavorful cuisine of Turkey. Even if you can't pronounce the dishes, the meat and fish here come sprinkled with an array of spices that will excite your senses while gentle Arabic music plays overhead. Cocktails will leave you with a comfortable buzz as you move on from the candlelight of this restaurant to the bars and clubs nearby.

[M]Ledru-Rollin or [M]Bastille. Walk south on av. Ledru-Rollin and take the 1st right onto rue de Charenton. [$] Entrées €7-11.50. Plats €13.50-17. Open M-Sa noon-2:30pm and 7-11:30pm. Traditional dancers on Sa nights.

L'EBAUCHOIR BISTRO, TRADITIONAL $$$$

45 rue de Citeaux ☎01 43 42 49 31 www.lebauchoir.com

L'Ebauchoir is a Parisian classic that has been serving up traditional French food for years, and the crowd here is as clean cut as the decor. Excellent for a celebratory meal or just an extra relaxing, somewhat fancy dinner, L'Ebauchoir is worth a long evening out.

[M]Faidherbe-Chaligny. Walk west on rue du Fauberg St-Antoine toward Bastille and turn left onto rue de Citeaux. Across from Siffleur de Ballons. i Credit card min. €25. [$] Entrées €8-15. Plats €17-22. Dessert €7-8. Open M 8pm-11pm, Tu-Th noon-2:30pm and 8-11pm, F-Sa noon-2:30pm and 7:30pm-11pm.

LA BAGUE DE KENZA PATISSERIE, ALGERIAN $

106 rue St-Maur ☎01 43 14 93 15 www.labaguedekenza.com

La Bague de Kenza is Candyland incarnated. Stacks upon stacks upon stacks of carefully designed sweets shaped like pears, watermelons, roses, and other, more ambiguous forms will make your mouth water. The restaurant has a few good lunch options, but the main attractions here are the pastries.

[M]Rue Saint-Maur. Walk west, away from the cemetery, on av. de la République. i Credit card min. €16. 7 other locations; check website for details. [$] Pastries €1.40-3.50. Open in summer M-Th 9am-10pm, F 2:30-9pm, Sa-Su 9am-10pm; in fall, winter, and spring M-Th 9am-10pm, F 2-9pm, Sa-Su 9am-10pm.

KATMANDOU CAFE INDIAN $$

14 rue de Bréguet ☎01 48 05 36 36; www.katmandou.fr

Specializing in everything spicy, this Indian restaurant has six types of naan and curry for those who want their taste buds slowly singed off. To wash it down, order a lassi with mint, banana, or rose and mango.

➡ [M]Bréguet-Sabin. Cross Canal St-Martin on rue Sedaine, turn left onto bd Richard Lenoir, and turn right onto rue de Bréguet. [$] Plats €9.50-13. Prix-fixe menu €12. 10% discount for takeout. ⏰ Open M-Sa noon-2:30pm and 7-11:30pm, Su 7-11:30pm.

MORRY'S BAGELS AND TOASTS BAGELS $

1 rue de Charonne ☎01 48 07 03 03

Those who miss the towering *grattes-ciel* of NYC should stop at Morry's for heated bagels topped with pastrami, cream cheese, avocado, or salmon. While the young clientele probably don't recognize the picture of a young Bob Dylan, they do know budget eats when they see them.

➡ [M]Bastille. Walk down rue du Faubourg St-Antoine and turn left onto rue de Charonne. [$] Bagels €3-5.90. Desserts €1.50-3.40. ⏰ Open M-Sa 8:30am-7:30pm.

BARBERSHOP BISTRO $$

68 av. de la République ☎01 47 00 12 85

For a Parisian restaurant, Barbershop manages the rather impressive task of making French food seem out of place, since everything else here seems to have come straight from Jamaica. Enjoy your beef in Roquefort sauce or roasted Camembert while pictures of Bob Marley watch over you. DJs take the theme further by spinning soul and reggae tunes during dinner.

➡ [M]Rue St-Maur. [$] Plats €10-18. Prix-fixe menu €13. ⏰ Open M-Sa noon-3pm and 8-11pm, Su noon-4pm.

LE DALLERY BISTRO $$

6 passage Charles Dallery ☎01 47 00 11 72

"French" and "hole in the wall" don't always go together, but this bistro combines them perfectly with express menus of grilled beef, lamb, or *salade paysanne* (€11) with dessert and coffee. The smell alone is enough to make you wander in from the main street.

➡ [M]Ledru-Rollin. Take av. Ledru-Rollin north, turn right onto rue de Charonne, and then left onto passage Charles Dallery. [$] Express menu €11. Regular menu €12. ⏰ Open M-Sa noon-8pm.

LE TOUAREG AFRICAN $$

228 rue de Charenton ☎01 43 07 69 49

Le Touareg will throw you across the Mediterranean before you realize what you ordered—unless you're familiar with Moroccan cuisine, you won't notice. The *couscous méchoui* piles up with *merguez*, vegetables, and lamb, while their bowls of *chakchouka* (a spicy vegetable and egg dish) are big enough to bathe in. But these spicy dishes might make you sweat, so we suggest having pitchers of water handy.

➡ [M]Dugommier. [$] Lunch menu €12. Plats €12-17. ⏰ Open M-Sa noon-3pm and 7pm-midnight.

CAFE DE L'INDUSTRIE CAFE $$

16 rue St-Sabin ☎01 47 00 13 53

Though the coffee is one of the major draws here, the cafe expands its repertoire to include traditional French dishes (*plat du jour;* €10), including a selection of sliced meats and tartines for those who just want to nibble as they down cheap wine. If the Cubist artwork starts to morph, we suggest slowing down on the wine.

➡ [M]Breguet-Sabin. [$] Plats €9-13. Desserts €2.50-6. ⏰ Open daily 10am-2am. Kitchen closes at 12:30am.

LE BAR À SOUPES SOUP BAR $

33 rue de Charonne ☎01 43 57 53 79 www.lebarasoupes.com

This soup bar offers a pick-me-up for anyone feeling under the weather or a little homesick. Their lunch menu has basic soups like lentil and, for those whose hearts flutter when they hear "mmm mmm good," tomato soup. Giant paintings of vegetables match the equally large portions of soup. The rotating menu ensures that no two days are exactly the same.

❦ Ⓜ*Ledru-Rollin. Take av. Ledru-Rollin north and turn left onto rue de Charonne.* Ⓢ *Soups €5-6. Lunch menu €9.80.* 🕐 *Open M-Sa noon-3pm and 6:30-11pm.*

BODEGA BAY   SOUTH AMERICAN $$
116 rue Amelot   ☎01 47 00 13 53 www.bodega-bay.fr
Bodega Bay might seem like a cheesy throwback to TexMex and gringos, but you can skip over the nachos and fajitas for the more authentic grilled swordfish and bitter chocolate cake. If you're wondering why there's a large mural of a space invasion, we couldn't figure it out either.

❦ Ⓜ*Oberkampf. Follow the traffic on rue de Crussol and turn left onto rue Amelot.* Ⓢ *Plats €13-14. Prix-fixe menu €12.* 🕐 *Open M-F noon-3pm and 6pm-midnight, Sa 6pm-midnight.*

PAUSE CAFE   CAFE $$
41 rue de Charonne   ☎01 48 06 80 33
Hipster glasses are an unofficial pre-req for working here. People climb over themselves to get a seat on the large outdoor terrace and peruse the basic menu of salads, beer, tartare, and honey-glazed duck breast. It's run-down chic, but it was cool enough to be featured in the film *Chacun Cherche Son Chat*, which we suspect is the main reason people come here.

❦ Ⓜ*Ledru-Rollin. Take av. Ledru-Rollin north and turn left onto rue de Charonne.* Ⓢ *Plats €8-11.* 🕐 *Open M-Sa 8am-2am, Su 9:30am-9pm. Kitchen open M-Sa noon-midnight, Su noon-5pm.*

MONTPARNASSE AND SOUTHERN PARIS

Many restaurants across southern Paris serve up ethnic cuisine in a quiet setting that feels a whole country away from the ever-crowded streets in the center of the city. Restaurants around the Montparnasse Tower can either be unforgettable finds or have mediocre food despite attractive decor, so choose wisely. Neighborhoods around the lower half of **boulevard Raspail** in the 14ème serve more traditional French cuisine, while the **Quartier de la Butte-aux-Cailles** and **Chinatown** in the 13ème offer obscure foreign dishes for next to nothing.

🎖 **LE TROQUET**   SPANISH, FUSION $$$$
21 rue François Bonvin   ☎01 45 66 89 00
If you have to eat at sweaty kebab takeout spots for a week to afford this, just do it—it's worth the splurge. Original recipes developed under the supervision of master chef Christian Ethebest have their origins in traditional Basque cuisine, specifically from the Béarn region. The menu is only written on chalkboards that the waiters will bring to your table. You can pay *à la carte* for an item if you ask, but you should really splurge on a three-course meal: seriously, with *entrées* fit for a king, *plats* fit for the king's mother, and souflées as big as the king's mother's toy dog, you will want to try everything. With all these plates leaving the kitchen at super speed, it can get real steamy in here, but the wait staff will be happy to hang your coat on the rack, and you will be enjoying the food too much to notice you might be breaking a sweat.

❦ Ⓜ*Sèvres-Lecourbe. Walk down bd Garibaldi 2 blocks and turn right onto rue Francois Bonvin and continue about ½ block.* Ⓢ *Lunch menu €30. Dinner menu €32. Entrées €8, plats €18. Desserts €7.* 🕐 *Open Tu-Sa noon-2pm and 7:30-10:30pm.*

🎖 **ATELIER AUBRAC**   TRADITIONAL $$$$
51 bd Garibaldi   ☎01 45 66 96 78
This cool traditional French restaurant is a carnivorous cavern. With hefty plates full of the kind of meat you'd expect a lumberjack or quarterback to enjoy, Atelier Aubrac is a place you want to come to with an empty stomach. If you're not sure what to order, have a chat with the gregarious chef, and he'll be happy to talk

to you about pretty much anything. Lunchtime tends to bring in a professional crowd, but the clientele gets more diverse at dinner.

 # [M]Sèvres-Lecourbe. Walk northwest on bd Garibaldi; the restaurant is on the right. [$] Entrées €7 10. Plats €15-27. ⏰ Open M-F noon-2:30pm and 7:30-10:30pm, Sa 7-10:30pm.

LE DIX VINS — TRADITIONAL $$$

57 rue Falguière ☎01 43 20 91 77 www.ledixvins.fr

Le Dix Vins is a subtle little restaurant with modest decor that packs a mean punch in the kitchen. In 2010, the restaurant won a prize from the prestigious *Confrerie Gastronomique de la Marmite d'Or* for its fine cuisine. Candlelit tables with single roses make for a romantic setting, and everyone knows that cheese and wine are aphrodisiacs (right?), so you know what to do.

 # [M]Pasteur. Walk southwest on bd Pasteur (with the Montparnasse Tower to the left), then turn right onto rue Falguière. [$] Menu €19.50. ⏰ Open M-F noon-2pm and 8-11pm, Sa 8-11pm.

CHEZ GLADINES — BASQUE $

30 rue des 5 Diamants ☎01 45 80 70 10

What Chez Gladines lacks in decoration (beyond a prominent Basque flag) it makes up for by sticking to its separatist roots. Customers constantly line up to enjoy *cassoulets* and *piperade* (scrambled eggs with vegetables).

 # [M]Place d'Italie. Take bd Auguste Blanqui away from pl. d'Italie and turn left onto rue des 5 Diamants. [$] Assiettes €4-7.90. Plats €8.90-12. Cash only. ⏰ Open daily noon-3pm and 7-10:30pm.

AU BRETZEL — ALSATIAN $$

1 rue Léopold Robert ☎01 40 47 82 37

This is a more upscale Alsatian restaurant that still serves affordable *flammekeuche* (a kind of thin pizza). Come here to settle down in the carved wood chairs next to murals of German and French towns. The huge *flammekeuche* can be shared and are some of the most traditional in Paris, despite decor that feels like the inside of a cuckoo clock.

 # [M]Vavin. Walk down bd du Montparnasse away from the tower and turn right onto rue Léopold Robert. [$] Flammekeuche €8.50-10. Prix-fixe menu €18. ⏰ Open M 7:30-10:30pm, Tu-Sa noon-2pm and 7:30-10:30pm.

PHO 14 — VIETNAMESE $

129 av. de Choisy ☎01 45 83 61 15

If you only eat in one place in Chinatown, make it Pho 14. A local favorite that draws starving students and penny-pinching barmen, Pho 14 (not to be confused with Pho 13 next door) serves huge bowls of *pho* beef (flank steak in spicy soup with rice) for next to nothing. This restaurant usually has a line out the door at night, so try to arrive on the early or late side of dinner.

 # [M]Tolbiac. Walk east on rue de Tolbiac and turn left onto av. de Choisy. [$] Pho €6-10. ⏰ Open daily 9am-11pm.

LE FILIPPO — ITALIAN $$$$

54 rue Cambronne ☎01 43 06 19 73 www.lefilippo.com/en

Le Filippo will leaving you feeling as rich as the old suits lunching next to you without robbing you of every hard-earned penny from your two-figure hourly wage. The colorful but elegant decor, complete with purple and brass hues, accents the spotless wine glasses adorning every table. You can't go wrong ordering anything on this menu, but the risotto is a house favorite. It's worth the few extra euro to sample as many dishes as you can—enjoy spending a long evening savoring every last bite of your meal.

 # [M]Cambronne. Walk up bd Garibaldi to its intersection with rue de la Croix Nivert, then take a sharp left onto rue Cambronne and continue past the Hotel Ibis Paris. Le Filippo is about 3-4 blocks down. i Free Wi-Fi. [$] Lunch menu €16, complet €22. Entrées €9-14. Risotto €14-17. Meat, fish, and other plats €15-24.

TY BREIZ
CREPERIE $$

52 bd de Vaugirard ☎01 43 20 83 72 www.tybreizcreperieparis.fr

Ty Breiz gloats about its supposedly best crepes in Paris, and we'll take them at their word. A hot waft of savory and sweet will hit you like a bus as soon as you open the door, and once you step inside, you won't want to leave. Couples and friends gather here to share a particularly delightful selection of one of France's finest culinary inventions. The rustic interior is decorated with old family portraits and will make you feel right at home. That is, if your home is an 18th-century French farmhouse. Bring a handful of friends and share your food—there are too many delicious options to have just one.

✦ ⓜPasteur. *About 2 blocks down bd Pasteur at its intersection with bd de Vaugirard.* ⓢ *Crepes €6-12.* ⓒ *Open Tu-Sa 11:45am-2:45pm and 7-11pm.*

AU ROI DU CAFÉ
CAFE, TRADITIONAL $$$

59 rue Lecourbe ☎01 47 34 48 50 www.auroiducafe.com

With its homey atmosphere, Au Roi du Café is the ideal spot to share brunch with friends on a rainy day. Diners here are in no hurry to be anywhere but in the company of their comrades while feasting on delicious food and puffing on a never-ending supply of cigarettes. The terrace is covered and heated, but the chairs inside are more comfortable, the walls brighter, and the conversation lighter.

✦ ⓜSèvres-Lecourbe. *About 2 blocks down rue Lecourbe after its intersection with bd Garibaldi.* ⓢ *Salads €10.50. Plats €11.50. Happy hour mixed drinks €4.* ⓒ *Open daily 11am-11pm. Happy hour 6-8pm. Su brunch 11am-3:30pm.*

SAMAYA
LEBANESE $

21 bd de Grenelle ☎01 45 77 44 44 www.samayaparis.com

If you need some nourishment before or after the tiresome visit to the Eiffel Tower, head to Samaya for a falafel sandwich or shawarma wrap. The food here is freshly made and fully flavorful, unlike the fare at some Mediterranean restaurants that can somehow manage to make boring meals out of interesting ingredients. See for yourself the fresh ingredients laid out in aluminum bowls alongside mouth-watering desserts. The interior of this restaurant is spacious and relaxed and will be a relief from the huge crowds at the Eiffel, but most people take their food to go.

✦ ⓜBir-Hakeim. *On the northern side of the street across from the Metro stop.* ⓢ *Entrées €6. Plats €14. Sandwiches to go €5. Menus €15-24.* ⓒ *Open daily 10am-midnight.*

CRÊPERIE DE LA BUTTE AUX CAILLES
CREPERIE $$

33 rue Bobillot ☎01 45 80 07 07 www.creperiebutteauxcailles.sitew.com

La Butte aux Cailles *crêperie* cooks up sweet and savory crepes in a rustic, barn-like building. The smell of the crepes alone will have your head rising, even if you don't opt for the crepes made with your choice of rum, whiskey, or other draught of choice. This is a great place to enjoy a sweet treat sitting down with the family rather than on-the-go from one of the countless crepe stands lining the streets of Paris.

✦ ⓜPlace d'Italie. *Walk down rue Bobillot for just a few minutes; the creperie is on the left.* ⓢ *Crepes €3-10.* ⓒ *Open M 7-10pm, Tu-Sa noon-4pm and 7pm-10pm.*

LE SAMSON
TRADITIONAL, MEDITERRANEAN $$$

9 rue Jean-Marie Jego ☎01 45 89 09 23

Le Samson offers traditional French cuisine in a less than traditional setting. Inside the fire-engine red building, you'll find booths made of old jeans and a decorative rooster watching over the restaurant and wonder who let your crazy Aunt Gertrude decorate the place. Despite the questionable decor, Le Samson offers hefty portions of tasty French food. Be sure to let your adventurous traveler spirit loose and try some *escargot.*

⇄ [M]Place d'Italie. Follow rue Samson off of rue de la Butte-aux-Cailles. Go up the stairs and turn left, passing a playground on the right. Continue straight between the buildings; Le Samson is on the right with a bright red storefront. 💲 Lunch menu €13-17, complet €22. Entrées €6-12. Plats €12-16. Cheese plate €6. ⏰ Open M-Sa noon-2:30pm and 6:30-11:30pm.

TANDOORI INDIAN $$

10 rue de l'Arrivée ☎45 48 46 72 www.restaurant-indien.com

Tandoori will have all of your senses buzzing. The food will set your taste buds on fire with flavor, while the wooden Indian carvings on the walls create a sight for the eyes. Meanwhile, families laughing and diners *mmm*ing every bite will dance on your ears as the mixing aromas of incense and spices will fill your nose.

⇄ [M]Montparnasse-Bienvenue. With your back to the tower and the mall in front of you, rue de l'Arrivée is the street running along the left-hand side of the mall. Tandoori is in the middle of the block. 💲 Naan €3-6. Tandoori €10-16. Lunch menu €10-12. Dinner menu €22. Entrées €6-9. ⏰ Open Tu-Su noon-2:30pm and 6:30-11pm.

TANG FRÈRES SUPERMARKET $

48 av. d'Ivry ☎01 45 70 80 00

This Chinatown staple is the place to stock up on your basic groceries like rice, kidneys, and fresh sting ray. Check out some other debatable items at the meat counter, or take the safe route and hit the instant noodles aisle.

⇄ [M]Port d'Ivry. Walk northwest up av. d'Ivry. ℹ 6 other locations in Paris. 💲 Tsingtao beer €1. Kikkoman soy sauce €2. ⏰ Open M-F 10am-8:30pm, Sa 9:30am-8:30pm.

CHEZ PAPA 14 TRADITIONAL $$

6 rue Gassendi ☎01 43 22 41 19

Specializing in cuisine from the wine production regions of southwestern France, Chez Papa serves cheap foie gras, salads, and *cassoulets.* Don't let the low-hanging peppers, grapes, and spices hit you in in the head as you're being seated.

⇄ [M]Denfert Rouchereau. Walk toward Cimetière Montparnasse on rue Froidevaux. The restaurant is at the intersection of rue Froidevaux and rue Gassendi. 💲 Entrées €5-7. Plats €9-12. Prix-fixe menu €12. ⏰ Open daily noon-3pm and 6pm-midnight.

LES TONTONS BISTRO $$

3 rue des Gobelins ☎08 99 69 76 21

Designed after an old-style bistro with mirrors to make it appear larger, Les Tontons specializes in steak and tartare. You can even order bone marrow. If steak isn't your thing, choose from desserts like tiramisu with strawberry tagada or Nutella cake.

⇄ [M]Les Gobelins. 💲 Lunch menu €13. Dinner menu €16. ⏰ Open M-Sa noon-2:30pm and 7-10:30pm.

MUSSUWAM AFRICAN $$

33 bd Arago ☎01 45 35 93 67 http://mussuwam.fr

Mussuwam serves traditional Senegalese food that provides a spicy break from the creamy and cheesy fare of French establishments. Some of the dishes are listed in a strange dialect that makes us wonder if Senegalese is its own language. Dinner is too pricey to bother, but if you keep an open mind, their lunch menu changes daily and costs a fraction of the regular prices.

⇄ [M]Les Gobelins. ℹ Lunch menu Tu-F. 💲 Lunch menu €16. Dinner and weekend menu €25. ⏰ Open Tu-Th noon-3pm and 7-10:30pm, F-Sa noon-10:30pm

LES TEMPS DES CERISES TRADITIONAL $$

18 rue de la Butte-aux-Cailles ☎01 45 89 69 48

One of several outrageous menu options at Les Temps des Cerises is a *pot-au-feu* with a mix of pig cheek and duck. Waiters joke with each other and clients and are happy to point you in the direction of more obscure French dishes.

⇄ [M]Place d'Italie. 💲 Entrées €7.50-11. Plats €10-17. Lunch menu €9.20. ⏰ Open M-F 11:45am-2:10pm and 7:15-11:45pm, Sa 7:15-11:45pm.

AUTEUIL, PASSY & BATIGNOLLES

The upscale restaurants in the 16ème are certainly good, but you will only find moneyed Parisians eating there. The 17ème, on the other hand, has countless high quality yet affordable restaurants. **Rue des Dames,** located in the 17ème, is a temptress that will seduce your nose into doing things it wouldn't normally do, so if you're not sure what you want, take a stroll down this road or up **rue des Batignolles**—or along any of the nearby side streets—and follow your nose.

LE SCHEFFER
BISTRO $$$

22 rue Scheffer
☎01 47 27 81 11

Despite being within walking distance from Trocadéro, where tourists flock by the thousands to see the view of the Eiffel Tower from the Palais de Chaillot, Le Scheffer is almost entirely frequented by locals. Red checkered tablecloths and a meager display of posters on the walls make this place look like every other classic bistro in Paris, but the food sets it apart. Chef Gilles Epié has been cooking up some of the best traditional French meals for 20 years, and before opening Le Scheffer in Paris, he cooked for America's stars at his restaurant in Hollywood. Luckily, the prices here are affordable enough for us common folk to be able to enjoy the bounty of this French culinary genius.

✦ ⓂTrocadéro. With your back to the Palais de Chaillot, head left down av. Doumer and turn right onto rue Scheffer. The restaurant is on the right close to the corner. ⓢ Entrées €6.50-7. Plats €14-19. Dessert €5-9. ⌚ Open M-Sa noon-2:30pm and 7:30-10:30pm.

LE PATIO PROVENÇAL
TRADITIONAL $$$$

116 rue des Dames
☎01 42 93 73 73 www.patioprovencal.fr

Come away with me...to Le Patio Provençal. Located in a romantic, relaxing setting that seems to always be dusted in a faint twilight, this restaurant will soothe your worries and satisfy your appetite with delicious and immaculate food. Norah Jones, meanwhile, will serenade your indoor garden dinner if the mouth-watering scents of pasta, meat, fish, and fresh vegetables aren't seductive enough. Be sure to leave enough room for all three courses—you won't want to miss out.

✦ ⓂVilliers. Follow rue de Levis away from the intersection and turn right onto rue des Dames. ⓢ Entrées €9. Pasta and salads €16. Plats €17-20. Desserts €8. ⌚ Open M-Sa noon-2:30pm and 7-11pm.

3 PIÈCES CUISINE
TRADITIONAL $$

25 rue de Chéroy
☎01 44 90 85 10

3 Pièces Cuisine keeps things simple with (surprise!) just three types of cuisine on its brief menu: burgers, tartines, and salads. The restaurant itself is more visually exciting than the one-page menu, with every wall and tabletop painted red, green, purple, or yellow and bright artwork hanging on the walls. The mojito is a local favorite here, as is the whole restaurant, so get here on the earlier side if you want to snag a table from the hungry locals.

✦ ⓂVilliers. Head east down bd de Batignolles (which is bd de Courcelles in the other direction) and take a left onto rue de Chéroy. The restaurant is on the next corner on the left. ⓢ Burgers €10-13. Tartines €6.50-7.50. Salads €9-9.50. ⌚ Open daily 8:30am-1:30am.

JOY IN FOOD
VEGETARIAN $$

2 rue Truffaut
☎01 43 87 96 79

Joy in Food apparently finds joy in a select list of food, seeing as the restaurant has only six *entrées* and three *plats* options. But the dessert menu is longer than any other section, so we know where this restaurant's priorities are, and we're okay with it. However seemingly sparse the menu, the food is top quality vegetarian and customers leave happy. The bright blue façade welcomes lunchers into a peaceful, plain, but homey dining room for a tasty midday meal.

✦ ⓂPlace de Clichy. Walk down bd des Batignolles and turn left onto rue Lecluse, then right onto rue des Dames. ⓢ Entrées €4-6. Plats €9. Desserts €4. Menus €11, €14. ⌚ Open M-F noon-2:30pm.

food

LA PLACE DU VILLAGE

TRADITIONAL $$$

68 rue des Dames

☎01 43 87 72 27

With traditional red and white checkered tablecloths, old ladies sipping on *café*, and a waitress enjoying a glass of wine, you know that La Place du Village is the real deal. Although the decor and atmosphere are so traditionally French that it almost feels like the whole place is staged, the food here is as authentic as it gets. Have real French *escargots*, and we promise you won't be disappointed.

✦ ⓜRome. Walk north on rue de Rome and turn right onto rue des Dames. *i* Free Wi-Fi. ⓢ Lunch menu €14. Entrées €7-8. Salads €12-13. Fish and meat €14-17. ◙ Open M 7-11pm, T-Sa noon-3pm and 7-11pm.

ÉTOILE DU KASHMIR

INDIAN $$$

1 rue des Batignolles

☎01 45 22 44 70

Glowing purple, yellow, and green lights accentuate the intricate wood carvings on the walls of this restaurant. But if you're beginning to think you've landed in the middle of Mardi Gras, the pungent smell of curry will shock your senses and remind you that you are, in fact, at an Indian place. Whatever you order, the *haute gastronomie Indienne* will seduce your taste buds like a charmer does his snake.

✦ ⓜRome. Walk east on bd des Batignolles, then turn left onto rue des Batignolles. Étoile is close to the corner on the left. *i* 10% discount on takeout. ⓢ Lunch menus €7.50-11.50. Dinner menus €15-21. Entrées €5-7.50. Plats €8-11. ◙ Open M-Sa noon-3pm and 6:30-11:30pm, Su 6:30-11:30pm.

LA FOURNÉE D'AUGUSTINE

BOULANGERIE $

31 rue des Batignolles

☎01 46 47 42 44

It's no mystery why La Fournée d'Augustine won Paris's Medaille d'Or in 2004. Dragging customers in by the nose with the delicious aroma of freshly baked pastries, this boulangerie is everything you thought Paris would smell like: butter, chocolate, and heaven in general. Don't be fooled, though—it may look like every other *boulangerie* in Paris, but baguettes, *pain de chocolat*, and pastries have never tasted this good.

✦ ⓜRome. Walk east toward pl. de Clichy and turn left onto rue des Batignolles. *i* 3 other locations in the 2ème, 11ème, and 14ème. ⓢ Donuts €0.60. Loaf of brioche €4.60. Baguette sandwiches €4-4.50. ◙ Open M-Sa 7:30am-8pm.

LA VILLA PASSY

CAFE $$

4 Impasse des Carrières

☎01 45 27 68 76

Tucked away from the main roads in the 16ème, this cafe allows you and your date to swoon under the ivy-covered seating on pink-and-white cushioned benches. Or you can get the same theme inside, since the plants and fountains make the interior look like an outdoor courtyard. La Villa Passy is a bit more expensive than most restaurants, but if you're looking for the 16ème at its best, your search is over.

✦ ⓜLa Muette. Walk in the direction of traffic (toward the Seine) down rue de Passy. Impasse des Carrières is the 5th street on the left, and the restaurant is at the end of the alley. ⓢ Plats €15-19. Su brunch (salad, omelette, croissants, and coffee) €25. ◙ Open Tu-F noon-3pm and 7-11pm; Sa noon-4pm and 7-11pm; Su noon-4pm.

CAFÉ DES PETITS FRÈRES DES PAUVRES

CAFE $

47 rue des Batignolles

☎01 42 93 25 80

It's not so impressive in the food department, but this cafe is among the most affordable around: the €1.50 breakfast includes croissants, jam, and coffee. If that doesn't do it, some of the ▨**cheapest coffee in Paris** (€0.45) will surely make you fall in love. The older regulars and staff are quick to chat and welcome you into their artsy community. In the afternoon, stop by to see local performances by poets, singers, and bands, plus the occasional movie showing.

✦ ⓜPl. de Clichy. With your back to Montmartre, walk down bd des Batignolles 3 blocks and turn right onto rue des Batignolles. The cafe is 3 blocks down on the left. ◙ Open M 9am-12:30pm and 2-6pm, Tu 9am-12:30pm, W-Th 9am-12:30pm and 2-6pm, F 9am-12:30pm and 2-5pm, 1st and 3rd Sa each month 9am-12:30pm.

food in the fast lane

Even Paris, a city filled with fine dining, isn't immune to the fast-food invasion. If *escargots* are a little too slow for you, get in the fast lane to some of these cheap joints.

- **QUICK BURGER.** Although it's a clear rip-off of McDonald's, Parisians prefer it to the original, even if they can't get a *Royale* with cheese.

- **FLUNCH.** The chain was named after a *portmanteau* between "fast food" and "lunch," which is now French slang meaning "to eat on the go" *(fluncher)*. The food is cooked in minutes at the grill, including the steak, green beans, and potatoes meal. We're not sure if that gives the cook enough time to determine whether the steak is *"rosé"* or *"à point,"* so dine at your own risk.

- **BRIOCHE DORÉE.** This chain patisserie sells all the usual tarts, morning croissants, and lunchtime baguettes. Located in some Metro stations, these identical shops mass manufacture pastries and are only redeemed by their gleaming glass cases and over-the-top gilded signs. After all, presentation is everything.

LE MANOIR   BRASSERIE $$
7 rue des Moines   ☎01 46 27 54 51
A local favorite (if the packed terrace of chattering Parisians didn't give it away), this restaurant and cafe attracts laid-back 17ème residents. To keep up with high demand in the summer months, the owner makes a habit of expanding his outdoor seating well into the public sidewalk.
✈ ⓂBrochant. With your back to the post office, walk down av. de Clichy 1 block and turn right on rue des Moines. The restaurant is 3 blocks down and on the left. *i* Free Wi-Fi. Ⓢ Plats €10-20. 2-course lunch €12. Su brunch €20. ☪ Open daily 7:30am-2am.

LES FILAOS   AFRICAN $$$
5 rue Guy de Maupassant   ☎01 45 04 94 53 www.lesfilaos.com
The first joint in Paris to specialize in Mauritian cuisine, Les Filaos provides an ethnic touch to the 16ème restaurant scene. *Tit ponches* (rum punches; €5) are made fresh behind the straw hut bar. Curries (€15-16) can be made as spicy as you like, and be sure to save room for the coconut tarts. Saturday night *soirées* feature live Mauritian dancers.
✈ ⓂRue de la Pompe. Walk towards the RER station Henri Martin, and turn left on bd Émilie Augier. Walk 1 block and turn left on rue Guy de Maupassant. The restaurant is on the left. Ⓢ Prix-fixe lunch €20; dinner €35. ☪ Open Tu-F noon-2pm and 7-10pm, Sa 7-10:30pm.

ROSIMAR   SPANISH $$$$
26 rue Poussin   ☎01 45 27 74 91 www.restaurant-rosimar.com
With white cushioned chairs and blue and shiny brass accents, this place will make you feel like you're dining on the shores of the Mediterranean. Although it attracts the kind of clientele that can afford a seaside villa, Rosimar serves up some of the best fish and Spanish delicacies in Paris. The unusually quiet room makes it feel like there's nothing special going on here, but you will change your mind as soon as you taste the food.
✈ ⓂMichel-Ange Auteuil. Walk up rue Girodet to rue Poussin. Ⓢ Entrées €8-14. Plats €18-23. Menu €38. ☪ Open M-Tu noon-2:30pm, W-F noon-2:30pm and 7-10pm, Sa 7-10pm.

MARCHE DE BATIGNOLLES   MARKET $
96 bis rue Lemercier
One of the many indoor markets throughout Paris, the Marche de Batignolles has everything you might find in a regular grocery store, except it's better because

this isn't your typical supermarket. Fruits, vegetables, flowers, olives, fish, and meat can be found at various counters inside the market. Vegetarians will be happy with the selection here, but Peter Cottontail or Trix fans should tread lightly around the meat freezers, where you might see a whole skinned rabbit laid out next to the sausages.

✱ ⓂBrochant. Entrances also on rue Brochant and 5 rue Fourneyron. 🕙 Open Tu-F 8:30am-1pm and 2:30-8pm, Sa 8:30am-8pm, Su 8:30am-2pm.

LE CLUB DES 5   DINER, AMERICAN $$
57 rue des Batignolles   ☎01 53 04 94 73 www.leclubdes5.fr

This should be your go-to place when you're really craving an American burger—or just curious about the French take on American pop culture and the diner experience. The walls are covered with pop culture icons like Superman and Michael Jackson, and the realistic diner stools will have you thinking you're back in the USA. But then you see the menu. We bet you've never seen *cocottes* or *tournedos de boeuf* on a diner menu, but their MEGACHEESEBURGER screams authenticity. It's spelled in all CAPS, after all.

✱ ⓂPl. de Clichy. With your back to Montmartre, walk 3 blocks down bd des Batignolles and turn right on rue des Batignolles. The cafe is 2 blocks down on the left. ⓢ Lunch plats €11; entrée and plat €14; entrée, plat, and dessert €17. Dinner plats €16-20. Brunch €24. 🕙 Open daily 11:30am-2:30pm and 7:30-11pm. Brunch served Sa-Su noon-4pm.

BATIGNOLLES ORGANIC PRODUCE MARKET   MARKET $
bd de Batignolles

Stretching across bd de Batignolles every Saturday morning, the Batignolles Organic Produce Market is a delectable jumble of singing shoppers, hats, bottles of apple cider, scarves, loaves of bread, and obscenely large hunks of cheese, not to mention organic fruits and vegetables. Construct a gourmet picnic with ease and schlep it to the nearby Square des Batignolles.

✱ ⓂRome. On the traffic divider along bd des Batignolles, at the border of the 8ème and 17ème. ⓢ Prices vary widely. Sugar crepes €1.70. Box of strawberries €6. 🕙 Open Sa 9am-2pm.

MONTMARTRE

Montmartre has tons of great food options at relatively reasonable prices, considering how popular it is with tourists. That being said, the better options are farther out from the crowds around ⓂAnvers, where the pickpockets become more scarce. There are lots of creative and ethnic restaurants here, so skip the boring bistros and brasseries and pick something that looks interesting.

🔲 REFUGE DES FONDUS   FONDUE $$$
17 rue des 3 Frères   ☎01 42 55 22 65

Refuge des Fondus really is a refuge—both from the tourist crowds at the Sacré-Cœur and from the often monotonous Parisian bistro dinner experience. Diners are packed along two long, communal tables where you can share meat or cheese fondue with your friends and neighbors. Refuge lays on the quirk with wine served in baby bottles and walls covered in chalk-written notes of gratitude from happy customers. If you love to eat cheese dipped in more cheese and don't mind washing it down with wine, then Refuge des Fondus is the place to be.

✱ ⓂPigalle. Walk east on bd de Clichy and turn left onto rue des 3 Frères. The restaurant is up the hill on the left. ⓢ Menu €21. 🕙 Open daily 7pm-2am.

🔲 BODEGA   CAFE, SANDWICHES $
54 rue Ordener

Bodega is discretely tucked into a narrow crevice along the busy rue Ordener, but it shouldn't be missed. If hot, fresh deliciousness had a scent, it would come from Bodega, so just follow your nose if you're having trouble finding it. The specialty foods here are the sandwiches that come out hot, hot, hot, and stuffed full of fresh ingredients. To make things even better, these healthy helpings of yummy will only set you back €5. The place is tiny and only has two beautifully mosaicked patio tables barely large enough for two people to share, so it's probably best to take your sandwich *à emporter*.

✈ Ⓜ*Marcadet-Poissonniers. Located down rue Ordener; turn left facing the Mairie, and the cafe is on the left.* Ⓢ *Sandwiches €4.50-5. Plats du jour €5-9.* ⌚ *Open M-Sa noon-10pm.*

LE PERROQUET VERT   BISTRO $$$
7 rue Cavallotti   ☎01 45 22 49 16 www.perroquet-vert.com

This French bistro is named after a book by Marthe Bibesco, a scandalous writer from the 1920s (don't worry, we had to Wikipedia her too). After Le Perroquet Vert's opening, it became a source of inspiration for Picasso and Edith Piaf. While we can't promise artistic talent after eating here, we can promise one of the oldest bistros in Montmartre (where bistros originated) with traditional French fare like veal and market fish with chorizo sauce. Enjoy your food while sitting in red velvet chairs and waiting for an epiphany. Try to dine here during the week, as the weekend selection is pricey.

✈ Ⓜ*Place de Clichy. Walk up av. de Clichy for 3 blocks. Turn right onto rue Capron, walk 1 block, and turn left onto rue Cavallotti.* Ⓢ *Entrées €8. Plats €16-17. Weekday lunch menu €14; weekend €29.* ⌚ *Open M-Sa 12:15-2:30pm and 7:30-10:30pm.*

RESTAURANT SEÇ   TURKISH $$
165 rue Ordener   ☎01 42 51 18 46 http://restaurant-sec.com

This upscale Turkish restaurant serves one hell of a lunch menu, with choices like stuffed peppers, kebabs, and grilled meatballs. But be sure not to miss the Middle Eastern take on yogurt and honey—after all, it is the region that invented.

✈ Ⓜ*Jules Joffrin. With your back to the church, walk to the left of the triangular building and walk up rue Ordener. The restaurant is on the left.* Ⓢ *Entrées €4-7. Plats €10-14. Lunch menu €15.* ⌚ *Open M-Sa 11:30am-3:30pm and 6:30pm-midnight.*

DJERBA CACHER CHEZ GUICHI   GRILLED MEAT $$
76 rue Myrha   ☎01 42 23 77 99

Chez Guichi is about as rough around the edges as the gritty neighborhood it's in, and the clientele and sweaty men in front of the grill may seem a bit gruff, but don't be scared off by the local crowd. Eat in and stay to pick some bones clean while watching a soccer match; alternatively, you can pick out what you want from the freezer and take your freshly-grilled meat to go.

✈ Ⓜ*Château Rouge. Exit the Metro, turn around, and take the 1st left onto rue Myrha. Chez Guichi is on the left.* Ⓢ *Sandwiches €6.50-11. Plats €9.* ⌚ *Open M-F noon-11:30pm and Su noon-11:30pm.*

LE CARAJAS   BRAZILIAN $$$
24 rue des 3 Frères   ☎01 42 64 11 26 carajas.free.fr

Le Carajas serves delicious traditional Brazilian food in an oddly decorated, close-quarters dining room. The strange cartoon of girls in bikinis in the back is a bit weird, but the photos and postcards of Brazil are more visually appealing. Even if you're sitting among strangers, you'll enjoy your meal here; the food is flavorful and the portions are just right, so you'll feel satisfied but not too stuffed.

✈ Ⓜ*Anvers. Exit the Metro and turn around to walk west on bd de Rochechouart, then turn right onto rue des 3 Frères; the restaurant is up the hill on the right. Or* Ⓜ*Abesses.* Ⓢ *Entrées €5-7. Plats €12-16.50. Dessert €6. Menu €25.* ⌚ *Open daily noon-11pm.*

LE REFLET DU MIROIR   CREPERIE, INTERNATIONAL $
161 rue Ordener   ☎01 42 62 23 97 www.lerefletdumiroir.fr

If you stare into the mirrors that decorate this "creperie," you'll probably have a confused look on your face. These aren't your average crepes, and it's not your average creperie. Drawing inspiration from around the world, Le Reflet du Miroir uses chutney from London or shredded parmesan from Italy and puts

food

them in French wrapping. Apparently beside themselves with what to do with American cuisine, they gave up and served plain ol' burgers (€11).

 # [M]Jules Joffrin. With your back to the church, walk to the left of the triangular building and up rue Ordener. [S] Crepes €8-10; deluxe crepes €11. Plats €4-12. ⏰ Open Tu-F 7-10pm, Sa noon-10pm, Su 7-10pm.

BUTTES CHAUMONT & BELLEVILLE

This neighborhood has some of the best African, Turkish, and Asian food in the city. **Rue de Belleville** has the cheapest options, but be careful when walking around this area after dusk.

LA BOULANGERIE PAR VÉRONIQUE MAUCLERC BOULANGERIE, PATISSERIE

83 rue de Crimée ☎01 42 40 64 55

Baking its divine bread in one of only four remaining wood-fired ovens in France, Véronique uses only organic ingredients in her creations. Oh, and she may cook the best damn chocolate chip cookie you've ever had. On the surface, the only difference between this *boulangerie* and every other one you'll find in Paris is that it's large enough to fit more than four people at a time. But we would readily wait outside in the sun for our turn to get a treat from Véronique. Be sure to stop by the *salon de thé* tucked in the back for a spoil-me-rotten Sunday brunch.

 # [M]Laumière. Walk northeast on av. Jean Jaurès, then turn right onto rue de Crimée; the boulangerie is near the end of the block on the right. [S] Chocolate chip cookies €2.10. Chocolate tarts €3.80. Lemon meringue tarts €4.10. ⏰ Boulangerie open Tu-F 9am-2pm and 3:30-8pm. Salon de thé open Tu-Sa 9am-5:30pm.

L'ATLANTIDE NORTH AFRICAN $$$

7 av. Laumière ☎01 42 45 09 81 www.latlantide.fr

With traditional North African rugs decorating the floor and driftwood walls dividing the restaurant into a few separate rooms, L'Atlantide will take you away from Paris for the evening. The dining experience here is specific to the Berber people that occupy various parts of Northern Africa, including Morocco, Libya, Algeria, and Tunisia, among others. Take a mini-vacation and get lost in the dim lighting, unforgettable couscous, and relaxing atmosphere.

 # [M]Laumière. Walk south down av. de Laumière toward the park. L'Atlantide is near the end of the road on the right. [S] Entrées €6-8. Couscous €13-19.50. Tajines €13-16.50. ⏰ Open M-F 7-11:30pm, Sa-Su 12-2:30pm and 7-11:30pm.

MASSAI MARA AFRICAN $

66 rue Armand Carrel ☎01 42 08 00 65 www.massaimara.fr

For students, €5 at lunch gets you whatever the chef whips up, a drink, and a seat in one of the low leather-backed chairs. Fried plantains, rice, and white fish topped with some spicy sauce are some of the staples.

 # [M]Jaurès. [S] Plats €8-13. Student lunch menu €5. ⏰ Open daily noon-3pm and 7-11pm.

LAO SIAM VIETNAMESE $$

48 rue de Belleville ☎01 40 40 09 68

While most of the dishes here are cheap, Lao Siam sneaks a few more euro from your wallet by charging separately for rice (€2.20). The decor is nothing fancy, and paper napkins leave no room for pretension. But the food speaks louder than the decor, and the place is generally packed. The *filet du poisson* with "hip-hop sauce" (€8.80) is not to be missed. They also feature very tasty and salty duck selections.

 # [M]Belleville. [S] Entrées €7-11. Plats €6.80-22. Beer €3.50. Wine by the bottle €11-55. ⏰ Open daily noon-3pm and 7-11pm.

PIZZA AND PASTA ITALIAN $$

36 av. Jean Jaurès ☎06 64 25 28 61

Although the interior of this restaurant is about as noteworthy as the wall color in the budget hotel you're probably staying at, the food is worth bragging about.

A mom-and-pop family restaurant with authentic Sicilian food, this plainly named restaurant knows what it's doing and how to do it right. Steaming plates of pasta and hefty pizzas will fill you up and leave you with a satisfied stomach and a big smile.

✚ ⓜJaurès. Walk northeast on av. Jean Jaurès away from the river; the restaurant is on the right. ⓢ Entrées €3.50-9. Pasta €6-9. 40cm pizzas €7.50-11.50. ⓓ Open M-Sa 11am-10pm. Closing time may vary.

L'ILIADE   GREEK, TURKISH $$
59 rue de Belleville   ☎01 42 01 19 22

Recently discovered and only known to a select group of restaurateurs, this Greek and Turkish fusion establishment maintains the old-world feel with walls covered in rugs and serves lamb dishes with traditional Turkish yogurt to central Parisian clientele.

✚ ⓜBelleville. ⓢ Plats €13-18. Chef specials €15-23. Lunch menu €13; dinner menu €22. ⓓ Open M-Sa noon-3:30pm and 6:30-11pm.

nightlife

You may have told your parents, professors, and prospective employers that you're traveling to Paris to study the differences between Monet and Manet (hint: it's not just one letter), but after 52 years in the business, we at *Let's Go* know it isn't just art that draws the young and the restless to Europe. If you're traveling to drink and mingle, Paris will not disappoint you. The nightlife here is debaucherous, and there's something for everyone. Bars are either chic cafes bursting with people-watching potential, party joints all about rock and teen angst, or laid-back local spots that double as havens for English-speakers. Clubbing in Paris is less about hip DJs and cutting-edge beats than it is about dressing up and being seen. Drinks are expensive, so Parisians usually stick to the ones included with the cover. Many clubs accept reservations, which means there's no available seating on busy nights. It's best to be confident (but not aggressive) about getting in. If dancing the night away isn't your thing, Paris is home to just as many pubs and bars that host live music on a regular basis and generally have more reasonably priced drinks. Bars in the 5ème and 6ème draw international students and backpackers, while Châtelet-Les Halles attracts a slightly older set. The Marais is the center of Parisian GLBT nightlife. Just remember: if you are in Paris to party, use the buddy system or have a backup plan for getting back to your hostel just in case you miss the Metro. Drunk people are easy targets for pickpockets, muggers, and other city slime, so don't put yourself in a vulnerable position.

ÎLE DE LA CITÉ AND ÎLE ST-LOUIS

Far from a party spot, the islands are a bit of a nightlife wasteland. If you're looking for a quieter terrace to share a beer and conversation, this is your spot. Tourists tend to clear out of les Îles after dark, so the pace is comfortably slower here. The bars are a lot more fun and a lot less expensive on either side of the bank in the neighboring 4ème and 5ème.

▨ LE LOUIS IX   CAFE, BRASSERIE
25 rue des Deux-Ponts   ☎01 43 54 23 89

The islands are quiet. And so is the rough-looking bearded man in the corner who's working on his third or fourth *pastis* at this local bar. While the clientele may be the kind that go to bed at 8:30pm, it's a good place to debate whether to go to the Latin Quarter or Marais over a pint of blond beer.

✚ ⓜPont Marie. ⓢ Wine €3.50-4.60. Beer €3.80-5. Aperitifs €3.80-4.50. ⓓ Open daily 7:30am-8:30pm.

L'ANNEKE   BRASSERIE

5 bd du Palais   ☎09 61 27 53 02

L'Anneke is a quiet neighborhood watering hole that is a pleasant spot for a happy hour drink. After that, get a €2 beer to go. There's not much going on here except for some late afternoon nibbling and chatter, so save your nightlife energy for the walk north of the Seine.

✢ Ⓜ*Cité. Turn left on bd du Palais from the Metro.* Ⓢ *Lunch €10-12. Beer €2-5. Coffee €1-2. Sandwiches €3-5.* 🕒 *Open daily 7am-8pm.*

ESMERALDA   BRASSERIE

2 rue du Cloître Notre-Dame   ☎01 43 54 17 72 www.lesmeralda.com

Esmeralda is a rest stop for tired tourists traveling between islands. The terrace has a nice view of the shenanigans on the bridge and a handful of lost drunk people. If you find yourself with a case of the munchies before midnight, a crepe stand on the terrace is reasonably priced compared to the drinks here.

✢ Ⓜ*Cité. Located on the eastern corner of Île de la Cité.* Ⓢ *Wine €5-6. Beer €5-7. Mixed drinks €8.50. Crepes €2.50-5.50.* 🕒 *Open in summer daily 7:30am-11pm.*

LE SOLEIL D'OR   BRASSERIE

15 bd du Palais   ☎01 43 54 22 22

With overpriced drinks and underwhelming, faux-modern seating, Le Soleil d'Or is somewhat disappointing. The view of the Seine and this brasserie's convenient location at the end of the bridge can be counted among its virtues, but we think it's best to trek just a few steps further to the other establishments on this island.

✢ Ⓜ*Cité. Turn left down bd du Palais from the Metro; the brasserie is on the corner.* Ⓢ *Beer €5-6. Mixed drinks €6-8. Crepes €5-9. Pizza €9.50-13.* 🕒 *Open daily 11am-11pm.*

CHÂTELET-LES HALLES

The bars in Châtelet are close together and easy to find. This neighborhood has its fair share of GLBT bars (though it's no Marais) and smaller establishments that are packed until dawn. Watch yourself around Les Halles: the area is a prominent location for pickpockets.

▩ FROG AND ROSBIF   PUB

116 rue St-Denis   ☎01 42 36 34 73 www.frogpubs.com

One of seven "Frog" pubs in France, Frog and Rosbif tosses a dash of Britishness over the French nightlife scene. A cardboard cutout of the queen herself watches over the raucous merriment and beer-swilling football fans from atop the bar. Many French locals and tourists alike come here for a quick trip to the UK to escape the sometimes monotonous nightlife nearby. Don't miss the chance to watch a game here with rowdy Brits, and be sure to sample one of the Frog's six homemade microbrews. Whatever you're drinking, expect lively conversation from the chipper bartenders, whose emphatic singing will surely let their presence be known.

✢ Ⓜ*Étienne-Marcel. Just off rue de Turbigo.* ℹ *Quiz nights Su 8pm unless there's a soccer game. Try a pint Th €4.50-5.* Ⓢ *Happy hour pints €5, otherwise €6.50.* 🕒 *Open daily noon-2am. Happy hour 5:30-8pm.*

▩ BANANA CAFÉ   BAR, CLUB, GLBT

13 rue de la Ferronerie   ☎01 42 33 35 31 www.bananacafeparis.com

Situated in the heart of Châtelet, Banana Café proclaims itself the most popular GLBT bar in the 1er, and rightly so. The club suits a wide range of clientele that range from the somewhat reticent patrons who occupy the terrace, to the erotic dancers/strippers stationed outside. Head downstairs after midnight for a piano bar and more dance space. There are weekly theme nights like "Go-Go Boys," which takes place Thursday through Saturday from midnight to dawn.

✢ Ⓜ*Châtelet. Walk 3 blocks down rue St-Denis and turn right onto rue de la Ferronerie.* Ⓢ *Cover F-Sa €10; includes 1 drink. Beer €5.50. Mixed drinks €11. Happy hour pints €3; mixed drinks €4.* 🕒 *Open daily 5:30pm-6am. Happy hour 6-11pm.*

THE THISTLE PUB
PUB

112 rue St-Denis   ☎01 40 26 33 20 www.the-thistle.com

The Thistle is a local favorite that offers cheap drinks and kilted men to enjoy them with. This is definitely a spot for the regulars, but all noobs are welcome to try to conquer Sunday night trivia or Monday night "Shithead" tournaments. Be sure to brush up on your pub trivia and card-playing mastery before you arrive—liquid prizes are at stake!

✦ ⓂÉtienne Marcel. Walk up rue Turbigo, away from Les Halles, and turn left onto rue St-Denis. *i* Quiz night Su 8:30pm. Shithead tournament M 8pm. Ⓢ Beer €4-7. Mixed drinks €8. Shots €4. ☒ Open M-Th 3pm-2am, F-Sa noon-2am, Su 3pm-2am. Happy Hour weekdays 3-8pm.

LE REX CLUB
CLUB

5 bd Poissonnière   ☎01 42 36 10 96 www.rexclub.com

Le Rex Club was the first in Paris to introduce electronic music to the scene, and more than 20 years later, it still holds its own against other late-late-night competitors. With a tiered dance floor, dark lighting, and bass that will make your ears throb, Le Rex Club is the place for those who like to have a seriously outrageous Saturday night of dancing and sweating. The club also redefines "fashionably late" by not opening until midnight, and even then the crowd doesn't really start to rev up until 2am, so time your pregame accordingly.

✦ ⓂBonne Nouvelle. Walking west on bd Poisonnière, the club is one the left. *i* Coat check €2, bag check €4. Ⓢ Cover €10-15. Shots €5. Beer €6-6.50. Champagne €12. ☒ Open Th 11:30pm-7am, F-Sa midnight-7am.

LE SUNSIDE, LE SUNSET
JAZZ CLUB, BAR

60 rue des Lombards   ☎01 40 26 21 25 www.sunset-sunside.com

A jazz club with a great reputation, Le Sunside, Le Sunset is very popular with American and English expats and tourists. Le Sunside and Le Sunset are actually two separate venues in the same location. Underground Le Sunset offers small red leather stools under a tiled, tunnel-like ceiling that leads to the small stage in the back. Le Sunside feels a bit more open but is about as narrow as Le Sunset, so get there early if you want a good seat. Be sure to try one of the specialty mojitos at Le Sunside.

✦ ⓂChâtelet. Walk north on rue St-Denis and turn left onto rue des Lombards; the bar is on the right. Ⓢ Cover sometimes free, never more than €25; the price goes down the later you show up. Students €2-3 discount. ☒ Open daily 6pm-2am. Happy hour 5-8 pm. Concerts M-Sa 8pm-1am.

LE CLUB 18
CLUB, GLBT

18 rue Beaujolais   ☎01 42 97 52 13 www.club18.fr

Flashing lights and pop, house, and dance beats make for a wild night in this intimate (read: tiny), almost exclusively gay bar. Couches and mirrors line the walls, which means getting cozy with your neighbor is guaranteed. Younger crowds don't show up until after 1 or 2am.

✦ ⓂPalais Royal-Musée du Louvre. Follow rue de Richelieu and turn right onto rue de Montpensier. Follow rue de Montpensier around the Jardin du Palais Royal until rue Beaujolais. Ⓢ Cover €10; includes 1 drink. Mixed drinks €6-9. ☒ Open W midnight-6am, F-Sa midnight-6am.

LA CHAMPMESLÉ
CLUB, GLBT

4 rue Chabanais   ☎01 42 96 85 20 www.lachampmesle.com

This welcoming lesbian bar is Paris's oldest and most famous. Head under the rainbow for discussions on art, books, and current events. Josy, the owner, still works the bar, knows almost every customer by name, and enthusiastically promotes the bar's late-night spectacles (which, when they happen, are at 2am). The crowd is friendly; straight folk are warmly welcomed. The club hosts weekly cabaret shows and monthly art exhibits.

✦ ⓂPyramides. Walk up av. de l'Opéra and turn right onto rue des Petits Champs. After a few blocks, turn left onto rue Chabanais. *i* Cabaret shows Sa 10pm. Ⓢ Beer before 10pm €5, after €7. Mixed drinks €8-10. ☒ Open M-Sa 4pm-3am.

BAR N'IMPORTE QUOI BAR

16 rue du Roule ☎01 40 26 29 71 www.nimportequoi.fr

Almost anything goes at this bar that's normally packed on the weekends. Bras hang above the bar, possibly as a result of the "le boob shot" policy (flash the bartender for a free shot; women only). The downstairs doubles the size of the bar, alleviating some of the crowds. American sports are shown on Sunday nights, and early in the week draft beer is €5 all night—anything to keep people knocking 'em back.

🧭 ⓂLouvre-Rivoli. Walk against traffic on rue de Rivoli and turn left onto rue du Roule. $ Shots €3. Beer €7-8. Mixed drinks €8.50. Happy hour mixed drinks €5.50. ⏰ Open M-W 6pm-4:30am, Th-Sa 6pm-5:30am, Su 6pm-4:30am. Happy hour 6-8pm.

AU DUC DES LOMBARDS JAZZ CLUB

42 rue des Lombards ☎01 42 33 22 88 www.ducdeslombards.com

With a holding capacity of just 80 people, this club makes for an intimate night of food, refreshments, and music. There are two shows six nights a week, so come early for dinner and stay the whole night, or stop by for the later show. The restaurant and club inside are the epitome of jazz, with dark walls and carpeting, low tables, leather chairs, a big black piano, and some serious mood lighting.

🧭 ⓂChâtelet. Walk north on rue St-Denis and turn right onto rue des Lombards; Au Duc is on the corner. ℹ Live music M-Sa 8 and 10pm. Buy tickets online or at the door. $ Cover €25-40; students usually get €3 discount. Wine €6-8. Mixed drinks €12-18. ⏰ Open M-Sa 5pm-2am.

LE BAISER SALÉ JAZZ CLUB, BAR

58 rue des Lombards ☎01 42 33 37 71 www.lebaisersale.com

This jazz bar is not the stereotypically hip, pretentious place you imagine. Housing African jazz and local alternative bands, Le Baiser Salé offers a quieter night for the partying type, with people intensely dancing in the packed upstairs lounge. Le Baiser Salé will please hipsters and their mainstream friends alike.

🧭 ⓂChâtelet. Take rue St-Denis 2 blocks and turn left onto rue des Lombards. ℹ Tickets available at FNAC stores and online. Free jam sessions M at 10pm, 1-drink min. $ Cover €12-22. Beer €6.50. Mixed drinks €9.70. Happy hour beer €4-5; mojitos €4.50; mixed drinks €7. After 10pm, €1.30 increase on all drink prices. ⏰ Open daily 5pm-6am. Happy hour 5:30-8pm.

THE MARAIS

There are about as many bars and clubs in the Marais as there are people, and the establishments you'll find here are just as diverse as the crowds. A simple walk up **rue Vieille du Temple** is a sure-fire way to find exactly the spot you're looking for, whether it be a chest-thumping club, a casual cafe, or a coolly lit modern lounge.

👍 **RAIDD BAR** BAR, CLUB, GLBT

23 rue Vieille du Temple ☎01 42 77 04 88

If you want a penis or just want to see one, come here. Sparkling disco balls light up Raidd Bar, as do the muscular, tank-topped torsos of the sexy male bartenders. After 11pm, performers strip down in the glass shower built into the wall (yes, they take it all off). There's a notoriously strict door policy: women aren't allowed unless they are outnumbered by (gorgeous) men.

🧭 ⓂHôtel de Ville. $ Beer €6.50. Mixed drinks €10. Happy hour beer €4.20; mixed drinks €4.50. ⏰ Open M-Th 5pm-4am, F-Sa 5pm-5am, Su 5pm-4am. Happy hour 5-11pm.

👍 **STOLLY'S** BAR

16 rue Cloche Percé ☎01 42 76 06 76 www.cheapblonde.com

This small Anglophone hangout takes the sketchy out of the dive bar, but leaves the attitude. The pitchers of cheap blonde beer (€14) ensure that the bar lives up to its motto: "Hangovers installed and serviced here." Come inside, have a pint, and shout at the TV with the decidedly non-trendy, tattoo-covered crowd.

✈ Ⓜ St-Paul. *From the Metro, turn right onto rue Pavée and then left onto rue du Roi de Sicile. Turn left onto rue Cloche Percé.* Ⓢ *Beer pints €5-6; 1.5L €13. Mixed drinks €6.50-8. Happy hour pints and mixed drinks €5.* 🕐 *Open M-F 4:30pm-2am, Sa-Su 3pm-2am. Happy hour 5-8pm. Terrace open until midnight.*

LE YONO   BAR, CLUB
37 rue Vieille du Temple   ☎01 42 74 31 65 www.leyono.fr

It's easy to walk past Le Yono, as it's set back from the street through a stone corridor that makes for a grand entrance to this cave-like club. The bar area is big and open and makes a great space for chatting on weekdays, but on weekends the real party is downstairs. The mosaics on the walls and bar light up the room, packed with students dancing along with DJs that rock the house with electronic beats. Make sure to check the performance schedule ahead of time; once or twice a month, some lucky live music acts will get to perform even further into the depths of the bar in a room that feels like a cave (only with better lighting and without bats and dripping stalactites).

✈ Ⓜ Hôtel de Ville. *Walk against traffic on rue de Rivoli and turn left. Or from* Ⓜ St-Paul, *walk with traffic on rue de Rivoli and turn right.* 𝒊 *Live music 2-3 times per week. Downstairs open F-Sa.* Ⓢ *Mixed drinks €10-11. Happy hour mixed drinks €5.50-6. Mojitos 10-12. Beer €4-4.50. Tapas Th-Sa €5-9.* 🕐 *Open M 6pm-midnight, Tu-Sa 6pm-2am, Su 6pm-midnight.*

O'SULLIVAN'S REBEL BAR   BAR
10 rue des Lombards   ☎01 42 71 42 72 http://chatelet.osullivans-pubs.com

A tattooed take on an Irish bar, O'Sullivan's Rebel Bar makes Paris's chain bars look like classy English tea rooms. The bartenders serve drinks so quickly that they sometimes use the water gun to cool off (or to squirt shots directly into their mouths). Come on the weekends when the music is loud and the crowd is rowdy.

✈ Ⓜ Hôtel de Ville. *Walk up rue du Renard and turn left onto rue de la Verrerie, which becomes rue des Lombards.* Ⓢ *Pints €4-5.30. Mixed drinks €7-9; cocktail of the evening €5.* 🕐 *Open M-Th 5pm-2am, F-Sa 5pm-5am, Su 5pm-1am. Happy hour 5-9pm.*

OPEN CAFÉ   BAR, GLBT
17 rue des Archives   ☎01 42 72 26 18 www.opencafe.fr

Popular almost to the point of absurdity, this GLBT-friendly bar draws a large crowd of loyal, mostly older male customers. Though women are welcome, they will slowly find themselves outnumbered as the ever-expanding sea of Y-chromosomes grows later in the evening.

✈ Ⓜ Hôtel de Ville. 𝒊 *½-price beer 6-10pm. ½-price champagne 10pm-close.* Ⓢ *Beer €3.80. Mixed drinks €7.90.* 🕐 *Open M-Th 11am-2am, F-Sa 11am-4am.*

LE KOMPTOIR   BAR
27 rue Quincampoix   ☎01 42 77 75 35 www.lekomptoir.fr

Head to this tapas bar for the cheapest happy hour pints and cocktails in the Marais. Le Komptoir's distinctive backward "K" in its name hints at its backward behavior of cheap drinks, free entry to Thursday and Fridays concerts, and catering to the businessmen who come for afternoon shakes.

✈ Ⓜ Hôtel de Ville. *In the pl. Michelet. Walk up rue du Renard, turn right onto rue St-Merri and then left onto rue Quincampoix.* 𝒊 *Jazz concerts Th 9pm. Pop rock concerts F 9pm.* Ⓢ *Beer €6.60. Mixed drinks €8. Happy hour beer €4, mixed drinks 2 for 1. Concerts free.* 🕐 *Open Tu-Su 10am-2am. Happy hour 6-8:30pm.*

LE DÉPÔT   CLUB, GLBT
10 rue aux Ours   ☎01 44 54 96 96 www.ledepot.com

Le Dépôt is a gay club that revolves around sex—literally. Winding passages lead to dance floors that shoot off into private rooms. Meanwhile, porn stars get off on mounted TVs. A steady stream of men and boys filter in at all hours, hoping for success in the designated "cruising" area. Women, as a rule, are not allowed.

⇆ [M]Étienne-Marcel. Follow the traffic on rue Étienne-Marcel, which becomes rue aux Ours. $ Cover M-Sa before 9pm and Su before 4pm €8.50; increases incrementally after that. ⏰ Open daily 2pm-8am.

LE PICK-CLOPS BAR

16 rue Vieille du Temple ☎01 40 29 02 18

With colorful halogen lights highlighting the bright mosaic tiles that dot the floors and walls, Le Pick-Clops adds a splash of color to Paris's nighttime scene, which often become a blur of monochromatic, coffee-colored brasseries. This local favorite is a great setting for upbeat conversation and drinks, with to-die-for menu items that make this place even more appetizing. Try the aromatic duck confit or one of the creative salads, like the Inca with lentils, quinoa, and avocado.

⇆ [M]Hôtel de Ville. Walk against traffic on rue de Rivoli and turn left. $ Plats €9.50-16. Beer €4-4.50. Mixed drinks €8.20. Wine €3.80-4.80. Drinks €0.50 extra after 10pm. ⏰ Open daily 7am-2am.

OKAWA BAR, LOUNGE, CABARET

40 rue Vieille du Temple ☎01 48 04 30 69 www.okawa.fr

This trendy bar doubles as a coffee shop and offers limited seating but free-flowing fun. Be sure to come here for Wednesday night cabaret, where the lady-boys may have you looking twice. GLBT and straight crowds enjoy the cool lighting and low mood music of the ground floor bar, but the real party is at the downstairs bar and oh-so-fabulous stage. The room fills up fast, though, so it's best to make a reservation in advance and make sure you don't miss out on some fabulous song and dance.

*⇆ [M]Hôtel de Ville. Walk against traffic on rue de Rivoli and turn left. **i** DJ on T and W. Cabaret on W: dinner 8:30pm, show 10:30pm. $ Happy hour beer €3.50-3.70, wine €3.50-4. ⏰ Open M-Th 10am-2am, F-Sa 10am-4am, Su 10-2am. Happy hour 7-10pm.*

L'APPAREMMENT CAFÉ BAR, LOUNGE, CAFE

18 rue des Coutures St-Gervais ☎01 48 87 12 22

L'Apparemment has sophisticated decor, including dark wood paneling and comfortable leather chairs, which it complements with a relaxed and hip young crowd. During the week you'll run into more professionals who come here for an evening drink, but on weekends, this cafe fills up with young people. Lounge on one of the huge couches or grab a board game and see how many drink names you can spell out on the Scrabble board. You could easily spend a whole night here, so if you get hungry, try one of the tapas or a make-your-own salads.

*⇆ [M]Chemin Vert. From bd Beaumarchais, turn right onto rue St-Gilles, right onto rue de Thorigny, and left onto rue des Coutures St-Gervais. **i** After Work Night once per month (bottom shelf champagne €5 per glass). $ Mixed drinks €9.50. Salads €12.50 for 4 ingredients, €14 for 5 ingredients, €15.59 for 6, €17 for 7, +€1.50 each additional. ⏰ Open M-Sa noon-2am, Su noon-midnight.*

ANDY WAHLOO BAR

69 rue des Gravilliers ☎01 42 71 20 38 www.andywahloo-bar.com

The walls may be covered with pictures of African women, but the clientele certainly dresses less conservatively. Andy Wahloo, which means, "I have nothing" in a certain Moroccan dialect, serves ambitious mint cocktails with chutney and banana liqueur (€10-14). DJs on Wednesdays start the weekend early with a mix of '90s rap, dance, and some salsa.

⇆ [M]Arts et Métiers. Follow rue Beaubourg for 2 blocks and turn left onto rue des Gravilliers. $ Mixed drinks €9-13. ⏰ Open Tu-Sa 5pm-2am.

LA BELLE HORTENSE WINE BAR

31 rue Vieille du Temple ☎01 48 04 71 60 www.cafeine.com

As a self-proclaimed literary bar/gallery/cafe, La Belle Hortense draws an older crowd for light reading, poetry, art exhibitions, and the occasional glass of wine. You could probably do this for much cheaper in your hotel lobby, but the atmosphere at La Belle Hortense is more intellectual.

[M]St-Paul. Walk with traffic on rue de Rivoli and turn left onto rue Vieille du Temple. $ Wine €3.50-9. ⏰ Open daily 5pm-2am.

bare it all

Don't be surprised to find statues or advertisements of topless, bottomless, or completely nude people on the streets of Paris. At Fontaine de l'Observatoire, visitors will find three fully disrobed statues of women atop the fountain. On Paris billboards, Yves Saint Laurent created a new ad for M7, a cologne for men, that featured a full-frontal naked model. In this city, the human body is seen as art rather than a promiscuous eyesore, so don't snicker, giggle, or react in typical *American Pie* fashion.

LATIN QUARTER AND ST-GERMAIN

The Latin Quarter and St-Germain neighborhoods are where you'll find the majority of Paris's students spending their intellectual (or not so intellectual) nights out. **Rue Mouffetard** has the cheapest bars in the city and is always flooded with students and backpackers. Wander down **rue de la Montagne Sainte-Geneviève** if you're looking for places where you'll be able to speak English (this is where Parisians come to practice their Anglophone skills).

LE 10 BAR BAR

10 rue de l'Odéon ☎01 43 26 66 83

Although the exterior of Le 10 Bar may make you think it's time for an upgrade, the 1950s posters advertising old plays and cabarets you'll find inside will quickly change your mind. The antiquely dusty interior of this local watering hole, along with the jukebox that croons Édith Piaf and Aretha Franklin, will make you feel like you've taken a step back in time. The bar itself is tiny but serves up big rounds of drinks to locals who gather here to start the evening with an intellectual discussion that will eventually turn into a drunken giggle-fest. Head downstairs to the basement where Ernest Hemingway used to come to write inspired tales after amorous encounters with his mistress who lived above the bar. Although we don't recommend trespassing above the bar in search of a lover, you may feel that literary love is in the air at Le Bar 10; memorize a few lines of French poetry and flirt the night away.

*[M]Odéon. Walk south where the road splits into 3 forks and take the middle fork; Le 10 Bar is on the right. **i** Cash only. Basement opens at 9:30pm. $ Beers €4.50-6.50. Mixed drinks €8. ⏰ Open daily 6pm-2am. Happy hour 4-8pm.*

L'ACADÉMIE DE LA BIÈRE BAR

88 bd de Port-Royal ☎01 43 54 66 65 www.academie-biere.com

With 12 beers on tap and 150 bottled varieties, L'Académie de la Bière is as serious about its brews as students are about getting sloshed on a Saturday night. The bar itself is minuscule, but the extensive patio (which is covered and heated, depending on the weather) is filled end-to-end with those spirit-seeking students. Most drinkers come to L'Académie to study the brews, but any smart student knows not to drink on an empty stomach—the steaming hot plates of mussels and fat burgers lined with fries are hard to ignore.

[M]Vavin. Walk southeast on bd du Montparnasse as it turns into bd du Port-Royal. The bar is on the left. $ Beer €6-11.50. Salads €11. Mussels €7-9. Plats €9-16. ⏰ Open M-Th 10am-2am, F-Sa 10am-3am, Su 10am-2am.

👍 **LE VIOLIN DINGUE** BAR, CLUB

46 rue de la Montagne Ste-Geneviève ☎01 43 25 79 93

Known as "le VD" to locals, this bar has some of the cheapest happy hour drinks, and it's open the latest. Upstairs feels like a pub with a strong American influence (they show American football, after all). After 1am, though, it floods with young French locals who swarm to get into the huge downstairs club, where the latest pop blasts against the vaulted stone ceilings until 5am.

➡ [M]Cardinal Lemoine. Walk uphill on rue du Cardinal Lemoine and turn right onto rue Clovis. Walk 1 block and turn right onto rue Descartes. When you hit the plaza, the bar is on the left. [S] Beer €6. Mixed drinks €7-10. Happy hour beer €3, mixed drinks €4. Prices increase €1.50 after 1:30am. ⏰ Open daily 8pm-5am. Happy hour 8-10pm

👍 **LE FIFTH BAR** BAR

55 rue Mouffetard ☎01 43 37 09 09

The prized possession of rue Mouffetard, this bar is frequented by students and international travelers—the popularity shows on the scratched-up bar and stools. The drinks are cheap, and there is a sitting area in the back and a small dance floor downstairs that you might confuse with a sweatbox.

➡ [M]Place Monge. Walk down rue Monge and turn right onto pl. Monge. Keep going as it turns into rue Ortolan and turn right onto rue Mouffetard. The bar is on the left. [S] Shots €4. Beer €5.50. Mixed drinks €7-10. Happy hour specials €1-3 cheaper. ⏰ Open M-Th 4pm-2am, F-Sa 4pm-6am. Happy hour 4-10pm.

LE CAVEAU DES OUBLIETTES JAZZ BAR

52 rue Galande ☎01 46 34 23 09

Le Caveau des Oubliettes draws in the younger, jazz-loving that keeps this club hipper than most of its counterparts. Upstairs, students enjoy sipping cocktails and engage in intellectual conversations over drinks and cigarettes. In the basement, where long ago prisoners *(les oubliettes)* were left locked up and forgotten, patrons forget about their worries and enjoy the vibes of the music and a variety of drinks from the second bar.

➡ [M]St-Michel. From bd St-Michel, walk away from the Seine, turn left onto rue St-Séverin, and continue across rue du Petit Pont until it turns into rue Galande. Le Caveau is on the left. i Jam sessions: Soul on W, Funk on Th, Blues on F. Free concerts on F-Sa. [S] Beer €5.50-6. Mixed drinks €10. ½-price during happy hour. ⏰ Open daily 5pm-4am. Happy hour daily 5-6pm.

LA POMME D'EVE BAR, CLUB

1 rue Laplace ☎01 43 25 86 18 www.lapommedeve.com

The only South African bar in Paris, La Pomme d'Eve is a night owl's hangout that explodes around 2am when the rest of the bars close. Ask George to make you a "Springbuck" (Amarula and Get 27; €5) then mingle under the zebra skin with local bartenders (French and international) who flock here after work.

➡ [M]Cardinal Lemoine. Walk uphill on rue du Cardinal Lemoine and turn right onto rue Clovis. Walk 1 block and turn right onto rue Descartes. Walk until the plaza, turn uphill, walk 1 block, and take the 1st right. The bar is on the left. [S] Beer €6.50. Mixed drinks €7-12. Happy hour beer and mixed drinks €5. ⏰ Open Tu-Su 8pm-5am. Happy Hour 6-9:30pm.

FINNEGAN'S WAKE IRISH PUB

9 rue des Boulangers ☎01 40 51 01 73 www.finneganswakeparis.com

Named for James Joyce's famous novel, Finnegan's Wake is one of Paris's most authentic Irish pubs. Only Irish bands play here (although don't expect Flogging Molly to be taking down the house), and the dark wood interior successfully supplants the rustic Irish pub feel in the middle of a quiet French neighborhood. Head here for student discounts on Thursdays or Wednesday night karaoke; if you really want to impress the lassies, show off your vocals while doing your best Irish jig.

✈ ⓜ*Jussieu. With your back to the big science building, walk straight up the hill on rue des Boulangers; the pub is near the top, on the left.* ⓘ *Happy hour M-Sa 4-8pm. Karaoke W 9pm-midnight. Student night (beer €3, mixed drinks €5) Th. Occasional live concerts.* ⓩ *Pints €5. Mixed drinks €7.* ⓩ *Open M-Th 6am-2am, F-Sa 6pm-4am. Happy hour daily 5-9pm.*

LE CAVEAU DE LA HUCHETTE   JAZZ BAR
5 rue de la Huchette   ☎01 43 26 65 05 www.caveaudelahuchette.fr

In the past, the Caveau was a meeting place for secret societies and leaders of the Revolution; downstairs, you can still see the prison cells and execution chambers that were once occupied by the victims of Danton and Robespierre. Today, a healthy mix of locals, tourists, students, and expats floods this deep underground cavern regularly for more friendly nights of music and dancing. Unlike at most jazz clubs where the performances are the main attraction, patrons here are more concerned about dirtying up their dance shoes and breaking a sweat as saxophones and basses croon through the night.

✈ ⓜ*St-Michel. Exit at bd St-Michel and walk away from the river, then turn left onto rue de la Huchette.* ⓘ *Live music 10pm-2am. Dance lessons offered in salsa, tango, swing, and rock at nearby locations; call ☎06 76 63 25 24 or email danse@swinghouse.net for details.* Ⓢ *Cover M-Th €12, F-Sa €14, Su €12; students under 25 €10. Beer €6-8. Mixed drinks €8-10.* ⓩ *Open M-W 9:30pm-2:30am, Th-Sa 9:30pm-dawn, Su 9:30pm-late.*

AUX TROIS MAILLETZ   JAZZ BAR
56 rue Galande   ☎ 01 43 25 96 86 www.lestroismailletz.fr

Aux Trois Mailletz is a triple-threat of piano, cabaret, and jazz concerts. Downstairs, the stage is set for mellow jazz or steamy cabaret, while upstairs, a piano sits next to the bar while a beautiful French girl sings along. Everyone at the bar seems to enjoy singing along, too, although we prefer just to hear the chords from the lyrical seductress. This place will fill up quickly with jazz enthusiasts, students, and local beer enthusiasts on the weekends, so come a bit early if you want to enjoy the never-ending music spilling out of this place.

✈ ⓜ*St-Michel. Walk along the river against traffic on quai de Montebello, then turn left onto rue du Petit Pont, then left again onto rue Galande.* Ⓢ *Cover for downstairs club F-Sa €20. Beer €7-10. Wine €7.50. Entrées €8.50-11.50. Meat €15.50-24.50.* ⓩ *Restaurant and cabaret open 7pm-5am.*

FUBAR   BAR
5 rue St-Sulpice   ☎01 40 51 82 00 www.fubarparis.fr

Martini drinkers with ironed clothes and good posture prefer this cocktail lounge. The bar comes alive on Thursday nights, when a slightly more rugged student crowd floods the place for happy-hour discounts that last all night, and again on Friday for a DJ that will leave electronic beats throbbing in your ears long after you head home. Come here if you're feeling extra-posh or want an excuse to wear that tight leather skirt that may get you some sideways looks at Le 10 Bar.

✈ ⓜ*Odéon. Walk south to where the road splits into 3 forks, take the right-hand fork, and then turn right onto rue St-Sulpice; Fubar is on the left.* ⓘ *Happy hour noon-10pm; all night for students on Th. Tu Quiz Night. DJ on F.* Ⓢ *Beer €3-6.* ⓩ *Open daily 6pm-2am.*

THE BOMBARDIER   PUB
2 pl. du Panthéon   ☎01 43 54 79 22 www.bombardierpub.fr

This laid-back traditional British pub has one of the best locations in Paris, right behind the Panthéon between rue Mouffetard and rue Ste-Geneviève. Come for the cask ale, hang out with expats, and see where the night takes you. The Bombardier is not recommended for the faint of heart—everyone at this pub goes hard.

✈ ⓜ*Cardinal Lemoine. Walk uphill on rue du Cardinal Lemoine and turn right onto rue Clovis. Walk 2 blocks and turn right onto pl. du Panthéon.* ⓘ *Student happy hour night on M. Trivia Su 9pm.* Ⓢ *Beer €5.50-6. Mixed drinks €8. Happy hour beer €4.50-5, mixed drinks €7.* ⓩ *Open daily noon-2am. Happy hour 5-9pm.*

nightlife

WOS (WIDE OPEN SPACES) BAR

BAR

184 rue St-Jacques ☎01 43 54 30 48 http://wosbar.com

No matter where you come from, this ironically tiny bar has drinks from your home country. Priding itself on being a true international bar, it's possible to go around the world without leaving your barstool. While mostly Anglophone, WOS is also popular with French and other Europeans. *Soirées* on the weekend will take you back to college with toga- and beach-themed parties, including free shots for those in costume.

✦ *RER B: Luxembourg. Walk on bd St-Michel toward the Seine, turn right onto rue Soufflot toward the Panthéon, and take the 3rd right onto rue St-Jacques. The bar is 1 block down on the right.* *i Trivia on M (winner gets a bottle of liquor). Student night on Th.* Ⓢ *Beer €5.50-7. Happy hour shots €4.* Ⓒ *Open M-Th 4pm-2am, F-Sa 4pm-5am, Su 4pm-2am. Happy hour 4-8pm.*

THE LONGHOP

BAR, CLUB

27 rue Frédéric Sauton ☎01 43 29 40 54 www.long-hop.net

By day, the Longhop is a large sports bar with pool tables and couches. But, at night, everything is moved out for college-themed *soirées* ("Wild Nights") aimed at backpackers and the locals trying to get with them.

✦ Ⓜ*Maubert-Mutualité. Exit the Metro and cross the street toward the Seine. The bar is on the right.* Ⓢ *Beers €5-6. Mixed drinks €7-10.* Ⓒ *Open daily 4pm-2am.*

INVALIDES

While there aren't a lot of hopping clubs and bars in this area, there are a few gems that are geared toward the thinky-artsy types than the more party-hardy travelers. Most of the brasseries here stay open until 8 or 9pm (especially in summer, when it stays light outside past 10pm); find them around rue Ste-Dominique. Head to the **Champs de Mars** if you're looking for a free hangout; you'll find it overflowing with revelers playing guitar and bocce, exploring the subtleties of each other's faces (read: PDA), and generally having a grand old time. However, some travelers do report that despite seeing droves of youths drinking in public in this area, such activities are illegal.

LE CONCORDE ATLANTIQUE

CLUB

23 quai Anatole France ☎01 40 56 02 82 www.bateauconcordeatlantique.com

Take a three-story club with themed *soirées*, add copious amounts of booze deals, and stick it right on the Seine. You have just imagined Le Concorde Atlantique. This boat/nightclub keeps going until 4 or 5am. *Soirées* are shamelessly promoted, often with cover charges that include free drinks and the occasional ladies' night. The deals don't end there: the website **www.parisbouge. com** is an invaluable resource here, giving out cheap tickets and drink passes to save travelers as much as 50%.

✦ Ⓜ*Assemblée Nationale, right on the Seine in between Pont de la Concorde and walking bridge Solferino.* Ⓢ *Cover from €10-20, includes (sometimes up to 5) free drinks. Some nights men pay extra €5-10 and must pay online before.* Ⓒ *Open Tu-Sa 8pm-4am (unless it's a special soirée, which occur occasionally on Su).*

O'BRIEN'S

PUB

77 rue Ste-Dominique ☎01 45 51 75 87

This no-fuss, get-drunk Irish pub has landed incongruously in an otherwise posh neighborhood. Clientele tends to be local Parisians rather than Anglophones. Beers are reasonably priced, but most people come for the big-screen TV.

✦ Ⓜ*La Tour-Maubourg. Walk with traffic down bd de la Tour-Maubourg, then turn left onto rue Ste-Dominique.* *i Live music every 2-3 months. Plays all major rugby and soccer games, some others.* Ⓢ *Beer €4-6. Happy hour pints €5.90.* Ⓒ *Open M-F 5pm-2am, Sa 2pm-2am, Su 5pm-2am; opens early on game days. Happy hour M-F 5-8pm.*

CLUB DES POÈTES RESTAURANT, LOUNGE

30 rue de Bourgogne ☎01 47 05 06 03 www.poesie.net

If you want to drink and feel cultured, this restaurant-by-day and poetry-club-by-night is exactly what you're looking for. It brings together an intimate community of literati for supper and sonnets as local actors and singers take to the stage for improv poetry readings from around the world. Despite giving off a slightly intimidating hipster vibe, the crowd is well versed in English and welcomes visitors and travelers to cram in next to them on the long L-shaped table.

⇄ [M]Varenne. Walk towards Pont d'Alexandre III on bd des Invalides, turning right onto rue de Grenelle. Walk 1 block to rue de Bourgogne and turn left. The club is on the right. ℹ Poetry readings M-Sa 10pm. $ Prix-fixe entrée-plat or plat-dessert €10-25. Wine €6 per glass. ⏰ Open for lunch M-F noon-3pm. In the evening arrive between 8-10pm for dinner or drinks. Kitchen open until 10pm. No entry after 10pm.

CHAMPS-ÉLYSÉES

Glam is the name of the game at the trendy, expensive bars and clubs of the 8ème. Dress up and bring some attractive friends or a fat wallet—it's going to be a pricey night out.

👍 **LE QUEEN** CLUB

102 av. des Champs-Élysées ☎01 53 89 08 90 www.queen.fr

Le Queen is a renowned Parisian institution where drag queens, superstars, tourists, and go-go boys get down and dirty to the mainstream rhythms of a 10,000-gigawatt sound system. Open all night, every night, Le Queen has *soirées* for just about every party demographic you can think of, as long as you can make it past the bouncer. Be prepared to show ID to gain entrance to this flashy disco with a light-up dance floor, which features theme nights that includes the occasional gay *soirée*.

⇄ [M]Georges V. ℹ Disco Night on M. Ladies Night on W; no cover for women 11:30pm-1am. Live DJ on F. $ Cover €20; includes 1 drink. Drinks €10. ⏰ Open daily 11:30pm-6am.

LE SHOWCASE CLUB

under Pont Alexandre III, Port des Champs Élysées ☎01 45 61 25 43 www.showcase.fr

One of the most popular clubs with the bohemian bourgeoisie in Paris (a.k.a. kids with money), Le Showcase's limited operation days and even more limited entrance make it nearly impossible to get in without some good-looking friends. To be sure you'll make it in, get on the "guest list" by registering your name for free online, then dance 'til dawn in this dungeon-esque club.

⇄ [M]Champs-Elysées-Clemenceau. ℹ Entrance typically free before midnight. Register for free on their website or Facebook page to be added to the guest list. $ Cover €10-15. Beer €9. Mixed drinks €15. ⏰ Open F-Sa 11pm-dawn.

THE FREEDOM BAR

8 rue de Berri ☎01 53 75 25 50

The Freedom might not have the decor or class of the rest of the neighborhood, but it makes up for it in sheer party spirit (we mean both kinds of "spirit"). Student Night has the cheapest shooters in all of Paris.

⇄ [M]George V. Walk away from the Arc de Triomphe and turn left down rue de Berri. ℹ Student Night on Th. Ladies night F-Sa 11pm-5am. $ Shots €5. Beer €6. Mixed drinks €8-9. Student Night shots €2.50; beer €4. Ladies Night cocktail and shot €6. ⏰ Open M-Th 5pm-2am, F-Sa 5pm-5am, and Su 5pm-2am.

LE SENS UNIQUE WINE BAR

47 rue de Ponthieu ☎01 43 59 76 77

In an area writhing with girls who don't know how to walk in their 5in. stilettos and guys who spend as much time on their hair as their outfit, Le Sens Unique manages to keep it classy—and we mean really classy. A small wine bar with dried vines wrapped over the bar and chalkboards and street signs decorating the walls, this mellow local hideout is almost entirely devoid of tourists. The gentle and bright owner welcomes everyone with open arms to sample hand selected fine wines from his hometown of Périgourdine, in the Bordeaux region of southern France. Although the wines here aren't super cheap and only a few are sold by the glass, the quality of the drinks and the relaxing atmosphere are well worth the price. Be sure to try some of the fresh cheeses and cold meat, too.

*# [M]Franklin D. Roosevelt. Walk up the Champs-Élysées toward the Arc de Triomphe, turn right onto rue La Boétie, then left onto rue de Ponthieu. Or [M]George V. Walk down the Champs-Élysées away from the Arc de Triomphe, turn left onto rue de Berri and right onto rue de Ponthieu. **i** Beaujolais Nouveau 3-day wine tasting event starts the 3rd Th in Nov. $ Wine €4.50-6. ⏰ Open M-F 10am-2am, Sa 4pm-2am. Kitchen open noon-midnight.*

THE BOWLER BAR, RESTAURANT

13 rue d'Artois ☎01 45 61 16 60 www.thebowler.fr

The Bowler's upscale clientele will make you rethink the stereotypical British pub. With (relatively) cheap drinks in the heart of the 8ème it's hard to say no, especially to the weekly Quiz Night or live music. The large interior bar plays sports (tennis, cricket, rugby, and, of course, soccer are the popular ones) as patrons debate whether they are going to continue their night elsewhere or camp out and relax here.

*# [M]St-Philippe du Roule. Walk down rue de la Boétie toward the Champs and turn right onto rue d'Artois. The Bowler is on the left. **i** Live music M 7pm. Quiz Night on Su. $ Beer €6-9. Mixed drinks €9-12. Happy hour beer and mixed drinks €5. Brunch €10. ⏰ Open M-F noon-2am, Sa-Su 1pm-2am. Happy hour M-F 5-7pm, Sa-Su 1pm-2am. Brunch Sa-Su 1-3:30pm.*

CHARLIE BIRDY BAR, RESTAURANT

124 rue de la Boétie ☎01 42 25 18 06 www.charliebirdy.com

This is the most flashy member of the Parisian Charlie Bird chain. Catering to middle-aged Champs locals, this bar tries to foster a club environment (and trust us, it has enough booze to be one), but the booths and barstools draw people from the floor to sit, drink, and attempt to talk over the disco music.

*# [M]Franklin D. Roosevelt. **i** Happy hour drinks ½ price. $ Wine €4.50-6.50. Beer €7.50-9. Mixed drinks €9-12. Salads €11-15. Burgers €13-17. ⏰ Open daily noon-5am. Happy hour M-F 4-8pm.*

BUDDHA-BAR BAR, RESTAURANT

8 rue Boissy d'Anglas ☎01 53 05 90 00 www.buddhabar.com

Apparently too cool for overdone trends like capital letters, buddha-bar is billed as the most glamorous watering hole in the city—Madonna tends to drop by when she's in town. If you're sufficiently attractive, wealthy, or well-connected, you'll be led to one of the two floors of candlelit rooms, where you will be surrounded by the hypnotic "global" rhythms. A two-story Buddha watches over the chic ground-floor restaurant, while the luxurious upstairs lounge caters to those looking to unwind in style with one of the creative mixed drinks. A solid contingent of "atheist drinkers" think buddha is overrated.

*# [M]Madeleine. Find the front of La Madeleine, turn around, and take the angled left onto bd Malesherbes, then take the 1st left onto rue Boissy d'Anglas. **i** No shorts or flip-flops; dress to impress. $ Mixed drinks €17-21. ⏰ Open daily noon-2am.*

OPÉRA AND CANAL ST-MARTIN

The area around [M]**Grands Boulevards** stumbles its way into the daylight hours each morning with the drunkest of the drunk. Unsurprisingly, this is also where many pickpockets and muggers pounce on their inebriated prey, so keep to the major streets and avoid heading to the Metro on back alleys in the 10ème late at night.

CORCORAN'S IRISH PUB, CLUB

23 bd Poissonnière ☎01 40 39 00 16 www.corcorans.fr

You could say Corcoran's is a typical Irish pub, except for the part where it turns into a hoppin' nightclub Thursday-Saturday nights. A flurry of French and English speakers alternately populate the dance floor, so if you're looking to play it smooth in your native tongue, throw back a Guinness (good luck) and party like a rock star at Corcoran's, where you'll find the best of both worlds. Don't show up too sloshed if you want the bouncers to let you in.

⇆ [M]Grands Boulevards. Upon exiting the Metro, look for the green awning. ***i*** *Other locations in the Bastille, St-Michel, and Clichy areas. $ Shots €4. Mixed drinks €8. Beer €6.50-7. Happy hour mixed drinks €6, pints €5. ⏰ Open daily 9am-dawn. Happy hour M-F 5-9pm.*

AU BOUQUET DU NEUVIÈME BAR, CLUB

24 rue St-Lazare ☎01 42 80 11 59 www.facebook.com/lebouquet

On weekdays Au Bouquet du Neuvième is simply a Franco-Italian bistro serving its customers delicious cuisine and playing host to a few football and rugby fans. The story changes on Friday nights, however, when DJs and live bands set up to entertain the droves of just-a-bit-older-than-a-student students letting loose and shaking it to popular hits.

⇆ [M]Notre Dame de Lorette. With your back to Notre Dame de Lorette, turn right and walk a few blocks, then turn right onto rue St Lazare. ***i*** *F students get 20% off drinks. $ Beer €5. Entrées €5.50-6. Plats €8.50-12.50. ⏰ Open M-Th 8am-9pm, F 8am-2am.*

LE BREBANT CAFE, BAR

32 bd Poissonnière ☎01 47 70 01 02

Of all the bars in this concentrated nook around [M]Grands Boulevards, Le Brebant has the privilege of occupying the largest corner of the intersection, thereby outdoing all its neighbors in size and noise. Most visitors listen to the music and watch drunk people from the patio, but inside there is a dance floor fitted with smoke machines and flashing lights to accentuate the booming bass. For those too disoriented to make it down the steps to the dance floor or too drunk to buy another drink, a small dance party can often be spotted on the corner of the street just outside.

⇆ [M]Grands Boulevards. Across from Corcoran's. ***i*** *DJ on F-Sa. $ Happy hour mixed drinks and beer €6. ⏰ Open daily 7pm-6am.*

L'ATMOSPHÈRE BAR

49 rue Lucien Sampaix ☎01 40 38 09 25

L'Atmosphère has the cheapest beer in the 10ème—or at least the cheapest you can find at 1:30am. An older, laid-back crowd sits on the raised terrace overlooking the canal. When they thin out around 1am, 20-somethings flood the place for beer and cocktails and take up the everlasting effort to keep the bar open past closing time.

⇆ [M]Jacques Bonsergent. Walk down bd de Magenta and turn left onto rue Lancry. When you get to the canal, turn left and walk 2-3 blocks; the bar is on the left. ***i*** *Live music some nights. $ Beer €2.50-5. ⏰ Open Tu-F 10am-2am, Sa 2pm-2am, Su 2-9:30pm.*

LE PACHYDERME BAR, RESTAURANT

2 bis bd St-Martin ☎01 42 06 32 56

More of a lounge bar than a party spot, this African-themed joint has statues of elephants and black leather love seats inside and a huge heated terrace outside. We would make some jokes about low lighting and elephants, but it's mean to pick on the overweight.

⇆ [M]Strasbourg St-Denis. 3 blocks toward pl. de la République, on the left. $ Beer €6.80. Mixed drinks €9.70; "Cocktail of the moment" €7. Entrées €14-19. Plats €17-25. ⏰ Open daily noon-1:30am.

ECLIPSE CAFE CLUB, BAR

12 rue du Château d'Eau ☎01 42 00 15 41

The party here depends on the size of the crowd. On a calm night, it's just some local youth drinking on the terrace with the bartenders and listening to music. When it gets packed, tables are moved and dancing gets going, aided by the cheap pints and cocktails.

[M]Jacques Bonsergent. Walk down bd de Magenta toward pl. de la République, turn right on rue de Lancry, and then left on rue du Château d'Eau. The bar is on the left. $ Pints and mixed drinks €5. ⏰ Open daily 6pm-2am.

LE VERRE VOLÉ RESTAURANT, BAR

67 rue Lancry ☎01 48 03 17 34

You'll need a reservation to dine here, but not if you just want to drink. While you won't hang out here all night, this great location on the canal is the perfect spot to mingle with young Parisian hipsters over a glass of one of the restaurant's many wines.

[M]Jacques Bonsergent. Walk down bd de Magenta and turn left onto rue de Lancry; it's just before the canal. $ Wine from €5. Beer €5.50. Entrées €5-6. Plats €10-11. ⏰ Open Tu-Su noon-3:30pm and 6:30-11:30pm.

BASTILLE

Nightlife in the 11ème has long consisted of Anglophones who drink too much and the French who hide from them, but the two groups seem to be warming up to each other a bit. With a few exceptions, **rue de Lappe** and its neighbors offer a big, raucous night on the town dominated by expats and tourists, while establishments along **rue Oberkampf, rue Amelot,** and **rue Thaillandiers** are more eclectic, low-key, and local. All four streets are worth your time, even if you only have one night in the area. **Rue Faubourg St-Antoine,** meanwhile, is a world of its own, dominated by enormous clubs that only let in the well-dressed. The clubs overflow onto the streets, so feel free to hop from one to the next all night—just know that it won't be cheap.

LE BARON ROUGE WINE BAR

1 rue Théophile Roussel ☎01 43 43 14 32

Le Baron Rouge is a lively wine bar with a 45 bottle selection of reds and whites that are all cheap and will leave you saying, "Yes, I'll have another glass." An easy going and young-at-heart crowd gathers here to enjoy several glasses with cheese and laughter.

[M]Ledru-Rollin. Walk south with traffic on av. Ladru-Rollin, then turn left onto rue de Prague. Turn left with traffic onto rue Traversière. i Credit card min. €15. $ Wine €1.50-3.60. ⏰ Open Tu-F 10am-2pm and 5-10pm, Sa 10am-10pm, Su 10am-4pm.

SIFFLEUR DE BALLONS WINE BAR

34 rue de Citeaux ☎01 58 51 14 04 www.lesiffleurdeballons.com

Siffleur de Ballons, a wine bar with a light atmosphere, successfully pulls off the casual, unpretentious vibe that many wine bars attempt and fail to create. The white walls and white bar top keep things bright, especially in the second room, where wine bottles line the shelves floor to ceiling. Siffleur offers 250 bottles of all natural, organic wine accompanied by organic meats, cheeses, and Alsatian jam. The owners here keep close relationships with all of their producers, and there is no stone left unturned in their quest for the best in wine pairing.

[M]Faidherbe-Chaligny. Walk west on rue du Fauberg St-Antoine toward Bastille, then turn left onto rue de Citeaux. The bar is across from L'Ebauchoir. $ Wine €3.50-6. Food €6-14. ⏰ Open Tu-Th 10:30am-3pm and 5:30-10pm, F-Sa 10:30am-3pm and 5:30-11pm.

FAVELA CHIC
BAR, CLUB

18 rue du Faubourg du Temple   ☎01 40 21 38 14 www.favelachic.com

A Franco-Brazilian joint, Favela Chic is light on the Franco and heavy on the brassy Brazilian. Wildly popular with locals, this restaurant-bar-club is covered in palm trees, Mardi Gras masks, and sweaty gyrating bodies.

ⓂRépublique. *Walk down rue du Faubourg du Temple and turn right into the arch at no. 18; the club is on the left.* Ⓢ *Cover F-Sa €10; includes 1 drink. Beer €5.50-6. Mixed drinks €9-10.* ☺ *Open Tu-Th 8pm-2am, F-Sa 8pm-4am.*

LE POP-IN
BAR, ROCK CLUB

105 rue Amelot   ☎01 48 05 56 11 www.popin.fr

Le Pop-In takes the pretension out of hipster and replaces it with booze. Hosting (almost) nightly concerts and open mic nights, this mix of punk rock, Swedish metal, and British pop attracts the dreadlocked and skinny-jeaned.

ⓂSt-Sebastien-Froissart. *i Open mic night on Su. Check website for concerts.* Ⓢ *Beer €2.80-5.50.* ☺ *Open daily 6:30pm-1:30am. Happy hour 6:30-9pm.*

CHEZ ALPHONSE
BAR

12 rue St-Bernard   ☎01 40 09 81 53

You know it's a good time when the owner is hammered. Dark red lights accent a heavy bass from the DJ that cranks out hip-hop, rap, electro, and funk. Parisians come here to enjoy a night among friends, but they will be more than willing to mingle with travelers, too.

ⓂFaidherbe Chaligny. *Walk west on rue du Fauberg St-Antoine and turn right onto rue St-Bernard. i DJs on Th-Su.* Ⓢ *Beers €2.50-3.50. Mixed drinks €7.* ☺ *Open daily noon-2am.*

ZÉRO ZÉRO
BAR

89 rue Amelot   ☎01 49 23 51 00

There is just barely space to turn around in this itsy-bitsy bar that is covered wall to wall with layers of graffiti, stickers, and other vandalistic mediums. The space is so small and so tightly packed, we think there may be a running competition to see who can get the sweatiest and the drunkest by the end of the night. DJs frequent this bar as much as the locals and spin free shows three nights a week.

ⓂSt-Sebastien-Froissart. *Walk south on bd Beaumarchais and turn left onto rue St-Sébastien, then right onto rue Amelot. i DJs on W, Th, Sa.* Ⓢ *Beer €3-4. Mixed drinks €6.50-8.50.* ☺ *Open daily 6pm-2am. Happy hour 6:30-8:30pm.*

WAX
CLUB

15 rue Daval   ☎01 40 21 16 16

Wax is a rare Parisian miracle—a place that is actually fun to dance in and almost free (you have to buy at least one drink to stay, though). Housed in a concrete bunker, the club is packed on the weekends with young locals and tourists. On Tuesdays they host a "soirée groove," making them some of the only people in the world who use the word "groove" unironically.

ⓂBastille. *Take bd Richard Lenoir and turn right onto rue Daval. i Mandatory coat check F-Sa €1.50. "Soirée groove" on Tu. House and techno on Sa-Su.* Ⓢ *Beer €4-6. Mixed drinks €10.* ☺ *Open W-Th 5pm-2am, F-Sa 5pm-5am.*

LE MÉCANIQUE (ONDULATOIRE)
BAR

8 passage Thiéré   ☎01 43 55 16 74 www.myspace.com/lemecanique

Come to Le Mécanique ready to rock because this place is fixin' to roll. A grungy crowd mixes with hard rockers to a serious variety of music, including garage, new wave, metal, and techno. Live concerts and DJs bring crowds to the cavernous basement for light dancing and mouth-to-ear conversation. Although this place may be more suited for the Mohawks, leather jackets, and pierced eyebrows, all types are welcome to party here.

⇄ [M]Bastille. Walk up rue de la Roquette and turn right onto passage Thiéré. Le Mécanique is on the right. $ Beer €4-6. Mixed drinks €7-8. ⏰ Open M-Sa 6pm-2am. Live concerts every night starting between 7:30 and 10pm.

BAZAR EGYPTIEN HOOKAH BAR

29 rue de Lappe ☎01 43 14 04 41

This Egyptian hookah bar is a great place to start the night with cheap drinks, bottles of Kir (€25), and shisha. The terrace is where the students usually hang out, but the interior is made to look like a Bedouin cave (except with strong ventilation to get the smoke out). Lamps, carpets, and North African trinkets provide sparkly distraction while pop music plays in the lounge area, until it suddenly switches to abrasive Middle Eastern music before close.

⇄ [M]Bastille. Take rue de la Roquette and turn right onto rue de Lappe. $ Mixed drinks €4.50-7.50. ⏰ Open daily 4pm-midnight

LE KITSCH BAR

10 rue Oberkampf ☎01 40 21 94 41

This might be the most random collection of objects that we've ever seen on a single wall—particularly the garden gnome next to the tie-dyed porcelain cow next to the Virgin Mary. It is Le Kitsch, after all. Priding itself on the nonsense factor, this bar named its signature drink, a mojito-cum-slushy, Shrek (€7.50). The bar attracts a more laid-back local crowd—or as laid-back as they can be in this weird establishment.

⇄ [M]Oberkampf. $ Beer €3. Mixed drinks €7.50; happy hour mixed drinks €5. ⏰ Open daily 5:30pm-2am. Happy hour 5:30-9pm.

BARRIO LATINO CLUB

46/48 rue du Faubourg St-Antoine ☎01 55 78 84 75 www.buddha-bar.com

Barrio Latino reminds us of a modern remake of *Scarface:* well-dressed clientele, Latin music broken up with house and techno, and tables filled with G-men watching over a raging five-story party. Enthusiastic and aspiring salsa dancers shake it in various corners and on tables (despite security's best efforts to dissuade them). The giant dance floor heats up around 11pm, but you'll pay a lot to get buzzed enough to fit in.

⇄ [M]Bastille. $ Cover Th-Sa €20. Beer €6.50-9. Mixed drinks €12-14. Shooters €6.50. ⏰ Open daily noon-2am.

SOME GIRLS BAR BAR

43 rue de Lappe ☎01 48 06 40 33

No, it's not a strip joint. It's actually a rock-themed bar that proudly plays the Rolling Stones and other bands from the '60s-'90s in a thoroughly confused, kitschy setting of neon lights, leopard skins, and palm trees. Take advantage of the happy hour that lasts until 10pm, then make your way out before another favorite song convinces you to stay.

⇄ [M]Bastille. Walk down rue de la Roquette and turn left onto rue de Lappe. $ Pints €5. Mixed drinks €7-9. Happy hour mixed drinks €5. ⏰ Open M-Sa 9pm-2am. Happy hour 7-10pm.

MONTPARNASSE AND SOUTHERN PARIS

The central area around the Montparnasse Tower and the train station is mostly filled with generic, somewhat inauthentic cafes, but the further you wander from this area, the more likely you are to find some local hotspots. A handful of floating bars litter the eastern end of the Seine near Chinatown, and **Butte-aux-Cailles** has super cheap hippie bars. The absolute highlight for anyone between the ages of 18 and 80 is **Cafe Oz.**

■ BATOFAR
BOAT, BAR, NIGHTCLUB, CONCERT VENUE

Across from 11 quai Francois Mauriac ☎01 53 60 17 00 www.batofar.org

You might feel like T-Pain at this nightclub, which occupies the lowest level of a boat and leads a quadruple life as a nightclub, concert venue, restaurant, and bar. Ideally located on the quiet eastern end of the Seine, the Batofar brings the area alive at night with its live concerts and bangin' DJs. If you're not interested in sweaty dancing and singing and bumpin' 'n' grindin', hit the bar on the breezy top level of the boat, or head for shore and relax on the patio, also known as *La Plage*, where you can enjoy fresh rum punch made with pineapple, oranges, mangos, or cranberries. Locals love this increasingly popular locale as much as the savvy backpackers who know it exists.

❦ ⓂQuai de la Gare. Go to the Seine and down the stairs to the riverbank, then turn right so the river is on your left. Walk about 5min. *i* Happy hour 5-7pm. DJ every night and after concerts. Concerts usually start 7pm or later. Tickets can be bought at the door, usually €3-25. Ⓢ White sangria €5. Punch €6. Mixed drinks €10. Tapas €5. ☒ Open daily noon-late. Patio on the bank (La Plage) open May-Sept noon-1am, brunch on Su. Terrace on the boat open daily 6pm-midnight. Happy hour Oct-Apr 6-8pm; May-Sept 5-7pm. Restaurant open Tu-Sa noon-2:30pm and 7:30-11:30pm.

■ CAFE OZ: DENFERT ROCHEREAU
BAR

3 pl. Denfert-Rochereau ☎01 47 38 76 77 www.cafe-oz.com

Opened in May 2011, the newest and largest iteration of this Australian chain is rumored to have the largest terraces in Paris. After midnight, the older crowd vacates and the massive interior becomes packed with young bodies dancing on tables, stairs, or wherever there is room. Things are kept cool by the drafty 30 ft. ceilings. Despite Oz's size, the palm fronds above the bar and walls covered in boomerangs still make you feel like you're in a packed hut on the beach of Queensland.

❦ ⓂDenfert-Rochereau, behind the RER station. *i* Snacks served until midnight. Ⓢ Shooters €5. Beer €7-8. Mixed drinks €10. Happy hour mixed drinks €6. ☒ Open M-Tu noon-2am, W noon-3am, Th noon-4am, F-Sa noon-5am, Su noon-2am. Happy hour 5-8pm.

L'ENTREPÔT
BAR, RESTAURANT, CINEMA, GALLERY

7-9 rue de Francis de Pressensé ☎01 45 40 07 50 www.lentrepot.fr

L'Entrepôt packs a powerful punch with a bar that hosts four concerts a week, a restaurant with a massive garden, a three-screen cinema, and a constantly changing art gallery. Start with a piping hot traditional French meal at the restaurant, then enjoy a night of funk, rock 'n' roll, jazz, or blues. If that somehow bores you, head to the gallery to contemplate photography, paintings, or sculptures. If you're looking for a tamer night, hit the cinema where you will likely find a film that you can't find anywhere else in Paris. Whatever mood you're in, expect a good time.

❦ ⓂPlaisance. Walk north on rue Raymond Losserand about 3 blocks and turn left onto rue de Francis de Pressensé; l'Entrepôt is on the right. *i* Concerts W-Sa nights. Ⓢ Beer €3-4. Mixed drinks €10-12. Wine €3.50-4. Concert cover charge €5-10. Entrées €7.50-9. Plats €15.50-20.50. Lunch menu €16. Brunch €26. ☒ Bar open M-Sa 9am-1:30am, Su 9-10:30pm. Restaurant open daily noon-2:30pm and 7-11pm. Brunch Su 11:45am-2:45pm. Cinema opens in the afternoon.

LA FOLIE EN TÊTE
BAR

33 rue de la Butte-aux-Cailles ☎01 45 80 65 99 www.lafolieentete.blogspot.com

Decorated with musical instruments, street signs, and newspaper clippings announcing Bob Marley concerts, this reggae bar has one of the cheapest happy hours in the neighborhood. Hipsters, poets, and broke students keep it packed until closing.

❦ ⓂPlace d'Italie. From pl. d'Italie, follow rue Bobillot. Turn right onto rue de la Butte-aux-Cailles and follow it as it turns right. Ⓢ Beer €5-6. Mixed drinks €7. Happy hour mixed drinks €5. ☒ Open M-Sa 5pm-2am, Su 6pm-midnight. Happy hour 5-8pm.

nightlife

SPUTNIK BAR

14-16 rue de la Butte aux Cailles ☎01 45 65 19 82 www.sputnik.fr

Don't expect to find any fur coats, thick accents, or Russians mixing you their best vodka tonics here. Sputnik does, however, manage to attract its own eclectic mix of hipsters, soccer fans, and intellectual locals. While smokers puff away on the quiet terrace, other patrons lounge and swap stories in another corner, and the floaters fall somewhere in between. Find your spot(nik) in the crowd or bop around and see how many social circles you are capable of penetrating.

 # [M]Corvisart. Follow the signs to Butte aux Cailles, south of the Metro stop. i Free Wi-Fi. $ Shots €3. Mixed drinks €8. Happy hour drinks €5. ⏰ Open M-Sa 2pm-2am, Su 4pm-2am.

LE MERLE MOQUER BAR

11 rue de la Butte aux Cailles ☎01 45 65 12 43

Capturing the spirit of the neighborhood with its eclectic mix of color block walls, uneven stools, spray-painted doors, and a rather random selection of art, this bar is a little funky and not at all fussy. The naked lady and her pig friend painted near the door are here to offer you a plastic patio chair and welcome you to the best dance place on the street.

 # [M]Corvisart. Follow the signs to Butte aux Cailles, south of the Metro stop. $ Drinks €4-6. Happy-hour pints €3.50, rum punch €4. ⏰ Open M-Su 5pm-1:30am. Happy hour 5-8pm.

THE BOOTLAGERS SPORTS BAR

73 quai Panhard et Levassor ☎01 44 23 79 75 www.thebootlagers.com

Nothing says "sports bar" like baseball and students. The Bootlagers has several TVs and wall-sized projector playing every American sport, along with some rugby and soccer, and caters to the university students who gather here to drink away their studying sorrows. Photos of Times Square and New York taxis decorate the walls. Don't expect a thumpin' DJ to show up here after the games, though; the apartments upstairs keep this bar pretty hushed later in the evening.

 # [M]Quai de la Port. Go toward the Seine and turn right so the river is on your left. Walk about 8min. i Free Wi-Fi. $ Beer €3-5. Mixed drinks €8. Wine €3-3.50. Happy hour drinks €1-5. Entrées €4-5. Burgers €11-12. Plats €10-18. ⏰ Open M-Sa 10am-11:30pm.

LA DAME CANTON BAR, CONCERT VENUE

Porte de la Gare ☎01 53 61 08 49 www.damedecanton.com

A quirky alternative to all those land-locked watering holes, this pirate-ship-inspired concert venue is a seizure-inducing collection of fishing nets, musical instruments, postmodern takes on the *Mona Lisa*, and small Chinese lamps. The floor slopes, the patrons rock dreds, and the burly bartenders serve Pirate Punch (€3) and cocktails (€7.50) in plastic cups. The view of the Seine is spectacular, and the mix of soul funk, hip hop, and reggae demonstrates excellent taste.

 # [M]Quai de la Gare. i Live concerts Tu-Sa 8:30pm. $ Cover €5-10. Mixed drinks €7.50. ⏰ Open Tu-Th 7pm-2am, F-Sa 7pm-5am.

LE REDLIGHT CLUB

34 rue du Départ ☎01 42 79 85 46 www.leredlight.com

If you love wild clubbing, come to Le Redlight, 'cos it doesn't get much crazier than this. Formerly known as—and sometimes still referred to as—l'Enfer (Hell), Le Redlight has a two-floor dance area that makes you think Hell might be kind of fun. Guys should come dressed up and accompanied by women if possible, since the bouncers are tough, even by Parisian standards.

 # [M]Montparnasse Bienvenue. $ Cover €20; includes 1 drink. Mixed drinks €6-8. ⏰ Open W-Sa midnight-6am, Su midnight-noon.

AUTEUIL, PASSY & BATIGNOLLES

Just like the food, the nightlife in these *arrondissements* tends to be cheaper, younger, and chiller in the 17ème than in the 16ème, where you'll find a bevy of overpriced bars and nightclubs. The farther south you go in the 16ème the more residential and less fun it gets, so we suggest you stick to the more walkable and likeable Batignolles.

🏮 LE BLOC   CAFE, BAR
21 rue Brochant   ☎01 53 11 02 37

This white-walled bar looks plain and boring on the outside but has a fully charged personality that greets you as you walk inside. Walls are decorated with quirky photographs, and there's a nook under the stairs with a cramped but comfortable array of lounge chairs, including a creatively redesigned shopping cart (yes, it is somehow comfortable). Whether you decide to park it there or head to the spacious patio or loft upstairs for a quieter meal, expect to run into a lot of friendly Parisians gathering for their nightly rendezvous.

🚇 ⓂBrochant. *From the Metro, walk straight onto rue Brochant.* **i** *Free Wi-Fi.* ⓈMixed drinks €7. Salads €8-11.50. 🕐 Open daily 8:30am-2am.

L'ENDROIT   BAR, CAFE
74 rue Legendre   ☎01 42 29 50 00

L'Endroit is French for "the place," and this is definitely the place to be. The Parisians who gather here suck down pint-sized mojitos and laugh carelessly over a shared pack of cigarettes. Chowing down on massive burgers accompanied by even more massive salads seems to be a popular activity as well. Although this may not sound too different from any other bar or cafe in the city, L'Endroit has been doing it for 25 years, so they've obviously gotten something right.

🚇 ⓂRome. *Walk north up rue Boursault; the restaurant is on the corner adjacent to the church.* **i** *Brunch Sa-Su 11am-4:30pm.* ⓈMixed drinks €9 and €12. Tapas €8-12. Salads €13.50-17.50. 🕐 Open M-Th 11am-2am, F-Sa 11am-5am, Su 11am-2am.

JAMES JOYCE PUB   BAR
71 bd Gouvion-St-Cyr   ☎01 44 09 70 32 www.kittyosheas.com

The James Joyce Pub is one of only a few truly authentic Irish pubs in Paris. The owner is what one might call a true Joyce fanatic—James Joyce memorabilia lines the walls of the bar, and the majority of the building was commissioned straight from the motherland, including some beautiful stained glass. While the pub attracts mostly an after-work business crowd during the week and gets quieter on the weekends, it's still a great place to chill out and speak English for a while.

🚇 ⓂPorte Maillot. *Exit at bd Gouvion-St-Cyr and walk toward the tall building on the left. The pub is on the right.* ⓈBurgers €14-16.50. Pint €7-7.50. Whiskey and scotch €7-18. 🕐 Open daily 11am-2am. Last call 1:30am. Kitchen open until 11pm.

FROG XVI   BAR
110 bis av. Kleber   ☎01 47 27 88 88 www.frogpubs.com

One of several English Frog pubs across Paris, Frog XVI is the trendier cousin of the more authentic Frog and Rosbif (see **Nightlife,** the Marais). With two levels, modern decor, and a DJ that plays three nights a week, this is the place where you can dance the night away with friends while drinking a homemade micro-brew. The crowd here is a healthy mix of young locals and tourists, which means this place can fill up quickly, so plan your arrival accordingly, especially on a game day.

🚇 ⓂTrocadéro. ⓈBeer €7 per pint, €5 happy hour pint. 🕐 Open daily noon-2am. Happy hour M-F 5:30pm-8pm.

THE HONEST LAWYER
BAR

176 rue de la Pompe   ☎01 45 05 14 23 www.honest-lawyer.com

The happy hour packs this bar, a throwback from the American Prohibition era and the fleet of alcoholic expats it sent to Paris. Cram into the small round tables with your friends if you're not feeling pretentious enough for the rest of the neighborhood.

♯ ⓜVictor Hugo. Walk down av. Victor Hugo away from the Arc de Triomphe and turn left at rue de Longchamp. Go 1 block and turn right onto rue de Pompe; the bar is at the corner with rue de Montespan. Ⓢ Beer €5.50. Happy hour mixed drinks €6. ☼ Open M-F 7:30am-2am, Sa 10am-2am, Su 7:30am-2am. Happy hour daily 5:30-8:30pm.

LA GARE
BAR

19 Chaussée de la Muette   ☎01 42 15 15 31 www.restaurantlagare.com

Once a train station, La Gare is now a trendy bar and favored hang-out spot of the wealthy young locals. Try the heated terrace seating over the old train platforms or warm up by the fire in the inner lounge. If you still have your youth, head out to cheaper, more fun places before midnight (or even 11pm).

♯ ⓜMuette. Ⓢ Wine €5.50. Martinis €5.50. ☼ Open daily noon-2am.

DUPLEX
CLUB

2 bis av. Foch   ☎01 45 00 45 00 www.leduplex.com

Stories of this late-night disco make their way around Paris, and we mean that in an infamous way. The three-story subterranean club plays mostly R&B and hip-hop and stays packed until dawn with young people looking to hook up.

♯ ⓜCharles de Gaulle-Étoile. ½ a block from the Circe. ⓲ Women enter free before midnight on F. Ⓢ Cover (includes 1 drink) Tu-Th €15, F-Sa €20, Su €15. Drinks M €8, Tu-Th €9, F-Sa €11, Su €9. ☼ Open Tu-Su midnight to dawn.

SIR WINSTON
BAR, CLUB

5 rue de Presbourg   ☎01 40 67 17 37

If you want the 16ème experience (note: you don't) put on your best shirt and shoes and head to this dimly lit jazz and lounge bar and slink into the leather chairs. Comfy? Good. Now pay €9 for a beer. For the martini lovers, this place does have €5.50 martinis *du moment*. Fortunately, if you're into drinking martinis, you'll probably be dressed up already.

♯ ⓜKleber. Walk toward the Arc de Triomphe and turn right onto rue de Presbourg. The bar is on your right. Ⓢ Wine €5. Pints €9. ☼ Open daily 9am-4am.

frenchism

If you hear a few familiar words while in Paris, even though you don't speak French, don't be alarmed; the adoption of English words here is both a common and controversial phenomenon. *Le hamburger, le jogging,* and *le weekend* are all words that French-speakers use regularly. As the digital age introduced words like "podcast," "email," and "Wi-Fi," French has struggled to keep up with English in the creation of new terminology. Most French people find it easiest to simply say "podcast" or "Wi-Fi" (pronounced *"wee-fee"*), but French cultural purists feel that this is an outrage. Enlisting French linguists at the Académie Française, nationalists associated with the stubborn Ministry of Culture have started a movement to invent new French words for the influx of new terms. Podcast becomes "*diffusion pour baladeur,*" and Wi-Fi is "*acces sans fil a l'internet.*" It's a valiant crusade, but Wi-Fi is just so much easier to say.

paris

MONTMARTRE

With sex shops and strippers galore, Montmartre can be sketchy at night. But if you look past all the shenanigans, there are a handful of good bars in the area. **Boulevard de Clichy** and the blocks just north of it have fewer tourists, and the local bars here are a blast. Just remember to be careful how much you drink and have a plan for getting home if you plan to stay after the Metro stops running for the night.

LE RENDEZ-VOUS DES AMIS   BAR

23 rue Gabrielle   ☎01 46 06 01 60 www.rdvdesamis.com

You know you're in for a night of debauchery when the owners and bartenders drink more than the customers, pounding shots and beers at random. The customers have the advantage of drinking from "giraffes," which are 3 ft. tall, 3L cylinders from which you pour your own beer. Patrons rock out to house music and occasional live guitar jams. Cigarettes are sold out front on an informal basis, but don't bring your drink outside—the burly but friendly bouncer will have words for you. Don't arrive too drunk, either: the subsequent hike from Ⓜ Abbesses is slightly less challenging than Everest.

‡ Ⓜ Abbesses. Exit the Metro and walk up rue la Vieuville and follow it as it curves right and then left. Continue (literally) up rue Drevet until you reach rue Gabrielle. Ⓢ Beers €2.30-7; pitchers €7. Mixed drinks €6. Giraffes €20. Tapas and snacks €7. Ⓩ Open daily 8am-2am.

L'ESCALE   BAR

32 bis rue des 3 Frères   ☎01 46 06 12 38

Young folk cram around the small tables of this tiny bar, and the owner proudly proclaims on their Facebook page that L'Escale and its strong drinks—for example the pint-sized mojitos (€4.50)—are the number-one enemy of the police. There's generally a guest DJ playing house music on Sunday nights (and you thought Sunday was boring).

‡ Ⓜ Abbesses. Exit the Metro and walk up rue la Vieuville and follow it as it curves right and then left. The bar is straight ahead at the intersection with rue des 3 Frères. Ⓢ Mixed drinks €4.50. Ⓩ Open daily 2pm-2am. Happy hour 4-10pm.

L'EPOQUE   KARAOKE BAR

38 bd de Clichy   ☎01 42 52 36 00

Whether you've got pipes like Adele (you don't) or can't distinguish between a sharp and a flat, you can test your vocal skills at L'Epoque. If you're brave enough to get behind the mic, claim your spot in line quickly, especially on the weekend, as L'Epoque is always packed. With some unusually talented regulars, the competition here gets stiff. But don't be bashful—the whole bar will sing along if you pick a crowd pleaser, and even an €8.50 pint won't stop singers from getting blitzed and joining in.

‡ Ⓜ Pigalle. Cross pl. Pigalle to the far side of bd de Clichy and walk left with the park on the left. ⓲ Credit card min. €15. Ⓢ Beer €5. Mixed drinks €11-13. Ⓩ Open daily 10am-5am.

L'ART SCENIK CAFÉ   BAR

48 bd de Clichy   ☎01 42 57 38 70

The energy is always turned up at L'Art Scenik. With loud music that changes genre every night, drinkers come to swing their hips to salsa, nod their heads to funk, or pump their fists to electro. This is a popular spot for pub crawls in the area and rightfully so, as everyone here is smiling and having a grand ol' time. You can take your drink outside to the patio, but don't leave without taking the time to dance the night away. If there is a soccer game on, expect the place to be packed with crazy fans.

‡ Ⓜ Pigalle. Crossing pl. Pigalle to the far side of bd de Clichy and left with the park on the left. ⓲ Live music once every month. Ⓢ Mixed drinks €8. Pint €6.50, happy hour €3.50. Ⓩ Open Tu-Sa 5pm-5am. Happy hour 5-7pm.

nightlife

THE HARP SPORTS BAR

118 bd de Clichy ☎01 43 87 64 99 http://harpbar.com

Home to the Celtics Supporters Club (no, not Boston—it's a Scottish soccer team), this traditional pub shows live sporting events featuring the team it clearly supports, as displayed by the bright green flag on the ceiling. Famous with expats who have been regulars for years, you can usually stop by The Harp for a relaxing pint, assuming the bar isn't filled with losing fans screaming at the TVs.

⇆ [M]Blanche Sarl. Walk 1 block past the Moulin Rouge. The bar is on the right. $ Beer €4; Guinness €6. Mixed drinks €6. ⏰ Open daily 5pm-2am.

HÉLICE BAR BAR

50 rue d'Orsel ☎01 46 06 24 70

This bar has more of an indie rock scene than most of the clubs and bars in Paris, and is famous for its super cheap beer. The bartenders provide snacks to keep patrons from falling over too fast as they jam to local bands on Thursday nights.

⇆ [M]Abbesses. Walk downhill on rue des Abbesses until you get to rue des Martyrs. Though this is not a straight intersection, keep going as straight as you can onto rue d'Orsel. The bar is on the left. $ Beer pints €3.50-5. Mixed drinks €5. ⏰ Open Tu-Sa 6pm-2am.

LE BEL-AIR BAR

6 rue Germain Pilon ☎01 42 54 92 68 www.myspace.com/lebelair

Everyone is friends with everyone here, so don't start making trouble in this neighborhood, even your auntie and your uncle are at the Bel-Air. This is the local spot where people walk in and make the rounds, greeting friends and pals at every table. Drinkers here enjoy cheap happy hour pints, and the house specialty are candy shots made with Smirnoff and Smartie-like sweets.

⇆ [M]Abbesses. Walk against traffic on rue des Abbesses and turn left onto rue Germain Pilon. $ Mixed drinks €4-7. Happy hour pints €3. ⏰ Open M-Sa 6pm-2am. Happy hour 6-10pm.

CHEZ JULIEN BAR

2 rue Lepic ☎01 42 64 21 20

Drinkers come to Chez Julien for a quiet night of drinks and simple bar food. Posters from the '60s and some old albums decorate the walls, making for a cool, chill vibe. Otherwise, there's not much going on. Come to Chez Julien if you've had too many wild nights in the Red Light District and need a calmer evening to recharge.

⇆ [M]Blanche. Cross pl. Pigalle to the far side of bd de Clichy and walk left with the park on the left; then turn right onto rue Lepic. i "Dead Hour" W 10:30-11pm, €2.50 shots. $ Mixed drinks €7-8. ⏰ Open daily noon-2:30pm and 7pm-midnight.

a whole new world down there

Every street in Paris has an equivalent address in the underground sewer system, equipped with more than 1300 mi. of tunnels, pipelines, and waterways. All the corners within the sewers have street signs that mirror the ones on the surface—perhaps Parisians were preparing for a sunless, underground lifestyle on the off chance they all turned into vampires.

In actuality, the layout is thanks to architect Eugène Belgrand efforts to reduce waste in the growing city. He enlarged the size of the drains, increased the sewer system, and built pipelines that, if stretched out, would run from Paris to Istanbul. Unfortunately, with one stinky problem solved, another arose. Since its construction, several robbers—affectionately nicknamed the "termite gangs"—have attempted to break into banks and shops after digging their way from the sewers into the buildings above.

LE FOURMI   BISTRO, BAR

74 rue des Martyrs   ☎01 42 64 70 35

Le Fourmi has one redeeming quality: the place is huge. At La Fourmi, you can bring a large group of friends; everyone will have a chair to sit on, and you can enjoy the personal space that we know you cherish so dearly. The place has a cool feel, with brass-colored walls, a chandelier made of empty wine bottles, and some mean mojitos.

⚑ ⓂPigalle. Cross pl. Pigalle to the far side of bd de Clichy and walk right with the park on the right.
i Live music once every month. Ⓢ Beer €5.30. Mojito €6.90. ⚅ Open M-Th 6pm-2am, F-Sa 6pm-4am.

BUTTES CHAUMONT & BELLEVILLE

Bars in 19ème and 20ème can be fun and cheap, as the locals are slightly less interested in tourists than in other areas of the city. If you are going to go this far out at night, it's probably best to stick with friends and use a buddy system.

ABRACADABAR   BAR

123 av. Jean Jaurès   ☎01 42 03 18 04 www.abracadabar.fr

Abracadabar brings the magic each night with live music performances; what's even more enchanting is that you won't have to pay a dime to enjoy them. The young local crowd here comes for the rock 'n' roll, reggae, funk, and more. Drinkers who want to enjoy the tunes without busting their eardrums can relax in the front room from the bar and a few tables scattered around a small statue of angelic babies. Otherwise most people can be found outside enjoying a smoke and some quieter conversation.

⚑ ⓂLaumière or ⓂOurcq. From both Metro stations, follow av. Jean Jaurès as it gets wider and the lanes divide. Ⓢ Beer €3.50-7. Mixed drinks €7. Concerts free. ⚅ Open daily 6pm-5am.

LOU PASCALOU   BAR, CAFÉ

14 rue des Panoyaux   ☎01 46 36 78 10 www.cafe-loupascalou.com

Definitely one of the local favorites in this area, Lou Pascalou will almost certainly be more crowded than all of its neighbors. Parisians come here to enjoy a warm evening on the large patio or weekly events like concerts, improv shows, jam sessions, photo exhibitions, and more. The tiled mosaic yellow floors and walls are brightened by collage paintings of guitarists and an energetic crowd.

⚑ ⓂMénilmontant. Walk south on bd de Ménilmontant and turn left onto rue des Panoyaux. Lou Pascalou is around the corner on the right. Ⓢ Beer €3-5. Mixed drinks €5-7. ⚅ Open daily 9am-2am.

ROSA BONHEUR   BAR, GLBT

2 av. de la Cascade   ☎01 42 00 00 45 www.rosabonheur.fr

If there is one place in this neighborhood that we recommend you start your night, it's Rosa Bonheur. This bistro bar is located within the confines of the Parc Buttes Chaumont, and is right near the Metro. Now that we have security out of the way (thank you, bouncers), it's also in an adorable, almost colonial-style building that emerges from the trees of the park. Rosa hosts lots of community service and charity events for GLBT rights and environmental awareness as well as Paris's *Silence de Danse*, where you put on headphones, dance, and look really funny.

⚑ ⓂBotzaris. Ⓢ Shots €4. Beer €5. Mixed drinks €9. ⚅ Open W-Su noon-midnight. Last entry 11pm.

OURCQ   BRASSERIE, TEA HOUSE

68 quai de la Loire   ☎01 42 40 12 26

Adjust your sense of "nightlife" to more of a "happy hour" and come here during the day (after a visit to the Cité des Sciences et de L'Industrie, for example). The drinks are cheap and the brasserie doubles as a tea house with books and board games.

⚑ ⓂLaumière. Ⓢ Wine €2-3. Beer €2.50-4. Mixed drinks €5. Ⓢ Open W-Th 3pm-midnight, F-Sa 3pm-2am, Su 3-10pm.

arts and culture

The question "What is art?" will inevitably lead to a debate that involves a list of thousands of possible answers. While you'll no doubt trudge through a museum or two, seeing live music, dance, theater, or cabaret will clue you in to what constantly molds and shapes French culture. A trip to the Opéra Garnier, comic relief at the Odéon Théâtre, or late-night wining and dining at the Moulin Rouge are all possibilities for total cultural immersion and will leave you with more memories than that one night on the Mouffetard. If this sounds boring to you (hopefully it doesn't, but we cater to all tastes), you'll be pleased to know that Paris's concerts can get just as rowdy as its clubs. You can see everything from Doors tribute bands to obscure French hip-hop (only the intrepid type should try this). Especially for those under 26, tickets can be absurdly cheap wherever you choose to attend. Whether you have a solid grasp of French or are a novice who just laughs along with everyone else, you'll definitely leave feeling a bit more cultured.

THEATER

Theater in Paris can be difficult to grasp. Both comedies and tragedies are performed in ruthlessly quick French, and you'll often learn as much about what's going on from audience reactions as you will from what you see and hear. The theater at **Odéon** offers a respite from the confusion if you happen to speak German or Spanish (or prefer to read French subtitles). Thankfully for those under 26, you'll be paying less than the price of a meal or movie ticket for a show that is infinitely more sophisticated than watching *X-Men* dubbed in French.

ODÉON THÉÂTRE DE L'EUROPE LATIN QUARTER AND ST-GERMAIN

2 rue Corneille ☎01 44 85 40 40 www.theatre-odeon.fr

The Odéon is a classically beautiful theater: gold lines the mezzanine and muted red upholstery covers the chairs. Many plays are performed in foreign languages with French translations shown above on a screen. Despite the fact that this is the mecca of Parisian theater, the prices are stunningly reasonable and standing tickets are dirt cheap. The under-26 crowd can score the luxury of a seat for the same price, so save your young legs—watching foreign performances of *Measure for Measure* or *La Casa de Fuerza* takes enough energy already.

 # [M]Odéon. i Limited number of rush tickets available night of the show. [$] Shows €10-32, under 26 €6-16. Rush tickets €6. ⏰ Performances generally M-Sa 8pm, Su 3pm.

THÉÂTRE DE LA VILLE CHÂTELET-LES HALLES

2 pl. du Châtelet ☎01 42 74 22 77 www.theatredelaville-paris.com

Since the '80s, the Théâtre de la Ville has become a major outlet for avant-garde dance, and it's been attracting art students ever since. One recent show was entitled "Walking next to our shoes…intoxicated by strawberries and cream, we enter continents without knocking." An open mind is a must.

 # [M]Châtelet. Walk down rue de Rivoli toward Hôtel de Ville. [$] Tickets €24, under 30 €13. ⏰ Box office open M 11am-7pm, Tu-Sa 11am-8pm.

THÉÂTRE DU CHÂTELET CHÂTELET-LES HALLES

1 pl. du Châtelet ☎01 40 28 28 40 www.chatelet-theatre.com

A staple of the first *arrondissement* since 1862, the majestic Théâtre du Châtelet is an easy place to find entertainment in Paris (we know, there's hardly anything to do in this city). The Châtelet hosts operas, ballets, and a variety of other musical performances, from the Orchestra National de France to Bobby McFerrin.

 # [M]Châtelet. Walk down rue St-Denis; the theater is on the right. [$] Tickets from €10. Last-minute discounts if shows haven't sold out. Under 28, 65 and older, and unemployed discounts available for some shows. ⏰ Box office open daily 2:30-7pm, open 1hr. before show.

LE VIEUX COLOMBIER

LATIN QUARTER AND ST-GERMAIN

21 rue du Vieux Colombier   ☎01 44 39 87 00   http://vieux.colombier.free.fr

Located in one of Paris's snobbiest neighborhoods, Le Vieux Colombier almost closed in the 1970s; the city brought it back in 1986 and classified it as a historical monument. It now hosts a wide range of plays, but most nights are basically just actors and directors talking about their lives, which ends up surprisingly similar to stand-up comedy. Plays typically fall on the left end of the political spectrum, as the upper-class clientele ironically takes a liking to plays on social welfare *(La Pluie d'été)* or the failure of the family unit *(La Noce)*.

✢ Ⓜ*St-Sulpice.* Ⓢ *Tickets €26-39, under 26 €12.* ☒ *Shows W-Sa 7-8pm, Su 4pm.*

CABARET

🗺 LE LAPIN AGILE

MONTMARTRE

22 rue des Saules   ☎01 46 06 85 87   www.au-lapin-agile.com

Halfway up a steep, cobblestoned hill that American tourists describe as "just like San Francisco," Le Lapin Agile has been providing savvy Parisians and tourists with music, dance, and theater since the late 19th century. The tiny theater was a hotspot of the 20th-century bohemian art scene—Picasso and Max Jacob are on the list of people who cabareted here.

✢ Ⓜ*Lamarck-Coulaincourt. Follow rue St-Vincent to rue des Saules.* Ⓢ *Tickets €24, students under 26 €17; includes 1 drink. Drinks €6-7.* ☒ *Shows Tu-Su 9pm-2am.*

BAL DU MOULIN ROUGE

MONTMARTRE

82 bd de Clichy   ☎01 53 09 82 82   www.moulin-rouge.com

Ever since Christina and Co.'s music video, the only thing people associate with the Moulin Rouge is that universal question, *"Voulez-vous coucher avec moi?"* But the world-famous home of the can-can isn't just about sex; it's also about glam and glitz. Since its opening in 1889, the Moulin Rouge has hosted international superstars like Ella Fitzgerald and Johnny Rey, and it now welcomes a fair crowd of tourists for an evening of sequins, tassels, and skin. The shows remain risqué, and the tickets prohibitively expensive. The late show is cheaper, but be prepared to stand if it's a busy night.

✢ Ⓜ*Blanche Sarl.* 𝒊 *Elegant attire required; no shorts, sneakers, or sportswear.* Ⓢ *9pm show €102, 11pm show €92; includes ½-bottle of champagne. 7pm dinner and 9pm show €150-180. Occasional lunch shows €100-130; call for more info.* ☒ *Dinner daily 7pm. Shows daily 9 and 11pm.*

CAVEAU DE LA RÉPUBLIQUE

THE MARAIS

1 bd St-Martin   ☎01 42 78 44 45   www.caveau.fr

It's mostly Parisians at this 100-year-old venue for political satire, and understandably so—the comedians are ruthlessly witty and speak quickly. If you don't really speak French and think Sarkozy is a cool guy, you'll probably find the *tour de champs*—made up of six separate comedy and song acts—excruciatingly long, and not very funny.

✢ Ⓜ*République.* 𝒊 *Tickets sold up to 6 days in advance.* Ⓢ *Tickets Tu-Th €32, students €15; F-Su €39/19.* ☒ *Box office open M noon-6pm, Tu-Sa noon-7pm, Su noon-4pm. Shows from mid-Aug to June Tu-Sa 8:30pm, Su 3:30pm.*

CINEMA

The French love movies. They go to the cinema almost every week, and conversations are peppered with references to local art films and box-office hits. Hit up *La Fête du Cinéma* in June, when patrons pay for one full-price ticket and only €3 for each additional movie; also keep an eye out for the *Palme d'Or*, which is almost as prestigious as the Best Picture Oscar. Paris has cinemas on almost every corner, but some notable ones include **La Pagode** and **L'Arelquin.** Anglophones should look for "VO" when selecting English-language films, as they are in *version originale.*

arts and culture

L'ARLEQUIN

LATIN QUARTER AND ST-GERMAIN

76 rue de Rennes   ☎01 45 44 28 80

A proud revival theater, L'Arlequin mixes modern French films with selections from a pool of international award-winners. Three films are featured each week, undoubtedly decreasing the prevalence of adolescent movie-hopping. Some films are in English, but the vast majority are in French.

⚑ ⓂSt-Sulpice. Ⓢ *Full price €9.50; M-Th students, under 18, and over 60 €7; F-Su under 18 €7.*

CINÉMATHÈQUE FRANÇAISE

BASTILLE

51 rue de Bercy   ☎01 71 19 33 33 www.cinematheque.fr

Though it's had some problems settling down (it's moved over five times, most recently in 2005), the Cinémathèque Française is committed to sustaining film culture. A must-see for film buffs, the theater screens four to five classics, near-classics, or soon-to-be classics per day; foreign selections are usually subtitled. The cinema also features multiple movie-related exhibits, which include over 1000 costumes and objects from the past and present world of film.

⚑ ⓂBercy. Ⓢ *€7, ages 18-26 and seniors €5, under 18 €4. ☼ Ticket window open M from noon to last showing, W-Sa from noon to last showing, Su from 10am to last showing. Exhibits open M noon-7pm, W-Sa noon-7pm, Su 10am-8pm.*

ACTION CHRISTINE

LATIN QUARTER AND ST-GERMAIN

4 rue Christine   ☎01 43 33 85 78 www.actioncinemas.com

This small theater plays American flicks from the 1930s to the '70s, like *African Queen, Bedlam,* and (of course) *King Kong.* This is a nice way to escape the heat, but if you want to escape tourists, try the other location entitled *Le Desperado* (23 rue des Écoles ☎01 43 25 72 07).

⚑ ⓂOdéon. Follow rue de L'Éperon and turn right onto rue St-André des Arts. Turn right onto rue Grands Augustins and then left onto rue Christine. *i Films in English with French subtitles. Ⓢ €8, under 20 €6. ☼ Shows 2-10pm.*

GAUMONT OPÉRA

CHÂTELET LES-HALLES

38 bd des Italiens   ☎0 892 696 696 www.cinemagaumont.com

Gaumont Opéra is one of 13 AMC-style cinemas in Paris, but this one is the most centrally located. Catch up on the biggest American blockbusters or practice your French by reading the subtitles.

⚑ ⓂOpéra. Walk east on bd des Capucines, which turns into bd des Italiens. *i Le Pass is a €20 per month annual card that allows unlimited entrance to movies and allows you to bring a friend who will pay just €6 for their ticket. Ⓢ Tickets €10.70, students €8.10. ☼ Open daily 10am-last showing, usually midnight.*

MUSIC

You can find live music in almost any bar, club, or boat on the Seine, but for true venues that make the House of Blues look tame, head to the party centers of Montmartre and Bastille. Any band that's worth seeing comes to Paris, and if you happen to be around during the summer, these concerts are popular with backpackers and local groupies.

ELYSÉE MONTMARTRE

MONTMARTRE

72 bd Rochechouart   ☎01 44 92 45 36 www.elyseemontmartre.com

Following a worryingly common trend among Montmartre venues, this concert hall burned down in March 2011 but was reopened in early 2012. Famous since 1807 and known to Anglophones for the Roots's song *You Got Me*, this concert hall has hosted the likes of David Bowie, Counting Crows (they recorded their debut album here), and Pendulum. Boxing matches are also held here when the rockers aren't around.

⚑ ⓂAnvers. Ⓢ *Tickets €14-45. ☼ Opens at 11:30pm for all shows.*

LE BATACLAN BASTILLE

50 bd Voltaire ☎01 43 14 00 30 www.le-bataclan.com

In French, *bataclan* is slang for "stuff" or "junk." In French music culture, Bataclan means a packed 1500-person Chinese pagoda that hosts alternative rock bands like Oasis, Blur, Jeff Buckley, and MGMT. The craziest venue in Bastille, Le Bataclan attracts a more local crowd since, for some reason, the French fall in love with more obscure bands (who are usually cheaper than those playing at Elysée Montmartre).

⚐ [M]Oberkampf. [S] Tickets start at €15. ⏰ Open Sept-July.

LA CIGALE MONTMARTRE

120 bd Rochechouart ☎01 49 25 81 75 www.lacigale.fr

La Cigale is a historic stop for most contemporary music tours. Expect Doors tribute bands, lesser known artists like Ziggy Marley, or French rock and hip-hop groups you haven't heard of. Prices are often lower than larger venues and attract locals instead of travelers, but don't rule out a mob of tourists when they hear that the Red Hot Chili Peppers are making an appearance.

⚐ [M]Pigalle. ℹ Reserve online. [S] Tickets generally €20-35.

POINT EPHÉMÈRE OPÉRA AND CANAL ST-MARTIN

200 quai de Valmy ☎01 40 34 02 48 www.pointephemere.org

Point Ephémère tends to attract the tattooed crowd that thinks black is the new green and smokes to be ironic. Bringing in lesser-known bands from France, Belgium, the UK, the US, and elsewhere, young people crowd the 300 person concert hall four or five days a week. And because in Paris it's not cool unless it's artsy, outside the concert hall is a bar, restaurant, and art expo space, with artists' residences upstairs.

⚐ [M]Louis Blanc. Walk down rue Louis Blanc toward the canal. Entrance is on the canal side, not the street. ℹ Buy tickets at the box office inside Point Ephémère in advance, online, or at the door. Don't walk back alone after dark. [S] Concerts €10-16. Lunch menus €10 and €18. Dinner à la carte. ⏰ Bar open M-Sa noon-2am, Su 1-9pm. Restaurant open daily noon-2:30pm, 8-11pm. Brunch Sa and Su until 4pm.

OPERA AND DANCE

There's more to opera in Paris than *The Phantom of the Opera* would have you believe. Performances usually have more singing than they do public murders. You can go black tie, but leave the white mask at home.

PALAIS GARNIER (OPÉRA GARNIER) OPÉRA AND CANAL ST-MARTIN

pl. de l'Opéra ☎08 92 89 90 90 www.operadeparis.fr

You can tour it during the day, but going at night is a whole different ball game. The chandeliers dim, the stage lights up, and you are thrown back to the *fin de siècle* with ballet performances ranging from Tchaikovsky's traditional *Swan Lake* to a tribute to Jerome Robbins of *West Side Story*. Although the Opéra Garnier confusingly no longer performs operas, its ballets, recitals, chamber music concerts, and choral performances still draw crowds who come to behold the beauty of both the building and the music.

⚐ [M]Opéra. ℹ Tickets usually available 2 weeks before the show. Rush tickets go on sale 1hr. before show. [S] Tickets generally €7-160. ⏰ Box office open M-Sa 10:30am-6:30pm.

OPÉRA BASTILLE BASTILLE

pl. de la Bastille ☎08 92 89 90 90 www.operadeparis.fr

Although considered Opéra Garnier's "ugly" other half, the Opéra Bastille has been the primary home of the Paris Opera since 1989. Matching its tiered glass exterior and geometric interior, the Opéra Bastille puts on classical pieces with a modern spin—there may not be gilded columns, but the breathtaking performances more than compensate. The 2013 season will include productions of Wagner's *Rheingold, Die Walküre,* and *Götterdämmerung* as well as Amilcare's *La Gioconda.*

✈ ⓂBastille. *i Tickets can be purchased online, by mail, by phone, or in person. Rush tickets 15min. before show for students under 25 and seniors. ⓈTickets €5-180. 🕐 Box office open M-Sa 10:30am-6:30pm.*

OPÉRA COMIQUE
CHÂTELET-LES HALLES

5 rue Favart
☎01 42 44 45 46 www.opera-comique.com

Opéra Comique is opera lite for drama dieters. The genre of opera here breaks up the singing with spoken drama, giving your ears much needed time-outs from all that musical trilling. Founded in 1714 to give theater-goers an alternative to the predominantly Italian operas of the time, this company has produced operas composed by Berlioz and Bizet and also premiered Debussy's only opera. ✈ ⓂRichelieu-Drouot. *Walk down the bd des Italiens and turn left onto rue Favart. ⓈTickets €6-115. Cheapest tickets are limited visibility and are usually available until the show starts. 15% discount sometimes available for last-minute tickets. 🕐 Box office open M-Sa 11am-7pm, Su 11am-5pm.*

journées du patrimoine

The third weekend of September in Paris is the annual celebration of European Heritage Days when public and private heritage sites open their doors to the public. Get an exclusive look at the Élysée Palace (the White House of France) and the Sénat (French Parliament), plus a number of embassies, ministries, and even backstage at some theatres. Public sites are free, but private destinations may charge a small fee.

paris

shopping

"Shopping" and "Paris" are almost synonymous. But the excessive wealth of the Champs-Élysées and Île St-Louis are not for the faint of heart—they're for the rich. The many antiques, rare books, and tempting tourist traps you find across the city could easily empty pockets. No one likes credit card debt, so we recommend the vintage shops and quirky boutiques in the youthful Marais and Bastille areas. Happily, thrift stores in Paris are the anti-Salvation Army—good-as-new Oscar de la Renta and Chanel are drastically marked down to more manageable prices. Despite the snobby *maitre d*'s and constant critiques of American foreign policy, the French are as fascinated by US culture as the US is by theirs. Perhaps because of this, Paris has a higher concentration of jazz music stores and vintage record shops than most American cities. If you take your music like you take your men (retro and coated in vinyl), then you'll be right at home.

BOOKS

The French love reading almost as much as they love film, museums, and art. Some of the best insights into why the French put autodidacts on a pedestal can be seen in these stores. Be sure to check out the most famous of the city's bookstores, **Shakespeare and Co.**

📖 ABBEY BOOKSHOP
LATIN QUARTER AND ST-GERMAIN

29 rue de la Parcheminerie
☎01 46 33 16 24 www.alevdesign.com/abbey

Clear your afternoon if you're going to Abbey Bookshop—you'll need the time. Set in a back alley, the sheer number of books is a bit overwhelming, whether they're shelved or stacked on the floor. This Canadian-owned shop probably has what you're looking for, and if not, they'll order it for you. Plus, they carry *Let's Go*—they've obviously got the right idea.

✈ ⓂCluny-La Sorbonne. Follow rue Bouteberie and turn left onto rue de la Parcheminerie. *i* Books in English and other languages available. 🕐 Open M-Sa 10am-7pm.

🞖 GIBERT JEUNE   LATIN QUARTER AND ST-GERMAIN
pl. St-Michel   ☎01 56 81 22 www.gibertjeune.fr

If you're studying abroad in Paris, this is probably where you'll want to buy your textbooks—Gibert Jeune carries over 300,000 titles. By the time you're through shopping here, you'll look like a real *savant parisien.* And it's air-conditioned, which can be a welcome change during the Parisian summer.

✈ ⓂSt-Michel. 🕐 Open M-Sa 9:30am-7:30pm.

🞖 L'HARMATTAN   LATIN QUARTER AND ST-GERMAIN
16, 21, 21 bis, 24, and 25 rue des Ecoles   ☎01 46 34 13 71 www.harmatheque.com

Doubling as a specialty bookstore and its own publisher, L'Harmattan has a wide range of genres, though none are in English. There are a number of stores all in the Latin Quarter, each one with a different theme or specialty, like the *Librairie Internationale* (16), *Librairie Sciences Humaines* (21 bis), and *La Boutique de l'Histoire* (24). There is also a section with a selection of films from the US, England, China, and Africa, among others.

✈ ⓂCluny-La Sorbonne. Walk with traffic down bd St-Germain, turn right onto rue St-Jacques, then turn left onto rue des Écoles. *i* 9 locations in Paris each with a different specialty all in the Latin Quarter and St-Germain. 🕐 Open Tu-Sa 10am-12:30pm and 1:30-7pm.

🞖 SHAKESPEARE AND CO.   LATIN QUARTER AND ST-GERMAIN
37 rue de la Bûcherie   ☎01 43 25 40 93 www.shakespeareandcompany.com

See **Sights**.

✈ ⓂSt-Michel. Take quai de Montebello toward Notre Dame and turn right onto rue St-Jacques. Rue de la Bûcherie is on the left. 🕐 Open daily 10am-11pm.

POP CULTURE SHOP   BASTILLE
23 rue Keller   ☎01 43 55 34 68 www.myspace.com/popcultureshop

Pop Culture Shop is focused on a specific kind of pop culture: comic books. Shelves upon shelves of comic books make this a geek's gold mine in Bastille's shopping district. The shop is only a few years old, but the owner's collection has been in the works for many more. Find all your Batman and Green Lantern classics as well as some less mainstream names.

✈ ⓂBastille. Walk down rue de la Roquette and turn right onto rue Keller. ⑤ C3PO action figure €32. The Avengers from €4. 🕐 Open M 2-7:30pm, Tu-Sa 11am-7:30pm.

SAN FRANCISCO BOOK CO.   LATIN QUARTER AND ST-GERMAIN
17 rue Monsieur le Prince   ☎01 43 29 15 70 www.sanfranciscobooksparis.com

San Francisco Book Co. is a quaint little English-language bookshop filled floor to ceiling with used books. Find some contemporary fiction or mysteries, or ask the gentle owner from Lincoln, Nebraska, about his more rare finds. You may not guess that among the Jodi Picoult novels and Michelin travel guides lie first edition copies of James Joyce's *Ulysses* or prints of Latin classics from the 17th century.

✈ ⓂOdéon. From the intersection, walk down rue Dupuytren. Turn left at the end of the street onto rue Monsieur le Prince. 🕐 Open M-Sa 11am-9pm, Su 2-7:30pm.

LADY LONG SOLO   BASTILLE
38 rue Keller   ☎09 52 73 81 53 www.ladylongsolo.com

Offering an assortment of counter-cultural books that range from anti-colonial diatribes to ⬛**The Communist Manifesto,** Lady Long Solo stocks all form of left-leaning print, including guides to the wonders of medical marijuana. Thank Marx and his ideas of price controls, since books here are some of the cheapest in the city.

✈ ⓂBastille. Follow rue de la Roquette until rue Keller. ⑤ Books as low as €2. 🕐 Open daily 2-7pm.

LES MOTS À LA BOUCHE   THE MARAIS

6 rue Ste-Croix de la Bretonnerie   ☎01 42 78 88 30 www.motsbouche.com

Logically located in the Marais, this two-story bookstore offers mostly GLBT literature, photography, magazines, and art, with everything from Proust to guides on lesbian lovemaking. Straight guys could probably learn a few pointers from that last one, too. The international DVD collection is somewhat hidden in the corner of the bottom level (€7-25); titles range from the artistic to the pornographic.

⚨ ⓂHôtel de Ville. *Take a left onto rue Vieille du Temple and a left onto rue Ste-Croix de la Bretonnerie.* 🕭 *Open M-Sa 11am-11pm, Su 1-9pm.*

CLOTHING

Parisians know how to dress well. It's in their blood. If you want to dress like them, you don't have to drain your bank account—or as they say in French, *"fais chauffer ta carte bleu"* ("heat up your credit card"). **Galeries Lafayette** is the French equivalent of Macy's and will save you time and money, not to mention the embarrassing experience of being asked to leave Louis V. For everything vintage, from pre-WWII garb to totally radical Jeff Spicoli get-ups, head to the Marais and Bastille. **Les Halles** are also a mega complex of stores that sell everything from clothing to music and provide all that your average supermall has to offer.

📓 **FREE 'P' STAR**   THE MARAIS

8 rue Ste-Croix de la Bretonnerie   ☎01 42 76 03 72 www.freepstar.com

Enter as Plain Jane and leave a star—from the '80s or '90s, that is. Choose from a wide selection of vintage dresses (€20), velvet blazers (€40), boots (€30), and military-style jackets (€5) that all seem like a good idea when surrounded by other antiquated pieces, but require some balls to be worn out in the open. Dig around the €10 jean pile and €3 bin for ripped jeans that died out with Kurt Cobain.

⚨ ⓂHôtel de Ville. *Follow rue de Renard and turn right onto rue St-Merri, which becomes rue Ste-Croix de la Bretonnerie.* ***i*** *There are 2 other locations at 61 rue de la Verrerie (☎01 42 78 076) and 20 rue de Rivoli.* ⑤ *Credit card min. €20.* 🕭 *Open daily noon-10pm.*

---

six ways to dress french

Although Paris is known to be the world's most fashion-conscious city, individuality rarely rears its head. Blending in with the locals means keeping your day-glo American Apparel tights at home and doing as the Parisians do.

- **THE FUR COAT.** The concept of animal cruelty seems to be ignored in Parisian fashion; practically everyone wears a woodland creature at some point during the winter season.

- **THE SCARF.** It's unclear whether Parisians use the *écharpe* as a mere fashion statement, or if they're just morbidly afraid of wind.

- **THE WEDGE HEELS.** Called *escarpin*, the pump isn't just for 30-something cougars dressing too young for their age. High heels are a defining staple in a woman's daily outfit, and even prepubescent Parisian Lolitas sport them.

- **THE NONDESCRIPT LEATHER BAG.** If your forearm isn't raised and your fingers aren't ready to snap at a moment's notice, get out of town.

- **OXFORD LACE-UP SHOES.** In the city where Hemingway began *A Farewell to Arms*, it's not really surprising that the choice of footwear would be equally intellectual.

- **THE PERPETUAL FROWN.** Because being happy is *très* tacky.

paris

SOBRAL
LES ÎLES

79 rue St-Louis-en-l'Île   ☎01 43 25 80 10 www.sobraldesign.fr

Brazilian artist Sobral is inspired by nature and makes all of his products with natural elements. Tiny Eiffel Towers, bangle bracelets, and elaborate necklaces are all made from natural resin infused with colors and objects. The prices here may be a bit out of reach, but it's a fun place to window shop. After all, Sobral only has three locations outside of Brazil, and this is one of them.

🚇 ⓂPont Marie. Walk across the bridge and continue straight, then turn right onto rue St-Louis-en-l'Île. Ⓢ Eiffel Tower earrings €25. Mirrors from €110. 🕐 Open daily 11am-7:30pm.

LE GRAIN DE SABLE
LES ÎLES

79 rue St-Louis-en-l'Île   ☎01 46 33 67 27 www.legraindesable.fr

The women here craft handmade, Kentucky Derby-worthy hats at a table right in the middle of the shop. Tight budgets may be better suited to splurge on Italian leather bags (from €34), a nice leather watchband (€28), or some playful polkadot sunglasses (€10).

🚇 ⓂPont Marie. Walk across the bridge and continue straight, then turn right onto rue St-Louis-en-l'Île. Ⓢ Hats €30-155. 🕐 Open M 11am-7pm, Tu 3-7pm, W-Su 11am-7pm.

GALERIES LAFAYETTE
MONTPARNASSE AND SOUTHERN PARIS

40 bd Haussmann   ☎01 42 82 34 56 www.galerieslafayette.com

While Galeries Lafayette has your acronymic clothing brands for men and women, their own brand sells for nearly 60% of the price. For guys who can't quite rock deep V-necks and three-quarter length pants, come here for more subdued button-ups.

🚇 ⓂChaussée d'Antin-La Fayette. 🕐 Open M-W 9:30am-8pm, Th 9:30am-9pm, F-Sa 9:30am-8pm.

FORUM DES HALLES
CHÂTELET-LES HALLES

Les Halles   ☎01 44 76 96 56 www.forumdeshalles.com

Like most of Paris's monuments, the history of Les Halles is closely tied to the whims of French royalty and, later on, politicians. Descend into the pits of one of Paris's storied historical sites to discover its bastard American child: a 200-boutique shopping mall, three movie theaters, the Gap, H&M, and Franck Provost.

🚇 ⓂChâtelet-Les Halles. 🕐 Open M-Sa 10am-8pm.

PRINTEMPS HAUSSMANN
OPÉRA AND CANAL ST-MARTIN

64 bd Haussmann   ☎01 42 82 50 00 www.printemps.com

Founded in 1865, this *grand magasin* has over 44,000 sq. m of space and brands from bargain basement to luxury. While the prices are slightly higher than other malls, you get the added benefit of shopping in a historical site and being seen among semi-fashion conscious Parisians.

🚇 ⓂHavre-Caumartin. 🕐 Open M-W 9:35am-8pm, Th 9:35am-10pm, F-Sa 9:35am-8pm.

VINTAGE

🏷 COME ON EILEEN
BASTILLE

16-18 rue des Taillandiers   ☎01 43 38 12 11

This vintage paradise has a plethora of options for the trendy and the hipster. With shiny shoes of the Dorothy variety and dresses appropriate for Halloween, this little shop has costume items scattered among the everyday pieces.

🚇 ⓂVoltaire or ⓂBastille. Walk up rue de la Roquette; rue des Taillandiers is about halfway between the 2 stops. Ⓢ Prices start at €10. 🕐 Open M 11am-8:30pm, Tu 2-8:30pm, W-Th 11am-8:30pm, F 11am-7pm, Su 2-8pm.

🏷 MAMIE SHOP
OPÉRA

73 rue de Rochechouart   ☎01 42 82 09 98

Right next door to Mamie Blue, Mamie Shop offers a bigger selection and a little more flair. The shop feels a bit like Willy Wonka's version of a clothing store, with spaces narrow enough for just one person to fit at a time but with so many rooms and clothing you could get lost. Sadly there are no glass elevators for sale, just some interesting articles of clothing. Mamie Blue specializes in clothing from the '20s-'70s, and we're thinking the prices might be a little over-adjusted for inflation. ⚐ Ⓜ*Anvers or Barbès. From bd de Rochechouart, turn onto rue de Rochechouart, which is located between the 2 Metro stops.* **i** *Will tailor clothing.* Ⓢ *Men's jackets from €30. Dresses €40-175.* ⚑ *Open M 3-8pm, Tu-Sa 11am-1:30pm and 3-8pm.*

MAMIE BLUE   OPÉRA
69 rue de Rochechouart   ☎01 42 81 10 42 www.mamie-vintage.com
Mamie Blue takes shoppers back to the '20s with its diverse and thorough collection of vintage clothes. You can find everything here, from men's naval jackets to women's flapper dresses. ⚐ Ⓜ*Anvers or Barbès. From bd de Rochechouart, turn onto rue de Rochechouart, which is located between the 2 Metro stops.* **i** *Also does restorations.* Ⓢ *Men's jackets from €30. Dresses €40-175.* ⚑ *Open M 2:30-7:30pm, Tu-Sa 11:30am-1:30pm and 2:30-7:30pm.*

COIFFEUR   MARAIS
32 rue de Rosiers   ☎01 40 27 04 98
Coiffeur packs a big selection of vintage items into a tight space. With everything from belts to shoes to plaid flannels to leather jackets, you're sure to find something that appeals to your taste even if it requires some hanger shuffling. ⚐ Ⓜ*Saint-Paul. Walk with traffic down rue de Rivoli and turn right onto rue Pavée, then turn left onto rue des Rosiers.* Ⓢ *Shirts and purses from €5.* ⚑ *Open daily 11am-9pm.*

FRIP'IRIUM   MARAIS
2 rue de la Verrerie   ☎01 40 29 95 57
Frip'irium is one of many vintage shops in the Marais, but one that is not afraid to make fun of itself. There is a nice selection of soccer jerseys and dresses on the racks, but the walls are a bit more entertaining. With old-school, one-piece bathing suits stapled to the back wall, a couple of mariachi dresses up high, and prom dresses from nightmares past in the window, Frip'irium isn't afraid to flaunt its goofy side. ⚐ Ⓜ*Hôtel de Ville. Walk away from the river on rue du Renard, then turn right onto rue de la Verrerie.* Ⓢ *Belts and ties €5. Shirts from €5.* ⚑ *Open Tu-Sa 1-9pm.*

ADÖM   BASTILLE
35 and 56 rue de la Roquette   ☎01 48 07 15 94 or 01 43 57 54 92
Think of every canonical high school film you've ever seen: *Fast Times at Ridgemont High, The Breakfast Club, Napoleon Dynamite.* The selection at Adöm seems to be pulled straight from the wardrobe departments of all of them. Cowboy boots, acid-wash jeans, and letterman jackets are in ample supply. It's, like, totally awesome, duh. ⚐ Ⓜ*Bastille. From the intersection, walk down rue de la Roquette.* **i** *Women's store at 56, men's at 35.* Ⓢ *Women's Levis from €20. Men's pants from €30.* ⚑ *Open M-Sa 11am-8pm and Su 3-8pm.*

MUSIC

🎵 CROCOJAZZ   LATIN QUARTER AND ST-GERMAIN
64 rue de la Montagne-Ste-Geneviève   ☎01 46 34 78 38
Everything is jazz jazz jazz-ied up here in this little store, which is packed wall to wall with records, CDs, and DVDs. Album covers and posters of jazz greats like Miles Davis and Louis Armstrong watch approvingly over the store. The cigar-smoking jazz buffs who run this joint will find you whatever you need without batting an eye. ⚐ Ⓜ*Maubert Mutualité. Walk south on rue de la Montagne-Ste-Geneviève toward the Pantheon; Crocojazz is just before the Pantheon on the right.* Ⓢ *Records from €10. CDs from €3.* ⚑ *Open Tu-Sa 11am-7pm.*

paris (margin)

CROCODISC
LATIN QUARTER AND ST-GERMAIN

40/42 rue des Ecoles   ☎01 43 54 33 22 www.crocodisc.com

Specializing in soul and funk, with its second store next door selling contemporary rock and electro, Crocodisc has everything you might need on disc and vinyl. With the faint smell of slow-burning cigars and stacks of old records, Crocodisc sets the mood just right.

⚐ ⓂMaubert-Mutualité. Ⓢ CDs €1-15. Records €2-18. 🕐 Open Tu-Sa 11am-1pm and 2-7pm.

LA CHAMUMIÈRE À LA MUSIQUE
LATIN QUARTER AND ST-GERMAIN

5 rue de Vaugirard   ☎01 43 54 07 25 www.chaumiereonline.com

If listening to Mozart's "Così Fan Tutte" at Così (see **Food**, Latin Quarter and St-Germain) left you hungry for more classics, head to Le Chamumière, where you will find everything there is to be desired. From Chopin to Prokofiev, La Chamumière has CDs, DVDs, and multi-disc sets to keep your ears happy for years.

⚐ ⓂOdéon. Walk south and take the left fork onto rue Monsiuer le Prince. Or RER Luxembourg. Walk north on St-Michel away from the garden, and take the angle left up rue Monsieur le Prince. Ⓢ CDs from €2. Occasional happy hour deals 5:30-7:30pm, select 20% discounts. 🕐 Open M-F 10am-7:30pm, Sa 10am-8pm, Su 2-8pm.

BORN BAD RECORD SHOP
BASTILLE

17 rue Keller   ☎01 43 38 41 78 www.bornbad.fr

Born Bad is a spacious shop with a generous selection of records of many genres: reggae, funk, soul, garage, alternative, rock, whatever you'd like. The owner is a big fan of garage, so you may find the selection slightly biased, but there's still a lot to find in this bad to the bone shop.

⚐ ⓂBastille. From the intersection, walk down rue de la Roquette, then turn right onto rue Keller. Ⓢ Records from €10. 🕐 Open M-Sa noon-8pm.

MONSTER MELODIES
CHÂTELET-LES-HALLES

9 rue des Déchargeurs   ☎01 40 28 09 39

From jazz to ska and from Bieber to Ziggy Marley, Monster Melodies probably carries what you're looking for. The lower level houses well over 10,000 used CDs.

⚐ ⓂChâtelet. Follow rue des Halles and turn left onto rue des Déchargeurs. 🕐 Open M-Su 11am-7pm.

SPECIALTY

PALAIS DES THÉS
MARAIS

64 rue Vieille du Temple   ☎01 48 87 80 60 www.palaisdesthes.com

Le Palais des Thés lives up to its name with a grand offering of teas. Tea experts travel to 20 countries in Asia, Africa, and South America to find the highest quality teas. By personally traveling to each tea estate, the owners of this tea Mecca are able to ensure fair trade and labor practices in the places they buy from. Teas can be as inexpensive as €3-4 or as pricey €100 for 100g. Describe your preferences and tastes to the welcoming staff, and they will point you in the direction of the tea that best fits your needs (and your pocketbook).

⚐ ⓂSt-Paul. Walk up rue Malher as it turns into rue Payenne. Turn left onto rue des Francs Bourgeois, then turn right onto rue Vieille du Temple. 𝒊 4 other locations around the city. Ⓢ Tea €3.50-120 per 100g. 🕐 Open M-Sa 10am-8pm.

PYLÔNES
ÎLE DE LA CITÉ AND ÎLE ST-LOUIS

57 rue St-Louis-en-l'Île   ☎01 46 34 05 02 www.pylones.com

A colorful collection of amorphous shapes and colors, Pylônes is the store version of the Pompidou. It sells things you'll impulsively buy, never need, but always marvel at, like cheese graters topped with doll heads (€18). More useful

shopping

(but just as fun) items include cigarette cases (€12) and espresso cups (€6). The artful objects are fun to look at even if you don't buy anything.

✦ ⓂPont Marie. **i** *5 other locations around the city.* Ⓢ *Cups €6. Wallets €24.* ⊡ *Open daily 10:30am-7:30pm.*

🏆 LA GRANDE ÉPICERIE DE PARIS   INVALIDES
38 rue de Sèvres   ☎01 44 39 81 00 www.lagrandeepicerie.fr

If a Parisian supermodel took on the form of an *épicerie* (supermarket), she'd be this one. Snooty Invalides women saunter up and down the aisles for the best (or most expensive) cheeses, wines, and Nespresso coffee makers. There is an aisle of American candy and products, but it exists mainly for the locals to cluck their tongues as they walk down. La Grande Épicerie de Paris is better for picking up a bottle of wine and some chocolate than a whole list of groceries, as the prices are as out of reach as the model.

✦ ⓂVaneau. ⊡ *Open M-Sa 8:30am-9pm.*

CAILLES DE LUXE   BASTILLE
15 rue Keller   ☎09 53 02 65 22 www.caillesdeluxe.com

When the owners of this glam little shop decided they were fed up with quality jewelry costing a fortune, they decided to go into the business themselves. Bright colors and geometric shapes mark the staples of this shop, while some more unusual pieces include skull heads and toy cars adorning rings and necklaces. This is definitely a place for the ladies, so guys might want to find a nice place to sit for a while.

✦ ⓂVoltaire. *Walk southwest on rue de la Roquette and turn left onto rue Keller; the store is about halfway down on the left.* Ⓢ *Earrings from €9. Rings from €5.* ⊡ *Open Tu-Sa 11am-8pm.*

LA PETITE SCIERIE   ÎLE DE LA CITÉ AND ÎLE ST-LOUIS
60 rue St-Louis-en-l'Île   ☎01 55 42 14 88 lanetitescierie.fr

This is where you can find the perfect gift for that wacky foie gras friend or French expat you know. Their traditionally made foie gras comes from a handful of farms in central France, and is sold only in this store. Ask nicely and the owner is more than happy to let you taste the oh-so-delicious fattened goose liver. You didn't know what foie gras was? Sorry for ruining that for you.

✦ ⓂPont Marie. ⊡ *Open Jan-Nov M 11am-7pm, Th-Su 11am-7pm; Dec daily 11am-7pm.*

CINE REFLET   LATIN QUARTER AND ST-GERMAIN
14 rue Monsieur le Prince   ☎01 40 46 02 72 www.cinereflet.fr

Film buffs and serial movie-quoters, gather 'round. Cine Reflet holds a comprehensive collection of literature entirely devoted to the movies— cinematography, film reviews, plot synopses, and genre analyses. For those of you who enjoy the movies for the simplicity of visual appeal, great movie posters from famous films like *Scarface* and *Apocalypse Now* are also up for grabs. Be sure to check out the 1950s film projector at the front of the store.

✦ *RER Luxembourg. Walk north up bd St-Michel away from the park and take the angled left onto rue Monsieur le Prince.* Ⓢ *Posters €18.* ⊡ *Open M-Tu 1-8pm, W 1-7:30pm, Th-Sa 1-8pm.*

LE MARCHÉ AUX FLEURS   MARAIS
pl. Louis-Lépine

The flower market at the center of Île de la Cité brings a welcome scene of green and freshness to the city streets. Go traditional and buy your sweetheart a dozen roses or a wild orchid. Or go vogue and opt for a birdhouse, a lantern, or a rare tree from Madagascar.

✦ ⓂCité. ⊡ *Open M 10am-6:30pm, W-Su 10am-6:30pm.*

paris

excursions

VERSAILLES
☎01 30

Less than a 30min. train ride (or a 15min. death commute by scooter) from the center of Paris is a town famous for a single house. "House" might be an understatement. Your history books will tell you that this palace was hated just as much as the Bastille, but thankfully its beauty (and we can only assume massive tourism potential) saved it from the raging mob. Versailles is about as modest as the man who built it—the ultimate arrogant Frenchman, the "Sun King," Louis XIV. He had plenty of time to pimp his 580m-long crib, too, over his 72-year rule. The city surrounding the château mainly serves as another suburb for wealthy Parisian families. Some things never change.

Orientation

Versailles is a blessing for the navigationally challenged. In the middle of the **place d'Armes** sits the massive **Château de Versailles,** with **avenue de Paris** extending from the center. Crossing av. de Paris is **avenue de l'Europe,** which leads to the train stations Rive Droite and Rive Gauche (corresponding to the terminus locations in Paris). Av. de l'Europe also crosses through **place de Notre Dame,** where you can find banks, a large open air market, and cheaper creperies. For a daytrip, you won't go beyond the two avenues, whose intersection holds the tourist office.

Sights

🏛 **CHÂTEAU**

☎01 30 83 78 89 www.chateauversailles.fr

Though the Sun King's palace boasts a whopping 51,200 sq. m of floor space, the 10 million lowly serfs that visit the château every year are granted access to only a small percentage of it. After a walk through the **Musée de l'Histoire de France,** which—surprise!—briefly recounts French history, visitors are shepherded down the halls in a single direction. The museum's 21 rooms feature stunning depictions of the royal family, including a smaller copy of Rigaud's famous portrait **Louis XIV** with those sexy red-heeled shoes that would have made Dorothy blush. (Louis was notoriously short and always wore heels like it was Friday night.) Up the main staircase to the right is the two-level chapel, built in 1710, where the king heard mass. Here God competed with the Sun King for attention, as the court came for the privilege of watching the king pray. It might have worked well for Louis XIV, but his grandson and selfish Austrian wife should have done a lot more praying.

The luxurious **State Apartments**—which include the king's bedroom, the **Room of Abundance,** the **Apollo Salon,** and the famed 🪞**Hall of Mirrors**—are through the hallway. The bed, like the man, is incredibly short. Curtains encircle the bed, inspiring some interesting questions about his self-esteem in the boudoir. The Apollo Salon houses the Sun King's throne, 3m tall, which enabled the king to tower over his subjects and enjoy the view of the beautiful fresco of himself on the ceiling (we've made enough over-compensation jokes already). As if the Apollo Salon wasn't narcissistic enough, the sumptuous Hall of Mirrors exemplifies the King's need to look at himself. Lined with the largest mirrors 17th-century technology could produce and windows that overlook the grand gardens outside, the room served as a reception space for great ambassadors. Today, it can be rented out for a Napoleon-sized fortune (we mean small, as in his stature, not large, as in his coffers).

excursions

The **Queen's Bedchamber** (which cannot be rented out; keep holding out for the Lincoln Bedroom), where royal births were public events to prove the legitimacy of heirs, is much less ornate than the king's, but almost exactly as the queen left it on October 6, 1789. Not to worry though; from what we could tell, they changed the sheets.

Ⓢ *€15, under 18 and EU residents 18-25 free; includes audio guide. "Passport" €18, under 18 and EU residents 18-25 free; allows entry to the château, Trianon palace, and Marie Antoinette's estate. Nov-Mar 1st Su each month free. ☼ Château open Tu-Su Apr-Oct 9am-6:30pm, last entry 5:30pm; Nov-Mar 9am-5:30pm, last entry 4:50pm.*

GARDENS

When you have a big-ass house, you need a big-ass garden to go with it—otherwise it just looks silly. The château gardens are an impressive 800 hectares (if you aren't fluent in hectares, just know that they're huge) and are filled with fountains and rows upon rows of hedges. A visit to the gardens is included with the price of admission to the château, so go look at the pretty shrubbery. During **Les Grandes Eaux Musicales,** almost all the fountains are turned on at the same time, and chamber music booms from among the groves—but you'll pay extra to experience that.

Ⓢ *Free. Grandes Eaux Musicales €8, under 18 €6, under 6 free. ☼ Gardens open daily Apr-Oct 8am-8:30pm; Nov-Mar 8am-6pm. Grandes Eaux Musicales Apr-Oct Sa-Su 11am-noon and 3:30-5:30pm.*

TRIANONS AND MARIE ANTOINETTE'S HAMEAU

Contrary to what officials will tell you, the walk up to Trianons and Marie Antoinette's Estate does not take 25min. Less ambitious sightseers are overwhelmed by the prospect of leaving the main area, which makes for a quieter and infinitely more pleasant Versailles experience for those willing to make the trip. Within Marie Antoinette's house are numerous examples of her self-importance. Her bedroom had riggings that could raise mirrors to obscure the windows at the turn of a crank—a need for privacy rarely seen in modern France. Entrance to the compound was strictly forbidden; even the king had to ask for permission. The little Austrian was so secluded that the tables in the dining rooms were designed to be lowered and raised from the floor, since it must have been so annoying for her to have to actually *see* the servants. While the tables are no longer there, you can still see the lines in the marble where the plans used to be. In an apparent misread of Rousseau's ideas on the simple life of reclusion (heavy on reclusion, completely lacking in simple), Marie Antoinette had the gardens commissioned to include a 12-building compound with a dairy farm, gardener's house, mill, and swan-filled lake. Simplicity is relative when you're a queen.

If you're surprised by the unnecessary opulence of Marie Antoinette's Estate, bear in mind that she was just following precedent. The **Grand Trianon** served as Louis XIV's château-away-from-château when the stress of Versailles became too much to bear. It also served as a nice place to house his mistress(es) and (up to) seven illegitimate children by Madame de Montespan alone. Still luxurious, but nowhere near the size of Versailles, this is the palace of the super-wealthy average Joe.

Ⓢ *€10, under 18 and EU residents 18-25 free. ☼ Open Tu-Su Apr-Oct noon-6:30pm; Nov-Mar noon-5:30pm. Last entry 40min. before close.*

Food

Eating in Versailles is less expensive than you would expect, considering the three million tourists that visit each year. Restaurants and vendors jack up the price about €1-2 for the privilege of eating where the kings once did, but prices outside the gilded gates are more reasonable. Packing a lunch is recommended, but if you don't want to schlep it from Paris, stop by a market or the deli below.

◩ MAISON BEAUDET   DELI $

4 rue Maréchal Foch

This small gourmet deli supplies the cheapest of the cheap sandwiches as well as
a selection of wines, cold self-serve pasta, deli meats, and pretty much anything
you would need for a picnic.

❦ *Turn left facing the Mairie and it will be on your left.* ⑤ *Sandwiches €3.50. Sandwich, dessert,
and soda €6.* ⏰ *Open Tu-Su 9am-6pm.*

Essentials

PRACTICALITIES

- **TOURIST OFFICES:** Get maps, hotel and market information, and a complete city guide (even
  though you're probably just going to the Château). Also provides travel advice for visitors with
  disabilities. (2 bis av. de Paris ☎01 39 24 88 88 www.versailles-tourimse.com ❦ Corner of
  av. de Paris and av. de l'Europe. ⏰ Open Apr-Sept M 10am-6pm, Tu-Su 9am-7pm; Oct-Mar M
  11am-5pm, Tu-Sa 9am-6pm, Su 11am-5pm.)

- **PHARMACIES:** English spoken with Dr. Elizabeth Kennedy. (rue de la Pourvoirerie ☎01 39 50
  09 23 ❦ Corner of rue Marechal Foch and rue de la Pourvoirerie ⏰ Open M 10am-8pm, Tu
  8:30am-8pm, W-Th 9am-8pm, F 8:30am-8pm, Sa 9am-7:30pm.)

- **ATMS: HSBC.** (18 rue du Maréchal Foch ⏰ Open 24hr.)

GETTING THERE

RER trains beginning with "V" run from St-Michel Notre Dame to the Versailles Rive
Gauche station. From Gare St-Lazare, trains run to Gare Versailles Rive Droite,
which is on the opposite side of the town, and equidistant from the Château as the
other train station. From Montparnasse, trains arrive at Gare de Chantiers, which is
the farthest from the Château. Buy a round-trip ticket, as ticket lines in Versailles are
long. Buy your RER ticket before going through the turnstile to the platform; when
purchasing from a machine, look for the **Île-de-France ticket** option. While a Metro
ticket will get you through these turnstiles, it won't get you through RER turnstiles
at the other end and could ultimately result in a significant fine. (⑤ Round-trip €5.80.
⏰ 30-40min., every 20min. from 4:50am-12:15am.)

GETTING AROUND

Versailles is entirely walkable for what you want to see; it's almost like they anticipated the tourists when they built it. Any bus that goes to the city center will stop
next to the Château, but you can walk to and from most points of interest in 10min.

CHARTRES   ☎02 37

Were it not for a holy scrap of fabric, Chartres might still be a sleepy hamlet. But the
cloth that the Virgin Mary supposedly wore when she gave birth to Jesus somehow
ended up here, making Chartres a major medieval pilgrimage center. The majestic
cathedral that towers over the city isn't the only reason to visit; the *vieille ville* is also
a masterpiece of medieval architecture, which almost makes you forget the zooming
highways that have encroached upon it.

Orientation

To reach the **Cathédrale** from the train station, walk straight ahead down **avenue Jehan de
Beauce** to **place de Châtelet** and look up. You'll see the Cathedral and the **place de la Cathédrale**
and quickly comprehend that the church isn't the only show in town. Don't make the
mistake of asking a local where the Cathedral is; you'll get laughed at or severely snarked.
The **Musée des Beaux-Arts** and other prominent sights are located behind the Cathedral.
La Maison Picassiette is a little farther, about 10min. away from the *vieille ville* by taxi.
Chartres's medieval tangle of streets can be confusing, but getting lost is enjoyable.

Sights

Is the cathedral the best show in town? Obviously, yes. It even offers three attractions in one. It attracts the historical buffs with its crypt, the pilgrims with its relics, and the athletes with its giant, I-dare-you-to-climb-me tower. Just try to break up your sightseeing with some non-cathedral attractions as well.

LA CATHÉDRALE NOTRE-DAME DE CHARTRES

LA CATHÉDRALE CHURCH

18 cloître Notre-Dame ☎02 37 21 75 02

The Cathédrale de Chartres is quite possibly the best-preserved medieval church in Europe, having miraculously escaped any major damage during its nearly 1000 years of existence. While Notre Dame's statues were beheaded, this architectural wonder survived the French Revolution and two world wars unscathed. This was after earlier cathedrals on this site were destroyed by fire, though, so we guess they earned a bit of good luck. Most attribute the church's ability to escape revolutionaries and the Nazis to its housing of the **Sancta Camisa,** the cloth that the Virgin Mary wore while giving birth to Jesus. Donated by Charles the Bald, so named for his lack of hair (or his full head of it—historians still can't decide if the name was ironic), the Sancta Camisa attracts thousands of sick Catholics hoping that it will heal their ailments. It's on display in the back of the church and alternates between the three chapels. If you're having trouble finding it, just look for the mob of non-praying tourists.

Other must-sees include the 176 stained-glass windows that date from the 13th century. They were preserved through both world wars by the heroic and extremely savvy town authorities, who carefully dismantled all the windows and stored them in Dordogne until the fighting was over. The glass designs are characterized by a stunning color known as "Chartres blue," which has not been successfully reproduced in modern times. The windows of Chartres often distract visitors from the treasure below their feet: a winding labyrinth pattern that is carved into the floor in the rear of the nave. The labyrinth originally served as a pilgrimage substitute—by following this pattern on their hands and knees, the devout would enact a symbolic voyage to Jerusalem, and then still have time to be home by dinner. Commitment loophole? Maybe.

*# In pl. de la Cathédrale. **i** English tours of the cathedral begin outside the gift shop in the cathedral. 1hr. English audio tours available at the gift shop require ID. $ Free. English tours €10, students and children €5. Audio tours for cathedral €4.20; for choir loft €3.20; for both €6.20. ⏰ Open daily 8:30am-7:30pm. English tours M-Sa noon and 2:45pm.*

TOUR JEHAN-DE-BEAUCE TOWER

Only the in-shape and non-claustrophobic can climb the narrow, 300-step staircase to the cathedral's north tower, but those who do shall receive wealth and fame—in reality, just a really stellar view of the city and the surrounding valley. If you can't make it all the way to the top, the first viewing platform offers a slightly obstructed but nonetheless impressive panorama.

$ €7, ages 18-25 €4.50, under 18 free. ⏰ Open May-Aug M-Sa 9:30am-noon and 2-5:30pm, Su 2-5:30pm; Sept-Apr M-Sa 9:30am-noon and 2-4:30pm, Su 2-4:30pm.

LA CRYPTE CRYPT

Visitors may enter the 110m subterranean crypt only as part of a guided tour. Chapels within the crypt alternate between Gothic and Romanesque styles and house the original statues from the facade. You are led to the foundation stone of the church, where two priests and the Sancta Camisa miraculously survived for three days during one of the most destructive fires to afflict the Cathedral.

Parts of the crypt, including the well in which Vikings tossed the bodies of their victims during raids, date back to the ninth century.

ℹ *30min. tours in French leave from the store opposite the cathedral's south entrance at 18 cloître Notre-Dame. English leaflets are available at La Crypte store.* 💲 *€2.70, students €2.10, under 7 free.* ⏰ *Tours Apr-Oct M-Sa 11am, 2:15, 3:30, and 4:30pm; Su 2:15, 3:30, and 4:30pm. Tours Nov-Mar M-Sa 4:15pm, Su 11am. Additional 5:15pm tour June 22-Sept 21.*

OTHER SIGHTS

👍 **MAISON PICASSIETTE** MUSEUM

22 rue du Repos ☎02 37 34 10 78

After buying this plot of land at 22 rue du Repos, the owner (in a fit of recycling savvy) decided to make intricate mosaics out of pieces of broken and discarded glass that he found. If you thought mosaics only come on floors and walls, think again. At Maison Picassiette, chairs, tables, lamps, stoves, and even the doghouse are covered with depictions of the cathedral and biblical scenes that could make good color blindness tests. Apart from a slight headache, you'll leave with a new understanding of hot glue that will shame every macaroni art project your mother ever put up on the fridge.

⇄ *Well outside the city center, it is most accessible by taxi, which can be found in pl. de la Cathédrale or pl. Pierre Sémard.* 💲 *€5.20, students and under 26 €2.60, under 18 free.* ⏰ *Open Jul-Aug M 10am-6pm, W-Sa 10am-6pm; Oct-Apr M 10am-noon and 2-6pm, W-Sa 10am-noon and 2-6pm.*

MUSÉE DES BEAUX-ARTS MUSEUM

29 cloître Notre-Dame ☎02 37 90 45 80

The former Bishop's Palace, the beautiful and creaky building which is now home to this museum, is a little more impressive than the collection itself. The museum deals with the medieval history of Chartres, including a temporary exhibit on ★**dragons** and their most famous slayer, St. George (sorry, Buffy). It also houses 15th- through 19th-century European paintings, suits of armor, and a sword collection.

⇄ *Across the street from the cathedral.* 💲 *Permanent collection €3.10, under 18 and seniors €1.60. Permanent collection and temporary exhibits €5.10/€2.60.* ⏰ *Open May-Oct M 10am-noon and 2-6pm, W-Sa 10am-noon and 2-6pm, Su 2-6pm; Nov-Apr M 10am-noon and 2-5pm, W-Sa 10am-noon and 2-5pm, Su 2-5pm. Last entry 30min. before close.*

CENTRE INTERNATIONAL DU VITRAIL MUSEUM

5 rue du Cardinal Pie ☎02 37 21 65 72 www.centre-vitrail.org

The Centre International du Vitrail is strangely located in a medieval tithe barn dating from the 12th century. It might not be the ideal setting for a stained-glass museum, but it's there nonetheless. Exhibits explain the process that creates the windows and the evolution of the craft from the Middle Ages until the modern day. Expect a lot of debate on why they can't replicate that special blue in the cathedral.

⇄ *Across the street from the cathedral.* 💲 *€4, students and under 26 €3.* ⏰ *Open M-F 9:30am-12:30pm and 1:30-6pm, Sa 10am-12:30pm and 2:30-6pm, Su 2:30-6pm.*

Food

Food in Chartres really only caters to the tourist population, so falling into a tourist trap is inevitable. While your cheapest option is always to picnic, there are some calmer joints that don't attract the hordes of pilgrims.

ÉPICERIE DE LA PLACE BILLARD GROCERY STORE $

19 rue des Changes ☎02 37 21 00 25

Épicerie de la Place Billard is a friendly, inexpensive grocery store that sells all the picnic basics, though there isn't much green space in Chartres to eat it on. The store also sells over 40 flavors of *limonade* (€5).

⇄ *3 blocks southeast of the cathedral.* ⏰ *Open M-Sa 6:30am-7:30pm, Su 6am-6pm.*

LE PICHET 3 RESTAURANT, GROCERY STORE $$

19 rue du Chevel Blanc ☎02 37 21 08 35 www.wix.com/francechartres/lepichet3

Combining a boutique and restaurant (to maximize buying impulses), this restaurant will have you torn between ordering stewed duck and buying colorful scarves, beads, and photos of the city. Or you could just give up and chill with a coffee on the second-floor terrace of this split-level establishment.

🧭 Exit pl. de la Cathédrale to the west (on rue de l'Horloge) then turn left onto rue du Chevel Blanc. $ Lunch menu €14. Plats €11-15. 🕐 Open daily 11am-6pm.

LE MOULIN DE PONCEAU TRADITIONAL $$$

21 rue de la Tannerie ☎02 37 35 30 05 www.moulindeponceau.fr

Le Moulin de Ponceau has about 20 tables that snake along the tranquil Eure River and up rue de la Tannerie, just 5min. from the cathedral. Think of your ideal farm-inspired countryside meal and you'll begin to imagine their lamb covered in rosemary gravy, sweetbreads, and olive polenta. While the prices are more Parisian than practical, the dining experience is entirely worth it.

🧭 From the cathedral, follow rue des Acacias down to the river. Once over the river, turn left onto rue de la Tannerie. $ Entrées €12. Plats €19. Desserts €10. Prix-fixe menus €29-39. 🕐 Open Tu-Sa noon-3:30 and 7-10:30pm, Su noon-3:30pm.

Nightlife

There's not much excitement in Chartres at night, especially during the week. Tourists are generally a bit older than the lively expat crowd in Paris, so don't expect much beyond a refreshing drink before your train ride back. If you do find yourself here at night, check out **L'Académie de la Bière.** (8 rue du Cheval Blanc ☎02 37 36 90 07 🧭 On pl. de la Cathédrale, across the street from the cathedral. $ Beers €4-6. 🕐 Open M-Th 6pm-1am, F-Sa 6pm-2am.)

Essentials

PRACTICALITIES

- **TOURIST OFFICES:** The **Office de Tourisme de Chartres** provides maps and books accommodations. (pl. de la Cathédrale ☎02 37 18 26 26; www.chartres-tourisme.com 🕐 Open M-F 9am-1pm and 2-6pm, Sa 10am-1pm and 2-6pm.)
- **TOURS:** English-language walking tours are available at the tourist office. ($ €6, under 12 €4. 🕐 1hr., Jul-Aug Tu 2:30pm.) Audio tours of the *vieille ville* are also available. ($ €5.50, 2 for €8.50. 🕐 1hr.)
- **CURRENCY EXCHANGE: Currency Exchange Office.** (Parvis de la Cathédrale ☎02 37 36 42 33 🕐 Open Mar-Oct M-Sa 9am-5pm.)

EMERGENCY

- **POLICE: Hôtel de Police.** (57 rue du Docteur Maunoury ☎02 37 23 42 84 🧭 Follow rue Collin d'Harleville to pl. des Épars and continue onto rue du Docteur Maunoury.)
- **LATE-NIGHT PHARMACIES: Pharmacie Desprez Buis.** (49 rue Soleil d'Or ☎02 37 36 02 63 🕐 Open 24hr.)
- **HOSPITALS/MEDICAL SERVICES: Louis Pasteur Hospital.** (4 rue Claude Bernard ☎02 37 30 30 30 ℹ English-speaking doctors.) For a closer but French-speaking hospital, go to 34 rue du Docteur Maunoury, near the police station.

GETTING THERE

Chartres is accessible by frequent **trains** from Gare Montparnasse, on the Nogent-le-Rotrou line. ($ €30, ages 12-24 €22, under 12 €5. ⏰ 1hr.)There are two SNCF trains per hour during the summer; pick up a schedule ahead of time, as times are frequently irregular (thanks, striking workers). The train station in Chartres is located at pl. Pierre Sémard. (☎02 37 84 61 50)

GETTING AROUND

Chartres is a very walkable city, with most of its worthwhile sights clustered around the cathedral. The Maison Picassiette is the main exception and is most accessible by **taxi.** We suggest Taxi 2000. (pl. Pierre Sémard ☎02 37 36 00 00) If you ever get lost, look up—the cathedral is visible from almost everywhere in the town, so you can easily find your way back to the center.

essentials

PRACTICALITIES

- **TOURIST OFFICES: Bureau Central d'accueil** provides maps and tour information and books accommodations. (25 rue des Pyramides ☎01 49 52 42 63 www.parisinfo.com 🚏 [M]Pyramides. ⏰ Open daily May-Oct 9am-7pm; Nov-Apr 10am-7pm.) Also located at Gare de Lyon (☎01 43 33 24 ⏰ Open M-Sa 8am-6pm); Gare du Nord (☎01 45 26 94 82 ⏰ Open daily 10am-6pm); Gare de L'est (⏰ Open M-Sa 8am-7pm). Tourist kiosks at [M]Champs Élysées-Clemenceau, [M]Cité in front of Notre Dame, [M]Hôtel de Ville inside the Hôtel de Ville, [M]Anvers, and [M]Bastille. All offices and kiosks have tourist maps; Metro, bus, and RER maps; and walking guides to Paris produced by the Paris Convention and Visitors Bureau. Most hotels and hostels also offer these resources for free.
- **TOURS: Bateaux-Mouches** offers boat tours along the Seine. (Port de la Conférence, Pont de l'Alma ☎01 42 25 02 28 www.bateaux-mouches.fr 🚏 [M]Alma-Marceau or Franklin Roosevelt. *i* Tours in English. $ €11.50, under 12 €5.50, under 4 free. ⏰ Cruise about 70min. Apr-Sept M-F every 20-45min. 10:15am-11pm; Oct-Mar M-F 11am-9pm, Sa-Su 10:15am-9pm every 45-60min.)
- **GLBT RESOURCES: Paris Gay Village.** (63 rue Beaubourg ☎01 43 57 21 47 www.parisgayvillage.com 🚏 [M]Rambuteau. *i* English spoken. ⏰ Open M 6-8pm, Tu-Th 3:30-8pm, F 1-8pm, Sa 1-7pm.) SKOPIK map can be found at most tourist offices. Map of GLBT friendly establishments throughout Paris.
- **STUDENT RESOURCES: Centre d'Information et de Documentation pour la Jeunesse** provides information on temporary work, job placement, tourism info, and housing for students studying in Paris. (101 quai Branly ☎01 44 49 12 00 www.cidj.com 🚏 [M]Bir-Hakeim. ⏰ Open Tu-F 1-6pm, Sa 1-5pm.)
- **TICKET AGENCIES: FNAC.** (74 av. des Champs-Élysées ☎08 25 02 00 20 www.fnacspectacles.com 🚏 [M]Franklin D. Roosevelt. Forum des Halles [M]Châtelet/Les Halles *i* There are various other FNAC stores throughout Paris; check the website for more locations. ⏰ Open M-Sa 10am-11:45pm, Su noon-11:45pm.)
- **INTERNET: American Library in Paris** has computers and internet access for members or guests with day passes. (10 rue du Général Camou ☎01 53 59 12 60 www.americanlibraryinparis.org 🚏 [M]École Militaire. ⏰ Open Tu-Sa 10am-7pm, Su 1-7pm. Jul-Aug T-F 1-7pm, Sa 10am-4pm.) There is also free Wi-Fi at **Centre Pompidou** and in its **Bibliothèque Publique d'Information.** (pl. Georges Pompidou, rue Beaubourg 🚏 [M]Rambuteau or Hôtel de Ville.

⏰ Center open M 11am-9pm, W-Su 11am-9pm. Library open M noon-10pm, W-F noon-10pm, Sa-Su 11am-10pm.)

- **POST OFFICES: La Poste** runs the French postal system (www.laposte.fr). There are many post offices in Paris that are generally open M-F 8am-7pm and Sa 8am-noon. The most centrally located post offices are in **Saint-Germain** (118 bd St-Germain ➡ [M]Odéon. ⏰ Open M-F 8am-8pm, Sa 9am-5pm.) and **Châtelet-Les Halles.** (1 rue Pierre Lescot ➡ [M]Les-Halles. ⏰ Open M-F 8am-6:30pm, Sa 9am-1pm.) The **Paris Louvre** post office is also easily accessible. (52 rue du Louvre ➡ [M]Louvre-Rivoli. ⏰ Open 7:30am-6pm.)

EMERGENCY

- **POLICE:** ☎17. **Préfecture de la Police.** (9 bd Palais ☎01 58 80 80 80 ➡ [M]Cité. Across the street from the Palais de Justice. ⏰ Open 24hr.)
- **CRISIS LINE: SOS Help!** is an emergency hotline for English speakers. (☎01 46 21 46 46)
- **DOCTORS:** ☎36 24.
- **AMBULANCE (SAMU):** ☎15
- **FIRE:** ☎18
- **LATE-NIGHT PHARMACIES: Pharmacie Les Champs.** (84 av. des Champs-Élysées ☎01 45 62 02 41 ➡ [M]Franklin Roosevelt. ⏰ Open daily 24hr.) **Grande Pharmacie Daumesnil.** (6 pl. Félix Eboué ☎01 43 43 19 03 ➡ [M]Daumesnil. ⏰ Open daily 24hr.) **Pharmacie européenne.** (6 pl. de Clichy ☎01 48 74 65 18 ➡ [M]Pl. de Clichy. ⏰ Open daily 24hr.) **Pharmacie Première.** (24 bd de Sébastopol ⏰ Open daily 8am-2am.)
- **HOSPITALS/MEDICAL SERVICES: American Hospital of Paris.** (63 bd Victor Hugo and 84 bd de la Saussaye. ☎01 46 41 25 25 www.american-hospital.org ➡ [M]Port Maillot then bus 82 to last stop Hôpital Américain. Or Ponte de Neuilly then bus #93 to Hôpital Américain.) **Hôpital Bichat.** (46 rue Henri Huchard ☎01 40 25 80 80 ➡ [M]Porte de St-Ouen.)

GETTING THERE

How you arrive in Paris will be dictated by where you are traveling from. Those flying across the Atlantic will most likely end up at **Paris-Charles de Gaulle,** one of Europe's main international hubs. If flying from within Europe, it will probably be cheaper for you to fly into **Orly.** Though it hardly counts as arriving in Paris, flying into **Beauvais** from other European cities will often save a lot of money even if you count the €15 75min. shuttle ride into the city. RER lines, buses, and shuttles run regularly from all three airports to Paris; however, time and price vary with the airport. With its confusingly endless number of train stations, Paris offers options for both those coming from within France and those who are traveling by train from the rest of Europe.

By Plane

PARIS-CHARLES DE GAULLE (CDG)

Roissy-en-France, 23km northeast of Paris ☎01 48 62 22 80 www.adp.fr

Most transatlantic flights land at Aéroport Paris-CDG. The two cheapest and fastest ways to get into the city from Paris-CDG are by RER and by bus. The RER train services Terminals 1, 2, and 3. The RER B ($ €9.25, includes Metro transport when you get off the RER) will take you to central Paris. To transfer to the Metro, get off at Gare du Nord, Châtelet-Les Halles, or St-Michel. The **Roissybus** (☎01 49 25 61 87 $ €10 ⏰ 35min., every 15-20min. during day, 20min. at night) departs from Terminals 1 and 3 and arrives at Opéra.

ORLY (ORY)

Orly, 18km south of Paris ☎01 49 75 15 15 www.adp.fr

Aéroport d'Orly is used by charters and many continental flights. From Orly Sud Gate G or Gate I, platform 1, or Orly Ouest level G, Gate F, take the **Orly-Rail** shuttle bus to the Pont de Rungis/Aéroport d'Orly train station, where you can board the RER C for a number of destinations in Paris, including St-Michel, Invalides, and Gare d'Austerlitz. Another option is the RATP 🚌**Orlybus** (☎08 36 68 77 14 $ €6.90 ⏰ 30min., every 15-20min.), which runs between Metro and RER stop Denfert-Rochereau and Orly's south terminal. RATP also runs **Orlyval** (☎01 69 93 53 00 $ VAL ticket €8.30 or VAL-RER ticket €10.75), a combination Metro, RER, and VAL rail shuttle that is the fastest way to get to the city. The VAL shuttle goes from Antony (RER B) to Orly Ouest and Sud. Buy tickets at any RATP booth in the city or from the Orlyval agencies at Orly Ouest, Orly Sud, and Antony. See www.aeroportsdeparis.fr for maps of transportation between Orly and different locations in Paris.

BEAUVAIS (BVA)

Tillé, 85km north of Paris ☎08 92 68 20 66 www.aeroportbeauvais.com

Aéroport de Paris Beauvais serves **Ryanair, EasyJet, Wizair,** and other budget airlines. The **shuttle bus** leaves from Paris-Beauvais and goes to Porte Maillot in Paris, where you can take the Metro to the city center (☎03 44 11 46 86 www.aeroportbeauvais.com ℹ Tickets must be purchased in arrival lounge. $ €15 ⏰ About 75min., departs every 20-25min. after flight arrivals). To get back to Beauvais, arrive 3¼hr. before flight time at the Pershing parking lot, near the Hotel Concorde La Fayette at Porte Maillot and purchase tickets on the bus.

By Train

SNCF (www.sncf.fr) sells train tickets for travel within France and offers *la Carte 12-25*, which, for a one-time €50 fee, guarantees reduced prices of up to 60% if you want to hop around France. If you're traveling to France from another country, check out **Rail Europe** (www.raileurope.com). Thalys offers reduced prices for those under 26. **Gare du Nord** (112 rue de Maubeuge) is the arrival point for trains from northern France and Germany as well as Amsterdam ($ From €65 ⏰ 3½hr.), Brussels ($ From €50 ⏰ 1hr.), and London ($ €50-120 ⏰ 2½hr.). **Gare de l'Est** (78 bd de Strasbourg) receives trains from eastern France and southern Germany, Austria, Hungary, Munich ($ €125-163 ⏰ 9-10½hr.) and Prague ($ €118-172. ⏰ 12-15hr.). **Gare de Lyon** (20 bd Diderot) has trains from: Florence ($ €135-170 ⏰ 9-12hr.); Lyon ($ €60-70 ⏰ 2hr.); Marseille ($ €45-70 ⏰ 3-4hr.); Nice ($ €100 ⏰ 5½hr.); and Rome ($ €177-200 ⏰ 12-15hr.). **Gare d'Austerlitz** (85 quai d'Austerlitz) services the Loire Valley and the Iberian peninsula, including Barcelona ($ €135-170 ⏰ 7-12hr.) and Madrid ($ €220-300 ⏰ 12-13hr.). **Gare St-Lazare** (13 rue d'Amsterdam) will welcome you from northern France, while **Gare Montparnasse** (17 bd Vaugirard) is the destination of trains from northeastern and southwestern France.

GETTING AROUND

By Metro

In general, the Metro is easy to navigate, and trains run swiftly and frequently. Pick up a colorful map at any station. Metro stations themselves are a distinctive part of the city's landscape and are marked with an "M" or with "*Métropolitain.*" The earliest trains start running around 5:30am, and the last ones leave the end-of-the-line stations (the *portes de Paris*) at about 12:15am during the week and 2:15am on Friday and Saturday. In general, be at the Metro by 1am if you want to take it home at night. Connections

how to metro

You'll hear it a thousand times: keep your Metro ticket until you exit. If you don't, you may well be caught and, according to French punishment, be horribly shamed in public as well as having to pay a fine. Here are some other Metro tips to be aware of.

- **NO SMOKING:** But that doesn't mean people won't light up while on the exit escalator.

- **MONEY ISSUES:** Unless you have a European credit card, bring coins. Change machines are notoriously hard to find, and shops are not quick to change your €10 note. We've seen many a tear over this problem in the early morning when the red eye from JFK comes in.

- **CONNECTIONS:** The Metro is designed so you only need to make one transfer to get anywhere in the city. But don't be silly—following this rule might mean traveling halfway across the city in the wrong direction just to change just to change lines. Instead, brush up on your pronunciation of "*correspondence,*" swallow your obsession with efficiency, and take the multiple connections in significantly less time.

to other lines are indicated by orange *correspondance* signs, and exits are marked by blue *sortie* signs. Transfers are free if made within a station, but it's not always possible to reverse direction on the same line without exiting. Hold onto your ticket until you exit the Metro, and pass the point marked **Limite de Validité des Billets;** a uniformed RATP *contrôleur* (inspector) may request to see it on any train. If you're caught without a ticket, you must pay a €40 fine on the spot. Don't count on buying a ticket late at night, either—some ticket windows close as early as 10pm, and many close before the last train arrives. It's a good idea to carry one more ticket than you need, although large stations have ticket machines that accept coins. Tickets cost €1.70 per journey, although it's much more useful to buy a *carnet* of 10 tickets for €12.70. You can also buy unlimited Metro passes for 1 day (€9.75), 2 days (€15.85), 3 days (€21.60), or 5 days (€31.15) that service the Metro, buses, and RER Zones 1-3. If you're going to be in Paris longer, ask the ticket office at the big stations about a week- or month-long unlimited **Navigo Pass.** You will need a passport photo to attach to the ID, and then your Navigo Pass will be able to scan into Metro stops. The week-long pass starts on Monday.

When it's getting really late, your best chance of getting the train you want is heading to the biggest stations like Gare du Nord, Gare de l'Est, and Châtelet-Les Halles. However, these stations are often full of tourists and pickpockets, so stay alert when traveling at night or avoid it altogether. If you must travel by public transport late at night, get to know the Noctilien bus (see below). When in doubt, take a taxi.

By RER

The RER *(Réseau Express Régional)* is the RATP's suburban train system, which passes through central Paris and travels much faster than the Metro. There are five RER lines, marked A-E, with different branches designated by a number. The newest line, E, is called the Eole *(Est-Ouest Liaison Express)* and links Gare Magenta to Gare St-Lazare. Within central Paris, the RER works just like the Metro and requires the same ticket for the same price (if you have to transfer from the RER to the Metro or vice versa, however, you will need another ticket). The principal stops within the city that link the RER to the Metro, are Gare du Nord, Nation, Charles de Gaulle-Étoile, Gare de Lyon, Châtelet-Les Halles, St-Michel, and Denfert-Rochereau. The electric signs next to each track list all the possible stops for trains running on that

paris

track. Be sure that the little square next to your destination is lit up. Trips to the suburbs require more expensive tickets that can also be bought at the automatic booths where you purchase Metro tickets. You must know what zone you're going to in order to buy the proper ticket. In order to exit the RER station, insert your ticket just as you did to enter and pass through. Like the Metro, the RER runs 5:30am-12:30am on weekdays and until 2:30am on weekends, but never wait until 2:30am to get to the Metro or RER. Again, if you must travel by public transport late at night, get to know the Noctilien bus.

By Bus

Although slower than the Metro, a bus ride can be a cheap sightseeing tour and a helpful introduction to the city's layout. Bus tickets are the same as those used for the Metro and can be purchased in Metro stations or from bus drivers (€1.70). Enter the bus through the front door and punch your ticket by pushing it into the machine next to the driver's seat. Inspectors may ask to see your ticket, so hold on to it until you get off. When you want to get off, press the red button so the *arrêt demandé* (stop requested) sign lights up. Most buses run daily 7am-8:30pm, although those marked **Autobus du nuit** continue until 1:30am. The **Noctilien** runs all night (daily 12:30am-5:30am) and services more than 45 routes throughout the city, so if you plan to use this frequently, get a map of the routes in a Metro station and study it. Hard. Look for bus stops marked with a moon sign. Check out www.noctilien.fr or inquire at a major Metro station or Gare de l'Est for more information on Noctilien buses. Complete bus route maps are posted at the bus stops, while individual lines only give out maps of their own routes. Noctilien #2 runs to all the major train stations along the periphery of the city, while #12 and #13 run between Châtelet and Gare de Montparnasse.

By Taxi

Traveling by taxi in Paris can be intimidating. Parisian taxis usually have three fares that change based on the time of day and day of the week. Rush hours and early morning hours on the weekends are the priciest, whereas morning to midday fares on weekdays are the cheapest. Fares are measured out by the kilometer and only switch to waiting time if a trip is over an hour. The pick-up base charge is €2.20 and minimum fare is €6.20. Each additional person after three passengers costs €3, and each additional piece of luggage after the first costs €1. A typical 20min. taxi ride costs €12-20, and a 40min. ride can be as much as €50. Taxis are easily hailed from any major boulevard or avenue, but stands are often outside major Metro intersections. If the taxi's green light is on, it is available. From the airport, prices skyrocket to around €80-100. It's never a bad idea to ask for a receipt at the end of your trip in case of dispute or lost property.

By Bike

If just don't feel like walking or gambling with timetables, bike rentals may be for you. There are many **Vélib'** stations around the city where you can rent a public bike for prices ranging from free (under 30min.) to €7 (up to 2hr.). You can return the bike at any Vélib' station. Before you leave, check to see if your destination has open spots, as machines won't feel bad if you're late and can't find somewhere to park. Stations at the top of hills are generally open, and those at the bottom are typically not; spots near major tourist destinations and the quais are often a safe bet. You must have a credit card with a chip on it to use the automatic booths where you can rent a bike. Note that the Velib' machine will request a €150 hold on your card that will be withdrawn in the event of a damaged or lost bike. **Paris Bike Tour** also offers bike rentals for €20 for a 24hr. period; each extra day costs €10 (38 rue de Saintonge ☎01 42 74 22 14 ☒ Open 9:30am-6:30pm). The bad news is they also require a €250 deposit and a copy of your photo ID.

paris 101

450 BCE.
The Celts migrate to France from Switzerland and Austria. Many settle and become known as Gauls.

250 CE.
St. Denis picks up his freshly severed head from the ground and proceeds to march 10km while preaching a sermon (just your everyday post-beheading stuff).

1163-1345.
Notre Dame Cathedral is constructed. After years of house-hunting, Quasimodo finds a home.

1387.
The city of Paris builds its third ever bridge, Pont St-Michel. Though the bridge is popularly called Pont Neuf, it soon becomes old, and 200 later a new Pont Neuf is constructed.

HISTORY

Unfortunately, Woody Allen has declined to share with us the secrets of Parisian time travel, but perhaps this outline of the city's rich history will help you figure out where you'd like to go if you ever starred in a remake of *Midnight in Paris*.

Caesar Salad With a Side of Celt (250 BCE-250 CE)

Once upon a time, around 250 BCE, a small tribe called the Parisii settled on the Left Bank of the Seine River. Not finding the much-hyped haven for bohemians and boutiques they'd come for, the Parisii went for the next best option and created a tiny fishing village, Lutetia. In 52 CE, **Julius Caesar,** pugnacious as ever, brought his army of overachieving Romans to conquer the place. The Parisii put up a valiant fight under their determined leader, Vercingétorix, but (as with most people who faced the Romans) ultimately succumbed to defeat at the Battle of Alesia. The victorious Romans sent their interior decorators in and outfitted the previously sleepy Lutetia with a forum, palaces, baths, temples, theaters, and an amphitheater. The revamped village was so hot it nearly became the new Rome of the Roman Empire. It was everything the Parisii had dreamed of and more, but, alas, they were already gone.

Christianity, which was at the time rapidly gaining popularity across Europe, arrived in Paris in the third century CE. The budding religion was not, however, an immediate hit. Though Paris's first bishop, **Saint Denis,** managed to convert some when he first came to the city to build churches and Christianize the locals, the people rose up against him. They decapitated Denis in 250 CE, a year that marks the advent of what would become a trend throughout Parisian history. What can we say? The city loves her guillotine.

Huns Hate Paris in the Springtime (250-1000)

In the fourth century, the city was renamed Paris after those first eager tourists cum founders. In spring of 451, yet another conqueror came to town: **Attila the Hun.** In response to the imminent attack, the recently christened Parisians did what they'd been taught—they prayed. Remarkably, the story goes, the prayers and works of penance led by **Sainte Geneviève** repelled Attila and his men from their city and on to Orléans (where they ultimately had the Roman and Visigoth armies to thank for their defeat). Geneviève was then named a patron saint of the city.

In 508, Clovis, King of the Franks, named Paris his kingdom's capital; in the 700s, the title was stripped from the city as the capital was moved northeast to Aachen. In 800, the Pope crowned **Charlemagne,** King of the Frankish people, as Holy Roman Emperor after expanding the empire to cover nearly all of central and western Europe. In 987, **Hugh Capet,** the Count of Paris and no relation to the Hugo Cabret of recent cinematic fame, became King of France, and Paris once again became the country's capital.

Paint it Black (1000-1643)

Then the students came. As it turns out, they invaded Paris almost a millennium before the well-known student uprisings of 1968. Under Philip II (this guy *was* related to Hugh Capet, and he reigned from 1180-1223), the University of Paris became a center of education in Europe; the king also built churches and a highly protected castle, known today as the **Louvre.** Philip extended city walls and paved streets, reorganized state infrastructure, and furthered Paris as a commercial center. Things were going well until the **Black Death** came along in 1348 and ruined it all. The disease killed as many as 800 people per day, which effectively stunted the city's hitherto rapid development.

Under the leader **Étienne Marcel,** Paris became an independent commune in 1358. In 1407, civil war swept through Paris, and in 1430, the English won control of the city for the following six years of the **Hundred Years' War.** In 1572, around 10,000 Protestants were murdered in the **Saint Bartholomew's Day Massacre**—the worst moment of the long religious conflict brought on by the Reformation.

Occupy Versailles: We Are the 98% (1643-1799)

Unfortunately for the French aristocracy, this was not the end of unrest in Paris. Perhaps due to **Louis XIV's** obscenely luxurious lifestyle during his rule (1643-1715) and his grandson's wife's suggestion that those short on bread should eat cake instead, the lower strata of French society (the Third Estate, which comprised 98% percent of French citizens) decided it was time to do something. In June of 1789 they formed the Assemblé Nationale, and by mid-July they'd stormed the Bastille prison. While it is difficult to say for sure just why the protesters chose to attack the Bastille on July 14th, some have speculated that they wanted their grandchildren to one-up America's July 4th and figured this was their best shot.

Three years later, the monarchy crumbled. Those early years of the revolution would eventually be viewed as glory days. Once **Maximilien Robespierre** and his Committee of Public Safety came to the foreground at the dawn of the 1790s, things really got exciting. In 1793, Max and friends decided to ensure the safety of Louis XVI, Marie Antoinette, and around 3000 others by politely offing their heads. (Told you it was a trend!)

Shorty Breaks it Down (1799-1914)

Fed up with Robespierre's unhealthy reliance on the guillotine and the ineffectiveness of those who followed him, **Napoleon Bonaparte** overthrew the revolutionary government in 1799. Rewriting the constitution and issuing his own standardized

1429.
A 17-year-old girl named Joan (of Arc) single-handedly saves France. The English execute her and throw her remains into the Seine.

1578-1607.
The real Pont Neuf is constructed. A year later, it's still not new. Parisian authorities vow to choose a better name next time.

1643-1715.
King Louis XIV collects 1000 wigs during his reign.

1793.
After carrying out the revolution, the National Assembly decides to take exotic animals out of private hands and move them to Paris, where they form a menagerie at the Jardin des Plantes. Like Matt Damon, they bought a zoo.

paris 101

paris

1889.
The famed cabaret Moulin Rouge opens for business. Debauchery ensues, and Nicole Kidman nabs a singing gig.

1900.
The Paris Métro system opens during Paris's World's Fair.

1969.
America's greatest wannabe Frenchman, Joe Dassin, records the infinitely catchy "Aux Champs-Élysées," about the city's great boulevard. All who hear it get it stuck in their heads for a minimum of two years.

1998.
France hosts the FIFA World Cup, and the French win the final in Paris. They party like it's 1999.

2006.
Even more people fall in love with the City of Lights after the premier of the movie *Paris, je t'aime.*

"Napoleonic Code," Napoleon's ambitions were larger than he was. In 1804, he managed to convince people that naming himself Emperor was totally consistent with the ideals of the revolution, then proceeded to create a physical empire so vast it extended, at its height, from Spain to Russia. In 1813, Napoleon was defeated by the Sixth Coalition (an alliance comprised of Austria, Prussia, Russia, the United Kingdom, Portugal, Spain, Sweden, and a number of German states) and was exiled to the island of Elba. Basically, Elba was the beginning of the end for old Boney. Though Napoleon managed to escape the island within a year and work his way back to the throne, he was defeated once and for all in 1815 at the **Battle of Waterloo**. Napoleon was banished yet again, this time to the tropical island of Saint Helena, where he is rumored to have spent the last of his balmy days sipping piña coladas on the white sand beach until he died of stomach cancer or foul play in 1821.

The next hundred years witnessed another period of development for Paris, with innovations in technology, infrastructure, and culture, as well as a healthy smattering of revolutions. Napoleon's nephew even showed up and ruled for 18 years as **Napoleon III**, transforming the city of Paris by clearing out the neighborhoods of the old center and replacing them with today's grand boulevards. His partner in crime in the endeavor was one **Baron Haussmann**. You can thank this duo for the scenic finish to the Tour de France as well as the virtual strip mall *de luxe* that is now the Champs-Élysées (more on that later).

Guns and Republics (1914-Present)

While the stalemate on the Western Front prevented the German forces from reaching Paris in WWI, the French were not so lucky the second time around. Hitler's forces occupied the city from 1940-44. Most of Paris's historical buildings and monuments were spared from the destruction of WWII, but over half a million French citizens were not so fortunate.

In 1958, undaunted by the failure of its first four republics, France officially began its next chapter as a nation, creatively titled the Fifth Republic. The country nearly gave way to a sixth in May 1968 when student demonstrations took over the streets of Paris, eventually escalating into a nationwide general strike. The crisis passed, however, and since then the French government has demonstrated an uncharacteristic stability, minus a few hiccups here and there. (We're looking at you, Bettencourts.)

The Fifth Republic replaced the traditional parliamentary government structure with a semi-presidential system, in which both a prime minister and a president take administrative lead of the government. The president, who in France wields significantly more visible authority than the prime minister, is currently **François Hollande,** a member of the French Socialist party who replaced right-wing former president **Nicolas Sarkozy** (also known as Carla Bruni's husband) in 2012.

In Paris, the position of mayor has been held since 2001 by **Bertrand Delanoë**. Today, 12 million Parisians make up about a fifth of France's total population, and one in four Parisians are between the ages of 13 and 30. With over 300,000 students, Paris also ranks among the most populated and most popular university cities in Europe. And, as in its early years, Paris is still very much a capital city, home to a wide variety of food, cultures, and people from across France, North Africa, and the world.

CUSTOMS AND ETIQUETTE

How to Make Friends

Everyone knows the stereotype of the unfriendly, pretentious Parisian. But if you exhibit basic manners, most will simply label you as a foreigner and remain civil. Of course, Parisians define basic manners somewhat more extensively than the average American. Basic etiquette requires that you greet everyone that you interact with as *monsieur* or *madame*. It is common to kiss once on each cheek when greeting a friend, but a handshake is usually acceptable upon first introduction. Simply saying please *(s'il vous plaît)* and thank you *(merci*—adding *beaucoup* is optional) will earn you respect. While you should at least try to communicate *en français*—*bonjour*, *bonsoir*, and *pardon* are your three favorite words starting now—engaging in faux-French banter *Flight of the Conchords*-style may or may not get you what you're looking for. Even if you do attempt to speak French, Parisians will almost invariably respond in English, so don't expect to be fluent by the time you leave, and don't be afraid to declare that you simply *ne parle pas français*.

How to Get By

At a restaurant, waiters will not bring you the bill unless you ask for it. Don't let the ghosts of French teachers past tell you otherwise—it is, in fact, *passé* to refer to your waiter as *garçon*, or boy. A simple *pardon, monsieur!* should get his attention without emasculating the poor guy, and when you're ready for the check, you can request *l'addition* (don't forget to say please!). Though **tips** are usually included in the check, most customers add an extra five percent to go directly to the waiters. A 2008 law banned smoking in restaurants and bars, so don't test your luck. Beware of crazy driving in the capital—even the childhood "look both ways" lesson may not always cut it in Paris, especially in the always busy Place de la Concorde. Most public restrooms are free, and many self-clean after every use, so be sure to get out of there fast unless you also want a shower.

Table Manners for Dummies

After hearing your mother repeat proper table manners for the billionth time, your younger self was pretty annoyed. "No one's going to terminate a friendship over the occasional elbow on the table," you thought. Well, you were wrong. "Just wait until you get to Paris," your mother thought. She was right. At a meal in this noble city, don't even think about eating before someone says, "*Bon appétit!*" If invited to a dinner party, it's polite to send flowers to the host beforehand, and be prepared to clean your plate completely; not only did your mother tell you to eat your veggies, but it is bad form to leave any food uneaten, as it can be seen as an insult to the cook rather than a reflection of your appetite (or lack thereof). Resist the temptation to fill wine glasses up to the top, no matter how delicious the *vin*—keep in mind that refills are often readily available. Although knives and forks are used to eat almost everything (even fruit), don't think about touching a knife to your salad leaves, since it is inexcusably offensive. And while the French generally abhor finger food, do not cut a baguette on the table—tear it or face social exile for the rest of your stay in Paris. You may (rightfully) insist that these customs are somewhat prissy, to which we can only bid thee good luck and assure you that you are one step closer to fitting in. Or, at the very least, not being sneered at.

FOOD AND DRINK

Rich, Rich, and Richer

You're entitled to think that snails and frogs are gross, but you have to admit that France is a center of gastronomic innovation, and as the capital of that capital, Paris has the best of the best. Here, you'll dine on the most delicious Provençal bouillabaisse and the tastiest Breton *galette*. The wine's not bad either. Sure, French culture is known for food rich enough to put you into cardiac arrest on the spot, but that doesn't necessarily translate into supersized portions. The French are known for their focus on taste and quality rather than quantity.

French meals need not always be multiple courses. A typical day begins with a small breakfast, which isn't called *petit déjeuner* ("small lunch") for nothing. Don't expect Belgian waffles (for that, see **Brussels 101,** Food and Drinks). Instead, go for toast or pastries and coffee. (Ask for an Americano if you're not into the fancy stuff.) Lunch is usually served anywhere between noon and 3pm, and many restaurants in Paris serve reasonable *prix-fixe* meals that let you sample several dishes. Many Parisians eat simple lunches of salads, sandwiches on baguettes, crepes, *croques-monsieur* (a fancy-pants version of a grilled cheese with ham), or heavier meat dishes. Dinner is usually a similar affair, with somewhat bigger portions and dessert. A full French meal is a bigger, multi-step ordeal: it begins with an *entrée* of *hors d'oeuvres* (appetizers) with an aperitif; then comes the *plat principal*, which is usually a main fish or meat dish with sides; salad typically comes after the *plat principal;* a cheese plate is often served after the main dish; dessert ends the meal, along with coffee. Wine is served during dinner. The type of wine will depend on your budget, your meal, and your level of pretentiousness.

Vegetarians in Paris

We get it. You like animals, you want to save the world, whatever. But it's only fair that we warn you—while being a vegetarian in Paris is certainly a viable possibility, it's going to get you more raised eyebrows than accommodating nods. Many restaurants don't have any vegetarian options beyond salads on their standard menus, but most will prepare a simple omelette if you ask nicely. Forget being a vegan if you want to experience any semblance of authentic French cuisine. Since Paris is a major world city, of course there are some crunchier options for the vegan set, but asking us to visit France without eating a crepe is like Jay-Z without Kanye.

SPORTS AND RECREATION

It turns out that Paris is a great place to watch professional sporting events. For starters, the grand av. des Champs Élysées is the annual endpoint for the **Tour de France,** where spectators line up each year to watch Lance Armstrong win. Paris also hosts the **French Open** tennis tournament, known locally as the Roland Garros tournament. The tournament, held exclusively on red clay courts, takes place in May and June. (And what better way to experience tennis than in the country that invented the game?) The outskirts of the city are home to the **Palais Omnisports de Paris Bercy,** an arena of epic proportions that accommodates a wide variety of professional sporting events, from martial arts to basketball to wrestling. If you're interested in actually playing sports while in Paris, try your luck at joining a friendly game of **Boules,** known alternately as Petanque or Bocce, in a park like le Jardin du Luxembourg. (You may find that many of these games are actually quite serious, in which case you wouldn't want to endanger your life by asking to join. Just watch instead.) If soccer (known in French as **football**) is more your style, many parks have pickup games in which the bolder types can participate, while others can just buy a ball and play their own game.

ART AND ARCHITECTURE

Pop! Goes My Art

Paris has drawn its fair share of artists to its decorated avenues, and it has some of the world's greatest collections to prove it. The **Louvre** holds more than 35,000 works that range from antiquity to modernity. Highlights include the ancient Greek statue *Venus de Milo*, the famous *Mona Lisa* by Leonardo da Vinci, and the world's highest concentration of angry security guards telling tourists not to take pictures. The **Musée de Cluny** showcases medieval art, including the 15th-century tapestry *La Dame à la Licorne* ("The Lady and the Unicorn"). For Belle Époque (late 19th through early 20th centuries) fans, the **Musée d'Orsay** houses an outstanding collection of Impressionist and post-Impressionist art; the small **Musée de l'Orangerie** has an amazing room, paneled by wall-sized Monet water lily paintings; its neighboring **Galerie nationale du Jeu de Paume,** located in the building that once housed Napoleon III's tennis courts, features a great deal of photography and installation art; and the **Musée Rodin** showcases many of the sculptor's best works. If you're interested in modern and contemporary art, the **Musée National d'Art Moderne** is devoted to just that.

Epoch Building

Paris is an amalgam of architectural (and historical and artistic and political, but we've already covered those) periods, and it's safe to say that a product of each epoch adds its own (dare we say, epic) style to the city. The oldest examples can be traced back to ancient Rome, with what Romans may be best known for: roads and ruins. Rue Saint-Jacques, which they built in what is now the fifth *arrondissement*, exists to this day (re-paved, thankfully), and the stone amphitheater, **Arènes de Lutèce,** dates back to the first century CE. During the medieval period, the Gothic style developed, with flying buttresses suspending intricate stained glass windows and pointed arches, evident in the cathedrals of **Notre Dame** in Paris and **Chartres** a bit farther afield. Renaissance architecture focused more on proportion and balance, and from there emerged the Baroque style, best exemplified by the extravagant palace and grounds of **Versailles.** The decorative Rococo style, which emulated grotto rock and shells, developed in the early to mid-18th century. Both the **Hôtel de Matignon** and the **Hôtel d'Evreux,** the residences of the prime minister and president of France respectively, employ the Rococo style in their architecture. Neo-classicism, an homage to Greek and Roman architecture, was popularized in the late 18th and early 19th centuries. It resulted in constructions like the **Panthéon** and the **Arc de Triomphe.** In the late 19th century, Napoleon III also had Baron Georges-Eugène Haussmann renovate the streets of Paris: the city can thank him for the wider boulevards and balconied apartment buildings that are such standard Parisian features today. The Industrial Revolution sparked Art Nouveau architecture, which took its designs from patterns in the natural world. For an example, look up and wave hello to the **Eiffel Tower,** built for the 1889 Exposition Universelle.

HOLIDAYS AND FESTIVALS

With its eclectic history, Paris can compete with any European city for having the most obscure holidays and festivals. Aside from the standard Christian holidays like Christmas, New Year's Day, Easter, Ascension Day (May), and the Assumption (August 15), the city's festivals are unique. Keep in mind that museums and other monuments usually close on some of these dates.

HOLIDAY OR FESTIVAL	DESCRIPTION	DATE
Fashion Week	A week of fashion shows, complete with new styles by the world's most famous designer labels.	usually late January
Carnival	Over 500 years old, this city carnival gives residents an excuse (as if you need one) to wear masks and parade through the streets.	early March
VE Day	A celebration of the Allied victory over Germany in World War II. Festivities include a parade on the Champs-Élysées.	May 8
Fête de la Musique	Free concerts and performances are given throughout the city.	June 21
Gay Pride Parade	Parades and presentations celebrate Paris's GLBT community.	mid-June
Bastille Day	This national holiday commemorates the storming of the Bastille in 1789. Kick it off with the *Bal du 14 Juillet*, a giant dance party the night before, and end by watching fireworks over the Eiffel Tower.	July 14
Armistice Day	A holiday that celebrates the armistice signed between the Allies of World War I and Germany	November 11
Beaujolais Nouveau Wine Festival	A nationwide celebration of the release of Beaujolais Nouveau wine; bar-hopping and drinking ensue.	November 15

paris

AMSTERDAM

Tell someone you're going to Amsterdam, and you'll be met with a chuckle and a knowing smile. Yes, everyone will think you're going for the hookers and weed, but there's much more to Amsterdam. The Netherlands's permissive attitudes are the product of a long history of liberalism and tolerance that dates back far before the advent of drug tourism and prostitutes' unions. A refuge for Protestants and Jews in the 16th and 17th centuries, Amsterdam earned tremendous wealth as the center of a trading empire that stretched from the New York (sorry: New Amsterdam) to Indonesia. The city's wealth served as an incubator for the artistic achievements of the Dutch Golden Age and the economic and political birth of modern Europe. Today, Amsterdam is a diverse and progressive city as famous for its art museums and quaint canal-side cafes as for its coffeeshops and prostitution.

As you stroll the streets, savor the culture and vitality of this pretty city. You can walk or bike it in a day, moving from the peaceful canals of the Jordaan to the gaudy peepshows of the Red Light District. Old trading money lives on in graceful mansions, while, a few blocks away, repurposed squats house clubs and cinemas. Whether you're obsessed with van Gogh, want to dance all night at GLBT clubs, or always wanted to learn all about the history of fluorescent art, you're guaranteed to have a good time in Amsterdam.

greatest hits

- **LEID THE WAY.** Leidseplein (p. 240) has possibly the highest concentration of great bars and clubs you'll find anywhere. Except perhaps for its clubbing cousin, Rembrandtplein (p. 242).

- **MUSEUMPLENTY.** The area around Museumplein features not one, but two of the world's greatest art museums. Relive the Dutch Golden Age at the Rijksmuseum (p. 219) or stop and smell the sunflowers at the Van Gogh Museum (p. 218).

- **CENTRAAL PERK.** Amsterdam's coffeeshops are like no others in the world. No matter what your tastes, a visit to just one is sure to be an enlightening experience (p. 250).

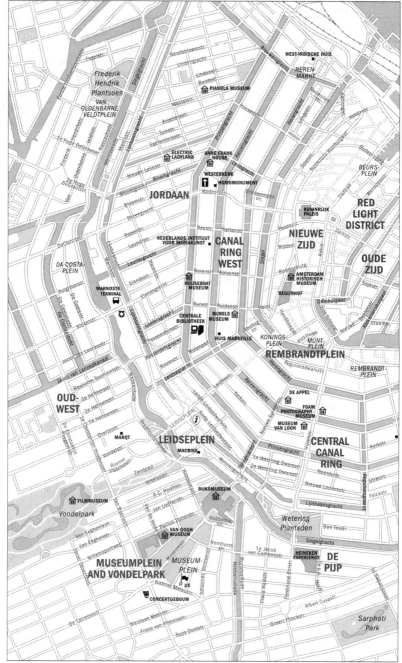

amsterdam

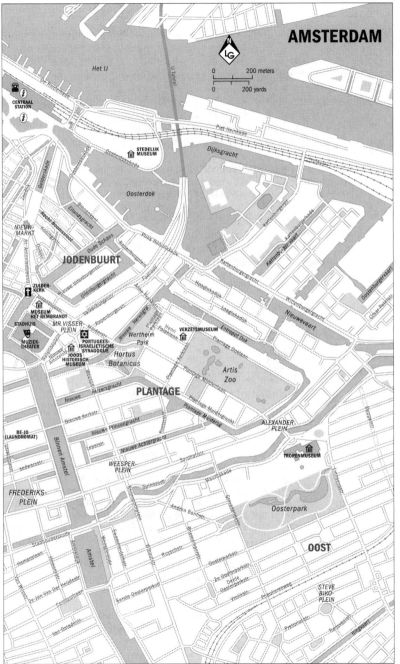

AMSTERDAM

Het IJ

CENTRAAL STATION

STEDELIJK MUSEUM

Piet Heinkade

Dijksgracht

Oosterdok

NIEUW MARKT

JODENBUURT

ZUIDER-KERK

MUSEUM HET REMBRANDT

STADHUIS

MR VISSER-PLEIN

MUZIEK-THEATER

PORTUGEES-ISRAELIETISCHE SYNAGOGUE

JOODS HISTORISCH MUSEUM

VERZETSMUSEUM

Wertheim Park

Hortus Botanicus

Artis Zoo

PLANTAGE

BE-JO (LAUNDROMAT)

ALEXANDER PLEIN

TROPENMUSEUM

WEESPER-PLEIN

FREDERIKS-PLEIN

Oosterpark

OOST

STEVE BIKO-PLEIN

student life

It's hard to think of a city anywhere in the world that is as friendly to students as Amsterdam. Though not a college town in the pure sense, it's hard to go one block (or canal) without a couple of students whizzing by on bicycles. Grownups in charge of Amsterdam's cultural output have taken note: anyone under 26 can purchase a **Museumjaarkaart** at half price for unlimited access to Amsterdam's numerous museums. The **Muziektheater** offers student rush tickets to opera and classical ballet performances, and the English comedy house **Boom Chicago** admits four students for the price of one every Wednesday. If you're too afraid to cozy up to the hottie in the plush seat next to you, hostels dotted throughout the town foster their own close communities. Once your advances are successful, bring your date to dinner at **'Skek** in Oude Zijd, where you'll receive a 33% discount by showing a student ID. This might be the only place in the world where people try to borrow IDs from people under 21.

Of course, the most (in)famous attraction in Amsterdam is its nightlife. If you're forced to skip the coffeeshops because of your nationality, don't worry: the parties rage nightly in **Leidseplein** and **Rembrandtplein**, while the central areas like the **Red Light District** offer a seedier, but uniquely "Amsterdam," experience. Those who'd prefer not to dance with 40-year-olds should head to **Dansen bij Jansen,** a student-only nightclub in Nieuwe Zijd.

orientation

call me!

The phone code for Amsterdam is ☎020.

The first step to getting a handle on Amsterdam's geography is to understand its canals. The Singel wraps around the heart of the Centrum, which is made up from east to west of the Oude Zijd, Red Light District, and Nieuwe Zijd. Barely 1km in diameter, the Centrum's skinny streets overflow with bars, brothels, clubs, and tourists—many of whom won't leave this area during their whole stay in Amsterdam.

The next set of canals, running in concentric circles, are Herengracht, Keizergracht, and Prinsengracht (hint: "gracht" means "canal," so if you're looking for a "gracht" street and you don't see water, you're lost). These enclose a somewhat classier area filled with locals, tasty restaurants, and plenty of museums (some very worthwhile, others completely ridiculous). Rembrandtplein and Leidseplein, the twin hearts of Amsterdam's and party scene, are also nestled here.

To the east of the canal ring are Jodenbuurt and Plantage, the city's old Jewish quarter. Moving southwest you get to De Pijp, an artsy neighborhood filled with immigrants and hipsters, then Museumplein and Vondelpark, home to the city's largest park and most important museums. Working back north to the west of the center you'll find Oud-West and Westerpark, two largely residential neighborhoods that are experiencing a boom in popularity and culture. In between Westerpark and the canal ring is the reliably chic Jordaan. Finally, to the north, in between Jordaan and Centraal Station, lies Scheepvaartbuurt, the city's old shipping quarter.

OUDE ZIJD

Many will delight in telling you that the Oude Zijd ("Old Side") is in fact newer than the Nieuwe Zijd ("New Side"). That doesn't really say much about the character of the neighborhood, which is sandwiched between the wild Red Light District and the more relaxed, local-dominated Jodenbuurt, and which feels like a balance between the two. A mini-kinda-Chinatown stretches along the northern part of **Zeedijk,** which spills into **Nieuwmarkt,** a lovely square dominated by a medieval ex-fortress. The bars and cafes lining Nieuwmarkt's perimeter are popular places for tourists and locals to rub elbows over a beer. Farther south is **Kloveniersburgwal,** a canal lined with genteel 17th-century buildings (many now occupied by the University of Amsterdam). Fancier hotels and cafes start to replace the tourist-traps and faux-British pubs where the canal hits the Amstel.

RED LIGHT DISTRICT

Once defined by the sailors who frequented Amsterdam's port, the Red Light District dates back to the 13th century, when business-savvy ladies began to capitalize on the crowds of sex-starved seamen. Today, the only sailors you'll find are the fake ones in the gay porn and costume shops, but the sex industry still flourishes here. The neighborhood is remarkably well regulated and policed, but this is definitely no Disneyland (though the number of families sightseeing here might surprise you). The **Oudezijds Achterburgwal,** with its live sex shows and porn palaces, is the Red Light's major artery. The streets perpendicular to this main thoroughfare are lined with girl-filled windows, stretching to **Oudezijds Voorburgwal** and **Warmoesstraat.** Some sex stores and theaters have set up camp on these western streets, but for the most part they provide bars for male tourists to get liquored up before venturing through one of the neon-lit doors. Those not looking for prostitution can still carouse in the Red Light District's endless sea of bars and coffeeshops. You'll also find an immense army of the infamous Dutch public urinals, as well as the type of traveler who feels comfortable using them. To see the hedonism at its peak, come on a Friday or Saturday night; for a less overwhelming visit, try strolling through on a weekday afternoon.

SCHEEPVAARTBUURT

Scheepvaartbuurt, which would create quite a round on *Wheel of Fortune,* is Amsterdam's old shipping quarter. It was traditionally a working-class neighborhood with a lot of immigrants and had a reputation as one of the rougher parts of the city. Nowadays, despite looking difficult to pronounce (it's actually not that bad…it's like "shape-fart-burt"), Scheepvaartbuurt is a pleasant area full of young people and largely devoid of tourists. Remnants of the neighborhood's salty seadog past—like bronze propellers, anchors, and steering wheels—dot the sidewalks, and you can almost detect a faint whiff of the sea breeze that once blew ships to this shore. There aren't any real sights, but it's worth a visit for the local shops that line **Haarlemmerplein,** which becomes **Haarlemmerdijk** as you move east toward residential Westerpark.

CANAL RING WEST

The Canal Ring West lies around—spoiler alert—a ring of three canals: the **Herengracht, Keizersgracht,** and **Prinsengracht** (helpful hint: they go in alphabetical order from the center of the city toward the west). It extends from Brouwersgracht in the north down to the Leidseplein. Chock-full of grand canal houses and quaint houseboats, the neighborhood provides a nice escape from the more crowded Nieuwe Zijd next door. Three major sights draw visitors: the **Anne Frank House, Westerkerk,** and the **Homomonument.** The ▨**Nine Streets,** small lanes running from the Prinsengracht to the Singel, south of Raadhuisstraat, are packed with more unique stores and vibrant cafes than we can fit in this guidebook.

orientation

CENTRAL CANAL RING

The Central Canal Ring tends to get overshadowed by its neighbors: Museumplein outshines its sights, Rembrandtplein and Leidseplein outdo its nightlife, and De Pijp offers a more exciting culinary scene. However, this neighborhood—the area from **Leidsestraat** to the **Amstel,** bordered on the north by the **Singel** and on the south by **Weteringschans**—enjoys the best parts of its surrounds without suffering their crowds, high prices, and soul- and cash-sucking tourist traps. **Utrechtsestraat** in particular offers lively cafes, restaurants, and stores, all frequented by a mix of locals and tourists, while the **Golden Bend** boasts some of Amsterdam's most impressive architecture. Along the Southern border, **Weteringplantsoen** and **Frederiksplein** provide some small but pretty green spaces to stop and rest your feet.

LEIDSEPLEIN

The Leidseplein, an almost exclusively commercial rectangle south of the Central Canal Ring, has a polarizing effect on those who pass through it, inspiring either devotion or disapproval. It's a busy, touristy part of town that lies in the area between the Nassaukade, Spiegelgracht, Prinsengracht, and Leidsegracht. During the day, the square is packed with street performers and promoters for pub crawls and other assorted evening entertainments. At night, the revelry continues in a bath of neon light and cheap beer. The few streets running through the Leidseplein's interior are packed with ethnic restaurants, theaters, bars, and clubs. Among the sushi and salsa, there are also a number of very Dutch establishments to be found. Numerous transport connections, including the elusive night bus, make this neighborhood a convenient as well as fun part of town. There are no sights to speak of, though look out for the enigmatic inscription *"Homo sapiens non urinat in ventum "* ("A wise man does not piss into the wind") on the pillars above **Max Euweplein Square.** While many Dutch will frown in pity if you spend much of your trip here, the best part about Leidseplein is that some of those frown-bearers will secretly be living it up here all weekend, too.

REMBRANDTPLEIN

For our purposes, the Rembrandtplein neighborhood comprises the square itself, the area stretching from Herengracht to the Amstel, and the part of Reguliersdwarstraat between Vijzelstraat and the Bloemenmarkt. Once upon a time (a.k.a. the late 17th century), the area now known as Rembrandtplein was home to Amsterdam's butter market *(Botermarkt)*. The construction of a few hotels in the 20th century brought tourists, and with the tourists came booze (and euro-trance). With a few noteworthy exceptions, food and accommodations in Rembrandtplein often cost more than they're worth. The real reason to come here is the nightlife. Rembrandtplein's bars and clubs are as popular and numerous as in the Leidseplein, but tend to be larger and more exclusive, with more locals and GLBT establishments. Europe's largest LCD TV screen, located above Amsterdam's largest club, **Escape,** lights up the square at night. From the middle of the square, **Rembrandt van Rijn** looks benevolently down at the madness. When you get tired of bar-hopping, take a rest in nearby **Thorbeckeplein,** a grassy stretch of trees, named for Johan Rudolph Thorbecke (1798-1872), known colloquially as the first prime minister of the Netherlands. Thorbeckeplein is also the name of a song written by the popular Dutch singer Robert Long about a bittersweet gay love affair.

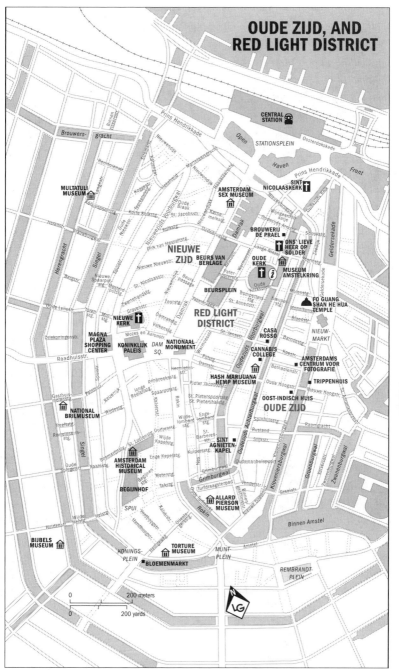

OUDE ZIJD, AND RED LIGHT DISTRICT

CENTRAL STATION

STATIONSPLEIN

Prins Hendrikkade

Open Haven

Oosterdokskade

Front

Prins Hendrikkade

SINT NICOLAASKERK

Brouwers-gracht

MULTATULI MUSEUM

AMSTERDAM SEX MUSEUM

BROUWERIJ DE PRAEL

ONS' LIEVE HEER OP SOLDER

NIEUWE ZIJD

BEURS VAN BERLAGE

OUDE KERK

MUSEUM AMSTELKRING

Singel

BEURSPLEIN

FO GUANG SHAN HE HUA TEMPLE

NIEUWE KERK

RED LIGHT DISTRICT

NIEUW-MARKT

CASA ROSSO

AMSTERDAMS CENTRUM VOOR FOTOGRAFIE

MAGNA PLAZA SHOPPING CENTER

KONINKLIJK PALEIS

DAM SQ.

NATIONAAL MONUMENT

CANNABIS COLLEGE

HASH MARIJUANA HEMP MUSEUM

TRIPPENHUIS

Raadhuisstr.

OOST-INDISCH HUIS

OUDE ZIJD

NATIONAL BRILMUSEUM

Singel

SINT AGNIETEN-KAPEL

AMSTERDAM HISTORICAL MUSEUM

BEGIJNHOF

ALLARD PIERSON MUSEUM

SPUI

Rokin

Binnen Amstel

BIJBELS MUSEUM

TORTURE MUSEUM

MUNT PLEIN

REMBRANDT PLEIN

KONINGS-PLEIN

BLOEMENMARKT

Amstel

0   200 meters

0   200 yards

orientation

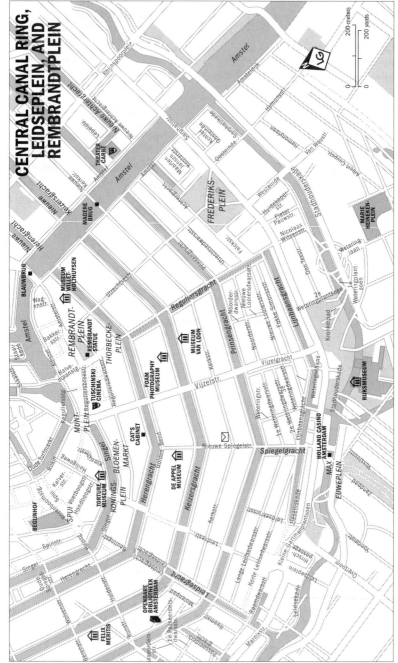

CENTRAL CANAL RING,
LEIDSEPLEIN, AND
REMBRANDTPLEIN

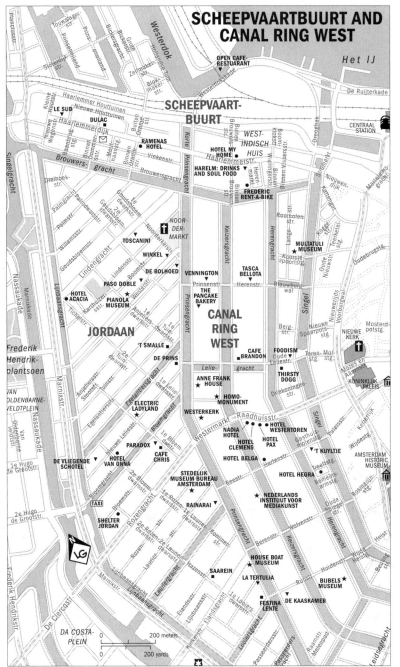

SCHEEPVAARTBUURT AND CANAL RING WEST

Het IJ

OPEN CAFE-RESTUARANT

De Ruijterkade

SCHEEPVAART-BUURT

CENTRAAL STATION

LE SUD

DULAC

RAMENAS HOTEL

WEST-INDISCH HUIS

HOTEL MY HOME

HARELM: DRINKS AND SOUL FOOD

FREDERIC RENT-A-BIKE

NOOR-DER-MARKT

MULTATULI MUSEUM

TOSCANINI

WINKEL

DE BOLHEED

VENNINGTON

TASCA BELLOTA

PASO DOBLE

THE PANCAKE BAKERY

HOTEL ACACIA

PIANOLA MUSEUM

JORDAAN

'T SMALLE

DE PRINS

CANAL RING WEST

CAFE BRANDON

FOODISM

Frederik Hendrik-plantsoen

ANNE FRANK HOUSE

THIRSTY DOGG

VAN OLDENBARNE-VELDTPLEIN

HOMO-MONUMENT

ELECTRIC LADYLAND

WESTERKERK

NADIA HOTEL

HOTEL WESTERTOREN

HOTEL CLEMENS

HOTEL PAX

'T KUYLTJE

AMSTERDAM HISTORIC MUSEUM

PARADOX

CAFE CHRIS

HOTEL BELGA

DE VLIEGENDE SCHOTEL

HOTEL VAN ONNA

HOTEL HEGRA

STEDELIJK MUSEUM-BUREAU AMSTERDAM

NEDERLANDS INSTITUUT VOOR MEDIAKUNST

TAXI

RAINARAI

SHELTER JORDAN

HOUSE BOAT MUSEUM

SAAREIN

LA TERTULIA

BIJBELS MUSEUM

FESTINA LENTE

DE KAASKAMER

DA COSTA-PLEIN

0   200 meters

0   200 yards

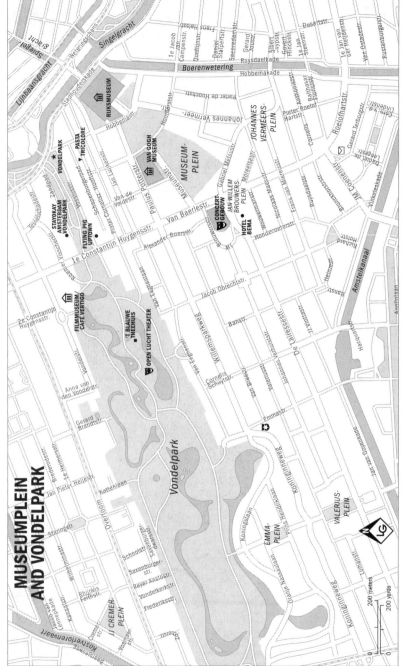

MUSEUMPLEIN AND VONDELPARK

amsterdam

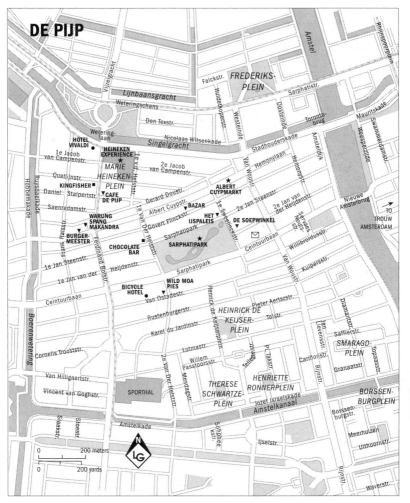

DE PIJP

FREDERIKS-
PLEIN

orientation

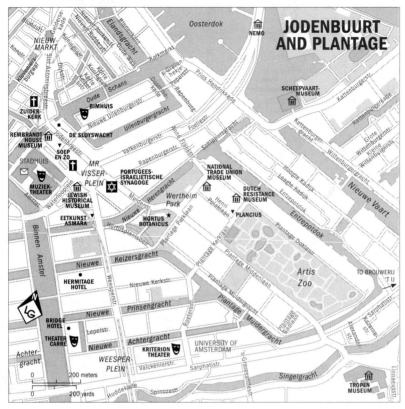

JODENBUURT AND PLANTAGE

Oosterdok

NEMO

SCHEEPVAART-MUSEUM

Nieuwe Vaart

NIEUW-MARKT

ZUIDER-KERK

BIMHUIS

Oude Schans

REMBRANDT HOUSE MUSEUM

DE SLUYSWACHT

SOEP EN ZO

STADHUIS

MR VISSER-PLEIN

MUZIEK-THEATER

JEWISH HISTORICAL MUSEUM

PORTUGEES-ISRAELIETISCHE SYNAGOGE

NATIONAL TRADE UNION MUSEUM

DUTCH RESISTANCE MUSEUM

Entrepotdok

Wertheim Park

EETKUNST ASMARA

HORTUS BOTANICUS

PLANCIUS

Artis Zoo

TO BROUWERIJ 'T IJ

Binnen Amstel

Nieuwe Keizersgracht

HERMITAGE HOTEL

Nieuwe Prinsengracht

Plantage Muidergracht

BRIDGE HOTEL

THEATER CARRE

Nieuwe Achtergracht

KRITERION THEATER

UNIVERSITY OF AMSTERDAM

Achter-gracht

WEESPER-PLEIN

TROPEN MUSEUM

Singelgracht

0   200 meters

0   200 yards

amsterdam

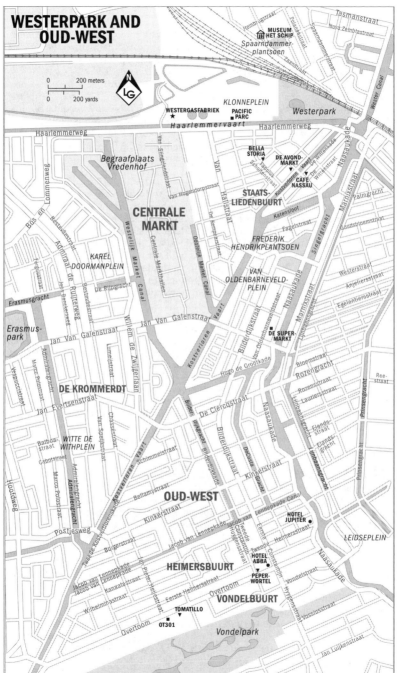

WESTERPARK AND OUD-WEST

Tasmanstraat
Nova Zembiastraat

MUSEUM
HET SCHIP
Spaarndammer-
plantsoen

0   200 meters
0   200 yards

N
LG

KLONNEPLEIN

WESTERGASFABRIEK
★

PACIFIC
■ PARC

Westerpark

Haarlemmervaart

Haarlemmerweg

Haarlemmerweg

Begraafplaats
Vredenhof

BELLA
STORIA ▼

DE AVOND-
MARKT ■

STAATS-
LIEDENBUURT

CAFÉ
NASSAU ▼

Palmgracht

CENTRALE
MARKT

Katensloot

Fagelstraat

Goudsbloemstraat

KAREL
DOORMANPLEIN

FREDERIK
HENDRIKPLANTSOEN

Westerstraat

De Rijpgracht

Am_liersstraat

Erasmusgracht

VAN
OLDENBARNEVELD-
PLEIN

Egelantiersstraat

Erasmus-
park

Jan Van Galenstraat

Jan Van Galenstraat

DE SUPER-
MARKT ■

Bloemstraat

Rozengracht

Ree-
straat

Hugo de Grootkade

Rozenstraat

Laurierstraat

DE KROMMERDT

Jan Evertsenstraat

De Clercqstraat

Elands-
straat

Elands-
gracht

WITTE DE
WITHPLEIN

Cabotstraat

OUD-WEST

Kinkerstraat

HOTEL
JUPITER ●

LEIDSEPLEIN

Postjesweg

Kinkerstraat

Jacob van Lennepkade

HOTEL
ABBA ▼

HEIMERSBUURT

PEPER-
WORTEL ▼

VONDELBUURT

TOMATILLO ■

Overtoom

OT301

Overtoom

Vondelpark

Jan Luijkenstraat

orientation

NIEUWE ZIJD

Older than the Oude Zijd (but home to a church that's younger than the Oude Kerk, thus explaining the neighborhoods' confusing name swap), the Nieuwe Zijd offers a mix of history, culture, and a whole lot of tourists. **Damrak**, its eastern edge, stretches from **Centraal Station** to **Dam Square** and then turns into **Rokin.** These are some of the busiest streets in the city, full of souvenir shops and shawarma stands; they're best tackled on foot, as this is the one part of Amsterdam where bikes don't rule the road. As you head west to **Spuistraat,** the streets become less crowded and more hip. **Kalverstraat,** one of the city's prime shopping streets for centuries, is now home to department stores and international chains. The Nieuwe Zijd is tourist central, full of huge hostels and coffeeshops, and you're much more likely to run into drug-ready backpackers and elderly tourists taking pictures than any locals.

JORDAAN

Once a staunchly working-class neighborhood, the Jordaan has been transformed into one of Amsterdam's prettiest and most fashionable areas. It provides a nice escape from the overwhelming hordes of tourists in the Red Light District to the east and has more energy than the more residential Westerpark to the (what do you think?) west. Streets are narrow, canals are leafy, and gabled houses are clumped together in colorful rows. You won't find any of Amsterdam's most famous sights here (well, except for ▨**Electric Ladyland**), but the Jordaan's restaurants and cafes are not to be missed. Establishments in the northern part of the neighborhood are more often filled with locals, while tourists tend to wander over from Westermarkt into the area near **Rozengracht.**

WESTERPARK AND OUD-WEST

Westerpark is a residential neighborhood northeast of the main city center; its eponymous park is a serene stretch of green that makes for a pleasant break from the urban jungle. It has a loyal and vocal community—just don't expect to hear any English—and is becoming increasingly popular among young people and artists, bringing ever-exciting cultural projects and nightlife to its streets. South of Westerpark lies the Oud-West, still dominated by locals but with a few large streets (**Kinkerstraat** and **Overtoom** in particular) that keep the area busy with their small ethnic cafes and cheap chain stores. The northern part of Oud-West is a little grungy, but the area farther south—north of Vondelpark, close to the Leidseplein—is probably the most tourist-friendly part of the neighborhood.

MUSEUMPLEIN AND VONDELPARK

Museumplein and Vondelpark lie just south of the main canal ring, close to the city center yet somewhat removed from its hectic disposition. Vondelpark is a gorgeous green space with some fine hostels not far from the excitement of Leidseplein and the ethnic eateries of the Oud-West. Museumplein, meanwhile, feels distinctly different from the rest of the city, attracting older and more affluent tourists than the backpacker-swarmed areas to the north. **P. C. Hooftstraat** is lined with designer stores like Prada and Tiffany—the number of fancy French brasseries reflects the cash thrown around here. But just because you're young and on a budget doesn't mean you should shy away. Museumplein is a large, grassy field lined with some of the best museums in the world—no visit to Amsterdam is complete without a trip to the **Van Gogh Museum** and **Rijksmuseum.** Most of the tourist-friendly action is sandwiched between Stadhouderskade to the north and Van Baerlestraat (which contains the Museumplein tram stop) to the south. Come here to get some space, culture, and class—three things that feel far away when you're downing Heinekens with the masses in a hostel bar on Warmoesstraat.

DE PIJP

De Pijp ("duh pipe") may lack history and sights, but it more than makes up for that with modern culture. A mix of immigrants, students, and artists creates a haven of excellent ethnic restaurants, fun cafes, and relatively inexpensive housing. **Albert Cuypstraat** hosts the city's largest open-air market, along with a cluster of cafes, clothing stores, and cheap eats. Intersecting Albert Cuypstraat to the west is **Ferdinard Bolstraat,** which is home to a high concentration of restaurants and leads to the avoidable **Heineken Experience.** Still a little bit rough around the edges, De Pijp has all the charm of the Jordaan in a much younger and more urban environment.

JODENBUURT AND PLANTAGE

A high concentration of sights and museums is the real draw here, but don't overlook the few excellent restaurants and small bars. The open space in these neighborhoods is a great antidote to the over-crowded city center. Jodenbuurt, centered around **Waterlooplein,** was historically the home of Amsterdam's Jewish population. Plantage, home to wide streets and numerous parks, stretches around Jodenbuurt to the east. Most commercial establishments can be found on the streets near the **Artis Zoo** or near the **Rembrandt House.**

accommodations

When lodging in Amsterdam, chances are you'll either be staying in a big backpacker hostel or a small hotel in a converted canal house. For the most part, anything you find in the city center is a decent option, but there's a huge range of value—some rooms are simply small white boxes with a bed, while others are lovingly decorated with attention to cozy details or an interesting theme. To get the most for your euro, consider staying in one of the neighborhoods outside of the main canal ring. If you didn't come to Amsterdam to find a 24hr. party, avoid hostels in the Red Light District. If you came to get down all day and all of the night, centrally located hostels, often with late-night bars attached, will provide plenty of opportunities to meet fellow travelers with similar missions.

Room rates fluctuate according to season and day of the week. The closer you get to the cold of winter, the cheaper your room will be—except for the days surrounding Christmas and New Year's, when prices skyrocket. While we don't advise showing up without having booked a room, especially during the summer, owners with too many unoccupied beds have been known to radically slash prices at less busy times.

OUDE ZIJD

The Oude Zijd isn't home to as many accommodations as the nearby Red Light District or Nieuwe Zijd, but it's home to two of the city's best.

✉ SHELTER CITY   HOSTEL $

Barndesteeg 21   ☎020 625 32 30 www.shelter.nl

Shelter City is a large Christian hostel (with no religious requirements for guests) in the heart of the Oude Zijd. All rooms are single-sex, most with shared baths, a few with ensuites. The beds are a bit reminiscent of those in army barracks, but the well-decorated common spaces—including a cafe, breakfast room, and courtyard garden—encourage guests to make new friends. Shelter City is popular with a wide array of young backpackers, from the quiet museum lover to the rabid party-goer.

⚐ Ⓜ*Nieuwmarkt. Just off the southwestern edge of the square.* ⓘ *Breakfast included. Free Wi-Fi. No drugs or alcohol allowed.* ⓢ *Beds €15-34. Discounts available for longer stays.* ⚑ *Security 24hr.*

STAYOKAY AMSTERDAM STADSDOELEN (HI) HOSTEL $

Kloveniersburgwal 97 ☎020 624 68 32 www.stayokay.com/stadsdoelen

Enjoy professional, upbeat staff and some cushy amenities rarely found in hostels: washing and drying machines, a TV room complete with foosball table, and a substantial breakfast including fruit and cornflakes (different varieties of cornflakes!). Rooms are plain and clean in this huge hostel—with over 150 beds, look here when your whole Varsity Marching Band needs a place to stay in Amsterdam. Located in an old canal building in a tranquil part of the Oude Zijd, this hostel is nearer to Jodenbuurt but still just a short walk from Dam Square, the Red Light District, and Rembrandtplein.

 # Tram #4, 9, 16, 24, or 25 to Muntplein. Walk down Nieuwe Doelenstraat; Kloveniersburgwal is on the right over the bridge. i Breakfast included. Free Wi-Fi. [$] Co-ed or single-sex 8- to 20-bed dorms €15-30, depending on season and day. Private rooms €39-70. HI discount.

RED LIGHT DISTRICT

Sure, this neighborhood is obsessed with sex, but the high concentration of hotels and hostels on Warmoesstraat means that there is an industry for the less red-blooded traveler as well. These are great places to stash your pack and go unabashedly wild with fellow backpackers. While the prices vary seasonally, rates in the Red Light District also tend to fall drastically in the middle of the week.

THE GREENHOUSE EFFECT HOTEL HOTEL $$$

Warmoesstraat 55 ☎020 624 49 74 www.greenhouse-effect.nl

The Greenhouse Effect has some of the nicest rooms in Amsterdam, definitely miles above average for the Red Light District. Each room is decorated according to its own whimsical theme: there's "1001 Nights," with gauzy wall hangings and an exotic chandelier; the "Sailor's Cabin," done up ship-shape with deep blue walls and brass accents; and the "Outer Space" room, with a translucent neon green light-up sink, to name a few. Guests receive discounts at the bar below and the coffeeshop next door.

 # From Centraal Station, walk south on Damrak, turn right onto Brugsteeg, and left onto Warmoesstraat. i Breakfast included. Most rooms have ensuite bath. Free Wi-Fi in the bar. [$] Singles €65-75; doubles €95-110; triples €130.

DURTY NELLY'S HOSTEL HOSTEL $

Warmoesstraat 115-117 ☎020 638 01 25 www.durtynellys.nl

A popular hostel over a convivial pub, Durty Nelly's boasts co-ed dorms that are (ironically) very clean. The rooms aren't terribly spacious, but they feel more cozy than cramped. Guests receive a discount at the pub below.

 # From Centraal Station, walk south on Damrak, turn right onto Brugsteeg, and right onto Warmoesstraat. i Breakfast included. Free Wi-Fi. Large lockers available. [$] 4- to 10-bed dorms €25-50.

HOTEL WINSTON HOSTEL, HOTEL $$

Warmoesstraat 129 ☎020 623 13 80 www.winston.nl

Hotel Winston feels more modern and continental than the other boozing-and-snoozing complexes on the street, thanks in part to the attached sleek bar and trendy club. Always busy, Winston fills up fast with backpackers and young people. It's not the cheapest place on the block and doesn't have the most interesting rooms, but it's perfect for larger groups and those who prefer the club scene to the pubs connected to most of Winston's competitors.

 # From Centraal Station, walk south on Damrak, turn right onto Brugsteeg, and right onto Warmoesstraat. i Breakfast included. Free Wi-Fi. [$] Dorms €32-40; singles €73-95; doubles €88-114.

MEETING POINT YOUTH HOSTEL HOSTEL $

Warmoesstraat 14 ☎020 627 74 99 www.hostel-meetingpoint.nl

Meeting Point's low prices and location near Centraal Station make it popular with young backpackers. Be warned: anarchy frequently reigns in the 24hr. bar downstairs. Female travelers take note that there are no single-sex dorms, and the hostel tends to attract a rowdier crowd that isn't suited for the faint of heart. Those looking for peace and quiet would do best to look elsewhere.

*⇆ From Centraal Station, turn left onto Prins Hendrikkade, right onto Nieuwebrugsteeg, and right onto Warmoesstraat. **i** Breakfast €2.50. Lockers provided, lock rentals €2 per stay. Free Wi-Fi. [$] 18-bed dorms €18-25; 8-bed €25-30.*

OLD NICKEL HOTEL HOTEL $$$

Nieuwebrugsteeg 11 ☎020 624 19 12 www.oldquarter.com/oldnickel

At the northern tip of the Red Light District, Old Nickel remains close to the activity but maintains some peace and quiet for guests. The nature wallpaper and plaid coverlets on the beds can almost fool you into thinking you're in a British country inn—the pub downstairs certainly adds to that impression. Slanted ceilings add a nice sense of coziness to the rooms on the top floor.

*⇆ From Centraal Station, turn left onto the far side of Prins Hendrikkade and right onto Nieuwebrugsteeg. **i** Breakfast included. All rooms have shared bath. Free Wi-Fi. [$] Singles €50-75; doubles €60-85.*

NIEUWE ZIJD

The Nieuwe Zijd is packed with accommodations, making it easy to stumble straight from Centraal Station into your room. Hotels here tend to be pricey, but top-notch hostels abound.

FLYING PIG DOWNTOWN HOSTEL $

Nieuwendijk 100 ☎020 420 68 22 www.flyingpig.nl

A lively bar, a comfy smoking lounge, and spacious dorms make this party hostel a perennial favorite among backpackers. The youthful staff and frequent events—like live DJs, drink specials, and televised sports games—help to drive a social atmosphere. Guests are referred to as "piggies," but don't worry, it's meant to be endearing. Queen-sized bunk beds (perfect for couples, "special" friends, or maybe even "just friends") are available in some dorms and must be booked for two people.

*⇆ From Centraal Station, walk toward Damrak. Pass the Victoria Hotel and take the 1st alley on the right, which leads to Nieuwendijk. **i** Breakfast included. Towels included. Kitchen available. Free Wi-Fi. Computers available. [$] 4-to 18-bed dorms €20-30. Significant discounts online and in the low season.*

AIVENGO YOUTH HOSTEL HOSTEL $

Spuistraat 6 ☎020 421 36 70 www.aivengoyouthhostel.com

Aivengo isn't just one of the closest hostels to Centraal Station; it's also one of the nicest. Deep colors and gauzy purple curtains give some dorms a decadent, *Arabian Nights* vibe, while others have clean, crisp interiors that are more reminiscent of Ikea. A mix of bunks and normal beds fills the large and sociable dorms. Somewhat humorously (misogynously, some might say), the all-female dorms are the only ones equipped with kitchens—other dorms include only a fridge and microwave. Two private doubles are also available, one with a roof terrace and a hot tub.

*⇆ From Centraal Station, walk down Martelarsgraacht and keep straight onto Hekelveld, which becomes Spuistraat. **i** Free Wi-Fi. Computers available. [$] Summer dorms €20-35; winter from €12. Private rooms €70-110.*

BOB'S YOUTH HOSTEL HOSTEL $

Nieuwezijds Voorburgwal 92 ☎020 624 63 58 www.bobsyouthhostel.nl

A slightly hippie-er counterpart to the Flying Pig, Bob's Youth Hostel attracts flocks of young travelers who enjoy lounging in the graffiti-filled bar and strumming their guitars outside on the steps. The dorms are decorated with cheeky, colorful murals by visiting artists. An apartment with a kitchen and bath is available for two or three people. Though it used to operate on a first-come-first-serve, ultra-free-spirit-style system, the new management now accepts reservations in advance.

🧭 From Centraal Station, go down Martelaarsgracht and bear left as it becomes Nieuwezijds Voorburgwal. ℹ Breakfast included. Wi-Fi €3 per hr., €4 per day. Computers available. $ 4- to 16-bed dorms €25-35; apartment €90-120. ⏰ Bar open until 3am.

HOSTEL AROZA HOSTEL $

Nieuwendijk 23 ☎020 620 91 23 www.aroza.nl

Trippy murals in the halls give this place definite charm, although the "Don't Worry, Be Sexy" signs might be a little too charming for some tastes. The downstairs bar is a popular hangout and features a guestbook and colored pencils for guests to record their visit for future generations, or just so they can amuse themselves after an evening of bar-hopping.

🧭 From Centraal Station, turn right, left at Martelaarsgracht, and right onto Nieuwendijk. ℹ Breakfast included. Lockers included. Single-sex and co-ed dorms available. Free Wi-Fi. Computer with internet in the bar. $ Dorms €25-30.

HOTEL BROUWER HOTEL $$$

Singel 83 ☎020 624 63 58 www.hotelbrouwer.nl

If you want to know what it's like to live in an old Dutch canal house, Hotel Brouwer is your best bet (and value). Each room is named for a Dutch artist, but the "Bosch" room, a small double, is the real delight, with antique furniture in the living room and a traditional box bed set into the wall. The other rooms, which all overlook the pretty Singel Canal, are less distinctive but still spacious and well decorated. All of them make for a nice change of pace from the seedier hostels and hotels of the Nieuwe Zijd.

🧭 From Centraal Station, cross the water, turn right onto Prins Hendrikkade, and left onto Singel. ℹ Breakfast included. Free Wi-Fi. $ Singles €60; doubles €95.

HOTEL GROENENDAEL HOTEL $$

Nieuwendijk 15 ☎020 624 48 22 www.hotelgroenendael.com

This conveniently located hotel offers some of the cheapest singles in the city. The simple rooms include large windows and a few small terraces.

🧭 From Centraal Station, turn right, go left at Martelaarsgracht, and turn right onto Nieuwendijk. ℹ Breakfast included. Reservations by telephone only. Free Wi-Fi. $ Singles €35; doubles €60; triples €90.

SCHEEPVAARTBUURT

Scheepvaartbuurt lacks the stellar hostels of nearby Nieuwe Zijd, but it does have one of the best hotels in the city.

👍 **FREDERIC RENT-A-BIKE** HOTEL $$

Brouwersgracht 78 ☎020 624 55 09 www.frederic.nl

Three homey and uniquely decorated rooms, each named after a different artist, sit at the back of Frederic's bike-rental shop. The Mondrian room steals the show with a double 👍**waterbed** and a 👍**hot tub** in the brightly tiled bathroom. Frederic also rents out a number of houseboats and apartments throughout the area. The supremely helpful owners know the city inside-out and will enthusiastically dispense some of the best Amsterdam advice you can find. They also have some great stories to tell; make sure to ask about their experiences with other luminaries of the travel-writing world.

🧭 From Centraal Station, turn right, cross the Singel, and walk 2 blocks down Brouwersgracht. ℹ Breakfast included with hotel rooms. Small rooms have shared bath. $ Smaller rooms as singles €40-50; as doubles €60-70. Mondrian room €90-100. Houseboats €100-225, with 15% reservation fee.

HOTEL MY HOME HOTEL $$$

Haarlemmerstraat 82 ☎020 624 23 20 www.amsterdambudgethotel.com

This place has been around for a while, as you can tell by their prime piece of internet real estate. The rooms are small and simple, but the yellow walls and patterned bedspreads brighten things up a bit. The relaxed common space includes a pool table. Most rooms are private, but some dorms are available.

🪧 From Centraal Station, turn right, cross the Singel, and walk down Haarlemmerstraat. i Breakfast included (and includes more than toast!). Free Wi-Fi. $ Doubles €55-70; triples €84-99; quints €140-65.

RAMENAS HOTEL HOTEL $$$

Haarlemmerdijk 61 ☎020 624 60 30 www.hotelramenas.nl

Near Haarlemmerplein, Ramenas sits above a cafe of the same name. The rooms are nothing special, but the low ceilings and wooden window frames embrace the cozier side of Amsterdam. Ramenas Hotel isn't a terrible option if more interesting hotels are booked.

🪧 Tram #3 to Haarlemmerplein. Cross Haarlemmerplein to reach Haarlemmerdijk, then continue walking east. Reception is in the cafe downstairs. i Breakfast included. Some rooms with bath. Free Wi-Fi. $ Singles €50-75; doubles €60-100. Additional 5% tourist tax.

CANAL RING WEST

Raadhuisstraat is a row of hotel after hotel, making it a great place to try and find a private room if everywhere else is full. Many hotels are more charming than the busy traffic below might suggest (although almost all have mountainous Amsterdam staircases, so if your grandma is coming along, you might want to spare her). For a quieter and more picturesque location, try one of the accommodations on the **Nine Streets.**

👍 **HOTEL CLEMENS** HOTEL $$

Raadhuisstraat 39 ☎020 624 60 89 www.clemenshotel.com

Every room in this small hotel is decorated with French-patterned wallpaper and tiered curtains, many revealing great views. Some have cushioned window seats, and all have both a fridge and a safe. Enjoy breakfast on the balcony with a view of Westerkerk. Best of all, Hotel Clemens is a great value.

🪧 Tram #13, 14, or 17 to Westermarkt. Walk across the bridge; it's on the right. i Breakfast included. Free Wi-Fi. $ Singles €40-60; doubles €60-120; triples €120-150.

👍 **NADIA HOTEL** HOTEL $$$

Raadhuisstraat 51 ☎020 620 15 50 www.nadia.nl

Nadia Hotel boasts luxurious rooms with thick red bedspreads, large windows, and built-in wooden shelves. The gorgeous breakfast room is full of hanging plants and a baller view of Westermarkt. The double overlooking the canal will make you feel like you're on a **boat.** Some deluxe rooms have balconies and views of the canal or Westerkerk. All rooms have desks, coffee and tea makers, safes, and ensuite bathrooms.

🪧 Tram #13, 14, or 17 to Westermarkt. Walk across the bridge; it's on the right. i Breakfast included. Free Wi-Fi. Computer available. $ Singles €50-90; doubles €65-100.

HOTEL WESTERTOREN HOTEL $$

Raadhuisstraat 35B ☎020 624 46 39 www.hotelwestertoren.nl

The most exciting room here is the seven-person ensemble, which has two lofted double beds, a single bed underneath, and another double against the opposite wall. Have fun building a fort with your friends—it definitely beats the average hostel. Each room is decorated with traces of the old luxe charm that once characterized this canal house (think red curtains, floral bedspreads, and romantic paintings).

🚊 *Tram #13, 14, or 17 to Westermarkt. Walk across the bridge; it's on the right.* *i* *Breakfast included, and can be delivered to your room. Free Wi-Fi. All rooms have fridges. Some rooms have balconies.* Ⓢ *Singles €40-60; 7-person room €35 per person (must be booked as a group).*

HOTEL PAX
HOTEL $$

Raadhuisstraat 37B ☎020 624 97 35 www.hotelpax.nl

The common spaces in Hotel Pax are brightly painted and decorated with mirrors and prints, giving it a much nicer feel than most budget hotels in the neighborhood. The no-frills rooms are outfitted with plain metal-frame beds but are spacious and airy.

🚊 *Tram #13, 14, or 17 to Westermarkt. Cross the bridge and it's on the right.* *i* *Computer available for a fee. All rooms have cable TV.* Ⓢ *Singles from €35; doubles €60-90; quads €120-150.*

HOTEL BELGA
HOTEL $$

Hartenstraat 8 ☎020 624 90 80 www.hotelbelga.nl

Tucked among hip cafes and quirky shops on one of the Nine Streets, this cannabis-friendly hotel remains popular with young travelers. The rooms are large, if a bit plain, but abstract floral paintings brighten up the white walls. Some rooms have slightly slanted floors, which can seem either charming or disorienting depending on your degree of dyspraxia.

🚊 *Tram #13, 14, or 17 to Westermarkt. Cross Keizersgracht, make a right, and then a left onto Hartenstraat.* *i* *Breakfast included. Free Wi-Fi.* Ⓢ *Singles with shared bath €45-55; doubles €60-100.*

CENTRAL CANAL RING

Stay in the Central Canal Ring if you're looking for private rooms in a relatively quiet atmosphere. You'll still be close to the action of Museumplein, Leidseplein, and Rembrandtplein, but you won't have to pay the hefty surcharge that can accompany the short stumbling distance.

HEMP HOTEL
HOTEL $$$

Frederiksplein 15 ☎020 625 44 25 www.hemp-hotel.com

Each of Hemp Hotel's rooms has a different geographic theme—the Caribbean, Tibet, and India are all represented—brought to life by hemp fabrics, handmade wood carvings, and vibrant pictures. The Hemple Temple bar downstairs serves a dozen varieties of hemp beer, along with drinks derived from less infamous crops. If you don't mind stained carpets and unpainted wood, it's a great place to hang out and meet chilled-out travelers. Book far in advance—there are a surprising number of travelers who are very excited about showering with hempseed soap and eating hemp rolls for breakfast.

🚊 *Tram #4, 7, 10, or 25 to Frederiksplein. Walk diagonally across the square.* *i* *Breakfast included. Free Wi-Fi.* Ⓢ *Singles €60; doubles €70, with bath €75.*

THE GOLDEN BEAR
HOTEL $$$

Kerkstraat 37 ☎020 624 47 85 www.goldenbear.nl

Since 1948, this has been Amsterdam's premier gay hotel (about 75% of the guests are male, though women and straight guests are certainly welcome). Besides the fun atmosphere, the hotel is notable for its welcoming staff and well-decorated rooms—if you're lucky, you might get the one with fur on the wall.

🚊 *Tram #1, 2, or 5 to Keizersgracht. Continue down Leidsestraat and turn right.* *i* *Breakfast included. Free Wi-Fi.* Ⓢ *Singles with shared bath €65-70; doubles €73-90, with bath €90-130.*

HOTEL KAP
HOTEL $$

Den Texstraat 5B ☎020 624 59 08 www.kaphotel.nl

Hotel Kap is an especially attractive option in the summer, when you can eat breakfast or relax in the leafy garden out back. The rooms have high ceilings and large windows, though the furnishings are rather plain. It's one of the best deals you'll find in this neighborhood and a good place to look if other hotels are booked, even if the single "student rooms" are a bit cramped.

Tram #4, 7, 10, 16, 24, or 25 to Weteringcircuit. Walk down Weteringschans, turn right onto 2e Weteringplantsoen, and left onto Den Texstraat. i Breakfast included. Singles have shared bath, doubles have shared or ensuite bath; all rooms have private showers. Wi-Fi €5 per stay. [$] Singles €40-65; doubles €60-95.

HOTEL ASTERISK HOTEL $$$

Den Texstraat 16 ☎020 624 17 68 www.asteriskhotel.nl

Hotel Asterisk offers well-priced rooms in a great location, a pocket of calm between touristy neighborhoods. Rooms with good furniture, pretty paintings, and nice curtains are kept very clean. The simpler twins and singles might feel a little small, but the deluxe rooms with bath are quite spacious.

Tram #4, 7, 10, 16, 24, or 25 to Weteringcircuit. Walk down Weteringschans, turn right onto 2e Weteringplantsoen, and left onto Den Texstraat. i Breakfast included. Free Wi-Fi. [$] Singles €59-68; doubles €60-79, deluxe €89-129.

LEIDSEPLEIN

The best hotels in the Leidseplein are found down **Marnixstraat** and around the bend of the **Leidsekade.**

BACKSTAGE HOTEL HOTEL $$

Leidsegracht 114 ☎020 624 40 44 www.backstagehotel.com

Popular with musicians in town for shows at nearby clubs, the decor at Backstage adheres to a concert-venue theme: backboards are made to look like trunks, lamps resemble spotlights, lights have drum lampshades, and some rooms have dressing tables that even Lady Gaga would envy. Some suites are quads and quints big enough to house the whole band. Autographed concert posters line the walls and stairways, and reception is accompanied by a bar, pool table, and piano. Open-mic nights are held every Tuesday, and the staff are happy to talk up Amsterdam as well as the hotel's concert schedule. Guitars are available for jamming, and there's also Guitar Hero for pretend jamming.

Tram #1, 2, or 5 to Leidseplein. Head away from the square toward Leidsegracht. i Most rooms with private bath. Free Wi-Fi. Computer available. [$] Singles €35-85; doubles €50-150; quints €150-250.

FREELAND HOTEL $$$

Marnixstraat 386 ☎020 622 75 11 www.hotelfreeland.com

The small, 17-room Freeland feels miles apart from the crowds and grit of the Leidseplein, though the neighborhood's bustling center is just a block away. Rooms are airy and floral, and each one is stocked with amenities like DVD players and coffee makers. Ask if the special double with a sunroom is available. Book early, as this place's charm isn't a well-kept secret.

Tram #1, 2, 5, 7, or 10 to Leidseplein. Or #7 or 10 to Raamplein. i Breakfast included. Free Wi-Fi. [$] Singles €55-82; doubles €75-125.

INTERNATIONAL BUDGET HOSTEL HOSTEL $

Leidsegracht 76 ☎020 624 27 84 www.internationalbudgethostel.com

This place is popular with students and backpackers, yet still significantly toned down from the Red Light District's party hostels. Maybe things are quieter because everybody is too busy partying outside the hostel in the bars just across the canal. Each dorm has four single beds and lockers. Two private doubles (with shared bath) are also available. The lounge has couches, a TV, and vending machines. Breakfast (€3-8) is served until noon in the canteen.

Tram #7 or 10 to Raamplein. Continue walking down Marnixstraat and turn left at the canal. Or, tram #1, 2, or 5 to Prinsengracht. Turn right and walk along Prinsengracht and then turn left after you cross the bridge. i Free Wi-Fi. [$] Dorms €20-32.

HOTEL QUENTIN   HOTEL $$

Leidsekade 89   ☎020 622 75 11 www.quentinhotels.com

Located in a beautiful renovated mansion overlooking the Leidsekade, this hotel sets itself apart with the funky, abstract furniture and posters of musicians (not to mention flat screen TVs) that fill its comfortable rooms. The hotel bar serves coffee, alcohol, and soft drinks.

✚ Tram #1, 2, 5, 7, or 10 to Leidseplein. Walk down Marnixstraat and turn left at the canal; the hotel is around the bend. *i* Free Wi-Fi. Ⓢ Singles €35-55, with bath €40-60; doubles €50-85.

swimming with the fishes

Move over, Atlantis. Rather than searching for the fabled underwater paradise, Dutch architects and city engineers have taken matters into their own hands. In 2018, construction will begin on an underwater city buried under canals. The underwater buildings would mostly be used for parking, shopping, and entertainment. The architects, Zwarts & Jansma, claim the project will be completely eco-friendly, and that the air filtration techniques will improve Amsterdam's above-ground air. Objectors to the project oppose the idea of living like moles under the earth—but we're pretty excited by the idea of living like mermen and mermaids, to be honest.

REMBRANDTPLEIN

Rembrandtplein's reputation as a popular nightlife hotspot be both a blessing and a curse. On the one hand, living here means it's easy to stumble home after a long night; on the other, prices and noise levels can be high (especially on weekends).

HOTEL THE VETERAN   HOTEL $$

Herengracht 561   ☎020 620 26 73 www.veteran.nl

Hotel the Veteran is a bare-bones establishment, but all the essentials are here. The rooms are clean and cozy with floral bedspreads and wood paneling, which seems to be the go-to tactic for creating welcoming sleeping environments in this city. The hotel sits at the corner of a beautiful stretch of the Herengracht Canal and Thorbeckeplein's strip of bars. Be advised: to enter some rooms you must climb an external staircase next to a bunch of bars, which may be uncomfortable for some travelers returning to their rooms at night. That said, this is one of the cheapest places to stay around Rembrandtplein.

✚ Tram #9 or 14 to Rembrandtplein. At the corner of Thorbeckeplein and Herengracht. *i* Breakfast included. Singles all have shared bath; both shared and ensuite doubles available; triples all ensuite. Wi-Fi available. Ⓢ Singles €35-65; doubles from €50; triples and family rooms from €65.

CITY HOTEL   HOTEL $$$$

Utrechtstraat 2   ☎020 627 23 23 www.city-hotel.nl

City Hotel boasts large, clean rooms, brightly decorated with colorful bedspreads and oversized pictures of flowers. Some rooms have balconies, and those on the top floor have great views of Rembrandtplein and the rest of the city. Many of the rooms are made for five to eight people (some with bunk beds), but none feel cramped. The hotel is popular with groups of young backpackers, since you can find much better values if you're only looking for a double or triple (there are no singles). Breakfast is available—for an extra charge—in a chic dining area with red leather seats.

✚ Tram #9 or 14 to Rembrandtplein. City Hotel is off the southeast corner of the main square. *i* Breakfast €7.50 per day. All rooms have ensuite safe. Free Wi-Fi and free public computer in dining room. Ⓢ Doubles from €100; triples from €135; 6-person rooms €270.

HOTEL MONOPOLE HOTEL $$$

Amstel 60 ☎020 624 62 71

A few blocks removed from the madness of Rembrandtplein, this hotel has simple but pretty pastel rooms, many with canal views (ask ahead). Rooms have the added luxury of breakfast delivered to your door. There's also a cushy common space on the first floor.

*# Tram #9 or 14 to Rembrandtplein. Cut through one of the alleyways on the northern side of the square to get to the canal side. **i** Breakfast included. Free Wi-Fi. [$] Singles €65-105; doubles €75-125.*

JORDAAN

If you want to live like a local but not commute like one, camp out here.

SHELTER JORDAAN HOSTEL $

Bloemstraat 179 ☎020 624 47 17 www.shelter.nl

Smaller and in a quieter location than its sister hostel in the Oude Zijd, the Shelter Jordaan has the same excellent prices, clean facilities, and comfortable atmosphere. They cater to Christian travelers (though all are welcome), so the rooms are single-sex, and drugs and alcohol are forbidden. With speakers blaring an uninterrupted stream of Christian rock, this hostel isn't for everybody, but it's in a good location and feels safe. The rooms are large and bright, with colorful beds and lockers. The large cafe and garden provide cozy places to hang out and enjoy the free breakfast, which often features pancakes and French toast.

*# Tram #10 to Bloemstraat or tram #13, 14, or 17 to Westermarkt. Follow Lijnbaansgracht for 50m, then turn right onto Bloemstraat. **i** Breakfast included. All rooms with shared bath. Lockers available, though you'll have to bring your own lock or purchase one for €4. Free Wi-Fi. [$] 4- to 8-bed dorms €17-30.*

HOTEL VAN ONNA HOTEL $$

Bloemgracht 104 ☎020 626 58 01 www.vanonna.nl

The rooms on the top floor of this hotel are truly remarkable, with slanted ceilings, exposed wood beams, and views over the rooftops of the whole Jordaan. You'll need to hike up the stairs to reach them, but at least the staircase is lined with lovely black-and-white photos of the city. The rooms are impeccably clean, though the ones downstairs are dull compared to those upstairs.

*# Tram #10 to Bloemgracht or tram #13, 14, or 17 to Westermarkt. Cross Prinsengracht and turn right; Bloemgracht is 2 blocks away. **i** Breakfast included. Free Wi-Fi. [$] Singles €50; doubles €90; triples €135. Credit cards add 5%.*

HOTEL ACACIA HOTEL $$$

Lindengracht 251 ☎020 622 14 60 www.hotelacacia.nl

Tucked in a tranquil corner of the picturesque northern Jordaan, Acacia is nonetheless the epitome of bland and boring. Small studio apartments, which come with a kitchenette and living area, feel a little less institutional.

*# Tram #3 or 10 to Marnixplein. Cross the small canal and make a left onto Lijnbaansgracht; Acacia is on the right. **i** Breakfast included. All rooms with full bath. Free Wi-Fi. [$] Doubles €60-90; studios €70-110.*

WESTERPARK AND OUD-WEST

Westerpark is almost exclusively residential with relatively few accommodations. The section of the Oud-West closest to the Leidseplein has a smattering of small hotels, but make sure to bring a good pair of walking shoes or learn how to use the tram if you plan on staying out here. Accommodations cost about the same as their competitors closer to the canal ring, but they are far less crowded and noisy.

HOTEL JUPITER   HOTEL $$

2e Helmersstraat 14   ☎020 618 71 32 www.jupiterhotel.nl

This hotel sits on one of the small streets parallel to Overtoom, so it's close to transportation and grocery shopping but removed from the bustle and noise of the main thoroughfare. Rooms are sleek and bare, but they're only a 5min. walk from the Leidseplein. Breakfast is included, but the staff can be grouchy.

🚊 *Tram #3 or 12 to Overtoom or #1 tp 1e Con. Huygensstraat. Walk 2 blocks away from Vondelpark on 1e Con. Huygensstraat and turn right.* Ⓢ *High-season singles €54, with bath €64; doubles €74/99. Low-season singles €39/49; doubles €59/79. Triples and quads also available.*

HOTEL ABBA   HOTEL $$

Overtoom 116-122   ☎020 618 30 58 www.hotel-abba.nl

This probably isn't where you'd go to become a dancing queen—the rooms aren't much more than white walls and gray concrete. This "smoker-friendly" hotel has a very practical location right above an Albert Heijn supermarket. Cable TV (in every room) and breakfast are included. Free safety deposit boxes are available at reception, where the friendly staff will help you arrange trips and tours.

🚊 *Tram #1 to 1e Con. Huygensstraat. Above the Albert Heijn.* Ⓢ *High-season singles €50, with bath €60; doubles €70/85. Low-season singles €35/40; doubles €60/70.*

MUSEUMPLEIN AND VONDELPARK

You can get your hostel fix without facing the noise and crowds of the Centrum at one of Vondelpark's two excellent backpacker lodgings. Hotels in the neighborhood are removed from the city's best restaurants and bars, but they ooze residential luxury.

🏨 **STAYOKAY AMSTERDAM VONDELPARK**   HOSTEL $

Zandpad 5   ☎020 589 89 96 www.stayokay.nl/vondelpark

This is a huge hostel—the size makes it feel slightly institutional, but it's clean and well managed. Each room has its own bathroom (the larger rooms have two). Downstairs, an affordable bar with foosball tables, vending machines, and pool tables is a popular hangout. For the young backpacker clientele. The staff is happy to answer questions about the city, and with so many guests, it won't be hard to find some buddies to venture to nearby Leidseplein with you.

🚊 *Tram #1, 2, 5, 7, or 10 to Leidseplein. Walk across the canal toward the Marriott, take a left, then make a right onto Zandpad after 1 block.* 𝒊 *Breakfast included. Single-sex dorms available. Free Wi-Fi.* Ⓢ *2- to 20-bed dorms €20-34; singles €50-80.*

🏨 **FLYING PIG UPTOWN**   HOSTEL $

Vossiusstraat 46-47   ☎020 400 41 87 www.flyingpig.nl

We find it a little confusing that Flying Pig Uptown is actually south of Flying Pig Downtown (in Nieuwe Zijd), but then again, we can't quite wrap our heads around the fact that the Nile runs south to north—no matter. This is the original Flying Pig, and with a tranquil location across from Vondelpark, this winged swine is a little less rowdy than its younger sibling. Nevertheless, it's still phenomenally popular. The quality of the dorms vary—some are just plain walls and metal-frame bunks—but they're all comfortable and clean, and they have their own bathrooms. The downstairs boasts a bar with a TV lounge on one side and a smoking room on the other. With proximity to the Leidseplein, guests frequently start off here before going pubbing and clubbing.

🚊 *Tram #2, 3, 5, or 12 to Van Baerlestraat. Walk down Van Baerlestraat toward Vondelpark and turn right onto Vossiusstraat.* 𝒊 *Breakfast included. Linens and towel included. Free lockers. Free Wi-Fi. Kitchen available.* Ⓢ *Dorms €12-40.* 🕐 *Bar open until 3am.*

🏨 **HOTEL BEMA**   HOTEL $$

Concertgebouwplein 19B   ☎020 679 13 96 www.bemahotel.com

Just across from the stunning Concertgebouw and the major museums on the Museumplein, Hotel Bema boasts elegant rooms with high ceilings, crystal chandeliers, and old-fashioned floral wallpaper. Chambers on the ground floor have antique-style furniture to boot. They'll even deliver breakfast to your room. It's amazing that you can get such luxury at these prices, but no one seems to be arguing with it.

Tram #3, 5, 12, 16, or 24 to Museumplein. Walk down the left side of the Concertgebouw and cross the street. i Breakfast included. Free Wi-Fi. [$] Singles with shared bath €40-45; doubles €65-75, with bath €85-90.

HOTEL MUSEUMZICHT HOTEL $$$

Jan Luykenstraat 22 ☎020 671 29 54 www.hotelmuseumzicht.com

Staying here is a bit like staying in your cool grandmother's house—if your grandmother has a perfect view of the Rijksmuseum and serves a traditional Dutch breakfast every day. Old wooden furniture, oriental carpets, and decorative curtains adorn each room. Museumzicht caters to the individual or celibate traveler—there are no double beds, though twins can be pushed together.

Tram #2 or 5 to Hobbemastraat. Walk away from the Rijksmuseum and turn left onto Jan Luykenstraat. i Breakfast included. Free Wi-Fi. [$] Singles €55; doubles €75-85, with bath €85-125.

DE PIJP

Though far from the city center, De Pijp has character and easy transportation options, making it a good place to get a feel for local life in a hip up-and-coming neighborhood.

BICYCLE HOTEL HOTEL $$

Van Ostadestraat 123 ☎020 679 34 52 www.bicyclehotel.com

A certain current of yuppie environmentalism runs through De Pijp, so it's appropriate that this eco-conscious hotel is located here. We couldn't be happier: not only does the hotel have solar panels and a "green roof" (plants grow on it and it saves energy—the owners explain it better than we can), but the theme of clean freshness permeates the entire building. The rooms have lavender sheets and pastel prints on the walls, while large windows overlook leafy gardens and let in sun and fresh air. There are even some balconies to sit on. Plus, the per-day bike rental costs the same as a 24hr. transport ticket, so there's no excuse for you not to go green as well.

Tram #3, 12, or 25 to Ceinturbaan/Ferdinand Bolstraat. Continue 1 block down Ferdinand Bolstraat and turn left onto Van Ostadestraat. i Breakfast included. Free Wi-Fi. [$] Singles €35-70; doubles €40-85, with bath €60-120. Bike rental €7.50 per day.

HOTEL VIVALDI HOTEL $$$

Stadhouderskade 76 ☎020 577 63 00

Location is everything at this hotel, which sits at the northern end of the main part of De Pijp, across from the Central Canal Ring. The rooms are minimally furnished (don't worry, there's still a bed), but a few will surprise you with stained-glass windows and great canal views.

Tram #16 or 24 to Stadhouderskade. Walk toward the water, veer left, and Hotel Vivaldi is on the left. i Breakfast included. Free Wi-Fi. [$] Singles €45-120; doubles €60-150.

JODENBUURT AND PLANTAGE

Slightly removed from the city center (though in pocket-sized Amsterdam you're never really far from anything), staying here will give you a more local experience, but expect to pay a little (or a lot) extra for the tranquility.

BRIDGE HOTEL HOTEL $$$$

Amstel 107-111 ☎020 623 70 68 www.thebridgehotel.nl

The nicest hotel in this pricey neighborhood, Bridge's massive, comfortable rooms will easily accommodate you and all the shoes you didn't need to pack. The staff is eager to help you settle into what feels more like a modern

Amsterdam apartment than a hotel room (actual apartments with kitchens are also available). The location may feel remote, but you're really just across the bridge from Rembrandtplein.

🚋 Tram #9 or 14 to Waterlooplein or Mr. Visserplein. Walk down Waterlooplein toward the bridge and turn left onto Amstel. i Breakfast included. Free Wi-Fi. [$] Singles €85-115; doubles €98-140.

HERMITAGE HOTEL HOTEL $$$

Nieuwe Keizersgracht 16 ☎020 623 82 59 www.hotelhermitageamsterdam.nl

A new addition to the area, Hermitage has a younger feel than most of the neighboring hotels. Somehow managing to combine two of Amsterdam's predominant hotel aesthetics—modern minimalist and old-fashioned floral—Hermitage covers its walls in stylized silver-and-black flowered wallpaper for a cozy, but urban, feel.

🚋 Tram #9 or 14 to Waterlooplein or Mr. Visserplein. Walk down Waterlooplein toward the bridge, turn left onto Amstel, and then left onto Nieuwe Keizersgracht. i Breakfast €9. Free Wi-Fi. [$] Singles €44-90; doubles €55-120.

sights

Between the pretty old churches, quaint canals, and nightly showcases of revelry and debauchery, Amsterdam is a sight in itself. You can see and learn a lot about the city, even with zero euro. For a little more, you can see Museumplein's excellent art museums (showcasing everything from Northern Renaissance masterpieces to newer avant-garde works), modern photography exhibitions held in hip ex-squat studios and 14th-century churches, and a slew of museums and monuments devoted to remembering WWII. If you're dead set on shunning anything remotely highbrow, there are still plenty of things to see (like the Sex Museum and the Hash, Marijuana, and Hemp Museum). Drug-loving tourists shouldn't miss 👍**Electric Ladyland,** the First Museum of Fluorescent Art—more a trip than a sight, but still highly recommended.

If you're planning on visiting a number of museums, save some euro by investing in the Museumjaarkaart (www.museumjaarkaart.nl). For €40 (or €20 if you're under 26) you get free entrance to most museums in Amsterdam and the Netherlands for a whole year. With the Museumjaarkaart, there's nothing to stop you from popping into one of the many small and weird museums and then popping right back out if it's not up to snuff. You can't get the card at the tourist office (it's a great deal rarely advertised to tourists), but it's sold at some of the bigger participating museums.

OUDE ZIJD

While the best museums in Amsterdam are found elsewhere, the Oude Zijd is home to some worthwhile architecture and history. Make some erudite observations on these landmarks on your way to the Red Light District.

👍 **NIEUWMARKT** SQUARE

Dominated by the largest still-standing medieval building in Amsterdam, Nieuwmarkt is a calm square lined with cafes and bars, making it one of the best places in the city for some relaxed people-watching. Originally a fortress gate, **De Waag,** the 15th-century castle-like structure in Nieuwmarkt's center, has housed a number of establishments over the years, including a weighing house, a gallery for surgical dissections (Rembrandt's *The Anatomy Lesson of Dr. Tulp* depicts one such event), the **Jewish Historical Museum,** and, today, a swanky restaurant. Nieuwmarkt is beloved by tourists and locals alike: heavy rioting erupted in 1975 in response to a proposal to build a highway through the square.

Daily markets here sell everything from souvenirs to organic food, especially on weekends.

✣ ⓂNieuwmarkt. Or from Centraal Station walk 10min. down Zeedijk.

CENTRUM VOOR FOTOGRAFIE
GALLERY
Bethanienstraat 39   ☎020 622 48 99 www.acf-web.nl

Tucked in a small street between Nieuwmarkt and the Red Light District, this gallery showcases the work of young Dutch photographers, many just out of art school. Exhibits vary greatly in topic and quality, but since it's free, it's worth poking your head in if you're in the neighborhood. The center also holds lectures, workshops, and master classes—all in Dutch.

✣ ⓂNieuwmarkt. Walk south on Kloveniersburgwal and turn right. Ⓢ Free. ⌚ Open Th-Sa 1-5pm.

OOST-INDISCH HUIS
HISTORICAL SITE
Kloveniersburgwal 48

For almost two centuries, the *Vereenigde Oostindische Compagnie*, or Dutch East India Company—the world's first multinational corporation—wielded quasi-governmental powers and a whole lot of cash. Beginning in 1606, they set up shop in this building along Kloveniersburgwal. Its Dutch Renaissance design is a trademark of Hendrik de Keyser, the architect to whom the building has been (convincingly) attributed. Today, the University of Amsterdam occupies this national monument, and the students loitering and smoking outside take away much of the building's gravitas.

✣ ⓂNieuwmarkt. Kloveniersburgwal is on the southwestern edge of the square.

FO GUANG SHAN HE HUA TEMPLE
TEMPLE
Zeedijk 106-118   ☎020 420 23 57 www.ibps.nl

You can't miss this brightly painted, gabled building on Zeedijk. That's probably because it's Europe's largest palace-style Buddhist temple. Queen Beatrix herself officially opened the temple, associated with the Taiwan-based Fo Guang Shan Buddhist order, in 2000. The goals of the temple include both spiritual development and cultural exchange. Most travelers come to peek inside at the ornate Buddha statues, but there's really not much to see here.

✣ ⓂNieuwmarkt. Ⓢ Free. ⌚ Open Tu-Sa noon-5pm, Su 10am-5pm. Services Su 10:30am open to the public.

subprime tulip crisis

What can tulips tell us about the current global financial situation? A lot, actually. In 1593, tulips were brought from Turkey to the Netherlands, where they soon contracted the "mosaic" virus, which caused flames of color to develop on the petals. The colorful flowers became increasingly desirable, and, in just one month, tulips increased 20 times in value. At the height of tulip mania, you could trade a single tulip for an entire estate. Pubs turned into tulip exchanges at night, and people from all social strata staked their homes and livelihoods on the precious bulbs in a frenzy of what the Dutch call *windhandel,* or "trading in the wind"—speculating without any actual goods to back it up.

When the market inevitably crashed overnight in 1637, prices took a nosedive. A tulip was suddenly worth no more than an onion. The whole credit system fell apart and the Netherlands experienced a major depression whose reverberations were felt across Europe.

Today, Amsterdam hosts tours about tulip mania. Bankers and investors could definitely learn a thing or two from these pretty, but financially deadly, flowers.

SINT NICOLAASKERK   CHURCH

Prins Hendrikkade 73☎020 624 87 49 www.nicolaas-parochie.nl/nicolaaskerkamsterdam.html
If the austere Protestant churches around town are getting you down, head to
this relatively new (opened in 1887) Catholic one. Adrianus Bleijs designed the
church in a combination of neo-Renaissance and neo-Baroque styles. Murals
inside depict the life of St. Nicholas (the patron saint of sailors) and the cupola
(that's the dome-thingy), is the only glass cupola in the Netherlands. The organ,
designed by William Sauer, is also impressive in size and sound and can be heard
at one of the church's frequent concerts.

🏃 *2min. walk from Centraal Station; make a left when leaving Stationsplein.* 🕐 *Open to tourists
M noon-3pm, Tu-F 11am-4pm, Sa noon-3pm. Mass held throughout the week in Dutch, Latin, and
Spanish; check website for schedule.*

RED LIGHT DISTRICT

Many tourists treat the Red Light District as a sight in and of itself, wandering through
the crowded streets while pretending not to look at window prostitutes. But there
are plenty of other worthwhile opportunities for travelers to learn about parts of
Dutch history and culture that don't involve sex, drugs, and drunk frat boys.

🖼 OUDE KERK   CHURCH

Oudekerksplein 23   ☎020 625 82 84 www.oudekerk.nl
Since its construction in 1306, Oude Kerk, the oldest church in Amsterdam, has
endured everything from the Protestant Reformation to the growth of the Red
Light District, which today encroaches naughtily on its very square. (Case in
point: the bronze relief of a hand caressing a breast set into the cobblestones
outside.) Oude Kerk didn't escape all this history unscathed; during the
Reformation of 1578, the church lost much of its artwork and religious figures.
However, it remains a strikingly beautiful structure, with massive vaulted
ceilings and gorgeous stained glass that betray the building's Catholic roots.
You can occasionally hear concerts played on the grandiose **Vater-Muller organ,**
which dates back to 1724, but Oude Kerk is now used mainly for art and
photography exhibitions, including the display of the prestigious **World Press
Photo** prizewinners. Whether you come for the art, music, or the sanctuary, tread
lightly—you're walking on 35 generations of Amsterdam's dead.

🏃 *From Centraal Station, walk down Damrak, turn left onto Oudebrugsteeg, and right onto
Warmoesstraat; the next left leads to the church.* 𝒊 *Check the website for a calendar of
performances.* 💲 *€7.50; students, seniors, and under 13 €5.50; with Museumjaarkaart free.*
🕐 *Open M-Sa 10am-5:30pm, Su 1-5:30pm.*

🖼 ONS' LIEVE HEER OP SOLDER   MUSEUM

Oudezijds Voorburgwal 40   ☎020 624 66 04 www.opsolder.nl
The Ons' Lieve Heer op Solder ("Our Lord in the Attic") museum
commemorates a beautiful Catholic church...in an attic. Built by a
merchant in the 17th century, when Catholicism was officially banned
in the Netherlands, the church was once regularly packed with secret
worshippers. The museum includes three houses whose connected offices
house the church, featuring art and furniture from the period. In contrast to
the Catholic lavishness of Oude Kerk around the corner, Ons' Lieve Heer op
Solder highlights the more muted Catholicism of the post-Reformation era.
The church contains an impressive organ and a beautiful altarpiece by the
famous painter **Jacob de Wit,** but the real appeal is the understanding you'll
gain of broader trends in Dutch history and culture.

🏃 *From Centraal Station, turn left onto Prins Hendrikkade and then right onto Nieuwebrugsteeg.
Continue straight as Nieuwebrugsteeg becomes Oudezijds Vorburgwal.* 💲 *€7, students €5, under
18 €1, under 5 and with Museumjaarkaart free.* 🕐 *Open M-Sa 10am-5pm, Su 1-5pm.*

BROUWERIJ DE PRAEL
BREWERY

Oudezijds Voorburgwal 30   ☎020 408 44 70 www.deprael.nl

If you love beer but find yourself asking "what's a hops?" come get a quick and easy crash course with a tour of this favorite local brewery. All the beer is organic, unfiltered, and unpasteurized, and all are named after classic *levensliederen*, sappy Dutch love songs (aww). A brewery that does more than make beer, de Prael was founded by two former psychiatrists and now employs over 60 people with a history of mental illness. The attached store sells de Prael's beers and other merchandise.

⚑ *From Centraal Station, turn left onto Prins Hendrikkade and then right onto Nieuwebrugsteeg. Continue straight as it becomes Oudezijds Vorburgwal.* Ⓢ *Tour with 1 beer €7.50, with tasting menu €16.50.* Ⓓ *Brewery open M-F 9am-5pm. Tasting room open Tu-Su 11am-11pm.*

CANNABIS COLLEGE
MUSEUM

Oudezijds Achterburgwal 124   ☎020 423 44 20 www.cannabiscollege.com

Get your druggie "diploma" (a bachelor's in blunts? a master's in marijuana? a doctorate in doobies?) by taking a short quiz on all things cannabis. If you want cold, hard, sticky-icky facts, this is a repository of any information you could ever want to know about hemp and marijuana, especially regarding growing the plants themselves. Friendly volunteers, who are knowledgeable enough to provide training workshops to coffeeshop owners, are happy to answer questions about the history, science, and use of the drug. If you're dying to see some of the plants in person, check out the garden downstairs—otherwise, save the couple of euro and check out the pictures on their website. If you're looking for more kitsch, try the **Hash Marijuana Hemp Museum** just a few doors down (Oudezijds Achterburgwal 148; www.hashmuseum.com Ⓢ €9.).

⚑ *From Dam Sq., walk east on Dam and turn left onto Oudezijds Achterburgwal.* Ⓢ *Free. Garden €2.50.* Ⓓ *Open daily 11am-7pm.*

NIEUWE ZIJD

The Nieuwe Zijd (despite its name) is one of the oldest parts of the city. Go back in time at the Amsterdam Historical Museum, then get a rude awakening into the present at some of the area's gimmicky attractions, such as Madame Tussaud's and the Sex Museum.

NIEUWE KERK
CHURCH, MUSEUM

Dam Sq.   ☎020 638 69 09 www.nieuwekerk.nl

Built in 1408 when the Oude Kerk became too small for the city's growing population, the Nieuwe Kerk is a commanding Gothic building that holds its own amid the architectural extravaganza of Dam Sq. Inside, the church is all vaulted ceilings and massive windows. Don't miss the intricate organ case designed by Jacob van Campen, architect of the Koninklijk Palace. Today, the Nieuwe Kerk is the site of royal inaugurations (the most recent one being Queen Beatrix's in 1980) and some royal weddings (like Prince Willem-Alexander's in 2002). Most of the year, however, the space serves as a museum. Each winter, the church holds exhibits on foreign cultures, specifically focusing on world religions (recent topics have included Islam and Ancient Egypt). The space is also used for temporary exhibits by prominent Dutch museums like the Stedelijk and Rijksmuseum. Organ concerts are held here every Sunday, while shorter and more informal organ recitals are performed on Thursday afternoons.

⚑ *Any tram to Dam Sq. Nieuwe Kerk is on the northeastern edge of the square.* Ⓢ *€5, students €4, with Museumjaarkaart free. Organ concerts €8.50; recitals €5.* Ⓓ *Open daily 10am-5pm. Recitals Th 12:30pm. Concerts Su 8pm.*

AMSTERDAM SEX MUSEUM
MUSEUM

Damrak 18   ☎020 622 83 76 www.sexmuseumamsterdam.nl

Unless you were previously unaware that people have been having sex since mankind's origin, there's not much new information about sex or sexuality in this museum. (The brief "Sex Through the Ages" presentation is hilariously simplistic, though the elegant British-accented narration is priceless.) But let's face it: who needs information when you've got smut? Tons of pornographic photographs, paintings, and life-sized dolls fill the museum, along with models of various sexual icons: Marilyn Monroe with her skirt fluttering over the subway vent, a 1980s pimp, and even a **flasher** who thrills the audience every few seconds. The museum attracts crowds of tourists who react quite differently: some leave slightly offended by the hardcore porn-and-fetish room, some find the farting dolls funny, and others inexplicably insist on having their picture taken with one of the giant model penises. If you really want to see a parade of pictures of people having sex, you could just visit a sex shop in the Red Light District, but at least the Sex Museum charges a low rate for its high kitsch factor. Be warned: after you see (and hear) the mannequins of a Dutch girl giving a handjob in a public urinal, you may never look at those Dutch curlys the same way again.

From Centraal Station, walk straight down Damrak. i 16+. $ €4. ⏰ Open daily 9:30am-11:30pm.

AMSTERDAM HISTORICAL MUSEUM MUSEUM

Nieuwezijds Voorburgwal 359 ☎020 523 18 22 www.amsterdammuseum.nl

People, schmeople. This museum is about Amsterdam as a city. Through paintings, artifacts, and multimedia presentations, the museum's "Grand Tour" will show you how Amsterdam changed from 1350 to the present (spoiler: it changed a lot). Don't miss the room dedicated to Golden Age art and its stomach-churning paintings of anatomy lessons, which were apparently all the rage in the 17th century. Also fascinating is the corner that shows various city planning designs from the past century, driving home the fact that Amsterdam is an entirely man-made city. Only true history buffs will really be intrigued enough to read the placards about mercantile ships, but accessible and interesting temporary exhibits make up for some of the slower material. If you want to get to know the city a little better, this is a great place to start.

Tram #1, 2, or 5 to Spui/Nieuwezijds Voorburgwal. Head up Nieuwezijds Voorburgwal and the museum is on the right. $ €10, seniors €7.50, students and ages 6-18 €5, under 6 and with Museumjaarkaart free. Audio tour €4.50. ⏰ Open M-F 10am-5pm, Sa-Su 11am-5pm.

BEGIJNHOF COURTYARD, CHURCH

Begijnhof www.begijnhofamsterdam.nl

The Beguines were small groups of Catholic laywomen who took vows of chastity and chose to serve the Church, though they didn't retreat from the world and formally join a convent. After seeing this beautiful 14th-century courtyard, surrounded by the Beguines' homes, you'll agree that they made a good call: this is a pretty sweet crib. Tour groups, bicycles, and photographs aren't allowed, so take in the place's original tranquility. During the Alteration, the original chapel was turned into a Protestant place of worship. The women responded by using a secret Catholic church, the **Begijnhofkapel,** built within two of the houses. Today, the cute but unremarkable chapel is an English Presbyterian church (the Belgians would be livid) and is open to respectful visitors.

Tram #1, 2, or 5 to Spui/Nieuwezijds Voorburgwal. Walk down Gedempte Begijnsloot and the gardens are on the left. $ Free. ⏰ Open daily 9am-5pm.

DAM SQUARE SQUARE

Once upon a time, Amsterdam was just two small settlements on either side of the Amstel River. One day the villagers decided to connect their encampments with a dam. Since then, Dam Sq. has been the heart of the city, home to markets, the town hall, a church, and a weigh house (until Napoleon's brother had it torn down because it blocked his view). The obelisk on one end is the

Nationaal Monument, erected in 1956 to honor the Dutch victims of WWII. The wall surrounding the monument contains soil from cemeteries and execution sites in each of the Netherlands's 12 provinces, as well as the Dutch East Indies. Across from the monument, next to the Nieuwe Kerk, you'll find the **Koninklijk Palace** (www.paleisamsterdam.nl), where you can see what it's like to be Dutch royalty. Louis Napoleon took it over in 1808, deciding that the building (constructed in the 17th century as Amsterdam's town hall) would make an excellent fixer-upper. Since then, it has been a royal palace, although Queen Beatrix only uses it for official functions. Too bad—she's wasting a unique view of the crowds, street performers, and occasional concerts in the square below.

🚏 Tram #1, 2, 4, 5, 9, 13, 14, 16, 17, 24, or 25 to Dam (remember when we said this was the center of the city?). $ Palace €7.50; ages 5-16, over 65, and students €6.50; with Museumjaarkaart free. ⏰ Palace usually open noon-5pm; check website for details.

CANAL RING WEST

The Canal Ring West is home to a few must-see sights (the Anne Frank House and nearby Westerkerk should be near the top of your list) along with some wackier ones like the **Nationaal Brilmuseum** and the **National Spectacles Museum** (Gasthuismolensteeg; www.brilmuseumamsterdam.nl).

📷 ANNE FRANK HOUSE — MUSEUM

Prinsengracht 267 — ☎020 556 71 00 www.annefrank.nl

This is one of the most frequently visited sights in Amsterdam, and for good reason. It is the house where Anne Frank and her family lived in hiding from 1942 to 1944, when they were finally arrested by the Nazis. The well-organized museum route takes you through the family's hiding place, starting behind the moveable bookcase that masked their secret annex. Displays include pages of Anne's famous diary and a model of the rooms in 1942—Anne's father Otto requested that the museum not re-furnish the actual annex rooms after the Nazis seized all the original furnishings. Videos featuring interviews with those who knew the family make the story even more tangible. The end of the route includes information and interactive displays on contemporary issues in human rights and discrimination, reflecting the museum's mission as a center for activism and education as well as remembrance. This is one of the few museums in Amsterdam that opens early and stays open late, and we recommend you take advantage of it: the cramped attic gets packed with visitors in the middle of the day, and you'll want to be able to move around and take your time in such a thought-provoking place.

🚏 Tram #13, 14, or 17 to Westermarkt. Walk away from Keizersgracht down Westermarkt, then turn right onto Prinsengracht. $ €8.50, ages 10-17 €4, under 10 and with Museumjaarkaart free. ⏰ Open daily July-Aug 9am-10pm; Sept 1-14 9am-9pm; Sept 15-March 14 9am-7pm; March 15-June 9am-9pm.

📷 WESTERKERK — CHURCH

Prinsengracht 281 — ☎020 624 77 66 www.westerkerk.nl

Westerkerk's 85m tower, the Westerkerkstoren, stands far above central Amsterdam's other buildings. A 30min. guided tour to the top is a must. The patient staff will pause to accommodate your huffing and puffing until you finish the climb and step out to behold the best view in Amsterdam. The tower also houses 47 bells, one of which weighs in at an astonishing 7509kg. The church was completed in 1631, a gift to the city from Maximilian of Austria (whose crown can be seen on the tower) in thanks for the city's support of the Austro-Burgundian princes. The church's brick-and-stone exterior is a fine example of Dutch late-Renaissance architecture. Inside, its plain white walls and clear glass windows are typical of the clean Calvinist aesthetic. The only real decorations are the shutters on the organ, which were beautifully painted by Gerard de

Lairesse. The tower's carillon plays between noon and 1pm on Tuesdays, free organ concerts are held every Friday at 1pm, and the church hosts many other concerts throughout the year. Queen Beatrix and Prince Claus were married here in 1966, and Rembrandt is buried somewhere within the church—although no one seems to know exactly where. (Yeah, we don't know how they forgot where they put one of the most famous painters of all time either.)

✴ *Tram #13, 14, or 17 to Westermarkt. Walk away from Keizersgracht and turn right onto Prinsengradcht.* Ⓢ *Free. Tower tour €7.* Ⓓ *Open Apr-June M-F 10am-6pm, Sa 10am-8pm; July-Sept M-Sa 10am-8pm; Oct M-F 11am-4pm, Sa 10am-6pm. Tower tours every 30min.*

🏳️ HOMOMONUMENT   MONUMENT
Westermarkt   www.homomonument.nl

The Homomonument is the culmination of a movement to erect a memorial honoring homosexual victims of Nazi persecution, but it's also meant to stand for all people who have been oppressed for their sexuality. Designed by Karin Daan and officially opened in 1987, the monument consists of three pink granite triangles (in remembrance of the symbol the Nazis forced homosexuals to wear), connected by thin lines of pink granite to form a larger triangle. The Homomonument was designed to merge seamlessly with the daily life of the city, so it can be hard to discern under picnicking tourists and whizzing bikes. The first triangle points toward the Anne Frank House, symbolizing the past; it is engraved with the words *"Naar Vriendschap Zulk een Mateloos Verlangen"* ("such an endless desire for friendship"), a line from the poem "To a Young Fisherman" by the gay Dutch Jewish poet Jacob Israel de Haan (1881-1924). Another triangle is set down into the water of the Keizergracht and points toward the National War Monument in Dam Sq., representing the present. The raised triangle stands for the future and points toward the headquarters of the COC, a Dutch gay rights group founded in 1946 and the oldest continuously operating gay and lesbian organization in the world.

✴ *Tram #13, 14, or 17 to Westermarkt. The Homomonument is between Westerkerk and the Keizersgracht.* Ⓢ *Free.*

MULTATULI MUSEUM   MUSEUM
Korsjespoortsteeg 20   ☎020 638 19 38 www.multatuli-museum.nl

This museum is dedicated to the Netherlands's most famous writer, Eduard Douwes Dekker, who was born here in 1820. Dekker was better known by

enduring legacy

Multatuli was a rather unsuccessful lad, and after failing at school and a trade clerkship, he was carted off to Indonesia by his sea captain father. Here, he finally exhibited some talent in the civil service, rising through the ranks and marrying a baroness along the way. Disgusted by the abuses of imperialism, he eventually quit his job, returned to a penniless life in Europe, and wrote the autobiographical novel *Max Havelaar* to expose the evils of colonialism and the Dutch East India Company. Ironically, *Max Havelaar* became a massive hit, not due to its message of reform (which was largely ignored by the contemporary public) but because of Multatuli's entertaining, well-written prose. In time, the work came to be cited as one of the most important books to influence reform movements. Today, *Max Havelaar* remains the most popular Dutch novel, and has been translated into more than 40 languages. Multatuli is considered a crucial intellectual forefather to the atmosphere of tolerance for which the Netherlands is so famous today.

his pen name, Multatuli—Latin for "I have endured much." The dedicated proprietor of the museum, who cares passionately about Multatuli's legacy, will gladly tell everything about the author's life in the form of personal and funny stories. The free museum is worth a stop for literary fiends, those who want a quick brush-up on Dutch history, or those curious to learn more about the brain inside the enormous head replicated in the big statue over the Singel.

🚋 Tram #1, 2, 5, 13, or 17 to Nieuwezijds Kolk. Walk to the Herengracht and make a right. $ Free (but don't forget to tip the guide!). ⏰ Open Tu 10am-5pm, Sa-Su 10am-5pm.

NEDERLANDS INSTITUUT VOOR MEDIAKUNST MUSEUM

Keizersgracht 264 ☎020 623 71 01 www.nimk.nl

The Netherlands Media Art Institute puts on four 10-week exhibitions each year to showcase the works of Dutch and international artists who use film, video, the internet, and other media technology. If you're planning a visit, be prepared to invest some time, as pieces can sometimes run for 20min. or more, but most are interesting enough that you'll want to see the whole thing. The institute also runs a number of smaller exhibitions that involve more experimental performances and symposia. The museum is in the same building as the **Mediatheque,** which houses a huge collection of books and media pieces.

🚋 Tram #13, 14, or 17 to Westermarkt. Follow Keizersgracht and the museum will be on your right. $ €4.50, students and seniors €2.50. Mediatheque free. ⏰ Open Tu-F 11am-6pm, Sa and every 1st Su 1-6pm. Mediatheque open M-F 1-5pm.

CENTRAL CANAL RING

The grand buildings in the center of the canal ring, architectural landmarks themselves, house a few historical museums as well as art galleries that lean toward the avant-garde. For kitsch aficionados, come here for some of the quirkier museums in the city, such as the **Museum of Bags and Purses** (Herengracht 573 ☎020 524 64 52; http://www.tassenmuseum.nl).

★ **FOAM** MUSEUM

Keizersgracht 609 ☎020 551 65 00 www.foam.org

Foam—the Fotografiemuseum Amsterdam—showcases new photography, from gritty photojournalism to glossy fashion photos. Work by renowned and up-and-coming photographers is displayed in an expansive wood-and-metal space. Grab a coffee and try to blend in with the artsy students hanging out here.

🚋 Tram #4, 16, 24, or 25 to Keizersgracht. Foam is about 50m east of the stop. $ €8, students and seniors €5.50, under 12 and with Museumjaarkaart free. ⏰ Open M-W 10am-6pm, Th-F 10am-9pm, Sa-Su 10am-6pm. Cafe open daily 11am-5pm.

GOLDEN BEND ARCHITECTURE

Herengracht, between Leidsestraat and Vijzelstraat

If Amsterdam's tiny, teetering canal houses are beginning to make you feel claustrophobic, head to this scenic stretch of the canal ring, removed from the noisy center but still only 15min. south of Dam Sq. In the 17th century, expanding the canals meant the city needed wads of cash, so they allowed the rich to build houses twice as wide as before in order to encourage investment. Termed the "Golden Bend" for the wealth that subsequently flocked here, this stretch of former residences features Neoclassical facades and glimpses of sparkling chandeliers through latticed windows. Today, most of these former mansions are inhabited by banks, life insurance agencies, and a few very lucky (and very wealthy) residents. To get a peek inside one of the swanky buildings, you may have to stifle your suppressed fear of crazy cat ladies and visit **Cat's Cabinet** (Herengracht 497 ☎020 626 53 78; www.kattenkabinet.nl). This bizarre museum was created a Golden Bend house after the owner's beloved cat—fittingly named JP Morgan—passed away. For some reason, the apparently distraught owner felt the world needed a museum devoted to all things feline. For a less idiosyncratic peek inside, **Open Garden Days** each June allow visitors to tour many of the houses' gardens (for more info, check out www.opentuinendagen.nl).

🚊 Tram #1, 2, or 5 to Koningsplein. $ Cat's Cabinet €6, ages 4-12 €3. ⏰ Cat's Cabinet open M-F 10am-4pm, Sa-Su noon-5pm.

MUSEUM WILLET-HOLTHUYSEN — MUSEUM

Herengracht 605 ☎020 523 18 22 www.willetholthuysen.nl

Not technically on the "Golden Bend" but just as elegant and opulent, this building has been preserved by the Amsterdam Historisch Museum. The museum's goal is to demonstrate what wealthy Dutch life was like in the 19th century as seen through the eyes of **Abraham Willet** and **Louisa Willet-Holthuysen,** the house's last inhabitants. Visitors gawk and admire three floors of wealth on display, including the Willets' art collection and a stately garden. Those less interested in history might tire of all the tidbits from the meticulously chronicled lives of Louisa and Abe, but if you've got a few minutes and a Museumjaarkaart, the inside offers a new perspective on the famous canal houses. The house will leave you wondering if all the tall skinny abodes you trek past are this ridiculously grand.

🚊 Tram #9 or 14 to Rembrandtplein. Walk down Utrechtsestraat and turn left. $ €8, ages 6-18 €4, under 6 and with Museumjaarkaart free. ⏰ Open M-F 10am-5pm, Sa-Su 11am-5pm.

MUSEUM VAN LOON — MUSEUM

Keizersgracht 672 ☎020 624 52 55 www.museumvanloon.nl

The Van Loons have been so integral to this city's history, their family tree might as well be drawn on a map of Amsterdam. One of the earliest Van Loons was a founder of the Dutch East India Company, and since then many of his descendants have been mayors, political advisors, and the like. The powerful family donated this residence to serve as a museum, preserving a record of themselves and the city they thrived in. That said, this museum probably won't be too interesting to most visitors. If you want a look into the life of wealthy Amsterdammers of the past, you're better off going to the Museum Willet-Holthuysen.

🚊 Tram #4, 16, 24, or 25 to Keizersgracht. The museum is about 50m east of the stop. $ €8, students €6, ages 6-18 €4, with Museumjaarkaart free. ⏰ Open M 11am-5pm, W-Su 11am-5pm.

JORDAAN

👍 ELECTRIC LADYLAND — MUSEUM

Tweede Leliedwarsstraat 5 ☎020 420 37 76 www.electric-lady-land.com

Electric Ladyland, the "First Museum of Fluorescent Art," is a sight unlike any other. The passionate and eccentric owner, Nick Padalino, will happily spend hours explaining the history, science, and culture of fluorescence to each and every visitor who walks through the door. The museum consists of a one-room basement full of Padalino's own art and other artifacts, including rocks and minerals from New Jersey to the Himalayas that glow all kinds of colors under the lights. The most intriguing part, though, is the fluorescent cave-like sculpture that Padalino terms "participatory art." Don a pair of foam slippers and poke around the glowing grottoes and stalactites, flick the lights on and off to see different fluorescent and phosphorescent stones, and look for the tiny Hindu sculptures. Upstairs, you can buy your own fluorescent art and blacklight kits. When a tour is in progress, you may have to ring the doorbell for a few minutes, but trust us: it's worth any wait.

🚊 Tram #13, 14, or 17 to Westermarkt. Cross Prinsengracht and walk 1 block down Rozengracht, then make a right and walk a few blocks. The museum is just before you reach Egelantiersgracht. $ €5. ⏰ Open Tu-Sa 1-6pm.

STEDELIJK MUSEUM BUREAU AMSTERDAM (SMBA) MUSEUM

Rozenstraat 59 ☎020 422 04 71 www.smba.nl

There's no telling what you'll find at the Stedelijk Museum's project space, but it seems to usually be some kind of art. Local artists have the chance to showcase artwork in rotating exhibits; during *Let's Go*'s last visit it was "The Marx Lounge"—a red room with a table full of books on critical theory. Special lectures and movie screenings are also sponsored occasionally. Check the website for current events or simply take your chances and drop by—after all, it's free.

🚏 Tram #13, 14, or 17 to Westermarkt. Cross Prinsengracht, turn left, and walk 1 block. $ Free. ⏰ Open Tu-Su 11am-5pm.

HOFJES GARDENS, HISTORICAL SITE

The northern third of the Jordaan

Tucked behind the neighborhood's closed doors are some of the oldest and prettiest gardens in the city. *Hofjes* are courtyard gardens, surrounded by almshouses originally built to provide housing for impoverished old women. These old gardens are scattered throughout the Jordaan, and many are now open to the public. In the northern part of the Jordaan, at Palmgracht 28-38, you can find the **Raepenhofje,** and a few blocks down is the **Karthuizerhof** (Karthuizersstraat 21-131). This larger *hofje* has two flowering gardens dotted with benches and a pair of old-fashioned water pumps. Finally, head to Egelantiersgracht 107-145 for the **Sint-Andrieshof.** These gardens are surrounded by residences, so be quiet and respectful.

🚏 From Raepenhofje, take tram #3 to Nieuwe Willemstraat, cross Lijnbaansgracht, make a left, and turn right onto Palmgracht. $ Free. ⏰ Open M-Sa 9am-6pm.

PIANOLA MUSEUM MUSEUM

Westerstraat 106 ☎020 627 96 24 www.pianola.nl

Vying with **Electric Ladyland** for the title of Weirdest Museum in the Jordaan, Pianola began as a private collection and now fills a space on busy Westerstraat with a glimpse into early 20th-century music and culture. What's a pianola, you ask? Commonly referred to as a player piano, it's an upright piano that plays itself from paper rolls inserted into the instrument. The museum houses over 25,000 such rolls, most of which can be played on the museum's instruments. A 1920s feel pervades the exhibition, since that was the time when these instruments were at their most popular (though we expect a resurgence any day now). Regular concerts are held here; check the website or posters outside for details.

🚏 Tram #3 or 10 to Marnixplein. Cross Lijnbaansgracht and walk up Westerstraat. $ €5. ⏰ Open Su 2-5pm. Group visits by appointment.

poezenboot

At first, Henriette van Weelde was your typical cat lady. In 1966, she took in a family of stray cats she found across from her home. Then she took in another. And another. After a while, she realized she had a bit of a space issue–namely, too many cats, too little space. So, Henriette did the reasonable thing: she bought her feline friends a sailing barge. The cats never stopped coming, so she upgraded the boat a few times over the years. By 1987, the boat was named an official cat sanctuary. Today, it meets all the requirements for an animal shelter. The Poezenboot (Cat Boat) has room for 30 kitties, and they adopt out an average of 15 per month. If you find yourself looking for a different kind of pussy in Amsterdam, stop by to offer one a good home. (Sangel 38G ☎020 625 87 94; www.poezenboot.nl ⏰ Open M-Tu 1-3pm, Th-Sa 1-3pm.)

WESTERPARK AND OUD-WEST

Visitors to this area can relax in the park that gives the neighborhood its name, while art-lovers can check out two of the city's more idiosyncratic destinations, to the north and east of the park.

MUSEUM HET SCHIP   MUSEUM

Spaarndammerplantsoen 140   ☎020 418 28 85 www.hetschip.nl

This museum commemorates "The Ship," a housing project designed by Amsterdam School architect Michel de Klerk in 1919. Inspired by Socialist ambitions, de Klerk added unusual shapes and fanciful brickwork to his building, believing that Amsterdam's working class was overdue for "something beautiful." The first floor houses an old post office designed by de Klerk as well as a re-creation of what one of the original apartments looked like. Be sure to take the free tour, as knowledgeable staff can point out quirky details in the architecture that are otherwise easily missed. Across the street, a lunchroom serves food amid an exhibit of Amsterdam School photography and sculptures.

�︎ *Tram #3 to Haarlemmerplein. Walk across the canal toward Westerpark, up Spaarndammerstraat, then take a left onto Zaanstraat; the building will be a few blocks down the street.* ⑤ *€7.50, students €5, with Museumjaarkaart free.* ☼ *Open Tu-Su 11am-5pm. Tours every hr. 11am-4pm, though they can usually be joined late.*

WESTERGASFABRIEK   CULTURAL PARK

Pazzanistraat 41   ☎020 586 07 10 www.westergasfabriek.nl

Westergasfabriek, a so-called "cultural park" right next to Westerpark, serves as a center for local artists and trendy restaurants. Originally a 19th-century gasworks, its imposing brick buildings are now open to all manner of cultural projects, and currently house art studios and galleries, restaurants, theaters, and nightclubs. Check the website for upcoming showings and special events like film festivals, art showings, and market days.

🚶 *Just east of Westerpark. Tram #10 to Van Hallstraat. Cross the bridge and turn right to get to the main cluster of buildings.*

MUSEUMPLEIN AND VONDELPARK

The Museumplein is filled with museums—surprise! Plus, the beautiful **Concertgebouw**, at the southern end of Museumplein, is worth checking out even when the music isn't playing (see **Arts and Culture**).

🖼 VAN GOGH MUSEUM   MUSEUM

Paulus Potterstraat 7   ☎020 570 52 00 www.vangoghmuseum.nl

Van Gogh only painted for about a decade, yet he left a remarkable legacy of paintings and drawings. There's a lot more here than the pictures on the walls: one exhibit has a graphic novel depicting van Gogh's tumultuous personal life, while another details how the paintings have changed over the years with recreations of the masterpieces as the painter himself would've seen them. The museum dedicates considerable space to the artists who influenced van Gogh; including Toulouse-Lautrec, Gauguin, Renoir, Manet, Seurat, and Pissarro. On the flip side, there are paintings by some of the artists that van Gogh influenced, including Derain and Picasso. Of course, the highlight of the museum is its impressive collection of van Gogh's own work—the largest in the world—ranging from the dark, gloomy works like the *Potato Eaters* and *Skull of a Skeleton with Burning Cigarette* to the delicate *Branches of an Almond Tree in Blossom*. The exhibits are arranged chronologically, and wall plaques do an excellent job tracking the artist's biography alongside the paintings, concluding with the artist's descent into depression and suicide. We think this may be the best museum in

Amsterdam—unfortunately, so do a lot of other people. The lines can get pretty painful; to avoid them, reserve tickets on the museum's website or arrive when the crowds thin at around 10:30am or 4pm. But don't let the fear of crowds deter you—this is hands down one of the city's must-sees, and it's absolutely worth the wait.

Tram #2, 3, 5, or 12 to Van Baerlestraat. Walk 1 block up Paulus Potterstraat. $ €14, under 18 and with Museumjaarkaart free. Audio tour €5. Open M-Th 10am-6pm, F 10am-10pm, Sa-Su 10am-6pm. Last entry 30min. before close.

RIJKSMUSEUM — MUSEUM

Jan Luijkenstraat 1 — ☎020 674 70 00 www.rijksmuseum.nl

When you first see the commanding facade of the Rijksmuseum, it looks like the type of place you could get lost in for hours (if not days). When we visited, the museum featured art and artifacts from the Middle Ages through the 19th century, a comprehensive exhibit on Dutch history, and a collection of Asian art. There is also an enormous selection of furniture, Delftware, silver, and decorative objects (including two enormous **dollhouses** that probably cost more than some apartments). The exhibits on the ground floor trace the Netherlands's history as it grew from a small republic to a world power, commanding more than a fair share of the seas and international trade.

The heart of the museum, however, is the second-floor gallery of art from the Dutch Golden Age. Numerous landscapes, portraits, and still lifes—cheese figures prominently, typical Dutch—set the tone for 17th-century Dutch art, reflecting the same trends as the history lesson on the first floor. They pull out the big guns in a room full of beautiful works by **Rembrandt** and his pupils, evocative landscapes by Jacob van Ruisdael, and four luminous paintings by **Vermeer,** including *The Milkmaid.* The big finish is the room devoted to the **Night Watch,** probably Rembrandt's most famous painting. Only in Amsterdam would the old master be exhibited alongside a modern sculpture that looks like metal magic mushrooms hanging upside-down. Two audio tours are available to guide you through the museum: one is more traditional and led by the museum director, while the other is narrated by the Dutch artist, actor, and director Jeroen Krabbé, who gives a more personal view of the artists and paintings.

Tram #2 or 5 to Hobbemastraat. Alternatively, tram #7 or 10 to Spiegelgracht. The museum is directly across the canal. i Lines are shorter after 4pm. $ €12.50, under 18 and with Museumjaarkaart free. Audio tour €5. Open daily 9am-6pm.

VONDELPARK — PARK

Rolling streams, leafy trees, and inviting grass make the 120-acre Vondelpark central Amsterdam's largest and most popular open space. Established in the 1880s to provide a place for the city's residents to walk and ride, the park is now a hangout for skaters, senior citizens, stoners, soccer players, and sidewalk acrobats. Head here on the first sunny day of spring to see the whole city out in full force. The park is named after Joost van den Vondel, a 17th-century poet and playwright often referred to as the "Dutch Shakespeare." Vondelpark is also home to excellent cafes and an open-air theater (www.openluchttheater.nl), which offers free music and performances in the summer. If you're looking for a different sort of outdoor entertainment, you should know that in 2008 the Dutch police decided that it's legal to **have sex** in Vondelpark—so long as it's not near a playground and condoms are thrown away. Even without a bit of afternoon delight, this is still a delightful place to picnic and take a break from the bustling city.

Tram #2, 3, 5, or 12 to Van Baerlestraat. Walk down Van Baerlestraat to the bridge over the park and take the stairs down.

DE PIJP

De Pijp's sights are of a decidedly different variety than those in nearby Museumplein. Rather than staring at paintings you'll never own, haggle for wares at **Albert Cuypmarkt** (see **Shopping**). Or, instead of contemplating what life would be like in the Dutch Golden Age, find out what it's like being a bottle of beer at the **Heineken Experience.**

SARPHATIPARK PARK

In the 1860s, Amsterdam's chief architect was convinced that the center of the city would move south, and that this spot in De Pijp (then just marshlands and a windmill or two) would be the ideal place for Centraal Station. We all know how that one turned out (though we wonder what would have happened to the Red Light District if visitors couldn't stumble straight into it from the station). Not one to be deterred, the architect decided to build a park instead. Sarphatipark is fairly small, but its crisscrossing paths and central monument give it a genteel, 19th-century feel. It's rarely as crowded as Vondelpark, so you can have more grassy sunbathing space to yourself. The monument commemorates the park's namesake, the Jewish philanthropist and doctor Samuel Sarphati.

Tram #3 or 25 to 2e Van der Helstraat.

HEINEKEN EXPERIENCE MUSEUM

Stadhouderskade 78 ☎020 523 92 22 www.heinekenexperience.com

They can't call it a museum because it isn't informative enough, and they can't call it a brewery, because beer hasn't been made here since 1988. So, welcome to the Heineken "Experience." Four floors of holograms, multimedia exhibits, and virtual-reality machines tell you everything you'll ever want to know about the green-bottled stuff. Highlights include a ride that replicates the experience of actually becoming a Heineken beer. (There's something very Zen-alcoholic about the whole "in order to enjoy the beer you must BE the beer" idea.) In the end, this is a big tourist trap where you pay €15 to watch an hour of Heineken commercials. On the other hand, there's something quintessentially Dutch about the whole "experience"—these are, after all, the people who invented capitalism.

Tram #16 or 24 to Stadhouderskade, or tram #4, 7, 10, or 25 to Weterincircuit. From Weterincircuit, cross the canal and you'll see the building. $ €15. Open daily 11am-7pm. Last entry 5:30pm.

JODENBUURT AND PLANTAGE

Some lesser-known but still worthwhile museums fill Jodenbuurt, historically the city's Jewish Quarter and now home to several sights focusing on Jewish culture and identity. Spacious Plantage, meanwhile, is home to the Botanical Gardens and Artis Zoo.

VERZETSMUSEUM (DUTCH RESISTANCE MUSEUM) MUSEUM

Plantage Kerklaan 61 ☎020 620 25 35 www.verzetsmuseum.org

This museum chronicles the five years the Netherlands spent under Nazi occupation during WWII. The permanent exhibit centers on the question that people faced in this period, "What do we do?" In the early days of the occupation, many struggled to decide whether to adapt to their relatively unchanged life under Nazi rule or to resist. As time went on, the persecution of Jews, gypsies, and homosexuals intensified, and as repression grew, so did the resistance. The museum masterfully presents individuals' stories with interactive exhibits and an extensive collection of artifacts and video footage. The museum pays tribute to the ordinary Dutch citizens who risked (and often lost) their lives to publish illegal newspapers, hide Jews, or pass information to Allied troops. A smaller portion of the exhibit details the effects of the war on Dutch colonies in East Asia. Verzetsmuseum is well worth your time and money, even if you're not a history buff.

Tram #9 or 14 to Plantage Kerklaan. Across from Artis Zoo. $ €7.50, ages 7-15 €4, under 7 and with Museumjaarkaart free. Open M 11am-5pm, Tu-F 10am-5pm, Sa-Su 11am-5pm.

TROPENMUSEUM MUSEUM

Linnaeusstraat 2 ☎020 568 82 00 www.tropenmuseum.nl

In a palatial building that is part of the Koninklijk Instituut voor de Tropen (Dutch Royal Institute of the Tropics), this immense museum provides an anthropological look at the world's tropical regions from the distant past to today. A running theme throughout the exhibits is the complicated relationship between Europe and the tropics during the rise and fall of Western imperialism. An astounding collection of cultural artifacts like Thai bridal jewelry and African presidential folk cloths give a sense of life in these regions. An extensive portion of the first floor is devoted to the Dutch colonial experience in Indonesia (from the perspective of both the colonizers and colonized). There are also some cool interactive exhibits like drum kits to make early African music. That one's probably for the kids, but if you find yourself rocking out, we won't tell.

🚏 Tram #9, 10, or 14 to Alexanderplein. Cross the canal and walk left along Mauritskade. $ €9, students €5, under 18 and with Museumjaarkaart free. ⏰ Open daily 10am-5pm.

JOODS HISTORISCH MUSEUM (JEWISH HISTORICAL MUSEUM) MUSEUM

Nieuwe Amstelstraat 1 ☎020 531 03 10; www.jhm.nl

Four 17th- and 18th-century Ashkenazi synagogues were incorporated to form this museum dedicated to the history and culture of Dutch Jews. One part of the museum highlights the religious life of the community using artifacts (including a number of beautifully decorated Torahs), explanations of Jewish traditions, and videos that recount personal anecdotes. Another exhibit explores the history of the community between 1600 and 1900, from the first settlements in this unusually tolerant city to later struggles to gain full civil and political liberties. The period surrounding WWII is also covered. The museum holds two temporary exhibition spaces that host art shows. The JHM Children's Museum introduces kids to Jewish life and culture through the reconstruction of a typical Jewish family, with friendly Max the Matzo as their guide.

🚏 Trams #9 or 14 or ⓂWaterlooplein. Walk down Waterlooplein and turn right onto Wesperstraat. Nieuwe Amstelstraat is on the right. $ €9, students and seniors €6, ages 13-17 €4.50, under 13 and with Museumjaarkaart free. Special exhibits may cost extra. ⏰ Open daily 11am-5pm.

BROUWERIJ 'T IJ BREWERY

Funenkade 7 ☎020 622 83 25 www.brouwerijhetij.nl

What could be more Dutch than drinking beer at the base of a windmill? Even better, the beer brewed and served here is much, much tastier than the more internationally famous Dutch brands. Once a bathhouse, this building was taken over as a squat in the 1980s. Today, its brewers craft 10 organic, unfiltered, and non-pasteurized beers. You can try a glass or three of their wares at the massive outdoor terrace of the on-site pub, or at cafes and bars throughout the city. The brewers are proud of their selection, which ranges from a golden triple beer to a pilsner; proud of their brewery, which you can scope out on a free tour; and even prouder of their huge collection of beer bottles, purportedly one of Europe's largest.

🚏 Tram #10 to Hoogte Kadijk or #14 to Pontanusstraat. Head toward the windmill. $ Beer €2. ⏰ Pub open daily 3-8pm. Free brewery tours F and Su 4pm.

REMBRANDT HOUSE MUSEUM MUSEUM

Jodenbreestraat 4 ☎020 520 04 00 www.rembrandthuis.nl

Flush with success at the height of his popularity, Rembrandt van Rijn bought this massively expensive house in 1639. Twenty years later, after a decline in sales and failure to pay his mortgage, he was forced to sell it along with many of his possessions. His misfortune turned out to be a great boon for historians—the inventory of Rembrandt's worldly goods gave curators the ability to reconstruct his house almost exactly as it was when he lived there. Now visitors can see where Rembrandt slept, entertained guests, made paintings, sold paintings, and got attacked by his mistress after a fight over alimony (that would be the kitchen). The most interesting rooms are on the top floor: Rembrandt's massive studio (with many of his original tools) and the room where he stored his *objets d'art*—armor, armadillos, and everything in between. Paintings by his talented contemporaries and students adorn the walls, and the museum holds a collection of hundreds of Rembrandt's etchings. Guides reenact his etching and printing techniques on the third floor every 45min.

✈ Tram #9 or 14 or ⓂWaterlooplein. Walk down Waterlooplein, around the stadium, then turn right and continue until you reach Jodenbreestraat. The museum is on the right. ⓢ €9, with ISIC card €6, ages 6-17 €2.50, under 6 and with Museumjaarkaart free. ◫ Open daily 10am-5pm.

HORTUS BOTANICUS   GARDENS
Plantage Middenlaan 2A   ☎020 638 16 70 www.dehortus.nl
One of the oldest botanical gardens in the world, Hortus Botanicus began in 1638 as a place for growing medicinal herbs (no, not that kind). Now it's grown to include over 4000 species of plant life. Thanks to the Dutch East India company, the gardens gathered exotic species from all around the world, and some of those original plants (such as the Eastern Cape giant cycad) are still around today. The "crown jewels" section is the place to go to catch a glimpse of extremely rare species such as the *Victoria amazonica*, a water lily that only opens at dusk. Nicely landscaped ponds and paths make this a pleasant place to wander for an afternoon, and the butterfly house might be the closest you'll get to some steamy summer weather in Amsterdam.

✈ Tram #9 or 14 to Mr. Visserplein. Walk down Plantage Middenlaan. The gardens are on the right. ⓢ €7.50, seniors and ages 5-14 €3.50. Tours €1. ◫ Open July-Aug M-F 9am-7pm, Sa-Su 10am-7pm; Sept-June M-F 9am-5pm, Sa-Su 10am-5pm. Tours Su 2pm.

food

For some reason, when we think "Northern Europe," we don't think "awesome food." It's telling that in the vast world of Amsterdam restaurants, not too many of them actually serve Dutch cuisine. (Here's a quick run-down of what that looks like: pancakes, cheese, herring, and various meat-and-potato combinations.) Luckily, Amsterdam's large immigrant populations have brought Indonesian, Surinamese, Ethiopian, Algerian, Thai, and Chinese food to the banks of the canals. Finally, Amsterdam has this thing with sandwiches—they're everywhere, and they tend to be really, really good.

De Pijp, Jordaan, and the Nine Streets in Canal Ring West boast the highest concentration of quality eats, and De Pijp is the cheapest of the three. If you really want to conserve your cash, the supermarket chain Albert Heijn is a gift from the budget gods (find the nearest location at www.ah.nl). Keep in mind that most supermarkets close around 8pm. If you need groceries late at night (we can only guess why), try De Avondmarkt near Westerpark.

OUDE ZIJD

Zeedijk is overrun with restaurants, but if you shop around to avoid touristy rip-offs, you can land a great meal.

▨ **'SKEK**   CAFE, GLOBAL $$
Zeedijk 4-8   ☎020 427 05 51 www.skek.nl
A "cultural eetcafe" where students (with ID) get a 33% discount, Skek prepares healthy, hearty cuisine, with rotating options like a Japanese hamburger with wasabi mayonnaise, grilled vegetable lasagna, and braised eggplant. The interior is on a mission to be hip, with whimsical fantasy board games painted on the

tables, student art on the walls, and occasional live music. Come for the free Wi-Fi and student discount, stay for the not-bad food—just don't accidentally order the hamburger made out of carrots.

From Centraal Station, follow Prins Hendrikkade to Zeedjik. [$] Lunch dishes around €5-7. Dinner entrees around €13. Open M-Th noon-1am, F-Sa noon-3am, Su noon-1am.

LATEI CAFE $

Zeedijk 143 ☎020 625 74 85 www.latei.net

Colorful and eccentric, Latei is filled with mismatched furniture and interesting knick-knacks—which just so happen to all be for sale. But save your money for the simple, filling, and tasty food: sandwiches are made with artisan bread and the cafe's own olive oil and topped with fresh cheese or veggies. (Note: Dutch "sandwiches" usually only include one slice of bread.) Indian cuisine makes a guest appearance at dinner Thursday to Saturday nights.

[M]Nieuwmarkt. Zeedijk is along the northwestern corner of the square. [$] Sandwiches €3-5. Desserts €3-4. Open M-W 8am-6pm, Th-F 8am-10pm, Sa 9am-10pm, Su 11am-6pm.

BIRD THAI $$

Zeedijk 72-74 ☎020 620 14 42 www.thai-bird.nl

Zeedijk may be considered Amsterdam's Chinatown, but the best Asian restaurant in town might be this Thai eatery. Across the street from the main restaurant is a simpler snack bar version, which sells many of the same dishes for a few euro less. The menu is full of all your favorite Thai classics, including some special dishes from the northeast. *Let's Go* really likes their green curry.

[M]Nieuwmarkt. [$] Entrees €8-14. Snack bar cash only. Open daily 5-11pm. Snack bar open daily 2-10pm.

IN DE WAAG ITALIAN, DUTCH $$$

Nieuwmarkt 4 ☎020 452 77 72 www.indewaag.nl

Located inside De Waag, Nieuwmarkt's distinctive 15th-century castle, this restaurant presents quite the dining experience—with prices to match. During the summer, sit on the large terrace and admire the architecture and bustle of the square. When it's cold out, the modernized medieval interior, lit by hundreds of candles, is just as enticing. The food is Mediterranean with a Dutch twist—lots of lamb, beef, and fish, with some vegetarian pastas and polentas.

[M]Nieuwmarkt. [$] Lunch entrees €7.50-14; dinner entrees €18-22. Open daily 10am-1am.

RED LIGHT DISTRICT

Gluttony is one of the few sins you can't indulge in the Red Light District. There are plenty of snack shops selling plastic-looking pizzas and imitation falafel, though there are a few good, reasonably priced cafes. If you're looking for a quality meal, head next door to the Oude Zijd.

DE BAKKERSWINKEL CAFE $

Warmoesstraat 69 ☎020 489 80 00 www.debakkerswinkel.nl

This place is as cute and homey as the surrounding streets are neon and sordid. In the large pastel dining room, you can enjoy quiche, breakfast, or homemade sourdough bread and cheese. High tea is also available, with different combinations of scones, sweets, and sandwiches. Dessert here is a special treat, befitting the general decadence of the neighborhood.

From Centraal Station, walk down Damrak, turn left onto Oudebrugsteeg, and then right onto Warmoesstraat. [$] Sandwiches €4. Slice of quiche €5. Breakfast menus €6-12. High teas €14-40. Open Tu-F 8am-6pm, Sa 8am-5pm, Su 10am-5pm.

SI CHAUN KITCHEN CHINESE $

Warmoesstraat 17 ☎020 420 78 33

Chinese is probably the best deal for a substantial meal in the Red Light District, and Si Chaun is marginally cozier, cheaper, and tastier than many of its competitors. This place offers standard favorites like fried rice and noodle dishes alongside house specialties and plenty of vegetarian options.

From Centraal Station, walk down Damrak, turn left onto Oudebrugsteeg, and left onto Warmoesstraat. [$] Most entrees €7-12. Open daily 3-11:30pm.

NIEUWE ZIJD

Eating in the Nieuwe Zijd is less than ideal: the area is packed with overpriced, low-quality tourist traps. Try the southern half of **Spuistraat** or head to one of the shopping-center cafeterias nearby for a quick lunch. Otherwise, save your money and head to the Canal Ring West instead.

CAFE SCHUIM CAFE $

Spuistraat 189 ☎020 638 93 57

This artsy cafe offers a nice break from the neighborhood's usual big chains, with old movie posters adorning the walls and massive, padded leather chairs. Try the smoked chicken and avocado club for lunch, or the creative pasta or steak at dinner. Cafe Schuim is popular at night, too, when young professionals and hipsters crowd the bar and picnic tables outside. Live music and DJs perform a few times per month.

Tram #1, 2, 5, or 14 to Dam/Paleisstraat. Walk down Paleisstraat toward Singel and make a left onto Spuistraat. [$] Sandwiches €4-7. Pasta €9.50-13. Beer from €2.20. Open M-Th noon-1am, F-Sa noon-3am, Su 1pm-1am.

LA PLACE CAFETERIA $

Kalverstraat 203 ☎020 622 01 71 www.laplace.nl

In most parts of Amsterdam, cute cafes tend to be the best informal dining choice. In the Nieuwe Zijd, many of those cafes will charge €10 for a sandwich, so embrace the rampant commercialism and head to this immense multilevel cafeteria inside the giant **Vroom and Dreesmann** department store. You'll be rewarded with a vast, affordable buffet of pizza, pasta, salad, sandwiches, meats, and pastries. Grab a tray and help yourself, then head to one of several seating areas, including an outdoor terrace. Of the many cafeterias and food courts nearby, this is the biggest and the grandest.

Tram #4, 9, 14, 16, 24, or 25 to Muntplein. Note the giant V and D store, and enter through the Kalverstraat door. The entrance to the cafeteria is on the left. [$] Sandwiches €3-5. Pizzas €7. Entrees typically €3-8. Open M 11am-8pm, Tu-W 10am-8pm, Th 10am-9pm, F-Sa 10am-8pm, Su noon-8pm.

RISTORANTE CAPRESE ITALIAN $$

Spuistraat 259-261 ☎020 620 00 59

The service here is leisurely at best, but that just makes it feel more authentically Italian. With the massive wall mural of the Bay of Naples, you might even be convinced that you're a few countries to the south. Ristorante Caprese serves traditional Italian food done well, from the excellent tomato sauce to the organically raised meat.

Tram #1, 2, or 5 to Spui/Nieuwezijds Voorburgwal. Cross over to Spuistraat and turn right. [$] Pasta €9-14. Meat entrees €18-22. House wine from €4. Open daily noon-11pm.

SIE JOE INDONESIAN $

Gravenstraat 24 ☎020 624 18 30 www.siejoe.com

This unassuming Indonesian spot in the shadow of the Nieuwe Kerk is one of the best cheap options for a sit-down meal in the area. The limited menu contains a half-dozen rice dishes, some soups, and meat satays. For vegetarians, the *gado gado* (mixed vegetables and tofu in peanut sauce) is a good option.

From Dam Sq., walk up Nieuwezijds Vorburgwal and turn left onto Gravenstraat. Sie Joe is directly behind the church. [$] Entrees €6.75-9.25. Open M-W noon-7pm, Th noon-8pm, F-Sa noon-7pm.

dutch delicacies

Ordering a meal at a Dutch restaurant is no easy affair. The names of many Dutch dishes contain more letters than the dishes do calories. Educate yourself on the meanings of these common Dutch delicacies in order to ensure you get a sweet deal.

- **JAN-IN-DE-ZAL.** This "john in the bag" is no evil twin to SNL's "dick in a box." Also known as "plum duff," this dessert consists of a ball of dough stuffed with candied lemon peels and slices of roasted almonds, all cooked in a pot of boiling water. Before you ask, changing the name to "ball in a pot" probably wouldn't help with the sexual connotations.
- **BOERENJONGENS.** Is this just us, or does this all sound like sex stuff? Boerenjongens are just brandied raisins, and frequently appear at the bottom of a cup of eggnog.
- **KAPUCIJNERS.** This bean is not for cappuccino-lovers. Rather than deriving its name from any coffee drink, the pea-like Kapucijners gets its name from its color, which is reminiscent of the habits of Capuchin monks.
- **KIP MET SLAGROOMSAUS.** This isn't some Martian version of *When Harry Met Sally.* This dish, which translates to "chicken with whipped cream sauce," involves a light, airy cream usually made with onions or mushrooms.

SCHEEPVAARTBUURT

Haarlemmerstraat and **Haarlemmerdijk** are lined with restaurants, from cheap sandwich joints to upscale bistros. You'll have no problem finding somewhere to eat, but don't disregard the quality options off the main streets.

HARLEM: DRINKS AND SOUL FOOD AMERICAN $$
Haarlemmerstraat 77 ☎020 330 14 98

No, they didn't leave out a vowel: this place is the Dutch outpost of good ol' American soul food (or, at least, as close to it as you'll get in the Netherlands). At Harlem, you can indulge your culinary homesickness without the shame of being seen in a Burger King. Fill up on a variety of club sandwiches, soups, and salads at lunch or sup on dishes like fried chicken at dinner. As the night wears on, patrons stick around to imbibe and listen to the grooving soul and funk on the stereo, making Harlem one of Scheepvaartbuurt's livelier places come nightfall.

⇋ From Centraal Station, turn right, cross the Singel, and walk down Haarlemmerstraat a few blocks. Harlem is on the corner with Herenmarkt. [$] Sandwiches €5-8. Entrees €12-18. ⏰ Open M-Th 10am-1am, F-Sa 10am-3am, Su 10am-1am. Kitchen closes at 10pm.

OPEN CAFE-RESTAURANT MEDITERRANEAN $$
Westerdoksplein 20 ☎020 620 10 10 www.open.nl

This restaurant inhabits one of the coolest locations in Amsterdam—a renovated segment of a train bridge perched high above the water, between Westerdok and the IJ. You can sit in the glossy interior (lined with windows and green leather booths), on a walkway terrace, or on the sidewalk right by the water. The Mediterranean-style food is elegant and includes dishes like lamb ravioli, stewed oxtail, and sea-bass salad. Most dishes come in both half and full portions.

⇋ From Haarlemmerstraat, walk from Korte Prinsengracht through the tunnel under the train tracks and then cross the bridge. Open is on the right. [$] Sandwiches and salads €7-14. Half-entrees €7-14; full €14-22. ⏰ Open daily 10am-10:30pm.

LE SUD   VEGETARIAN, MEDITERRANEAN $
Haarlemmerdijk 118   ☎064 019 04 49 www.lesud.nl
This counter near Haarlemmerplein sells a variety of salads and vegetarian
sandwiches filled with things like hummus, grilled eggplant, and falafel. There's
also a tremendous array of deli items, including olives, cheeses, dolmades (stuffed
grape leaves), tapenades, and more hummus. Food is primarily for takeout.
☛ *Tram #3 to Haarlemmerplein. Cross Haarlemmerplein to reach Haarlemmerdijk, then continue
walking east.* ⑨ *Sandwiches €3. Salads €1.25-2.50 per 100g.* ⌚ *Open M-Sa 10am-6pm.*

CANAL RING WEST

This is one of the best places for high-quality eats in Amsterdam. The Nine Streets
area is packed with hip and delicious cafes.

▨ 'T KUYLTJE   SANDWICHES $
Gasthuismolensteeg 9   ☎020 620 10 45 www.kuyltje.nl
This no-frills takeout spot makes tremendous, filling Belgian *broodjes* (sandwich
rolls). The proprietor used to be a butcher, a fact which is immediately evident
from the fresh and flavorful meats (roast beef, pastrami, speck, etc.) hanging
from the ceiling.
☛ *Tram #1, 2, 5, 13, 14, or 17 to Dam/Radhuisstraat. Continue down Radhuisstraat and make a
left at the Singel.* ⑨ *Sandwiches €3-4.* ⌚ *Open M-F 7am-4pm.*

▨ TASCA BELLOTA   SPANISH $$
Herenstraat 22   ☎020 420 29 46 www.tascabellota.com
Spanish restaurants are hugely popular in Amsterdam, but few match the
quality and value of this tapas-and-wine bar. The menu features delicious dishes
like spicy lamb meatballs, peppers stuffed with lentils and Manchego cheese,
and dates with bacon. The interior is intimate, and its murals have a bullfighter
fetish that would put Hemingway to shame. Strongly recommended by locals,
Tasca Bellota also hosts live music some nights.
☛ *Tram #1, 2, 5, 13, or 17 to Nieuwezijds Kolk. Cross Spuistraat and the Singel and continue on
Herenstraat.* ⑨ *Small dishes €5-10.* ⌚ *Open Tu-Su 6-10pm.*

▨ DE KAASKAMER   CHEESE $$
Runstraat 7   ☎020 623 34 83 www.kaaskamer.nl
Wallace and Gromit's dream come true, this store is packed floor-to-ceiling
with hundreds of types of cheese. Hard cheese, soft cheese, French cheese,
Dutch cheese, red cheese, blue cheese—if you can make it out of milk, they
have it. Because man cannot live on cheese alone (though one ill-fated *Let's Go*
researcher tried it a few years back), the shop also sells wine, bread, olives, and
other cheese-complementing snacks. This is Holland: you want to go to a cheese
shop. Go to this one.
☛ *Tram #13, 14, or 17 to Westermarkt. Walk down Prinsengracht and Runstraat will be on the left.*
⑨ *Most cheeses €2-5 per 100g, €7-9 per 500g. Cash only.* ⌚ *Open M noon-6pm, Tu-F 9am-6pm,
Sa 9am-5pm, Su noon-5pm.*

THE PANCAKE BAKERY   DUTCH $$
Prinsengracht 191   ☎020 625 13 33 www.pancake.nl
Many swear that this canal-side restaurant serves the best pancakes in
Amsterdam. The menu has a dizzying list of sweet and savory options, from the
standard ham and cheese to international concoctions like the Indonesian (with
chicken, peanut sauce, and sprouts). Enjoy these flaky, gooey wonders in the
wooden interior or at a table by the water. The bakery also serves beer and
cherry jenever—because the only thing better than fat and happy is fat, happy,
and drunk.
☛ *Tram #13, 14, or 17 to Westermarkt. Turn right onto Prinsengracht.* ⑨ *Pancakes €7-14.* ⌚ *Open
daily noon-9:30pm.*

amsterdam

FOODISM
SANDWICHES, ITALIAN $
Oude Leliestraat 8
☎020 427 51 03 www.foodism.nl

This colorful little joint provides cheap, tasty food. The menu features creative sandwiches like chicken with mango chutney and hummus with alfalfa, as well as homemade pastas like chorizo and potato ravioli. Baked goods, breakfast, and soups are also served.

Tram #1, 2, 5, 13, 14, or 17 to Dam/Radhuisstraat. Continue on Radhuisstraat and turn right on the far side of the Singel; Foodism is on the left. ⑨ *Sandwiches €5.50. Pastas €10-12.* ⓧ *Open M-Sa noon-10pm, Su 1-6pm.*

VENNINGTON
CAFE $
Prinsenstraat 2
☎020 625 93 98

Vennington is an inexpensive, diner-esque restaurant that serves breakfast and lunch. There's nothing particularly gourmet going on here; it's just a place to get full and have a nice greasy meal for as few euro as possible. They have an extensive selection of sandwiches breakfast items, coffee, and shakes.

From the Westerkerk, walk up Prinsengracht and turn right. ⑨ *Sandwiches €2.50-7. Coffee from €1.50. Shakes €3-4.* ⓧ *Open daily 8am-5:30pm.*

CENTRAL CANAL RING

You'll eat well in the Central Canal Ring, where restaurants are affordable, tourist crowds are low, and you're never too far from Amsterdam's major sights. Try window-food-shopping down **Utrechtsestraat,** which is full of tasty ethnic eateries, Dutch cheese shops, and bakery fronts piled high with pastries—it's a little like food porn's answer to the Red Light District.

▨ ZUIVERE KOFFIE
CAFE $
Utrechtsestraat 39
☎020 624 99 99

There's an expression in Dutch, *"dat is geen zuivere koffie,"* which translates to, "that's no pure coffee," but really means something like, "that's totally suspicious." This cozy store is the opposite, offering good coffee and delicious homemade croissants, desserts, and sandwiches. The apple pie is a thing of beauty. Feel comfortably European while enjoying it all in the gorgeous garden seating area.

Tram #4, 16, 24, or 25 to Keizersgracht. Walk east on Keizersgracht and make a left onto Utrechtsestraat. ⑨ *Sandwiches €5. Apple pie €3.50. Drinks €2-4.* ⓧ *Open M-F 8am-5pm, Sa 9am-5pm.*

▨ GOLDEN TEMPLE
VEGETARIAN $$
Utrechtsestraat 126
☎020 626 85 60 www.restaurantgoldentemple.com

Golden Temple offers a new-age soundtrack, yoga classes, and a tiny roof terrace with sofas and Indian artwork. But none of that will matter once you taste the food. The dinner menu features vegetarian cuisine, from salads to Italian pizzas to Mediterranean *mezze.* The food is a bit on the pricey side, but Golden Temple takes its ingredients seriously, and the meals are delicious and filling.

Tram #4, 7, 10, or 25 to Fredericksplein. Walk diagonally through the square and up Utrechtsestraat. **i** *Free Wi-Fi.* ⑨ *Entrees €8-17.* ⓧ *Open daily 5-9:30pm.*

B&B LUNCHROOM
CAFE, SANDWICHES $
Leidsestraat 44
☎020 638 15 42

It's hard to walk by this storefront window heaped high with pastries and muffins and not drool with desire. Unlike so many bakeries in town, most people can actually afford to step inside this one and indulge. You can probably even afford a real meal too. Filling sandwiches feature healthy and tasty combinations like roast beef and "citron mayonnaise" or gorgonzola and asparagus. Soups and salads complete the extensive menu printed on blackboards across the store. In the afternoon, you may have to take your food to go, as the store gets busy with locals on lunch break.

Tram #1, 2, or 5 to Keizersgracht. The cafe is on the southwestern corner. ⑨ *Sandwiches €3.50-6. Salads €6.50-7.50.* ⓧ *Open daily 10am-6pm.*

LEIDSEPLEIN

Korte and Lange Leidsedwarsstraat are stuffed with restaurants of every kind. Most post menus and prices (and sometimes enthusiastic, soliciting hostesses) outside, making it a little easier to shop around and avoid rip-offs. For the best values, look for restaurants that have special set menus or daily deals, or just grab a sandwich and snack from a grocery store. At night, places like **Maoz** and **Wok to Walk** (both on Leidsestraat, toward Prinsengracht) stay open late and are surprisingly tasty and affordable.

BOJO INDONESIAN $$

Lange Leidsedwarsstraat 49 ☎020 643 44 43

Come here for great deals on delectable Indonesian cuisine. Bojo offers several special combo deals, including your choice of meat, noodle or rice dish, and a satay skewer (€10). The portions are ample, and the staff knows it—there's a note on the menu encouraging visitors to ask for a doggy bag. The bamboo walls and low-hanging lanterns will make you think you're oceans away from chilly Amsterdam.

Tram #1, 2, 5, 7, or 10 to Leidseplein. Walk down Leidseplein, turn left onto Leidsekruisstraat, and then left onto Lange Leidsekruisstraat. [$] Entrees €8-14. ⏰ Open M-F 4-9pm, Sa-Su noon-9pm.

DE ZOTTE BELGIAN $$

Raamstraat 29 ☎020 626 86 94 www.dezotte.nl

De Zotte is unusual among the infinite alcohol-focused establishments around the Leidseplein thanks to its attention to quality, not just quantity. It offers a wide selection of beers and a menu full of hearty Belgian food to go with them. Choose from steak, sausages, and pâté or cheese served with wonderful country bread. Less artery-clogging options like quiche are also available.

Tram #7 or 10 to Raamplein. Raamstraat is 1 block away from the Leidsegracht. Or tram #1, 2, or 5 to Leidseplein. Walk down Marnixstraat and Raamstraat is on the right after the canal. [$] Appetizers (some are filling enough to be a meal) from €3. Entrees €10-17. ⏰ Open M-Th 4pm-1am, Sa-Su 4pm-3am. Kitchen open daily 6-9:30pm.

THE PANTRY DUTCH $$

Leidsekruisstraat 21 ☎020 620 09 22 www.thepantry.nl

Designed to feel like an old Dutch living room, with traditional paintings and cozy wooden tables, The Pantry fills up with locals as well as tourists brave enough to try some authentic Dutch dishes, like salted herring and *boerenkoolstamppot* (mashed potatoes mixed with kale, served with a smoked sausage or meatball).

Tram #1, 2, 5, 7, or 10 to Leidseplein. Turn right onto Korte Leidsedwarsstraat; Leidsekruisstraat is on the left. [$] Entrees €12-17. ⏰ Open daily noon-9pm.

J. J. OOIJEVAAR DELI $

Lange Leidsedwarsstraat 47 ☎020 623 55 03

This is the place for the cheapest sandwiches on the Leidseplein—perhaps in all of Amsterdam. Rolls start at €1.30, and all kinds of fillings (cheeses, meats, vegetables, etc.) are available to stuff inside them. They also sell dirt-cheap grocery and convenience items.

Tram #1, 2, 5, 7, or 10 to Leidseplein. Walk down Leidseplein, take a left onto Leidsekruisstraat, and another left onto Lange Leidsekruisstraat. [$] Sandwiches €1.30-3.50. 6-pack of beer €6. ⏰ Open M-F 8:30am-6pm.

REMBRANDTPLEIN

Rembrandtplein, like the Leidseplein, is packed with enormous international restaurants and oversized cafes, but here there are fewer small, affordable eateries scattered into the mix. Below are the noteworthy exceptions.

VAN DOBBEN SANDWICHES $

Korte Reguliersdwarsstraat 5-9 ☎020 624 42 00 www.eetsalonvandobben.nl

An old-school deli and cafeteria that is everything most restaurants in Rembrandtplein are not: cheap, fast, and simple. The black and white ceramic tiling and chrome accents are a good match for the food's simplicity. Choose from a long list of sandwiches or a more limited selection of soups, salads, and omelets. We're not sure how this place stays in business, seeing as everywhere else nearby seems to charge five times as much, but keep it in mind when looking for a satisfying meal for under €10 in this neighborhood.

Tram #9 or 14 to Rembrandtplein. The easiest way to find the small street is to get onto Reguliersdwarsstraat heading away from Rembrandtplein, and then look for where the street veers off on the right. i Free Wi-Fi. $ Sandwiches €2.50-5. Open M-W 10am-9pm, Th 10am-1am, F-Sa 10am-2am, Su 11:30am-8pm.

RISTORANTE PIZZERIA FIRENZE ITALIAN $

Halvemaansteeg 9-11 ☎020 627 33 60 www.pizzeria-firenze.nl

The plentitude of pizzas and murals of Italian scenery on the walls will make you feel like you're actually in *Italia*. By no means is it the world's best pizza, but when you can get a huge pie for only €5-7, no one's complaining. With dozens of choices for both pizza and pasta, as well as some meat and fish dishes, Pizzeria Firenze is definitely one of the best values for a restaurant meal around Rembrandtplein.

Tram #9 or 14 to Rembrandtplein. Halvemaansteeg is the street to the left of the line of buildings with the giant TV screen. $ Pizza and pasta €5-11. House wine €2.50 per glass. Open daily 1-11pm.

ROSE'S CANTINA MEXICAN $$

Reguliersdwarsstraat 40 ☎020 625 97 97 www.rosescantina.com

A bright interior with salsa music and an outdoor patio make this a livelier option among the similarly overpriced restaurants around Rembrandtplein. They have a good selection of appetizers and standard Mexican entrees. The large bar serves up a long list of summery cocktails.

Tram #9 or 14 to Rembrandtplein or tram #1, 2, or 5 to Koningsplein. $ Appetizers €5.50-7.50. Entrees €14-21. Mixed drinks €7-9.50. Open M-Th 5-10:30pm, F-Sa 5pm-2am, Su 5-10:30pm. Kitchen closes F-Sa at 11pm.

JORDAAN

The Jordaan has very few truly budget food options, but few overpriced ones either. Establishments here are frequented more by loyal regulars than by tourists.

RAINARAI ALGERIAN $$

Prinsengracht 252 ☎020 624 97 91 www.rainarai.nl

The Algerian dishes at this small food counter change daily, and the staff will explain the day's offerings to you. A standard plate (get the medium) comes with generous servings of rice or couscous, a meat dish, and a vegetable dish, including items like spicy lamb meatballs, grilled asparagus, stuffed artichokes, and curry. Take-out is available, and serious fans can take home the store's cookbook or some Algerian spices from the mini grocery.

Tram #13, 14, or 17 to Westermarkt. Cross Prinsengracht and turn left. $ One medium entree plate €13.50. Open Tu-Su noon-10pm.

DE VLIEGENDE SCHOTEL VEGETARIAN $$

Nieuwe Leliestraat 162-168 ☎020 625 20 41 www.vliegendeschotel.com

With hearty dishes and generous portions, De Vliegende Schotel, "The Flying Saucer," is the perfect place to grab dinner after exploring **Electric Ladyland.** The organic and vegan-friendly menu changes seasonally, but often includes dishes like Ayurvedic curry, seitan goulash, or lasagna. You may have to wait

food

for your food—after all, it's prepared from scratch in the open kitchen by the eccentric old proprietor.

🚋 Tram #10 to Bloemgracht. Cross Lijnbaansgracht, turn left, and then right onto Nieuwe Leliestraat. $ Entrees €11-13. ⏰ Open daily 4-11:30pm. Kitchen closes at 10:45pm.

WINKEL CAFE $$

Noordermarkt 43 ☎020 623 02 23 www.winkel43.nl

It's all about the famous apple pie here, renowned across the city and served with a heap of fluffy whipped cream. Don't be surprised if every person inside has a plate of it. Enjoy your pie and the view from the outdoor patio, or step into the quaint interior and chat with locals. Not up for dessert? Winkel serves up sandwiches, soups, and stews, and occasionally hosts live music and dancing. Besides the pie, the food isn't too memorable, but it has a nice location and isn't too expensive.

🚋 Tram #3 or 10 to Marnixplein. Cross Lijnbaangracht, walk up Westerstraat, and make a left onto Noordermarkt Sq. $ Entrees €6-15. ⏰ Open M 7am-1am, Tu-Th 8am-1am, F 8am-3am, Sa 7am-3am, Su 10am-1am.

TOSCANINI ITALIAN $$$$

Lindengracht 75 ☎020 623 28 13 www.diningcity.nl/toscanini

Quite a few locals swear backward and forward that this is the best Italian food in Amsterdam. The menu is strongly authentic: instead of pizza, you'll find homemade pastas like ravioli with lemon and saffron, or *secondi* like pan-fried pork with *vin santo*. The bright, sky-lit interior lacks the gimmickry of faux-Italian trattorias the world over. Since it's been around for over 20 years, Toscanini is no longer a secret, so reservations are almost always required.

🚋 Tram #3 to Nieuwe Willemstraat. Cross Lijnbaansgracht to Willemstraat, turn right onto Palmdwarsstraat, and then left onto Lindengracht. $ Appetizers €11-15. Primi €8-15; secondi €18-23. ⏰ Open M-Sa 6-10:30pm.

breakfast sprinkles

Though the limited toast and jam in your hostel may suggest otherwise, the Dutch are pretty big on breakfast. They also have a fondness for desserts (name a culture that doesn't). In the 1930s, supposedly in response to a very persistent five-year-old boy who kept writing letters asking for a chocolate breakfast item, a Dutch company invented a great way to combine the two: *hagelslag*.

This confection is essentially chocolate sprinkles, but it provides a socially acceptable way to eat a ton of chocolate first thing in the morning: just sprinkle a thick layer of *hagelslag* on a piece of buttered toast. In addition to the original chocolate flavor, vanilla and fruit combinations exist. Still, legally, *hagelslag* must be over 35% cacao to be called *chocolat hagelslag*. Otherwise, the appropriate term is "cacao fantasy *hagelslag*"—which sounds like something unicorns eat.

WESTERPARK AND OUD-WEST

Some of the best-quality food can be found in these residential neighborhoods, where you're likely to be the only foreigner at the table.

TOMATILLO MEXICAN $

Overtoom 261 ☎020 683 30 86 www.tomatillo.nl

Fresh ingredients, generous portions, and prices perfect for the budget-conscious set Tomatillo apart from the rest of the ethnic fast-food eateries along Overtoom. Familiar Tex-Mex is prepared in an open-air kitchen, visible from the clean, crisp dining area. The food steers clear of the greasy, over-cheesiness of many gringo attempts at Mexican cuisine. The tacos are an especially good deal, consisting of two small tortillas and a heap of fillings that add up to a satisfying lunch. You may feel strange listening to "Georgia on Your Mind" while you eat, but the English menu makes this a good option in a neighborhood that's not always foreigner-friendly.

🚋 *Tram #1 to J. P. Heijestraat. Tomatillo is between Jan Pieter Heijestraat and G. Brandstraat, a block north of Vondelpark.* Ⓢ *Tacos €2.75-3.50. Burritos and tostadas €7.50-9.50. Desserts €2-4.* 🕐 *Open Tu-Su noon-9pm.*

BELLA STORIA   ITALIAN $$
Bentinckstraat 28   ☎020 488 05 99 www.bellastoria.info

For people who miss their Italian *nonna*'s home cooking (or missed out on having an Italian *nonna* entirely), this is the place to be. It's truly a family affair, run by a mother and her sons who chatter in Italian as they roll out dough. Since the restaurant sits in the middle of an extremely residential area, expect to have the place to yourself during a weekday lunch and to be surrounded by locals at dinner. The daily specials aren't always listed on the menu, so check the blackboard or ask the waitress when you come in.

🚋 *Tram #10 to Van Limburg Stirumplein. Facing Limburg Stirumstraat, Bentinckstraat is on your right.* Ⓢ *Pasta €10-17.* 🕐 *Open daily 10am-10pm.*

DE AVONDMARKT   GROCERY STORE $
De Wittenkade 94-96   ☎020 686 49 19 www.deavondmarkt.nl

One of the most frustrating things about the Netherlands can be the lack of 24hr. stores, but "The Evening Market" helps fill the bellies of night owls (at least until midnight). De Avondmarkt sells standard but high-quality groceries, wine, beer, cheeses, and prepared foods like lasagna. De Avondmarkt will also appeal to travelers looking for organic, cage-free, and vegan foods at affordable prices.

🚋 *Tram #10 to De Wittenkade. On the mainland side of De Wittenkade, at the corner of Van Limburg Stirumstraat.* 🕐 *Open M-F 4pm-midnight, Sa 3pm-midnight, Su 2pm-midnight.*

PEPERWORTEL   DELI $$
Overtoom 140   ☎020 685 10 53 www.peperwortel.nl

The type of bountiful gourmet market you'd expect to find in Italy or France, Peperwortel offers prepared foods such as quiche, pasta, hummus, soup, and more exotic dishes like Indonesian beef. A wide variety of vegetarian options and a good wine selection round out the menu. Limited seating is available outside, but the grass of Vondelpark a few blocks away makes for an even better table.

🚋 *Tram #1 to 1e Con. Huygensstraat. Peperwortel is on the corner of Overtoom and 2e Con. Huygensstraat.* Ⓢ *Entrees €9-14. Desserts €3. Wines from €7.* 🕐 *Open M-F 4-9pm, Sa-Su 3-9pm.*

CAFE NASSAU   CAFE, ITALIAN $$
De Wittenkade 105A   ☎020 684 35 62 www.cafenassau.com

Get your cute European cafe fix at this local favorite. Ingredients are fresh, and the helpful staff will guide you through the all-Dutch menu. Quaint outdoor patio furniture and picnic tables allow you to dine canal-side, and if you're lucky you can even land the table for two with the covered porch swing, perfect for taking that hostel romance to a classier level. Try the *broodje* (with spicy Italian sausage, grilled eggplant, parmesan, and arugula), sip on a Dutch coffee, or order a drink from the cafe's full bar.

🚋 *Tram #10 to De Wittenkade. At the corner of De Wittenkade and 2e Nassaustraat.* Ⓢ *Sandwiches from €5. Entrees €10-20.* 🕐 *Open M-Th 11:30am-midnight, F-Sa 11:30am-1am, Su 11:30am-midnight.*

food

MUSEUMPLEIN AND VONDELPARK

Museumplein seems to be the one area of Amsterdam that consistently attracts real grown-ups, so food here tends to be a bit pricey. A long day of museum-hopping can be strenuous though, and the 🍴**Albert Heijn** supermarket right behind the van Gogh museum is the place to refuel on the cheap.

🍴 **CAFE VERTIGO** — CAFE, MEDITERRANEAN $$

Vondelpark 3 — ☎020 612 30 21 www.vertigo.nl

Cafe Vertigo is housed in a remarkable, ornate building with a seemingly endless patio that makes it look like it should be more expensive than it is. On a summer day, there's no better place to enjoy a sandwich and a drink—except, perhaps, for the grass of Vondelpark itself. Sandwiches (like goat cheese with red onion compote) and soups (try the chickpea with lamb) make a great lunch. There's a full bar as well, so you can enjoy the atmosphere with just a drink too.

 # Tram #1, 3, or 12 to 1e Con. Huygensstraat/Overtoom. Walk down 1e Con. Huygensstraat, turn right onto Vondelstraat, and enter the park about 1 block down. The cafe is on the left. [$] *Soups and sandwiches €3.50-6.75. Entrees €12-20.* ⏰ *Open daily 10am-1am.*

🍴 **PASTA TRICOLORE** — ITALIAN $

P.C. Hooftstraat 52 — ☎020 664 83 14 www.pastatricolore.nl

If you want something a bit snazzier than Albert Heijn, Pasta Tricolore's front counter brims with a mouth-watering selection of salads, antipasti, lasagna, and desserts. You can also head to the back of the shop to order from a long list of Italian sandwiches (with filling combinations of salami, cheeses, and grilled vegetables). Limited seating is available, but it's nicest to take your meal to go and enjoy it in Vondelpark or Museumplein.

 # Tram #2 or 5 to Hobbemastraat. Walk down Hobbemastraat away from the Rijksmuseum and make a left onto P.C. Hooftstraat. [$] *Sandwiches and salads from €4.* ⏰ *Open M-Sa 9am-7pm, Su noon-7pm.*

DE PIJP

If you could somehow eat every meal in De Pijp, you would be a happy camper. In a radius of just a few blocks, you'll find a tremendous variety of cuisine dished up at significantly lower prices than in most other parts of the city. **Albert Cuypstraat** and **Ferdinand Bolstraat** are good places to start, but there are plenty of great options on side streets as well. Many of the bars in De Pijp also whip up surprisingly good food.

🍴 **CAFE DE PIJP** — MEDITERRANEAN $

Ferdinand Bolstraat 17-19 — ☎020 670 41 61 www.goodfoodgroup.nl

A catch-all local hostpot, Cafe De Pijp is usually swarmed with 20-somethings lingering over drinks, dinner, or more drinks. The menu has tapas-style offerings, like *merguez* (sausage) with Turkish bread and aioli, as well as more substantial dishes like eggplant parmesan. On weekend nights, DJs spin dance tunes to help you work off your meal.

 # Tram #16 or 24 to Stadhouderskade. Walk 2 blocks down Ferdinand Bolstraat. Cafe De Pijp is on the left. [$] *Entrees €5.50-8.* ⏰ *Open M-Th 3:30pm-1am, F 3:30pm-3am, Sa noon-2am, Su noon-1am.*

🍴 **HET IJSPALEIS** — ICE CREAM $

1e Sweelinckstraat 20 — ☎061 204 16 17

This is a gleaming white "Ice Palace" that looks awfully tempting on a hot day, especially after trawling through the crowds of Albert Cuypmarkt. They serve up about a dozen fresh, homemade flavors in cups or cones, along with coffee and tea if you get too chilly. Keeping to the neighborhood's hipster ambience, they offer exotic flavors like rooibos, but don't miss the stroopwafel ice cream.

 # Tram #16 or 24 to Albert Cuypmarkt. Walk through the market and turn right. [$] *Scoops from €1.10.* ⏰ *Open daily 11am-8pm.*

BAZAR MIDDLE EASTERN $$

Albert Cuypstraat 182 ☎020 675 05 44 www.bazaramsterdam.com

When the crush of Albert Cuypmarkt starts to feel a little overwhelming, pop into this church-cum-restaurant for inexpensive and tasty Middle Eastern. You can be basic with falafel or less basic with creative dinner specials like saffron veggie kebab. The vaulted ceilings are now decorated with Arabic Coca-Cola signs and old Dutch advertisements. Seating is available on the ground floor and in the old balconies above.

Tram #16 or 24 to Albert Cuypstraat. Walk through the market about 3 blocks. [$] Sandwiches and lunch entrees €4-10. Dinner entrees €12-16. ⏰ Open M-Th 11am-midnight, F 11am-1am, Sa 9am-1am, Su 9am-midnight.

WARUNG SPANG MAKANDRA INDONESIAN $

Gerard Doustraat 39 ☎020 670 50 81 www.spangmakandra.nl

Imperialism had more than a few downsides, but it was good at fostering new culinary combinations, like the Indonesian-Surinamese cuisine at this neighborhood favorite. Enjoy noodle and rice dishes, satays, and *rotis*—pancakes with meat and vegetable fillings—for incredibly low prices.

Tram #16 or 24 to Albert Cuypstraat. Walk 1 block north on Ferdinand Bolstraat and take the 1st left. The restaurant is on the left. [$] Entrees €5.50-9. ⏰ Open M-Sa 11am-10pm, Su 1-10pm.

DE SOEPWINKEL SOUP $

1e Sweelinckstraat 19F ☎020 673 22 83 www.soepwinkel.nl

Modern minimalism meets home cooking at this soup shop. Enjoy one of De Soepwinkel's six marvelous rotating soups (at least one is always vegetarian) inside the airy store or on the outside patio. They prepare quiches, tarts, and sandwiches as well.

Tram #3, 4, or 25 to Ceinturbaan/Van Woutstraat. Walk toward the park, turn right onto Sarphatipark, continue for 1½ blocks, and turn left onto 1e Sweelinckstraat. Alternatively, take tram #16 or 24 to Albert Cuypstraat. Walk a few blocks through the market and turn right onto 1e Sweelinckstraat. [$] Soups from €4. Menu with soup, a slice of quiche, and a drink €8.50. ⏰ Open M-F 11am-8pm, Sa 11am-6pm.

BURGERMEESTER BURGERS $

Albert Cuypstraat 48 ☎020 670 93 39 www.burgermeester.eu

Thankfully, the burgers here are better than the store's punny name (*burgermeester* is "mayor" in Dutch). This is something of a designer-burger bar—you can get a patty made from fancy beef, lamb, salmon, falafel, or Manchego cheese and hazelnuts, then top it with Chinese kale, truffle oil, or buffalo mozzarella. Burgers can be ordered normal-sized or miniature. They sell salads, too, but who goes to a burger joint for a salad?

Tram #16 or 24 to Albert Cuypstraat. Walk down the street away from the market. [$] Burgers €6.50-8.50. Toppings €0.50-1. ⏰ Open daily noon-11pm.

WILD MOA PIES PIES $

Van Ostadestraat 147 ☎064 291 40 50 www.pies.nu

We didn't know that New Zealand had much national cuisine, but apparently it does, and it's pie-centric. This Kiwi-owned store sells six types of meat pie (one made from real New Zealand beef) and three vegetarian types (we like the Three P's—pumpkin, sweet potato, and paprika). One large table is available if you want to eat your pies in the store, but you can also take them across the street to Sarphatipart.

Tram #3 or 25 to 2e Van der Helstraat. Walk 1 block south, away from the park. Von Ostadestraat is on the right. [$] Pies €3. ⏰ Open Tu-Sa 9am-5:30pm.

JODENBUURT AND PLANTAGE

[GLBT] EETKUNST ASMARA — ERITREAN $$

Jonas Daniel Meijerplein 8 ☎020 627 10 02

Jodenbuurt started out as a neighborhood of immigrants, and this East African restaurant is a testament to the area's continuing diversity. The menu consists of varieties of delicately spiced meat and vegetables, all served with delicious *injera*, a traditional spongy, slightly tangy bread. Each dish is accompanied by an assortment of lentils and other veggies, so one entree could feed two people. This is one of the best values around and a nice break from Amsterdam's unending parade of sandwiches.

⇄ Tram #9 or 14 or Ⓜ Waterlooplein. Walk down Waterlooplein and turn right onto Wesperstraat. Jonas Daniel Mieijerplein is on the right, 1 street after the Jewish Historical Museum. $ Entrees €9.50-11.50. Beer €1.50. ⏰ Open daily 6-11pm.

PLANCIUS — CAFE, SANDWICHES, FRENCH $$

Plantage Kerklaan 61A ☎020 330 94 69 www.restaurantplancius.nl

Right across from the zoo, Plancius is a stylish one-stop shop for everything from breakfast to after-dinner drinks. The menu rotates seasonally, but lunch always offers creative spins on the traditional sandwich, while dinner tends more toward formal French fare like lamb shank and shrimp croquettes.

⇄ Tram #9 or 14 to Plantage Kerklaan. $ Sandwiches €2.50-8.50. Appetizers €8. Entrees €15-19. ⏰ Open daily 11am-11pm. Lunch menu served until 6pm.

SOEP EN ZO — SOUP $

Jodenbreestraat 94A ☎020 422 22 43 www.soupenzo.nl

This small outpost of an Amsterdam chain serves fresh soups and a few salads. Soups come with bread and toppings like coriander and cheese. Take advantage of their outside patio when the weather's nice.

⇄ Tram #9 or 14 or Ⓜ Waterlooplein. $ Soups €3-7. ⏰ Open M-F 11am-8pm, Sa-Su noon-7pm.

nightlife

Experiencing Amsterdam's nightlife is an essential part of visiting the city. Sure, you can go to the Rijksmuseum and see a dozen Rembrandts, but there's nothing like stumbling out of a bar at 5am and seeing the great man staring down at you from his pedestal in the middle of Rembrandtplein. That square and its debaucherous cousin, Leidseplein, have all the glitzy clubs, rowdy tourist bars, and live DJs you could ever hope for. For a mellower night out, *bruin cafes* are cafe-pub combinations populated by old Dutch men or hipster students, depending on which neighborhood you're in. The closer you get to the Red Light District, the fewer locals you find, the more British bros on bachelor party trips you're forced to interact with. GLBT venues are a very visible and prominent part of Amsterdam's nightlife, and it's worth bearing in mind that in this city famous for tolerance, virtually every bar and club is **[GLBT] GLBT-friendly.**

NL20 is a free publication that lists the week's happenings—it's only in Dutch, but it's pretty easy to decipher the names of clubs and DJs. You can find it outside most stores, supermarkets, and tobacco shops. The English-language *Time Out Amsterdam* provides monthly calendars of nightlife, live music, and other events. It can be purchased at newsstands and bookstores.

OUDE ZIJD

Though the Oude Zijd is a little tamer at night than certain nearby neighborhoods, its close proximity to the Red Light District ensures consistent energy and some reveling tourists, especially along **Zeedijk.** If you're looking for a place to grab a drink here, both

Zeedijk and **Nieuwmarkt** are lined with pubs and cafe-bars. Follow the rainbow flags to find a smattering of ◙**GLBT** bars in the northern part of Zeedijk, near Centraal Station.

◙ **CAFE DE ENGELBEWAARDER** BAR
Kloveniersburgwal 59 ☎020 625 37 72 www.cafe-de-engelbewaarder.nl
The "Guardian Angel" Cafe takes its (exclusively) Belgian beer selection pretty seriously—and so should you. Located on the first floor of a canal house with a handsome, candle-lit seating area by the water, it's the perfect place to converse with artsy young locals. Despite the hipness, welcoming bartenders will gladly help you find the perfect drink. The walls inside are postered with advertisements for local goings-on that will bring you up to speed on all that's, well, going on.
✦ ⓜNieuwmarkt. *i* Live jazz Su 4:30pm. Occasional art showings; check website for details. ⓢ Beer from €3. ⓓ Open M-Th 11am-1am, F-Sa 11am-3am, Su 11am-1am.

◙ **HET ELFDE GEBOD** BAR
Zeedijk 5 ☎020 622 35 77 www.hetelfdegebod.com
For a country that produces so much beer, the Dutch can be surprisingly unpatriotic in their selections. Het Elfde Gebod is another all-Belgian-beer affair, this time with seven on tap and over 50 in bottles (many of which come served in their own special glasses). Don't worry if you're overwhelmed by the choices; the knowledgeable bartenders are happy to provide recommendations. The bar gets crowded on weekend nights with jolly, well-dressed locals.
✦ At the beginning of Zeedijk, near Centraal Station. ⓢ Beer from €3. Wine and spirits from €4. ⓓ Open M 5pm-1am, W-Su 3pm-1am.

CAFE DE JAREN BAR
Nieuwe Doelenstraat 20-22 ☎020 625 57 71 www.cafedejaren.nl
Popular with locals and tourists alike, Cafe de Jaren has an expansive interior and a two-tiered terrace overlooking the Amstel. It seems to be trying hard to be the coolest place in town, so it looks a lot more expensive than it is.
✦ Tram #4, 9, 16, 24, or 25 to Muntplein. Cross the Amstel and walk ½ a block. ⓢ Beer from €2.50. Wine from €3. Also serves lunch and dinner €15-20. ⓓ Open M-Th 9:30am-1am, F-Sa 9:30am-2am, Su 9:30am-1am.

CAFE "OOST-WEST" BAR
Zeedijk 85 ☎020 422 70 80
The Cafe "Oost-West" prides itself on being an old-fashioned pub where the jokes flow as freely as the booze. The music is unabashedly cheesy and often hilarious (we particularly enjoyed the Dutch techno cover of "Sweet Caroline"), which is just how the slightly rowdy crowd of older locals—often dressed in similarly ridiculous fashion—likes it.
✦ ⓜNieuwmarkt. ⓢ Beer from €2.50. ⓓ Open M-Th 11am-1am, F-Sa 11am-3am, Su 11am-1am.

RED LIGHT DISTRICT

Ah, the Red Light District at night. Most of the neon glow bathes **Oudezijds Achterburgwal** and the nearby alleyways. Farther over on **Warmoesstraat,** you can still get a twinge of the lascivious luminescence but will find fewer sex-related establishments. Especially on weekends, the whole area is filled with slow-moving crowds of predominantly male tourists. Despite getting very busy, the hotel bars on Warmoesstraat and Oudezijds Voorburgwal can be fun places to mingle with fellow backpackers. Despite police frequently strolling through, the area can turn into a meeting place for dealers and junkies late on weekends.

◙ **WYNAND FOCKINK** BAR
Pijlsteeg 31 ☎020 639 26 95 www.wynand-fockink.nl
Many people avoid small alleyways in the Red Light District for fear of up-close-and-personal contact with a red-lit window, but this one holds a unique draw—an over-300-year-old distillery and tasting room that makes the best

jenever in the city. Perfect for day-drinking, Wynand Fockink has no music, no flat screen TV, and not even any chairs: just rows of bottles on creaking shelves behind the small bar. Dozens of liquors are available, with flavorings like cinnamon, rose petals, bergamot, and strawberry. Most are complex blends with names like "Forget Me Not" and "The Bride's Tears," which often come with humorous histories. With as much focus on educating as getting crunk, this bar promises to answer all your burning questions about how the drinks are made—just ask the bartender or take a tour of the distillery.

⚥ *From Dam Sq., walk down Dam to Oudezijds Voorburgwal, make the 1st left, and turn left onto Pijlsteeg.* Ⓢ *Spirits from €2.50.* Ⓞ *Open daily 3-9pm. Tours in English Sa 12:30pm.* .

▨ DURTY NELLY'S PUB   IRISH PUB

Warmoesstraat 115-117   ☎020 638 01 25 www.durtynellys.nl

Right underneath Durty Nelly's Hostel, this pub attracts backpackers from upstairs, students from around the world, and drunkards from the official Red Light District pub crawl. There's plenty to keep you entertained, from watching international sports on the TVs to playing pool, foosball, and darts yourself. The atmosphere is fun-loving and rowdy, making it a great place for a pint or six. Durty Nelly's also serves standard pub food, including full Irish breakfast (which, big surprise, includes Guinness).

⚥ *From Centraal Station, go south on Damrak, turn right onto Brugsteeg, and turn onto Warmoesstraat.* ⓘ *Strict no-smoking policy (tobacco or otherwise).* Ⓢ *Beer from €2.* Ⓞ *Open M-Th 8am-1am, F-Sa 8am-3am, Su 8am-1am.*

HEFFER   BAR

Oudebrugsteeg 7   ☎020 428 44 88 www.heffer.nl

Heffer provides simple comforts for the sex-and-drugs-weary traveler: you can enjoy a pint from the decent beer menu, watch the game, and get a rare Red Light District view with no window ladies in sight. Heffer is a little bigger and less pub-like than most places in the area, reflecting its history as the old home of the city tax collector.

⚥ *From Centraal Station, walk down Damrak and turn left onto Oudebrugsteeg.* ⓘ *Comedy shows Sa; reservations recommended.* Ⓢ *Beer from €2.50.* Ⓞ *Open M-Th 10am-1am, F-Sa 10am-3am, Su 10am-1am.*

CAFE AEN'T WATER   BAR

Oudezijds Vorburgwal 2A   ☎020 652 06 18

Smack in the middle of the two busiest Red Light District drags, you'll be surprised by how relaxed you feel and how much Dutch you hear in Cafe Aen't Water. The drunkest and loudest of the Euro-tripping backpackers have been weeded out, making for a casual, quiet atmosphere. The large outdoor patio, which hugs a bend in the canal, is a perfect spot for sipping and people-watching.

⚥ *From Centraal Station, turn left onto Prins Hendrikkade, and right onto Nieuwebrugsteeg. Continue straight as it becomes Oudezijds Vorburgwal.* Ⓢ *Beer from €2.* Ⓞ *Open M-Th noon-1am, F-Sa noon-3am, Su noon-1am.*

CLUB WINSTON   CLUB

Warmoesstraat 129   ☎020 625 39 12 www.winston.nl

One of the largest and hippest of the many hostel bars and clubs on the block, Winston fills up with tireless dancers. There's also a lounge area across the dance floor, but people tend to stay on their feet. DJs spin everything from rock and metal to indie pop and hip hop—whatever people will get down to. Live acts sometimes play earlier in the evening; check their website for the schedule.

⚥ *From Centraal Station, go south on Damrak, turn right onto Brugsteeg, and left onto Warmoesstraat.* Ⓢ *Cover for live shows varies by event, usually around €5. Beer from €2.50.* Ⓞ *Hours vary by event, but usually open 9pm-4am.*

GETTO BAR, GLBT-FRIENDLY

Warmoesstraat 51 ☎020 421 51 51 www.getto.nl

A fun, everyone's-welcome cocktail bar crossed with a diner, Getto offers a phenomenal drink menu featuring homemade infused vodka (flavors range from vanilla to cucumber). The sedate atmosphere of this GLBT-friendly bar doesn't quite live up to its claims to "put the Cock in Cocktail."

⇆ From Centraal Station, go south on Damrak, turn right onto Brugsteeg, and left onto Warmoesstraat. ℹ DJ party Su from 5pm, includes special cocktail deals. $ Mixed drinks from €6; happy hour €4.50. ⏰ Open Tu-Th 4pm-1am, F-Sa 4pm-2am, Su 4pm-midnight. Happy hour Tu-Sa 5-7pm.

THE END BAR, KARAOKE

Nieuwebrugsteeg 32 ☎064 904 88 39 www.theendkaraoke.nl

The popularity of this karaoke emporium varies, so you may want to bring a group of friends or scope it out first to avoid performing for just the bartenders. If you've got the courage to sing, thousands of the cheesiest tunes await.

⇆ From Centraal Station, turn left onto Prins Hendrikkade and right onto Nieuwebrugsteeg. $ Beer from €2.50. ⏰ Open daily 9pm-4am.

jenever fever

Amsterdam may be famous for a certain kind of herbal intoxication, but don't let the siren call of coffeeshops prevent you from trying another one of Holland's delights: jenever. A juniper-based alcohol and ancestor of gin, jenever was first sold as a medicine, and then took off as a different kind of remedy once people figured out it tasted good and got you drunk.

Nowadays, some locals swear by a quick two shots of chilled jenever to get you ready for a night on the town. A more common method of imbibing it is a *kopstoot* ("headbutt"), which is a shot of jenever followed by a pint of beer. Most Dutch bars will have one or two generic jenever brands, but for a real authentic selection, head to the centuries-old distillery Wynand Fockink (Pijlsteeg 31-43 ☎020 639 26 95; www.wynand-fockink.nl) in the Red Light District.

NIEUWE ZIJD

The Nieuwe Zijd has some decent nightlife, but it's not very concentrated. **Spuistraat** is the place to go for artsier cafes and bars, while **Dam Square** and **Rokin** are lined with larger, rowdier pubs. The small streets in the southern part of the neighborhood are home to good beer bars and a couple of energetic clubs. However, with fewer people around, it can feel a little less safe at night than the jam-packed Leidesplein and Red Light District.

👍 **PRIK** BAR, CLUB, GLBT

Spuistraat 109 ☎020 320 00 02 www.prikamsterdam.nl

Voted both best bar and best gay bar in Amsterdam on multiple occasions, Prik attracts a mostly male crowd. Its atmosphere is about as light and fun as its name ("bubble" in Dutch—get your minds out of the gutter, English speakers). Come for cocktail specials all day Thursday and on Sunday evenings, or to hear DJs spin pop, house, and disco classics on the weekends.

⇆ Tram #1, 2, 5, or 14 to Dam/Paleisstraat. Walk down Paleisstraat and turn right onto Spuistraat. $ Beer from €2. Mixed drinks from €6. ⏰ Open M-Th 4pm-1am, F-Sa 4pm-3am, Su 4pm-1am. Kitchen open until 11pm.

BELGIQUE BAR

Gravenstraat 2 ☎020 625 19 74 www.cafe-belgique.nl

If you can muscle your way through to the bar—it tends to be packed in here, even on weekdays—you'll be rewarded by a choice of eight draft beers and dozens more Belgian and Dutch brews in bottles. "But I'm in the Netherlands," you say. "Should I really be at a bar called 'Belgium'?" Be quiet and enjoy your beer.

From Dam Sq., walk down Zoutsteeg. The bar is behind the Nieuwe Kerk, in between Nieuwendijk and Nieuwezijds Voorburgwal. $ Beer from €2.50. ⏰ Open daily 2pm-1am.

DANSEN BIJ JANSEN CLUB

Handboogstraat 11-13 ☎020 620 17 79 www.dansenbijjansen.nl

A student-only club, Dansen bij Jansen attracts students from the nearby University of Amsterdam as well as backpackers from local hostels. The music on the crowded dance floor is a slightly cheesy mix of Top 40, R&B, and disco. Upstairs, another bar offers a range of electronic music.

Tram #1, 2, or 5 to Koningsplein. Cross the canal, walk up Heiligeweg, and turn left onto Handboogstraat. ℹ Must have a student ID or be accompanied by someone who does. $ Cover M-W €2; Th-Sa €5. Beer from €2. ⏰ Open M-Th 11pm-4am, F-Sa 11pm-5am.

BITTERZOET BAR, CLUB

Spuistraat 2 ☎020 421 23 18 www.bitterzoet.nl

Not as reliably popular as the larger clubs to the south, Bitterzoet is one of the best parties you can find this close to Centraal Station. The crowd is mostly young people jamming to a steady mix of dance, bouncy house, smooth reggae, classic hip hop, and occasional live acts. There's a simple dance room with a cool balcony and smoking room upstairs, creating a generally unpretentious atmosphere.

From Centraal Station, walk down Martelaarsgracht, which becomes Hekelweg and then Spuistraat. $ Cover €5-8. Beer from €2. ⏰ Open M-Th 8pm-3am, F-Sa 8pm-4am, Su 8pm-3am.

GOLLEM BAR

Raamsteeg 4 ☎020 676 71 17 www.cafegollem.nl

This is not a bar for the indecisive. Beer aficionados from all across the city (and the world) flock to Gollem's slightly Gothic interior for the specialty brews. Way back in the '70s, this was one of the first cafes in Amsterdam to serve now-trendy Belgian beers. Nowadays, the bar offers over 200 varieties, with eight on tap. You can find Trappist ales, fruit lambics, doubles, triples—pretty much anything they make in Belgium with yeast and hops. They even have the famed **Westvleteren,** made by reclusive monks in incredibly small batches and only sold at the monastery itself.

Tram #1, 2, or 5 to Spui/Nieuwezijds Voorburgwal. Walk up Spui and turn left onto Raamsteeg. $ Beer from €2.50. ⏰ Open M-F 4pm-1am, Sa-Su 2pm-2am.

THE TARA IRISH PUB

Rokin 85-89 ☎020 421 26 54 www.thetara.com

This Irish pub is large enough to be called a complex. The Tara keeps multiple bars running, so the Guinness flows all night long. Different parts of the building have different themes—go from a hunting lodge to a downtown lounge without even stepping outside. It still attracts enough people for the tourists to be spilling out into the streets. Come here if you're determined to avoid any semblance of local culture.

Tram #4, 9, 14, 16, 24, or 25 to the Spui/Rokin stop. Walk a few blocks up Rokin. The Tara is on the right. $ Beer from €2.70. ⏰ Open M-Th 10am-1am, F-Sa 10am-3am, Su 11am-1am.

CLUB NL CLUB

Nieuwezijds Voorburgwal 169 ☎020 622 75 10 www.clubnl.nl

Club NL is a swanky lounge club with a surprisingly low cover. Patrons are slinkily dressed, and we advise you to spruce up a bit before trying to get in, especially later on weekend nights. Music goes from ambient house to more energetic dance tunes;

check their website for guest DJ appearances. The carefully crafted cocktail menu is just as image-conscious as the club itself, with delicious results.

Tram #1, 2, 5 or 14 to Dam/Paleisstraat. Walk east down Rozengracht and then right onto Nieuwezijds Voorburgwal. Club NL is south of the stop on Nieuwezijds Voorburgwal. $ Cover F-Sa €5. Beer from €2.50. Mixed drinks from €8. ⏰ Open M-Th 10pm-3am, F-Sa 10pm-4am, Su 10pm-3am.

SCHEEPVAARTBUURT

Nightlife in Scheepvaartbuurt isn't exactly happening. After dark, those who do stick around tend to congregate in the coffeeshops on **Haarlemmerstraat.** However, there are a few pleasant places to stop for a quiet drink.

DULAC — BAR

Haarlemmerstraat 118 ☎020 624 42 65 www.restaurantdulac.nl

This bar is popular with local and international students (maybe the 50% student discount on food helps with that). The exterior kind of blends into the background of Haarlemmerstraat, but follow the young Dutch kids to find it. You'll know you're in the right place if you find crazy sculptures and many miscellaneous objects inside. There's a nice garden terrace in the back.

From Centraal Station, turn right, cross the Singel, and walk down Haarlemmerstraat. $ Beer from €2.50. Entrees €10-18. ⏰ Open M-Th 3pm-1am, F 3pm-3am, Sa noon-3am, Su noon-1am.

CANAL RING WEST

The Canal Ring West doesn't go wild after sunset, but the pubs along the water are great places to grab a cheap beer and befriend some locals.

DE PRINS — BAR

Prinsengracht 124 ☎020 624 93 82 www.deprins.nl

De Prins attracts artsy types, young locals, and savvy tourists with its classic *bruin cafe* atmosphere. An extensive lunch and dinner menu complements the broad drink selection, which includes five beers on tap. Enjoy your brew at the canal-side seating or inside the wooden interior, which inexplicably features portraits of Al Pacino along with the usual pictures of Queen Beatrix.

Tram #13, 14, or 17 to Westermarkt. 2 blocks up Prinsengracht, on the far side. $ Beer €2-3.50. Liquor €3.50-5. ⏰ Open daily 10am-1am. Kitchen closes at 10pm.

THIRSTY DOGG — BAR

Oude Leliestraat 9 ☎064 512 22 72

A small bar in the Nine Streets that puts the extra "g" in "dogg," Thirsty Dogg is popular with young locals and the type of tourist who didn't come to Amsterdam to see art museums. The bar has an excellent selection of liquor, including six types of absinthe. During the week, the bartender dictates the music selection, which tends toward heavy hip hop; on some weekend nights a live DJ brings in trip hop and dubstep. Some travelers consider Thirsty Dogg a marijuana-friendly environment.

Tram #13, 14, or 17 to Westermarkt. Walk down Raadhuisstraat, turn left onto Herengracht, and then right onto Oude Leliestraat. $ Beer €2.50. Wine €3. Absinthe €4. ⏰ Open M-Th 4pm-1am, F-Sa 4pm-3am, Su 4pm-1am.

CAFE BRANDON — BAR

Keizersgracht 157 ☎065 434 71 36

The owners of this tiny bar took an 18-year hiatus when they won the lottery… twice in one year. Maybe they blew all the money, because Cafe Brandon has now reopened, much to the joy of the locals who pack it to the brim on weekends. A pool table fills the back room, and the walls are covered in Dutch memorabilia. Comfy outdoor seating includes benches with large cushions, but when this place fills up, most people just stand around looking hip.

Tram #13, 14, or 17 to Westermarkt. 1 block up Keizersgracht, on the corner with Leliegracht. $ Beer €2.50. ⏰ Open M-Th 11am-1am, F-Sa 11am-3am, Su 11am-1am.

CENTRAL CANAL RING

With the nightlife meccas of Leidseplein and Rembrandtplein at its corners, the Central Canal Ring doesn't have much in the way of its own nightlife. Given their proximity to the larger squares, **Spiegelgracht** and **Utrechtsestraat** house most of the neighborhood bars, including some decent places to have a quiet drink.

CAFE BRECHT CAFE, BAR

Weteringschans 157 ☎020 627 22 11 www.cafebrecht.nl

Cafe Brecht delivers everything you'd expect from a place named after a Marxist poet, playwright, and theorist (Bertolt Brecht). The cafe prides itself on its beer, which comes from an old Czech brewery, and most of the ingredients on the daytime soup-and-sandwich menu are organic and local. Brecht hosts free poetry readings and live music on the first Monday of each month. Though we aren't sure what exactly it has to do with a bar or German art, you can get a haircut here on Wednesdays.

🚋 Tram #7 or 10 to Spiegelgracht. Walk down Weteringschans and it's on the right. $ Beer from €2. ⏰ Open M-Th noon-1am, F-Sa noon-3am, Su noon-1am. Poetry nights start at 10:30pm.

MANKIND GLBT-FRIENDLY, BAR

Weteringstraat 60 ☎020 638 47 55 www.mankind.nl

In a quiet spot just a few blocks from Leidseplein and the Rijksmuseum, Mankind is an ideal bar to grab an afternoon or evening beer. Two outdoor patios, one facing Weteringstraat and the other adjacent to the canal, allow you to people-watch by land or by sea. Mankind draws local regulars but also caters to tourists with an extremely friendly staff happy to give recommendations. Mankind serves the usual menu of Dutch bar snacks (*bitterballen*, *tostis*, etc.) as well as a more substantial meal of the day. Though it's advertised as GLBT-friendly, the bar's crowd is not exclusively gay.

🚋 Tram #7 or 10 to Spiegelgracht. Walk down Weteringschans and turn left. $ Beer from €2. ⏰ Open M-Sa noon-11pm. Kitchen closes at 8pm.

LEIDSEPLEIN

"Leidseplein" roughly translates to "more diverse nightlife per sq. ft. than anywhere else in the city" (don't listen to anyone who feeds you a story about how it means something to do with a road to the city of Leiden). Some native Amsterdammers scoff at this area, considering it a sea of drunken British and American tourists. But the bars that cater to these liquored-up crowds are primarily confined to the Korte and Lange Leidsedwarsstraats. The rest of the area hosts some very hip and friendly bars as well as a few terrific nightclubs. You can also find several bastions of incredible live music scattered throughout the neighborhood, and, unless you're going to a big-name event at **Paradiso** or **Melkweg,** prices are extremely reasonable. Many establishments are just as full of locals as they are of tourists. If you want to be one of the revelers that gives the Leidseplein its bad name, check out the Leidseplein Pub Crawl (promoters lurk in the main square all day long).

👍 **WEBER** BAR

Marnixstraat 397 ☎020 622 99 10

Tremendously popular with young locals and a few stylish tourists, Weber is the place to be. Come early or late (after people have departed for the clubs) if you want to get a seat on a weekend night. Frilly red lampshades and vintage pornographic art give the place a cheeky bordello feel, complemented by jazzy French pop. But don't be fooled: this bar steers clear of the tawdriness that plagues so much of Amsterdam's nightlife.

🚋 Tram #1, 2, 5, 6, 7, or 10 to Leidseplein. Walk south of the main square and turn right onto Marnixstraat. $ Beer from €2.50. Spirits from €4. ⏰ Open M-Th 8pm-3am, F-Sa 8pm-4am, Su 8pm-3am.

PARADISO

CLUB, CONCERT VENUE

Weteringschans 6-8 ☎020 626 45 21 www.paradiso.nl

You can have a very good Friday in this former church. Paradiso began in 1968 as the "Cosmic Relaxation Center Paradiso," and its laid-back vibe (at least, as laid-back as you get in one of the city's most popular clubs) keeps this place true to its roots. The club generally attracts less well-known artists than nearby Melkweg, though it has played host to big names like Wu-Tang Clan and Lady Gaga. Check out the live music every day and club nights five nights per week—including *Noodlanding!* ("emergency landing!"), a party with "alternative dance hits" on Thursdays.

🚋 *Tram #1, 2, 5, 6, 7, or 10 to Leidseplein. Turn left onto Weteringschans.* 💲 *Cover for club nights €5-20. Concert tickets €5-20, plus €3 monthly membership fee.* 🕐 *Hours vary by event; check website for details.*

SUGAR FACTORY

CLUB

Lijnbaansgracht 238 ☎020 626 50 06 www.sugarfactory.nl

Billing itself as a *nachttheater*, Sugar Factory is, at its core, just a very sweet place to dance. Music is the main focus here: it tends to outshine that of larger clubs nearby, and includes house, electro, and "club jazz." Live music and DJs are accompanied by mind-bending video displays and dancers. The sizeable dance floor fills with a mix of young Dutch hipsters, older locals, and clusters of tourists. Check the website for upcoming events, though it's safe to assume that there's something going on Friday and Saturday from midnight to 5am.

🚋 *Tram #1, 2, 5, 6, 7, or 10 to Leidseplein. Turn down the small street to the left of the Stadsschouwburg theater.* 💲 *Cover varies depending on event; usually €8-12. Beer from €3. Mixed drinks €6.50.* 🕐 *Hours vary depending on event; check website for details.*

MELKWEG

CLUB, CONCERT VENUE

Lijnbaansgracht 234A ☎020 531 81 81 www.melkweg.nl

This club's name translates to "milky way," a pun on the fact that this cultural event is housed in an old milk factory. One of Amsterdam's legendary hotspots and concert venues, Melkweg hosts rock, punk, pop, indie, reggae, electronic…basically any type of music that exists in the big Milky Way has probably been played in this little one. Popular events sell out quickly, so keep an eye on the website if you're planning a visit. Club nights follow the concerts on Friday and Saturday. The building is also home to theater performances, photography exhibits, and a restaurant.

🚋 *Tram #1, 2, 5, 6, 7, or 10 to Leidseplein. Turn down the small street to the left of the Stadsschouwburg theater.* 💲 *Tickets €10-30, plus €3.50 monthly membership fee.* 🕐 *Hours vary depending on event, but concerts usually start at 8 or 9pm. Clubbing gets going around 11pm or midnight.*

DE PIEPER

BRUIN CAFE

Prinsengracht 424 ☎020 626 47 75

One of Amsterdam's oldest cafes, De Pieper lives in a building that's been around since the 17th century. The low ceilings and dark paneling reflect the building's age, but De Pieper also makes quirky nods to modernity, with strings of fairy lights and posters from performances at nearby venues. This is a place to escape from the bustle of the Leidseplein in a dark, subdued *bruin cafe* (though who comes to Leidseplein for that?).

🚋 *Tram #1, 2, or 5 to Prinsengracht or #7 or 10 to Raamplein. At the corner of Prinsengracht and Leidsegracht.* 💲 *Beer from €2.50.* 🕐 *Open M-Th 11am-1am, F-Sa 11am-3am.*

LUX

BAR

Marnixstraat 403 ☎020 422 14 12

Lux shares the three-tiered structure and extreme popularity of its sister bar, Weber (see above). It often attracts a slightly younger crowd, with a modern-chic atmosphere and electro-indie pop bumping over the speakers.

🚋 *Tram #1, 2, 5, 6, 7, or 10 to Leidseplein. Walk south of the main square and make a right onto Marnixstraat.* 💲 *Beer €2.50. Spirits from €3.* 🕐 *Open M-Th 8pm-3am, F-Sa 8pm-4am, Su 8pm-3am.*

nightlife

BOURBON STREET BLUES CLUB

Leidsekruisstraat 6-8 ☎020 623 34 40

One of the better touristy joints in the square, Bourbon Street is a bustling home to nightly live blues, soul, and funk shows. The walls are packed with memorabilia and photos from past events. They host jam nights on Monday, Tuesday, and Sunday, where all are welcome to bring their own instruments and play along (these tend to be high-quality, since if you're willing to haul your gear to the Leidseplein, you're probably pretty good).

🚋 Tram #1, 2, 5, 6, 7, or 10 to Leidseplein. Make a right onto Korte Leidsedwarsstraat and Leidsekruisstraat is on the left. $ Cover varies, but can be up to €5. Beer from €3. ⏰ Open M-Th 10pm-4am, F-Sa 10pm-5am, Su 10pm-4am. Music starts M-Th 10:30pm, F-Sa 11pm, Su 10:30pm.

PUNTO LATINO CLUB, SALSA

Lange Leidsedwarsstraat 35 ☎020 420 22 35

Punto Latino is a small salsa club that's popular on the weekends for fiery Latin music and dancing. It attracts a crowd of young tourists and older locals, many of Spanish or Latin origin.

🚋 Tram #1, 2, 5, 6, 7, or 10 to Leidseplein. $ Beer €2.50. ⏰ Open daily 11pm-4am.

REMBRANDTPLEIN

Rembrandtplein *is* its nightlife. Yeah, there's a pretty sweet statue of Rembrandt in the middle of this square, but if you were interested in the man himself, then you would be at one of Amsterdam's many fine museums, none of which can be found here. This is home to the art of looking good and getting down, not the art of the Dutch Renaissance. The square itself is lined with massive bars and clubs, while the streets that fan out from it are home to smaller establishments. **Reguliersdwarstraat,** known as "the gayest street in Amsterdam," is lined with a diverse array of gay bars and clubs, though many can be found on neighboring streets as well. Whatever you're looking for in nightlife can be found here: Irish pub, sleek bar, chic club, grungy dive, gay cafe, tourist dance party. Just walk around until you hear some music that you like. Rembrandtplein is conveniently serviced by night buses #355, 357, 359, 361, and 363; taxis also loiter around the main square at all hours.

👍 **STUDIO 80** CLUB

Rembrandtplein 17 www.studio-80.nl

Many swear that Studio 80 is the definition of nightlife in Amsterdam. A grungier alternative to the more polished clubs around Rembrandtplein, Studio 80 is extremely popular with students and young Dutch hipsters, and with good reason—the emphasis here is squarely on good music and good dancing. This is also where young Amsterdammers flock to have a wild night out on the town, and where in-the-know tourists come to get a taste of the action.

🚋 Tram #9 or 14 to Rembrandtplein. The entrance is next to Escape (see below), under the large balcony. $ Cover depends on the night, usually €6-10. Beer €2.50. ⏰ Open W-Th 11pm-3:30am, F-Sa 11pm-5am.

👍 **VIVE LA VIE** BAR, GLBT

Amstelstraat 7 ☎020 624 01 14 www.vivelavie.net

This long-established lesbian bar draws a diverse crowd of mostly young women and a few of their male friends. The atmosphere is refreshingly unpretentious, focusing on dancing and having a good time. The excellent drink selection includes the Clit on Fire shot (€4). Music ranges from indie rock and bluesy country in the early evening, toward more dance and hip hop as the night progresses.

🚋 Tram #9 or 14 to Rembrandtplein. $ Beer from €2.20. Spirits from €3. ⏰ Open M-Th 4pm3am, F-Sa 4pm-4am, Su 4pm-3am.

ESCAPE
CLUB

Rembrandtplein 11 ☎020 622 11 11 www.escape.nl

This is Amsterdam's biggest club, with a capacity for thousands. Although it may no longer be the hottest spot in town, it still draws reliably large crowds and excellent DJs. Escape is an institution—its hulking form dominates Rembrandtplein—and it has the cover and drink prices to match. The main dance floor features a massive stage (VIP area behind the DJ) and platforms scattered throughout for those brave enough to take the dancing spotlight. Upstairs, there's a lounge, another dance space, and a balcony from which to observe the bacchanalia below. The music varies depending on the DJ but generally tends toward house, electro, and trance. The crowd is a mix of droves of tourists and young-to-middle-aged Dutch. Lines can get long on weekends after 1am: some suggest that upping your style will increase your chances of getting in.

⚡ *Tram #9 or 14 to Rembrandtplein. Almost impossible to miss, under the huge TV screen.* Ⓢ *Cover €5-16. Beer from €2.60. Spirits €3.80-5.80.* ⌚ *Open Th 11pm-4am, F-Sa 11pm-5am, Su 11pm-4:30am.*

DE DUIVEL
BAR

Reguliersdwarsstraat 87 ☎020 626 61 84 www.deduivel.nl

Amsterdam's premier hip-hop joint has attracted the likes of Public Enemy, Cypress Hill, and Ghost Face, but even without famous guests, De Duivel remains a nighttime favorite, with expert DJs drawing a diverse group of music lovers. The intimidating stained-glass devil that gives the bar its name overlooks the small dance floor, but most patrons seem to be more interested in chilling and nodding their heads to the music than in showcasing their dance moves.

⚡ *Tram #9 or 14 to Rembrandtplein.* Ⓢ *Beer €2.50.* ⌚ *Open M-Th 10pm-3am, F-Sa 10pm-4am, Su 10pm-3am.*

MONTMARTRE
BAR, GLBT

Halvemaansteeg 17 ☎020 625 55 65 www.cafemontmartre.nl

A sinfully luxurious ⚑**Garden of Eden**-inspired interior provides the backdrop for this popular spot, regularly voted the best gay bar in Amsterdam. The crowd is dominated by gay men, but all are welcome. As the night wears on, the dancing heats up to Euro and American pop and bouncy disco. Special theme nights spice up each day of the week.

⚡ *Tram #9 or 14 to Rembrandtplein. Off of the northwest corner of the square.* Ⓢ *Beer from €2.50. Liquor from €3.50.* ⌚ *Open M-Th 5pm-1am, F-Sa 5pm-3am, Su 5pm-1am.*

LELLEBEL
BAR, GLBT

Utrechtstraat 4 ☎020 427 51 39 www.lellebel.nl

Outrageous drag queens preside over this bar just off the square, where the decor is as campy as the costumes. Lellebel plays host to a variety of theme nights—karaoke, "Transgender Cafe," Miss Lellebel contests, and a Eurovision party, to name a few—and attracts a mostly older, gay male crowd.

⚡ *Tram #9 or 14 to Rembrandtplein. Just off the southeast corner of the square. Karaoke on Tu. "Transgender Cafe" on W. Red Hot Salsa Night on Th.* Ⓢ *Beer €2.50.* ⌚ *Open M-Th 8pm-3am, F-Sa 8pm-4am, Su 8pm-3am.*

nightlife

bike 'n' beer

Want to drink beer, get to where you want to go, and be ecologically friendly, all at the same time? The Dutch seem to share the same extremely specific desires. The **Beer-Bike Bar** is a creation that allows 10-19 people to sit around a bar as they are pedaled through the streets. The multi-tasking and extremely in-shape bartender serves the drinks as he pedals the contraption.

Recently, there has been some backlash against the drink-while-you-go philosophy because of several accidents involving distracted beer-bikers. Thankfully, these concerns have influenced a new law requiring no more than 30 liters of beer on any bike bar, no matter how many people are riding. That means passengers may only drink half a keg en route to another bar—a tragedy, really.

JORDAAN

Nightlife in the Jordaan is much more relaxed than in Leidseplein or Nieuwe Zijd, but that doesn't mean it's not popular or busy. Establishments tend more toward cafe-bars or local pubs than clubs, though some excellent music can be found in the neighborhood's southern stretches. If you're looking to seriously mingle with the locals, try one of the lively-on-weekends places along **Lijnbaansgracht** and **Noordermarkt.**

FESTINA LENTE BAR

Looiersgracht 40B ☎020 638 14 12 www.cafefestinalente.nl

Looking something like a bar stuck in the middle of an elegant vintage living room, this spot is enduringly popular with fun and cultured young Amsterdammers who want to "make haste, slowly." Bookshelves line the walls, and games of chess and checkers are readily available—if you can find a spot to play. Poetry contests and live concerts are held often (check the website for details). The menu features *lentini*, small Mediterranean dishes, and an astonishing selection of bruschettas (on homemade bread!). No wonder it's always so crowded.

Tram #7, 10, or 17 to Elandsgracht. Go straight on Elandsgracht and turn right onto Hazenstraat; the bar is 2 blocks down on the corner. [$] Beer from €2. Wine from €3.30. Open M noon-1am, Tu-Th 10:30am-1am, F-Sa 10:30am-3am, Su noon-1am. Kitchen closes at 10:30pm.

SAAREIN BRUIN CAFE, GLBT

Elandsstraat 119 ☎020 623 49 01 www.saarein.info

A classic *bruin cafe* in the Jordaan tradition but with a GLBT focus, Saarein mainly attracts a local group of older lesbians, but no matter what your gender or orientation, you're sure to have fun. Saarein hosts a variety of events, including a pool competition every Tuesday and a bi-weekly "underground disco party."

Tram #7, 10, or 17 to Elandsgracht. Turn left onto Lijnbaansgracht and walk 2 blocks. i Free Wi-Fi, and a computer available. [$] Beer from €2. Open Tu-Th 4pm-1am, F 4pm-2am, Sa noon-2am, Su noon-1am.

'T SMALLE CAFE, BRUIN CAFE

Egelantiersgracht 12 ☎020 623 96 17

't Smalle was founded in 1780 as a spot to taste the products of a nearby *jenever* distillery. It's one of the most revered and popular *bruin cafes* in the city, but be warned: "revered and popular" can manifest itself in the form of stuffy middle-aged people chilling. Enjoy your drink or snacks like "Doritos with sauce" on the airy upper level of the old-fashioned interior, or, if you can get a spot, outside at one of the many tables lining Egelantiersgracht, one of the prettiest canals in Amsterdam.

Tram #13, 14, or 17 to Westermarkt. Cross Prinsengracht, turn right, and walk a few blocks. [$] Beer from €2. Wine and spirits €4-5. Open M-Th 10am-1am, F-Sa 10am-2am, Su 10am-1am.

CAFE CHRIS BAR

Bloemstraat 42 ☎020 624 59 42 www.cafechris.nl

Workers building the tower of the nearby Westerkerk used to stop here to pick up (and then probably spend) their paychecks—the bar first opened its doors in 1624, making it the oldest in the Jordaan. Come today to mingle with the local after-work crowd and let the gloomy dark wood interior transport you back in time to an era before electricity and indoor plumbing—okay, maybe not that far back.

⇞ Tram #13, 14, or 17 to Westermarkt. Cross Prinsengracht, turn right, and walk 1 block. $ Beer €3-5. ⏰ Open M-Th 3pm-1am, F-Sa 3pm-2am, Su 3-9pm.

WESTERPARK AND OUD-WEST

Large swathes of this area are dead at night, but you can brush shoulders with the locals for cheap if you know the right spots. Look for posters advertising weekend parties, as many of the establishments here keep irregular hours.

👍 **OT301** CLUB

Overtoom 301 www.ot301.nl

Home to everything even remotely entertaining—a temporary handicrafts store, a cinema, live music, yoga and acrobatic classes, a vegan restaurant, and excellent DJ parties on most weekend nights—OT301 provides an escape from the typical tourist to-do list. The building was occupied by squatting artists in the late '90s, and OT301 eventually became a destination for Amsterdam's hippest residents. A diverse and laid-back crowd congregates for OT301's parties, which feature music ranging from electro house to soul and funk.

⇞ Tram #1 to J. Pieter Heijestraat. ℹ Check the website for upcoming events, or just wander in and peruse the decorated handbills. $ Cover €3-5 most nights. ⏰ Hours vary depending on programming; check website for details.

PACIFIC PARC BAR, CONCERT VENUE

Polonceaukade 23 ☎020 488 77 78 www.pacificparc.nl

"Industrial honky-tonk" is the best phrase we can think of to describe this large bar on the end of the Westergasfabriek. Iron staircases and a massive stove in one corner recall the building's factory roots, while the cowhide coverings on the window shades will make you feel as if you're home, home on the range. The who-knows-what-the-hell-it's-made-of chandelier has to be seen to be believed. Spread out on plenty of tables and cushioned benches as you enjoy a drink amid a local late-20s crowd. There's also space for dancing to the blues and old-school country rock. Live music plays some nights as well, beginning at 11pm. Pacific Parc doubles as a restaurant during the day.

⇞ Tram #10 to Van Limburg Stirumstraat or Van Hallstraat. Either way, walk to the Haarlemmerweg and cross over; it's at the corner of the Westergasfabriek that is farthest from Westerpark. $ Beer from €2.50. Wine and spirits from €3. ⏰ Open M-Th 11am-1am, F-Sa 11am-3am, Su 11am-11pm.

MUSEUMPLEIN AND VONDELPARK

The museums don't often stay open past 6pm, so there's not much reason to come to Museumplein in the evening. Vondelpark has a handful of spots for grabbing a drink and enjoying the scenery, but if you're looking for a lively night out, you'd best head elsewhere.

'T BLAUWE THEEHUIS BAR

Vondelpark 5 ☎020 662 02 54 www.blauwetheehuis.nl

This bar looks a bit like a UFO that's just crash-landed on Earth. Alien or not, 't Blauwe Theehuis is probably the only bar in the city center where you can drink while surrounded by trees and greenery. Enjoy the view from the large circular patio outside or the terrace above.

🚊 *Tram #2 to Jacob Obrechtstraat. Enter Vondelpark, walk straight, cross the footbridge, and you should see the building ahead.* Ⓢ *Beer from €2.30. Spirits from €2.40. Wine from €3.* 🕐 *Open M-Th 9am-10:30pm, F-Sa 9am-midnight, Su 9am-10pm.*

DE PIJP

De Pijp does laid-back hipster bars with good beer, good food, and good company—and it does them very well.

🎇 CHOCOLATE BAR   BAR
1e Van Der Helststraat 62A   ☎020 675 76 72 www.chocolate-bar.nl

While most bars in the neighborhood have a cafe vibe, Chocolate Bar is more like a cocktail lounge. The long, glossy bar and seating area peppered with small, chic tables make the place classy. An outdoor patio with couches and picnic tables provides a prime place to survey the De Pijp scene. On weekends, DJs spin laid-back dance tunes inside.

🚊 *Tram #16 or 24 to Albert Cuypstraat. Walk 1 block down Albert Cuypstraat and turn right.* Ⓢ *Beer from €2. Mixed drinks €7.* 🕐 *Open M-Th 10am-1am, F-Sa 10am-3am, Su 11am-1am.*

TROUW AMSTERDAM   CLUB
Wibautstraat 127   ☎020 463 77 88 www.trouwamsterdam.nl

Housed in the former office building of the newspaper *Trouw*, this complex includes a restaurant, exhibition space, and club. It's gritty, industrial, and extremely popular with local students. The music ranges from dubstep to house and more; check the website for specific events. If you just can't stop partying, you'll be please to know they occasionally host after-parties beginning at 6am.

🚊 *Tram #3 or Ⓜ Wibautstraat. Walk a few blocks south on Wibautstraat and watch out for a giant white office building that says "Trouw" on the upper corner.* Ⓢ *Cover €10-17.* 🕐 *Open F-Sa 10:30pm-5am (sometimes Th and Su as well). Check website for specifics.*

KINGFISHER   BAR
Ferdinand Bolstraat 24   ☎020 671 23 95

One of the bars responsible for the initial cool-ification of De Pijp, Kingfisher hasn't let the popularity go to its head. They've got a good selection of international beers and a spacious wood interior. It gets crowded on weekend nights, but on a sunny afternoon you should still be able to grab one of the coveted outside tables.

🚊 *Tram #16 or 24 to Stadhouderskade. Walk 1 block down Ferdinand Bolstraat.* Ⓢ *Beer from €2.* 🕐 *Open M-Th 11am-1am, F-Sa 11am-3am, Su noon-1am.*

JODENBUURT AND PLANTAGE

This is not the neighborhood for rowdy nightlife. If you're looking for a big night out, you'd do better to head to nearby Rembrandtplein or Nieuwmarkt.

🎇 DE SLUYSWACHT   BAR
Jodenbreestraat 1   ☎020 625 76 11 www.sluyswacht.nl

This tiny, tilting 17th-century building houses the kind of bar you'd expect to find on a lone seacoast, not a bustling street. The outdoor patio sits right above the canal, with giant umbrellas ready in case it starts to rain. When it gets really inclement, the plain wooden interior is invitingly snug. This bar is perfect for day-drinking and people-watching, with a good selection of draft and bottled beers.

🚊 *Tram #9 or 14 or Ⓜ Waterlooplein. Walk north from the stop and turn left onto Jodenbreestraat.* Ⓢ *Beer €2-4.* 🕐 *Open M-Th 11:30am-1am, F-Sa 11:30am-3am, Su 11:30am-7pm.*

arts and culture

Amsterdam offers a whole host of cultural attractions, many of which are very affordable. The music, film, and arts festivals that take place throughout the summer—along with countless top-notch underground music venues—make the city an absolute paradise for art-lovers. In a city where the most cutting-edge photography exhibits are held in a 17th-century canal house, the performing arts in Amsterdam predictably run the gamut from traditional to bizarre. Many establishments provide significant student discounts or rush tickets so that, even on a budget, you can take a trip to the theater or see the famed Concertgebouw, which some say has the best acoustics in the world.

CLASSICAL MUSIC AND OPERA

Classical music is a strong presence in Amsterdam thanks to the various high-caliber orchestras and innovative chamber ensembles that call this city home. Churches (especially the **Oude Kerk**) regularly hold organ and choral concerts and are particularly nice in the summer, when a lot of the concert halls close. Use this guide to begin your exploration of Amsterdam's arts scene, but, as with nightlife, keep an eye out for posters advertising upcoming events.

CONCERTGEBOUW — MUSEUMPLEIN AND VONDELPARK

Concertgebouwplein 2-6 — ☎020 573 05 73 www.concertgebouw.nl

Home to the highly renowned **Royal Concertgebouw Orchestra,** this performance space boasts some of the best acoustics in the world. They manage to fit in 900 concerts each year—primarily classical but also some jazz and world music. You can catch rehearsal concerts for free on Wednesdays at 12:30pm during the summer.

Tram #3, 5, 12, 16, or 24 to Museumplein. i Guided tours available. $ Varies by concert, but generally €15-100. ⏰ Ticket office open M-F 1-7pm, Sa-Su 10am-7pm.

MUZIEKTHEATER — JODENBUURT AND PLANTAGE

Waterlooplein 22 — ☎625 54 55 www.het-muziektheater.nl

This large complex in Jodenbuurt is the best place in Amsterdam to see opera and classical ballet—it's the home turf of both the **Netherlands Opera** and the **Dutch National Ballet.** Muziektheater also hosts performances by visiting companies and some more modern works. Rush tickets are available for students 1½hr. before curtain for the ballet (€10) and opera (€15).

[M]Waterlooplein. $ Most tickets €15-100. ⏰ Box office open early Sept-July M-Sa 10am-6pm, Su 11:30am-2:30pm, and before curtain on performance days. Check for information about free summer concerts.

MUZIEKGEBOUW AAN'T IJ — JODENBUURT AND PLANTAGE

Piet Heinkade 1 — ☎020 788 20 00 www.muziekgebouw.nl

This is the prime spot in the city for cutting-edge classical music. In addition to their main concert hall, performances are also held in a smaller hall that houses a newly renovated, 31-tone Fokker organ. They clearly have the interests of young people at heart, as they set aside a certain number of "Early Bird" tickets (€10) for those under 30. If you miss out on those, you can still try to get under-30 rush tickets (also €10) 30min. before performances.

Tram #25 or 26 to Muziekgebouw Bimhuis. Make a hairpin turn around the small inlet of water to get to the theater. $ Most tickets €18. ⏰ Box office open from mid-Aug to June M-Sa noon-6pm.

LIVE MUSIC

It's not hard to find great live music in Amsterdam. Many local artists tend toward electronic, techno, and house music, but you'll find home-grown bands and international indie, punk, pop, and hip-hop acts as well. Small jazz and blues joints can be found throughout the city. Leidseplein and the Oud-West boast particularly high concentrations of quality venues, ranging from large all-purpose clubs and concert halls to cozy bars and repurposed squats. In the summer, festivals explode in Amsterdam and the surrounding cities, often centered around electronic or reggae (Amsterdam has this thing with reggae, we can't imagine why). Check the websites of major venues, look for posters around the city, and consult the newspapers *NL20* or *Time Out Amsterdam* for the most up-to-date listings.

DE NIEUWE ANITA WESTERPARK AND OUD-WEST

Frederick Hendrikstraat 111 ☎064 150 35 12 www.denieuweanita.nl

De Nieuwe Anita's popularity exploded recently when people realized that the cushy room at the front wasn't just some tasteful person's private living room. It's actually a great bar filled with creative and intellectual types, with a super-cool music room attached. American and Dutch underground and indie bands draw gangs of young local hipsters, while more diverse crowds show up for cheap movie screenings and readings.

Tram #3 to Hugo de Grootplein. Or take tram #10, 13, 14, or 17 to Rozengracht. Head north on Marnixstraat, make the 1st left before the Bloemgracht stop, cross the canal, and make another left at the traffic circle. $ Usually €5-10. ⏰ Hours vary; check website for details.

MELKWEG LEIDSEPLEIN

Lijnbaansgracht 234A ☎020 531 81 81 www.melkweg.nl

Melkweg is a legendary venue for all kinds of live music as well as clubbing.

Tram #1, 2, 5, 6, 7, or 10 to Leidseplein. Turn down the small street to the left of the Stadsschouwburg theater. $ Tickets generally €10-30; €3.50 monthly membership required. ⏰ Hours vary, but concerts usually start around 8 or 9pm.

PARADISO LEIDSEPLEIN

Weteringschans 6-8 ☎020 626 45 21 www.paradiso.nl

Paradiso hosts shows by everyone from big-name pop acts to experimental DJs.

Tram #1, 2, 5, 6, 7, or 10 to Leidseplein. Take a left onto Weteringschans. $ Tickets usually €5-20; €3 monthly membership required. ⏰ Hours vary; check website for details.

ALTO LEIDSEPLEIN

Korte Leidsedwarsstraat 115 ☎020 626 32 49 www.jazz-cafe-alto.nl

Amsterdam's most respected jazz joint, Alto is small, dark, and intimate. Look for the giant saxophone outside. With a loyal following and nightly performances by renowned artists, this place fills up quickly, so show up early to get a good seat.

Tram #1, 2, 5, 6, 7, or 10 to Leidseplein. Korte Leidsedwarsstraat is in the corner of the square. ⏰ Open M-Th 9pm-3am, F-Sa 9pm-4am, Su 9pm-3am. Music starts daily at 10pm.

COTTON CLUB NIEUWE ZIJD

Nieuwmarkt 5 ☎020 626 61 92 www.cottonclubmusic.nl

Cotton Club is an old and storied jazz club on the edge of Nieuwmarkt. Come every Saturday between 5 and 8pm to hear free concerts by the house band (often joined by special guests). There are occasionally other shows, but for most of the week this is just a relaxed place to enjoy a drink.

[M]Nieuwmarkt. $ Beer from €2.50. Weekly concerts are free. ⏰ Open M-Th noon-1am, F-Sa noon-2am, Su noon-1am.

MALOE MELO LEIDSEPLEIN

Lijnbaansgracht 163 ☎020 420 45 92 www.maloemelo.nl

This small bar with a simple stage seems more like New Orleans than Amsterdam. Maloe Melo is run by a father and son team—the dad sometimes joins performers on the accordion. There's live music every night and frequent jam sessions throughout the week. This is a good place to hear some decent blues along with a smattering of jazz and country.

🚋 Tram #7, 10, or 17 to Elandsgracht. Walk up the Jordaan side of Lijnbaansgracht a few blocks. $ Weekend cover to music room €5-7.50. Beer from €2. ⏰ Open M-Th 9pm-3am, F-Sa 9pm-4am, Su 9pm-3am. Music room opens 10:30pm.

THEATER AND COMEDY

Traditional theater and musicals don't have the same presence in Amsterdam as they do in many other cities. The comedy scene is perhaps more varied and vibrant. For entertainment you can picnic to, don't miss the **Open Air Theater** in Vondelpark in July.

👍 **BOOM CHICAGO** LEIDSEPLEIN

Leidseplein 12 ☎020 423 01 01 www.boomchicago.nl

Boom Chicago is the place for extremely popular improv comedy with plenty of audience participation. English-only shows manage to poke fun at Dutch as well, which you'll probably appreciate after spending a while in Amsterdam. Wednesday is student night: up to four students can get in using one regular ticket.

🚋 Tram #1, 2, 5, 7, or 10 to Leidseplein. At the far corner of the square. $ Tickets €20-25. ⏰ Most shows begin 8 or 9pm; check website for details.

COMEDY THEATER RED LIGHT DISTRICT

Nes 110 ☎020 422 27 77 www.comedytheater.nl

The three comedy troupes based here offer standup in both Dutch and English. Comedy Theater sometimes host international guests as well. Open-mic nights take place a few times per month, so start practicing now. Jokes at the expense of Germans will probably go down well.

🚋 Tram #4, 9, 14, 16, 24, or 25 to Spui/Rokin. Cross the canal and make a left onto Nes. $ Most tickets up to €20. ⏰ Shows start between 7:30 and 9pm. Box office open W-Th 5:30-8:30pm, F-Sa 5:30-11:30pm.

STADSSCHOUWBURG LEIDSEPLEIN

Leidseplein 26 ☎020 624 23 11 www.ssba.nl

A prime spot for catching theater in Amsterdam and the base for the **Holland Festival** in June, Stadsschouwburg also hosts opera and dance performances. The attached cafe that spills out onto the Leidseplein is almost as popular as the theater itself.

🚋 Tram #1, 2, 5, 7, or 10 to Leidseplein. $ Tickets €10-20. ⏰ Box office open M-Sa noon-6pm.

FILM

It's easy to catch a wide variety of old, new, and totally out-there films in Amsterdam. Most English-language movies are screened with Dutch subtitles. Look out for film festivals in the summer, like EYE institute's **North by Northwest.**

👍 **EYE INSTITUTE** MUSEUMPLEIN AND VONDELPARK

Vondelpark 3 ☎020 589 14 00 www.eyefilm.nl

This elegant theater at the edge of Vondelpark mostly shows new indie flicks from around the world. They also play classics, organize retrospectives on important actors and directors, and host occasional exhibits. The institute also has an extensive library, located across the street.

🚋 Tram #1, 3, or 12 to 1e Con. Huygensstraat/Overtoom. Walk down 1e Con. Huygensstraat, turn right onto Vondelstraat, and enter the park about a block down. The Institute is on the left. $ Screenings €8, students and with Museumjaarkaart €6.70. ⏰ Open M-F 9am-10pm, Sa-Su from 1hr. before the 1st show to 10:15pm. Library open M-Tu 1-5pm, Th-F 1-5pm.

PATHE TUSCHINSKI REMBRANDTPLEIN

Reguliersbreestraat 26-28 ☎020 626 26 33 www.tuschinski.nl

One of Europe's first experiments with Art Deco design, this 1921 theater maintains its original luxury but now boasts better technology. Watch new Hollywood releases from the comfort of some of the biggest, cushiest seats you'll ever sit in. Catch artsier fare at the **Tuschinski Arthouse** next door.

Tram #9 or 14 to Rembrandtplein. Walk down Reguliersbreestraat, and you'll see the cinema on the right. $ Tickets €7.80-10. Open daily from 11:30am.

surprise cinema

Pop-ups come in bad (porn ads when your dad looks over your shoulder) and good (birthday cards with $50 stuffed inside) flavors. Cinema41, a pop-up movie theater, definitely falls in the latter category. The smallest cinema in the world, Cinema41 is open to anyone at anytime—just email cinema41@golfstromen.nl to make a reservation. You'll receive an email with the exact location of the theater. The movies vary, but expect to see some classics. At a mere €3, including soda and popcorn, it's a great way to spend a rainy Amsterdam afternoon.

SAUNAS AND SPAS

Saunas and spas fall into two categories: those intended for indulgent pampering, and gay saunas where people go to indulge in the other pleasures of the flesh. It should be fairly obvious which are which, but, if you want to be sure, a quick Google search never hurt anyone.

SAUNA DECO CANAL RING WEST

Herengracht 115 ☎020 623 82 15 www.saunadeco.nl

Inside a stunning Art Deco interior (with ornaments from the original Le Bon Marché store on rue de Sèvres in Paris), bathers enjoy a sauna, steam room, plunge bath, and spa offering services from massages to facials. The patio garden and lounge beds make it the perfect place to relax even on dry land. All bathing is unisex.

Tram #1, 2, 5, 14, or 17 to Nieuwezijds Kolk. Walk east, cross the Singel, and turn left onto Herengracht. $ Sauna €21. Towel rental €2. 25min. massage €30; 55min. €55. Cash only. Open M noon-11pm, Tu 3-11pm, W-Sa noon-11pm, Su 1-7pm.

THERMOS LEIDSEPLEIN

Raamstraat 33 ☎020 623 91 58 www.thermos.nl

Thermos is one of the oldest and largest gay saunas in Europe. Its day and night branches were recently fused together into one complex, making it possible to stay from lunchtime till breakfast the next day (although you'd likely get pretty pruney). It has a Finnish sauna, Turkish steam bath, whirlpool, swimming pool, video room, private rooms, beauty salon, bar, and restaurant. Depending on the season, there may be a lot of tourists, but Thermos generally attracts a slightly older clientele.

Tram #7 or 10 to Raamplein. ***i*** *16+. Men only. $ €19.50, under 25 and over 65 €10. Open daily noon-8am.*

COFFEESHOPS

Once upon a time, Amsterdam allowed tourists from far and wide to flock to its canals for cheap, legal drugs at its famous "coffeeshops." But those days have come and gone, as Dutch officials are now limiting the purchasing and use of legal marijuana to Dutch citizens. New regulations aside, coffeeshops and the relative permissibility of soft drugs in the Netherlands provide a fascinating window into Dutch culture and society. The listings that follow represent but a small introduction to the vast world of Amsterdam coffeeshops. The exact impact of the new regulations is hard to predict at the time of publishing, so we encourage you to do some research if you're interested in learning more about coffeeshops. Finally, though we may list a number of coffeeshops, *Let's Go* does not recommend drug use in any form.

PARADOX JORDAAN

1e Bloemdwarsstraat 2 ☎623 56 39 www.paradoxcoffeeshop.com

Come to this local gem for the product, and stay for the chill atmosphere. The walls and furniture are covered in oddball art (one table is adorned with a painting of a bare-breasted, two-headed mermaid), while bongs, vaporizers, and bowls are on hand. Select from over a dozen types of weed and an usually broad selection of joints. A helpful menu describes the effects of each variety, making it easy to get exactly what you want. If you're still confused, the staff is happy to help.

Tram #13, 14, or 17 to Westermarkt. Cross Prinsengracht and continue on Rozengracht, then turn left onto 1e Bloemdwarsstraat. $ Joints €3-5; weed €5.50-11 per g; hash €7-15 per g; space cakes €6. ⏰ Open daily 10am-8pm.

AMNESIA CANAL RING WEST

Herengracht 133 ☎020 427 78 74

Amnesia is a well-regarded coffeeshop with a gorgeous canal view and high-quality products, highlighted by nine Cannabis Cup winners. There's also a large coffee bar for those who prefer the stimulating effects of caffeine to those of the other drugs on offer.

Tram #1, 2, 5, 13, 14, or 17 to Dam/Radhuisstraat. Continue along Radhuisstraat and turn right onto Herengracht. $ Joints €4-6; weed €8.50-13 per g; specialty brands €13-17 per g. ⏰ Open daily 10am-1am.

AZARIUS CENTRAL CANAL RING

Kerkstraat 119 ☎020 489 79 14 www.azarius.net

The best thing about this smartshop (a shop that sells psychoactive drugs rather than marijuana) is its knowledgeable staff, who are eager to answer any questions about their products. They sell magic truffles, salvia, herbal XTC, and other herbs and extracts as well as cannabis seeds and various smoking

move over, mushrooms

Holland may have a reputation as the land where "anything goes," but every country has its limits. In December 2008, in an effort to save face internationally, the government outlawed magical mushrooms. Dutch smartshops have lived up to their name, out-smarting the ban by turning instead to truffles. Also known as Philosopher's Stones, truffles can be eaten raw like mushrooms, and, because they contain the same hallucinogenic compounds (psilocin and psilocybin), they have a similar psychoactive effect. Some truffles might make you laugh, while others will give you a more mystical or contemplative high, and some will have you seeing brightly colored kaleidoscopic patterns everywhere you look. *Let's Go* never recommends drug use, but if you are considering trying truffles, talk to the people at the smartshop about the safest way to experience them.

paraphernalia. If you can't find what you're looking for, Azarius also runs the world's largest online smartshop.

🚋 *Tram #1, 2, or 5 to Prinsengracht. Walk 1 block up Leidsestraat and make a right onto Kerkstraat.*
Ⓢ *Truffles €10-14.* 🕐 *Open in summer daily noon-9pm; in fall, winter, and spring M-Tu noon-9pm, Th-Sa noon-9pm.*

DE TWEEDE KAMER
Heisteeg 6

NIEUWE ZIJD
☎020 422 22 36

It looks like a regular Dutch *bruin cafe*, but don't be fooled—De Tweede Kamer has one of the most extensive menus of any coffeeshop in Amsterdam, categorized by type, smell, flavor, and quality of the high. Plus, there's something fun about smoking in a store named after one of the Dutch chambers of Parliament.

🚋 *Tram #1, 2, or 5 to Spui/Nieuwezijds Voorburgwal. Walk down to Spui, up Spuistraat, and turn left onto Heisteeg.* Ⓢ *Joints €3-9; weed €4-13 per g; hash €8-40 per g; space cakes and muffins €6.* 🕐 *Open daily 10am-1am.*

TWEEDY
2e Constantijn Huygensstraat 76

MUSEUMPLEIN AND VONDELPARK
☎020 618 03 44

Tweedy is located just a short walk from a classy museum (the Van Gogh Museum), a beautiful park (Vondelpark), and a repurposed squat (OT301). Hit all of them plus this coffeeshop in one day and you'll see just about everything that matters in Amsterdam. Tweedy's selection is small but cheap and includes quality favorites like White Widow. A steady stream of reggae will join you in the relaxing basement-like smoking area.

🚋 *Tram #1 to 1e Con. Huygensstraat or tram #3 or 12 to Overtoom. Walk down Overtoom and turn left onto 2e Con. Huygensstraat.* Ⓢ *Joints €3.50; weed €5-11 per g; hash €6-10 per g.* 🕐 *Open daily 11am-11pm.*

THE BUSH DOCTOR
Thorbeckeplein 28

REMBRANDTPLEIN
☎020 330 74 75

This small store boasts two floors and outdoor seating that spills out onto Thorbeckeplein. The drug menu caters to the serious and experienced smoker, making it one of the best places to try specialty strains of weed and hash. Not only does the Bush Doctor have a variety of its own potent mixes, various fruity options, and organic wares, but they also carry half a dozen kinds of the infamous ice-o-lator hash. The best part of this shop is its location, just a short distance away from Studio 80 and the other clubs of Rembrandtplein, and not too far from the bars in Leidseplein.

🚋 *Tram #9 or 14 to Rembrandtplein. Thorbeckeplein is across the square from the giant TV screen.* Ⓢ *Joints €4-6; weed €7.50-12.50 per g; hash €10-12 per g, ice-o-lator €22-55 per g; space cakes €7.* 🕐 *Open daily 9am-1am.*

shopping

With shopping, as with pretty much everything else, Amsterdam accommodates both snooty European intellectuals and renegade rasta men. The Nine Streets just south of Westerkerk are packed with vintage stores and interesting boutiques. Haarlemmerstraat, in Scheepvaartbuurt, is an up-and-coming design district. For more established brands, look to Kalverstraat, with its string of international chains and large department stores. For something really pricey, P. C. Hooftstraat, near Museumplein, is home to all the big-name designers. On the other end of the spectrum, markets like Albert Cuypmarkt and Waterlooplein offer dirt-cheap and, at times, flat-out bizarre clothing and other miscellaneous wares.

CLOTHING AND JEWELRY

SPRMRKT JORDAAN

Rozengracht 191-193 ☎020 330 56 01 www.sprmrkt.nl

Too cool for school (or for vowels, at least), this large store in the Jordaan sells excruciatingly hip streetwear for men and women. The store-within-the-store, SPR+, sells even nicer designer pieces.

⚐ Tram #10, 13, 14, or 17 to Rozengracht/Marnixstraat. Walk a few blocks down Rozengracht; the store is on the right. ⏰ Open Tu-W 10am-6pm, Th 10am-8pm, F-Sa 10am-6pm, Su noon-6pm.

STUDIO 88 DE PIJP

Gerard Douplein 88 ☎770 65 84 www.fashionstudio88.nl

Sometimes it feels like affordable Albert Cuypmarkt isn't a deal, because you won't even wear the clothes. The items at Studio 88 might not have the same rock-bottom prices, though the overstock and sample attire let you get high-end pieces for a fraction of the original cost. The store mostly carries women's clothes, with a few racks of men's things in the back and a small selection of kid's attire.

⚐ Tram #16 or 24 to Albert Cuypstraat. Walk 1 block up (toward the canal) and turn right onto Gerard Doustraat. The store is up 2 blocks on the right. $ Shirts around €20. Dresses around €40. ⏰ Open M 1-6pm, Tu-F 11am-6pm, Sa 10am-6pm.

VEZJUN JORDAAN

Rozengracht 110 www.vezjun.nl

Vezjun is a small store that specializes in clothing from young, independent Dutch designers. The clothes are occasionally a little out there, but they are well constructed, fresh, and modern. You can be sure no one else will be wearing the same thing at the next party—but you'll be paying for that peace of mind.

⚐ Tram #10, 13, 14, or 17 to Rozengracht/Marnixstraat. Walk a few blocks east on Rozengracht; the store is on the left. $ Dresses €70-90. ⏰ Open Tu-F noon-7pm, Sa 11am-6pm.

got wood?

Wooden shoes may sound bizarre, but this is Amsterdam, so obviously that isn't stopping them. The traditional shoes can be traced back to the Germanic tribes who were the original occupants of the Netherlands. Over a century ago, they were used to protect the feet of factory workers, miners, and farmers. Known as *klompen*, these clogs can withstand almost anything that would threaten a worker's feet with harm, including sharp objects and acid.

You're not likely to find a native strolling the city in this old-fashioned style, but they are still a common (and cliché) souvenir among tourists. And some people do indeed wear them while working in the garden or on the farm. Have a green thumb yourself? Take a pair home and garden like the Dutch.

BOOKS

THE BOOK EXCHANGE OUDE ZIJD

Kloveniersburgwal 58 ☎020 626 62 66 www.bookexchange.nl

The Book Exchange stocks a tremendous inventory of secondhand books, ranging from New Age philosophy to poetry. They have a particularly large selection of paperback fiction. The knowledgeable expat owner is more than happy to chat at length with customers. As the name suggests, the shop also buys and trades books.

⚐ From Nieuwmarkt, cross to the far side of Kloveniersburgwal and turn left. ⏰ Open M-Sa 10am-6pm, Su 11:30am-4pm.

AMERICAN BOOK CENTER NIEUWE ZIJD

Spui 2 ☎020 625 55 37 www.abc.nl

A centrally located English-language bookstore with a wide range of new and classic titles, American Book Center also has an excellent selection of maps of Amsterdam, from the simple to the more-detailed-than-you-could-ever-have-need-for.

🚋 Tram #1, 2, or 5 to Spui/Nieuwezijds Voorburgwal. It's on the northern edge of the square. ℹ 10% discount for students and teachers with ID. ⏰ Open M 11am-8pm, Tu-W 10am-8pm, Th 10am-9pm, F-Sa 10am-8pm, Su 11am-6:30pm.

THE ENGLISH BOOKSHOP JORDAAN

Lauriergracht 71 ☎020 626 42 30 www.englishbookshop.nl

This small, cozy shop in the Jordaan draws a vibrant community of regulars who enjoy coffee, tea, and fresh pastries while browsing the wide selection of English-language books. The store hosts events like writing workshops, a monthly book club, and the quirky 👍**literary Trivial Pursuit.**

🚋 Tram #10, 13, 14, or 17 to Rozengracht/Marnixstraat. Cross Lijnbaansgracht, turn right, and then left onto Lauriergracht. ⏰ Open Tu-Sa 11am-6pm.

ANTIQUES AND VINTAGE CLOTHING

The **Nine Streets** area in Canal Ring West is the place to find quirky stores selling antiques and vintage swag. For slightly cheaper options, check out the smaller stores on **Haarlemmerstraat.**

👍 **LAURA DOLS** CANAL RING WEST

Wolvenstraat 7 ☎020 624 90 66 www.lauradols.nl

Laura Dols specializes in vintage gowns, including taffeta prom dresses, fluffy shepherdess numbers, and things you could actually get away with wearing outside of the house. It also sells shoes, bags, and old-school lingerie (including some awesome metallic bras).

🚋 Tram #1, 2, or 5 to Spui/Nieuwezijds Voorburgwal. Walk west to the far side of Herengracht, turn right, and then left onto Wolvenstraat. $ Most dresses €30-60. ⏰ Open M-W 11am-6pm, Th 11am-9pm, F-Sa 11am-6pm, Su 1-6pm.

👍 **PETTICOAT** JORDAAN

Lindengracht 99 ☎020 623 30 65

Come to Petticoat for a good selection of secondhand men's and women's clothing, some from fairly upscale brands. It's unusual to find such an affordable option in the Jordaan, or anywhere in the city for that matter.

🚋 Tram #3 to Nieuwe Willemstraat. Cross Lijnbaansgracht, turn right, and then left onto Lindengracht. $ Tops from €10. Bottoms from €15. ⏰ Open M 11am-6pm, W-F 11am-6pm, Sa 11am-5pm.

LADY DAY CANAL RING WEST

Hartenstraat 9 ☎020 623 58 20 www.theninestreets.com/ladyday

An established go-to spot for '50s, '60s, and '70s vintage style, Lady Day offers a massive collection of men's and women's clothes: tweed jackets, cocktail dresses, bathing suits, sweaters, tops, scarves, and much more. Most of the clothes are still quite fashionable, and the things that aren't are still really cheap.

🚋 Tram #13, 14, or 17 to Westermarkt. Walk down Radhuisstraat to the far side of Keizersgracht, make a right, and then turn left onto Hartenstraat. $ Dresses around €25. Sweaters €20. Scarves €1. ⏰ Open M-W 11am-6pm, Th 11am-9pm, F-Sa 11am-6pm, Su 1-6pm.

MARKETS

👍 **ALBERT CUYPMARKT** DE PIJP

Albert Cuypstraat

Stretching almost half a mile along the length of Albert Cuypstraat, this is the most famous market in the city. Need a motorcycle helmet, sundress, and cinnamon all in one afternoon? Albert Cuypmarkt is the place to go. The clothes can be hit or miss, but for produce or knick-knacks, it's a great option. Rows of stores behind the market stalls sell similar items at slightly higher prices (though the clothes are a bit more wearable). Be sure to come early if you want to see the full display—some vendors start packing up as early as 4pm.

🚋 *Tram #16 or 24 to Albert Cuypstraat. ⏰ Open M-Sa 9am-6pm.*

🛍 NOORDERMARKT   JORDAAN
Noordermarkt   www.boerenmarktamsterdam.nl
This organic market pops up every Saturday in a picturesque northern corner of the Jordaan to sell produce, cheese, baked goods, herbs, homeopathic remedies, and some hippie-esque clothes. Noordermarkt is a great place to shop or browse when you can't afford the Jordaan's classy indoor boutiques.

🚋 *Tram #3 to Nieuwe Willemstraat. Cross Lijnbaansgracht, walk up Willemstraat, turn right onto Brouwersgracht, and then right onto Prinsengracht. The market is about a block down. ⏰ Open Sa 9am-4pm.*

DAPPERMARKT   OUTSKIRTS
Dapperstraat   www.dappermarkt.nl
Dappermarkt exudes the vibrant local flavor of Amsterdam East, blending the city's old charm with the cultures of its North African and Middle Eastern immigrant communities. Come here to find vegetables, spices, cloth, furniture, clothes, and more at cheaper prices than the touristy markets in the city center. It's near Oosterpark, just south of Plantage.

🚋 *Tram #3 or 7 to Dapperstraat. Walk south on Wijttenbachstraat and make the 1st right onto Dapperstraat. ⏰ Open M-Sa 9am-5pm.*

MUSIC
Smartshops and larger coffeeshops often have wide selections of drug toys, from pipes to bongs to one-hitters in all colors, shapes, and sizes. Amsterdam also has some excellent music stores and quirky secondhand music can be found at some of the markets.

🛍 CONCERTO   CENTRAL CANAL RING
Utrechtsestraat 52-60   ☎020 623 52 28 www.platomania.eu
Multiple storefronts make up this huge complex with the biggest music selection in Amsterdam. Concerto sells almost every genre imaginable as well as records, DVDs, and secondhand CDs. It's also a great place to check out flyers and posters for upcoming concerts and festivals. You can even purchase some show tickets here.

🚋 *Tram #4, 7, 10, or 25 to Frederiksplein. Walk diagonally across the square and up Utrechtsestraat. ⏰ Open M-W 10am-6pm, Th 10am-9pm, F-Sa 10am-6pm, Su noon-6pm.*

SOUTH MIAMI PLAZA   DE PIJP
Albert Cuypstraat 116   ☎020 662 28 17 www.southmiamiplaza.nl
Come here for a fine selection of pop, blues, reggae, R&B, world music, and a special section of Dutch classics (trust us, browsing the covers alone is a worthwhile endeavor). They also have plenty of DVDs. Bargain bins hold an eclectic mix of CDs that start at just €1.

🚋 *Tram #16 or 24 to Albert Cuypstraat. Walk through the market and the store is on the right. ⏰ Open M-Sa 10am-6pm.*

VELVET MUSIC   JORDAAN
Rozengracht 40   ☎020 422 87 77 www.velvetmusic.nl
Velvet carries the latest releases and older music in virtually every genre, with an especially good selection of the diverse kinds of sounds that get lumped together as "indie." Smaller than Concerto, but less overwhelming to navigate, the shop also buys use music and has a large selection of vinyl.

🚋 *Tram #13, 14, or 17 to Westermarkt. Cross Prinsengracht and walk down Rozengracht. ⏰ Open M noon-6pm, Tu-Sa 10am-6pm.*

shopping

cannabis cup

Don't you hate having to choose between smoking weed and going to a sweet convention? Yeah, we've never had that dilemma before either, but the Cannabis Cup is a solution to this non-existent problem. If you're in Amsterdam in late November, head to the PowerZone club for the opportunity to see everything from seeds to weed to famous supporters of the counterculture. Plus, every year at the Expo, *High Times* magazine inducts a new celebrity into its Counterculture Hall of Fame. What do Bob Marley, Bob Dylan, Tommy Chong, and Cheech Marin have in common? Exactly what you think.

essentials

PRACTICALITIES

- **TOURIST OFFICES: VVV** provides information on sights, museums, performances, and accommodations. They also sell the **I Amsterdam** card, which gives you unlimited transport and free admission to many museums for a set number of days. For other transportation information, you're better off going to the **GVB office** next door. The lines at the office by Centraal Station can be unbearably long, so unless you need information right after you step off the train, try the one in Leidseplein instead. (Stationsplein 10 ☎020 201 88 00 www.iamsterdam.com ✚ Across from the eastern part of Centraal Station, near tram stops 1-4. ✪ Open July-Aug daily 9am-7pm; Sept-June M-Sa 9am-6pm, Su 9am-5pm.) Other locations at **Schiphol Airport** (Aankomstpassage 40, in Arrival Hall 2 ✪ Open daily 7am-10pm) and **Leidseplein 26.** (✪ Open M-F 10am-7:30pm, Sa 10am-6pm, Su noon-6pm.)

- **GLBT RESOURCES: GAYtic** is a tourist office that specializes in GLBT info, and is authorized by the VVV. (Spuistraat 4 ☎020 330 14 61 www.gaytic.nl ✚ Tram #1, 2, 5, 13, or 17 to Nieuwezijds Kolk. Walk 1 block west to Spuistraat; the office is inside the Gays and Gadgets store. ✪ Open M-Sa 11am-8pm, Su noon-8pm.) **Pink Point** provides information on GLBT issues, events, and attractions in the city, and sells all kinds of GLBT souvenirs. (Westermarkt, by the Homomonument ☎020 428 10 70 www.pinkpoint.org ✚ Tram #13, 14, or 17 to Westermarkt. ✪ Open daily 10am-6pm; reduced hours in winter.) **Gay and Lesbian Switchboard** provides anonymous assistance for any GLBT-related questions or concerns. (☎020 623 65 65 www.switchboard.nl ✪ Operates M-F 2-6pm.)

- **LAUNDROMATS: Rozengracht Wasserette** sells detergent and provides self-service and next-day laundry. (Rozengracht 59 ☎020 063 59 75 ✚ Tram #13, 14, or 17 to Westermarkt. Cross Prinsengracht and walk a few blocks down Rozengracht. ⑨ Wash €8, dry €7. ✪ Open daily 9am-9pm.) **Powders Laundrette.** (Kerkstraat 56 ☎062 630 60 57 www.powders.nl ✚ Tram #1, 2, 5, 7, or 10 to Leidseplein. Walk up Leidsestraat and make a right. *i* Detergent for sale. Wi-Fi. ⑨ Wash €4.50 per hr.; dry €0.50 per 11min. 5kg wash, dry, and fold €10. ✪ Self-service open daily 7am-10pm. Full-service open M-W 8am-5pm, F 8am-5pm, Sa-Su 9am-3pm.)

- **INTERNET: Openbare Bibliotheek Amsterdam** provides free Wi-Fi and free use of computers that can be reserved through the information desk. (Oosterdokskade 143 ☎020 523 09 00 www.oba.nl ✚ From Centraal Station, walk east, sticking close to the station building. You'll cross a canal, and the street will become Oosterdokskade. ✪ Open daily 10am-10pm.) **The Mad Processor** is popular with gamers. (Kinkerstraat 11-13 ☎020 612 18 18 www.madprocessor.nl ✚ Tram #7, 10, or 17 to Elandsgracht. Cross Nassaukade onto Kinkerstraat. *i* Computers with Skype. Fax machines and scanners available. ⑨ Internet €1 per 30min. Printing €0.20 per page. ✪ Open daily noon-2am.)

- **POST OFFICES:** The main branch can deal with all of your postal needs, plus it has banking services and sells phone cards. (Singel 250 ☎020 556 33 11 www.tntpost.nl 🚏 Tram #1, 2, 5, 13, 14, or 17 to Dam. Walk on Raadhuisstraat away from the square and turn left onto Singel. The post office is in the basement. ⏰ Open M-F 7:30am-6:30pm, Sa 7:30am-5pm.) You can also buy stamps and send packages from any store that has the orange and white TNT sign (including many grocery stores and tobacco shops).
- **POSTAL CODES:** Range from 1000 AA to 1099 ZZ. Check the TNT website or http://maps.google.nl to find out the code for a specific address.

EMERGENCY

- **EMERGENCY NUMBER:** ☎112.
- **POLICE: Politie Amsterdam-Amstelland** is the Amsterdam police department. Dialing ☎0900 8844 will connect you to the nearest station or rape crisis center. The following stations are located in and around the city center. **Lijnbaansgracht.** (Lijnbaansgracht 219 🚏 Tram #7 or 10 to Raamplein. Walk 1 block south and turn left onto Leidsegracht. ⏰ Open 24hr.) **Nieuwezijds Voorburgwal.** (Nieuwezijds Voorburgwal 104-108 🚏 Tram #1, 2, 5, 13, or 17 to Nieuwezijds Kolk. Walk 1 block down Nieuwezijds Voorburgwal, away from Centraal Station. ⏰ Open 24hr.) **Prinsengracht.** (Prinsengracht 1109 🚏 Tram #4, 7, 10, or 25 to Fredericksplein. Walk north diagonally through the square, up Utrechtsestraat, and turn right onto Prinsengracht. ⏰ Open 24hr.) From outside the Netherlands, you can call the Amsterdam police at ☎+31 20 559 91 11.
- **CRISIS HOTLINES: Telephone Helpline** provides general counseling services. (☎020 675 75 75 ⏰ Operates 24hr.) **Amsterdam Tourist Assistance Service** provides help for victimized tourists, generally those who have been robbed. They offer assistance with transferring money, replacing documents, and finding temporary accommodations. (Nieuwezijds Voorburgwal 104-08 ☎020 625 32 46 www.stichtingatas.nl 🚏 Tram #1, 2, 5, 13, or 17 to Nieuwezijds Kolk. Walk 1 block down Nieuwezijds Voorburgwal. It's inside the police station. ⏰ Open daily 10am-10pm.) **Sexual Abuse Hotline** provides information and assistance to victims of domestic violence, abuse, and rape. (☎020 611 60 22 ⏰ Operates 24hr.)
- **LATE-NIGHT PHARMACIES: Afdeling Inlichtingen Apotheken Hotline** provides information about which pharmacies are open late on a given day. (☎020 694 87 09 ⏰ Operates 24hr.) You can also check posted signs on the doors of closed pharmacies to find the nearest one open in the area. There are no specifically designated 24hr. pharmacies, but there are always a few open at any given time.
- **HOSPITALS/MEDICAL SERVICES: Academisch Meidisch Centrum** is one of two large university hospitals in Amsterdam. Located southeast of the city, past the Amsterdam Arena stadium. (Meibergdreef 9 ☎020 566 91 11 www.amc.uva.nl 🚏 Bus # 45, 47, 355 or metro trains 50 or 54 to Holendrecht. Hospital is directly across. ⏰ Open 24hr.) **Tourist Medical Service** provides doctor's visits for guests at registered hotels and runs a 24hr. line to connect tourists to non-emergency medical care. (☎020 592 33 55 www.tmsdoctor.nl ⏰ Operates 24hr.)

GETTING THERE

By Plane

Schiphol Airport (AMS) is the main international airport for both Amsterdam and the Netherlands. (☎020 900 01 41 from the Netherlands, +31 207 940 800 from elsewhere; www.schiphol.nl) It's located 18km outside the city center. The easiest way to reach Centraal Station from the airport is by train. ($ €4.20. ⏰ 15-20min.; 4-10 per hr. 6am-1am, 1 per hr. 1am-6am.) The train station is located just below the airport; you can buy tickets at machines with cards or coins, or from the ticket counter with cash. Buses also leave from the airport, which can be useful for travelers staying outside the city center. Bus #370 passes by Leidseplein, and other buses travel to Amsterdam and neighboring towns.

By Train

Within the Netherlands, the easiest way to reach Amsterdam is by train, which will almost certainly run to **Centraal Station**. (Stationsplein 1 ☎020 900 92 92; www.ns.nl) Trains arrive from The Hague (Ⓢ €10.20 ⓩ 1 hr., 3-6 per hr. 4:45am-12:45am), Rotterdam (Ⓢ €13.40 ⓩ 1hr.; 3-8 per hr. 5:30am-12:45am, 1 per hr. 12:45am-5:30am), and Utrecht (Ⓢ €6.70 ⓩ 30min.; 4 per hr. 6am-midnight, 1 per hr. midnight-6am). International trains from Belgium and Paris are operated by **Thalys** (www.thalys.com), which runs trains from Brussels (Ⓢ €29-69 ⓩ 2hr., 1 per hr. 7:50am-8:50pm) and Paris (Ⓢ €35-120 ⓩ 3hr.).

You'll need to shop around for the best deals on trains to Amsterdam from other major European cities. Check Rail Europe (www.raileurope.com) to compare prices for most companies. Like Dutch trains, all international trains run to the glorious potpourri of travelers known as Centraal Station. Train ticket prices range from €100-300 depending on the destination and rise rapidly as the date of departure approaches.

By Bus

While buses aren't a great way to get around the Netherlands, they can be cheaper for international travel. **Eurolines** (☎020 560 87 88 www.eurolines.com) is the best choice, and runs buses from Brussels (Ⓢ €25, under 25 €19 ⓩ 3-4½hr., 7-12 per day) and Bruges (Ⓢ €25, under 25 €19 ⓩ 5hr., 1 per day) to the **Amsterdam Amstel station,** which is connected to the rest of the city by Metro and tram #12.

If you want to travel to Amsterdam by bus from major cities such as London (Ⓢ €42), Munich (Ⓢ €42), and Paris (Ⓢ €84), you will almost definitely have to go through Brussels, Bruges, and the above-mentioned stops on the way. Eurolines often has deals for those who book in advance.

GETTING AROUND

Tram, bus, and Metro lines extend out from Centraal Station, while more trams and buses cross those routes perpendicularly, or circumnavigate the canal rings. Trams are generally the fastest and easiest mode of transport in Amsterdam, serving almost all major points within the city center. The Red Light District and Oude Zijd only have stops on their northern or southern ends. Buses are good if you are heading outside of the center or to more residential parts of the city, though trams extend to some of these as well. The Metro is rarely useful for tourists, as it only goes down the eastern side of the city and has few stops within the center.

Tickets and information can be found at **GVB.** (☎020 460 60 60 www.gvb.nl ⚓ On Stationsplein across from the eastern end of Centraal Station next to the VVV tourist office. ⓩ Open M-F 7am-9pm, Sa-Su 10am-6pm.) The lines here can be long, but it's the easiest place to buy transport tickets. The **OV-chipkaart** (www.ov-chipkaart.nl) has replaced the strippenkaart as the only type of ticket used on Amsterdam public transport. Disposable tickets can be purchased when boarding trams and buses. (Ⓢ 1hr. ticket €2.60, 1- to 7-day tickets €7-30.) A personalized OV-chipkaart, featuring the owner's picture and allowing perks like automatically adding value when the balance is low, is a good option if you're staying in Amsterdam for an extended period of time. You're more likely, however, to get an anonymous card, which can be purchased for €7.50 (plus an extra €5 as a starting balance) and reloaded at machines located throughout the city (most visibly in major supermarkets like Albert Heijn).

You must both tap in and tap out with your chipkaart to avoid being charged for more than you actually travel. With the chipkaart, a ride on the bus, tram, or Metro costs €0.79 plus €0.10 per km. Most rides within the city center will cost around €1-2. Most transport runs 5am-midnight; after that, there are 12 night bus lines that run once per hour, twice per hour on weekend nights. An ordinary chipkaart does not work on night buses; you must buy special tickets (€4; 12 for €30) or one of the one- to seven-day passes.

Bike Rentals

[✓] FREDERIC RENT-A-BIKE SCHEEPVAARTBUURT

Brouwersgracht 78 ☎020 624 55 09 www.frederic.nl

In addition to rooms and general wisdom re: all things Amsterdam (see **Accommodations**), come here for bike repairs and rentals.

*🚋 From Centraal Station, cross the canal, make a right on Prins Hendrikkade, cross the Singel, turn left onto Singel, and then right onto Brouwersgracht. **i** Prices include lock and insurance. No deposit required, just a copy of a credit card or passport. $ Bike rentals €10 per day; €16 per 2 days; €40 per week; €100 per month. ⏰ Open daily 9am-5:30pm.*

BIKE CITY JORDAAN

Bloemgracht 68-70 ☎020 626 37 21 www.bikecity.nl

Rentals cost a bit more here than at other shops, but they are well worth it, because the bikes come free from the plastered advertisements attached to most rented bikes in the city. You may even be able to blend in as a local with one of Bike City's plain black rides.

*🚋 Tram #13, 14, or 17 to Westermarkt. Cross Prinsengracht, turn right, and then left onto Bloemgracht. **i** ID and deposit of a credit card or €50 required. $ Bike rentals from €10 per 4hr.; €13.50 per day; up to €43.50 per 5 days. Insurance €2.50 per day. ⏰ Open daily 9am-6pm.*

DAMSTRAAT RENT-A-BIKE RED LIGHT DISTRICT

Damstraat 22 ☎020 625 50 29 www.bikes.nl

Damstraat rents multiple kinds of bikes, including tandems, and also sells new and secondhand bikes.

*🚋 One of the many trams to Dam. Walk to the end of the square and make a left onto Damstraat. **i** Copy of credit card or ID and €25 deposit required. $ From €6.50 per 3hr.; €9.50 per day; €31 per 6 days. Sells bikes from €160. ⏰ Open daily 9am-6pm.*

amsterdam 101

You probably know Amsterdam as the center of tolerance for sex, drugs, and rock and roll whether you want to celebrate this, condemn this, or admit that it's the main incentive for your visit. Yes, you'll find all of those things here, but the Netherlands's legacy rests on two more profound pillars: innovation and internationalism. Between rocking their superiority on the seas and boasting some pretty impressive expertise on the easel, the Dutch have blazed (no, not that way) a trail through innovative terrain—or, well, water. Amsterdammers, as they're called, annexed 3000 square miles of land from the North Sea with a mind-boggling puzzle of dikes, canals, and pumps that would put a Rubik's cube to shame. Only a city with this much spunk could combine Amsterdam's mix of hedonism, world-class art, multicultural sophistication, and come-one, come-all openness. Maybe the old adage, "God created the world, but the Dutch created the Netherlands," says it all (or maybe that's all the beer talking). Come for the coffeeshops, but let the windmills blow you away.

HISTORY

Over Troubled Waters (1200-1648)

For the original inhabitants of this humble 13th-century village, making a living was fishy business. The town was located on the mouth of the Amstel River, where frequent flooding offset the gains its denizens made from fishing. Soon citizens grew tired of getting their feet wet and finally got around to building a dam. Thus sprang *Aemstelledamme* ("the dam on the Amstel"), which soon became an important harbor and seaport.

1275. The name Amsterdam makes its first appearance in a certificate exempting residents from a bridge tax. Discovering the euphoria (and lack of wet socks) of crossing a bridge for free, Amsterdammers build more than a thousand of them.

1452. The second large fire of the century tears through Amsterdam, burning over three quarters of the city and perhaps establishing its strong ties to smoke.

1593. Tulip-mania begins after the Dutch ambassador to Istanbul ships some of these babies back home. The original age of flower power begins.

1637. Some tulips are sold at a price 10 times the salary of a skilled laborer, but prices suddenly drop and all trade of the bulb-to-rule-them-all crashes soon after. Oops—enter tulip panic.

Amsterdammers then decided to net more income instead of fish and traded in their tackle boxes for some liter mugs: a booming beer trade was established in the city, vastly increasing its supply of cash money. Amsterdam also asserted itself with the central granary of the area and became the most significant city for trade in the Netherlands.

After the so-called **Miracle of Amsterdam**, an event that involved a dying man and some pretty spectacular vomit (probably best explained by locals), Amsterdam became a common site of pilgrimage for the Roman Catholics. Once the Dutch became subject to Spanish rule in 1506, however, they didn't find the high taxes and religious intolerance imposed by their faraway Catholic overlords particularly miraculous.

Amsterdam remained loyal to Spain in the early years of the Netherlands's rebellion but took the plunge in 1578 and joined the revolution on the side of Willem van Oranje. This sparked the **Eighty Years' War**, a pretty calm near-century dispersed with a few mercenary army invasions, a benevolent Blood Council, and some mutinies thrown in here and there. After a treaty in 1648, the Dutch finally established their own republic, built on the principle of religious tolerance.

Death By Gold (1649-1700)

The 17th century marked Amsterdam's **Golden Age**, as merchants built Amsterdam into the undisputed commercial hub of Northern Europe. Amsterdam's growth brought with it an increase in trade, military expansion, and a new Baroque trend in art. Sending ships from South Africa to Brazil to Japan, the **Dutch East India Company** showed its strength as the world's first multinational trading corporation, monopolizing and colonizing around the world. The city's new affluence and power encouraged a renaissance in art and architecture that gave birth to some influential painters like Rembrandt and Vermeer.

Alas, wealth was soon followed by the **Black Death,** which became a minor setback as it killed off about 10% off the population between 1663 and 1666. All was made well, however, by the sage advice of the city's mayors, who recommended tobacco smoke as a precaution against the disease and also warned citizens not to consume salad, spinach, or prunes.

Growing Pains (1701-1945)

Even as the center of an empire, however, Amsterdam wasn't safe from the threat of rival colonial powers looking to jack some of its swag, which led to a series of wars against rival colonial powers in the 18th century. Unfortunately for the city but quite luckily for the rest of the world, the Dutch turned out to be far better businessmen than soldiers. Things were no longer sailing smoothly in Amsterdam—everyone was talking about the economy, and political unrest was brewing. They lost many of their colonies to France and Britain, and when Belgium and Luxembourg broke off in

1830, the Kingdom of the Netherlands wasn't much of a kingdom anymore.

Amsterdam worked on getting back its mojo during the **Industrial Revolution,** but more development only led to more problems. Peasants, who had moved into the city from the countryside to follow new jobs, soon made up a militant socialist base, and violence between protestors and the police was just a day in the life.

Although the Netherlands managed to stay neutral during WWI, the country still faced a shortage of essentials (like food) and weren't able to escape a Nazi occupation during WWII. Throwing the city's tradition of religious tolerance into the Amstel, the Nazis sent more than 100,000 Jews in the city to concentration camps. Many Jews, including **Anne Frank,** were able to go into hiding, but the majority of Amsterdam's formerly robust Jewish community was decimated.

Magical Mystery Tour (1946-2000)

Amsterdam limped through its recovery after the war, but the city was reborn in the cultural revolution of the 1960s and '70s, during which time it became known as the *magisch centrum,* or "magical center," of Europe. The city legalized soft drugs while anarchists and squatters took to the streets and yuppies invaded old working-class neighborhoods. Amsterdam's economy transitioned its focus from industry to service, sparking the growth of wealth and finance in the city.

Amsterdam's demographics shifted along with this tide: nearly a third of the city's residents are immigrants, mainly from Turkey, North Africa, and Dutch colonies in the Caribbean. To mollify some of the cultural tension that accompanied this early immigration, strict social tolerance laws govern the city—accompanying tolerance of all other forms, as well.

Flashback (2000-Present)

This pervasive openness, however, has been closed down in recent years. Taming its reputation somewhat, Amsterdam shut down a third of the Red Light District's brothels in 2006 amid accusations of promoting criminality. In 2008, the central government ordered the city to shut down all coffeehouses located within 500m of school zones. And in a move that sucked all the fairytale out of everyday life, the cultivation and sale of magic mushrooms was banned in the same year.

CUSTOMS AND ETIQUETTE

So you're obviously expecting some culture shock in the Red Light District, but there's plenty more to look out for in your more "professional" encounters with Hollanders. A firm handshake is customary when introduced to someone, and close friends greet each other with three (yes, three) kisses, *comme le style français.* Men, we know you're hungry and growing and all that, but it's common to wait for women to be seated when sharing a meal.

Although soft drugs and prostitution are legal in Amsterdam, recent laws have cracked down on these activities, and abusers

1839. The Treaty of London officially recognizes Belgium and Luxembourg's independence from the Netherlands, limiting the country's modern borders. Amsterdam decides it can make waffles on its own.

1902. Nico Broekhuysen invents korfball, a controversial game allowing men and women to play on the same team. Scoring with the other team takes on a whole new meaning.

1988. Dutch law gives the green light to the red-light district: prostitution becomes a recognized occupation.

2001. Two Amsterdam grooms wed and become the world's first legally married same-sex couple.

amsterdam 101

and lawbreakers face harsh punishment. Hard drugs (read: not weed) are illegal, and as of late 2011, so is selling marijuana to foreigners. While coffeeshops continue to serve as a beacon of local culture, it's no longer legal to participate yourself.

Strangely, coffeeshops in Amsterdam are required to adhere to the requirements set by a recent tobacco ban, which means that customers are only allowed to smoke tobacco with their pot in a separate, specially designated tobacco room. Although you might be offered more attractive prices outside of these shops—say, during a casual midday stroll through the Red Light District—that guy with the trench coat whispering out to passersby probably isn't someone to trust. If you're tempted to experiment in Amsterdam, don't cross through the gate—stick with the all-natural, organic, grows-out-of-the-ground type of deal. Stay away from joy rides: DUIs are still uncool and illegal here. Try to keep your debauchery to a minimum and you'll be smooth-sailing. Please remember that *Let's Go* does not recommend drug use.

FOOD AND DRINK

The typical Dutch *ontbijt* (breakfast) consists of bread topped with cold cuts and slices of local cheese, complemented with a dab of *appelstroop* (a thicker syrup made from apple juice). If you're looking to satisfy that morning sweet tooth, top off your toast with some *hagelsag* (chocolate, anise, or fruit-flavored sprinkles). And a strong cup of *kaffie* (need a hint?) can always help kick off your day.

Lunch (we'll let you figure out the translation for that yourself) includes rolls, sandwiches, or soup at one of the city's cafes. *Erwtensoep* (pea soup) is a cold-weather favorite and often includes chunks of smoked sausage. You'll probably also encounter *uitsmijter*, or Dutch fried eggs, sunny-side up—for some reason, the name translates to "out-thrower" or "bouncer," as in the doorman at a club. A *broodje haring*, or herring sandwich, garnished with onions and pickles is particularly tasty (no, we're not kidding); you'll find one at various fish stands throughout the city.

Diner is served in Dutch homes at around five or six in the evening. A meat entree is traditionally accompanied by two veggie side dishes, but you might also see *stamppot* on the menu—this dish combines meat, vegetables, and gravy in a mash. Amsterdam also has an almost bizarre selection of international food, like Indonesian cuisine (a tasty relic and means of still capitalizing off Dutch colonialism), Middle Eastern joints, Chinese restaurants, and Argentinean steakhouses.

Fruit, yogurt, or a cold custard followed by more *kaffie* are common local desserts. It is helpful to know that cafes and bars are a packaged deal in the Netherlands—cafes serve *kaffie* by day and beer by night, so order a Heineken on its home turf, or sample some of the other famous Dutch pale lagers. A frosty *witbeer* (white beer) hits the spot after a long day of wandering the streets. Whatever your choice, do like the Dutch and *eet smakelijk* ("enjoy your meal").

SPORTS AND RECREATION

Feet and Balls

Unsurprisingly, soccer is Amsterdam's biggest professional sport. The **Amsterdamsche Football Club Ajax** (AFC Ajax—Ajax for short) was founded in 1900 and is named after the legendary Greek hero, who was famed for his ability to toss boulders and leap between ships. Don't fall for the allure, though: these athletes cannot do the same. But this is still a *voetball* team that anyone would be scared to confront in the center circle, and for good reason: the International Federation of Football History and Statistics ranked Ajax as the seventh most successful Eurpean club of the 20th century. So don your white shorts (anything but tightie-whities, please) and white jersey with a single vertical red stripe to cheer on the 4-time European Cup winners—but try to stay away from launching heavy rocks into the Amsterdam ArenA (not a typo). If you happen to be in the city during a World Cup year, though, you'd be better off sporting orange, the official color of the Netherlands National Football Team. As of 2011, the team was ranked #1 in the world by FIFA, despite the fact that they've never actually won a World Cup title.

Teammates

Amsterdam is the birthplace of **korfball,** a hybrid of basketball and soccer that requires each team be composed of four men and four women (talk about playing games with the other sex). Players score points by tossing a grippy soccer ball and bouncing it into the other team's *korf* (basket), attached to a 3m-high pole. The court is divided in half, with two men and two women of each team playing side by side, so all face-offs are man-on-man or woman-on-woman—quite the potential for a girl-fight.

When it burst onto the scene in 1902, korfball generated some controversy for mandating that men and women share the same field. Players suffered accusations of immorality, especially since female uniforms displayed lewd bare knees and ankles (the horror!). Today korfball fans play in 57 countries, including the US, but the Netherlands has won every World Championship title since the competition's inception in 1978, with the exception of 1991, when Belgium triumphed.

ART AND ARCHITECTURE

You could say the Dutch have some experience when it comes to art. Dutch painters, after all, spurred the departure from the Gothic style of the Middle Ages, sparked the Northern Renaissance, and perfected oil painting—you know, just a few notable achievements short of finding the cure to cancer.

The First Dutch Masters

Jan van Eyck is sure to top any list of Amsterdam's best-known painters. In the 15th century, he was one of the first artists to use oil paint as a medium, and he impressed the world with renderings of detailed architecture and realistic portraits of subjects in long, multicolored robes. (Okay, Jan, we get it, you're pretty good.) Keep your eyes peeled for reproductions of Amsterdam's most beloved knocked-up lady in green, featured in **The Arnolfini Portrait**. Van Eyck's paintings are prized in museum collections around the world, but you can find a select few on display at the **Rijksmuseum**.

Although he probably could have been famous for bearing one of the most obscure names in history, **Hieronymous Bosch** decided to follow his artistic whims and left behind the Flemish style of van Eyck. His passion for originality carried him toward the cloud of Surrealism some 400 years before the larger Surrealist movement really got off the ground in the early 20th century. Notable for their departure from traditional technique, Bosch's paintings might call into question his mental stability—those fantastical demons and hellish punishments just aren't your average scene, man. This guy was either uncomfortably preoccupied with Hell, or he did some serious sinning in his spare time.

Reforming and Performing

During the **Protestant Reformation** of the 17th century, the Church stopped funding religious paintings, liberating artists from all the cumbersome Catholic symbolism. Dutch painters turned their gaze down from the heavens, up from Hell (thank God, no pun intended), and right into the realm of the living. Many small paintings commissioned by bourgeois Flemish families depicted small, laughing children with kittens, their great-great uncles and entire extended families, and other semi-laughable portraits—the kind that could substitute for today's embarrassing home videos.

The undisputed star of this Dutch Golden Age has to be **Rembrandt Harmenszoon van Rijn**. Rembrandt, as he is conveniently called, was marked for his masterful realism and the illusion of movement in the scenes he depicted. Initially celebrated by his compatriots, Rembrandt ended up alienating his clientele by taking an experimental turn and was forced to declare bankruptcy and die in poverty. Fortunately, his reputation endured better than his finances—try to get up close and personal for some quality time with **The Night Watch** and **Landscape with a Stone Bridge 2** at the Rijksmuseum.

Rembrandt's contemporary **Johannes Vermeer** is celebrated for creating windows into everyday 17th-century life. Among Vermeer's most renowned works is **Girl with a Pearl Earring,** widely hailed as the *Mona Lisa* of the north. Scarlett Johansson might be attractive in that movie, but this painting is probably worth putting down the remote and getting your butt over to the **Mauritshuis Gallery** in The Hague.

Caution: Falling Pianos

Amsterdam itself is something of an architectural miracle. The city's many waterways forced architects to get creative: canalside houses were built with many large windows to keep the weight of the buildings from sinking them into the ground, and tight quarters resulted in resorting to the tall and skinny. On the city's winding and characteristically narrow streets, homes were often built at terrifying angles so that large furniture could be hoisted through windows without hitting other buildings. Watch your head as you wander narrow alleys—not just for falling sofas, but for the hooks that served as pulleys to get them inside, which still stick out from just about every canal house.

HOLIDAYS AND FESTIVALS

HOLIDAY OR FESTIVAL	DESCRIPTION	DATE
Amsterdam International Fashion Week (AIFW)	A week of invitation-only catwalks and hoity-toity gatherings alongside public exhibitions and disco parties. Think *The Devil Wears Prada*, and show off your finest attire.	Late January
The Queen's Birthday	A day of national pride, chock-full of orange clothing and street parties galore. Although Queen Beatrix was actually born in January, she decided to keep the holiday on the springtime birthday of the previous queen, her mother.	April 30, or April 29 if the 30th is a Sunday
World Press Photo Exhibit	Oude Kerk hosts this celebration of the world's best photojournalism, combining disturbing images of warfare with the serene beauty of the natural world.	Late April to mid-June
WWII Remembrance Day	A solemn day to remember the victims of WWII from the Netherlands. Two minutes of silence are observed at 8pm.	May 4
Liberation Day	A day of public festivities to celebrate the country's liberation from the Nazi occupation.	May 5
National Windmill Day	The country's ever-proud windmills throw open their doors to the public, holding special and often educational events.	The second Tuesday of May
Amsterdam Gay Pride	Three days of tolerance and partying, featuring parades and street festivals for all sexual orientations.	Early August
Aalsmeer Flower Parade	Flower floats, flower art, and flower power in the world's tulip capital.	Early September
High Times Cannabis Cup	One long tokefest—at the end of this festival, the best hash and weed receive awards.	November
Sinterklaas Eve	On this night, the Dutch Santa Claus supposedly delivers candy and gifts to nice children. According to not-at-all-questionable local lore that suggests Santa might not be allowed within 200 yards of a school zone, the naughty children are kidnapped.	December 5

BRUSSELS

After wining and dining in Paris or weeding a few too many gardens in Amsterdam, many students only visit Brussels for a couple of nights as an obligatory stepping stone on the way to the next best thing. Yes, Brussels is a small city, but it's not the effective capital of Europe for nothing. Nowhere else in the world is it perfectly acceptable (and sometimes expected) to include chocolate- and ice cream-covered waffles, french fries with mayonnaise, rum- and champagne-flavored chocolates, and no less than one cherry-flavored beer in your daily diet. If that's not enough, throw in some *stoemp*—a heart attack on a plate of mashed potatos, cream, bacon, and usually a hunk of meat—between visiting three different publicly displayed (and revered) statues that involve public urination (it must be all that beer).

But don't be fooled into thinking that nourishment and laughable art are all that Brussels has to offer. A closer look at this colorful cultural center will reveal a city with an appreciation for art, music, and history (even history that is humble enough to admit its mistakes). Museums that won't leave your head drooping in boredom abound (don't miss the **Musée Royal de l'Armée et d'Histoire Militaire**—it's free!), and even the Metro is its own art museum: works of nearly every medium in adorn the stations. If the typical city museum tour is still not enough for you, visit any one of a number of the city's parks, four of which are located in or near the city center, and you will forget that you're in a city at all.

greatest hits

- **WAX PHILOSOPHIC.** Grab a glass of strawberry wine and talk philosophy at Goupil le Fol (p. 295).

- **LAND OF PLENTY.** Visit Fritland for fries so good you'll want to bitch-slap Ronald McDonald for claiming his are better (p. 287).

- **PUT ON YOUR BOWLER HAT.** Dive into a surrealist dreamland at the Magritte Museum (p. 280).

- **HANDSOME MANSION.** Slightly removed from the city center, the Horta Museum is an Art Nouveau architectural masterpiece of loopy iron railings, stained glass, and mirrors (p. 280).

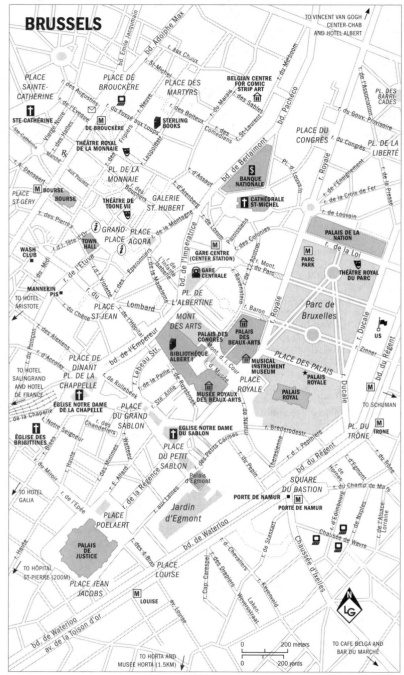

BRUSSELS

TO VINCENT VAN GOGH
CENTER-CHAB
AND HOTEL-ALBERT

PLACE
SAINTE-
CATHERINE

STE-CATHÉRINE

PLACE DE
BROUCKÈRE

PLACE DES
MARTYRS

BELGIAN CENTRE
FOR COMIC
STRIP ART

PL. DES
BARRI-
CADES

STERLING
BOOKS

DE BROUCKÈRE

THÉÂTRE ROYAL
DE LA MONNAIE

PLACE DU
CONGRÈS

PL. DE LA
LIBERTÉ

PL. DE LA
MONNAIE

BANQUE
NATIONALE

PLACE
ST-GÉRY

BOURSE

BOURSE

THÉÂTRE DE
TOONE VII

GALERIE
ST. HUBERT

CATHÉDRALE
ST-MICHEL

PALAIS DE LA
NATION

WASH
CLUB

GRAND-
PLACE

TOWN
HALL

PLACE
AGORA

GARE CENTRE
(CENTER STATION)

PARC
PARK

THÉÂTRE ROYAL
DU PARC

MANNEKIN
PIS

TO HOTEL
ARISTOTE

GARE
CENTRALE

PLACE
ST-JEAN

Lombard

PL. DE
L'ALBERTINE

Parc de
Bruxelles

MONT
DES ARTS

PALAIS DES
CONGRÈS

PALAIS DES
BEAUX-ARTS

US

TO HOTEL
SALINGRAND
AND HOTEL
DE FRANCE

PLACE DE
DINANT

PL. DE LA
CHAPPELLE

BIBLIOTHÈQUE
ALBERT I

MUSICAL
INSTRUMENT
MUSEUM

PLACE
ROYALE

PLACE DES PALAIS

PALAIS
ROYALE

PALAIS
ROYAL

ÉGLISE NOTRE DAME
DE LA CHAPELLE

MUSÉE ROYAUX
DES BEAUX-ARTS

ÉGLISE DES
BRIGITTINES

PLACE
DU GRAND
SABLON

ÉGLISE NOTRE DAME
DU SABLON

PL. DU
TRÔNE

TRONE

TO HOTEL
GALIA

PLACE
DU PETIT
SABLON

Palais
d'Egmont

SQUARE
DU BASTION

PLACE
POELAERT

Jardin
d'Egmont

PORTE DE NAMUR

PORTE DE NAMUR

PALAIS
DE
JUSTICE

TO HÔPITAL
ST-PIERRE (200M)

PLACE JEAN
JACOBS

PLACE
LOUISE

LOUISE

Chaussée de Wavre

Chaussée d'Ixelles

N

LG

TO HORTA AND
MUSÉE HORTA (1.5KM)

0   200 meters
0   200 yards

TO CAFE BELGA AND
BAR DU MARCHÉ

brussels

In a city with this much beer, it's not surprising that there's a group of students on every corner. Any bar you visit in Lower Town is pretty much guaranteed to be packed with students on the weekends, but **Delerium** in particular draws an enormous local and international crowd with their world-famous selection of beers and similarly infamous cocktail lounge. If you're looking to escape the tourist crowd, **Pl. Flagey** is a young adult favorite for its classic bars, performance spaces, and proximity to one of the largest Belgian universities, the Université Libre de Bruxelles.

Once you've cured your hangover, Brussels still has a lot to offer the student traveler. Fashion-forward youth pass the daylight hours at **rue Neuve,** the main shopping street in Brussels, which features department and chain stores that are much cheaper than those found on av. Louise. Students spend their afternoons lounging in the outdoor bars and cafes just west of the Bourse, calmly sipping beers and occasionally leaving their seats to purchase fries from nearby vendors. Those who don't want to splurge €5 on a beer at a bar can pick up drinks at a convenience store and take them to the Parc du Cinquantenaire, where groups of students relax on the lawn in sight of the triumphal arch. If high culture gives you that drunk slap-happy feeling, **BOZAR** offers tremendous student discounts on everything from art exhibitions to classical music concerts. Edgy concerts at the **Botanique** will force you into close contact (literally) with other students who pile in to listen to little-known bands; with lounge spaces and bars, the venue is a great place to connect with other hip young people over the next big thing in music.

orientation

orientation

The center of Brussels is roughly split between **Upper Town,** on the hill, and **Lower Town,** at the foot of that hill. These neighborhoods bleed into each other a bit, but the clear heart of the city is the **Grand Place** in Lower Town. These areas are encircled by a guitar-pick shaped loop of main roads and part of the Metro. The biggest Metro stops that serve this area are **Gare du Nord** in the north, Arts-Loi in the east, Place Louise in the south, **Gare du Midi** in the southwest, and Comte de Flandre in the west, with **Gare Centrale** smack-dab in the middle. Going east of Arts-Loi will take you to **Place Schuman,** the neighborhood that houses the EU and its parliamentary big-wigs along with the grand Parc du Cinquantenaire/Jubelpark and some of the city's coolest museums. South of the city center is **Louise,** best known for its shopping, and Place Flagey, where a picturesque pond is dotted with funky bars. These four areas—Upper and Lower Town in the center, Place Schuman in the east, and Louise in the south—make up the meat of Brussels. A bit farther northwest, at the end of the Metro, is **Heysel,** where you will find some of Brussels's more concentrated tourist traps, including the Atomium (which, however tourist trappy, you should still see).

call me!

The phone code for Brussels is ☎02.

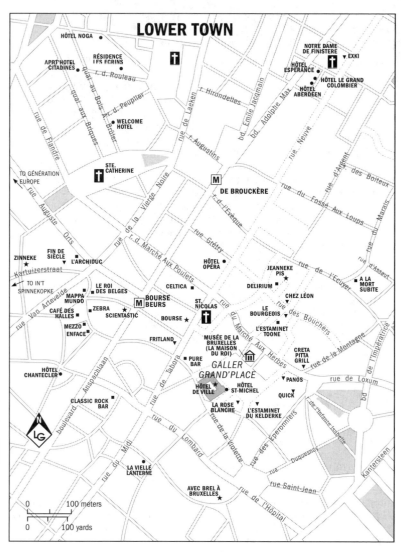

LOWER TOWN

Brussels is not a huge tourist destination, but those who do visit tend to stay near the **Grand Place**, or "Grand Plaza," where the **Musée de la Ville** (city museum) and the **Hôtel de Ville** (town hall) are located. The busy Grand Place is the heart of Brussels, where you will find the best of the city's waffles, chocolate, and tourists, but venturing away from this center and through the smaller, winding streets will allow you to really experience the city. ◪**Manneken Pis** is a straight shot from the Grand Place down **rue de L'Etuve;** going farther east and south will lead you into the Upper Town. Northwest of the Grand Place, **boulevard Anspach,** accessible by Metro stop Bourse, is a diagonal

brussels

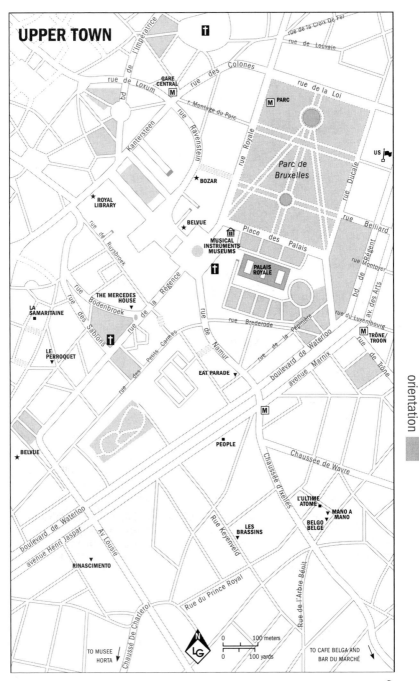

UPPER TOWN

- ✝
- GARE CENTRAL Ⓜ
- Ⓜ PARC
- US 🚩
- ★ BOZAR
- ★ ROYAL LIBRARY
- ★ BELVUE
- 🏛 MUSICAL INSTRUMENTS MUSEUMS
- ✝ PALAIS ROYALE
- THE MERCEDES HOUSE ▼
- LA SAMARITAINE ■
- ✝
- LE PERROQUET ▼
- EAT PARADE ▼
- Ⓜ TRÔNE/ TROON
- Ⓜ
- BELVUE ★
- PEOPLE ■
- L'ULTIME ATOME ▼
- MANO A MANO ▼
- BELGO BELGE ▼
- LES BRASSINS ■
- RINASCIMENTO ▼

Parc de Bruxelles

Place des Palais

rue de la Croix De Fer
rue de Louvain
rue des Colones
rue de Loxum
bd de l'Impératrice
rue de Ravenstein
r. Montage du Pere
rue Royale
rue de la Loi
rue Ducale
rue Belliard
rue de Montoyer
bd de Régent
av. des Arts
rue du Luxembourg
Kantersteen
rue de Pursbroek
rue de Bodenbroek
rue de la Régence
rue des Sablons
rue des Petits-Carmes
rue de Namur
rue Brederode
rue de la Pépinière
boulevard de Waterloo
avenue Marnix
rue de Tigne
Chaussée de Wavre
Chaussée d'Ixelles
Rue Keyenveld
Boulevard de Waterloo
avenue Henri Jaspar
Av. Louise
Chaussée De Charleroi
Rue du Prince Royal
Rue de l'Arbre Bénit

TO MUSEE HORTA

TO CAFE BELGA AND BAR DU MARCHÉ

N LG

| 0 | 100 meters |
| 0 | 100 yards |

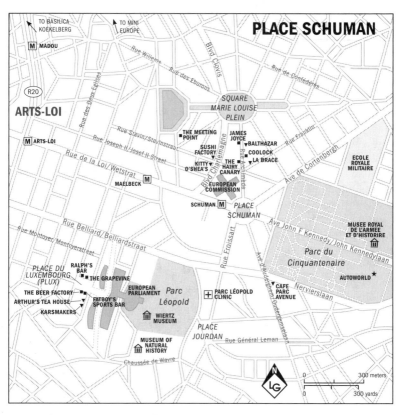

PLACE SCHUMAN

TO BASILICA KOEKELBERG

TO MINI EUROPE

Ⓜ MADOU

Rue Willems

Blvd Clovis

Rue des Eburons

Rue de Confederes

Ⓡ20

ARTS-LOI

Rue des Deux Eglises

Rue Joseph II/Josef II Straat

Rue Stevin/Stevinstraat

Ⓜ ARTS-LOI

Rue de la Loi/Wetstraat

Ⓜ MAELBECK

SQUARE
MARIE LOUISE
PLEIN

THE MEETING POINT

JAMES JOYCE

SUSHI FACTORY

BALTHAZAR

COOLOCK

KITTY O'SHEA'S

THE HAIRY CANARY

LA BRACE

Rue Franklin

EUROPEAN COMMISSION

Ave de Cortenbergh

ECOLE ROYALE MILITAIRE

SCHUMAN Ⓜ

PLACE SCHUMAN

Rue Belliard/Belliardstraat

Rue Montoyer/Montoyerstraat

PLACE DU LUXEMBOURG (PLUX)

RALPH'S BAR

THE GRAPEVINE

THE BEER FACTORY

ARTHUR'S TEA HOUSE

KARSMAKERS

EUROPEAN PARLIAMENT

FATBOY'S SPORTS BAR

Parc Léopold

WIERTZ MUSEUM

MUSEUM OF NATURAL HISTORY

Rue Froissart

Ave John F Kennedy/John Kennedylaan

Ave John F Kennedy/John Kennedylaan

Ave d'Auderghem/Oudergemselaan

PARC LÉOPOLD CLINIC

CAFE PARC AVENUE

Nerviersbaan

MUSEE ROYAL DE L'ARMEE ET D'HISTOIRE

Parc du Cinquantenaire

AUTOWORLD

PLACE JOURDAN

Rue Général Leman

Chaussée de Wavre

N

LG

0   300 meters

0   300 yards

that bisects the city where you will find basic needs like ATMs, pharmacies, and *alimentations*. Farther west of the Bourse and bd Anspach is **Place Saint-Géry,** home to most of Brussels's night owls. To the north is **rue Neuve,** a central shopping district filled with clothing outlets and fast food. Rue Nueve is flanked to the west by the beautiful neighborhood of **Sainte Catherine,** which is a bit pricey but still a welcome respite from the noise of the Grand Place.

UPPER TOWN

Upper Town is large enough that you might wonder why it's not just called "Everything That's Not Lower Town." It's divided into a number of smaller neighborhoods that wrap around the eastern and southern ends of Lower Town, each of which maintains a distinct personality despite rather blurred borders. These areas are home to Brussels's best museums and some fancy shopping—great places to spend the day before heading to the city center for an evening beer.

Unlike Lower Town, where the short blocks and unexpected turns may throw off foot travelers, it is the broad, traffic-laden streets and long city blocks that make Upper Town difficult to navigate by foot, so take advantage of the Metro and tram lines. Use the **Mont des Arts** and the **Place Royale** as your central anchors when navigating Upper Town. From there, the **rue Royale** will take you past the **Parc de Bruxelles** and many of the Upper Town's museums, galleries, and grand palaces, not to mention the Belgian Parliament. Be careful going much farther north than La

Botanique, especially at night; this area is unofficially known as Brussels's red light district. South of Place Royale are **boulevard de Waterloo** and **avenue de la Toison d'Or,** which hug the eastern edge of Upper Town and extend down to shopaholic heaven, **avenue Louise.** Boulevard de Waterloo becomes Boulevard du Midi, which takes you through **Marolles,** a generally avoidable neighborhood which poses a sharp contrast to the opulent av. Louise nearby.

PLACE SCHUMAN AND HEYSEL

Venturing outside the loose bounds of Upper and Lower Towns will take a few Metro stops, but it's worth leaving the busy city center for a day. Place Schuman (which typically refers to the Metro stop and its surrounding buildings) is just east of the city center and home to the **European Commission** and **European Parliament.** The area is much nicer than central Brussels but consequently is populated almost entirely by Eurocrats and doesn't really cater to the student crowd or the student budget. Parc du Cinquantenaire Jubelpark is a few steps farther east of Place Schuman and houses the **Musée Royal de l'Armée et d'Histoire Militaire** and **Autoworld,** which are definitely worth visiting after a picnic in the big park. To the south of Place Schuman is the European Parliament and Place du Luxembourg (or P'Lux), which feeds and waters all the tired politicians.

On the opposite side of town, northeast of the city center, is **Heysel,** the last major stop on the Brussels Metro. It seems far but only takes 20min. to reach and is worth the ride if only to see the **Atomium,** the signature structure from the 1958 World Expo. **Mini-Europe** is a fun little excursion if you're feeling the need to get in touch with your inner child.

accommodations

Accommodations in Brussels fill up quickly, especially during the week. The EU Parliament attracts Europe's elite and the pricey, bougie hotels that come with them. Most student-friendly accommodations are located slightly north of the **Grand Place** and are within walking distance of Lower Town. This is definitely where you want to stay if there is availability, especially if you're only in Brussels for a short period. Hotels will get more expensive in Upper Town, and the neighborhoods will generally get more unsafe for solo travelers the further south you get; try to avoid staying in the **Marolles** in the south or north of **Botanique** if possible. Many hostels and hotels will tell you to book online for the best rates, but we suggest just calling ahead when you want to make a reservation. There is no clearly defined high or low season in Brussels, although prices drop significantly in July and August, when Parliament is on vacation.

LOWER TOWN

2GO4 HOSTEL HOSTEL $$

99 bd Emile Jacqmain ☎02 219 30 19 www.2go4.be

2go4 is a haven for young solo travelers and students thanks to its strict no-large-groups policy. Shared spaces like the funky common room and the well-trafficked, well-stocked communal kitchen make for good opportunities to meet your fellow travelers. Amenities like individual reading lights and power outlets, plus the convenient location, make up for the street noise and substandard showers.

[M]Rogier. Follow bd d'Anvers and turn left onto bd Emile Jacqmain. i Linens included. Towels available for rent. Max. 6 people per group. Free Wi-Fi. Computers available. $ Dorms €21-29; singles €50-55. ⏰ Reception 7am-1pm and 4-10pm.

SLEEP WELL
HOSTEL, HOTEL $$

23 rue du Damier ☎02 218 50 50 www.sleepwell.be

Sleep Well has hostel and hotel components. Both are bright, cheerful, and cheap, and they share huge common areas (featuring colorful murals, foosball tables, pool tables, and comfy couches) and a popular bar. The hostel, though, has an inconvenient lockout between 11am and 3pm.

✦ ⓂRogier. *Follow rue Neuve and turn left onto rue de la Blanchisserie. Rue du Damier is on your right.* ⓲ *Breakfast and linens included. Towels available for rent. Wi-Fi €1 per 30min. Computer use free.* ⓢ *Dorms €20-24; singles €36; doubles €54.* ⓩ *Reception 24hr. Lockout 11am-3pm.*

HOTEL ESPERANCE
HOTEL $$$$

1-3 rue du Finistère ☎02 219 10 28 www.hotel-esperance.be

Concealed above a French style brasserie, Hotel Esperance has decorated each of its 11 rooms with bright blocks of color, meaning you could find yourself dozing in a calming blue room or trying to sleep amid garish purple walls. Each room, however, is furnished with grand chairs or desks, and the beds come with enough pillows to keep a family of 20 comfortable. A bit less lavish than its counterparts, this hotel will still provide comfort at a low price. Breakfast can be enjoyed in the very quaint dining area that also serves as a restaurant in the evening.

✦ ⓂDe Brouckère. ⓢ *Free Wi-Fi. Breakfast €10.* ⓢ *Doubles €80; triples €110.* ⓩ *Reception 24hr. Check-in 3pm. Check-out 11am.*

HOTEL OPERA
HOTEL $$$

53 rue St Grétry ☎02 219 43 43 www.hotel-opera.eu

Although "Hotel Opera" may bring to mind the sounds of shrill Italian bravado, this hotel is wonderfully quiet despite being just a couple blocks from the bustling Grand Place. The warmly colored rooms, complete with flowery peach quilts, are reasonably sized for a reasonable price, but it is the location that's absolutely prime. Sing your way toward the Lower Town nightlife or hum yourself a sweet lullaby and fall into a peaceful, blissfully quiet slumber.

✦ ⓂBourse. *Walk north on bd Anspach about 3 blocks, turn right onto rue St Grétry; the hotel is on the corner across from La Monnaie.* ⓲ *Free Wi-Fi. Breakfast included.* ⓢ *Singles €75-89; 1-bed doubles €89-99; 2-bed doubles €99-119; triples €119-139; quads €139-159. Special rates if you book online.* ⓩ *Reception 24hr.*

WELCOME HOTEL
HOTEL $$$$

23 quai Bois à Brûler ☎02 219 95 46 www.brusselswelcomehotel.be

Get ready for the cheesy plug: Welcome Hotel is not just a hotel, it's an experience. Cliché? Yes. True? Yes. The manager of this immaculate establishment spent time traveling the world and has used souvenirs from his sojourns to decorate his 17-room hotel, leaving each room with a different country theme. While visiting Brussels by day, guests here can fall asleep in Bali, Marrakesh, Cuba, or even the Silk Road. Bon voyage!

✦ ⓂSte-Catherine. ⓲ *Free Wi-Fi. A/C. Breakfast included. Pets allowed. Jacuzzi baths in some rooms. Gold Card available for return customers free of charge; guarantees at least €10 off the next visit. Family room available for up to 8 people; call for rates.* ⓢ *Singles €95; doubles €135, deluxe €155; suites €240. Discounted rates in July and Aug and when occupancies are low.* ⓩ *Reception 7am-11pm.*

HOTEL LE GRAND COLOMBIER
HOTEL $$$

8 rue du Colombier ☎02 223 25 58 www.hotelseurop.com

Sharing reception with Hotel Aberdeen (see below), Hotel le Grand Colombier is the better of the two adjoining hotels on this little side street. The rooms are some of the largest you will find in this price bracket; many even come with marble fireplaces (of the purely decorative variety). The colorful decor inside makes up for the building's less interesting exterior, and the rooms facing the street have a brilliant view of the mural outside.

🍴 Ⓜ*Rogier. Just off of rue Neuve.* 𝒊 *Free Wi-Fi. Breakfast €5.* Ⓢ *Singles €49-59; doubles €59-69; triples €75-89. Rates go down in July and Aug.* 🕐 *Reception 24hr.*

HOTEL ABERDEEN   HOTEL $$$
4 rue du Colombier   ☎02 223 52 58 www.hotelseurop.com

Hidden down a tiny side street, Hotel Aberdeen shares reception with Hotel Colombier (see above). The hotel has less character than Colombier but provides spacious rooms with wood floors, plush beds, and a view. Cheaper rooms with a little less comfort are available for a reduced price. Lucky for those hoping to snag some souvenirs, Hotel Aberdeen hugs Brussels's busy shopping district.

🍴 Ⓜ*Rogier. Just off of rue Neuve.* 𝒊 *Free Wi-Fi. Breakfast €5.* Ⓢ *Singles €65; doubles €75; triples €95.* 🕐 *Reception 9am-6pm. Check-in 2pm. Check-out noon.*

HELLO HOSTEL   HOSTEL $$
1 rue de l'Armistice   ☎47 193 59 27 www.hello-hostel.eu

Apart from their addiction to "Radio Nostalgie," this hostel is pretty great. It's not the most centrally located hostel, but it is right next to the Metro. The airy and spacious rooms are popular with young backpackers.

🍴 Ⓜ*Simonis (Leopold II). The hostel is down the street from the Godiva chocolate factory.* 𝒊 *Breakfast and linens included. Free Wi-Fi and computer use.* Ⓢ *Dorms €21-27.*

RÉSIDENCE LES ECRINS   HOTEL $$$
15 rue du Rouleau   ☎02 219 36 57 www.lesecrins.com

Though a small hotel, Résidence Les Ecrins provides plain but spacious rooms and a quiet neighboring street that offers patrons an ideal location in the Ste-Catherine neighborhood. Although this is a no-frills place, with such reasonable prices in a wonderful area, it's hard to find anything to complain about.

🍴 Ⓜ*Ste-Catherine.* 𝒊 *Free Wi-Fi. Breakfast included.* Ⓢ *Singles €50, "standard" €85; doubles €60/95; triples €110; quads €125; suites €135.* 🕐 *Reception 8am-10pm.*

HÔTEL SAINT-MICHEL   HOTEL $$$$
15 Grand Place   ☎02 511 09 56 www.hotelsaintmichel.be

Given that it's the only hotel actually located in the Grand Place, Hôtel St-Michel could charge a lot more than it does for its rooms. Justifiably, rooms with a view of the Grand Place cost a bit more than those without, but most rooms are about the same size and have been renovated within the last year. The gregarious owner will gladly satisfy all your needs and answer any question with a smile; you will be happy to see a welcoming face after tiresome days and nights gallivanting about your new backyard—the very heart of Europe's capital.

🍴 Ⓜ*Bourse. Located in the Grand Place (about 2 blocks behind Bourse).* 𝒊 *Free Wi-Fi; €5 per day when rates are discounted July-Aug. Breakfast included.* Ⓢ *With view singles €150, discounted €109; doubles €185/120. Without view singles €138/80; doubles €150/98. Extra bed €23.* 🕐 *Reception 24hr.*

APRT'HOTEL CITADINES   APARTMENTS $$$
51 quai Bois à Brûler   ☎02 221 14 11 www.citadines.com

If you're preparing for a long stay in Brussels, or maybe just looking to stay in more comfortable digs, Citadines will sort you out. Each of the three areas of the building—aptly named Brussels, Strasbourg, and Luxembourg—provide studios and apartments (a studio with an additional bedroom), each of which is available in standard or deluxe. The longer your stay, the cheaper your daily rate, so these accommodations are really only ideal for long-term travelers.

🍴 Ⓜ*Ste-Catherine.* 𝒊 *Free Wi-Fi. Breakfast €14. Book online for best rates.* Ⓢ *Studios for up to 2 people from €90; apartments for up to 4 people from €140. Rates change frequently; call or check online.* 🕐 *Reception 24hr.*

accommodations

LA VIEILLE LANTERNE   B&B $$$$

29 rue des Grands Carmes   ☎02 512 74 94 www.lavieillelanterne.be

While an awning that reads "La Vieille Lanterne" suggests your arrival at "The Old Lantern," you'll have to make your way through a lace and Manneken Pis souvenir shop to reach this six-bedroom B&B. Accessed by a dizzyingly narrow spiral staircase tucked in the back of the building, you can *pis* away your concerns when you reach the small but comfortable rooms that offer a view of Brussels's favorite public urinator. The little intersection where this B&B is located is heavy with foot traffic but remains secure—only hotel guests can access the building after the doors lock at 8pm.

✦ Ⓜ*Bourse. Walk south on bd Anspach 1 block, turn left onto rue du Lombard, walk 3 blocks, and turn right onto rue de l'Etuve. Across the intersection from Manneken Pis.* **i** *Free Wi-Fi. Breakfast included.* Ⓢ *High-season singles €90; doubles €95; triples €125. Low-season singles €76-78; doubles €86-90; triples €105-112.*

UPPER TOWN

◪ JACQUES BREL   HOSTEL $$

30 rue de la Sablonnière   ☎02 218 01 87 www.laj.be

Surprisingly lively, Jacques Brel provides a modern bar and lounge in its reception area. Rooms are comfortable, priced for budget travelers, and not nearly as boring as the exterior suggests. The hostel is conveniently located right near the action of Upper Town, a 20min. walk from the Grand Place.

✦ Ⓜ*Botanique. Head south down rue Royale (away from Botanique) and take the 1st left.* **i** *Breakfast and linens included. Reserve 4 weeks in advance. Free Wi-Fi and computer access.* Ⓢ *6- to 8-bed dorms €21; 3- to 5-bed dorms €23; singles €36. Over age 25 add €2.* ⚅ *Reception daily 7am-midnight. Lockout 10am-3pm.*

BRUEGEL   HOSTEL $$

2 rue Haute   ☎02 511 04 36 www.youthhostels.be

Bruegel has one of the most important amenities a hostel can have: a hoppin' bar. It looks like a watering hole you'd find in the city center and stays open until all the guests have gone to bed, so you can finish up your night with some dancing and karaoke. Each of the three floors has a lounge or seating area with free Wi-Fi.

✦ Ⓜ*Gare Central. Head west along bd de l'Empereur. Bruegel is opposite the skate park.* **i** *Linens included. Free Wi-Fi.* Ⓢ *3- to 4-bed dorms €20; singles €32. More expensive for over age 25.* ⚅ *Reception daily 7-10am and 2pm-1am. Lockout 10am-2pm.*

HOTEL STALINGRAD   HOTEL $$$

117 av. de Stalingrad   ☎02 511 11 32 hotel.stalingrad@skynet.be

We're not sure why Hotel Stalingrad chose to name itself after the scariest place to room and board in Europe, but fear not: there are no ◪**Red Guards** at the entrance, and the staff's a lot sweeter than Lenin and his Commie chums. This small hotel in Marrolles has small but not overly cramped rooms, and the decor is bright and cheerful compared to other hotels nearby. If you're expecting a quiet room with a view, though, prepare to be disappointed: with the train station nearby, this neighborhood is pretty noisy. And just so you know, no, you can't see Russia from your room if you stay here.

✦ Ⓜ*Gare du Midi. At the big intersection with the overpass, the hotel is on the northwest side of the tracks, on the middle corner before the overpass.* **i** *Breakfast €5. Free Wi-Fi.* Ⓢ *Singles €60; doubles €75.* ⚅ *Reception 24hr. Check-in and check-out noon.*

VINCENT VAN GOGH CENTER—CHAB
HOTEL $

8 rue Traversière
☎02 217 01 58 www.chab.be

This hostel has a welcoming interior lobby full of natural light, and high ceilings open up the narrow rooms. Low rates and no curfew or lockout make up for this hostel's lack of flair. The Vincent Van Gogh Center is located in a quiet neighborhood, so if you plan to paint the Lower Town red, find a group of hostel friends and head to the nearby Metro stop.

♯ ⓂBotanique. Head north along rue Royale, past La Botanique, then turn right onto rue Traversière. Main building and reception are on the right; another building with dorms is located across the street. ⓘ Free Wi-Fi. Breakfast and linens included. Ages 18-35 only. Max. stay 7 days. ⓢ 8- to 10-bed dorms €19.50; 6-bed dorms €21.50; 4-bed dorms €23; 3-bed dorms €29; singles €35; doubles €54-56. Ⓚ Reception 24hr. Check-in 2pm. Check-out 10am.

HOTEL ARISTOTE
HOTEL $$$

5 av. de Stalingrad
☎02 513 13 10

Come to Aristote to question your own existence or ponder why hotel rooms in Europe are so darn tiny. Find something to muse over, as the simple, generic rooms at this hotel don't offer much in the way of philosophical stimulation. But with a location on the quieter end of av. de Stalingrad, Hotel Aristote hosts a pleasant and peaceful atmosphere for patrons.

♯ ⓂGare du Midi. Walk about 6 blocks up av. de Stalingrad; the hotel is on the left before the big intersection. ⓘ Free Wi-Fi. Breakfast €6. ⓢ Singles €45; doubles €55. Ⓚ Reception 24hr. Check-in after 2pm. Check-out noon.

HOTEL SABINA
HOTEL $$$

78 rue de Nord
☎02 218 26 37

A little guest house with comfortable common spaces and small but pretty singles, Hotel Sabina is located near some of the major Upper Town sights.

♯ ⓂBotanique. Head south along rue Royale, then turn left up rue de la Sablonnière, which leads to rue de Nord on the right. ⓘ Breakfast included. Free Wi-Fi. ⓢ Singles €40-70. Ⓚ Reception daily 7am-11pm.

HOTEL DE FRANCE
HOTEL $$$

21 bd Jamar
☎02 522 79 35 www.hotel-de-france.be

Hotel de France might be a little confused about what country it's in (it happens to the best of us), but this cheap hotel will wake you up in the morning with its bright, white corridors and peachy air freshener. Overbearing perfume and institutional corridors aside, the rooms are bright, cheerful, and will keep you comfortable. Although the bathrooms aren't the biggest you'll find in Brussels, the reasonable rates make staying here completely bearable.

♯ ⓂGare du Midi. At the big intersection with the overpass, Hotel de France is on the northwest side of the tram tracks; turn left onto bd Jamar, and the hotel is on the right. ⓘ Free Wi-Fi. Breakfast €5. Book online for free breakfast. ⓢ Singles €49-69; doubles €59-79. Ⓚ Reception 24hr. Check-in noon.

HOTEL ALBERT
HOTEL $$$$

27-29 rue Royale Ste Marie
☎02 217 93 91 www.hotelalbert.be

Despite the dodgy paint job in some rooms and the dim hallway lighting, Hotel Albert has reasonably sized rooms that put you close to Brussels's main museum district. Apart from being located in a quiet neighborhood set just north of downtown Brussels, this hotel doesn't offer up much else.

♯ ⓂBotanique. Head up rue Royale, past Le Botanique; the hotel is on the other side of Église Royale Ste-Marie. ⓘ Free Wi-Fi. Breakfast €7.50. ⓢ Singles €70; doubles €95; triples €129; quads €149. Ⓚ Reception 24hr. Check-in 2pm. Check-out noon.

accommodations

Fortunately or unfortunately, *Manneken Pis* is not one of those expressions in a foreign language that sounds hilarious but would be insensitive to mock—it means precisely what you might expect. Literally translated as "The Little Man Peeing," *Manneken Pis* is one of Brussels' most celebrated landmarks. The current bronze version of the *Manneken Pis*, which has been around since 1619, was designed by Jerome Duquesnoy, but it is commonly held that a stone version of the statue existed before the current bronze model, perhaps dating as far back as 1388.

There's a boatload of stories about how *Manneken Pis* came into being. One story recounts the exploits of the 2-year-old Belgian Lord Godfrey III of Leuven, whose troops were fighting against the Berthouts of Grimbergen; the precocious tot, who was hung from a tree in his cradle in order to inspire his troops, proceeded to pee on the Berthouts, who eventually lost the battle. Another version of the story involves a wealthy merchant who, on a visit to Brussels with his family, lost track of his son; miraculously, his son was found joyfully urinating in a small garden, and the wealthy merchant commissioned the sculpture in celebration of being reunited with his mischievous offspring.

Regardless of how it got there, *Manneken Pis* is absolutely worth seeing when traveling in Brussels. Located on the corner of rue de l'Étuve and rue du Chêne, the statue is often dressed in an elaborate costume, of which there are over 800. The costumes, which are changed multiple times a week, commemorate important dates in Belgian history, celebrate members of the Belgian working class, or represent the national dress of countries whose tourists regularly pass through the city. Unsurprisingly, there are times when water is not the only thing spouting forth from *Manneken Pis,* as the fountain is occasionally transformed into an elaborate beer-tap, much to the delight of passers-by (soon to be passers-out).

Due to the statue's high profile, it has been stolen 7 times, but has each time been returned safely to its fountain-top perch. For everyone's sake, make sure that *Manneken Pis* is the only one peeing into his fountain—control your intake of Belgian beer and ensure that you do not become the drunken tourist who defaces this important piece of Belgian heritage. It's only cute if you're bronze.

brussels

HOTEL GALIA   HOTEL $$$

15-16 pl. du Jeu de Balle   ☎02 502 42 43 www.hotelgalia.com

This hotel is perfect for bargain hunters, but not necessarily because of the prices or the hotel itself. Hotel Galia is, however, ideally situated near the daily Marolles flea market, which starts up around 4am—when the best deals in the city can be found. Once you've snagged that €3 antique necklace, you can take your pre-sunrise purchase back to the hotel and catch up on sleep in the small but well-furnished rooms. The open terrace area is also a great place to watch the hagglers in the market. Keep an eye out for the rendition of Tintin that guards the reception desk.

✈ Ⓜ*Louise. Head along rue des Renards until you hit pl. du Jeu de Balle.* ℹ *Free Wi-Fi.* Ⓢ *Singles €65-75; doubles €75-85; triples €90-105; quads €120-140.*

sights

Brussels is definitely underrated in the things-to-see category. Aside from its notorious and unusual statues and the **Grand Place**, Brussels has a diverse array of museums and several lovely city parks that are worth your time. The **Musée Royal de l'Armée et d'Histoire Militaire** in Place Schuman has a huge collection of war paraphernalia, including an impressive collection of planes and vehicles. **Autoworld,** located right across the way, offers a fun history lesson whether or not you're actually into cars. **Mini-Europe** is a bit gimmicky but still a fun time, and the **Atomium** is simply a must-see. Parc Leopold and the Square Marie Louise Plein are beautiful respites from the city noise. So while you definitely shouldn't miss everyone's favorite urinating boy, don't let anyone fool you into thinking that's all there is to see in Brussels.

LOWER TOWN

The Lower Town has most of Brussels' famous sights. Avoid most of the museums (they tend to be rip-offs) and instead spend your time exploring the charming side streets around the Grand Place.

▧ MANNEKEN PIS   STATUE
Intersection of rue de l'Étuve and rue du Chêne

Prepare to be both amused and underwhelmed by the icon of Brussels—a 2ft. tall statue of a little boy peeing into a pond. Don't ask us what it means (his actual origins are unknown); all we know is that he is continually swamped with giggling tourists and that he likes to celebrate certain national holidays and events. He even indulges in the weird happenings and habits of Brussels—hundreds of Elvis fans once congregated at his feet as he was dressed in blue suede shoes and a white jacket. For true insight into the enigma that is the Manneken, start up a conversation with the souvenir vendor directly in front of the sight—he's been there for over 20 years and has some interesting stories to tell.

🔆 *Head southwest from the Grand Place along rue de l'Étuve. The Manneken is 3 blocks down.*

i *Check the vendor's calendar to see what the Manneken Pis will be wearing and when.*

GRAND PLACE   SQUARE
Grand Place

The historic center of Brussels is a grand place known, naturally, as the Grand Place. Soak up the grandeur in one of the square's many cafes, where you can sip coffee and watch tourists rush through with their cameras. Many of them are too focused on what's in front of them to look up—that's a mistake, as the really worthwhile, intricate architecture is actually above you. Grand Place really lets down its hair at night, so make sure to return once the sun goes down, when the famous **Guildhall buildings,** including the **Hôtel de Ville** and the **Maison de Roi,** are dramatically illuminated. During mid-August, the Grand Place is home to the "Flower Carpet," which sees green-thumbed Belgians use colorful native flora to create a remarkable display.

🔆 Ⓜ*Bourse. Head straight down rue de la Bourse, which leads to the northeast corner of the square.*

MUSÉE DU CACAO ET DU CHOCOLAT   MUSEUM
9-11 rue de la Tête d'Or   ☎02 514 20 48 www.mucc.be

What's more Belgian than peeing statues? Chocolate, that's what. Opened in 1998 by Jo Draps, the daughter of one of the founders of Godiva, the Musée du Cacao et du Chocolat is a chocoholic's dream (or worst nightmare, if it's Lent). Fresh milk chocolate is churned in the entrance, and the back room allows you to watch a chocolate chef work his magic. As far as magic goes, seeing a bunny appear out of chocolate is about as remarkable as seeing one appear out of a hat, but no experience can possibly be bad when you're surrounded by this much chocolate.

✈ ⓂBourse. *Head straight down rue de la Bourse, which leads to the northeast corner of the Grand Place. The museum is just south of the Grand Place.* Ⓢ *€5.50; students, seniors, and ages 12-16 €4.50; under 12 free with parent.* ⓒ *Open Tu-Su 10am-4:30pm.*

MUSÉE DE LA VILLE DE BRUXELLES (LA MAISON DU ROI)   MUSEUM
Grand Place   ☎02 279 43 50 www.bruxelles.be

The dignified building that houses the Musée de la Ville de Bruxelles is arguably a bigger deal than the museum itself. La Maison du Roi (King's House) was built in the 13th century to both demonstrate the power of the Belgian prince and serve as an economic center for the city. After being rebuilt and renovated, the building now houses exhibits on the history of the Brussels, the renovation of the city, and even pays special homage to the infamous **Manneken Pis.** Make sure to check out the stone remains from the original building on the first floor and the room with model replicas of 13th-century Brussels. The highlight of this grand museum, however, has to be the display on the top floor, which features the numerous outfits that the Manneken Pis has worn throughout the ages. Look for the little boy's firefighter, bee-keeper, and Welsh guard get-ups, or peruse the many cultural outfits that have been presented to the statue as gifts from other countries.

✈ *In the northeast corner of Grand Place.* Ⓢ *€4; students, seniors, and groups €3; children €2. Under 18 free on weekends.* ⓒ *Open Tu-W 10am-5pm, Th 10am-8pm, F-Su 10am-5pm.*

HÔTEL DE VILLE   HISTORIC BUILDING
Grand Place   ☎02 279 20 10

Dating from the Middle Ages, the Hôtel de Ville's Gothic tower can be seen from anywhere in Brussels and is one of the city's most photographed sights. Be sure to get a look inside via one of the guided tours. The main courtyard features two grand fountains of Poseidon near the entrance, and the tour will take you around some of the building's most beautiful rooms. On weekends, it is common to see weddings taking place at the Hôtel de Ville, so keep an eye out for a bride and groom posing on the balcony for photos (then do the typical tourist thing and snap your own shot of the happy couple).

✈ ⓂBourse. Next to Tourist Info. Ⓢ €5, students and seniors €3. ⓒ Tours W 3pm, Su 10am and 2pm.

AVEC BREL À BRUXELLES   MUSEUM
11 pl. de la Vieille Halle aux Blés   ☎02 511 10 20 www.jacquesbrel.be

What would Brussels be without an entire museum dedicated to its most beloved *chanteur* Jacques Brel? Avec Brel À Bruxelles offers two methods to get to know Monsieur Brel: *J'aime l'accent Bruxellois,* an audio-guided walking tour of Brussels, and *J'aime les Belges,* an exhibition inside the actual museum. The walking tour explores Brel's Brussels and the places that inspired him for the first 24 years of his life, while the exhibition is a series of five rooms that feature videos of interviews with and about Brel. Beware, you culturally-immersed traveler you: the exhibition is about one hour and 15min., and the city tour is about two hours and 40min., so Avec Brel À Bruxelles should probably be reserved for those who have particularly a keen interest in one of Europe's most popular French singers.

✈ ⓂGare du Central Bruxelles. *Walk southeast on rue Duquesnoy about 3 blocks to the roundabout, then walk straight across and continue southeast; the museum is on the corner at the next turnstile.* ⓘ *Audio tours in French only. Written guides available in English.* Ⓢ *Exhibition and audio tour €5. Walk and audio tour €8.* ⓒ *Exhibition open July-Aug daily 10am, last entry 5:30pm; Sept-June Tu-F 10am-6pm, Sa-Su noon-6pm.*

JEANNEKE PIS   STATUE
Off rue des Bouchers

The poor lonely sister of Manneken Pis is locked away behind bars (albeit pretty ones) down a tiny alleyway and isn't even listed by the Tourist Office in its official

brussels

guides—where are women's rights activists when you need them? Jeanneke Pis shows no shame as she squats down to do her business in a small pond. Conceived by Denis Adrien Debourvrie in 1985, the statue doesn't actually urinate anymore, but local lore has it that if you toss a coin in Jeanneke's puddle, the little girl will bring you luck. So throw a penny in the pond for good fortune and feminism.

☞ Ⓜ*Bourse. Just off rue des Bouchers. Take a right after Chez Léon.*

ÉGLISE SAINT-NICOLAS
CHURCH

1 rue au Beurre ☎02 513 80 22

This grand church was built around 1000 years ago, when the city of Brussels was founded, but all that remain of the original edifice are some 12th-century archways and the main nave from the 13th century. The far transepts house three ornate altars. The first is dedicated to the Virgin Mary and encrusted in gold; the second is the High Altar, built in Louis XVI style; the third, on the far right, is dedicated to St. Nicolas himself. The most recent addition to the church was made during its last renovation in 1956, when Guy Chabrol designed a stunning stained glass window depicting the Assumption of the Virgin Mary.

☞ Ⓜ*Bourse. Just behind the Bourse building.* Ⓢ *Free.* 🕔 *Open daily 10am-4pm.*

BOURSE
HISTORIC BUILDING

Palais de la Bourse, bl. Anspach

By the 19th century, Brussels was ready for an upgrade. And we're not talking about the cell phone kind. As part of a commercial and architectural renewal plan, the city traded its oh-so-glamorous butter market for a stock market, and today's Bourse is still home to the Belgian Stock Exchange. Designed by LP Suys, this Neo-Renaissance building lies on Brussels's busy commercial thoroughfare, **boulevard Anspach.** Nowadays, the steps to the Stock Exchange are often the camping ground for some of Brussels's less desirable inhabitants, but Auguste Rodin's lion sculptures and impressive ornamentation are usually squatter-free. Although visitors aren't allowed inside, be sure to check this place out as you walk by or pose for a quick photo-op.

☞ Ⓜ*Bourse.* 𝒊 *Not generally open to casual visitors.*

ÉGLISE SAINTE-CATHERINE
CHURCH

pl. Ste-Catherine 50 ☎02 513 34 81

This regal church lies at the north end of pl. Ste-Catherine and is the crowning jewel of its peaceful little neighborhood. The original 12th-century chapel went the way of the butter market (see **Bourse,** above) and was rebuilt and expanded in the 19th century. The current church was in turn threatened with demolition in the 1950s, when city officials wanted to replace it with a parking lot. Fortunately, the building was saved, but the renovations it so desperately needs have yet to be completed. The church, however, remains beautiful and worth a visit. Inside, you will find a rather impressive 15th-century statue of the Virgin and Child, which locals rescued in 1774 after Protestants tried to chuck it down the Seine.

☞ Ⓜ*Ste-Catherine.* Ⓢ *Free.* 🕔 *Open M-Sa 10am-5pm, Su 10am-mid-afternoon.*

ZINNEKE
STATUE

rue de Chartreux

Seriously, Brussels? This humorous addition to the city's peeing posse is, to say the least, a rather absurd sight to behold. At the intersection of rue des Chartreux and rue du Vieux Marché, there's a bizarre statue of a dog doing his business on a post. Tom Frantzen, a Flemish sculptor, is the barking mad creator of the Zinneke, which is supposed to embody the irreverent spirit of the city. Perhaps it just means people (and dogs) in Brussels really just can't hold it in.

☞ Ⓜ*Bourse. Head down rue Auguste Orts and take the 1st left onto rue des Charteux. The Zinneke is on the corner of the street.*

ÉGLISE NOTRE DAME DE FINISTÈRE CHURCH

rue Neuve ☎02 217 52 52

It's not every day that you find a delicately restored 18th-century church sandwiched between an H&M and a McDonald's, but this is Brussels, after all. Église Notre Dame de Finistère is situated in the center of Brussels' bustling commercial area and boasts a lavish Baroque interior. The church's grand altar portrays Moses holding the 10 Commandments, and artwork from the 16th-18th centuries depicts various religious moments. For those who enjoy organ music, the church offers free concerts on Mondays for all to enjoy.

🚏 ⓂDe Brouckère. Head east along rue du Fossé aux Loups and turn left onto rue Neuve. ⏰ Free. ⏰ Open daily 10am-5pm. Organ concerts M 12:45-1:30pm.

SCIENTASTIC MUSEUM

Bourse metro station ☎02 732 13 36 www.scientastic.be

Don't be put off by the location of this brilliant museum—although many of Brussels's homeless hang around in the Bourse Metro station, this museum's a load of kid-friendly fun. Head downstairs and follow the large, colorful signs to Scientastic, which looks a bit like a fortune teller's tent. The museum's goal is to make science interactive and accessible for both kids and adults, but travelers who don't have children might find Scientastic less than enchanting. The good news is that adults can try a "freebie" visit before deciding to pay for entrance. If you do visit, make sure you check out the Manneken Pis recreation to discover how water actually flows, and experiment around with color shadows. The very comical 👍**mirror performance** demonstrates the magic of reflections, as the tour guide uses various illusions to appear to float, shrink, explode, and even stab himself.

🚏 ⓂBourse. Head toward the Anspach exit and follow the signs for Scientastic. ℹ English-speaking tour guides and English walkthrough guide available. $ €7.90, under 26 and seniors €5.30. ⏰ Open M-Tu 10:30am-5:30pm, W 2-5:30pm, Th-F 10:30am-5:30pm, Sa-Su 2-5:30pm.

UPPER TOWN

The Upper Town has many of Brussels's best sights: big museums, pretty palaces, and beautiful greenery. If you happen to be in town on the first Wednesday of the month, you're in luck—many of the museums are free in the afternoon.

👍 **MAGRITTE MUSEUM** MUSEUM

3 rue de la Régence ☎02 508 32 11 www.musee-magritte-museum.be

René Magritte may not be the most famous painter in the Musées royaux des Beaux-Arts collection, but he's certainly one of the most interesting. The paintings of this master of Surrealism question the relationship between words, images, and reality. He's beloved in this country for pulling off the rare feat of being both famous and Belgian. Start your tour at the glass elevator, where Magritte paintings on the opposite wall blur together eerily as the elevator rushes by. Make sure to check out the collection of hand-drawn images—compiled by Magritte, Scutenaire, Hamoir, and Nougé—in which each of the friends took turns drawing a different limb or cross-section of the human form without looking at what their colleagues had previously drawn. These might just be the world's most valuable round of telephone Pictionary.

🚏 ⓂParc. Walk south down rue Royale. $ €8, seniors €5, students €2, under 19 and 1st W of each month after 1pm free. Audio tour €4. Combined ticket with Musées Royeaux des Beaux-Arts €13, students €3. ⏰ Open Tu 10am-5pm, W 10am-8pm, Th-Su 10am-5pm.

👍 **HORTA MUSEUM** MUSEUM

25 rue Américaine ☎02 543 04 90 www.hortamuseum.be

Once the home of influential architect Victor Horta, this tiny museum now pays homage to its namesake. With four floors and an attic, the museum features Horta's famous Art Nouveau style that transitions and flows throughout the house. Admire the beautiful central stairwell and stained glass, in particular. The house can only fit about 45 people inside at a time, which means you might have to stand in line to get in; the beauty of the house and the tranquility of its secluded gardens, however, are well worth the wait.

☞ ⓜLouise. Walk south on av. Louise, turn right onto Chausee de Charleroi, walk 5-10min. (about 7 blocks), and turn left onto rue Americaine; the museum is on the right. *i* No photography. ⓢ Adults €7, students and seniors €3.50, under 12 €2.50. ⓢ Open Tu-Su 2-7:30pm.

🖼 **CATHÉDRALE DES SAINTS MICHEL ET GUDULE**   CATHEDRAL
15 rue du Bois Sauvage   ☎02 217 85 45   www.cathedralestmichel.be
Perhaps the grandest cathedral in Brussels, Saint Michel et Gudule expects respectful silence from all its visitors. Blabbermouths have no fear: when you hear the grand organ mysteriously playing from the lofty stretches above, you'll have no problem shutting up. The original foundations of the building date back to the ninth century (more recent areas of the foundation can be seen in the crypt for €1, or for free by peeking from the glass panels in the floor above). 11th-century architecture snobs didn't like its original design, so the church was rebuilt in the Gothic style over the next three centuries. As you wander through the splendor of the Catholic cathedral, gaze up to the saintly statues guarding the walls. Each holds a symbolic item—St. Philippe, for example, holds the book of knowledge, while St. Peter clutches a set of golden keys.

☞ ⓜGare Centrale. ⓢ Free. Crypt €1. Free choir concerts throughout the year. 🕑 Open M-F 7:30am-6pm, Sa-Su 8:30am-6pm. Mass in French Su 10, 11:30am, and 12:30pm.

MUSÉE DU JOUET   MUSEUM
24 rue de l'Association   ☎02 219 61 68   www.museedujouet.eu
The slogan of this toy museum is *un musée qui s'amuse*—"a museum that will amuse you." Although valuable items are stored behind glass cabinets, this haphazardly thrown together museum is a messy jumble of toys and screaming kids. While children will have a blast here, those who are traveling sans-rugrats might not find themselves as enthused. Many of the exhibits, however, feature toys from days gone by, so if you're feeling particularly keen to relive your childhood, check out the marionette puppet area, teddy bear school, and toy robot section.

☞ ⓜBotanique. Walk south on rue Royale; museum is the first left after Av. Galilee. ⓢ €5.50; students, children, and seniors €4.50; family €18. 🕑 Open daily 10am-noon and 2-6pm.

MUSICAL INSTRUMENTS MUSEUM (MIM)   MUSEUM
2 montagne de la Cour   ☎02 545 01 30   www.musicalinstrumentsmuseum.be
If you have the slightest interest in music, the history of instruments, or just cool art deco buildings, you should get yourself on down to MIM. This museum just celebrated its 10th anniversary, and the 10 floors of its collection features impressive interactive exhibits, though not every floor has something to look at. A large glass elevator leads to the top floors and the rooftop restaurant, which boasts a panoramic view of the city (see **Food,** Upper Town). The main exhibits move from the fourth floor downward and host interactive displays on keyboards, strings, and western art music—there's even a sound lab. The most ingenious part of the museum is the audio tour, which, instead of being vocal, is just 🎵music. They even select an Instrument of the Month, highlighting equipment a bit more exotic than the piano or the violin.

☞ ⓜParc. *i* Permanent collection free 1st W of each month after 1pm. ⓢ €5, under 26 and over 64 €4, under 13 free. Audio guide free with admission. 🕑 Open Tu-F 9:30am-5pm, Sa-Su 10am-5pm. Last tickets sold 4:15pm.

PARC DE BRUXELLES   PARK
Between Belgian Parliament and Royal Palace
Walk the perimeter of Brussels's most beautiful park to view the **Palace of the Nation** and other monuments, or head inside for the trees and foliage. The wide green

patches, benches, and fountains make the park an ideal place for a picnic lunch, or just to rest your feet after a busy morning walking around the museums.

⚡ Ⓜ*Parc. Look around you, it's everywhere.* ⏰ *Open daily 7am-11pm.*

CENTRE BELGE DE LA BANDE DESINÉE   MUSEUM
20 rue des Sables   ☎02 219 19 80 www.cbbd.be

Don't expect to find Marvel or DC on the shelves of this comic book museum, dedicated to the likes of Tintin and Boulle and Bill. If these names mean nothing to you, then you might as well not bother. The Moomins currently rule the roost in this exhibition space...okay, if that name's also running blanks for you, then this definitely isn't the museum for you. But if those names excite you to your inner international-comic-book-nerd core, then the Centre Belge de la Bande Desinée may be your new home. With a Smurf statue, a bust of Tintin, and the famous red-and-white rocket from the Tintin series all in the lobby, the comic book excitement begins before you even get into the permanent collection. The display is continually changing, but you can expect classic French and Belgian comic strips in both original and remastered form. Real comic book nerds head downstairs to the library, where you can read as many comics as you want, or pop next door to the bookshop where you can purchase your own to take home with you.

⚡ Ⓜ*Rogier.* ⏰ *€8, ISIC card holders and ages 12-18 €6, under 12 €3.* ⏰ *Open Tu-Su 10am-6pm. Reception closes at 5:30pm.*

MUSÉES ROYAUX DES BEAUX-ARTS   MUSEUM
3 rue de la Régence   ☎02 508 32 11 www.fine-arts-museum.be

The Musées royaux des Beaux-Arts, attached to the Magritte Museum, holds a vast collection split between modern and ancient works. The modern arts section displays mind-boggling works from the 19th through 21st centuries, including provocative paintings and sculptures that will either fascinate you or make you wonder why you bought a ticket. Head upstairs for the ancient arts; highlights include works by Reubens, Jacque-Louis David's famous *The Death of Marat*, and a permanent exhibit on "Art and Finance." Before you leave, make sure to visit the adjacent ◪**Garden of Sculptures.**

⚡ Ⓜ*Parc. Walk south down rue Royale.* Ⓢ *€8, students €5, under 18 and 1st W of each month after 1pm free. Combined ticket with Magritte Museum €13, students €3.* ⏰ *Open Tu-Su 10am-5pm. Last entry 4pm.*

BOZAR   EXHIBITION SPACE
23 rue Ravenstein   ☎02 507 82 00 www.bozar.be

A center of innovation and discovery, Bozar puts on exhibitions ranging from art, to history, to geographical concerns. The modern arts space holds numerous exhibitions at once, as well as a cinema and different music festivals. Although the 2011 season had yet to be announced at time of printing, you can expect exhibits along the lines of 2010's "Visionary Africa," which celebrated the culture and heritage of African countries through its art. For a great view of the city, head up to the roof of the building once you exit, past the Bozar studios, and along the metal staircase.

⚡ Ⓜ*Parc.* Ⓢ *Generally €5-10, but admission depends on event. Student rates available.* ⏰ *Box office open July-Aug M-F 11am-5pm; Sept-June M-Sa 11am-7pm. Exhibits open Tu-W 10am-6pm, Th 10am-9pm, F-Su 10am-6pm.*

BELVUE   MUSEUM
7 pl. des Palais   ☎070 22 04 92 www.belvue.be

Through a selection of videos, artwork, and even '60s clothing models, the BelVue's grand exhibits will better acquaint you with Belgian history. The permanent collections are chronological, beginning in 1830, with Belgium's Independence and ending with Brussels's current position as the "capital of Europe." Although it appeals most to the history buffs, it has some contemporarily relevant exhibits—including one on the developments of the EU since WWII—and temporary exhibitions that have ranged from "Brussels, A City With a View" to "Celebration Tables."

✂ ⓜParc. Ⓢ €5, ages 18-25 €3, under 18 free. Combined ticket with Coudenberg Palace €8/5/ free. 🕓 Open Tu-F 10am-5pm, Sa-Su 10am-6pm.

PALAIS DE JUSTICE   HISTORIC BUILDING
pl. Poelart

Enter the Palace of Justice, the building with the golden roof perched on high above Lower Town, and you will be thrown into a world of powdered wigs and black capes. Lawyers sweep past the gawking tourists, who are allowed to explore some of the ancient corridors and lobby areas. As Belgium's supreme court of law, this is very much a functioning courthouse, so do adhere to the "private" door signs. Stand in the grand lobby and admire the stately staircases and intricately designed hallway. A walk down the stone stairwell on the south side will take you outside, near a glass elevator that offers a great view of the city as it descends.

✂ ⓜLouise. 🕓 Open M-F 10am-5pm. Ⓢ Free.

PALAIS ROYALE   PALACE
pl. des Palais   ☎02 551 20 20

This ornate palace was once the location of the ancient Coudenberg Palace and is now one of Brussels' grandest buildings. Although the palace only opens for tours during July and August, it's still worth venturing down to the gates to admire the beautiful gardens and try to distract the guards on duty—we think they're not allowed to blink. At night, the palace is beautifully lit and provides the perfect backdrop for a **photo.** If you do go for a tour, you will see some very impressive chambers, including the magnificent Throne Room, drawing rooms, and a majestic Hall of Mirrors.

✂ ⓜParc. Ⓢ Free. 🕓 Open July-Aug; exact times subject to change. Check ahead on the Belgian tourist office website (www.opt.be).

ÉGLISE ROYALE SAINTE-MARIE   CHURCH
pl. de la Reine   ☎02 218 06 93 www.lescoteaux.be

This grand and lavish church is only open for a couple hours each day, but if you are in the area at the right time, make sure you take advantage of the free tour. Église Royale Ste-Marie is a foreboding figure in the Brussels's skyline, and although the interior isn't as impressive as the exterior, the altar is beautiful and the architecture extremely impressive. However, the red light district that surrounds the church is less than appealing, so perhaps Sainte Marie is best admired from afar.

✂ ⓜBotanique. Pass Botanique on the left; the church is straight ahead at the end of rue Royale. Ⓢ Free. 🕓 Open after Easter-Oct 31 Tu-F 11am-1pm, Sa-Su 2:30-5pm; Nov 1-Easter Sa-Su 2:30-4pm. Mass Tu-Th 8pm, Su 9:30am in French. Guided tours 1st Su of each month, 2:30pm in French.

LE BOTANIQUE   BOTANICAL GARDENS
236 rue Royale   www.botanique.be

These beautiful gardens provide the ideal spot to catch a bit of sun or take a break from sightseeing. Le Botanique has a concert venue on its terrace where up-and-coming artists put on free shows.

✂ ⓜBotanique. Ⓢ Free. 🕓 Open daily Oct-Apr 8am-5pm; May-Sept 8am-8pm.

PLACE SCHUMAN AND HEYSEL

🖼 MUSÉE ROYAL DE L'ARMÉE ET D'HISTOIRE MILITAIRE   MUSEUM
3 Parc du Cinquantenaire   ☎02 737 78 33 www.klm-mra.be

This grand museum is absolutely massive, and you can easily get lost among the weapons and swords on display here. The aviation hall is the largest part of the museum; you'll spend most of your time here, where light aircraft from WWI and WWII abound, including the legendary Dakota and a Hunter MK6 that you can actually walk through. History buffs and war nerds could easily spend a couple of hours here, but those of you who aren't impressed by generations of war technology, uniforms, equipment, and strategy may want to just do a quick in-and-out while at the nearby park.

➥ ⓂSchuman. Head through the Arcade du Cinquantenaire; the museum is on the left, through the parking lot and across from Autoworld. $ Free. Audio guides €2-3. ⏰ Open Tu-Su 9am-noon and 1-4:45pm. Aviation hall open Tu-Su 9am-4:45pm. Sky Cafe open 11am-4pm.

👍 PARC DU CINQUANTENAIRE — PARK

This park's **Arcade Cinquantenaire** looks like a cross between the Arc de Triomphe and the Brandenburg Gate, so take some pictures of it and try to convince your gullible/clueless friends that you went to Paris or Berlin (for bonus points, use two different photos of it and convince them you went to both). A walk east along the park will bring you to **Autoworld,** the **Musée Royal de l'Armée et d'Histoire Militaire,** and the **Musées Royaux d'Art et d'Histoire**—which means that, even if it rains, you have some shelter (we recommend the free Military Museum). This park is less crowded, though perhaps also less grand, than the Parc de Bruxelles.

➥ ⓂSchuman. At the end of rue de la Loi.

AUTOWORLD — MUSEUM

11 Parc du Cinquantenaire ☎02 736 41 65 www.autoworld.be

Take a spin through Autoworld for a historical tour of the motorcar and a large display of some of the world's oldest and newest automobiles. Racing cars, WWI jeeps, and futuristic models sit side-by-side in what looks like a converted car warehouse. Even if you don't know a Chrysler from a Clio, this museum is a fascinating look into the evolution of modern transportation. Some cars switch out on a monthly basis, so there is always something old and new to see.

➥ ⓂSchuman. Head through the Arcade du Cinquantenaire; Autoworld is on the right, across from the Military Museum. $ €6, students €4.70, ages 6-13 €4, under 6 €2.25. ⏰ Open Apr-Sept 10am-6pm; Oct-Mar 10am-5pm.

ATOMIUM — MONUMENT

Sq. de l'Atomium ☎02 475 47 77 www.atomium.be

For some, the Atomium is a horrific eyesore in the Brussels skyline; for others, it's a stroke of architectural genius. Built for the 1958 World Expo, André Waterkeyn designed this monument to resemble the atom of an iron crystal—just 165 billion times bigger. The resulting structure is over 100m high, and you can reach the top at the astounding pace of 5m per second in Europe's fastest elevator (although this isn't the first place we've found that makes that claim). The top of the Atomium offers a panoramic view of the city, as well as a restaurant and cafe, a permanent exhibition on the '58 Expo and the Atomium's construction, and temporary exhibits on science and European culture.

➥ ⓂHeysel. $ €11, students and ages 12-18 €8, ages 6-11 €4, under 6 free. Audio tour €2. ⏰ Open daily 10am-6pm. Last entry 30min. before close.

MINI-EUROPE — INTERACTIVE PARK

Bruparck ☎02 474 13 11 www.minieurope.eu

If you can't afford to visit as many different countries as Europe holds, or if you have a serious Napoleon complex that needs attention, Mini-Europe will satisfy your needs. Although you are likely to run into tourist-trapped families or hooligan kids on a scavenger hunt for their class field trip, Mini-Europe is a fun way to mix up the sightseeing and museum routine. Blue buttons at each display will play that country's national anthem and usually cause some sort of entertaining activity among the country's mini-people, mini-cars, mini-boats, or mini-bulls and -toreadors. Be sure to go on a day with good weather and take some pictures with the Atomium in the background for some serious optical illusions.

➥ ⓂHeysel. Ⓜ €13.80, under 12 €10.30. Combination tickets with Atomium €23.10, under 18 €20.30, under 12 €15.20. ⏰ Open daily July-Aug 9:30am-8pm; Sept 9:30am-6pm; Oct-Jan 10am-6pm; mid-Mar to June 9:30am-6pm.

MUSÉES ROYAUX D'ART ET D'HISTOIRE
MUSEUM
10 Parc du Cinquantenaire   ☎02 741 72 11 www.mrah.be

The vast collections of Brussels's Museum of Art and History come mainly from the world's ancient civilizations, with particularly impressive collections of Aztec, Roman, Egyptian, and ancient Islamic art. It's worth a visit if you're in the neighborhood and like art history, or if you just want gawk at the massive Easter Island stone head. Most displays are in French and Dutch.

✦ ⓜ*Schuman. In the far southwest corner of Parc du Cinquantenaire.* ⓢ *€5, students and under 18 €4.* ⓞ *Open Tu-F 9:30am-5pm, Sa-Su 10am-5pm.*

BASILICA KOEKELBERG
BASILICA
1 parvis de la Basilique   ☎02 421 16 67 www.basilicakoekelberg.be

The Basilica Koekelberg is the fifth largest church in the world, a number that becomes increasingly daunting as you get closer and closer to its impressive façade. From the Simonis Metro station, you will have to trek across the long rectangular park to reach the church, but it's worth taking the time to enjoy a lazy stroll through the canopy of trees that line this area. Once inside, the interior of the church is somewhat underwhelming given that there are equally impressive churches on just about every other street corner in Europe. The real reason to visit the basilica is for the panoramic view of Brussels from the top of this monstrous building.

✦ ⓜ*Simonis.* ⓘ *Guided tours available by reservation.* ⓢ *View €4, students €3.* ⓞ *Open daily in summer 9am-5pm; in winter 10am-4pm. Last admission to view 30min. before close.*

MARIE-LOUISE PLEIN
PARK
Formerly a marshy swamp, the Marie-Louise Plein is now a park, complete with endearing ducks and a massive fountain in the center of the lake. The dirt paths lead to segmented corners of the grass that are ideal for a game of soccer with your chums or a quiet picnic with your lover. A walk around the border of the park and through the streets to the north provides a prime example of Brussels's Art-Nouveau houses, which were built to make the area more appealing to the affluent crowd moving to the city at the beginning of the 20th century.

✦ ⓜ*Schuman. Walk north on rue Archimede, which leads to the central square of the park.* ⓢ *Free.*

PARC LÉOPOLD
PARK
rue Belliard

Parc Léopold sits right at the foot of the European Parliament; pick a perch on the grassy banks and watch the Eurocrats rush by in their fine suits, scarfing down lunch on the way back to the office. The less manic locals take to the grass to relax and snack, especially on *frites* bought from pl. Jourdan just a few meters away. The park was the location of Brussels Zoo until, in 1876, all the animals died; Brussels's historians remain fuzzy on the details. Today the only animals here are the pigeons who will try to share your lunch—and the stuffed animals in the Natural History Museum at the top of the hill.

✦ ⓜ*Schuman.* ⓢ *Free.* ⓞ *Open daily until 10pm.*

WIERTZ MUSEUM
ART GALLERY
62 rue Vautier   ☎02 648 17 18 www.fine-arts-museum.be

Formerly the home and studio of Antoine Wiertz himself, this small house is now a museum that honors his life and studio, in conjunction with the Musée des Beaux Arts in Upper Town. As you climb the steps to the entrance, you get the feeling that this gallery isn't going to be too overwhelming, but a step into the studio is enough to knock the wind out of you, with some of Wiertz's most fantastic and apocalyptic works towering above you. All the work in this room is positioned in the exact spot where Wiertz painted it, while the smaller salon on the left side of the exhibit houses some of his smaller pieces and sketches. Many of these pieces are routinely sent off to temporary exhibits in Paris and the rest of the world, so it is not uncommon for some of his smaller works to be missing from the collection. A brochure will set you back €1.50, but if you talk to the curator, she'll tell you anything you want to know.

♯ ⓂSchuman. *Head through Parc Léopold and follow the signs to rue Vautier.* Ⓢ *Free.* 🕐 *Open Tu-F 10am-noon and 1-5pm. Open Sa-Su by appointment for groups only.*

EUROPEAN PARLIAMENT   GOVERNMENT BUILDING
60 rue Wiertz   ☎02 284 21 11 www.europarl.europa.eu

Most of the tour here involves watching a portable video that closely resembles a PBS special, so if you tend to snooze through that kind of thing, grab a coffee beforehand. While the tour itself can get dull, the building and the ambience are still impressive (and if nothing else, they let you keep the headphones). If you're lucky (or good at planning), you'll get to see Parliament when it's actually in session. During debates, look for the translators working in real time in each of the 23 official EU languages.

♯ ⓂSchuman. *Walk through Parc Léopold and head to the northeast corner. Look for the visitors' entrance sign on rue Wiertz.* Ⓢ *Free.* 🕐 *Tours M-Th 10am and 3pm, F 10am, Sa-Su 10am and 3pm. It's best to arrive 15min. early.*

NATURAL HISTORY MUSEUM   MUSEUM
29 rue Vautier   ☎02 627 42 38 www.naturalsciences.be

If you're looking to keep the kids entertained, or if you just love dino-skeletons and stuffed 🔳**mammals,** this museum should be on your list. Belgium has had a strong connection to dinosaurs since the very first fossilized skeleton was discovered there in the 19th century; it is now on display in this museum. The North and South Pole exhibits are also entertaining, with stuffed polar bears and penguins ideally positioned for photo-ops. Temporary exhibits are often geared toward kids, so the permanent displays are probably more worth your time. Don't miss the extensive shell collection, where you may come across local art students sketching and painting these intricate specimens.

♯ ⓂSchuman. *Head through Parc Léopold and follow the signs to rue Vautier.* Ⓢ *€9, students €8, ages 6-17 €6.50, under 6 free. Free for teachers with ID. Free every first W of the month after 1pm.* 🕐 *Open during the school year Tu-F 9:30am-5pm, Sa-Su 10am-6pm; summer Tu-Su 10am-6pm.*

PLACE SCHUMAN   GOVERNMENT BUILDINGS
Place Schuman

As you stand in the center of this horrific roundabout, you may wonder what's so special about it. Surprisingly, this hopelessly congested area is where all of the EU's important decisions are made. The European Commission, the governing body that must approve laws made by members of the European Parliament, is located in the cross-shaped building on the square. So is the European Council building, which locals say looks like a sandwich with glass in the middle. Take a moment to note the importance of this bizarre location before leaving to wander through the prettier parks and squares of the EU district.

♯ ⓂSchuman. Ⓢ *Free.*

food

Even though it's the capital of the EU, Brussels does not have capital prices. With *friteries* and waffle joints on every other corner, in addition to the traditionally meat-and-potato heavy Flemish diet, don't expect to tighten the notches on your belt any time soon. Most restaurants have outdoor terraces, and the weather is almost always pleasant enough to enjoy the fresh air. Tourist traps are sprinkled about the more authentic places, but it's not too hard to distinguish between the rip-offs and the real deal.

LOWER TOWN

The Lower Town offers some of the best places to get all your artery-clogging cravings met. There are also plenty of touristy rip-offs, most of which are centered on the **rue des Bouchers**. For late-night munchies or a meal on the run, try the **rue du Marché aux Fromages,** just off the Grand Place—it's sometimes called the "rue des pittas" or "kebab street."

▓ FRITLAND   FRITERIE $

49 rue Henri Maus   ☎02 514 06 27

Forget about arteries: we'll gladly wash down as many fistfuls of creamy, mayonnaise-dipped French fries with as many cans of blonde Belgian beer as we like, *merci beaucoup.* Especially when the whole thing only costs €5 per round (seriously, €3 for a mountain of fries and sauce, €2 for the beer). Take your fries to go or sit outside and tip the one-man, Beatles/Bob Dylan cover band down the street if his acoustic musings make your meal of cardiac arrest all the more enjoyable.

❦ Ⓜ*De Brouckere. Head northwest on rue de l'Evêque and turn left onto bd Anspach. Turn left onto rue des Pierres; Fritland is on the left.* Ⓢ *Beer €2. Fries €3. Chicken kebab €3.* ⏲ *Open M-Th 11am-1am, F-Sa 11am until dawn, Su 11am-1am.*

▓ MOKAFE   CAFE $

9 Galerie du Roi   ☎02 511 78 70

Tucked inside the fancy (and expensive) Galerie du Roi is the charming Mokafe, a cafe specializing in waffles—not the €1 sugarballs sold around Mannekin Pis, but the proper Belgian kind, served on a real plate with powdered sugar on top. You'll be dining with locals, a few tourists, and the biggest waffle snobs of them all: little old Belgian ladies. Entrees can be pricier, but lunch items and snacks tend to be affordable.

❦ *From the Grand Place, take the rue de la Colline on the eastern side to reach the Galerie du Roi. It looks like a shopping center inside a palace.* Ⓢ *Sandwiches €2-4. Waffles €3-5.* ⏲ *Open daily 7am-8pm, but hours are flexible.*

▓ CRETA PITTA GRILL   GREEK $

6 rue du la Montagne   ☎0474 97 34 22

When the cooks bring out your pita pocket, you may scoff at the deceptively small size, thinking they have mistaken your appetite for that of a child. You will soon discover, however, that great things come in small packages. Hot and fresh, these pockets make for great drunk food or a delicious midday snack. If you are still feeling slighted by the size, though, a pita will only set you back about €4, so you can always try for a more hefty helping of food with one of the *assiettes* options.

❦ *From Grand Place, take the northeast corner to rue du Marché aux Herbes. Across from Panos and to the right. i Takeout available.* Ⓢ *Pitas €3.50-5. Salads €7-10. Plats €8-14.* ⏲ *Open daily 11:30am until dawn.*

▓ IN'T SPINNEKOPKE   TRADITIONAL, BELGIAN $$$

1 pl. Jardin aux Fleurs   ☎02 511 86 95 www.spinnekopke.be

Spinnekopke (that's "spider's head" in Flemish) might not sound like an appetizing name for a restaurant. But once you take in this rustic tavern's candlelit tables and crowds of locals, you'll know that you've stumbled across something very exciting. Green-aproned waiters will attend to your table with the utmost attention. For a really tasty meal, try one of the many sauces available for their steak (steak €17.50, with sauce €3), including a brilliant cheese, limbek beer, and cream sauce.

❦ Ⓜ*Bourse. Head down rue Orts and turn left onto rue des Charteux, which leads to pl. du Jardin aux Fleurs. i English menus available.* Ⓢ *Plats €12-25. Desserts €6-9. Beers €2.50-5.* ⏲ *Open M-F noon-3pm and 6-11pm, Sa-Su 24hr.*

food

FIN DE SIÈCLE
BELGIAN $$

9 rue des Charteux   ☎02 513 51 23

Don't let the borderline pornographic prints of greased up hands caressing female lady parts turn you off (or on). We assume those aren't the hands cooking your food. Aside from the uncomfortable choice of wall art, Fin de Siècle is a perfect gem. With a small patio, a deep interior, and high ceilings, Fin de Siècle caters to a relaxed, intimate crowd of regulars looking to enjoy a respite from the rowdy bar scene of nearby pl. St Géry. So sit back, relax, and nurse a cold beer while enjoying some excellent cuisine.

✦ ⓂBourse. Head down rue Auguste Orts and take a left onto rue des Charteux. ⑤ Plats €12-19. ⓀOpen daily in the evening until late.

FRITERIE TABORA
FRITERIE $

4 rue de Tabora

The absurd thing about the whole "freedom fries" episode (okay, one of the many absurd things about the whole "freedom fries" episode) was that fries aren't French: they're Belgian. Their fresh *frites* are fried twice and served with your choice of sauce (mayo is the way to go local). Tabora slso serves Flemish fast-food classics like *bitterballen* and *krokets*, but with such huge portions, a large *frites* could easily count as lunch—yeah, you just ate a meal entirely of French fries, but when they're this good, why would you want anything else?

✦ ⓂBourse. Adjacent to Église St-Michel. ⑤ Small €1.80; large €2.30. Sauce €0.50. ⓀOpen daily 10am-6am.

CHEZ LÉON
FRITES $$$

18 rue des Bouchers   ☎02 511 14 15 www.chezleon.be

This popular restaurant spans several storefronts along the very busy rue des Bouchers and is always a safe option when choosing somewhere to dine. Although there is nothing too exciting or particularly noteworthy about Chez Léon, its 11-page menu and homemade beer will keep things interesting. A family place, expect to find plenty of regulars and locals eating here.

✦ ⓂDe Brouckere. Walk 1 block south down bd Anspach to rue Grétry and turn left. Continue down rue des Brouchers; Chez Léon is about 3 blocks in, across from Le Bourgeois. ⑤ Meat dishes €10-20. Fish €17-27. Kids under 12 with parents eat free. ⓀOpen M-Th 11:30am-11pm, F-Sa 11:30am-11:30pm, Su 11:30am-11pm.

LA ROSE BLANCHE
TRADITIONAL $$

11 Grand Place   ☎02 513 64 79

Grab a window seat at La Rose Blanche and enjoy ogling at tourists in the Grand Place below while savoring this restaurant's traditional wood-fired meat and fish dishes. An old-fashioned restaurant located in a rustic, two-story house, La Rose Blanche specializes in meaty goodness, including lamb or pork accompanied by an array of veggies for just €9.

✦ In the far south corner of the Grand Place, just past the tourist office. ⑤ Lunch €9. Express lunch €13. Entrées €5-14. Plat €13-25. Daily special €9. ⓀOpen daily 11am-11:30pm.

CHAO CHOW CITY
CHINESE $

89-91 bd Anspach   ☎02 512 82 83

A large Cantonese-style restaurant just south of Bourse, Chao Chow City has tasty food and the best lunch deal in Brussels. The daily special (€3.80 for lunch and €5.80 for dinner), usually served with lightning speed, turns hordes of hungry, budget-savvy tourists and locals into happy, bloated customers.

✦ ⓂBourse. Head south on bd Anspach, toward the Bourse building. ⑤ Most plats €7-8. ⓀOpen daily 11am-midnight.

brussels

LE BOURGEOIS TRADITIONAL, FRITERIE $$$

17 rue des Bouchers ☎02 511 84 45

Though its name suggests otherwise, this cozy little restaurant is anything but pretentious. The doorway is decorated with small sailing ships and guarded by the naughty Manneken Pis; students and local seniors lunch side-by-side next to a burning log fire. At only €12, Le Bourgeois's daily set menu is a great price for two courses and comes with a wide variety of choices. The restaurant also serves up the classic *moules frites* (€17-19). The cheeky waiters will try to impress you with their English, so be sure to laugh at their jokes.

*[M]De Brouckere. Walk 1 block south down bd Anspach to rue Grétry and turn left. Continue down rue des Brouchers; the restaurant is about 3 blocks down, across from Chez Léon.* *[$] Lunch €12. Plats €12-22. Mussels €17-19. Fish €22-28.* ⏰ *Open daily noon-midnight.*

L'ESTAMINET DU KELDERKE TRADITIONAL

15 Grand Place ☎02 511 09 56 www.restaurant-estaminet-kelderke.be

A evening seat on the terrace may just be the highlight of L'Estaminet du Kelderke. Watch tourists trudging through the illuminated Grand Place while chowing down on the house special, *moules frites*, which come in a very large (and apparently bottomless) bucket. The waiters are dressed to the nines and provide quality service that won't cost a fortune. The mood here can get very romantic, so we suggest you treat that special someone (or maybe just a new hotel friend you've been crushing on) to a night of indulgence and nice views of the Grand Place.

*[M]Bourse. In the northwest corner of the Grand Place.* *[$] Entrées €6.50-15. Plats €10-25.* ⏰ *Open daily noon-11pm.*

EXKI ORGANIC, FAST FOOD $

78 rue Neuve ☎02 219 19 91 www.exki.com

Exki is the perfect spot to grab and go or order and sit. The wall of refrigerated items has sandwiches, salads, wraps, fresh fruit, and health foods galore. Freshly cooked soups, quiches, and lasagna are also available in individual portions. Prices are lower if you get takeout, but the free Wi-Fi may compensate for the higher eat-in prices. Regardless, the food here is good and quick. Exkis are scattered about Brussels, but this is the main location and offers plenty of indoor and outdoor seating.

*[M]Rogier. Head down rue Neuve; the restaurant is about 2 blocks down on the right.* ***i*** *Free Wi-Fi.* *[$] Hot and cold drinks €1-3. Prepared dishes €4-6.50.* ⏰ *Open M-F 8am-7pm, Sa 9am-7pm.*

PUBLICO BELGIAN $$$

32 rue des Chartreux ☎02 503 04 30 www.publicobxl.be

This spacious restaurant combines traditional food with a modern atmosphere. The staff will happily guide travelers through the menu of classic Belgian dishes, including *stoemp* (sausage and mashed potatoes), various meat stews, and a good selection of vegetarian options. The weekday *prix-fixe* menu, which gives you a *potage*, choice of entree, and coffee for €11.50, is a good deal.

*[M]Bourse. Walk straight down rue Jules Van Praet, turn right onto rue Orts, then take a quick left onto rue des Chartreux.* *[$] Plats €9-16.* ⏰ *Open daily 11am-midnight. Kitchen open M-F noon-3pm and 6pm-midnight, Sa noon-midnight, Su noon-3pm and 6pm-midnight.*

QUICK FAST FOOD $

101 rue du Marché aux Herbes ☎02 511 47 63 www.quick.be

This French fast food chain looks just like a McDonald's, but with fancier salads and burgers that actually look and taste like burgers. But just because the food here is quality doesn't mean you'll have to pay an arm and a leg for it; Quick is easy on a budget, especially if you can snag the student discount. While there are Quicks scattered throughout the city, this one is most central and has free Wi-Fi.

*[M]Bourse. From Grand Place, take the northeast corner to rue du Marché aux Herbes and turn right.* ***i*** *Free Wi-Fi.* *[$] Burger combo €5-6; 2 burgers, maxi fry, and maxi soft drink €7 with student ID. Other meals €6.40-7.30. Salads €6.* ⏰ *Open daily 10am-11pm.*

PANOS BAKERY $

85 rue du Marché aux Herbes ☎02 513 14 43 www.panos.be

Panos is a not-so-hidden gem just steps beyond the Grand Place. Here, fresh ingredients are used to make deli sandwiches of different sizes and ready-to-grill panini that you can select from the display case. A filling and tasty meal with a refreshing cold drink here can easily cost you less than €8; if you have room left in your stomach, there will certainly be room left in your wallet for a sweet pastry or a loaf of bread to take home.

➤ [M]Bourse. From Grand Place, take the northeast corner to rue du Marché aux Herbes; the bakery is on the corner on the right. [$] Deli sandwiches €2-4. Pastries €0.50-2. ⏰ Open daily 6:30am-7pm.

UPPER TOWN

Eating in the Upper Town on a budget takes a mix of determination, flexibility, and creativity. If you're near the **Place de la Liberté,** a number of convenience stores carry snacks and sandwich fixings for a picnic in the **Parc de Bruxelles.** In the southern part of Upper Town, the area around **Place Flagey**—though far from the city center—boasts a number of interesting and moderately priced eateries.

👍 **EAT PARADE** SANDWICHES $$

87 rue de Namur ☎02 511 11 95

The only procession here is the line of Brussels's businessmen stretching out the door, and if you can make it past the packed crowd to the counter of this cozy lunchtime joint, you'll see why they're eager to be part of the spectacle. Whether you choose from the house list of sandwiches and soups or pick out the incredibly fresh ingredients yourself, do as the locals do and take your *chef d'œuvre* to the nearby Parc de Bruxelles for the perfect summer picnic in front of the Royal Palace. One bite of the Normand sandwich (brie, arugula, apple slices, *sirop de Liège*, walnuts; €3.70) and you'll be calling the mayor to pitch in for a celebratory float.

➤ [M]Port de Namur. Walk northwest on rue du Namur; Eat Parade is on the next corner after the big intersection. [$] Sandwiches €4. ⏰ Open M-F 7am-3:45pm, Sa 9:30am-4pm.

👍 **LE PERROQUET** SALADS AND PITA $$

31 rue Watteeu ☎02 512 99 22

If you're starting to feel weighed down by all those fries and waffles drowned in chocolate, head to Le Perroquet for a vegetable cleanse. The menu, with its 33 different salads and 72 varieties of pita, was created in collaboration with a dietician, and the servings, though generous, are healthy enough to keep your cardiologist at bay. Butterfly chairs make the quiet terrace a great place to enjoy a drink, while the marble tables and checkered tile inside provide a nice setting for a meal with your health-conscious significant other.

➤ [M]Louise. Head northwest on av. de la Toison d'Or; at the roundabout, take the 3rd exit onto rue des Quatre Bras; continue onto pl. Poelaert. At the next roundabout, take the 2nd exit onto rue de la Régence and turn left onto rue Van Moer. Continue onto rue Watteeu; Le Perroquet is on the left. ℹ €12 min. credit cards. [$] Pitas €6.50-7.50. Salads €9.50-15. Mixed drinks €7.50-9.50. ⏰ Open M noon-11:30pm, Tu-W noon-midnight, Th-Sa noon-1am, Su noon-11:30pm.

THE MERCEDES HOUSE BRASSERIE $$$

22-24 rue Bodenbroek ☎02 400 42 63

Looking for a way to combine your love of cars with some fine Belgian dining? This brasserie is part of the Mercedes House, which showcases Mercedes-Benz cars, and is an ideal location for a coffee or light lunch. Hot drinks are available and can be enjoyed on the terrace outside, where you can also admire the shop's crop of shiny cars. At lunchtime, you can sample traditional dishes that won't drive away with your money, but if you want to take a different kind of spin, order a bottle of champagne at €50 a pop.

➤ [M]Parc. [$] Entrées €11.50-15.50. Plats €15.50-24. ⏰ Open M-F 11:30am-3pm.

DELIZ SPRL DELI $
34 rue du Congrès ☎02 203 93 13 www.deliz.eu
A welcome respite from the expensive brasseries of the area, this bright deli offers sandwiches, pastas, and omelets that make for a fresh and filling meal before hitting up the major museums nearby.
☴ Ⓜ*Parc. Walk north on rue Royale and turn right onto rue du Congrès.* Ⓢ *Sandwiches €2-3.50. Omelets €6-8. Pasta €9.* Ⓚ *Open M-F 9am-3pm.*

MANO À MANO ITALIAN $$
8 rue St-Boniface ☎02 502 08 01
The St-Boniface area has become a popular lunch and dinner spot for businessmen and Brussels's younger crowd. Along this line of eateries, Mano à Mano whips up traditional Italian dishes—the smells that dance out of the kitchen alone are likely to give you a foodgasm. And once you see the ridiculously reasonable prices, you may just have to come more than once. The interior has an open, truly Italian feel to it, but the terrace is really the place to eat. Tables here are in high demand, so you may want to arrive earlier; most travelers, however, agree that Mano à Mano is well worth the wait.
☴ Ⓜ*Port de Namur. Walk down Chausée d'Ixelles about 4 blocks, turn left onto rue Solvay and right onto rue St-Boniface. Located between L'Ultime Atome and Le Belgo Belge.* Ⓢ *Pasta €8.50-13. Pizza €10-14.* Ⓚ *Open M-F noon-2:30pm and 7-11pm, Sa-Su 7-11pm.*

RESTAURATION NOUVELLE TRADITIONAL $$$
2 rue Montagne de la Cour ☎02 502 95 08 www.restauration-nouvelle.be
Feel seriously swanky high atop the Museum for Musical Instruments at this futuristic-looking restaurant. Ascend the 10 stories in the glass elevator—reminiscent of *Charlie and the Chocolate Factory*—and be seated by penguin-like waiters. On a sunny day, make sure to request an outdoor seat. The view of Brussels from above is breathtaking; you can see as far as the Atomium and the Grand Place.
☴ Ⓜ*Parc. Enter through the museum and head up in the elevator.* Ⓢ *Plats €10-19.* Ⓚ *Open M-W 10am-4pm, Th-Sa 10am-4pm and 7-11pm, Su 7-11pm.*

LES BRASSINS TRADITIONAL $$
36 rue Keyenveld ☎02 512 69 99 www.lesbrassins.com
Les Brassins is the ultimate hole in the wall; impress that cute Australian hostel friend with your knowledge of local digs and treat them to a meal at this intimate little spot. Located on a quiet and fairly empty street, Les Brassins is perfect for a casual but romantic date or a family dinner. Belgian fare is served nonstop, and vintage beer signs on the warm yellow walls will tell you what's best to wash down your *stoemp* with. Les Brassins is also just a few doors down from the childhood home of Audrey Hepburn (a plaque marks the address of her birthplace), so if that Australian also happens to be a film and fashion buff, you're welcome.
☴ Ⓜ*Porte de Namur. Head southwest on av. de la Toison d'Or, turn left onto rue des Chevaliers, and continue when it turns into rue Keenveld; the restaurant is on the left.* 𝒊 *Cash only.* Ⓢ *Entrées €6.50-13.50. Plats €9.50-21. Drinks €2-7.50.* Ⓚ *Open daily noon-midnight.*

LES SUPER FILLES DU TRAM BURGERS $$
22 rue Lesbroussart ☎02 648 46 60
This is of the more colorful places around the Pl. Flagey area, with murals of a dream-like Brussels skyline being destroyed by monsters and a massive monkey. Their burgers come stuffed with delicious fillings and a side of *frites* in a little flower pot. If you fancy a burger challenge, try to finish the Big Joe, which overflows with bacon, cheese, pickles, onions, BBQ sauce, and a special house sauce (€12).
☴ *Bus #60, 71, or 83 to Flagey. Walk west down rue Lesbroussart.* Ⓢ *Tartines €9-12. Burgers and salads €10-14.* Ⓚ *Open M-Sa 10am-11pm, Su 11am-5pm. Kitchen open M-Sa noon-3pm and 6-11pm, Su 11am-5pm.*

food

LE BELGO BELGE TRADITIONAL $$$

20 rue de la Paix ☎02 511 11 21 www.belgobelge.be

This modern, chic-looking restaurant serves small but filling plates of Belgian classics like *stoemp* to Eurocrats, businessmen, and expats. The calm setting features artwork on the walls that celebrates the heritage of Brussels (note the large, three-paneled painting of babies holding the Belgian flag).

➜ ⓂPort de Namur. Walk down Chausée d'Ixelles about 4 blocks, turn left onto rue Solvay and right onto rue St-Boniface; the restaurant is on the next corner. [$] Entrées €5-12.50. Plats €13.50-20. ⏰ Open M-F noon-2:30pm and 6pm-midnight, Sa-Su noon-midnight.

IL RINASCIMENTO ITALIAN $$

14 rue Jourdan ☎02 534 75 20

Mamma mia, it's a pizza! And a delicious, authentically Italian €10 pizza, at that. Il Rinascimento brings the homey aroma of basil and parmesan to a street frequented by stuffy Stepford wives who sip *vino* after a rough day of shopping at Galerie Porte Louise. Not only can you enjoy a true Italian meal without burning a hole in your wallet, but the meal is also preceded by a cheese plate, olives, and mini-beets in addition to the traditional bread basket. Can you say *Mamma mia?* Oh wait, we already did.

➜ ⓂLouise. Walk south on av. Louise, take the 1st right onto rue Jourdan; the restaurant is about halfway down on the left. [$] Pizza €10-€18. Pasta €10-18.50. ⏰ Open Tu-Su noon-3pm and 6-11:30pm.

PLACE SCHUMAN AND HEYSEL

Place Schuman and Heysel boast lots of fancy restaurants that cater to Eurocrats and upscale tourists, but the budget traveler can find relief in the abundance of supermarkets. If you keep your eyes open, you can find some affordable cafes and kebab stands to hold you over until you head back to the city center.

👍 **ANTOINE'S** FRITERIE $

1 pl. Jourdan

Around lunchtime, crowds of businessmen, children, students, and tourists descend on Brussels's oldest *friterie* for large, piping-hot portions of some of the city's best *frites*. Many people head to grassy Parc Léopold to enjoy their fries alfresco.

➜ ⓂSchuman. Pl. Jourdan is just off rue Froissart. [$] Frites €2-2.20. Sauce €0.50. ⏰ Open M-Th 11:30am-1am, F-Sa 11:30am-2am, Su 11:30am-1am.

👍 **CHEZ MOI** PIZZERIA, BAR $

66 rue du Luxembourg ☎02 280 26 66

Avoid the expensive eateries in and around the EU area and join the young workers devouring their delicious (and dirt-cheap) pizza slices on the grass of pl. du Luxembourg. Chez Moi offers a daily menu of classic flavors (mushroom, pepperoni, etc.).

➜ ⓂMaelbeek. Turn left onto rue de la Loi after exiting the station. Take the 1st left onto rue de Trèves, walk 4 blocks, then turn right onto pl. du Luxembourg. Head right across the square to get to rue du Luxembourg. ℹ Takeout and delivery available. [$] Slices €2-3.50. ⏰ Open M-W 11am-11pm, Th-F 11am-midnight.

CAFÉ PARC AVENUE CAFE $$$$

50 av. d'Auderghem ☎02 742 28 10 www.parc-avenue.be

Eating out in the EU area can be expensive. Fortunately, this upscale cafe has a €16 lunch special that includes the *entrée* and *plat* of the day. It may not sound like much, but after mounds of greasy fries and sweet waffles, this meal will leave you feeling as satisfied and as slick as the suits lunching next to you.

➜ ⓂSchuman. Walk toward the park and to the right; the cafe is on the corner of rue Belliard and av. d'Auderghem. [$] Entrees €8-12. Salads €12-14. Plats €16-34. ⏰ Open M-F 11am-2:30pm and 6:30-11pm.

PITTA HOUSE JOURDAN

KEBAB, PITA $

43 pl. Jourdan · ☎02 231 09 86

The perfect place for a quick dinner or greasy kebab, Pitta House is a welcome alternative to the fancy restaurants of the area. The patio offers a chance to spy on the Eurocrats in pl. Jourdan without having to empty your wallet for the privilege.

✈ Ⓜ*Schuman. Pl. Jourdan is down rue Froissart.* Ⓢ *Most dishes €6-9.* ⏰ *Open M-Th 11am-3am, F-Sa 11am-4am, Su 11am-3am.*

KARSMAKERS

BAGELS $

20 rue de Trèves · ☎02 502 02 26 · www.karsmakers.be

Although the bagels here may not hold a candle to H&H, the fresh ingredients and creative combinations add plenty of flavor to an American favorite. Monthly spread specials like guacamole with yellow pepper and homemade red bean add some variety to your pastrami standby. You will certainly be sharing your meal among well-ironed Eurocrats taking a generous lunch break to discuss extremely important matters—red or white wine with that salmon bagel? Nonetheless, this naturally lit cafe offers packed tables in the front for political eavesdropping or low, soft couches in the back for people-watching.

✈ Ⓜ*Troon. Walk straight down rue du Luxembourg and turn right when you hit Parliament.* Ⓢ *Bagels €5-8.* ⏰ *Open M-F 7am-6pm, Su 10am-4pm.*

RESTO SIMBA

AFRICAN $

13 Chausée de Louvain · ☎02 203 54 53 · www.lsctraiteur.be

Take a seat among the African art and statues and dive into some African cuisine at Resto Simba, located inside the Musées Royaux d'Art et d'Histoire. Dishes include Madagascar chicken, *scampi nin* (a Kenyan curry), and *Croq'Simba* (chicken in palm nut sauce)—though something tells us that dish isn't called "Simba" back in its homeland.

✈ Ⓜ*Madou. Turn right upon exiting the station, then the 1st right.* Ⓢ *Sandwiches €3. Toasted baguettes €5.50-7.50. Plats €7.80-16.20.* ⏰ *Open Tu-Su noon-3pm.*

CAPOLINO'S

ITALIAN $$$

69 pl. Jourdan · ☎02 230 37 51

Capolino's plentiful selection of pizza and pasta makes it one of the cheaper options among the many expensive restaurants in this "lunching" square. Make sure to grab a wicker chair in the garden out back to feel extra classy. This is one of those rare places where the pizza is made exactly how you want it, so don't be afraid to ask.

✈ Ⓜ*Schuman. Pl. Jourdan is just down rue Froissart.* 𝒊 *8% discount for takeout.* Ⓢ *Pizza €8.70-14. Pasta €10-16.* ⏰ *Open M-Th noon-2:30pm and 6:30-11pm, F-Sa noon-2:30pm and 6:30-11:30pm, Su 6:30-11pm.*

LA BRACE

PIZZERIA $$$

1 rue Franklin · ☎02 736 57 73

With its bright red-brick walls and matching stone ovens, La Brace has a classic, family-friendly feel but also retains a romantic Italian atmosphere. The menu here is extensive, but you really don't have any choice but to get a pizza; it's a bit large for one person, but you'll greedily devour it on your own anyway. Despite La Brace's large interior and sizeable terrace, seats are taken and mouths are full nearly all the time at this popular restaurant, so reservations will be an added assurance that your pizza cravings will not go unanswered.

✈ Ⓜ*Schuman. Walk north on rue Archimède; the pizzeria is on the corner of rue Franklin.* Ⓢ *Pizzas €10-14. Pastas €12-14. Plats €12-25.* ⏰ *Open M-Sa noon-3pm and 6-11:30pm.*

KITTY O'SHEA'S IRISH PUB

PUB $$$

42 bd Charlemagne · ☎02 280 27 33 · www.kittyosheas.eu

Although Kitty O'Shea's may not be as authentic an Irish pub as James Joyce (see **Nightlife**), it still serves great food for even greater prices given the area.

As per usual for Place Schuman, the crowd here will be suited up, but fat wallets and penny pinchers alike come for hearty meals and even heartier laughs.

⇞ Ⓜ Schuman. Go around the left side of the European Commission building; the pub is on the corner. $ Entrées €4-7. Plats €9.50-15.50. Beer €3-5.50, happy hour €2. ⏰ Open daily noon-1am. Happy hour M 5-10pm. Brunch Sa-Su 1-6pm.

THE SUSHI FACTORY SUSHI $$

44 bd Charlemagne ☎02 230 74 32 www.sushifactory.be

If you fancy something a little 💬**fishy,** or if you're just craving a Japanese salad, then this sushi shop is just what the doctor ordered. The sushi here is made fresh only twice a day, so don't wait until the 11th hour to get your fix, as they may close early when the second batch of sushi has all been snatched up. Seating here is limited, so sit outside on the terrace or get your sushi to go.

⇞ Ⓜ Schuman. Walk west on rue de la Loi, away from the park, and turn right onto bd Charlemagne. The restaurant is on the next corner across the street. Across from Kitty O'Shea's. ℹ Delivery and takeout available. $ Entrées €3.50-5. Plats €7-16. Soup, salad, 4 pc. sushi €10. Soup, salad, 7 pc. sushi €12. ⏰ Open M-Sa 11:30am-8:30pm. Takeout available until 9pm.

nightlife

We encourage you to sample as many 🍺**good Belgian brews** as humanly possible, but remember: the Metro stops at midnight. Don't forget to plan around it, particularly if you want to club your way through the Upper Town area or the classier Place Schuman. The cheapest and most popular bars are in Lower Town, which features a decent mix of tourist traps and well-kept local secrets. Pl. St-Gery is the well-populated bar strip of 20-something Belgians looking to share a beer with friends along with the same demographic of foreigners looking for a raging time. Be careful of pickpockets in this area. Upper Town nightlife is less vibrant and more expensive, with bars and lounges full of 30-somethings in abundance but fewer options for students (even the students of Brussels University migrate en masse to the Lower Town for their nightly fix). For a more "European" experience, head to Place Schuman or Place du Luxembourg (that's PLux to the Eurocrats), where young men in suits will undoubtedly ask you what you do and how much you make. Don't be put off by this attitude; they are a friendly bunch in the EU.

LOWER TOWN

The Lower Town has the liveliest nightlife in Brussels, with a mix of tourist traps, cozy cafes, grimy pubs, and well-kept local secrets.

👍 **DELIRIUM** BAR

4A Impasse de la Fidélité ☎02 514 44 34 www.deliriumcafe.be

If you want to party hard in Brussels, Delirium is the place to do it. While its immense popularity means that all of the drunkest tourists (and Belgians) will be here, Delirium is a big enough place that you won't mind. Shenanigans and revelry abound, and with a selection of more than ☐**2000 beers,** this bar provides the opportunity to get drunk on new brews every night. We recommend asking one of the expert bartenders for a recommendation; otherwise, grab a menu, close your eyes, and pick whatever your finger lands on first. But beware: these beers are strong (10% alcohol), so exercise caution when you go out—it's not called Delirium for nothing.

⇞ Ⓜ De Brouchere. Walk south on bd Anspach 1 block, turn left onto rue Grétry, and continue about 2 blocks; the bar is on the left. $ Beer €2-6. ⏰ Open daily 10am-4am.

👍 **L'ESTAMINET TOONE** PUB

Impasse Schuddeveld 6 ☎02 511 71 37 www.toone.be

You are likely to run into a chill, older crowd at l'Estaminet Toone, but occasional live music, marionettes dangling from the ceiling, and laughter keep this place light-hearted and young. This tavern neighbors le Royal Théâtre Toone, where you can enjoy an evening marionette show before heading down to the bar for some brews. The bar is accessed through a long tunnel, so although it may get a bit noisy inside, the hubbub from rue des Bouchers is (thankfully) drowned out. Enjoy drinks with close friends in one of the three rooms or out on the patio.

🚶 ⓂDe Brouckère. *Walk 1 block south on bd Anspach to rue Grétry and turn left. Continue down rue des Brouchers; a big sign over the road points to Toone, on the right.* *i* *Cash only.* ⓢ *Beers €2.50-6.50.* 🕑 *Open Tu-Su noon-midnight.*

BONNEFOOI   BAR
8 rue des Pierres   ☎048 762 22 31 www.bonnefooi.be
Bonnefooi is one of Brussels's most pleasant bars, and it attracts a steady stream of young tourists to its unobtrusive side street near Bourse. It's not as wild as its 8am closing time might suggest, but it is a great place to relax at the end of a night of partying. Check the board inside the bar for the schedule of nightly events, which include acoustic concerts, DJ dance parties, and jazz performances.

🚶 ⓂBourse. *Just off of bd Anspach.* ⓢ *Beer €2-4. Mixed drinks €7.* 🕑 *Open daily 6pm-8am.*

GOUPIL LE FOL   BAR
22 rue de la Violette   ☎02 511 13 96
This eclectic *estaminet* is one of the Lower Town's best finds. A sign outside explains that the bar will not serve Coca-Cola to its patrons (except as a vehicle for alcohol). Step inside and you'll be enveloped in a world of revolution, literature, and art. Goupil le Fol is packed with an intellectual crowd of alternative students and older art-lovers, and the owner, Abel, counts the Princes of Spain and Belgium among his patrons.

🚶 ⓂBourse. *From the Grand Place, head down rue des Chapeliers and turn left onto rue de la Violette.* ⓢ *Beer €3-6.* 🕑 *Open daily 6pm-6am.*

CAFÉ DES HALLES   BAR
pl. St Géry 1   ☎475 94 33 81 www.cafedeshalles.be
Cafe des Halles is the IKEA of Brussels's bars, with a sampling of setups for every nighttime style. Take your drink from the bar to the terrace that surrounds most of the building to the makeshift dance floor for some chest-thumping beats. For a backyard barbecue feel, check out the low hammock chairs that swing over AstroTurf. A huge obelisk that once marked the center of Brussels now divides the main floor of this bar into two parts. The building was originally built over the obelisk as a market before being converted into one of the city's cultural headquarters and a favorite haunt for night crawlers.

🚶 ⓂBourse. *Head south on bd Anspach, take the 1st right onto rue des Pierres, and follow it to pl. St-Géry. Des Halles is the rectangular brick building in the center.* ⓢ *Drinks €3-8.* 🕑 *Open daily 10am-1am.*

LE ROI DES BELGES   CAFE, BAR
35 rue Jules Van Praet   ☎02 513 51 16
With its two separate floors, Le Roi des Belges offers patrons a couple different nighttime experiences. The ground floor has your typical small tables, small bar, and small cafe chatter, while the loft-style second floor atop a spiral staircase offers a thumpin' cocktail bar and a quieter back room with swings for seating. For a more home-grown evening, stick to the ground floor bar (which is more like an open kitchen), where the bartenders will cook just about anything you ask for. If you're in the mood for some beats, head upstairs to the cocktail bar, where conversation is drowned out by blaring dance music.

🚶 ⓂBourse. *Turn right onto rue Jules Van Praet; the bar is on the corner, across from Mappa Mundo and Cafe des Halles.* *i* *DJ on F-Sa.* ⓢ *Beer €3-5. Mixed drinks €8.* 🕑 *Ground floor open M-Th 9am-2am, F-Su 9am-3am. Cocktail bar open daily 4pm until late.*

nightlife

MUSIC LOUNGE
JAZZ CLUB

50 rue des Pierres ☎02 513 13 45 www.themusicvillage.com

One of Brussels's hippest jazz bars, Music Lounge attracts an audience of all ages with a wide range of concerts (tending to veer toward traditional jazz). The relaxed atmosphere and artsy clientele provide a chill setting to begin or end the night.

⚓ Ⓜ*Bourse. Just off of the Grand Place.* 𝒊 *50% student discount with ID.* Ⓢ *Cover €7-20. Drinks €2-7.* 🕑 *Doors open at 7pm. Concerts start M-Th 8:30pm, F-Sa 9pm, Su 8:30pm.*

MAPPA MUNDO
PUB

2-6 rue du Pont de la Carpe ☎02 514 35 55

From the outside, Mappa Mundo looks like a small, disappointing pub filled with English tourists looking to recreate their local watering holes back home. But if you can escape the tourists in the front rooms and head upstairs or to the little wooden caverns out back, you will find brighter lights, booths, an impressive view of busy pl. St Géry, and a generally comfortable setting where you can enjoy a few drinks with good friends. Mappa Mundo claims to be one of Brussels's oldest and most popular bars, and its authentic feel lives up to that reputation.

⚓ Ⓜ*Bourse. Turn right onto rue Jules van Praet; the pub is on the next corner, across from Le Roi des Belges.* 𝒊 *Brunch F-Su 11am-3pm.* Ⓢ *Beer €2-4. Mixed drinks €8.* 🕑 *Open M-Th 11am-2am, F-Su 11am-3am.*

ZEBRA
BAR

35 pl. St Géry ☎02 511 09 01 www.zebrabar.be

Although Zebra may look just like all the other bars in pl. St Géry, its one notable difference is its sound. With tunes that range from a selection of Beatles hits to live contemporary music that sets up in the front corner of the bar twice a week, this bar draws a young crowd looking to enjoy a few beers and chill conversation on the terrace.

⚓ Ⓜ*Bourse. Turn right onto rue Jules van Praet, then left at pl. St Géry; the bar is across from Café des Halles.* Ⓢ *Beer €3-4. Mixed drinks €7.* Ⓢ *Open M-Th 11am-1am, F-Su 11am-2am.*

MEZZO
BAR

18 rue Borgval ☎02 511 33 25 www.mezzo.be

This large modern corner bar is tourist-friendly without being tourist-trappy. The left side of the room is divided by a long bar, which leaves just enough room to gather around the bar chairs, while the right side is wider and has tables lining the walls. Regardless of where you sit, the English-speaking bartenders and very reasonable drink prices will make you feel at home.

⚓ Ⓜ*Bourse. Turn right onto rue des Pierres; the bar is on the left, on the corner across from Cafe des Halles and next to Enface.* Ⓢ *Beer €2-4. Mixed drinks €7.50.* 🕑 *Open M-Th 4pm-2am, F-Sa 4pm-6am, Su 4pm-2am.*

ENFACE
BAR

1-3 rue St Géry ☎02 502 00 57 www.enface.be

Although the seating here may feel cramped and narrow, a three-sided island bar opens up the room and offers enough space that you won't have to step on your drunk companions to ask for a drink. This corner bar draws patrons of different ages, but regardless of whether you run into your friends or your dad's friends, the Top 40 music and dancing in the large back room appeals to everyone.

⚓ Ⓜ*Bourse. Turn right onto rue des Pierres; the bar is on the corner on the opposite left.* Ⓢ *Beer €2-3. Mixed drinks €7-9. 3 shots €11, 6 shots €20. Tapas €4-7.* 🕑 *Open M-Sa 3pm-2am.*

CLASSIC ROCK BAR
BAR

55 rue Marché au Charbon ☎02 512 15 47 www.rockclassic.be

While you won't find any bats in this cave-like grunge bar, you will discover plenty of ponytailed, jean-clad rockers. Classic Rock Bar caters to a specific

brussels

audience, but it is not unwelcoming to explorers who might be looking for something new for the night. Mingle with local-head bangers, play a round of foosball, or shoot to the very back of the cavern for a quieter atmosphere at the Blindway Cocktail Bar, complete with comfortable couches and some extra-strong concoctions.

➔ Ⓜ Bourse. Walk south on bd Anspach, turn left onto rue du Lomard, then right onto rue Marche au Charbon. $ Drinks €3-8.50. ⏰ Open daily 8pm-6am.

À LA MORT SUBITE BAR

7 rue Montagne-aux-Herbes Potagères ☎02 513 13 18 www.alamortsubite.com

Despite its name (which translates to "Sudden Death" in English), À la Mort Subite is alive and thriving but might not be hoppin' enough to satisfy younger travelers. Boasting an older, more sober crowd, evenings here are decidedly tamer than most other bars in town. If your parents just arrived in Brussels, take them here for a real Belgian beer among real Belgian beer drinkers. Otherwise, head back toward rue des Bouchers, where the nightlife has a little more vitality.

➔ Ⓜ Bourse. From the Grand Place, head up to the Galleries St-Hubert; the bar is through the galleries on the corner. $ Mixed drinks €2-4. Beer €3-5. Sandwiches €4.50-7. ⏰ Open M-Sa 11am-1am, Su noon-midnight.

L'ARCHIDUC JAZZ BAR

6 rue Antoine Dansaert ☎02 512 06 52 www.archiduc.net

Dating back to before WWI, L'Archiduc is renowned for its jazz concerts and Art Deco interior. Though the prices are a little higher than other bars in the areas (expect to pay between €4 and €12), the intricate and historic decor make those few extra euro worth it. Grab a spot in the gallery-style balcony area for a good spot of people watching; L'Archiduc draws a good mix of locals and jazz-loving tourists. On weekends, the bar doesn't really pick up until 11pm, so we recommend paying L'Archiduc a visit near the end of your night for a classy drink or two.

➔ Ⓜ Bourse. Head down rue Orts, which leads to rue Antoine Dansaert. ℹ Free concerts May-Aug M 11pm. $ Drinks €3-12. ⏰ Open daily 4pm-5am.

UPPER TOWN

Apart from one of the city's best clubs, Upper Town nightlife tends to be less vibrant and more expensive than in the Lower Town. Even the students of Brussels University work up the energy to migrate en masse to the Lower Town for their nightly fix. Bars and lounges for 30-somethings are in abundance, but head elsewhere to find young people.

👍 **FUSE** CLUB

208 rue Blaes ☎02 511 97 89 www.fuse.be

Fuse proudly proclaims itself "Best Belgian Club Ever." That might be overdoing it, but it is one of Brussels's biggest and liveliest clubs, with pounding music and drinks that will make even the worst dancing excusable.

➔ Ⓜ Port de Hal. Head north on bd du Midi, then turn right onto rue Blaes. $ Cover Sa before midnight €6, after midnight €11. Drinks €4-10. ⏰ Open on club nights Th-Sa 11pm-late.

👍 **LA FLEUR EN PAPIER DORÉ** PUB

55 rue des Alexiens ☎02 511 16 59 www.lafleurenpapierdore.be

A mix of older locals and young artsy types crowd this historic pub just off of the Sablon area. Now protected by the Belgian government, it counts the artist Magritte and Tintin-author Hergé among its former clientele. Temporary art exhibits fill the kooky space, making for a nice break from the monotonous profusion of Irish pubs and dark taverns.

➔ Ⓜ Gare du Midi. $ Beer €2-7. ⏰ Open Tu-Sa 11am-midnight, Su 11am-7pm.

THE FLAT
LOUNGE, BAR
12 rue de la Reinette   ☎02 502 74 34 www.theflat.be

A hip and trendy lounge bar, The Flat replicates the experience of drinking in an upscale London or New York City apartment: hang out in the spacious living room, a dining area, a grand bathroom, even a bedroom. Downstairs, a DJ mixes house, electro and Top 40 Thursday through Saturday.

✦ ⓂPort de Namur. Cross the roundabout and turn left onto rue Ste-Anne. ⓈDrinks €3-10. ☼ Open W-Sa 6pm-2am.

L'ULTIME ATOME
BAR, BRASSERIE
14 rue St Boniface   ☎02 511 13 67

This brasserie, like several others in the area, has a nonstop kitchen but is primarily a drinker's haven. With 85 beers on the menu and a great selection of delicious noms, too, L'Ultime Atome is likely to quench your thirst and provide fuel for a good time. The bar is frequented by Dutch-speaking Belgians and plenty of Eurocrats. Solo travelers be warned: the local crowd and dearth of tourists can mean service will be difficult to attract.

✦ ⓂPort de Namur. Walk down Chausée d'Ixelles about 4 blocks and turn left onto rue Solvay; the bar is on the next corner on the right. Ⓢ Beer €2-4. Mixed drinks €7. Wine €2.50-7. Appetizers €10-13. Entrees €9-17. ☼ Open M-Th 11am-12:30am, F-Sa 11am-1am, Su 11am-12:30am.

CAFÉ BELGA
BAR
18 pl. Flagey   ☎02 460 35 08 www.cafebelga.be

Located across from a beautiful pond and central plaza, Café Belga takes up an entire street corner. Most of the local patrons congregate outside on the sprawling terrace, and some even take their drinks a bit further to benches closer to the water. A healthy mix of Belgians, Eurocrats, and expats, the crowd is the primary draw here and provides a refreshing break from the more tourist-heavy areas of the city.

✦ ⓂPort de Namur. Walk about 1.5km south on Chausée d'Ixelles; the bar is across from the pond. Or tram to pl. Flagey; the bar is on the northeast corner of the plaza. 𝒊 Free Wi-Fi. Free jazz concerts on Su. Ⓢ Beer €2-5. Mixed drinks €7. Sandwiches €4. Salads €7-7.50. ☼ Open M-Th 8am-2am, F-Sa 8am-3am, Su 8am-2am. Terrace open until 1am.

LA SAMARITAINE
CABARET, BAR
16 rue de la Samaritaine   ☎02 511 33 95 www.lasamaritaine.be

As you descend the steep steps down an alley off Sablon Square, you'll know you aren't headed into any ordinary cabaret. La Samaritaine looks a bit like a converted wine cellar, and you can hear the music from down the street. This underground bar is a fantastic local favorite frequented by the young, the old, and the artsy, all of whom cheer on songs, dance numbers, and theatrical performances in cavernous rooms. You can catch *a cappella* concerts and other live performances while enjoying some remarkably cheap drinks (cocktails only €6). Some tickets sell out quickly, so check online and call in advance to reserve your spot at Brussels's most interesting cabaret.

✦ ⓂCentral Station. Walk southwest on bd de l'Empreur, turn left onto rue Lebeau, right onto rue Joseph Stevens, left onto rue des Pigeons, and right onto rue Samaritaine. 𝒊 Seats not occupied by 8:10pm will be given away. Ⓢ Tickets €15, students €10. Book in advance. Drinks €2-8. ☼ Doors open on performance nights at 7:30pm, usually W-Sa. Shows at 8:30pm but may vary, check program.

BAR DU MARCHÉ
BAR, CAFE
12 rue Antoine Dewitte   ☎02 644 04 00 www.bardumarche.be

This smoky bar caters to the type of cool crowd that won't be seen without a cigarette in hand and the latest fashion staple in their wardrobe. Arts and philosophy are more likely to be the topic of conversation here than sports or politics, and the 20-somethings seem to all be regulars and travel in groups that might be difficult for a lone traveler to penetrate. The bar has a very artsy vibe and is a great place to hang out with friends or just grab a mid-afternoon coffee.

✦ Ⓜ️*Port de Namur. Just off of pl. Flagey, via Chausée d'Ixelles.* *i* *Free Wi-Fi. Free jazz concerts on Su.* Ⓢ *Beer €2-4. Mixed drinks €7.* 🕐 *Open M-W 10am-2am, Th-Sa 10am-3am, Su 10am-2am. Happy hour M-W 10-11pm, Th-Sa 11pm-midnight, Su 10-11pm.*

PEOPLE
BAR

11 av. Toison D'Or   ☎02 511 64 05 www.peoplebar.be

Imagine all the people, sharing drinks in peace. At People, there are all kinds of people boozing together in peace—from Eurocrats to students to expats—although the throbbing DJ booth isn't exactly quiet. Outside, patrons can relax at tables and enjoy cocktails while people-watching; inside, the party and plenty of dancing get going to the beats of various remixed tracks.

✦ Ⓜ️*Port de Namur. On the southeast side of av. Toison d'Or.* Ⓢ *Beer €2.50-4.50. Mixed drinks €8.50-9.50. Tapas €3.50-5. Bottle service €85-150.* 🕐 *Open daily noon-1am.*

KARAOKE SABLON
KARAOKE BAR

34 rue St-Anne   ☎02 512 40 94 www.karaokesablon.be

This smokey karaoke bar off a side alley in the Sablon area is full of locals and specializes in French music, so you can expect to hear tone-deaf renditions of Edith Piaf as often as you hear the Beatles. This quirky bar will put a smile on your face, even if you just sit and watch the regulars.

✦ Ⓜ️*Louise. From the Église Notre Dame du Sablon, head toward the roundabout and turn right onto rue st. Anne.* Ⓢ *Drinks €3-6.* 🕐 *Open Tu-Sa 9pm-4am.*

PLACE SCHUMAN AND HEYSEL

Place Schuman isn't the most lively of places for the student traveler, but it is the place to network and exchange business cards. Expect expats, businessmen, and EU workers as well as an awful lot of English speakers, especially during the week. Things will get very quiet on the weekends.

🏴 JAMES JOYCE
IRISH PUB

34 rue Archimède   ☎04 7162 05 80

If you show up to James Joyce solo, never fear—you will surely depart among (new) friends. This pub caters a bit more to the middle-aged crowd than the student scene, but as some travelers might say, every hour is happy hour here. The only Brussels bar with a full dartboard, a smoke room, and a reading corner with books that include (you guessed it) *Ulysses,* James Joyce ensures that there will be no shortage of conversation topics. So let your stream of consciousness run wild, have a pint of Guinness, and make some new friends.

✦ Ⓜ️*Schuman. Walk north on rue Archimède 1½ blocks. James Joyce is on the left just past the Hairy Canary.* *i* *Bartenders will make mixed drinks on request but no fancy mixed drinks. Live music 1st Th of each month.* 🕐 *Beer €3-5.* 🕐 *Open M-Th 5pm-late, F 5pm-7am, Sa noon-7am, Su noon-late.*

🏴 OLD OAK IRISH PUB
IRISH PUB

26 rue Franklin   ☎02 735 75 44

This jolly Irish pub has an unpretentious atmosphere that draws in fewer men in suits with BlackBerries and more young Europeans. Old Oak also hosts special events like a pub quiz on Monday nights.

✦ Ⓜ️*Schuman. Follow rue Archimède and turn right onto rue Franklin.* Ⓢ *Drinks €2-5.* 🕐 *Open daily noon-1am.*

SOHO
CLUB

47 bd du Triomphe   ☎02 649 35 00 www.soho-club.be

Soho is one of Brussels's liveliest clubs, despite being situated near the EU district. The 20-something crowd on the gigantic dance floor is a welcome break from the older Eurocrats found in the area. Expect a wide variety of music and theme nights.

✈ Ⓜ*Hankar. Head west on Chaussée de Wavre and turn left onto rue de la Chasse Royale, then right onto bd du Triomphe.* *i* *The Hankar stop is serviced by the night bus.* Ⓢ *Cover €10. Drinks €5-10.* Ⓩ *Open Th-Sa 11pm-late.*

FAT BOY'S SPORTS BAR   SPORTS BAR

5 pl. du Luxembourg   ☎02 511 32 66 www.fatboys-be.com

Fat boys don't frequent the TV screens of this bar—unless, perhaps, they're showing a sumo wrestling championship, which is completely possible. The owner of this bar boasts of over 7000 sports channels, with 11 screens inside and two outside; the result is as many as five live games showing simultaneously. Patrons can watch almost every major sporting event here, be it soccer, American football, baseball, or cricket; if there's a game on that you want to catch, Fat Boy's will be showing it. Hockey will draw Canadians and Americans in droves, while you can expect a whirlwind of Romance languages when it's Italy vs. Spain in the World Cup.

✈ Ⓜ*Troon. Walk straight down rue du Luxembourg; the bar is in the plaza, right in front of the European Parliament.* *i* *Credit card min. €15.* Ⓢ *Beer €2.50-5.50. Mixed drinks €8-8.50.* Ⓩ *Open daily 11am-late.*

THE MEETING POINT   PUB

49 rue du Taciturne   ☎02 230 28 02 www.themeetingpoint.be

The Meeting Point pumps some life into a generally desolate nighttime scene in the EU area. This bar is one of the few in Brussels that has theme evenings, including Ladies Night on Tuesdays and Karaoke on Fridays. Even if the colored strobe lights and amateur DJ don't live up to your fist-pumping standards, this place will do the trick in a neighborhood where the competition is virtually non-existent.

✈ Ⓜ*Maelbeek.* *i* *Free drinks for ladies Tu. DJ Th-F. Karaoke F.* Ⓢ *Beer €2-5. Mixed drinks €7.* Ⓩ *Open daily 10am-late.*

COOLOCK CAFÉ   PUB

55 rue Archimede   ☎479 45 48 53

In an area known for its stuffy and moneyed clientele, CooLock Café is a safe haven for students. The young crowd flocks here on weekends for billiards, trivia, sports games, and general debauchery while the rest of the town tucks into bed by 9pm. CooLock is the pub that's like your favorite older brother: it's laid-back, does what it wants, and is effortlessly cool.

✈ Ⓜ*Schuman. Walk north on rue Archimède 1½ blocks; the pub is on the right.* *i* *Cash only. Pool €1 per game.* Ⓢ *Beer €3-5. Mixed drinks €6.50-7.50.* Ⓩ *Open daily noon-late.*

THE HAIRY CANARY   ENGLISH PUB

12 rue Archimède   ☎02 230 13 36

The chipper clientele and service are what attract many people to this English pub, but unfortunately the crowd here is a bit subdued for most students in search of a raging evening. Don't expect to be met with enthusiasm if you try to order a round of Irish car bombs, but in proper English fashion, the barman will be at your service (albeit with a subtle nod of distaste). Don't get us wrong, no one here is rude, in fact it's quite the opposite. Just know that the Hairy Canary is a place for joyful cheers and quiet beers, so leave your drunk goggles for another night.

✈ Ⓜ*Schuman.* Ⓢ *Beer €2.50-5. Mixed drinks €7.* Ⓩ *Open daily noon-late.*

RALPH'S BAR   BAR

13 pl. du Luxembourg   ☎02 230 16 13 www.ralphsbar.be

Ralph's Bar attempts to up the already high-class ante of pl. du Luxembourg with modern decor, a blue-lit interior, and bass-thumping house music. It's less rough-and-tumble than its more pub-style neighbors across the way, but this bar still offers a good time and attracts a younger crowd looking to do more than discuss politics.

✢ ⓂTroon. *Walk straight down rue du Luxembourg; the bar is in the plaza, right in front of the European Parliament.* *i* *DJ on F.* Ⓢ *Beers €4-4.50. Mixed drinks €8.* ⓐ *Open daily 10am-1am.*

THE GRAPEVINE   BAR
11 pl. du Luxembourg   ☎02 280 00 17 www.the-grapevine.be
This place has certainly made it through the grapevine; European workers mob this bar for a drink and a quick bite to eat after work. The Grapevine's outdoor seating overflows onto the property of the bar next door, which seems to attract fewer visitors (the Eurocrats clearly know something we don't). The interior resembles a French brasserie more than a modern Belgian bar, so ditch the beer for wine and mingle. Make sure you're carrying some business cards, as the Grapevine is an ideal place to network.

✢ ⓂTroon. *Walk straight down rue du Luxembourg; the Grapevine is in the plaza right in front of the European Parliament.* *i* *Students get €0.50 discount on drinks with ID.* Ⓢ *Lunch €10. Entrées €7-13.50. Plats €10.50-18. Beer €2.50-4.* ⓐ *Open daily 9am-midnight.*

THE BEER FACTORY   BAR
6 pl. du Luxembourg   ☎02 513 38 56 www.brasserie-beer-factory.be
One of the more relaxed bars in this bustling square, the Beer Factory can be summed up by the vintage picture of a man grinning over a generous pint on the wall. Although we're not entirely certain why this place calls itself the Beer Factory, given its short beer list and lack of specialty brews, this bar does have a cool, rounded bar topped with a large oven hood that makes it look like a brewery.

✢ ⓂTroon. *Walk straight down rue du Luxembourg; the bar is in the plaza, right in front of the European Parliament.* *i* *Credit card min. €10. Takeout available.* Ⓢ *Entrées €4-6. Tapas €3-5. Plats €10-18. Beer €2-5. Mixed drinks €7-8.* ⓐ *Open M-F 10am-midnight. Kitchen open noon-10:45pm.*

arts and culture

Brussels is a hotbed of theater, popular music, and opera and hosts numerous music and film festivals throughout the year. Make sure you pick up the free weekly culture publication, **Agenda**, from the Tourist Office or the free magazine, **BruXXL** (available in English), both of which print schedules of all the best arts and culture events in the city.

OPERA

THÉÂTRE ROYALE DE LA MONNAIE   LOWER TOWN
pl. de la Monnaie   ☎070 23 39 39 www.lamonnaie.be
Brussels's Opera House featured numerous sold-out shows in 2012, including *La Traviata* and *Così fan Tutte*. Performances at this theater range from classical opera to chamber music. Student rush tickets and discounts of up to 50% are available, but performances sell out quickly, especially in June.

✢ ⓂDe Brouckère. *i* *Box office at 23 rue Léopold.* Ⓢ *Tickets from €20.* ⓐ *Box office open Tu-Sa 11:30am-5:30pm.*

THEATER

▨ BEURSSCHOUWBURG   LOWER TOWN
20-28 rue Auguste Orts   ☎02 550 03 50 www.beursschouwburg.be
A haven for up-and-coming artists, the Beursschouwburg hosts modern theater productions along with film and documentary screenings, dance performances, and temporary art installations. On Wednesdays, they host a free, student-oriented show with the superb title SHOW, which stands for "Shit Happens on Wednesday."

✢ ⓂBourse. Ⓢ *€12, students €10.* ⓐ *Box office open M-F 10am-6pm.*

THÉÂTRE ROYAL DU PARC
UPPER TOWN
3 rue de la Loi ☎02 505 30 30 www.theatreduparc.be

If you're game for a laugh, then get yourself down to the Parc and pick up a ticket to see a variety of performances. The early 2013 season includes *Sherlock Holmes* (a reenactment of the classic detective story with puppets), *Around the World in 80 Days, Oedipus*, and *Les Misérables*.

♯ ⓜTroon. *Walk toward the park and to the left; the theater is in the corner of the park.* Ⓢ *Tickets €5-30. Student tickets €9.50.* ⓩ *Box office open Sept-May M-Sa 11am-6pm, Su 11am-5pm; June and Aug Tu-F 11am-6pm. Closed all of July.*

CIRQUE ROYAL
UPPER TOWN
81 rue de l'Enseignment ☎02 217 23 00 www.cirque-royal.org

Cirque Royal isn't actually a circus, but given its wide range of shows, it's surprising that a circus doesn't make it onto the docket. Expect to see comedies, ballets, popular French and European singers, operas, and traditional theater gracing the stage. Prices and student discounts for individual shows depend on the visiting company.

♯ ⓜMadou. *Cross the big intersection and head west on rue du Congrès. Walk 2 blocks and turn left onto rue de l'Ensignment; Cirque Royal is on the left.* Ⓢ *Prices vary by show.* ⓩ *Box office open M-F 10am-6pm.*

BOZAR
UPPER TOWN
18 rue Ravenstein ☎02 507 82 00 www.bozar.be

Bozar isn't just a brilliant sight to visit during the day for its exhibits—it also hosts visiting artists and performances in dance, music, theater, and film throughout the year. Expect quality cultural events to match the stunning political exhibits. For more information, make sure you grab a copy of the Bozar Magazine, which lists the venue's current offerings.

♯ ⓜParc. *i Ticket prices vary. Student discounts offered.* ⓩ *Box office open July-Aug M-F 11am-5pm, Sept-June M-Sa 11am-7pm.*

THÉÂTRE DE LA TOISON D'OR
UPPER TOWN
396-398 Galeries de la Toison d'Or ☎02 510 05 10 www.ttotheatre.be

Located inside one of Brussels's busy shopping malls, Le Théâtre de la Toison d'Or offers lively plays and comedies. They have been showing performances of *The Vagina Monologues* for several years now, and the 2013 season will include shows such as *Purgatoire* and *Ciao Ciao Bambino*.

♯ ⓜLouise. *Walk down Chausee d'Ixelles about 2.5 blocks; the theater on the right in the Galeries Toison d'Or. i Doors open at 7pm, performances start at 8:30pm.* Ⓢ *€22, seniors €20, students €10. Every first Monday of the month €16, students €8. Package deals available.* ⓩ *Box office open M 10am-4pm, Tu-F 10am-6pm, Sa 2-6pm.*

THÉÂTRE VARIA
PLACE SCHUMAN
78 rue Sceptre ☎02 640 82 58 www.varia.be

Varia is sure into variety, and it offers a plethora of experimental theater and dance performances that will keep you on your toes, including a Woody Allen production and an ice show. The company has two venues, so make sure that you turn up to the right one: Petit Varia is at 154 rue Gray, and Grand Varia is at 78 rue Sceptre.

♯ ⓜSchuman. Ⓢ *Tickets €17-20, students €10-12, seniors €12-25.* ⓩ *Box office open Tu-F 1-7pm, Sa 2:30-7pm.*

CONCERT VENUES

LE BOTANIQUE
UPPER TOWN
bd du Jardin. 29-31 Botanique ☎02 218 37 32 www.botanique.be

The Botanical Gardens make for a beautiful stroll during the day, but things get a little raunchier at night, when the grand building that towers above the gardens hosts some of the best concerts in the city. Three different stages provide an intimate performance space for artists from the UK, continental Europe, and on occasion the US; past heavyweight performers include Ellie Goulding, Marina and the Diamonds, and Kate Nash. Brussels's student crowd can't get enough of Le Botanique, and in recent years it has become the city's most popular venue for live music.

☘ ⓂBotanique. *i* Buy tickets online. Some tickets available at the door. Ⓢ Prices vary by show. 🕐 Box office open daily 10am-6pm.

L'ANCIENNE BELGIQUE   LOWER TOWN
110 bd Anspach   ☎02 548 24 24 www.abconcerts.be

L'Ancienne Belgique is one of the coolest concert venues in Brussels and is regularly mobbed by local students. Performances range from alternative to rock to pop; in 2012, Shantel, Yeasayer, Fun., and Grizzly Bear all graced the stage. Regular free concerts are another plus, so make sure you check out what's happening at this awesome venue.

☘ ⓂBourse. *i* Box office at 25 rue des Pierres. Ⓢ Generally free; some concerts around €10. 🕐 Box office open M-F 11am-6pm.

CINEMAS

STYX   UPPER TOWN
72 rue de l'Arbre Bénit   ☎02 512 21 02 www.cnc-cinema.be

Styx has just two theaters, each seating fewer than 40 people. Films here are screened after their debut in Brussels theaters and include both foreign blockbusters and independent films. Each year Styx sponsors a series of film screenings recommended by foreign film associations.

☘ ⓂLouise. *i* Films always screened in original language. Subtitles usually in French or Dutch. Ⓢ Tickets €5. 🕐 Screenings generally M-F 7 and 9pm; Sa 5, 7, and 9pm; Su 3pm.

UGC   LOWER TOWN
38 pl. du Brouckère   www.ugc.be

If you want to catch the latest Hollywood blockbuster in French or Dutch, then you might want to check out the UGC; the above address is their main location, but there's also a smaller complex located at 8 av. de la Toison d'Or (ⓂLouise).

☘ ⓂDe Brouckère. *i* Unlimited UGC card activation fee €30, then €18.90 per month. Available to anyone, used for unlimited movie admissions. 12-month min. Ⓢ Tickets €5-10. 🕐 Open daily from 10am until last showing.

KINEPOLIS   HEYSEL
Laken 1020   ☎02 474 26 00 www.kinepolis.com

If you're looking for a movie and it's not showing at Kinepolis, chances are it won't be showing at any other mainstream cinema in Belgium. This huge multiplex has 24 screens and shows almost every current blockbuster from Europe and America. Each movie is played in its original language, so you can sit back and practice your language skills or reminisce about home at an English-language film.

☘ ⓂHeysel. *i* To get a student discount, order a Kinepolis student card online. Ⓢ Tickets €9.50, 3-18 years old €8.50, students €6.90. 🕐 Open daily from 9am until last showing. First showing at 2pm.

FESTIVALS

COULEUR CAFÉ   MUSIC FESTIVAL
www.couleurcafe.be

Jessie J and Sean Paul headlined the Belgian music festival here in 2012, though the rest of the performances were dominated by French and Belgian artists. The music festival draws in young people from all over Europe; many of its performances focus on fusion music and Afro-Caribbean sounds. Packed with

arts and culture

as many old hippies as teenagers in cutoff T-shirts, the festival completely takes over an old fairground in northeast Brussels. Couleur Café celebrated its 20th festival in 2010, and is set to continue going strong in 2013.

Ⓢ *1-day ticket €36, 3-day €81; with camping €97.* ☒ *Last weekend in June.*

FÊTE DE LA MUSIQUE   OUTDOOR CONCERT
                                                      www.fetedelamusique.be

Considered by some to be a national holiday (it's actually treated as such in France), the Fête de la Musique is an annual jackpot for music lovers that features a variety of musical styles and performers. Stages are set up by the Royal Palace throughout the city, and the musicians perform around the clock.

Ⓢ *Free.* ☒ *3rd weekend in June.*

BRUSSELS JAZZ MARATHON   JAZZ FESTIVAL
                                                  www.brusselsjazzmarathon.be

The Brussels Jazz Marathon sets up five outdoor stages in the Grand Place, Ste-Catherine, Sablon, Marché aux Poissons, and Fernard Cock, and provides free jazz shows for all to enjoy. Expect fusion, modern, and traditional jazz from both venerated musicians and up-and-coming stars.

Ⓢ *Free.* ☒ *Late May.*

BRUSSELS SUMMER FESTIVAL   MUSIC FESTIVAL
                                                              www.bsf.be

The 10-day Brussels Summer Festival regularly draws music fans from across Europe, and will be in its 12th installment in August 2013. Big European names hit the stage and entertain the mainly student crowd on outdoor and indoor stages; your ticket gets you in to all the performances in the city center. Tickets can be bought online or from FNAC stores (www.fnac.be) or at www.ticketnet.be.

Ⓢ *Presale €35. One day pass €12.50-17.50.* ☒ *10 days in mid-Aug.*

shopping

In many ways, Brussels is a shopaholic's paradise, with everything from big chains to tiny boutiques. The biggest shopping district is the **rue Neuve** in Lower Town, while the area around **Louise** in Upper Town has more upscale fashion shops (and some affordable options too). At the end of the **rue du Marché aux Herbes** is a daily market selling jewelry, produce, and clothing. Similar markets pop up around the **Gare du Midi,** but the unrivaled lord of the flea markets here is the **Marolles.**

The city is also loaded with gorgeous chocolate and candy shops. If you're looking to stock up on Belgian chocolate, your best bet is to do as the locals do and hit up a supermarket. The **GB** has a particularly great selection; head to their conveniently located branch just north of Bourse off bd Anspach to pick up that edible souvenir—Mom will never know the difference.

SHOPPING MALLS

GALERIE PORTE LOUISE   UPPER TOWN
235 Galerie de la Porte Louise   ☎02 2 512 97 12

Galerie Porte Louise is where the rich and fashion-forward find the goods to line their walk-in closets. Budget travelers will probably just want to window-shop here, but it may be worth it to splurge on a nice leather bag. The mall stretches from corner to corner and has shops you can enter from the street, while the interior can be accessed from entrances on av. Louise, av. de la Toison d'Or, and pl. Stephanie.

✤ Ⓜ*Louise.* ☒ *Open M-Sa 6:30am-9:30pm (most shops open from 9am), Su 9am-9pm.*

CLOTHES

GOOD VIB'S
LOWER TOWN

14 rue de Riches Claire ☎02 502 35 81 www.goodvibs.be

Bright walls and Bob Marley will draw you into this smooth shop that sells soft Dirty Velvet tees with designs that manage to be vintage and cool without being outdated. You can shop for tees on the table and on the rack, or you can pretend you really are a cool vintage hipster by shopping for tees that are wrapped and lined up to look like vinyl albums. Don't be fooled, though—you're probably not as cool and hipster as you feel.

✦ ⓂBourse. Walk south on bd Anspach and turn right onto rue des Riches Claires; the store is on the left, just past Foxhole. ⓈMost T-shirts €25-35. Men's shoes €40-45. ☼ Open Tu-F 11am-7pm, Sa 11am-9pm.

RUE NEUVE
LOWER TOWN

rue Neuve

Rue Neuve is Brussels's main shopping district, a nice pedestrian thoroughfare blocked off to traffic. Big brand names, including H&M, Pull & Bear, Levi's, and Brussels's Galeria Inno Department Store, are tucked between the small cafes and mom-and-pop shops. On the weekends, the street becomes packed with students and local families looking for bargains.

✦ ⓂRogier or ⓂDe Brouckère. Rue Nueve is between the two Metro stops. ☼ Shops usually open M-Sa 10am-6pm. Some shops open Su.

FOXHOLE
LOWER TOWN

4 rue des Riches Claires ☎32 476 95 8 72 www.foxholeshop.com
6 rue des Renards ☎32 477 20 53 36

FoxHole is your place for secondhand vintage fashion. Offering the retro styles of yesteryear, this store avoids some of the more garish trends from the '70s and '80s, and the owner buys from specifically selected vendors.

✦ ⓂBourse. ⓈT-shirts and tanks from €5. Men's and women's shoes €15-50. ☼ Riches Claire open Tu-Sa 12:30-6:30pm. Des Renards open Th-Su 10am-6:30pm.

EPISODE
LOWER TOWN

28 rue de la Violette ☎02 513 36 53 www.episode.eu

For affordable vintage clothing, including '80s shell suits, a great range of hats, and stone-washed Levis, head up to Episode, a chain that has stores throughout Europe's major cities. Treat yourself to some plaid and a genuine gas mask.

✦ ⓂBourse. Walk east on rue des Pierres 3 blocks, and continue onto rue de la Violette 2 more blocks. ⓈWallets €5. Animal print scarf €2. Gas mask €10. High-top Converse sneakers €25. ☼ Open M 2-7pm, Tu 1-7pm, W-Sa 11am-7pm.

BELLEROSE
UPPER TOWN

5 Chaussée de Charleroi ☎02 539 44 76 www.bellerose.be

The flagship store of a small local chain, Bellerose has an expansive range of modern American vintage. Nothing's particularly cheap, but you'll definitely find yourself some very stylish and trendy clothes here. If you're after something "American" or just want a fashionable reminder of home, head here.

✦ ⓂLouise. ⓈFrom €20. ☼ Open M-Sa 10am-6:30pm.

CITY2
LOWER TOWN

123 rue Neuve ☎022 211 40 60 www.city2.be

While a trip to the characterless City2 probably won't be a highlight of your trip to Brussels, it may be your most practical stop. The mall includes H&M, Sports World, GB supermarket, and a variety of clothes, electronics, and jewelry shops.

✦ ⓂRogier. ☼ Open M-Th 10am-7pm, F 10am-7:30pm, Sa-Su 10am-7pm.

shopping

CHOCOLATE SHOPS

MAROLLES FLEA MARKET
LOWER TOWN

pl. Jeu de Balle

This is the biggest flea market in Brussels. You can find anything and everything on sale here, from pocket watches to plastic pins, taxidermied squirrels to ferret skins. The local vendors will happily bargain with you, but don't expect to out-haggle them—they're good. If you want to maximize your chances of finding treasure amid all the junk, make sure to get there shortly after the market opens. Be sure to get a big Belgian *broodje* from one of the vendors on the edge of the square.

⚑ Ⓜ Port de Hal. Follow bd du Midi to rue Blaes, turn right, and follow it to the pl. du Jeu de Balle. ⏲ Open daily 7am-3pm.

PLANÈTE CHOCOLATE
LOWER TOWN

24 rue du Lombard　　　　　　　　　☎02 511 07 55 www.planetechocolat.be

One of the most renowned chocolate shops in Brussels (and that's saying something), Planète Chocolate displays an infinite array of handmade chocolate creations, including detailed chocolate bouquets. Take a trip to the chocolate salon to watch the local Oompa-Loompas brew the house specialties, learn a little chocolate history, and try some of the creations.

⚑ Ⓜ Bourse. Ⓢ Chocolate salon €7. ⏲ Open M-Sa 10am-6:30pm, Su 11am-6:30pm. Demonstrations Sa and Su 4pm or by appointment.

LA MAISON DES MAÎTRES CHOCOLATIERS
LOWER TOWN

4 Grand Place　　　　　　　　　　☎02 888 66 20 wwww.mmcb.be

The craftsmen at La Maison des Maîtres Chocolatiers create scrumptious treats and sculpt their creations into increasingly eccentric shapes—we particularly enjoyed the life-sized chocolate baby in the window. Prices can be steep, but it's worth at least gawking at if you're in the neighborhood, if only to see the flowing waterfall of chocolate.

⚑ Ⓜ Bourse. ⏲ Open daily 10am-10pm.

BOOKS

▨ TROPISMES
LOWER TOWN

4 Galerie du Roi　　　　　　　　　☎02 512 88 62 www.tropismes.com

With uniform white bindings on most of the books, Tropismes looks a bit more like an archival library than a book shop. Composed of three levels of French novels, plays, and comics, along with a small break room with a couch, free water, and coffee, Tropismes can keep you busy for as long as you want. Any employee at one of the five info desks will be more than willing to help you find what you are looking for.

⚑ Ⓜ De Brouckère. Walk east down rue l'Ecuyer about 4 blocks, then turn right into Galerie du Roi. *i* 2nd location at 11 Galerie des Princes. ⏲ Open Tu-Th 10am-6:30pm, F 10am-7:30pm, Sa 10:30am-7pm, Su 1:30-6:30pm.

WATERSTONES
LOWER TOWN

71-75 bd Adolphe Max　　　　　　☎02 219 27 08 www.waterstones.com

One of the UK's biggest bookstores, this renowned English chain is currently staging a hostile takeover of Brussels's book scene. Though *Let's Go* never recommends *coups d'état*, we approve. You can find just about anything here, from magazines to newspapers to old and new classics. The English-speaking staff will happily advise you on a good read for your trip to Brussels. If you are staying in the long term, check out the Waterstones Brussels Facebook page for updates on monthly talks by authors and other speakers.

⚑ Ⓜ Rogier. Head south on bd Adolphe Max; the store is on the left. ⏲ Open M-Sa 9am-7pm, Su

10:30am-6pm.

PASSA PORTA LOWER TOWN

46 rue Antoine Dansaert ☎02 502 94 60 www.passaportabookshop.be

Passa Porta looks like a fashion studio for books. Despite its appearance, however, Passa Porta is filled not just with best sellers but also with an eclectic mix of cookbooks and beer and wine guides, a fun kids section, and a whole wall of travel books.

🏲 Ⓜ*Ste-Catherine. Walk toward the cathedral and turn right, walk 1 block, then turn left onto rue Antoine Dansaert.* 🕐 *Open M noon-7pm, Tu-Sa 11am-7pm, Su noon-6pm.*

BOZAR BOOKSHOP UPPER TOWN

15 rue Ravenstein ☎02 514 15 05 www.bozarshop.com

After exploring the fine arts exhibits at the Bozar Center, make sure to browse the thick stacks of books, postcards, and DVDs in the bookstore in the back.

🏲 Ⓜ*Parc.* 🕐 *Open daily 10am-10pm.*

MUSIC

JUKE BOX SHOP LOWER TOWN

165 bd Anspach ☎02 511 67 51 jukeboxshop@versadsl.be

Juke Box Shop is packed wall-to-wall and floor-to-ceiling with a huge selection of vinyls that go at 45rpm and those weird CD things (who uses those anymore?). Every musical taste is catered to here, but the shop's collection specializes in psychedelic, soul, *chansons*, and new-wave, making this store a little different from the others in the area.

🏲 Ⓜ*Bourse. Walk south on bd Anspach almost 3 blocks; the store is on the right.* Ⓢ *Sgt. Pepper's Lonely Hearts Band original vinyl €50.* 🕐 *Open M-Sa 11am-6pm.*

VEALS AND GEEKS LOWER TOWN

8 rue des Grand Carmes ☎02 511 40 14

Bring your old Dungeons and Dragons set—nerds rule here. Veals and Geeks stocks a small but carefully selected collection of records that range from the Beatles to Metallica but is better known for its secondhand Gameboys, band T-shirts, and DVDs.

🏲 Ⓜ*Bourse.* 🕐 *Open daily 11am-8pm.*

JEWELRY

BETTY DE STEFANO 20TH-CENTURY JEWELRY, DIAMONDS

17 rue Lebeau ☎02 511 46 13 www.collectors-gallery.com

Betty de Stefano travels the world looking for one-of-a-kind jewelry pieces to sell in her personal collection at this store. From diamond necklaces to sterling silver rings, not only are Betty's finds irreplaceable, but many of her pieces are also 20th-century antiques. Here, age comes not before beauty but with it, and unless you have a few hundred euro you just don't need, expect to window-shop.

🏲 Ⓜ*Gare Centrale. Walk southwest on Cantersteen and turn left onto rue Lebeau; the store is on the right.* Ⓢ *From €190.* 🕐 *Open W-Sa 11am-6pm, Su 11am-3pm.*

LUXIOL UPPER TOWN

221 Chaussée d'Ixelles ☎02 648 77 14

Still going strong after more than 20 years, Luxiol is a small but bright little shop with a diverse range of handmade jewelry from India and Thailand. Luxiol also specializes in classic wooden toys and precious stones.

🏲 Ⓜ*Port de Namur. Walk south on Chaussée d'Ixelles about 5-10min.* Ⓢ *Earrings from €3. Wood toys €8-25.* 🕐 *Open Tu-Sa 10:30am-6:30pm.*

shopping

LA VIE EST BELLE UPPER TOWN

4 rue Jules Bouillon ☎02 513 89 98

The earthy vibe that pervades this little shop is reflected in its jewelry collection, which is vaguely South Asian and very intricate; expect lots of greens, purples, and precious stones. Walk away with a small piece of Asia without actually leaving Brussels.

⇟ [M]Port de Namur. Walk south on Chaussée d'Ixelles about 4 blocks past Chaussée de Wavre, then take the angle left onto Atheneumstraat; the store is across the street at the corner. ⏰ Open Tu-Sa 11am-6:30pm.

excursion

BRUGES *brugge* ☎050

There's a reason you'll meet cute old couples on second honeymoons in Bruges: with its picturesque canals and narrow old houses, it looks a little like a fairy-tale land. Romantic Bruges is perhaps the best-preserved medieval city in Europe, with entire blocks dating back to the 12th and 13th centuries. The cobbled streets are often clogged with tourists wearing fanny packs and toting cameras; most congregate around the museums, which range from the history of the *frite* to Flemish art. It's easy to get caught in the tourist-trap side of Bruges, but if you step away from the town center and explore the side streets, you'll find cheap and tasty Flemish cuisine, shops selling beer glasses and proper Belgian lace, and quirky bars and pubs. Put in a little extra effort, and locals will happily share with you all of Bruges's ghost stories, weird secrets, and small-town charm.

Orientation

Thanks to its small size, Bruges is very easy to navigate. Getting lost in the city is more fun than worrying, since it takes only 10min. to get back on track. Bruges is surrounded by a canal which cuts through the center of the city, so if you do get lost, just follow the water. **The Markt** is the center of town, and is recognizable by the large **belfry tower,** which can be seen from almost any part of town. Four of Bruges's main roads emanate from the Markt: **St-Jakobstraat** to the northwest, **Vlamingstraat** to the northeast, **Wollestraat** to the southeast, and **Steenstraat** to the southwest. East of the Markt along Breidelstraat is **the Burg,** Bruges's other main square, which boasts the Town Hall and Holy Blood Chapel. **Hoogstraat** runs east from the Burg, while **Blezelstraat** runs south. You can easily find all destinations in Bruges from the Markt and the Burg.

Accommodations

Bruges draws a fair amount of young backpackers, so hostels are plentiful in the city center and just outside the city walls.

BAUHAUS HOSTEL, HOTEL $

133-145 Langestraat ☎050 34 10 93 www.bauhaus.be

This huge hostel, budget hotel, and bar complex spans 12 houses on one of Bruges's historic streets. The exterior may be medieval, but the rooms inside are definitely modern. Bauhaus has amenities galore: bike rental, Wi-Fi, laundry machines, lockers, printers, and "pod beds" with private curtains in most rooms. The lively bar is an excellent place to start the night—just try not to get lost in the labyrinth of corridors leading back to your room.

*⇟ From the Burg, head east along Hoogstraat, which leads into Langestraat. **i** Breakfast and linens included. Free Wi-Fi. $ 4- to 8-bed dorms €15-22; singles €30-34; doubles €38-50. ⏰ Reception 9am-11pm.*

SNUFFEL
HOSTEL $
47-49 Ezelstraat   ☎050 33 31 33 www.snuffel.be

This quirky hostel features odd touches like colorful cartoon murals and chain-operated showers. There are also some less novel comforts, like bike rental, laundry, a kitchen, and free walking tours of the city. The bar on the ground floor boasts chess and checker sets, sometimes hosts concerts, and attracts locals as well as travelers (practically unheard of for a hostel bar).

⚡ *From the Markt, head up St-Jacobstraat, which leads into Ezelstraat.* ℹ *Breakfast and linens included. Free Wi-Fi.* Ⓢ *4- to 12-bed dorms €16-22.* ⏰ *Reception 7:30am-midnight.*

PASSAGE
HOSTEL $
26 Dweersstraat   ☎050 34 02 32 www.passagebruges.com

Just a short walk from the center of town, Passage is situated above an old-fashioned Bruges restaurant. While the rooms lack the elegance of the attached "Grand Cafe," they have everything you need. Limited common spaces make it less social than other hostels in town.

⚡ *From the Markt, walk southwest and veer toward the right. Turn left onto Geldmuntstraat, which becomes Noordzendstraat. Dweersstraat is on the left.* ℹ *Breakfast €5. Free Wi-Fi.* Ⓢ *Dorms €16.*

Sights

The biggest sight in Bruges is, well, Bruges. You can probably allot most of your time to wandering around, taking pictures, and oohing and aahing. For indoor entertainment, Bruges is home to 16 museums, all run by the local **Musea Brugge** organization. You can buy a three-day combo ticket, which will get you into most of them (€15, under 26 €5), but most of the museums are small and anticlimactic, and not all of the best ones are included in the combo ticket. Bruges loves young people, leading to huge discounts for those under 26.

BELFORT
TOWER
7 Markt   ☎050 44 87 78 www.museabrugge.be

If you've bribed the weather gods into giving Belgium a cloudless day, the gorgeous view from the Belfort can extend all the way to the North Sea. Keep in mind that the 83m structure was built centuries before the age of elevators, so you'll have to climb a lot of stairs to get that photo-op. But the panoramic view over the entire city is well worth the huffing and puffing.

⚡ *In the Markt.* Ⓢ *€8, seniors €6, under 26 €4.* ⏰ *Open daily 9:30am-5pm.*

GROENINGE MUSEUM
MUSEUM
12 Dijver   ☎050 44 87 43 www.museabrugge.be

Bruges's best museum, the Groeninge Museum, features a collection of Flemish and Belgian art from the 15th to 20th centuries. We particularly enjoyed the Flemish Expressionists, who applied the famous style to the rural life of small-town Bruges. Admission includes access to the temporary exhibition in the **Arentshuis** and **The Forum,** Bruges's center for contemporary art.

⚡ *From the Markt, head south along Wollestraat and cross the bridge. Turn right onto Dijver and head through the archway on the left.* Ⓢ *€8, seniors €6, ages 6-25 €1.* ⏰ *Open Tu-Su 9:30am-5pm.*

CHURCH OF OUR LADY
CHURCH, MUSEUM
Mariastraat   ☎050 44 87 78 www.museabrugge.be

This church houses some of Bruges's most beautiful artwork, including one of the very few Michelangelo statues outside of Italy: the *Madonna and Child*, which sits on the Baroque altar at the south end of the church. Some visitors pray at its feet; others just whip out their cameras. The church itself is free, but if you're in the mood, you can pay to visit the museum to see some more 16th-century religious artwork as well the decorative tombs of Mary of Burgundy and

Charles the Bold. With a 122m steeple that dominates the Bruges skyline, the church is easy to find—when in doubt, look up.

From the Markt, head west along Secnstraat to Simon Stevenplein Sq. Head south down Mariastraat. The church is just before the bridge. $ Church free. Museum €2, students €1. Open M-F 9:30am-4:50pm, Sa 9:30am-4:40pm, Su 1:30-4:50pm.

HOLY BLOOD CHAPEL CHURCH

10 Burg ☎050 33 67 92

And now for something completely different…every afternoon from 2-4pm the faithful gather to pay their respects to the namesake of this small church: a vial containing what is purported to be the blood of Christ. There's not really anything to do here except see the blood, but if you're in Bruges in May you can catch the Holy Blood Procession, a 14th-century tradition in which the faithful reenact the passion and resurrection and parade the vial around the city. Those on a blood-seeing tour of Europe can add this to their itineraries right next to bullfighting and Jack the Ripper tours.

In the southwest corner of the Burg. i For more information about the procession, visit www.ticketsbrugge.be. $ Free. Open daily Apr-Sept 10am-noon and 2-6pm; Oct-Mar 10am-noon and 2-4pm.

Food

Bruges is brimming with restaurants—unfortunately, the local specialty is pawning small portions of overpriced food off on unsuspecting tourists. These places cluster around the Markt, but you know better than to fall into these traps. Instead, head a little farther out from the Markt to find a quality place, which will leave neither your wallet nor your stomach empty.

PAS PARTOUT TRADITIONAL $

1 Jeruzalemstraat ☎050 33 51 16 srpaspartout@busmail.net

Pas Partout was once a three-star Michelin restaurant where just looking at the menu cost a fortune. Then it was taken over and turned into a social service project, offering high-quality food to those who wouldn't normally be able to afford it. Well played, Bruges.

From the Burg, head east along Hoogstraat, cross the bridge, and continue onto Molenmeers. Turn left onto Jeruzalemstraat just past the laundromat, then continue to the end of the road. $ Meals €3-10. Open M-Sa 11:45am-2:15pm.

MÉDRAD TRADITIONAL $

18 Sint-Ammandstraat ☎050 34 86 84

It's hard to find better value anywhere in Bruges, let alone this close to the Markt. The specialty spaghetti with cheese, vegetables, and plenty of ground beef (€3) can easily make a light dinner for the hungry backpacker. Larger dishes are also just the way we like them: big, tasty, and inexpensive. This neighborhood favorite isn't a well-kept secret, so you may want to reserve a day ahead.

Just off of the Markt. $ Meals €2-10. Sandwiches €2.50-4. Spaghetti €3-5.50. Open Tu-Sa 11am-8:30pm, Su 12:30-8:30pm.

CAFÉ VLISSINGHE CAFE, BAR $$

2 Blakesstraat ☎050 34 37 37 www.cafevlissinghe.be

This isn't just any old Flemish eatery—it's the oldest Flemish cafe in Bruges. The best part: only the locals seem to know about it. The rustic kitchen and meticulously preserved 16th-century interior, hidden down a charming side street, make this place feel like a time warp. The menu will satisfy you with basic sandwiches and cheeses, while tasty entrees like lasagna are available for dinner.

From the Burg, head east along Hoogstraat, cross the bridge, and continue onto Molenmeers. Just past the laundromat, turn left onto Jeruzalemstraat. Blakesstraat is the 4th street on the left. $ Food €3.50-8. Drinks €2-7. Open W-Sa 11am-late.

MARKT FRITES FRITERIE $

The Markt, by the Belfort

Although these two *frite* sheds look like identical, there's actually a war of the *frites* being waged here. Both stands charge identical prices for small servings, but we reckon that the one on the left, **Sharsa,** has the slightly tastier fries. If the line is too long, the offerings at **Mi-resto** (on the right) aren't bad.

South corner of the Markt. $ Frites €2.25-2.75. Sauce €0.60. ⏰ Sharsa open July-Aug M-Th 10am-5am, F-Sa 9am-7am, Su 10am-5am; Sept-June M-Th 10am-3am, F-Sa 9am-7am, Su 10am-3am. Mi-resto open M-Th 9am-3am, F-Sa 9am-7am, Su 9am-3am.

Nightlife

Nightlife in Bruges is pretty easy-going; the only things open until 7am are the *frites* stands. Locals enjoy a quiet drink in hidden spots, while tourists congregate near the Markt to down pricey pints. For a more authentically Belgian experience, head to one of the bars below. This is a place to drink slowly and strike up conversations with the locals.

'T POATERSGAT BAR

82 Vlamingstraat www.poatersgat.com

Popular with locals, 't Poatersgat fills an underground passage that the owner claims used to be used by monks sneaking out of the nearby church and into the brothel at the end of the road. Nowadays, the rabbit-hole-like entrance (the door is embedded in the church wall) leads to a great place for a casual drink.

Vlamingstraat is just off the Markt. [i] Free Wi-Fi. $ Beer €2-5. ⏰ Open daily 5pm-late.

LUCIFERNUM BAR

8 Twijnstraat www.lucifernum.be

Lucifernum is one of Bruges's quirkiest treasures. Ring the bell of this stately old mayor's residence on Saturday night and you'll be ushered inside by Willy Restin, the tux-wearing proprietor and a local **Mephistopheles** (in a good way). Try your luck with the Cuban-style rum bar's strong but tasty mojitos, which you can enjoy indoors among Willy's trinkets or outside in the garden. On the first Saturday of each month, local expert Maria opens up an **Absinthe Bar.** Locals consider Willy's place a well-hidden gem, so be respectful—don't arrive too late and don't embarrass yourself.

From the Burg, head along Hoogstraat, turn left onto Kelkstraat, and right onto Twijnstraat. Ring the doorbell (indicated with a sign). [i] Leave your sneakers at the hostel: no sportswear or shorts. $ Rum Bar cover €5; includes 1 drink. Absinthe Bar cover €6; includes 1 drink. Drinks €5-6. ⏰ Open Sa 9pm-4am.

DE GARRE PUB

1 De Garre ☎050 34 10 29

They say no one just stumbles across De Garre—if you manage to find it, you were destined to visit. Located down a small alleyway between the Markt and the Burg, De Garre is the only place to sample the smooth and tasty De Garre beer (€3). This 12% beer is strong—so strong that they'll only let you have three in one sitting. The two-story seating area is typical of Belgian watering holes, and the cheese that comes with every beer helps the drinking along nicely.

De Garre is just off of Breydelstraat, in between the Markt and the Burg. $ Beer €2-3.50. ⏰ Open daily noon-midnight.

DE REPUBLIEK BAR

36 St-Jakobsstraat ☎050 34 02 29

De Republiek hosts a crowd of tourists, older locals, and local teenagers, who grab drinks here before heading to the cinema next door (that's pretty much all there is for kids to do around here). The mellow atmosphere and whimsical cocktails keep De Republiek a little less touristy than some of the bars closer to the Markt.

St-Jakobsstraat is off the northeast corner of the Markt. $ Beer €2.40-6. Mixed drinks €7.50. ⏰ Open daily 10:30am-3am.

Essentials

PRACTICALITIES

- **TOURIST OFFICES: In and Uit Brugge.** (Concertgebouw 34 't Zand ☎050 44 46 46 www.bruges.be/tourism ⏰ Open daily 10am-6pm.) A smaller branch is in the train station, **Stationsplein.** (⏰ Open M-F 10am-5pm, Sa-Su 10am-2pm.)
- **LUGGAGE STORAGE:** Available at the train station.
- **ATMS:** In the **Markt,** on **Vlamingstraat,** and in **Simosteviplein.**
- **INTERNET:** There's free Wi-Fi at the train station, at the bars of central hostels, and at a few bars like **'t Poatersgat** (see **Nightlife**).
- **LAUNDROMATS: Wash Casino.** (151 Langestraat $ Wash €4 per 8kg, dry €0.50 per 20min. ⏰ Open daily 6am-10pm.) **Wassaloon Happyram.** (10 Ezelstraat $ Wash €4 per 7.5kg., dry €1 per 15min. ⏰ Open daily 6am-10pm.)
- **POST OFFICES:** The central post office is at **5 Markt.** (☎050 33 14 11; www.depost.be ⏰ Open M-F 9am-6pm, Sa 9am-3pm.)
- **POSTAL CODE:** 8000.

EMERGENCY

- **POLICE:** The police headquarters are at **7 Hauwerstraat.** (☎050 44 88 44 🚏 From the Markt, exit on the northwest side and turn left onto Geldmuntstraat, which becomes Noordzandstraat. Turn left onto Vrijdagmarkt, then right onto Hauwerstraat.)
- **LATE-NIGHT PHARMACIES:** Call the 24hr. pharmacy hotline. (☎0900 10 500 ⏰ Operates 10pm-9am.)
- **HOSPITALS/MEDICAL SERVICES: Hospital AZ St-Jan.** (Riddershove 10 ☎050 45 21 11; www.azbrugge.be 🚏 Bus #13 to AZ Sint-Jan AV.)

GETTING THERE

Bruges is most easily reached by train. **Brugge Station** is located just outside of town, a 20-30min. walk from the center. (⏰ Ticket office open June-Aug daily 10am-7pm; Sept-May M-Sa 10am-6pm, Su 10am-7pm.) Public transportation runs from the station to the main squares all day. Trains arrive from Brussels ($ €13 ⏰ 50min.) and Paris ($ €47 ⏰ 2½hr., 3 per day). To reach Bruges from other major European cities, you will have to change at Brussels Midi/Zuid or Brussels Nord.

Bruges is also close to Brussels Airport and the budget-airline-beloved Brussels South Charleroi Airport, but you will need to go through Brussels to get to Bruges. See **Essentials,** Getting There later in this chapter for information on how to get from the airports to Brussels. **Eurolines** buses also connect Bruges to Amsterdam. ($ €25, under 25 €19. ⏰ 5hr., 1 per day.) To get to Paris, Rotterdam, or the Hague, you'll have to change in Brussels.

GETTING AROUND

Tiny Bruges is simple to navigate, and most visitors tackle the city by foot. Bikes can be useful, especially if you're hoping to explore farther afield. Try **Ropellier Bikes** at 26 Mariastraat. (☎050 34 32 62 $ €4 per hr., €8 per 4hr., €12 per day. ⏰ Open daily 9am-7pm.) **Bruges Bike Rental** offers a student discount on single-day rentals. (17 Desparsstraat ☎050 61 61 08 $ €4 per hr.; €6 per 2hr.; €8 per 4hr.; €12 per day, students €8. ⏰ Open daily 10am-10pm.)

De Lijn runs the bus system. (Stationsplein ☎070 220 200; www.delijn.be) Buses #1, 6, and 11 go from the station into the town center. Tickets are valid for 1hr. (€1.20 at the station booth, €2 on board). If you're staying a little out of the way and don't want to walk, you can call **Bruges Taxi Service** (☎050 33 44 55).

essentials

PRACTICALITIES

- **TOURIST OFFICES:** 👍**Use-it** makes maps especially for student travelers that are available for free at many hostels as well as at their office and on their website. The office staff can give advice on nightlife, food, shopping, GLBT life, and more. They also provide a list of festivals and events, have free internet (computers available), and free coffee. (8 Steenkoolkaai www.use-it.be ⇄ [M]Ste-Catherine. ⏰ Open M-Sa 10am-1pm and 2-6pm.) The **central tourist office,** in the east corner of the Grand Place ([M]Bourse), sells the **Brussels Card,** which includes free public transport, a city map, free museum access, and discounts at a few shops and restaurants for one, two, or three days (€24/34/40). There is also a second, less central office (2-4 rue Royale) and another at the central concourse of Gare du Midi (open daily 9am-6pm). (☎02 513 89 40 www.brusselsinternational.be ⏰ Open daily 10am-6pm.)
- **CURRENCY EXCHANGE: CBC Automatic Change ATMs.** (7 Grand Place ☎02 546 12 11 ⏰ Open 24hr. Also at [M]De Brouckere and [M]Gare du Midi.)
- **LAUNDROMATS: Washing 65.** (65 rue du Midi ⏰ Open daily 7am-9pm.) **Wash Club.** (68 rue du Marché au Charbon [$] Wash €3.80 per 8kg. ⏰ Open daily 7am-10pm. Detergent for sale in vending machine.)
- **INTERNET: CyberCafés.** (86 bd Émile Jacqmain [$] €1.50 per 30min. ⏰ Open daily 9am-10pm.) Free Wi-Fi is available at **McDonald's, Exki,** and **Quick** on rue Neuve.
- **POST OFFICES: Central Office.** (1 bd Anspach ⇄ [M]De Brouckère. ☎02 201 23 45 ⏰ Open M-F 8:30am-6pm, Sa 10am-4pm. Belgium €0.75, EU €1.09, other countries €1.29.)
- **POSTAL CODE:** 1000.

EMERGENCY

- **EMERGENCY:** For police, ambulance, or fire, call ☎100 or ☎101.
- **POLICE: Police headquarters** are located at 30 rue du Marché au Charbon. (☎02 279 77 11 ⇄ [M]Bourse. From the Grand Place, follow rue du Marché au Charbon from the northwest corner of the square. ⏰ Open 24hr.)
- **LATE-NIGHT PHARMACIES:** Pharmacies in Brussels rotate hours, so there will always be one reasonably close to you that's open late. Pharmacies will usually display hours on a sign. **Pharmacie Fripiers** is closest to the Grand Place. (24B rue des Fripiers ☎02 218 04 91 ⏰ Open M-F 9am-7pm, Sa 9:30am-7pm.) To find one open near you, visit www.servicedegarde.be or call ☎0800 20 600.
- **HOSPITALS/MEDICAL SERVICES:** The Saint-Pierre University Hospital has two locations. **Saint-Pierre University Hospital–Site César de Paepe** is a 10min. walk from the Grand Place. (11 rue des Alexiens ☎02 506 71 11 www.stpierre-bru.be ⇄ [M]Bourges. From the Grand Place, exit through the southernmost corner of the square and turn left onto rue des Alexiens.) **Saint-Pierre University Hospital (International Patients Service)** is to the south. (322 rue Haute ☎02 535 33 17 www.stpierre-bru.be ⇄ Tram #3, 4, 33, or 51 to [M]Porte de Hal. Head south on rue Haute. ⏰ Open 24hr.)

GETTING THERE

By Plane

The **Brussels airport** (BRU ☎090 07 00 00 www.brusselsairport.be) is 14km from the city center. Trains run between the airport and Gare du Midi every 20min. (€6-7 max; 5am-midnight). STIB bus #12 runs until 8pm, later on weekends and public holidays;

bus #21 runs every 30min. (5am-11pm, until midnight during the summer). **Brussels South Charleroi Airport** (CRL ☎090 20 24 90 www.charleroi-airport.com) is a budget airline hub 45km south of Brussels. A shuttle runs from the airport to Gare du Midi. (Ⓢ €13, round-trip €22. ⌚ Every 30min.)

By Train

Brussels has three main train stations: **Gare du Midi, Gare Centrale,** and **Gare du Nord.** All international trains stop at Gare du Midi, and most stop at Gare Centrale and Gare du Nord as well. Gare Centrale is the closest to the center and the Grand Place. Gare du Nord is in the north just past Botanique. Gare du Midi is in the southwest on bd du Midi. Brussels can be reached from Bruges (Ⓢ €12 ⌚ 30min.), Amsterdam (Ⓢ €43 ⌚ 3hr.), and Paris (Ⓢ €55-86 ⌚ 1hr. from ⓂMidi); trains also run from London (www.eurostar.com Ⓢ €60-240 ⌚ 2hr.). There are also normal commuter trains that run between Amsterdam and Brussels that you can board without advance booking, but you can (and probably should) book in advance.

GETTING AROUND

Getting around Brussels is cheap and simple on foot, especially in Lower Town. With skinny, winding streets that change names often (and often have two names to begin with), it's easy to get lost. Luckily, it's also easy to get found: look for tall signposts around Lower Town and the major museum districts of Upper Town. These will point you in the direction of major attractions and Metro stations and will even suggest whether to walk or take the Metro based on how far your destination may be. Cars rule the roads in Brussels, so bikes are only advisable for the truly brave. If you want to bike around Brussels, there are **villo** (bike rental) points located at key locations throughout the city; the first 30min. is free, but you pay incrementally for each 30min. thereafter (www.villo.be).

By Public Transportation

The Metro system rings the city, with a main **tram** running vertically through the middle and two other lines running east to west. There are 18 trams in total. The **bus** and tram system connects the various quarters of the city, and night buses service major stops on Friday and Saturday nights every 30min. until 3am. All public transport in Brussels is run by the **Société des Transports Intercommunaux Bruxellois (STIB).** (☎07 023 20 00 www.stib.be ⌚ System operates daily 5am-midnight.) The **Metro,** tram, and bus all use the same tickets. (Ⓢ €2, purchased inside vehicle €2.50; round-trip €3.50; day pass €6; 10-trip ticket €13.) It's a good idea to pick up a copy of the Metro map, which also contains information about transfers and night buses. The map is free and available at ticket counters and at the Gare du Midi.

By Taxi

After the Metro stops running, you can call **Taxi Bleus** (☎02 268 00 00), **Taxi Verts** (☎02 349 49 49), **Taxis Oranges** (☎02 349 43 43), **Autolux** (☎02 411 41 42), or **CNTU** (☎02 374 20 20). Official taxi signs are yellow and black. Taxi prices are calculated by distance (€1.66-2.70 per km), plus a fixed base charge (€2.40, at night €4.40). **Collecto** is a shared taxi system that has 200 pickup points in Brussels (☎02 800 36 36 www.collecto.org Ⓢ €6 ⌚11pm-6am. Call 20min. or more in advance).

brussels 101

HISTORY

The Chapel on the Island (695-979)

The area of central Belgium where Brussels lies has been a settlement since before settlement was even a word. However, the first mention of the area being called something similar to "Brussels" didn't occur until 695 CE, when St. Vindicianus referenced a place called "Brosella." The city's name originated from an Old Dutch translation of "home in the marsh." The city was officially founded in the year 979 by **Charles, the Duke of Low Lotharingia,** who was the expelled son of France's King Louis IV. Charles decided to build a "castrum"(fortress) around the settlement, thereby creating the city of Brussels.

Middle-Aged Rejuvenation (979-1500)

After the castrum was built, Brussels established itself as a central point of trade between Bruges, Ghent, and Cologne. During the city's heyday, Brussels was the main exporter of luxury goods such as fabrics and tapestries to places like Paris and Venice. The first set of walls were built around the city in the 11th century, which increased population growth by eliminating the need to guard one's home throughout the night and allowed citizens to pursue other late-night activities. During this time, Brussels was also a burgeoning center for many artists, including Rogier van der Weyden and Robert Campin.

You Say You Want a Revolution...or Five? (1500-1830)

Brussels, although well known today for its neutral diplomacy, has a history rife with bloodshed and uprisings. During Europe's Renaissance, Brussels was a hotspot for conflict between more powerful countries like Germany, Austria, and France. There were multiple changes of power in Brussels, from Holy Roman Emperor Maximilian I to Charles V to Isabella and Archduke Albrecht of Russia, who finally brought peace to the region. However, this peace didn't last long—King Louis XIV of France bombed the entire city in 1695 as part of the Nine Years War, destroying over 4000 buildings and leaving the Grand Palace in ruin. The city continued this pattern of conflict when French troops invaded in the mid-1700s during the War of Austrian Succession. Brussels remained under Austrian control from 1749 until 1795, when France captured and annexed the region. After breaking from the French in 1815, Brussels joined the United Kingdom of the Netherlands only to revolt in 1830. (It was after a showing of Auber's opera, *La Muette de Portici,* that the entire city of Brussels rose up and ousted the Dutch imposers.)

The Capital of the World (1830-present)

After taking back their city, the Belgians established **King Leopold I** as their leader in July 1831. This period became a time of great urban renewal after the **Covering of the Senne,** a project undertaken due to the enormous health hazards posed by the river. This allowed for more buildings to be constructed above the covered waterway. Brussels was occupied by Germany during both **World War I** and **World War II** and suffered a great deal of damage. However, the **Treaty of Brussels** in 1948 led to the initiation of a Western European defense cooperation. After WWII, Belgium separated into two semi-independent regions: Flanders, which is Dutch, and the Walloon Provinces, which are French (the city district of Brussels remained bilingual). The accepting and bicultural atmosphere that resulted from this split led to Brussels emerging as a prime choice for the capital of the European Union, as well as the headquarters of the North Atlantic Treaty Organization (NATO). This redefinition of Brussels as a cosmopolitan city helped the city's economy and industry. Brussels did, however, continue to have trouble trying to maintain its cultural identity while modernizing the urban areas. Brussels has hosted many world events, including the 1958 World Fair. As home to the EU and NATO, Brussels has had to contend with international crises such as the Rwandan Genocide, the Euro-Zone Crisis, and other calamities. Today the city remains focused on its place in the European Union and maintaining its global neutrality.

CUSTOMS AND ETIQUETTE
French or Dutch?
With both Dutch and French serving as official languages, the city of Brussels is a polyglot. However, due to the presence of many international organizations, dozens of languages are spoken around the city. The citizens of Brussels are skillful masters of language, and government proceedings take place in both national languages. So what do people speak in casual conversation? To prevent the domination of either French or Dutch, Belgian people from different regions will speak English while together, which makes it easy for English-speaking visitors to the city. In order to be polite, however, one should have a few Dutch or French phrases handy to show some appreciation for the local culture.

Meeting New People
Brussels is quite socially conservative compared to other prominent cities in Europe. A handshake is common for people who haven't met before, and after a relationship has been formed, three kisses on the cheek—starting on the left—will replace the handshake. Men never kiss other men and instead always shake hands (you aren't Spanish, after all). When visiting Belgians in their homes, it's polite to come bearing flowers or chocolates. But don't give white chrysanthemums, which are a symbol of death (unless, of course, that's the message you're meaning to convey), and flowers should be given in odd numbers (just never 13).

On the Street
Personal appearances and cleanliness are very important to the people of Brussels, who dress more conservatively and formally than is typical in the United States or the UK. People here are also less apt than those of other cultures to strike up a conversation in the middle of the road. That doesn't mean they won't help with directions if you ask, but it does mean they won't invite you back to their house for a beer or care about what you have to say. Also, because Brussels is a totally egalitarian society, over half the Parliament is made up of women, and women generally don't take their husbands' last names when they get married. Many people are also internationals, which means you can't walk down the street without any regard for your surroundings—any joke or comment that might be taken as rude or hurtful to a certain gender, race, or religion could very well fall on unappreciative ears.

FOOD AND DRINK
Beer
There are over 800 types of beer in Belgium, the most common varieties being Stella Artois, Jupiler, and Maes. Belgians consume over 150 liters of beer per capita each year. Thus, asking for wine in Brussels is like asking for a beer in Napa Valley. The brews in Brussels are varied, from fruit to wheat beers. Try the famous Kriek beer, made with cherries, or some fruit beers like raspberry, peach, grape, or even banana and pineapple. Each beverage is served in a beautiful and distinct glass, which means everyone can instantly recognize what everyone else is drinking in a bar.

brussels

Chocolate

Belgium is known for its chocolate, and the country produces 220,000 tons of the confection every year (which amounts to 22kg of chocolate per person every year). The world's biggest selling location for chocolate is the Brussels National Airport. The praline chocolate was invented here in 1912 by Jean Neuhaus. Brussels is also home to many chocolate and praline manufacturers such as Neuhaus, Leonidas, and Godiva.

Moules-Frites

This dish consists of mussels and French fries. The mussels are usually served in a big black pot and covered in delicious sauces such as white wine, herb, and cream and garlic. Belgians also claim to have invented French fries, which are very popular in Brussels and can be found on snack carts throughout the city. Unlike the French fry-ketchup combination that is popular in America, Belgian French fries are usually served with a mayonnaise sauce. Maybe the country's love of quality *frites* is why Belgium has the lowest proportion of McDonald's restaurants in the developed world (seven times less than that of the US).

Waffles

Called *gaufres*, Belgium is famous globally for its delicious waffles. Although waffles were technically invented in Ghent in 1839, Brussels is well known for this delectable breakfast treat. The Brussels special variation on this dish is big, light, and rectangular waffles that are usually eaten with toppings such as fruit or ice cream. But if you don't want to look like a tourist, it is well known that the true way to eat a waffle is by simply topping it with icing sugar. American visitors might also be surprised to learn that Belgian waffles are not just for breakfast—try them as a snack or for dessert after some *moules-frites*.

ARTS AND ARCHITECTURE

Museums

Brussels is home to over 80 museums, including the Museum of Modern Art, the Royal Museums of Fine Arts of Belgium, and the Magritte Museum. These boast the works of famous artists like Peter Paul Reubens, Anthony van Dyck, and Jacob Jordaens, three Flemish Baroque painters who brought prestige and celebrity to the world of Belgian art during the 17th century. Rene Magritte was another famous Brussels painter who employed the Surrealist technique in the early to mid-1900s.

Comics

Interestingly enough, Brussels also has four comic book museums, which pay homage to famous Belgian comics like Tintin, Lucky Like, and Gaston Lagaffe. Fun fact: the country of Belgium has more comic makers per square mile than anywhere in the world, with 884 currently registered. There are also comic strip murals throughout the city, so keep a look out for Tintin while you're out taking a stroll.

Architecture

The architecture of Brussels is mostly in the Art Nouveau style. There are a few medieval constructions such as the Grand Palace as well as more modern political institutions. The Art Nouveau style was brought to Brussels by local architect Victor Horta. Unfortunately, there was also a period of urban renewal that arose alongside the improvement of the economy and establishment of international organizations in Brussels. This was called Brusselization, which is now a term used by city planners to describe the overhaul of a historic city with unsightly modern buildings. In the

1960s and 1970s, architects were given unchecked power to build wherever and whatever they wanted in Brussels in attempt to make the city look "futuristic." It was during this unfortunate era that many of the city's historic and beautiful buildings were torn down.

Sculptures and Structures

A well-known structure called the **Atomium** was erected in Brussels for the World Fair of 1958. It is the shape of an iron crystal, magnified 165 billion times, and allows people to explore the inside of the atom through its system of escalators. Another very famous sculpture is the **Manneken Pis,** or "Little Man Pee" in Dutch. Erected in 1618, there are many legends surrounding this little boy who just gotsta go. One is that he was put in a tree when an approaching army was coming and fended them off by peeing on their heads. Another is that a little boy peed on a burning fuse and saved the city from a bomb. Basically, this boy was a great urinator and saved the day with his voidance. Today, there are many replications of this famous whizzer (including dog, girl, and chocolate versions) in other cities around the world.

HOLIDAYS AND FESTIVALS

HOLIDAY OR FESTIVAL	DESCRIPTION	DATE
Carnival	The national celebration before Lent lasts for a week prior to Ash Wednesday and is typically celebrated with costume parades, fireworks, and parties.	Second week in February
Europe Day	This holiday celebrates the date May 9, 1950, when the European Union was formed. Visitors get to tour the European Parliament, and there is entertainment and food in the streets.	May 9
Queen Elizabeth International Music Competition	This highly respected annual event features many violin, piano, voice, and composition performances across the city.	April-June 2013
Ommegang Pageant	A tradition since 1549, this annual celebration focuses on folklore and cultural heritage. Craftsmen and tradesmen dress in traditional garb for the pageant, which originated as a medieval religious ritual.	July
Meyboom Celebration	This event celebrates the anniversary of a wedding that took place in 1213. According to legend, the nuptials ambushed by a pack of fiends, and as a token of gratitude for the man who fought them off, every year a Maypole is erected in his honor.	August 9
Comic Strip Festival	An annual convention of over seventy comic book artists. There are also other events such as drawing sessions, workshops, and many refreshments.	January 2013

brussels

ESSENTIALS

You don't have to be a rocket scientist to plan a good trip. (It might help, but it's not required.) You do, however, need to be well prepared, and that's what we can do for you. Essentials is the chapter that gives you all the nitty-gritty you need to know for your trip: the hard information gleaned from 52 years of collective wisdom and several months of furious fact-checking. Planning your trip? Check. Where to find Wi-Fi? Check. The dirt on public transportation? Check. We've also thrown in communications info, safety tips, and a ✎phrasebook, just for good measure. Plus, for overall trip-planning advice from what to pack (money and as little underwear as possible) to how to take a good passport photo (it's physically impossible; consider airbrushing), you can also check out the Essentials section of www.letsgo.com.

So, flick through this chapter before you leave so you know what documents to bring, while you're on the plane so you know how you'll be getting from the airport to your accommodation, and when you're on the ground so you can find a laundromat to solve all your 3am stain-removal needs. This chapter may not always be the most scintillating read, but it just might save your life.

greatest hits

- **GET A VISA.** Put it on your spring-cleaning list, since you'll need to apply six to eight weeks in advance (p. 320).
- **DON'T SMUGGLE IN ANY DRUGS.** Um, duh. No one wants to end up in a French prison (p. 326).
- **SHIP SOUVENIRS HOME BY SURFACE MAIL.** Our thrilling "By Snail Mail" section will tell you how (p. 330).
- **BE AWARE OF LOCAL LAWS.** (p. 327).

planning your trip

- **PASSPORT:** Required for citizens of all countries.
- **VISA:** Required for non-EU citizens staying longer than 90 days.
- **WORK PERMIT:** Required for all foreigners planning to work in France, the Netherlands, or Belgium.

DOCUMENTS AND FORMALITIES

We're going to fill you in on visas and work permits, but don't forget the most important document of all: your passport, which must be valid 3 months beyond the end of your stay. **Don't forget your passport!**

Visas

Those lucky enough to be EU citizens do not need a visa to globetrot through France, the Netherlands, and Belgium. Citizens of Australia, Canada, New Zealand, the US, and other non-EU countries do not need a visa for stays of up to 90 days. Take note that this three-month period begins upon entry into any of the countries that belong to the EU's **freedom of movement** zone. For more information, see **One Europe** (below). Those staying longer than 90 days should apply for a longer-term visa; consult an embassy or consulate for more information.

Double-check entrance requirements at the nearest embassy or consulate of France, the Netherlands, or Belgium (listed below) for up-to-date information before departure. US citizens can also consult http://travel.state.gov.

Entering France, Belgium, or the Netherlands to study requires a special visa. For more information, see the **Beyond Tourism** chapter.

essentials

one europe

The EU's policy of freedom of movement means that most border controls have been abolished and visa policies harmonized. Under this treaty, formally known as the Schengen Agreement, you're still required to carry a passport (or government-issued ID card for EU citizens) when crossing an internal border, but, once you've been admitted into one country, you're free to travel to other participating states. Most EU states (the UK is a notable exception) are already members of Schengen, as are Iceland and Norway. In recent times, fears over immigration have led to calls for suspension of this freedom of movement. Border controls are being stregthened, but the policy isn't really targeted against casual travelers, so unless you've been traveling so long that you look like an illegal immigrant, you should still be able to travel with ease throughout Europe.

Work Permits

Admittance to a country as a traveler does not include the right to work, which is authorized only by a work permit. For more information, see the **Beyond Tourism** chapter.

french consular services

- **FRENCH CONSULATE GENERAL IN AUSTRALIA:** (Level 26, 31 Market St., Sydney NSW 2000 ☎02 92 68 24 00 www.ambafrance-au.org ✆ Open M-F 9am-1pm.)

- **FRENCH CONSULATE GENERAL IN CANADA:** (Level 10, 1501 McGill College, Montréal QC H3A 3M8 ☎514-878-4385 http://consulfrance-montreal.org ✆ Open M-F 8:30am-4:30pm.)

- **FRENCH EMBASSY IN IRELAND:** (36 Ailesbury Rd., Dublin 4 ☎1 277 50 00 www.ambafrance-ie.org ✆ Open for visa services M-Th 2-4pm, F 2-3pm.)

- **FRENCH EMBASSY IN NEW ZEALAND:** (34-42 Manners St., PO Box 11-343, Wellington 6142 ☎04 384 25 55 www.ambafrance-nz.org ✆ Open M-F 9:15am-1:15pm.)

- **FRENCH CONSULATE GENERAL IN THE UNITED KINGDOM:** (21 Cromwell Rd., London SW7 2EN ☎020 70 73 12 50 www.ambafrance-uk.org ✆ Call for hours.)

- **FRENCH EMBASSY IN THE UNITED STATES:** (4101 Reservoir Rd. NW, Washington DC 20007 ☎202-944-6000 www.ambafrance-us.org ✆ Call for hours.)

- **AUSTRALIAN EMBASSY IN PARIS:** (4 rue Jean Rey ☎01 40 59 33 00 www.france.embassy.gov.au ✆ Open M-F 10am-5pm.)

- **CANADIAN EMBASSY IN PARIS:** (37 av. Montaigne ☎01 44 43 29 00 www.france.gc.ca ✆ Open M-F 9am-noon.)

- **IRISH EMBASSY IN PARIS:** (4 av. Foch ☎01 44 17 67 00 www.embassyofireland.fr ✆ Open M-F 9:30am-noon.)

- **NEW ZEALAND EMBASSY IN PARIS:** (7 ter rue Léonard de Vinci, 75116 Paris ☎01 45 01 43 43 http://nzembassy.com/france ✆ Open M-F 9am-1pm and 2-5pm.)

- **UNITED KINGDOM EMBASSY IN PARIS:** (35 rue du Faubourg St-Honoré ☎01 44 51 31 00 ukinfrance.fco.gov.uk ✆ Open M-F 9:30am-1pm and 2:30-6pm.)

- **UNITED STATES EMBASSY IN PARIS:** (2 av. Gabriel ☎01 43 12 22 22 france.usembassy.gov ✆ Open M-F 9am-3pm. Appointment recommended.)

money

money

GETTING MONEY FROM HOME

Stuff happens. When stuff happens, you might need some money. When you need some money, the easiest and cheapest solution is to have someone back home make a deposit to your bank account. Otherwise, consider one of the following options.

Wiring Money

Arranging a **bank money transfer** means asking a bank back home to wire money to a bank in Paris, Amsterdam, or Brussels. This is the cheapest way to transfer cash, but it's also the slowest and most agonizing, usually taking several days or more.

dutch consular services

- **IN AUSTRALIA: Consulate General.** (Level 23, Westfield Tower 2, 101 Grafton St., Bondi Junction NSW 2022 Sydney ☎02 93 87 66 44 australia.nlembassy.org ⏰ Open M-F 10am-1pm.)

- **IN CANADA: Consulate General.** (350 Albert St., Ste. 2020, Ottawa, ON K1R 1A4 ☎877 388 24 43 www.netherlandsembassy.ca ⏰ Open M-F 9am-4:30pm. Appointment required.)

- **IN IRELAND: Embassy.** (160 Merrion Rd., Dublin 4 ☎01 269 34 44 www.ireland. nlembassy.org ⏰ Open M-F 9am-11:30pm.)

- **IN NEW ZEALAND: Embassy.** (Investment House, 10th fl., Wellington 6011 ☎04 471 63 90 www.netherlandsembassy.co.nz ⏰ Open M-Th 10am-12:30pm.)

- **IN THE UK: Embassy.** (38 Hyde Park Gate, London SW7 5DP ☎020 7590 3200 www. netherlands-embassy.org.uk ⏰ Open M-F 8:30am-noon, closed 1st and 3rd W each month. Appointment required.)

- **IN THE USA: Embassy.** (4200 Linnean Ave. NW, Washington, DC 20008 ☎877-388-2443 dc.the-netherlands.org ⏰ Open M-F 9:30am-12:30pm. Appointment required.)

Embassies in the Netherlands are situated in The Hague. The UK and the US have Consulate Generals in Amsterdam; their embassies do not offer consular services.

- **AUSTRALIAN CONSULAR SERVICES: Embassy.** (Carnegielaan 4, 2517 KH The Hague ☎070 310 82 00 www.netherlands.embassy.gov.au ⏰ Open M-F 9am-1pm.)

- **CANADIAN CONSULAR SERVICES: Embassy.** (Sophialaan 7, 2514 JP The Hague ☎070 311 16 00 www.canada.nl ⏰ Open M-F 9am-12:30pm.)

- **IRISH CONSULAR SERVICES: Embassy.** (Scheveningseweg 112, 2584 AE The Hague ☎070 363 09 93 www.irishembassy.nl ⏰ Open M-F 10am-12:30pm and 2:30-5pm.)

- **NEW ZEALAND CONSULAR SERVICES: Embassy.** (Eisenhowerlaan 77N, 2517 KK The Hague ☎070 346 93 24 www.nzembassy.com/netherlands ⏰ Open M-F 9am-12:30pm and 1:30-5pm.)

- **BRITISH CONSULAR SERVICES: Consulate General.** (Koningslaan 44, 1070 AL Amsterdam ☎020 676 43 43 www.britain.nl ⏰ Open M-F 9am-1pm. Appointment required.)

- **AMERICAN CONSULAR SERVICES: Consulate General.** (Museumplein 19, 1071 DJ Amsterdam ☎020 575 53 09 amsterdam.usconsulate.gov *i* All non-emergency visits require online appointment. ⏰ Open M-F 8:30-11:30am. Immigrant visa services available M-Tu 1:30-3pm, Th 1:30-3pm.)

essentials

Note that some banks may only release your funds in local currency, potentially sticking you with a poor exchange rate; inquire about this in advance. In general, bank transfers in Paris can be performed at post office banks *(La Banque Postale)*. **Banque de France** has some of the most competitive rates for international transfers in Paris; however, if your home bank has a relationship with a bank in Europe, make sure to use that bank, as the rate will often be better.

belgian consular services

- **IN AUSTRALIA: Embassy.** (19 Arkana St., Yarralumla, Canberra ACT 2600 ☎(0)2 62 73 25 01 www.diplomatie.be/canberra ☒ Open M-Th 9am-12:30pm and 1-4pm, F 9am-12:30pm and 1-3pm.)

- **IN CANADA: Embassy.** (360 Albert St. Ste. 820, Ottawa Ontario K1R 7X7 ☎613-236-7267 www.diplomatie.be/ottawa ☒ Open M-Th 9am-1pm and 2-3pm, F 9am-2pm.)

- **IN IRELAND: Embassy.** (2 Shrewsbury Rd., Ballsbridge, Dublin 4 ☎01 205 71 00 www.diplomatie.be/dublin ☒ Open M-F 9am-1pm and 2-3pm. Visa services available 9am-12:30pm.)

- **IN NEW ZEALAND: Consulate.** (Level 6 Leaders Building, 15 Brandon St., 6011 Wellington ☎04 499 91 70 ☒ Open T 2-4pm, Th 2-4pm and by appointment.)

- **IN THE UK: Embassy.** (17 Grosvenor Crescent, London SW1X 7EE ☎020 74 70 37 00 www.diplomatie.be/london ☒ Open M-F 9am-1pm and 2-5pm. Visa services open M-F 9am-1pm.)

- **IN THE USA: Embassy.** (3330 Garfield St. NW, 20008 Washington, DC ☎202-333-6900 www.diplobel.us ☒ Open M-F 9am-12:30 and 2-5pm. Visa services open 9:30am-12:30pm.)

- **AUSTRALIAN CONSULAR SERVICES: Embassy.** (6-8 rue Guimard, 1040 Brussels ☎02 286 05 00 www.belgium.embassy.gov.au ☒ Open M-F 8:30am-5pm. No visa section: visa services are handled by the Australian Embassy in Paris ☎01 40 59 33 00; www.france.embassy.gov.au.)

- **CANADIAN CONSULAR SERVICES: Embassy.** (2 Av. de Tervueren, 1040 Brussels ☎02 741 06 11 www.ambassade-canada.be ☒ Open M-F 9am-12:30pm and 1:30-5pm. Consular services open M-F 9am-noon. Afternoon hours for emergencies only.)

- **IRISH CONSULAR SERVICES: Embassy.** (180 Chaussée d'Etterbeek, 1040 Brussels ☎02 282 34 00 www.embassyofireland.be ☒ Open M-F 10am-1pm and 2-4pm.)

- **NEW ZEALAND CONSULAR SERVICES: Embassy.** (Level 7, 9-31 Av. des Nerviens, 1040 Brussels ☎02 512 10 40 www.nzembassy.com/belgium ☒ Open M-F 9am-1pm and 2-5:30pm.)

- **BRITISH CONSULAR SERVICES: Consulate General.** (Level 8, 9-31 Av. des Nerviens, 1040 Brussels ☎02 287 62 11 ukinbelgium.fco.gov.uk ☒ Open M-T 9am-12:30pm and Th-F 9am-12:30pm.)

- **AMERICAN CONSULAR SERVICES: Embassy.** (27 bd du Régent, 1000 Brussels ☎02 811 43 00 belgium.usembassy.gov ☒ Open M-Th 1:30-3:30pm, F 9-11am.)

money

Money transfer services like **Western Union** are faster and more convenient than bank transfers—but also much pricier. Western Union has many locations worldwide. To find one, visit www.westernunion.com or call the appropriate number: in Australia ☎1800 173 833, in Canada 800-235-0000, in the UK 0808 234 9168, in the US 800-325-6000, in France 0800 900 407, in the Netherlands 0800 022 8781, or in Belgium 0800 99 709. Money transfer services are also available to **American Express** cardholders and at selected **Thomas Cook** offices.

US State Department (US Citizens Only)

In serious emergencies only, the US State Department will help your family or friends forward money within hours to the nearest consular office, which will then disburse it according to instructions for a US$30 fee. If you wish to use this service, you must contact the Overseas Citizens Services division of the US State Department. (☎+1-202-501-4444, from US 888-407-4747)

WITHDRAWING MONEY

To use a debit or credit card to withdraw money from a cash machine (ATM) in Europe, you must have a four-digit Personal Identification Number (PIN). If your PIN is longer than four digits, ask your bank whether you can just use the first four or whether they'll need to issue you a new one. Credit cards don't usually come with PINs, so if you intend to hit up ATMs in Europe with a credit card to get cash advances, call your credit card company before leaving to request one.

ATMs are readily available throughout Paris, Amsterdam, and Brussels. They get the same wholesale exchange rate as credit cards, but there is often a limit on the amount of money you can withdraw per day. Depending on your domestic bank, there may be a surcharge of €1-5 per withdrawal. The most common banks are BNP Paribas, Crédit Agricole, HSBC France, and Société Générale in France; De Nederlandsche Bank, ABN AMRO Bank, Rabobank, and ING Bank N.V. in the Netherlands; and Dexia, BNP Paribas Fortis, ING Belgium, and KBC Bank in Belgium. Many have relationships with other international banks that will waive the surcharge if you withdraw from them. Check with your domestic bank to see if it has any such relationship before traveling to Europe. Always inform your domestic bank of your travel plans; this will prevent your card from being cancelled due to concerns over fraud while you're abroad.

the euro

Despite what many dollar-possessing Americans might want to hear, the official currency of 17 members of the European Union—Austria, Belgium, Cyprus, Estonia, Finland, France, Germany, Greece, Ireland, Italy, Luxembourg, Malta, the Netherlands, Portugal, Slovakia, Slovenia, and Spain—is the euro.

Still, the currency has some important—and positive—consequences for travelers hitting more than one eurozone country. For one thing, money-changers across the eurozone are obliged to exchange money at the official, fixed rate and at no commission (though they may still charge a small service fee). Second, euro-denominated traveler's checks allow you to pay for goods and services across the eurozone, again at the official rate and commission-free. For more info, check a currency converter (such as www.xe.com) or www.europa.eu.int.

TIPPING AND BARGAINING

A service charge is often added to bills in bars and restaurants in France, the Netherlands, and Belgium. Most people do, however, leave some change (up to €2) for sit-down services, and in nicer restaurants it is not uncommon to leave 5-10% of the bill. Tips in bars are very unusual. For other services, like taxis and hairdressers, a 10-15% tip is acceptable when not already included in the bill.

essentials

TAXES

As EU member states, France, the Netherlands and Belgium all require a **Value Added Tax (VAT)**, which is applied to a variety of goods and services and is included in the quoted price. This tax is generally levied at 19.6% in France, 19% in the Netherlands, and 21% in Belgium, although some goods are subject to lower rates. Non-EU visitors who are taking these goods home may be refunded this tax for purchases totaling over €175 per store. When making purchases, request a VAT form and present it at the *détaxe* booth at the airport. Goods purchased this way must be carried at all times while traveling, and refunds must be claimed within six months.

getting around

For information on how to get to Paris, Amsterdam, and Brussels and save a bundle while doing so, check out the Essentials section of **www.letsgo.com.** (In case you can't tell, we think our website's the bomb.) For information specific to a certain city, see the **Getting There** and **Getting Around** sections for that city.

BY PLANE

For small-scale travel on the continent, *Let's Go* suggests **budget airlines** like RyanAir or Wizzair. Be aware that budget airlines often service smaller airports that tend to be far removed from the city center, so plan on taking public transportation into the city rather than paying exorbitant cab fees. More traditional carriers have also made efforts to keep up with the budget revolution. The **Star Alliance Europe Airpass** offers low economy-class fares for travel within Europe to 220 destinations in 45 countries. The pass is available to non-European passengers on Star Alliance carriers, including Brussels Airlines. (www.staralliance.com) **EuropebyAir's** snazzy FlightPass also allows you to hop between hundreds of cities in Europe and North Africa. (☎+1-888-321-4737 www.europebyair.com $ Most flights US$99.)

In addition, a number of European airlines offer discount coupon packets. Most are only available as tack-ons for transatlantic passengers, but some are standalone offers. Most must be purchased before departure, so research in advance. For example, **oneworld,** a coalition of 10 major international airlines, offers deals and cheap connections all over the world, including within Europe *(www.oneworld.com).*

BY TRAIN

Trains in France, the Netherlands, and Belgium are generally comfortable, convenient, and reasonably swift. Make sure you are on the correct car, as trains sometimes split at crossroads. Towns listed in parentheses on European train schedules require a train switch at the town listed immediately before the parentheses.

You can either buy a **railpass,** which allows you unlimited travel within a particular region for a given period of time, or rely on buying individual **point-to-point** tickets as you go. Almost all countries give students or youths (under 26, usually) direct discounts on regular domestic rail tickets, and many also sell a student or youth card that provides 20-50% off all fares for up to a year.

Eurail offers the Eurail Benelux pass (www.raileurope.com/rail-tickets-passes/eurail-benelux-pass/index.html), a railcard offering five days in one month of unlimited use of rail networks in Belgium, the Netherlands, and Luxembourg for $151 to those under 26. For more information on rail passes check out the **Rail Resources** feature.

BY BUS

Though European trains and railpasses are extremely popular, in some cases buses prove a better option. Often cheaper than railpasses, **international bus passes** allow unlimited travel on a hop-on, hop-off basis between major European cities. **Busabout,** for instance, offers three interconnecting bus circuits covering 29 of Europe's best bus hubs. (☎+44 8450 267 514 www.busabout.com $ 1 circuit in high season starts at US$579, students US$549.) **Eurolines,** meanwhile, is the largest operator of Europe-wide coach services. We get misty-eyed just thinking about their unlimited 15- and 30-day passes to 41 major European cities. (☎020 560 8788 in the Netherlands, 02 274 1350 in Belgium www.eurolines.com $ High season 15-day pass €345, 30-day pass €455; under 26 €290/375. Mid-season €240/330; under 26 €205/270. Low season €205/310; under 26 €175/240.)

safety and health

GENERAL ADVICE

In any type of crisis, the most important thing to do is **stay calm.** Your country's embassy abroad is usually your best resource in an emergency; registering with that embassy upon arrival in the country is a good idea. The government offices listed in the **Travel Advisories** feature at the end of this section can provide information on the services they offer their citizens in case of emergencies abroad.

Drugs and Alcohol

Although mention of France often conjures images of black-clad smokers in berets, **France no longer allows smoking in public as of 2008.** The government has no official policy on berets. Similar laws have been passed in Belgium and the Netherlands, prohibiting people from smoking in bars, cafes, and nightclubs.

There is no drinking age in Paris, Amsterdam, or Brussels, but restaurants will not serve anyone under the age of 16, and to purchase hard alcohol you must be at least 18 years old. Though there is no law prohibiting open containers, drinking on the street is considered uncouth. Public drunkenness is also frowned upon and is a sure way to mark yourself as a tourist. The legal blood-alcohol level for driving in France is 0.05%, which is less than it is in the US, UK, New Zealand, and Ireland, so exercise appropriate caution if operating a vehicle in France.

When it comes to drugs other than alcohol, as is so often the case, things get a little more interesting. Possession of illegal drugs (including marijuana) in France or Belgium can result in a substantial jail sentence or fine. Police may arbitrarily stop and search anyone on the street. However, it hardly needs to be stated that attitudes toward conscience-altering substances are quite different between these two cities and Amsterdam. Hard drugs are completely illegal in all three countries, and possession or consumption of substances like heroin and cocaine will be harshly punished if caught. In the Netherlands, soft drugs like marijuana and mushrooms are tolerated, and you are very unlikely to face prosecution for using them. Consumption is confined to certain legalized zones, namely coffeeshops (for marijuana) and smartshops (for herbal drugs). Both are heavily regulated but very popular; the number of smartshops in particular has exploded in recent years. As of 2013, however, only residents of the Netherlands will be permitted to enter cannabis cafes and purchase marijuana. When visiting a coffeeshop or smartshop for the first time, it may be a good idea to take a sober friend with you. Even experienced drug users may be surprised at the hotbox effect created in shops where the fumes of several pot-smokers accumulate. Having a friend to guide you home could turn out to be helpful if not absolutely essential.

Prostitution

Just as with drugs, France, Belgium and the Netherlands have exceptionally different policies regarding prostitution. The sex industry is illegal in Belgium and probably always will be (Catholic morals live on). The "world's oldest profession" has, however, flourished in the Netherlands, particularly in the liberal capital of the world, Amsterdam. Prostitution in Amsterdam has always centered on what is today called the Red Light District, though it is practiced elsewhere in the city as well.

Legal prostitution in Amsterdam comes in two main forms. Window prostitution, which involves scantily clad women tempting passersby from small chambers fronted by a plate-glass window, is by far the most visible. Sex workers of this kind are self-employed and rent the windows themselves. Accordingly, each sets her own price. This form of commercial sex gave the Red Light District its name, as lamps both outside and inside the windows emit a red glow that, at night, bathes the whole area. Whether shopping or "just looking," be sure to show the women basic respect. Looking is fine and even expected, but leering and catcalling are absolutely uncalled for. Keep in mind that prostitution is an entirely legal enterprise, and windows are places of business. Most of the prostitutes whom you see belong to a union called "The Red Thread" and are tested for HIV and STIs, although testing is on a voluntary basis. Do not take photos unless you want to explain yourself to the angriest—and largest—man you'll ever see.

If you're interested in having sex with a window prostitute, go up to the door and wait for someone inside to let you in. Show up clean and sober; prostitutes always reserve the right to refuse their services. Anything goes as long as you clearly and straightforwardly agree to it beforehand. Specifically state what you want to get for the money you're paying—that means which sex acts, in what positions, and, especially, how much time you have in which to do it. Window prostitutes can set their standards; by no means are they required to do anything you want without consenting to it in advance. Negotiation occurs and money changes hands before any sexual acts take place. Always practice safe sex; a prostitute should not and will not touch a penis that is not covered by a condom. Don't ask for a refund if you are left unsatisfied—all sales are final. There is no excuse for making trouble; if anyone becomes violent or threatening with a window prostitute, she has access to an emergency button that sets off a loud alarm. Not only does it make an ear-splitting noise, but it also summons the police, who invariably side with prostitutes in disputes. If you feel you have a legitimate complaint or have any questions about commercial sex, head to the extremely helpful Prostitution Information Centre and talk it through.

Another option is the recently legalized brothels. The term usually refers to an establishment centered on a bar. There, women—or men—who are available for hour-long sessions will make your acquaintance. These brothels, also called sex clubs, can be pricey. They are also controversial, and in the last few years the authorities have sought to close brothels associated with trafficking and criminal gangs.

The best place to go for information about prostitution in Amsterdam is the **Prostitution Information Centre.** (Enge Kerksteeg 3, in the Red Light District behind the Oude Kerk, ☎020 420 7328 www.pic-amsterdam.com ☼ Open Sa 4-7pm. Available at other times for group bookings, call ahead.) Founded in 1994 by Mariska Majoor (once a prostitute herself), the center fills a niche, connecting the Red Light District with its eager frequenters. The center's staff can answer any question you might have, no matter how blush-worthy the query.

safety and health

SPECIFIC CONCERNS

GLBT Travelers

In Paris, **Le Centre Lesbien, Gai, Bi et Trans de Paris et Île-de-France** functions both as a counseling agency in and of itself, offering counseling and reception services for limited times during the week, and as the umbrella organization and formal location for many other GLBT resource organizations in Paris. (63 rue Beaubourg ☎01 43 57 21 47 ☞ ⓂRambuteau or ⓂLes Halles. ☒ Administrative reception open M 1-8pm, Tu 10am-1pm and 2-6pm, W 1pm-7m, Th-F 1pm-6pm.) In Brussels, the **Rainbow House** provides similar services. (3 rue de la Chauferette ☎32 (0)2 503 59 90 www. rainbowhouse.be ☞ ⓂBourse. ☒ Administrative reception open M-F 2pm-6pm.) In Amsterdam, the **COC organization** promotes safety and awareness and hosts events throughout the year. (Rozenstraat 14 ☎020 626 30 87 www.cocamsterdam.nl ☞ Tram 13, 14, 17 to Westermarkt. ☒ Open M-F 9am-5pm.)

Demonstrations and Political Gatherings

The French Revolution may have been in 1789, but the spirit of the revolution certainly hasn't died. Protests and strikes—or *grèves*, as the locals call them—are frequent in Paris and Brussels, and can be over anything from the minimum wage to Sarkozy's wardrobe choices, but violence does not often occur (unless he wears white after Labor Day). You may find yourself stuck in the city on the day of a transit strike (as one *Let's Go* researcher did), but who hasn't always wanted to ride a Vespa?

PRE-DEPARTURE HEALTH

Matching a prescription to a foreign equivalent is not always easy, safe, or possible, so if you take **prescription drugs,** carry up-to-date prescriptions or a statement from your doctor stating the medications' trade names, manufacturers, chemical names, and dosages. Be sure to keep all medication with you in your carry-on luggage. It is also a good idea to look up the French or Dutch names of drugs you may need during your trip.

Immunizations and Precautions

Travelers over two years old should make sure that the following vaccines are up to date: MMR (for measles, mumps, and rubella); DTaP or Td (for diphtheria, tetanus, and pertussis); IPV (for polio); Hib (for *Haemophilus influenzae* B); and HepB (for Hepatitis B). For recommendations on immunizations and prophylaxis, check with a doctor and consult the **Centers for Disease Control and Prevention (CDC)** in the US (☎+1-800-232-4636 www.cdc.gov/travel) or the equivalent in your home country.

keeping in touch

BY EMAIL AND INTERNET

Hello and welcome to the 21st century, where you're rarely more than a 5min. walk from the nearest Wi-Fi hot spot, even if you sometimes have to pay a few bucks or buy a drink for the privilege of using it. **Internet cafes** and free internet terminals are listed in the **Practicalities** section of each city. Fast food stores like Quick or McDonald's often offer free Wi-Fi. Hotels and hostels often provide internet access in common areas for free or at a small hourly rate. For lists of cybercafes in Paris, Amsterdam, and Brussels, check out www.cybercaptive.com.

Wireless hotspots make internet access possible in public and remote places. Unfortunately, they also pose security risks. Hotspots are public, open networks that use unencrypted, unsecured connections. They are susceptible to hacks and

essentials

"packet sniffing"—the theft of passwords and other private information. To prevent problems, disable "ad hoc" mode, turn off file sharing and network discovery, encrypt your email, turn on your firewall, beware of phony networks, and watch for over-the-shoulder creeps.

BY TELEPHONE

Calling Home

If you have internet access, your best—i.e., cheapest, most convenient, and most tech-savvy—means of calling home is probably our good friend 🔲**Skype** (www.skype.com). Calls to other Skype users are free; calls to landlines and mobiles worldwide start at US$0.023 per minute, depending on where you're calling.

For those still stuck in the 20th century, **prepaid phone cards** are a common and relatively inexpensive means of calling abroad. Each one comes with a Personal Identification Number (PIN) and a toll-free access number. You call the access number and then follow the directions for dialing your PIN. To purchase prepaid phone cards, check online for the best rates; www.callingcards.com is a good place to start. Online providers generally send your access number and PIN via email, with no actual "card" involved. You can also call home with prepaid phone cards purchased in Paris, Amsterdam, or Brussels.

Another option is a **calling card,** linked to a major national telecommunications service in your home country. Calls are billed collect or to your account. Cards generally come with instructions for dialing both domestically and internationally.

Placing a collect call through an international operator can be expensive but may be necessary in case of an emergency. You can frequently call collect without even possessing a company's calling card just by calling its access number and following the instructions.

Cellular Phones

In France, the Netherlands, and Belgium, mobile pay-as-you-go phones are the way to go. The largest carriers are **SFR, Base,** and **Orange,** and they are so readily available that even supermarkets sell them. Cellphone calls and texts can be paid for without signing a contract with a **Mobicarte** prepaid card, available at Orange and SFR stores, as well as tabacs. You can often buy phones for €20-40, which includes various amounts of minutes and 100 texts. Calling the US from one of these phones is around €0.80 a minute, with texts coming in at around €0.50.

keeping in touch

The international standard for cell phones is **Global System for Mobile Communication (GSM).** To make and receive calls in France, the Netherlands, or Brussels, you will need a GSM-compatible phone and a **SIM (Subscriber Identity Module) card,** a country-specific, thumbnail-size chip that gives you a local phone number and plugs you into the local network.

Many SIM cards are prepaid, and incoming calls are frequently free. You can buy additional cards or vouchers (usually available at convenience stores) to "top up" your phone. For more information on GSM phones, check out www.telestial. com. Companies like **Cellular Abroad** (www.cellularabroad.com) and **OneSimCard** (www.onesimcard.com) rent cell phones and SIM cards that work in a variety of destinations around the world.

BY SNAIL MAIL

Sending Mail Home from France and the Low Countries

Airmail is the best way to send mail home from Paris, Amsterdam , or Brussels. Write "airmail" or *"par avion"* or on the front. For simple letters or postcards, airmail tends to be surprisingly cheap, but the price will go up sharply for weighty packages. Surface mail is by far the cheapest, slowest, and most antiquated way to send mail. It takes one to two months to cross the Atlantic and one to three to cross the Pacific—good for heavy items you won't need for a while, like souvenirs that you've acquired along the way.

Receiving Mail in France and the Low Countries

There are several ways to arrange pickup of letters sent to you while you are in Paris, Amsterdam, or Brussels, even if you do not have an address of your own. Mail can be sent via **Poste Restante** (General Delivery) to Paris, Amsterdam, or Brussels, but it is not always reliable. Address Poste Restante letters like so:

Simone DE BEAUVOIR
Poste Restante
Paris, France

The mail will go to a special desk in the central post office of the city (52 rue du Louvre in Paris; Singel 250 in Amsterdam; av. Fonsny, Gare du Midi, in Brussels), unless you specify a local post office by street address or postal code. It's best to use the largest post office, since mail may be sent there regardless. Bring your passport (or other photo ID) for pickup; there may be a small fee. If the clerks insist that there is nothing for you, ask them to check under your first name as well. It is usually safer and quicker, though more expensive, to send mail express or registered. If you don't want to deal with Poste Restante, consider asking your hostel or accommodation if you can have things mailed to you there. Of course, if you have your own mailing address or a reliable friend to receive mail for you, that is the easiest solution.

TIME DIFFERENCES

France, the Netherlands, and Belgium are all 1hr. ahead of Greenwich Mean Time (GMT) and all observe Daylight Saving Time. This means that they are 6hr. ahead of New York City, 9hr. ahead of Los Angeles, and 1hr. ahead of the British Isles. In Northern Hemisphere summer they are 8hr. behind Sydney and 10hr. behind New Zealand, while in Northern Hemisphere winter they are 10hr. behind Sydney and 12hr. behind New Zealand. Don't get confused and call your parents when it's actually 4am their time!

Note that these countries change to Daylight Savings Time on different dates than others, so sometimes the time difference will be one hour off from what is stated here.

essentials

international calls

To call to or from France, the Netherlands, or Belgium, dial:

1. THE INTERNATIONAL DIALING PREFIX. To call from **France, the Netherlands, Belgium, Ireland, New Zealand,** or the **UK,** dial ☎00; from **Australia,** dial ☎0011; from **Canada** or the **US,** dial ☎011.

2. THE COUNTRY CODE OF THE COUNTRY YOU WANT TO CALL. To call France, dial ☎33; **the Netherlands,** dial ☎31; **Belgium,** ☎32; **Australia,** ☎61; **Canada** or the **US,** ☎1; **Ireland,** ☎353; **New Zealand,** ☎64; the **UK,** ☎44.

3. THE CITY/AREA CODE. The city code for Paris ☎1; for Amsterdam ☎020; for Brussels ☎02. If the first digit of the city code is a zero, omit the zero when calling from abroad.

4. THE LOCAL NUMBER.

climate

As pleasantly romantic as it is to think of springtime in Paris, *le printemps* doesn't last forever. Paris has a temperate climate with four seasons. The North Atlantic current keeps weather from approaching any extremes. Winters in Paris can be cold, but heavy snow is not characteristic of the City of Light. Springtime in Paris is definitely a lovely time of year, even if it does come kind of late. Flowers bloom, trees grow leaves—it's everything you've read about. Summers are comfortable for the most part, though some days in August will have you wishing you had picked a city closer to a beach. Fall is brisk but enjoyable as the city's foliage changes before your eyes.

Amsterdam and Brussels have similar climates that are mild, temperate, and unpredictable. As in much of Northern Europe, the mostly snow-free winters are chilly and wet, while the summers are warmish and wet. Basically, it's wet a lot. Hot summers are possible, but don't count on it. Rainfall is fairly consistent throughout the year, making a raincoat an essential thing to pack no matter what month you plan to visit. It's probably best not to complain about whatever the skies throw your way, since if you decided to travel to Amsterdam and Brussels, you clearly didn't come for the weather. Take another tour around the Rijksmuseum and forget the gray skies outside.

AVG. TEMP.(LOW/ HIGH), PRECIP.	JANUARY			APRIL			JULY			OCTOBER		
	°C	°F	mm	°C	°F	mm	°C	°F	mm	°C	°F	mm
Amsterdam	1/5	34/41	69	4/12	39/64	53	12/20	64/68	76	7/13	45/56	74
Brussels	-1/4	30/39	66	5/14	41/67	60	12/23	64/74	95	7/15	45/59	83
Paris	1/6	34/43	56	6/16	43/61	42	15/25	59/77	59	8/16	46/61	50

To convert from degrees Fahrenheit to degrees Celsius, subtract 32 and multiply by 5/9. To convert from Celsius to Fahrenheit, multiply by 9/5 and add 32. The mathematically challenged may use this handy chart:

°CELSIUS	-5	0	5	10	15	20	25	30	35	40
°FAHRENHEIT	23	32	41	50	59	68	77	86	95	104

climate

measurements

Like the rest of the rational world, France, the Netherlands, and Belgium all use the metric system. The basic unit of length is the meter (m), which is divided into 100 centimeters (cm) or 1000 millimeters (mm). One thousand meters make up one kilometer (km). Fluids are measured in liters (L), each divided into 1000 milliliters (mL). A liter of pure water weighs one kilogram (kg), the unit of mass that is divided into 1000 grams (g). One metric ton is 1000kg.

MEASUREMENT CONVERSIONS	
1 inch (in.) = 25.4mm	1 millimeter (mm) = 0.039 in.
1 foot (ft.) = 0.305m	1 meter (m) = 3.28 ft.
1 yard (yd.) = 0.914m	1 meter (m) = 1.094 yd.
1 mile (mi.) = 1.609km	1 kilometer (km) = 0.621 mi.
1 ounce (oz.) = 28.35g	1 gram (g) = 0.035 oz.
1 pound (lb.) = 0.454kg	1 kilogram (kg) = 2.205 lb.
1 fluid ounce (fl. oz.) = 29.57mL	1 milliliter (mL) = 0.034 fl. oz.
1 gallon (gal.) = 3.785L	1 liter (L) = 0.264 gal.

language

FRENCH

You hopefully won't be surprised to learn that the official language in Paris is French. English speakers will be happy to note that English is the most commonly taught foreign language in France, followed by Spanish and German. Although American tourists get a bad rap in Paris, many *parisiens*—especially the youngsters—are eager to speak English with foreigners. So when you start speaking French to a stranger on the street and they respond in English, don't take it personally. However, don't assume that everyone speaks English. Centuries of snootiness and making nasally sounds have made the French experts at turning their noses up at obnoxious monolingual tourists. The key is to try—*par politesse*—with whatever attempted French accent you can, some of the daily formalities of *"bonjour"* and *"merci"* if you want your *pain au chocolat.*

Pronunciation

Reading French can be tricky, but the table below should help you avoid some of the upturned noses.

PHONETIC UNIT	PRONUNCIATION	PHONETIC UNIT	PRONUNCIATION
au	o, as in "go"	ch	sh, as in "shoe"
oi	ua as in "guava"	ou	oo, as in "igloo"
ai	ay as in "lay"	å	ah, as in "menorah"

Phrasebook

ENGLISH	FRENCH	PRONUNCIATION
Hello!/Hi!	Bonjour!	bohn-jhoor
Goodbye!	Au revoir!	oh ruh-vwah
Yes.	Oui	wee
No.	Non	nohn
Sorry!	Désolé!	day-zoh-lay

essentials

EMERGENCY		
Go away!	Allez-vous en!	ah-lay vooz on
Help!	Au secours!	oh sek-oor
Call the police!	Appelez les flics!	apple-ay lay fleeks
Get a doctor!	Allez chercher un médecin!	ah-lay share-shay un mayd-sin
Police Station	Poste de Police	Exactly like you'd think.
Hospital	Hôpital	Ho-pee-tal
Liquor store	Magasin d'alcool	Maga-zahn dal-cool
FOOD		
Waiter/waitress	Serveur/serveuse	server/servers
I'd like...	Je voudrais	je voo-dray
Thank you!	Merci	mare-see
Check please!	L'addition, s'il-vous-plait!	Lah-dee-sion, seal-voo-play
Where is...	Où est...?	Oo ay

ENGLISH	FRENCH	ENGLISH	FRENCH
I am from the US/Europe.	Je suis des Etats-Unis/de l'Europe.	What's the problem, sir/madam?	Quelle est la problème, monsieur/madame?
I have a visa/ID.	J'ai un visa/une carte d'identité.	I lost my passport/luggage.	J'ai perdu mon passe-port/baggage.
I will be here for less than three months.	Je serai ici pour de moins trois mois.	I have nothing to declare.	Je n'ai rien à déclarer.
You are the woman of my dreams.	Vous êtes la femme de mes rêves.	Perhaps I can help you with that?	Peut-être je peux vous aider avec ça?
Your hostel, or mine?	Votre hôtel, ou le mien?	Do you have protection?	Avez-vous un préservatif?
I would like a round-trip ticket.	Je voudrais un billet aller-retour.	Where is the train station?	Où est la gare?
Can I see a double room?	Puis-je voir un chambre pour deux?	How much does this cost?	Combien ça coûte?
Where is the bathroom?	Où sont les toilettes?	Is there a bar near here?	Est-ce qu'il y a un bar près d'ici?
What time is the next train?	À quelle heure est le prochain train?	Do you have this bathing suit in another size?	Avez-vous ce maillot de bain dans une autre taille?
Can I have another drink please?	Puis-je prendre un autre boisson s'il vous-plait?	Please don't arrest me!	S'il vous plait, ne m'arrêtez pas!
I'm in a committed relationship.	Je suis dans une relation engagée.	You talkin' to me?	Vous me parlez?
It was like this when I got here.	C'était comme ça quand je suis arrivé(e).	I don't speak much French.	Je ne parle pas beaucoup de français.
I feel sick.	Je me sens malade.	Leave me alone!	Laissez-moi tranquille!
What time does reception close?	À quelle heure est-ce que la réception ferme?	I don't understand.	Je ne comprends pas.
Actually, I'm from Canada.	En fait, je suis Canadien(ne).	I didn't vote for him, I swear.	Je n'ai pas voté pour lui, je le jure.
Of course not!	Bah, non!	Does it inconvenience you if I...?	Est-ce que ça vous dérange si je...?
Do you have a map? I'm lost in your eyes.	Est-ce que tu as un plan? Je me suis perdu dans tes yeux.	Excuse me, I lost my phone number. Can I borrow yours?	Excuse-moi, j'ai perdu mon numéro de télé-phone. Est-ce que je peux emprunter le tien?

DUTCH

Dutch is the official language of the Netherlands, but in Amsterdam most natives speak English—and speak it well. Thanks to mandatory English education in schools and to English-language media exports, most locals have impeccable grammar, vast vocabularies, and a soft continental accent that makes conversing relatively easy. Knowing a few key Dutch words and phrases can't hurt, particularly in smaller towns where English is not spoken as widely. Dutch spellings frequently resemble German, but pronunciation is very different. To initiate an English conversation, politely ask, "Spreekt u Engels?" (SPRAYKT oo ANG-les?). Even if your conversational counterpart speaks little English, he or she will usually try to communicate, an effort you can acknowledge with the appropriate words of thanks: "Dank u wel" (DAHNK oo vell).

Pronunciation

For those of you willing to take on the vagaries of the Dutch language, we salute you. Here are a few tips that will at least set you apart from most tourists, even if every Dutch person will still immediately realize that you have no idea what you're saying. Most Dutch consonants, with a few notable exceptions, have the same sounds as their English versions, sometimes rendering Dutch into a phonetic version of English colored by a foreign accent. Vowels are a different story. The combinations "e," "ee," "i," and "ij" are occasionally pronounced "er" as in "mother." Here are the other counterintuitive pronunciations:

PHONETIC UNIT	PRONUNCIATION	PHONETIC UNIT	PRONUNCIATION
au, ou, or ui	ow, as in "now"	g or ch	kh, as in "loch"
oo	oa, as in "boat"	ie	ee, as in "see"
v	between f and v	j	y, as in "yes"
w	between v and w	ee, ij or ei	ay, as in "layer"
aa	a longer a than in "cat"	oe	oo, as in "shoo"
eu	u, as in "hurt"	uu	a longer oo than in "too"

Phrasebook

ENGLISH	DUTCH	PRONUNCIATION
Hello!/Hi!	Dag!/Hallo!	Dakh!/Hallo!
Goodbye!	Tot ziens!	Tot zeens!
Yes	Ja	Yah
No	Nee	Nay
Sorry!	Sorry!	SOR-ee!
My name is...	Mijn naam is...	Mayn nahm iss...
Do you speak English?	Spreekt u Engels?	Spraykt oo ANG-les?
I don't speak Dutch	Ik spreek geen Nederlands	Ik sprayk khayn NAY-der-lans
I don't understand	Ik begrijp het niet	Ik ber-KHRAYP het neet
Good morning!	Goedemorgen!	KHOO-der-mor-khern!
Good evening!	Goedenavond!	KHOO-der-na-fondt!
Please/You're welcome	Alstublieft	Als-too-BLEEFT
Thank you	Dank u wel	Dahnk oo vell
EMERGENCY		
Go away!	Ga weg!	Kha vekh!
Help!	Help!	Help!
Stop!	Stop!	Stop!
Call the police!	Bel de politie!	Bel der poh-LEET-see!
Get a doctor!	Haal een dokter!	Haal ayn DOK-ter!
I'm sick	Ik ben ziek	Ik ben zeek
I'm lost	Ik ben verdwaald	Ik ben ferd-VAHLDT
QUESTIONS		
Who?	Wie?	Vee?
What?	Wat?	Vat?
When?	Wanneer?	Van-AYR?
Why?	Waarom?	VAR-ohm?
Where is...?	Waar is...?	Vahr iss...?

essentials

How do I get to...?	Hoe kom ik in...?	Hoo kom ik in...?
...the museum	...het museum	...het muh-say-um
...the church	...de kerk	...de kerk?
....the bank	...de bank	...de bahnk?
...the hotel	...het hotel	...het ho-TEL
...the shop	...de winkel	...de VIN-kerl
...the market	...de markt	...de markt
...the consulate	...het consulaat	het kon-sul-AAT...
...the train station	...het station	het staht-see-OHN
...the bus stop	...de bushalte	de BUS-hahlter
...the tourist office	...de VVV	de fay fay fay
...the toilet	...het toilet	het tva-LET
What time is it?	Hoe laat is het?	Hoo laht iss het?
Do you have...?	Heeft u...?	Hayft oo...?
How much does this cost?	Wat kost het?	Vat kost het?
ACCOMMODATIONS		
I have a reservation	Ik heb een reservering	Ik hep ayn res-er-VAY-ring
Single room	Eenpersoonskamer	AYN-per-sohn-kah-mer
Double room	Tweepersoonskamer	TVAY-per-sohn-kah-mer
How much per night?	Hoeveel kost per nacht?	Hoo-FAYL kost het per nakht?
FOOD		
We have a reservation	We hebben gereserveerd	Vay HEP-bern kher-ay-ser-VAYRT
Waiter/waitress	Meneer/mevrouw	Mer-NAYR/me-FROW
I'd like...	Ik wil graag...	Ik vil krakh...
May I have the check/bill please?	Mag ik de rekening	Makh ik der Ray-kern-inkh

BELGIAN

Psych! Belgian isn't actually a language. There are three official languages in Belgium: Dutch, French, and German. Hardly anyone speaks German, so you don't really have to worry about that one. Dutch is more commonly known in Belgium as Flemish (conjuring up nasty thoughts of throat mucus). While about 60% of the country speaks Flemish as its first language, French is more prevalent in Brussels. French-speaking has been increasing for centuries in the formerly Flemish-speaking city, and the relationship between the two languages is extremely controversial. It's probably best not to ask locals why, as chances are they are pretty opinionated about it. But if you want to start up a rigorous political discussion, this might be the perfect place to start. Look out for lots of bilingual signs, although if you understand neither French nor Flemish you might not be able to tell the difference. Bear in mind that Belgian French and Flemish are not identical to the languages spoken in France and the Netherlands, and local vocabulary might be a little confusing to those who consider themselves competent in one or the other. Never fear, however, for Brussels, like Amsterdam, is a cosmopolitan city where many people speak English, particularly in large hotels and restaurants.

language

let's go online

Plan your next trip on our spiffy website, **www.letsgo.com.** It features full book content, the latest travel info on your favorite destinations, and tons of interactive features: read blogs from our trusty Researcher-Writers, browse our photo library, watch exclusive videos, check out our newsletter, find travel deals, follow us on Facebook, and buy new guides. Plus, if this Essentials wasn't enough for you, we've got even more online. We're always updating and adding new features, so check back often!

essentials

BEYOND TOURISM

If you are reading this, then you are a member of an elite group—and we don't mean "the literate." You're a student preparing for a semester abroad. You're taking a gap year to save the trees, the whales, or the dates. You're an 80-year-old woman who has devoted her life to egg-laying platypuses and whatever the hell is up with that. In short, you're a traveler, not a tourist; like any good spy, you don't just observe your surroundings—you become an active part of them.

Your mission, should you choose to accept it, is to study, volunteer, or work abroad as laid out in the dossier—er, chapter—below. We leave the rest (when to go, whom to bring, and how many changes of underwear to pack) in your hands. This message will **self-destruct** in five seconds. Good luck.

greatest hits

- **LEARN HOW TO LE COOK.** Master French culinary secrets in Paris (p. 340).
- **DON'T BOTHER LEARNING A LANGUAGE.** And teach English instead (p. 343).
- **LEARN HOW TO FARM.** In Paris (p. 342).

studying

It is not surprising that studying abroad has become a staple in the college experience. After all, when else can you get academic credit for eating too much bread in Paris, taking too many pictures of peeing statues in Brussels, or "studying botany" in Amsterdam? Studying in a foreign country is your chance to indulge in an exotic culture, become slightly less monolingual, and maybe even learn something.

UNIVERSITIES

Studying abroad at a university has a lot of appeal. Not only will you gain cultural knowledge (probably), but class abroad will likely be easier than classes at home. Additional perks include cultural excursions (yay field trips!) and people telling you your accent is cute.

Paris

ARCADIA UNIVERSITY

450 S Easton Rd., Glenside, PA, USA ☎1-866-927-2234 www.arcadia.edu/abroad

Offering both summer and semester-long programs at the American Graduate School in Paris, the Arcadia University study abroad program offers courses in French language as well as History and Diplomacy of France and Europe. Additional undergraduate programs include "Politics in Francophone Africa," and "Class of Cultures in Paris and France," among others. Go here if you're particularly keen to hear about French military losses from a French person.

i Guaranteed housing. $ Summer courses $7000; semester courses $17,550.

visa information

If you are only planning to study in France or the Netherlands for less than 90 days, you're in luck—residents of the US, do not need to have a visa for short-term stays. You will be able to travel to any Schengen country during those 90 days. However, if you plan to study in Belgium, you must obtain a short-term student visa; to do so, you'll need a passport (valid for 15 months), two visa application forms, three recent passport photos, a criminal history record, a medical certificate, proof of sufficient funds to cover the cost of your stay, and an attestation from an academic institution acknowledging that you are registered as a student. This can take several weeks, so we suggest going through this process about two months before your departure.

If you plan to study abroad for longer than 90 days—a semester, for example—you must jump through a few more hoops. While the process for Belgium remains the same, France and the Netherlands become more complicated. For France, citizens of the US must first register with Campus France (www.usa.campusfrance.org), and all applicants must present the same documents that are required by Belgium to obtain a long-term visa. You must also obtain a **carte de séjour** (residency permit) from the local police upon arrival. Similarly, in the Netherlands, your host institution must apply for a residence permit after you have arrived, and upon arrival of the permit, you must register with the local council.

For more information on visas and fees, visit the websites for the French embassy (☎www.ambafrance-us.org), Belgian embassy (☎www.diplobel.us), or Dutch embassy (☎http://dc.the-netherlands.org).

GLOBAL STUDENT EXPERIENCE

17752 Skypark Circle, Ste. 235, Irvine, CA, USA   ☎1-866-756-2443   www.gseabroad.com

Global Student Experience provides students with several options for studying abroad in Paris, including French and Language Culture programs at the University of Paris Sorbonne (for those of you who want to be understood by Parisians) and International Business programs at both the American Business School in Paris and the École Supérieur du Commerce Extérieur (for those who don't care if they can understand their professor).

Ⓢ *Semester program $13,895; trimester program $12,895; summer program $5000.*

CENTER FOR STUDY ABROAD

325 S. Washington Ave. #93, Kent, WA, USA   ☎1-206-583-8191
www.centerforstudyabroad.com

The Center for Study Abroad offers French language courses at the Paris Language Institute, art history and literature courses at the Sorbonne, and political science courses at the Catholic University of Paris. All programs include sightseeing and cultural excursions (field trips!).

i Enrollment begins every Monday. Ⓢ *$700 for one week; $900 for 4 weeks at the Sorbonne; Semester $2500. $1000 for 4 weeks at the Catholic University; $3000 per semester.*

Brussels

BRIDGE CONNECT ACT STUDY ABROAD

50 Alpha Dr., Elizabethtown, PA, USA   ☎1-717-361-6600   www.bca.org

If you want the complete Brussels experience, then Bridge Connect Act Study Abroad Brussels is just the right porridge for you (not too hot, not too cold). BCA runs semester long programs in which students study at Vesalius College—"a liberal arts institution partnered with Vrije Universieit"—while living with a host family (so you actually learn the language). Internships are also available if students are interested.

Ⓢ *$17,000 per semester; $32,200 per year.*

Amsterdam

IES ABROAD

35 N. LaSalle St., 15th Fl., Chicago, IL, USA   ☎1-312-944-1750   www.iesabroad.org

Unlike other fluffy, everything-is-planned-for-you study abroad programs, IES Abroad throws you directly into the fire in the best possible way. With IES Abroad, students have the opportunity to enroll directly in foreign universities in a program of their choice for either a semester or an academic year. If you are not so keen about discovering it all on your own, IES helps its students find the best program for them as well as housing and meal plans (*stroopwafels* anyone?)

i Information Office open M-F 8:30am-4:30pm. Ⓢ *Tuition starts at $22,700 per semester.*

LANGUAGE SCHOOLS

As renowned novelist Gustave Flaubert once said, "Language is a cracked kettle on which we beat out tunes for bears to dance to." While we at *Let's Go* have absolutely no clue what he is talking about, we do know that the following are good resources for learning French or Dutch.

Paris

ALLIANCE FRANÇAISE

101 bd Raspail 75270   ☎01 42 85 90 00   www.alliancefr.org/en

Located in the *coeur* (your first vocabulary word!) of Paris, the Alliance Française provides French language classes for all levels. In addition, the *grande école* offers workshops with different focuses ranging from dramatic theater (the true

studying

French language) to "the French Way of Life" (read: drinking and napping) to business (read: drinking and napping).

ℹ Office open M-T 8:30am-7pm; W-F 8:30am-6pm. $ €55 per individual workshop; €240 per week of intensive French; €59 registration fee.

INSTITUT DE LANGUE FRANÇAISE

6 rue Daubigny 75017 ☎01 45 63 24 00 www.study-french-in-paris.com

The year round Institut de Langue Française offers a wide range of programs, from traditional French classes to specialized courses focused on spelling, grammar, or conversation. A convenient feature of the ILF is the Au Pair Program, which provides language lessons at times accommodating the oh-so-jam-packed schedule of an au pair.

ℹ Open M-F 8:30am-6:30pm.

FRANCE LANGUE

14 rue Léonard de Vinci 75116 ☎01 45 00 15 www.en.france-langue.fr

If you are the type of the person that daydreams while staring out the window, then France Langue is the place for you—it's right across the river from the Eiffel Tower. If the sites are too tempting for a traditional classroom experience, you can sign up for one of France Langue's one-on-one French lessons instead. Classes vary in level and France Langue also offers classes on French art history, business, and hotel and tourism industry.

ℹ Open M-F 9am-5pm. Prices vary by program.

Brussels

EUROPA LANGUAGE SCHOOL

717A Chaussée de Waterloo 1180 ☎02 347 44 11 www.elsb.be

Europa Language School conducts classes for students of all levels in over 15 different languages, but if you want to make the most of your time in Brussels you should probably stick with French or Dutch. This non-profit organization offers both group and individual classes, and with a reference list that includes many foreign embassies, you know the classes are worth your while.

ℹ Open M-F 9am-2pm. $ €30-38 per hour.

Amsterdam

DUTCH AND SUCH

Nieuwe Kerkstraat 1bg 1018 DW ☎020 6221198 www.dutchandsuch.nl

With a name like Dutch and Such, how can you not take a class here? Founded by a native Dutch and English speaker, Dutch and Such allows you to take your language skills beyond "Dunglish" with elementary, intermediate, and individual classes.

$ €380 for 12 group lessons; €700 for 10 individual lessons.

COOKING CLASSES

Is there anything more French than losing a war? The answer you are looking for is "Yes—food." Luckily for you, there is a plethora of cooking schools in Paris. Tap into your inner Julia Child and learn how to make French classics like French onion soup or steak au poivre.

Paris

LA CUISINE PARIS

80 quai de Hôtel de Ville 75004 ☎01 40 51 78 81 www.lacuisineparis.com

What better way to enjoy the French cuisine than learn how to make it in one of the food capitals of the world? At La Cuisine Paris, you can learn how to make baguettes, croissants, and macaroons. If you would rather reap the benefits of fine dining without doing any of the work, La Cuisine Paris also offers "foodie walks" that take you to all of their favorite eateries in the city.

i Conducted in English and French. $ €65-90 per class.

COOK'N WITH CLASS

21 rue Custine 75018 ☎01 42 55 70 59 www.cooknwithclass.com

From what we at *Let's Go* have heard, ball gowns are the new aprons and the top hat is the new toque blanche. Located in the Monmartre section of Paris, Cook'n with Class offers 15 different five to six person classes at all hours of the day. (Well, mostly 9am-5pm, but at least you have options.)

i Conducted in English. $ €125-185 per class.

LES FILLES PLAISIRS CULINAIRES

85 rue Vanderschickstraat 1060, Brussels ☎02 534 0483 www.lesfillesplaisirsculinaires.be

Started by three *filles*, Les Filles Plaisirs Culinaires offers small monthly classes for men, women, and children, each with a different theme (the classes, not the children.) The primary principles of the organization are nutrition, social responsibility, creativity, and community (read: everyone eats scrumptious, healthy food at the same table after class.)

i Conducted in English. $ €50 per class.

volunteering

You might be thinking "Nobody volunteers in Europe. Europe is good; they don't need any help." False! Despite the reputation of being a wealthy, tourist destination, much of Europe—Paris, Brussels, and Amsterdam included—still needs help, particularly with historical conservation and social outreach programs for immigrants.

Volunteering can be a (relatively) cheap and engaging way to travel in Europe while getting to know people from around the world. Yes, most volunteer programs have enrollment costs, but these mostly cover room and board.

HISTORICAL RESTORATION

Paris, as beautiful and historical as it is, only remains that way because of historical preservation. Volunteering with a program that practices historical restoration will get you up close and personal with valuable artifacts like the *Mona Lisa*. Okay, maybe not the *Mona Lisa*, but at least you will be closer than the tourists trapped behind the barriers.

Paris

CHANTIERS HISTOIRE ET ARCHITECTURE MÉDIÉVALS

5-7 rue Guilleminot 75014 ☎01 43 35 15 51 www.cham.asso.fr

Chantiers Histoire et Architecture Médiévals (CHAM) offers two- to four- week restoration projects in Paris. Duties range from masonry work, stone-cutting (read: more masonry work), site clearing, archaeological surveys, and excavations. If you are into archaeological digs, then you are probably okay with roughing it for a few weeks, but just in case you aren't, CHAM provides camping-style accommodations.

$ €110 for two weeks; €15 registration fee.

ASSOCIATION POUR LA PARTICIPATION ET L'ACTION RÉGIONALE (APARE)

25 bd Paul Pon 84800, L'Isle-sur-la-Sorgue ☎04 90 85 15 www.apare-gec.org/EN

APARE offers historical restoration programs all over France for the "protection and enhancement of the natural and cultural assets." Work alongside professionals while learning about stonework and restoration and gaining an appreciation for Provençal and Mediterranean culture. Volunteers are expected to work 32 hours per week during the two- to three-week programs.

$ €100 for 2 weeks; €136 for 3 weeks; €25 registration fee.

ENVIRONMENTAL CONSERVATION

Save the (other side of the) planet. Volunteering with an environmental conservation organization in Europe can be both rewarding and allow you to see Europe from a different perspective. As Europe becomes more and more industrialized, farmland and farmhands are diminishing. This is where you come into play. Don't worry, European farmers won't use you as farmland, but they would very much like your help.

Paris

WORLD WIDE OPPORTUNITIES ON ORGANIC FARMING (WWOOF)

La Beaunaz 7450, Saint-Paul-en-Chablais   www.wwoof.org

Seeing as the amount of farmland in the heart of Paris is rather limited—all those self-important museums and that Eiffel Tower take up lots of space—you might not expect to find many farming opportunities in Paris. WWOOF offers volunteer opportunities around Paris and the rest of France. "WWOOFers," as they are affectionately called, receive free room and board in exchange for helping farmers with their daily tasks—everything from weeding the garden to selling the crops at a local market.

i Contact hello@wwoof.org with questions regarding WWOOF in France.

VOLUNTEERS FOR PEACE, INC.

7 Kilburn Street Suite 316 Burlington, VT, USA   ☎1-802-540-3060 www.vfp.org

Volunteers for Peace is an organization aimed at placing volunteers in environmental programs, archaeology programs, and groups that work with children and the elderly. Volunteers can either work in organized camps for two to three weeks or "create a personalized two-week to one-year international project."

Ⓢ $350 registration fee, plus an additional $200-500 for certain projects.

LANGUAGE PROGRAMS

The great thing about speaking English is that it's (almost) universal. Since you have read this far, you probably speak English and can put your language skills to use by volunteering in a foreign country as a teacher or translator.

Paris

GEOVISIONS - CONVERSATION CORPS FRANCE

63 Whitfield St., Guilford, CT, USA   ☎1-877-949-9998 www.geovisions.org

GeoVisions's group, Conversation Corps France, allows volunteers to live with and teach English to a family for one to three months. Seriously. You go to France. Live with a family. Expound your wisdom of the English language upon your host family for 15 hours per week. "Experience France and French culture in depth."

Ⓢ $1500-1675.

Brussels

NATO

www.nato.int

NATO (North Atlantic Treaty Organization) offers a year-long internship program in which volunteers are responsible for drafting and preparing official documents as well as attending and summarizing council and committee meetings. The aim of the internship is "to provide interns with an opportunity to learn from the NATO community and get a better understanding and a more balanced view of the Organization." Basically you will have a job and be an adult.

i Must be over 21 to apply, have completed at least 2 years of post-secondary school, and be proficient in English or French. Ⓢ €800 per month to defray the costs of housing and food.

more visa information

Regardless of whether or not you need a student visa, you will most likely need to obtain a **work permit** if you plan to work while studying in France, the Netherlands, or Belgium. These permits are generally applied for by your employer, meaning you should have already applied for a position before traveling overseas. Fees and requirements for the work permit vary by country, so visit each country's embassy website for more information about working abroad.

working

Can you speak English? Yes. Can you teach English? Maybe. Congratulations, you are qualified for a job on the international level. Teaching English is the most prevalent option for working abroad, but there are options in the mix, including au pair work and other teaching jobs. Despite the limited range of work abroad, there is never a shortage. You might even have an easier time finding a job than getting the visa.

LONG-TERM WORK

Teaching English

While there are many teaching opportunities abroad, there are some restrictions. Most teaching jobs are offered only at private language schools, as most schools prefer EU citizens who are also proficient in the language of that country. Additionally, most English teachers abroad are TEFL (Teach English as a Foreign Language) certified, though there are plenty of exceptions. Obtaining a long-term stay visa can be a challenge, especially if you are not an EU citizen. But there are still teaching jobs available for you if you're willing to jump through a few extras hoops to get there.

PARIS

INTERNATIONAL TEFL ACADEMY

916 Diversey Pkwy., Chicago, IL, USA ☎1-877-610-1337 www.internationalteflacademy.com

International TEFL Academy is based in Chicago but offers TEFL/TESOL certification courses around the world at its various locations so teachers can get trained and jump into a job immediately. International TEFL Academy helps its graduates find jobs through its extensive search engine.

$ $1350-2100 for TEFL/TESOL certification course. ⏰ 6-12 months, usually begin Sept or Oct.

GO ABROAD

324 E. Oak St., Fort Collins, CO, USA ☎1-720-570-1702 www.goabroad.com

If the name wasn't a giveaway, Go Abroad is a website where the main goal is to get you to the other side of the world as fast as possible. Go Abroad has extensive listings for both teaching jobs in Paris (as well as other locations) and TEFL certification programs, which ensures that you not only go the other side of the world but also arrive with the necessary qualifications.

BRUSSELS

OPEN CONTEXT LANGUAGE SCHOOL

rue du Grand Hospice 34a ☎02 218 30 66 www.opencontext.eu

This language school offers Dutch, French, English, German, and Spanish classes to students of all levels. While the school expects its teachers to have either relevant experience as a language trainer or an advanced degree in languages or pedagogy, teaching training courses are available.

i Applicants should send their CV to info@opencontext.be.

AMSTERDAM

OXFORD SEMINARS

244 5th Ave., Ste. J262, New York City, USA ☎1-800-799 1799 www.oxfordseminars.com

Oxford Seminars has got it all—TESOL/TEFL/TESL certifications courses, international teaching listings, visa information, and even tips for your first week of teaching. If they can't help you find the right teaching job in The Netherlands, then there probably aren't any available.

[i] *Open M-F 8:30am-10pm, Sa-Su 8:30am-5:30pm.*

Au Pair Work

Here are some very dry but super important au pair requirements. In France you must be 18-30 years old, unmarried, have no children, have basic knowledge of French, take a French course while in France, and have at least a high school diploma). In Belgium, you must have basic knowledge of the host family's language, be 18-25 years old, take a language course while in Belgium, stay no longer than one year, and work no more than four hours per day and 20 hours per week (nice life, eh?). Additionally, your host family must have health insurance for you and have at least one child under the age of 13 (because who wants to babysit a 15 year old?). In the Netherlands you must be 18-25 years old, unmarried, have no children, never previously resided in The Netherlands on a residence permit, and have basic knowledge of Dutch.

PARIS

AU PAIR PARIS

☎1-212-254-9779 www.aupairparis.com

The name pretty much says it all. You are looking to be an au pair in Paris, Parisians are looking for an au pair, and Au Pair Paris pairs up Parisians and au pairs. Now say that fast five times. Yeah, neither could we.

[$] *$150 application fee; $100 deposit (returned upon completion of the au pair program).*

BRUSSELS

GREAT AU PAIR

1329 HWY 395, Ste. 10-333, Gardnerville, NV, USA ☎1-800-935-6303 www.greataupair.com

Great Au Pair's website allows great au pairs and great families to pair up for an all-around great experience. Even if it sounds cheesy, it's true—Great Au Pair is one of the most trusted international job matching sites around, and since 2001, the company has helped more than one million families and caregivers find a match.

Amsterdam

NEW AU PAIR

www.newaupair.com

New Au Pair is an online meeting place where au pairs and families can connect. If you have specific requirements for being an au pair, New Au Pair has a specialized search engine called "My Perfect Family Wizard." No, you may not change your own family.

tell the world

If your friends are tired of hearing about that time you saved a baby orangutan in Indonesia, there's clearly only one thing to do: get new friends. Find them at our website, www.letsgo.com, where you can post your study-, volunteer-, or work-abroad stories for other, more appreciative community members to read.

INDEX

index

index

index

MAP INDEX

index

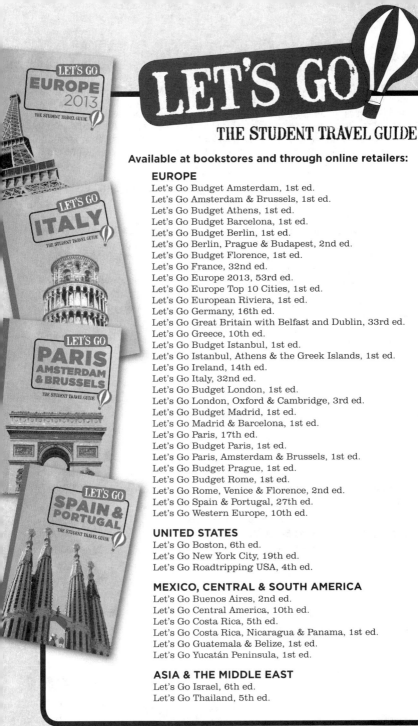

LET'S GO!

THE STUDENT TRAVEL GUIDE

Available at bookstores and through online retailers:

EUROPE
Let's Go Budget Amsterdam, 1st ed.
Let's Go Amsterdam & Brussels, 1st ed.
Let's Go Budget Athens, 1st ed.
Let's Go Budget Barcelona, 1st ed.
Let's Go Budget Berlin, 1st ed.
Let's Go Berlin, Prague & Budapest, 2nd ed.
Let's Go Budget Florence, 1st ed.
Let's Go France, 32nd ed.
Let's Go Europe 2013, 53rd ed.
Let's Go Europe Top 10 Cities, 1st ed.
Let's Go European Riviera, 1st ed.
Let's Go Germany, 16th ed.
Let's Go Great Britain with Belfast and Dublin, 33rd ed.
Let's Go Greece, 10th ed.
Let's Go Budget Istanbul, 1st ed.
Let's Go Istanbul, Athens & the Greek Islands, 1st ed.
Let's Go Ireland, 14th ed.
Let's Go Italy, 32nd ed.
Let's Go Budget London, 1st ed.
Let's Go London, Oxford & Cambridge, 3rd ed.
Let's Go Budget Madrid, 1st ed.
Let's Go Madrid & Barcelona, 1st ed.
Let's Go Paris, 17th ed.
Let's Go Budget Paris, 1st ed.
Let's Go Paris, Amsterdam & Brussels, 1st ed.
Let's Go Budget Prague, 1st ed.
Let's Go Budget Rome, 1st ed.
Let's Go Rome, Venice & Florence, 2nd ed.
Let's Go Spain & Portugal, 27th ed.
Let's Go Western Europe, 10th ed.

UNITED STATES
Let's Go Boston, 6th ed.
Let's Go New York City, 19th ed.
Let's Go Roadtripping USA, 4th ed.

MEXICO, CENTRAL & SOUTH AMERICA
Let's Go Buenos Aires, 2nd ed.
Let's Go Central America, 10th ed.
Let's Go Costa Rica, 5th ed.
Let's Go Costa Rica, Nicaragua & Panama, 1st ed.
Let's Go Guatemala & Belize, 1st ed.
Let's Go Yucatán Peninsula, 1st ed.

ASIA & THE MIDDLE EAST
Let's Go Israel, 6th ed.
Let's Go Thailand, 5th ed.

ACKNOWLEDGMENTS

CLAIRE THANKS: Haley, for being the best RM I could have asked for, a great friend, and a constant companion in the late-afternoon quest for Juicy Fruit. Michael, for being a peach, a late-night office buddy, and an ever-benevolent ME. Mallory, for overly-long dinners with Michael and for being a fantastic support in the great pursuit of the copyflow schedule. Heather, for being a champ and for taking good care of my gnome, Svindel, on the road. Sara, for hosting Let's Go fests and for having a velvet couch in her office. Thanks to everyone else at LGHQ for making the office a wonderful place to work. Thanks to Starbucks (obviously). And thanks always to my parental units for being supportive and generally awesome, even when I didn't call home enough.

HALEY THANKS: To the following entities, I give thanks: Juicy Fruit, Frasier, and coffee, three things without which I might now be a hollow shell of a person. Heather, for your curiosity and for your entertaining contributions to the list. John Green, for being my Internet father figure, and Mallory, who let me cling to her arm when I met him. Mark, for your excellent taste in beer. LGHQ, for making me happy to come to work each day! Lauren, Roland, and Emily, for exposing me to Asian fruits and for being brave in the face of rodents. Claire, for long chats and for knowing instinctively when it's time for a vending machine run. Michael, for nerding out with me and for your tireless patience and spirit. Love to Rotary Youth Exchange, for allowing me to see the world, and the friends I met abroad, who made me want to share it.

DIRECTOR OF PUBLISHING   Sara Plana
MANAGING EDITORS   Michael Goncalves, Mark Warren
PRODUCTION AND DESIGN DIRECTOR   Roland Yang
DIGITAL AND MARKETING DIRECTOR   Lauren Xie
PRODUCTION ASSOCIATE   Faith Zhang
MARKETING ASSOCIATES   Zi Wei Lin, Mariel Sena, Jess Stein

DIRECTOR OF IT   Calvin Tonini
PRESIDENT   Kirk Benson
GENERAL MANAGER   Jim McKellar

ABOUT LET'S GO

THE STUDENT TRAVEL GUIDE

Let's Go publishes the world's favorite student travel guides, written entirely by Harvard students. Armed with pens, notebooks, and a few changes of clothes stuffed into their backpacks, our student researchers go across continents, through time zones, and above expectations to seek out invaluable travel experiences for our readers. Because we are a completely student-run company, we have a unique perspective on how students travel, where they want to go, and what they're looking to do when they get there. If your dream is to grab a machete and forge through the jungles of Costa Rica, we can take you there. If you'd rather bask in the Riviera sun at a beachside cafe, we'll set you a table. In short, we write for readers who know that there's more to travel than tour buses. To keep up, visit our website, www.letsgo. com, where you can sign up to blog, post photos from your trips, and connect with the *Let's Go* community.

TRAVELING BEYOND TOURISM

We're on a mission to provide our readers with sharp, fresh coverage packed with socially responsible opportunities to go beyond tourism. Each guide's Beyond Tourism chapter shares ideas about responsible travel, study abroad, and how to give back to the places you visit while on the road. To help you gain a deeper connection with the places you travel, our fearless researchers scour the globe to give you the heads-up on both world-renowned and off-the-beaten-track opportunities. We've also opened our pages to respected writers and scholars to hear their takes on the countries and regions we cover, and asked travelers who have worked, studied, or volunteered abroad to contribute first-person accounts of their experiences.

FIFTY-THREE YEARS OF WISDOM

Let's Go has been on the road for 53 years and counting. We've grown a lot since publishing our first 20-page pamphlet to Europe in 1960, but five decades and 60 titles later, our witty, candid guides are still researched and written entirely by students on shoestring budgets who know that train strikes, stolen luggage, food poisoning, and marriage proposals are all part of a day's work. Meanwhile, we're still bringing readers fresh new features, such as a student-life section with advice on how and where to meet students from around the world; a revamped, user-friendly layout for our listings; and greater emphasis on the experiences that make travel abroad a rite of passage for readers of all ages. And, of course, this year's seven titles are still brimming with editorial honesty, a commitment to students, and our irreverent style.

THE LET'S GO COMMUNITY

More than just a travel guide company, *Let's Go* is a community that reaches from our headquarters in Cambridge, MA, all across the globe. Our small staff of dedicated student editors, writers, and tech nerds comes together because of our shared passion for travel and our desire to help other travelers get the most out of their experience. We love it when our readers become part of the *Let's Go* community as well—when you travel, drop us a postcard (67 Mt. Auburn St., Cambridge, MA 02138, USA), send us an email (feedback@letsgo.com), or sign up on our website (www. letsgo.com) to tell us about your adventures and discoveries.

For more information, updated travel coverage, and news from our researcher team, visit us online at www.letsgo.com.

If you are interested in purchasing advertising space in a Let's Go publication, please contact us at adsales@letsgo.com.

HELPING LET'S GO. If you want to share your discoveries, suggestions, or corrections, please drop us a line. We appreciate every piece of correspondence, whether a postcard, a 10-page email, or a coconut. Visit Let's Go at **www.letsgo.com** or send an email to:

feedback@letsgo.com, subject: "Let's Go Paris, Amsterdam & Brussels"

Address mail to:

Let's Go Paris, Amsterdam & Brussels, 67 Mount Auburn St., Cambridge, MA 02138, USA

In addition to the invaluable travel advice our readers share with us, many are kind enough to offer their services as researchers or editors. Unfortunately, our charter enables us to employ only currently enrolled Harvard students.

Maps © Let's Go and Avalon Travel
Design Support by Jane Musser, Sarah Juckniess, Tim McGrath

Distributed by Publishers Group West.
Printed in Canada by Friesens Corp.

ISBN-13: 978-1-61237-027-9
First edition
10 9 8 7 6 5 4 3 2 1

Let's Go **Paris, Amsterdam & Brussels** is written by Let's Go Publications, 67 Mt. Auburn St., Cambridge, MA 02138, USA.

Let's Go® and the LG logo are trademarks of Let's Go, Inc.

quick reference

YOUR GUIDE TO LET'S GO ICONS

👍	*Let's Go* recommends	☎	Phone numbers	➔	Directions
i	Other hard info	$	Prices	⏰	Hours

PRICE RANGES

Let's Go includes price ranges, marked by one to four dollar signs, in accommodations and food listings. For an expanded explanation, see How To Use This Book.

FRANCE AND BELGIUM	$	$$	$$$	$$$$
ACCOMMODATIONS	under €25	€26-45	€46-70	over €71
FOOD	under €10	€11-20	€21-32	over €33

AMSTERDAM	$	$$	$$$	$$$$
ACCOMMODATIONS	under €30	€31-50	€51-75	over €76
FOOD	under €10	€11-19	€20-29	over €30

IMPORTANT PHONE NUMBERS

The general emergency number throughout Europe is ☎112.

CITY	POLICE	FIRE	MEDICAL	ENGLISH CRISIS HELPLINE
PARIS	☎17	☎18	☎15	☎01 47 23 80 80
AMSTERDAM	☎112	☎112	☎112	☎09 00 07 67
BRUSSELS	☎101	☎100	☎100	☎02 648 40 14

USEFUL FRENCH AND DUTCH PHRASES

ENGLISH	FRENCH	DUTCH
Hi/Bye (Informal)	Ciao	Dag!/Hallo!
Good day/Hello	Buongiorno	Goedendag
Please	Per favore	Alstublieft
Thank you	Grazie	Dank u wel
Do you speak English?	Est-ce que vous parlez anglais?	Spreekt u Engels?

CURRENCY CONVERSIONS

These rates are current as we go to press.

AUS$1 = €0.83	€1= AUS$1.20	NZ$1 = €0.65	€1 = NZ$1.53
CDN$1 = €0.80	€1 = CDN$1.25	UK£1 = €1.26	€1 = UK£0.79
EUR€1 = €1	WOAH!	US$1 = €0.81	€1 = US$1.22

TEMPERATURE CONVERSIONS

°CELSIUS	-5	0	5	10	15	20	25	30	35	40
°FAHRENHEIT	23	32	41	50	59	68	77	86	95	104

MEASUREMENT CONVERSIONS

1 inch (in.) = 25.4mm	1 millimeter (mm) = 0.039 in.
1 foot (ft.) = 0.305m	1 meter (m) = 3.28 ft.
1 mile (mi.) = 1.609km	1 kilometer (km) = 0.621 mi.
1 pound (lb.) = 0.454kg	1 kilogram (kg) = 2.205 lb.
1 gallon (gal.) = 3.785L	1 liter (L) = 0.264 gal.